THE NEW HISTORY
OF LITERATURE

THE
VICTORIANS

THE NEW HISTORY OF LITERATURE

1. THE MIDDLE AGES Edited by W. F. Bolton
2. ENGLISH POETRY AND PROSE, 1540–1674 Edited by Christopher Ricks
3. ENGLISH DRAMA TO 1710 Edited by Christopher Ricks
4. DRYDEN TO JOHNSON Edited by Roger Lonsdale
5. LITERATURE OF THE ROMANTIC PERIOD Edited by David B. Pirie
6. THE VICTORIANS Edited by Arthur Pollard
7. THE TWENTIETH CENTURY Edited by Martin Dodsworth
8. AMERICAN LITERATURE TO 1900 Edited by Marcus Cunliffe
9. AMERICAN LITERATURE SINCE 1900 Edited by Marcus Cunliffe
10. THE ENGLISH LANGUAGE Edited by W. F. Bolton and David Crystal.

Volumes 5 and 7 will be published in 1988.

THE VICTORIANS

·

EDITED BY

ARTHUR POLLARD

Peter Bedrick Books
New York

First American edition published in 1987 by
Peter Bedrick Books
125 East 23rd Street
New York, NY 10010

Library of Congress Cataloging-in-Publication Data

The Victorians.
 (The New history of literature)
 Includes bibliographies and index.
 1. English literature—19th century—History and
criticism. I. Pollard, Arthur. II. Series.
PR463.V55 1987   820'.9'008   87–47750
ISBN 0–87226–130–1

Printed in Great Britain

10 9 8 7 6 5 4 3 2 1

CONTENTS

INTRODUCTION   vii

1 VICTORIAN THOUGHT   1
A. O. J. Cockshut

2 FAITH AND DOUBT IN THE VICTORIAN AGE   25
A. O. J. Cockshut

3 MATTHEW ARNOLD (and A. H. CLOUGH)   51
Kenneth Allott

4 DICKENS   81
Alan Shelston

5 SURTEES, THACKERAY AND TROLLOPE   111
Arthur Pollard

6 THE BRONTËS   145
Wendy A. Craik

7 MRS GASKELL AND GEORGE ELIOT   173
Barbara Hardy

8 VICTORIAN WOMEN PROSE-WRITERS   199
Marion Shaw

9 MID-VICTORIAN NOVELISTS   239
Sheila Smith and Peter Denman

10 FANTASY AND NONSENSE   287
Gillian Avery

11 LATER VICTORIAN NOVELISTS   307
Patrick M. Yarker and Owen Knowles

12 TENNYSON (and FITZGERALD)   361
John Killham

13 THE BROWNINGS   387
Isobel Armstrong

14 HOPKINS   413
    Norman H. MacKenzie

15 THE ROSSETTIS AND OTHER CONTEMPORARY POETS   435
    James Sambrook

16 ASPECTS OF THE *FIN DE SIÈCLE*   463
    Bernard Bergonzi

17 THE VICTORIAN THEATRE   483
    Cecil J. L. Price

    BIBLIOGRAPHY   499

    TABLE OF DATES   545

    INDEX   557

INTRODUCTION

It is difficult to characterize in brief compass a span of time as long as that in which Queen Victoria reigned over England and her realms beyond the seas. Not only did it cover so many years, but those years also witnessed political, economic, intellectual and scientific change previously unparalleled in British history. In his brilliant survey of the period, *The Victorian Frame of Mind*, W. E. Houghton cites many who felt themselves to be living in an age of transition (op. cit., p 1); 'an awful moment of transition' was Tennyson's phrase (quoted by Houghton, p 317). Writing of the 1840s, J. A. Froude declared:

It was an era of new ideas, of swift if silent spiritual revolution. Reform in Parliament was the symbol of a general hope for the introduction of a new and better order of things. The Church had broken away from her old anchorage . . . Among the middle class there was the Evangelical revival. The Catholic revival at Oxford had convulsed the university and had set half the educated men and women speculating on the authority of the priesthood as the essential meaning of Christianity . . . Physical science, now that it was creating railroads, bridging the Atlantic and giving proof of capacity which could no longer be sneered at, was forming a philosophy of the earth and its inhabitants, agitating and inconvenient to orthodoxy but difficult to deal with. Benthamism had taken possession of dominions which religion had hitherto claimed as her own, was interpreting morality in a way of its own, and directing political action.

(Carlyle's Life in London, 1891 edn, vol I, pp 310–11)

In the 1840s the half had not been told. By the end of the century Britain exercised 'dominion over palm and pine' with assurance and with a sense of responsibility that in retrospect looks both more beneficent and less self-interested than it was once fashionable to regard it. The Navy imposed a *pax Britannica* on many parts of the world. Trade and Christianity followed the flag. At home successive Reform Acts made democracy more and more a reality, and when after the 1867 Act it became necessary, in Robert Lowe's words, to 'educate our masters', universal elementary education was instituted in 1870. Science and technology together testified to man's adventure and achievement. Darwin and his associates gave man an entirely new view of himself and his place on earth, whilst technical advances extended and completed the revolution in industry that had begun in the previous century. These technical advances were themselves accompanied and in some ways made possible by the changes which brought into being the necessary commercial and financial structure of modern capitalism. Men confidently saw change as progress.

If progress is one Victorian watchword, freedom is the other. The twofold (and opposed) inspirations of the period, Utilitarianism, secular and rationalistic, and Evangelicalism, other-worldly and fideistic, agreed at least in their stress on individualism. Men must be free. As a result free trade replaced protection, government interference in industry and social organization was resisted, competition was extolled (though there were important contrary voices – see Houghton, op. cit., pp 191ff), the Dissenters opposed the claims of the Established Church, the Evangelicals emphasized the necessity of personal salvation, and some people found courage to espouse agnosticism. It all amounted in Arnold's phrase to 'doing as one likes'.

His was the most prominent of a series of dissentient voices. The contrasted ideal and threat that are represented in his title *Culture and Anarchy* remind us that, though it may have been an age of progress and achievement, the Victorian period was also an age of doubt and anxiety. The middle-classes were supreme. They were immensely self-confident, commercially successful, scornful of the old establishments of aristocracy and Church, but though they often showed a fine sense of social responsibility (they formed the backbone of the humanitarian movement – Mrs Gaskell is a fine literary example of their conscience in this respect), most of them failed to see the relevance of culture, of an organic view of society. They did not realize, sometimes indeed actively scorned, the importance of authority and traditional values. These modern 'Philistines' were blind to the 'sweetness and light' of the Hellenistic ideal, blinded in fact by their own subscription to a Hebraistic caricature, an arid Puritanism of narrow conduct and narrower dogma. Most Victorians would have accepted with Carlyle that *ernst ist das leben* (epigraph to *Past and Present* – from Schiller) (cf. their attitude to work), but there were some who thought that life need not be ugly as well. Amongst these, with Arnold, were to be found Newman with his appeal to the historic, authoritative Church, Carlyle in his cult of the hero and Ruskin with his vision of art and society. These several medievalisms were all lifelines in vain.

Hope was not fulfilled, confidence ebbed, and the last years of the century were marked by reaction, resignation and disillusion. Though men failed to realize it, the imperial heyday was passing and economic prosperity had gone beyond its peak. The old rigid social hierarchy had disappeared and in its place was social flux, the product of an individualism that issued in discontent and strife. The old certainties of faith had evaporated; those who continued to believe were, perforce, less sure and those who disbelieved were often unhappy. It all amounted to what Mark Pattison described as the 'present mood of depression and despondency' (*Fortnightly Review*, vol XXI, p 351). Tennyson was discouraged, Hardy gloomy, Shaw devastatingly critical, Wilde scintillatingly cynical. Arnold had lamented the age's 'sick hurry, its divided aims'; at its end it came to worse than this. It appeared to have lost all sense of purpose. There were sad ways by which the Victorian era seemed to have gained the whole world and lost its own soul. A period in which so many contrary forces interacted so intricately and energetically cannot fail to be interesting. Its writers, expressing the spirit of the age with all the resources of imagination, feeling and thought, abundantly reveal their response to their time and the effect it had upon them. In the following chapters an attempt has been made not to mention everybody but to cover both the major figures and others who, though less than major, yet have an interest and importance which demand that they should be considered.

1

VICTORIAN THOUGHT

A. O. J. Cockshut

To understand how people thought we need to know their feelings, their hopes and especially their fears. Of the early Victorians it is pre-eminently true that they pondered on the things that worried them, in some cases on the things that terrified them. For few, if any, of the great names is it useful to consider their thought as a closed intellectual system. The apparent exceptions – John Stuart Mill is one – have a way of proving only apparent while Newman, the man with the most finely-tempered speculative intelligence of them all, characteristically chose as his motto 'Cor ad cor loquitur'

The 1830s and early 1840s were a time of reaction against abstract theoretical solutions, or what Newman called 'paper systems'. The most striking fact about the literature of the 1840s is the entrance of industrial England, with its smoke, grime, misery and oppression, into serious literature. Carlyle, quickly followed by Disraeli, Dickens and Mrs Gaskell, and later by Ruskin, brooded on the life actually led by those who worked in the factories of Lancashire and by their children. Where the radicals at the time of the Napoleonic wars had talked of abstract rights, Disraeli talked of tommy-shops (in *Sybil*), and in *Hard Times* Dickens was soon to talk of a piston 'like the head of an elephant in a state of melancholy madness'.

The absence of any sign of serious interest in industrial society in literature before 1830, and its abundant presence after 1840 is deeply significant. For the Industrial Revolution was not, after all, a new thing. Arkwright, the pioneer of the spinning-mill, died in 1792, the year Shelley was born. But Shelley was too abstract, Wordsworth and Keats too introspective and personal, Byron too scornful and cosmopolitan, to give much attention to the consequences of what he did. The men of the new age were different, and Dickens, who was twenty-five when the Queen came to the throne, may stand as typical of the new interest in *facts* and the new distrust of reforms which were merely constitutional and legal and not administrative. What difference had the Reform Bill of 1832 really made after all the ardour and excitement that had gone into its making? We can find the answer in Trollope's political novels which show the social composition and the political instincts of the House of Commons still mainly aristocratic even in the 1860s.

But if the men of the new generation were very different from the Romantic poets in this respect, there were also ways in which they were like them. A very significant point which Wordsworth, Shelley, Carlyle and Dickens all have in common is a grudging, or at times a downright contemptuous attitude towards eighteenth-century literature and society. It is startling to find how cavalierly Coleridge could dismiss a great man like Samuel Johnson; and the portrait of Sir John Chester in Dickens's *Barnaby Rudge* (1841) shows a characteristic early Victorian view of eighteenth-century man. He is polished, gentlemanly, heartless and false. For the early Victorians, as for the Romantics, lack of heart, lack of natural feeling, is the ultimate transgression. Any form, any custom, any constitutional principle must be informed with living faith and love; otherwise it was merely, in Carlyle's words, that he loved to apply both to the French and English eighteenth century, 'buckram' or 'sham'. The early Victorians and the Romantics were alike, then, in their reverence for feelings, and what an unfriendly critic might call their hunger for sensation. But there is also a shift of emphasis. The early Victorians were seldom dreamy, and not markedly introspective. The feelings they cultivated were social, beginning with the primary family affections and stretching out to the unknown man at the bottom of the social pyramid. They did not always understand this man very well; the remedies they suggested for his lot were not always well-advised. But they always wanted to understand him and thought it their duty to try. In this connection the development of Ruskin's thought, with which we shall deal later, is significant. Here was a man naturally inclined to be egocentric, possessed of the strongest aesthetic sensibilities, and of the money and leisure to gratify them. Yet, under the influence of the *Zeitgeist* of the forties and fifties, he gradually turns his attention more and more to social questions and makes the most urgent, though largely ineffective, attempts to communicate with the poor and to benefit their lot.

To question *idées reçues*, to ask laws and customs to justify themselves, may be salutary, but for the enquiring mind it involves very awkward problems. Carlyle, Newman and Mill were all caught up in an agonizing search for origins and principles. Men of their age in that they jumped intuitively to affirmations derived from their deepest feelings, they were also men who felt the need, even the duty, to justify what they felt by study and argument. Sometimes this led them to modify their first instinctive affirmation, and when it did, the process was painful. This quest for origins, this need to justify established forms by showing their relevance to men's deepest emotional needs, is highly characteristic of early Victorian thinking. It is first clearly seen in two publications of 1833, four years before the Queen's accession, Carlyle's *Sartor Resartus* and Newman's first *Tracts for the Times*.

Carlyle is perhaps the easiest of all great Victorian figures to underrate today. His faults have often been pointed out, and can hardly be denied. He is turgid, repetitive, wilful and intemperate. He arrogates a divine prerogative of dividing the world into sheep and goats. It is frightening to see a man so absolutely sure that Cromwell was utterly right and Charles I was utterly wrong. But his importance, which it would be hard to overestimate, lies mainly in two things. Over and over again he was the first to ask the questions which soon became the general questions of the age. At the same time he was the strongest formative influence on the most talented of his younger contemporaries.

Sartor Resartus is a strange mixture, and has become in the course of time a mixture forbidding to most readers. Autobiographical fragments are interwoven with German philosophy, and a secular message is conveyed in the language of Calvinist preachers. German was a language not often studied in England in the 1830s, and part of Carlyle's authority (which is analogous to that of Coleridge in an earlier generation) sprang from an awed, ignorant respect for the translator of Goethe and the interpreter of unintelligible German metaphysics.

But Carlyle was not fundamentally Germanic. Above all, he was Scots. He was steeped from childhood in the stern, terrifying and thrilling world of Scots Calvinism. If in some ways his intellect wandered far from this, his feelings were formed for life in its crucible. His account of the conversion of the hero of *Sartor Resartus* to the 'Everlasting No' has the true accent of the old Calvinist preachers who did so much to form the Scottish national consciousness.

I asked myself: 'What *art* thou afraid of? Wherefore, like a coward, dost thou forever pip and whimper, and go cowering and trembling? Despicable biped! what is the sum-total of the worst that lies before thee? Death; and say the pangs of Tophet too, and all that the Devil and Man may, will or can *do* against thee! Hast thou not a heart; canst thou not suffer whatsoever it be; and as a Child of Freedom, though outcast, trample Tophet itself under thy feet, while it consumes thee? Let it come, then; I will meet it and defy it!' And as I so thought there rushed like a stream of fire over my whole soul; and I shook base Fear away from me forever. I was strong, of unknown strength; a spirit, almost a god. Ever from that time, the temper of my misery was changed: not Fear or whining Sorrow was it, but Indignation and grim fire-eyed Defiance.

Thus had the Everlasting No (das ewige Nein) pealed authoritatively through all the recesses of my Being, of my ME; and then was it that my whole ME stood up, in native God-created majesty and with emphasis recorded its Protest. Such a protest, the most important transaction in Life, may that same Indignation and Defiance, in a psychological point of view, be fitly called. The Everlasting No had said: 'Behold, thou art fatherless, outcast and the Universe is mine (the Devil's)'; to which my whole ME now made answer: '*I* am not thine, but Free, and forever hate thee!'

(Bk II, ch. 7)

If we wish to enter imaginatively into the world of an intellectual young man, born between (say) 1805 and 1820, we must try to understand the intense excitement he will have felt on first reading a passage like this. It appeared to cut through tedious philosophical disputes, to make anxieties, both intellectual and social, irrelevant. It appeared to reach out at one and the same time to the ultimate forces of the universe and to the deepest impulses in the human mind. Here was an answer.

Several points which were generally overlooked at the time became obvious later. The message was stirring, but it was vague. A later chapter of the book, it is true, was entitled 'The Everlasting Yea'. But this was just as vague and altogether less memorable. Carlyle was really setting a fashion which many later Victorians were to follow, of trying to use the language and emotional power of Christianity without accepting its doctrines. It would eventually become apparent that this was like trying to gather the fruit of a tree whose roots one had deliberately cut away. Meanwhile, the young responded to the deep earnestness of Carlyle, and they responded, too, to the fundamental idea embodied in the title *Sartor Resartus*. According to this, the fundamental verities of the universe were unchangeable, settled by Divine fiat for all eternity. These are represented in the figure by the unclothed body. The dress required by this body is the concepts, the language in which we try to speak of the eternal verities. This can and does change. The clothes wear out; and when this happens, there is a time of crisis and despair. For most people will try to pretend that the worn-out clothes are not really worn out. They will cling to what no longer has power to express the truth, and therefore no longer has power to save them. Hence the need for a new statement, a new set of clothes, a new batch of ideas, and, consequently, a new social order and a new way of living.

When this attractive idea is understood, it will be easy to see why Carlyle went on to write the history of the French Revolution. Published in 1837, *The French Revolution* is Carlyle's most important book, and it exercised a general philosophical influence which very few other historical works have attained. It was a detailed concrete illustration, backed with considerable learning, and an imaginative insight into character, and conducted with a moving eloquence, of the central idea of *Sartor Resartus*. It showed the old eighteenth-century order, in all its aspects, ecclesiastical, political, intellectual and social, irrevocably rejected by destiny, and the birth-pangs of a new civilization, full both of pain and hope. Carlyle's mind worked, like a poet's, primarily in images; and the master-images of *The French Revolution* are the volcano and the phoenix. A volcano is irresistible, and it comes at its appointed time, irrespective of all human efforts to prevent or delay it. So, for Carlyle, is the revolution. And what is it that is erupting? It is the people, the common people who, in the past, have been anonymous in history, have been sufferers rather than actors. Now, first in France, but later inevitably, everywhere, they will acquire power to make and overthrow monarchs and even, perhaps, to form the whole of society in their own image. This is Calvinism secularized. The vision is Calvinist in its sense of inevitability, which is at the same time a form of Divine Justice. The French Revolution is a judgment on a corrupt society, so that in one sense it is a punishment for collective sin. But it is an idea entirely foreign to Carlyle's thought that the Revolution could have been averted if aristocracies had been more generous or kings had been wiser. Sin and punishment are alike seen as inevitable. In true Calvinist fashion, Carlyle blames people for what they were inevitably destined to do.

But it is a secularized vision, because the Book of Revelation is no longer Scripture but History. In an earlier essay, Carlyle had stated this idea explicitly, calling history 'Universal Divine Scripture, whose "plenary inspiration" no man, out of Bedlam or in it, shall bring in question' ('On History Again,' *Fraser's Magazine*, No 41, 1833). Like many of Carlyle's ideas, this was a statement of great appeal in its stark simplicity, but essentially confusing in its wider implications. One knows who has won a game because there is a time limit. But in history there is no time limit. Did Cromwell 'win' and Charles I lose? Or did Charles I eventually triumph in the person of his son after Cromwell's death? Or did Cromwell win after all, because part of the change he effected in the constitution was permanent? Carlyle was later to compose three whole volumes of admiring comment on Cromwell's life and writings without seriously trying to answer these obvious questions.

More disturbing still, the plenary inspiration of history can carry the implication that success proves right. It is fair to say that in the sense Carlyle meant it the phrase 'Might is Right' was free from the taint of the worship of brutal power and vulgar success. He meant rather that the universe was so constituted that the right thing would be found to possess the most might, not that mere strength is the highest moral principle. But the idea, nevertheless, is a slippery one, capable of infinite degradation in the hands of millionaires and military dictators. Nor can Carlyle himself, especially in his later years, escape entirely free from the blame of unconsciously degrading it himself. The link of the idea with his assertion of the necessity of hero-worship is obvious. At first his conception of the hero included the hero of the realms of spirit and intellect. But he was always tempted to set up the simple strong man as admirable. He later wrote many volumes (1858–65) in praise of the tyrannical Frederick the Great; and as early as 1849 in the essay ominously entitled *The Nigger Question* he was asserting a fundamental distinction between master-races and slave-races.

This essay was written as a prelude to *Latter-Day Pamphlets* (1850), which mark a watershed of Carlyle's reputation. He had more than thirty years still to live, but his pre-eminence as sage and prophet never recovered from the damage inflicted by this sour and violent volume. After 1850 people came more and more to realize that Carlyle, for all his great literary gifts, was a negative prophet. His No was memorable, when his Yea was platitudinous or unintelligible, or even, in the treatment of some of his heroes, downright sycophantic. Carlyle in old age is the sad figure portrayed by Froude, who records:

'They call me a great man now', Carlyle said to me a few days before he died, 'but not one believes what I have told them.'
(*Thomas Carlyle*, new edn, 1896, vol II, p 495)

Younger than Carlyle by six years, Newman (like Mill) was one of the few thinkers of his generation powerful enough in mind to ignore the tidal pull of Carlyle's rhetoric. He was like him in that his fundamental assumptions were intuitive so that he, too, may be seen as one who developed the interior affirmations of the earlier Romantic writers. But he was like Carlyle in little else. Above all, he had the power that Carlyle lacked of bringing his subtle intelligence to bear upon his intuitions. Newman makes assumptions, but he is always able to state clearly exactly how much he is assuming. A deeply emotional temperament is checked and guided not only by deep learning but by a philosophical rigour of argument, in which Mill was his only peer among the thinkers of that age.

When in 1833 Newman began with his friends to compose the *Tracts* mentioned earlier, his primary assumptions were three; and of these two were to remain unchanged throughout his life, and one, under a long bombardment of reasoning and experience, was to change, with momentous consequences both for himself and for the future of the Christian churches in this country. The first assumption, which never wavered from the time of his Calvinist conversion at the age of fifteen, he described in his *Apologia* (1864) thus:

Isolating me from the objects which surrounded me, . . . confirming me in my mistrust of material phenomena, and making me rest in the thought of two and two only absolute and luminously self-evident beings, myself and my Creator . . .

(ch. 1)

In the fifth chapter he develops the idea thus:

Starting then with the being of a God, (which, as I have said, is as certain to me as the certainty of my own existence, though when I try to put the grounds of that certainty into logical shape I find a difficulty in doing so in mood and figure to my satisfaction,) I look out of myself into the world of men, and there I see a sight which fills me with unspeakable distress. The world seems simply to give the lie to that great truth, of which my whole being is so full; and the effect upon me is, in consequence, as a matter of necessity, as if it denied that I am in existence myself. If I looked into a mirror and did not see my face, I should have the sort of feeling which actually comes upon me, when I look into this living busy world, and see no reflexion of its Creator.

This kind of instinctive, primary devotion to religious causes is rare, and its association with the finest intellectual gifts is rarer still. Its association with the best fruits of literary culture is almost unique. (It is worth recalling that Matthew Arnold, whose religious position had nothing in common with Newman's, thought of him all his life as the epitome of the civilized intellect of Oxford.) All this makes it very difficult to do justice to Newman.

Newman's second assumption in 1833 was that the nature of this God in Whom he could not help believing was revealed in Christianity, and this was a religion both institutional and dogmatic. The mere sentiment of religion he calls 'a dream and a mockery'. This assumption also never changed. The third assumption, which did change, was that the proper home of this Catholic tradition and the proper seat of authority was to be found in the Church of England.

There is no space here to recount the gradual and painful stages of this change (see Newman, *Apologia pro Vita Sua*, 1864). But it is important to notice that it was more a change in the judgment of facts than in principles. Newman always held that the Catholic Church had authority because it was founded by Christ. The question was where to find the living voice of that authority in the nineteenth century. In this sense his original commitment to the Church of England, deep and fervent though it was, was conditional. Friends and allies like Keble, whose commitment was unconditional, found it hard to understand this and could be forgiven if, when he left the Church of England in 1845, they were unable to perceive the inner consistency of Newman's thought.

It is not easy for us to recapture the excitement or to feel the inherent importance of Newman's secession. Disraeli a quarter of a century later called his loss a blow from which the Church was still reeling. To understand this one needs to enter into the general unquestioning assumption of all parties in England that Protestantism in some form or other was the best of all religions and that England was clearly the best of all countries. The loss of Newman struck a triple blow. It was a blow at the intellectual superiority of Protestantism, for no one could doubt that Newman's was one of the finest and most theologically instructed of contemporary minds. It was a blow at the moral superiority of Protestantism. (Here, admittedly, Kingsley tried to draw a red-herring about Newman's sincerity across the path of evidence, but John Bull, however staunchly Protestant himself, was able, at least after the publication of the *Apologia*, to see that Kingsley was talking nonsense.) For Newman's selfless devotion to the cause of truth as he understood it did not admit of doubt. It was a blow at English insularity. It prepared the way for a new generation of intellectuals, whether Roman Catholic or High Anglican or agnostic, who were consciously European in their outlook, and, in some cases, like F. W. Faber, provocatively ultramontane and Italianate. A blow at insularity was thus a blow at what Arnold was later to call the philistinism of a great commercial country. The rapid growth of serious and discriminating interest in the arts bearing fruit eventually in such works as Pater's *The Renaissance* (1873) and J. A. Symonds's *History of the Italian Renaissance* (1875–86) can be traced in part to Newman's adhesion to a foreign ecclesiastical power.

Newman's literary power is best seen in the *Apologia*. The subtle complexity of his intelligence is best seen in *The Development of Christian Doctrine* (1845), which he wrote just before and published just after his reception into the Roman Church. It is a difficult book both in its material and its argument; great learning in early Christian history would be needed to follow every point. But it contains at its core an idea that can be expressed very simply. It is that an institution either grows or dies, and so, in the case of a dogmatic institution like a Church, the doctrines, too, must either grow or wither. Newman introduced a new term into the old debate between unchanging revealed doctrine and progressive ideological change according to the needs of the moment. As we have seen, Newman never doubted that religion involved dogma. By 'development' he did not mean change in the sense of abandoning the old in favour of the new; to hold that the original revelation could become outmoded was really to say that it had not been a revelation at all. 'Development' for Newman meant the gradual understanding of all the implications and corollaries of a fundamental principle. But he stressed that this process could involve very great changes in the appearance of things just as a root or seed does not *look* in the least like the full-grown tree or flower.

The importance of this idea for the future of Catholic theology was considerable. Its importance in general Victorian intellectual history was great, too. But it will be easier for us to see what it was when we have considered some of the alternative modes of thought. Meanwhile, we may briefly mention two other works of Newman. *The Idea of a University* (1852) shows Newman at his nearest point to Arnold. Indeed, *Culture and Anarchy* might be described as a satirical study of the social obstacles to the ideal of harmonious perfection of the intellect through study that Newman had proposed. *The Grammar of Assent* (1870), his most purely philosophical work, reveals his scepticism about abstract logic. He maintained that any study of the working of intellect must lean as much towards psychology as towards mathematics. The book is an enquiry into the way men actually reason and arrive at conclusions, and discovers profound differences between this and the arguments presented in text-books of logic. It is an extended comment on his saying on another occasion that reason is only the map of the mind's progress.

It is in this concreteness of approach that Newman differs most strongly from the one man in his generation who was his all-round intellectual, though not literary, equal. John Stuart Mill was the heir of an older tradition, anterior to the heritage of the Romantic poets of which we have been speaking. His father, James Mill, was the disciple and interpreter of Bentham, holding approximately the same relation to him in the eyes of the public as T. H. Huxley was later to have to Darwin. J. S. Mill, with his precocious intellectual powers, trained or overtrained by the extraordinary educational process later described in his autobiography, was the natural heir of the Benthamite tradition, and had already, before he came of age in 1827, a large share in the management of the new Benthamite organ, the *Westminster Review*. Mill has his niche in the history of philosophy as a technical discipline, especially through his *Logic* (1843), but his wider importance for us lies in his prolonged inner debate about the Utilitarian tradition in which he was bred, and in the fascinating, though fragmentary, record of the inner struggle that appeared in his published work. The Utilitarians were no exceptions to the general rule that men of the early nineteenth century were seeking for fundamental principles and origins to justify their practice. But they went markedly against the current in believing that a simple formula could cover every moral case. The celebrated principle of 'the greatest happiness of the greatest number', or felicific calculus, was the sole guiding principle of all their thought on morals, on politics, law and on administration.

Now, of course, adhering to a simple principle does not imply the possession of a simple mind or the use of simple methods of argument. Characteristically, the early Utilitarians were men of learning and heavy intellectuals, as a glance at the pages of the *Westminster Review* (to say nothing of Mill's account of his early study of Greek) will easily show. But the gulf between them and learned men of other schools, like Coleridge and Carlyle, was unbridgeable. Or was it? For one might say that the younger Mill spent his whole life trying to prove that it could be bridged.

It is obvious that the utilitarian principle if applied with rigour abolishes totally all right of appeal to instinct and tradition. The powerful conservative forces tapped by Burke and Coleridge had their origin in two ideas, which might be imprecise in their for-mulation, but which possessed a deep appeal to the feelings – the idea that society is like an organism or living body, not like a machine, and the idea that the human heart is a shrine of incomprehensible mysteries. Bentham and James Mill could see nothing in ideas of this kind but intellectual muddle and the self-interested special pleading of an aristocratic class and their intellectual satellites. One may say that the great debate between Bentham and James Mill on one side and Burke, Coleridge and Wordsworth on the other continued long after they were all dead, and indeed, it continues in some form to this day. It was (and is) a debate on which people take sides, as a rule, with a primary emotional commitment. J. S. Mill is almost alone in being deeply influenced by both sides.

He could not help being influenced by such a father; and though his personality was really very different from his father's, there are certain aspects of the father's thought that persist to the end in the writings of the son. There is a revealing similarity of prose-style. In each there is a kind of abstract precision. Their words are never formally unclear in their meaning, but they are often curiously remote from experience. Thus James Mill's *History of India* (1818) never gives any impression of what India looks like, feels like, smells like. It gives a very clear impression of the organization of the British administration. Similarly the son's most celebrated work, *On Liberty* (1859), masses the theoretical arguments for and against the liberty of the subject with consummate lucidity, but never gives any sign that the author felt deeply the experience of choosing, or had much curiosity about what Hopkins was later to call 'the selfless self or self' where fundamental choices are made.

For a full understanding of Mill the posthumous *Autobiography* (1873) is the key book, and any reader who came to it after reading all Mill's other works, as some of its first readers must have done, will experience a great surprise, a surprise which may help in the end to a salutary reinterpretation of what had gone before. He reveals that in 1826 he underwent a period of acute depression after asking himself whether, if all the utilitarian aims were realized, this achievement would be enough to make him happy. He continues:

An irrepressible self-consciousness distinctly answered, 'No!' At this my heart sank within me: the whole foundation on which my life was constructed fell down. All my happiness was to have been found in the continual pursuit of this end. The end had ceased to charm, and how could there ever again be any interest in the means? I seemed to have nothing left to live for.

(Autobiography, ch. 5)

A page or two later he adds the telling comment: 'To know that a feeling would make me happy if I had it, did not give me the feeling.'

He had no one to confide in, and eventually it was the reading of Wordsworth that initiated his recovery. Though Mill was much too modest to assume that his own case was of general importance, he came to see that he had accidentally stumbled at a very early age upon the central dilemma of Utilitarianism and on one of the key problems of the age. What is the use of a system that would work very well for certain imaginary creatures in human form, but will not work for men as they are? Mill spent his life worrying at this question. His deep reverence for his father, coupled with his own intellectual character, loving clearness and suspicions of mystery, forbade him ever to renounce Utilitarianism. Instead he pondered upon it, attempted to do what in strict logic was perhaps impossible, to make a synthesis of his father's system and others, even the most unlikely ally of all for a Utilitarian:

In the golden rule of Jesus of Nazareth, we read the complete spirit of the ethics of utility. To do as you would be done by, and to love your neighbour as yourself, constitute the ideal perfection of utilitarian morality.

(*Utilitarianism*, 1853, ch. 2, sec. 18)

We can only endorse the conclusion of one of Mill's most acute critics, Professor Plamenatz, who says, 'There is not much left of Benthamite Utilitarianism when Mill has completed his defence of it' (*The English Utilitarians*, 2nd edn, 1958, p 144).

To a large extent, as this last judgment will suggest, Mill was an unconscious rebel against his father's authority. His father regarded the passionate and sentimental relations between the sexes with contempt; the son believed his wife to possess superhuman gifts and virtues. The father had the usual Utilitarian distaste for art; the son's essay on poetry shows a romantic taste and treats poetry as a private voice of pure feeling, overheard by the reader rather than publicly presented by the poet (*Thoughts on Poetry*, 1833; revised 1859).

But in calling his rebellion unconscious I am far from implying a charge of timidity against Mill. There was one occasion when his lucid mind (for confusions in Mill's thought always have an emotional, never an intellectual cause) actively confronted the utilitarian dilemma. In his articles on Bentham and Coleridge Mill with great acuteness discerned the main lines of the future conflict of ideas. Bentham for him represents the practical effectiveness and the limitations of the purely rational mind. He is the 'great questioner of things established'. Coleridge represents the unconscious reserves of life hidden in traditions, institutions and feelings, of which the rational defence is either difficult or impossible. Mill is aware of his almost uniquely cross-bench position when he writes:

The limited philosophical public of this country is as yet too exclusively divided between those to whom Coleridge and the views which he promulgated or defended are everything, and those to whom they are nothing.
(*Mill on Bentham and Coleridge*, ed. F. R. Leavis, 1950, p 103)

Mill's voice in this essay is the most temperate in a debate that was not marked on the whole by temperance. Reading the great early Victorian writers, especially Carlyle, Dickens and Ruskin, one could derive the impression that Utilitarianism was a dead horse that everybody inexplicably insisted on flogging. Linked with Utilitarianism in their condemnations was a doctrine of great practical importance, 'political economy' or the economics of the great trading class. To some extent the connection was fortuitous. It is true that Mill wrote a book called *The Principles of Political Economy*. It is also true that, as with Utilitarianism, but more obviously, Mill eventually became a questioner, even a critic of the pure milk of Adam Smith's doctrine. But the loose general association between Utilitarianism and political economy aroused a new kind of public interest, and stirred into an angry controversial posture men like Dickens who would have allowed an abstract philosophical discussion to pass them by. *Hard Times* is not a fair book; but its critique of Utilitarian ethics and Manchester business theories is brilliant and memorable. Its fundamental assumption is the same as that which Mill, speaking in a much quieter tone, had found in Coleridge, that there is a non-rational element in human nature which makers of systems ignore at their peril. It is for this that the dying Mrs Gradgrind feebly gropes, as she takes upon her 'the dread solemnity of the sages and patriarchs' (*Hard Times*, Bk II, ch. 9)

But the horse that Dickens and others were flogging was dead only in a rather specialized intellectual sense. The debate was indeed one-sided, for Mill, whose loyalties, as we have seen, were ambiguous, was the only man of high intellectual stature who carried forward into the mid-Victorian period the tradition of Bentham and the early *Westminster Review*. But the practical man of the world does not worry about intellectual consistency so long as he is making a profit. The great political triumph of the Manchester School came in 1846 with the repeal of the Corn Laws, and the next twenty-five years were years of triumphant supremacy for the English businessman in the markets of the world. What did a commercial nation that had coal and iron in plenty, that led the world in the development of railways, need to worry about the grumbles of intellectuals or the satire of a great popular novelist? The first Utilitarians, as we have said, had been scholars and thinkers, but their system also had great advantage for people who were nothing of the kind. By shifting the basic Utilitarian principle a little, and using profit, not happiness, as the criterion (and does not profit make businessmen happy?), these people were able to pursue their ruthless commercial aims in the conviction that they had an unshakeable basis of moral and economic theory on which to build. Most of them were too unintellectual, and all of them were too busy to answer Dickens or Ruskin. Perhaps Arnold's *Culture and Anarchy* is the best place to look for an impression of this oddly uneven debate as it appeared at the time. For Arnold gives us a sketch of these shadowy opponents who were so powerful in their day, even if it is hardly a fair one. But to see how far the tendency to treat human nature as a laboratory-compound could go, one should glance through the works of Herbert Spencer with their ominous titles like *Social Statics*. Spencer is unreadable today, but his immense prestige in his time, which extended as far as Russia, is a clear proof that complete ignorance of human nature will not necessarily prevent a man from becoming an acknowledged expert upon it. It is a reminder, too, that Carlyle, Dickens and Ruskin were not tilting at windmills.

In a time of rapid change thinking men look to the past for help in understanding the present. Some of the fundamental controversies of the age were conducted in the form of arguments about the past. The French Revolution, the Glorious Revolution, the Civil War, the Reformation all played their part; Carlyle, Macaulay, Froude and others found very different lessons in these great events. But one thing they had in common. All the time they wrote about history, they were really arguing about the nineteenth century, and so their more perceptive readers understood them.

The French Revolution was the nearest and the most insistent of these great historical events. Everyone read Carlyle's great book, and many were stirred by it, but its central message was ambiguous. Did it really say that revolution was inevitable, because the world, led by France, was moving into a new democratic phase, in which monarchies and aristocracies must either agree to abdicate or else endure to be deposed by force? Or did it say that the French

Revolution was due to the inflexible selfishness of the French ruling classes so that the ruling powers in England could learn by the example and survive? Though terrible forebodings filled the minds of many in the 1840s, most people cautiously inclined to the second view. In this they were assisted, no doubt, by that hereditary feeling of superiority to the French in political and military affairs, which Tennyson so perfectly represented when he spoke of 'the red fool-fury of the Seine' and of freedom in England 'slowly broadening down'. There was a feeling expressed in Disraeli's *Coningsby* and *Sybil* that the new forces of organized labour were waiting for leadership from the educated and preferably from the aristocratic class. The comparative social peacefulness and increasing prosperity of the years from 1850 to 1890, coupled with the thoroughly ducal composition of the Cabinets of Disraeli and Gladstone as late as the seventies and eighties, showed that this was not an illusion. Dickens, who had read Carlyle with attention, helped to implant in all classes a horror of mob-law by the terrible power of the crowd scenes in *Barnaby Rudge* and *A Tale of Two Cities* and a suspicion of demagogic trade union leaders by his portrayal of the insincere Slackbridge in *Hard Times*. But it is easy to forget that at least until 1850 the thought of revolution was in the air, and that Chartism seemed a much more formidable phenomenon to the first readers of Carlyle's essay upon it than it was eventually to prove.

This apparent digression is necessary because the more celebrated doctrine of progress, and the accompanying evolutionary ideas, are misunderstood if they are imagined as having nothing to struggle against. Those who accepted them were just as often worried men snatching at comfort as they were the smug, comfortable men of later caricature. For Macaulay, the most coherent and persuasive of all preachers of progress, the French Revolution was something that had to be explained away as not relevant to England. Macaulay called in 1688 to redress the balance which Carlyle had disturbed with his terrible account of 1789, and worse of 1793.

The germ of the argument Macaulay was to present with such learned and lucid ease in his *History* of the reigns of James II and William III (1849–61) is to be found in his long review of Hallam's *History of England* published in September 1828. He had already thoroughly absorbed the Whig habit, which was so useful in calming an inflamed public opinion in 1832 and after, of presenting moderate, even conservative, views in language that sounds revolutionary. Thus he calls Strafford 'the lost archangel, the Satan of the apostasy', but the accusation against him is that he had formed a design against 'the fundamental laws of England'. A society that has fundamental laws, which it is impious to question, and which remain unchanged in the nineteenth century as in the seventeenth, must be in many respects a conservative society; and Macaulay's idea of progress is conservative in the sense that nothing is ever lost and no real change of direction in the line or aims of advance is ever envisaged. He is fond of the image of the child and the grown man for the early and later phases of a society's development. The vigour of his denunciation of democracy can still surprise those who have not grasped the inherently conservative character of Whiggism and have not measured the power and insistence of the fears that Carlyle had started by speaking of a new democratic age inaugurated by a blood-bath in France.

When Macaulay wrote his review of Hallam, and to some lesser extent still when he wrote his *History*, the accepted view of seventeenth-century history was that given by the history of David Hume. Hume had made a sharp distinction between the issues at stake in 1641 and the issues of 1688. In 1641, Hume, with judicious deliberation but in the end without any doubt, had sided with the Royalists, and his portrait of Charles I is notably sympathetic. But he treated the revolution of 1688 as an inevitable reaction to the reckless and unconstitutional actions of James II. Macaulay's aim was to break the traditional authority of Hume's antithesis and to represent that there had been a continuing inheritance of progressive and reactionary parties in the state from the Civil War down to the constitutional conflicts of 1832. Cromwell, the Whigs of the Exclusion Crisis in the time of Charles II, Charles James Fox and Lord John Russell are a strange team to carry the badge of uniformity, but Macaulay insists that they do so, for the strongest feature of his intellectual nature was a dislike of exceptions and anomalies. The great achievement of his *History*, which made it so popular in its time and makes it so readable today, is that, with its mass of detail and its genuine depth of learning, it still contrives to give an impression of simplicity. All the detail, in the end, is shown to be related to two great unchanging tendencies, the reactionary and the progressive, and these great tendencies, in turn, are for ever linked to the two great parties in the state, Tory and Whig. And before the terms were invented, the realities they describe were already at work in the Civil War struggle.

Bagehot, his most acute contemporary critic, complained of Macaulay's 'inexperiencing nature' and pointed out that his original ideas on Indian education had not been altered in the slightest degree as a result of visiting India (*Collected Works*, ed. N. St John Stevas, vol I, p 399). He imagined him saying that 'Hampden was preparing for the occasion in which I had a part' and wryly noted that he treated existing men as 'painful prerequisites of great-grandchildren.' All these charges, with a little allowance for the rights of witty exaggeration, are true, but Bagehot was the first to say that they did not dispose of Macaulay. The fallacies in Macaulay (I think we must agree that the Whig view of history contains fallacies) were fallacies that a large part of his audience would have accepted without him. It is very human to treat the past as a mere introduction to the present, for how can any time in which *I* was not alive be as interesting to me as the time in which I am? It is natural for the citizens of a country whose trade and warships circle the globe to suppose that they must be on the right lines and that future development must only be an increase in the scale of the benefits already attained. Macaulay endowed these natural, though quite fallacious, assumptions with a civilized pedigree. Read with care, the celebrated third chapter of the *History*, with its prolonged one-sided comparison of the England of 1685 to the England of his own day, does not appear, as it is often said to be, a materialistic performance. Macaulay is just as zealous for progress in the 'useless' pursuits of intellectual culture as he is for the improvement of machines. But he is, admittedly, much less successful in demonstrating that the first must always be linked to the second. For the student of the period the final thought on Macaulay may be that in an age of cloudy prophetic writings and works of obscure and troubled genius it is refreshing to encounter a mighty simplifier, whose meaning is never for a moment in doubt.

Turning to Macaulay's great successor in the art of historical narrative, J. A. Froude, one is reminded to praise also Macaulay's unfailing geniality of tone. Macaulay is often sweeping, and sometimes unfair, but he is never ungenerous. Froude's history of the sixty years from the fall of Wolsey to the Spanish Armada (1856–70) is a brilliant work, marred by an ungenerous worship of the strong triumphing over the weak. He tried to do for Henry VIII what Carlyle had done for Cromwell and he becomes ludicrous in an excess of barrister's zeal. To picture Henry, in his fifth marriage, as the innocent, pathetic victim of that designing harridan Catherine Howard and to represent the death penalty upon her almost as an act of lenity is to overstrain all ordinary credulity. Nevertheless, many of Macaulay's merits are recaptured. There is an extraordinary lucidity, an extraordinary power of arrangement in narrative form; and once again, the lesson Froude wished his readers to learn was a contemporary lesson. It was the same lesson that he tried to enforce in his Irish eighteenth-century history (1872–4). Froude offers a heady mixture of Carlylean hero-worship, English nationalism veering into racialism, and a kind of uncompromising secular Protestantism. I say secular Protestantism because it is not religious truth that is Froude's real concern. He believes that the Protestant system of belief leads on the whole to the growth of the civic virtues of veracity, courage and initiative, and that the Catholic system militates against these. Alternatively, he believes that Celts and Latins are naturally cowards, deceivers and sycophants, and that their traditional adherence to the Catholic system is an apt illustration of these congenital inferiorities. To a nation about to acquire, or already acquiring, great new tracts of land in many parts of the world, and determined to harden its conscience about its treatment of the Irish people, this reading of history had attractions.

Macaulay was a Whig and Froude was a Tory, but to a public taking its history in broad narrative doses and applying its lessons with the uncritical enthusiasm of the layman, both appeared to be saying similar things about the present and the future – that the new, the stronger, the more assertive nation or idea was also for that reason the better. The strength of this current of thought needs to be remembered in assessing the public reaction to the great scientific developments of the day.

Darwin was a very great man, whose achievements seem at least as important today as they did in his own time; as a general intellectual influence he has often been taken out of context, misunderstood or overestimated. The great scientific changes for which he may always stand as a representative had begun before the close of the eighteenth century, and it was geology that opened the way to the new view of the physical development of animals and men. Sir Charles Lyell in his *Principles of Geology* (1830–3) had drawn together a great mass of evidence for the very gradual development of the existing formation of the geological strata in the earth's crust and had drawn attention to the changing pattern of animal fossils in the different strata and the presence of the fossils of extinct animals in the lower strata. It gradually became apparent that the earth was vastly older than had been assumed in previous centuries, and that the fossil evidence suggested that man was a comparatively recent arrival upon the earth (See S. Toulmin and J. Goodchild, *The Discovery of Time*, 1965). Through the 1830s and

1840s these matters did not excite the general public interest that they were to claim later, but a few people, among whom Tennyson is notable for us, brooded long and deeply upon them. The sensitive mind was likely to receive two main impressions from the process. The first was that things became less solid, because they were set against a time-scale indefinitely increased. In past centuries people thought of a river as flowing and a tree as still; they thought of spring as transient but of the orderly progression of the seasons as unchangeable. Now they were forced to ask whether all material things were not transient, a point perfectly expressed in Tennyson's line 'The hills are shadows and they flow' (*In Memoriam*, CXXIII). The second impression, equally important, had to wait longer for its full impact. A shadowy sense of direction was given to non-human processes, astronomical or geological. Part of the importance of Darwin was that he gave stronger ground for extending this second impression to the animal world also. He first, after a quarter of a century of patient research, in *The Origin of Species* disposed of many of the stubborn scientific difficulties in supposing that one species could be descended physically from another. It has become fashionable for later writers, especially the authors of text-books, with their precious gift of hindsight, to ascribe all these difficulties to prejudice, and especially to a narrow reading of the book of *Genesis*. This is grossly unhistorical, as can easily be seen by a glance at two points (out of many that might be given.) The first is that Newman welcomed the *Origin* because of its interesting analogy with his own idea of development in intellectual and spiritual matters. The second is that Darwin himself was to the end of his life worried by certain apparent discrepancies and obvious scientific difficulties. The most obstinate of these was that raised by Lord Kelvin about the time required for Darwin's processes of mutation of types. This appeared to be much greater than Kelvin's perfectly lucid calculation of the age of the earth derived from the time of cooling could possibly allow. Neither Darwin nor Kelvin could guess that later scientists would be able to suggest a much greater age for the earth, because they would discover that the interior of the earth could generate its own heat and thus retard the cooling process. Just as old Test cricketers, sitting in the press-box, never miss a slip-catch, later commentators are apt to think they would easily have solved difficulties insoluble at the time. But though unable to meet all reasonable objections, Darwin was convinced that the weight of evidence was on his side. His *Descent of Man* (1871) set out in full the arguments in favour of believing that men were physically descended from more primitive animal ancestors, though part of its argument, once again, had been anticipated by Lyell in *The Antiquity of Man* (1863).

The effects of all this on the general current of thought were oblique and variable. No deductions of a strictly philosophical kind could be made, but habits of thought and modes of feeling were deeply influenced. For some the increase in the time-span of the imagined past intensified that sense of loneliness in the universe, which is one of the most disturbing sensations of civilized man. The most sensitive literary expression of this idea is to be found in the works of Thomas Hardy. Others used evolutionary ideas to provide a kind of cosmic backing to Macaulay's Whiggish argument, so on this side the result was a strengthening of the Broad Church school of liberal theologians of whom A. P. Stanley was the most acute and Benjamin Jowett, because of his immense educational influence, the most celebrated. The volume *Essays and Reviews* (1860), to which Jowett contributed an article on the interpretation of scripture, and Frederick Temple, later Archbishop of Canterbury, an article entitled 'The Education of the World', may be taken as representative of the strong but ill-defined impact of science on this school of religious thought. The title of Temple's article is especially revealing, comprehending in one large gesture progress à la Macaulay, the traditional religious idea of the Hebrew *preparatio evangelica* and a vague bow to immense aeons of pre-historic time in which the Divine purpose may have been at work in ways newly suggested by the scientists. There were others, though the most notable of them, Nietzsche, is outside the scope of this essay, who saw Darwinian evolution as a kind of delayed death-certificate for humanity as we know it, which would become, upon the arrival of the pre-destined new race, an anachronism, like the extinct creature in the lower fossil strata.

One thinker is worth a more special mention here, because, unlike the others, he found that the whole course of his intellectual life was changed and then directed anew by Darwin's discoveries. T. H. Huxley had all the gifts required for the more serious kind of popularization. He was pugnacious, lucid and well-informed. He scored some notable controversial successes against men of more powerful mind than his own, including Gladstone, when the latter ventured as amateurs into territory where Huxley was a professional. But more interesting than all this today is the impact of Darwinism on his own meditations about the world. This is best seen in the remarkable Romanes lecture delivered at Oxford in

1893 under the title *Evolution and Ethics*. In this lecture he announced the conclusion he had reached after more than thirty years of meditation on Darwin's theory and its consequences. It was simple, forceful and gloomy. He said that the evolutionary process, which must now be considered an unquestionable fact of nature, was unalterably opposed to the improvement of human civilization and even to the very existence of our moral institutions; but instead of saying, as others were saying, that we must accommodate our petty human ideas to the great cosmic forces revealed by the scientists, he said that we must fight the evolutionary process with all our strength in order to remain human at all. The more that mighty cosmic forces decreed that the weakest must go to the wall, the more we must tend with loving care our feeble grandmother or our crippled, sickly child.

Huxley's is not the last word on evolution and ethics, though his is the last notable voice raised within our period, but his lecture brings home forcibly a point of the highest importance that is very often overlooked. It is that Darwin's work does not for general human, philosophical purposes point in any direction at all. Once removed from the strictly zoological sphere and allowed to have free influence over thought and behaviour, Darwin's leading ideas become infinitely plastic. The highest common factor of what intelligent late Victorians found in Darwin is precisely nothing. Indeed, the testimony of the rocks and fossils formed thousands or millions of years ago was in this respect very like the testimony of the Civil War or the Middle Ages. Many a serious and learned seeker only found after careful study that his deepest instincts and convictions about life were clearly confirmed.

Yet the Victorian interest in the Middle Ages was of deeper significance than the interest in the Civil War and the Glorious Revolution. The latter were studied to derive certain contemporary lessons and to prove particular points. There was scarcely a serious wish to revive seventeenth-century civilization. With the Middle Ages it was different. The point is most easily seen in the imaginative writers. The seventeenth century, by common consent a rich and various contributor to our literary heritage, had practically no influence on the best writers (it was left to the poets of this century to use and adapt the poetic treasures left by Donne and Dryden), but medieval influence in various forms, devout, sociopolitical, decorative and erotic, is obvious in authors as different as Tennyson, Ruskin and Rossetti, while the influence on architecture and painting is stronger still.

An important source-book for various kinds of medieval influence is Pugin's *Contrasts* (1836) in which an architectural argument is cleverly woven with religious and social ones to show the superiority of medieval to modern culture, and especially to all classical or 'pagan' revivals in the modern world. But Pugin was no more able than Darwin to control the fortunes in the world of the ideas he had presented. Pugin saw the Middle Ages as tense, heroic and radically Christian and Catholic. Rossetti, partly following Keats, saw them as dreamy, langorous and deliciously unreal. Pugin, certainly, conceived himself to be making a real historical statement. So, on the whole, did Ruskin, while Tennyson was more concerned with finding a medieval image of the nineteenth-century dilemmas, and Rossetti cared little either for historical accuracy or for contemporary society. Nevertheless, all these and indeed all the different varieties of medievalizer had one very important thing in common. They all felt that the nature of the Victorian intellectual and social scene was such that the imagination could only grasp it obliquely. That is a point of prime importance about the society they lived in; and it is hasty to say that they must have been mistaken, and unfair to dismiss them all as escapists. The medieval cult, in all its forms, witnesses to the strain of living and thinking in a society where facts, theories and principles must have seemed to many sensitive people like an unintelligible whirl of atoms.

The most striking case of medieval interests leading to a prophetic reappraisal of, and attack on, Victorian society is that of Ruskin. It is impossible here to do justice to the complexities of his long career, which is apt to seem even longer than it was because of the variety of his interests, and intensity of his feelings, and the long despair of his final years. His early works are specialist studies in art criticism, and need not concern us here. His later works are tangled and obscure and darkened by mental instability, though he was incapable at any time of writing anything that was not obviously the work of an exceptional man. It was his middle period, especially the works of the 1860s, that made the most valuable contribution to the Victorian intellectual scene. *Unto This Last* (1860) was the first distinguished work containing an attack conceived in analytical and theoretical terms upon the economics of the Manchester school. The title, drawn from the parable of the labourers in the vineyard, corresponds exactly to the intention, to show the gulf between Christianity and *laissez-faire* economics. Ruskin solemnly accused the commercial classes of having set up a doctrine systematically opposed to the first principles of their professed religion. The history of the publication neatly illustrated the point. The *Cornhill Magazine* had just begun under Thackeray's editorship, and it combined great popularity with serious interest in ideas and in the arts. After three of Ruskin's essays had appeared the outcry against them became in Ruskin's own words 'too strong for any editor to endure', and the series had to be cut short. Had Ruskin, or anyone else, written attacks on the established religion of England, couched in the same decent and serious language as *Unto This Last*, the outcry would not have been strong enough to compel a friendly editor to such an extreme step. Ruskin's point was made. The Manchester doctrines were, in some sense, *more sacred* in the mind of the public than their professed religious beliefs.

Munera Pulveris (1863) is a fuller and perhaps more satisfactory statement of Ruskin's profound sense of the living inter-relation of religion, art, morality and economics. Ruskin was free from one of the chief difficulties felt by others in attacking *laissez-faire* capitalism. Its claim always was that it was on the side of freedom. The words 'Free Trade' had acquired, especially since the 1840s and the heroic days of the Corn Law debates, a special majesty of their own. Many people must have felt that the phrase was now consecrated as part of the tradition of *Magna Carta* and the precious personal rights of the citizen. But Ruskin had no difficulty about resisting this (rather specious) association, because he always believed it was more important to be right than to be free. He rejected altogether the idea that what the majority wants must be best, and he even went so far, in the fifth section of *Munera Pulveris*, as to compare an ill-informed democracy to a mass of beetles in Switzerland who tried to fly over a lake and all perished because they miscalculated the distance. His aim is always that the wisest and best should lead the weak and foolish. His radicalism had no trace of liberalism. He wanted the poor to have prosperity rather than the vote. Seen from this point of view, free trade becomes only the right of the rich and cunning to deceive the poor into spending what little money they have on shoddy goods. If one thinks of the poor man as a worker rather than as a consumer, the free-trade ethos comes in for an equally severe attack. To maintain his dignity a man needs to be a craftsman. (This is the original point of contact between Ruskin's original artistic interests and his social and economic ones.) The factory hand is not a craftsman, and his employer does not wish him to be one.

Ruskin replaces the current doctrine of freedom with a doctrine of society. Responsibility is mutual. The upper classes of England

and France are responsible for the shocking crimes perpetuated in the streets of the new urban societies, though nearly all of them would, as individuals, be incapable of taking part in them. In this way Ruskin opens the door to a general corporate choice exercised by the state in many activities (like town planning) where most of his contemporaries believed that no general policy was desirable.

A great part of the difficulty many people have in understanding Ruskin springs from this union of radical social doctrine with a rigid paternalism. (Perhaps the most extreme case of the latter is to be found in *Time and Tide* (1867), where he actually recommends that the right to marry should not be acquired simply by coming of age, but by the completion of a term of satisfactory service to the community.) We are conditioned by the state of affairs we know today to assume that a man who thinks in this way will be on the political right. Ruskin's thought shows that there is no necessary reason for such an assumption. When we see this we shall begin to understand how it was the man, who always claimed to be a high Tory of the old school, was execrated as a socialist at a time when this was generally felt to be an ugly word.

Ruskin typifies, sometimes in exaggerated form, many of the characteristics of the leading men of the age. Like Carlyle, Mill, Gladstone and so many more, he is, above all, a crusader and a deeply emotional man whose distinguished intellectual powers could never operate in a cool, rational spirit. Like them, too, he possessed a versatility and a breadth of learning which is simply astonishing to our own age. In the end the most stimulating thing about the Victorian intellectual scene is this: a great debate, intelligent and passionate, was conducted by brave men who neither despised the public, nor pandered to its lowest instincts.

2

FAITH AND DOUBT IN THE VICTORIAN AGE

A. O. J. Cockshut

It must seem strange to us now that the extremely moderate and in some ways conservative measure, the Reform Act of 1832, should have set so many alarm bells ringing. Yet those who saw in it a symbolic turning-point (the Utilitarians, Latitudinarians, High Churchmen) were not deceived. What was being signalled at that time later history abundantly confirmed: the end of the Anglican monopoly of power, influence and access to higher education, and the beginning of the lay 'liberal' state in which we live today. (I put the word 'liberal' in inverted commas because it seems to me that a state without principles and convictions is just as likely to be obscurantist and oppressive, indeed illiberal, as its predecessor.) If we want a convincing literary image of the change, we cannot do better than turn to *Felix Holt* (1866), which is set in the time of Reform Bill controversy. Here Mr Lyon, the Independent minister, challenges the Anglican incumbent to a public debate about Church establishment and other controverted issues. Eventually the Anglican, who is not used to arguing about convictions that have become second nature through a lifetime of family connections with the landed interest and a traditional rural order, fails to attend the debate and leaves the champing Independent disappointed at being denied his opportunity to deploy all his treasured arguments, but still master of the field. These things, as George Eliot might, but on this occasion did not, say, are a parable.

Catholic Emancipation (1829) was already a fact. It would be a whole generation more before the ancient universities ceased to be Anglican corporations; and it was not till 1911 that George V refused to insult millions of his subjects by taking the offensive anti-Catholic Coronation oath. Bradlaugh's claim to affirm as a member of the House of Commons (without professing faith in God) was nearly fifty years away. Change in England is often slow, but extraordinarily complete; the more perceptive of all schools saw all this foreshadowed in 1832, while the future Queen was still in the charge of governesses, and her raffish uncle, William IV, still lent a spurious air of an endlessly prolonged slack eighteenth century to the scene. We have only to go back fifteen or twenty years to Jane Austen's novels to find a world where Catholics, Dissenters, Jews and unbelievers do not impinge. The contrast was, and was felt to be, startling.

Of course there had been Catholics, Jews, Dissenters and unbelievers in Jane Austen's England. The point was that they were socially separate from the groups about whom she wrote; her characters knew of them, if at all, from books. Only a few years after 1832, the landscape was crossed by innumerable railway lines, which the most brilliant of the Broad Church school, Thomas Arnold, greeted as meaning the end of feudalism. He meant, I think, that the local separateness of a traditional rural society (Jane Austen again gives the most memorable image) could never be restored. The influence of London and the large towns would increase, class distinctions would become more commercial and less hereditary; above all, people would be more aware of others distant from them both in space and experience. The nation was about to be mixed together in a vast stew, exhilarating to some, alarming to others. This brought both opportunities and dangers to the upholders of every doctrine, but it brought only danger to any school of thought which depended on habit and tradition, rather than conviction and argument. Especially it brought danger to one particular Anglican school, the kind that cried 'Church and King, and down with the Rump' (Mrs Gaskell, *North and South*, ch. 5) and believed that the Church of England was the Church 'because by Law established'. The Oxford Movement saw this clearly, as did the Utilitarians, and some Broad Churchmen and Evangelicals. The Victorian age (especially but not exclusively in its educated élite) was an age of argument. Leading articles in *The Times*, quarterly periodicals, local debating societies and political meetings were all trying to convince the public. Ontario Moggs, the radical bootmaker in Trollope's *Ralph the Heir* (1871), and the more esoteric group described in *Daniel Deronda* (1876) are alike typical of the whole age.

The common link in all these different manifestations is earnestness, and a belief that people could be convinced by argument. And many people were convinced by argument. It was an age of many conversions, where each thinking person's opinions had their own history. The Gladstone of 1838 and of 1880, the

George Eliot of 1840 and 1870, the Mill of 1826 and 1860, the Manning of 1843 and 1870 all seem like totally different persons, at least if we think of their opinions and not of their personalities. The age was as dynamic intellectually as it was materially; and those, like Charlotte Yonge (say), who thought exactly the same in later life as they had in youth, were in danger of being left behind – left behind in rational argument, as their opponents might have said, or honourably refusing to join a senseless rush for novelty, as they might have said themselves. Either way they were at a disadvantage. Perhaps nothing is more emblematic of the nature of the mid-Victorian élite than the foundation in 1869 of the Metaphysical Society, where Anglicans, atheists and Catholics read papers on high speculative subjects, lacerating each other's arguments in a friendly, clubbable atmosphere.

But just as surely as it was an age of argument, it was an age of feeling. One of the few generalizations which would be almost accurate (none would be absolutely so) is that they were all capable of strong emotion, and expected their intellectual conclusions to be emotionally satisfying. Mill's crisis of 1826, described in his post-humous *Autobiography*, was, among other things, a revolt, deep in the heart, against the bloodless system-mongering of the previous age. Here the influence of Wordsworth was so pervasive that it could affect both Mill and Newman, opposite as their principles and conclusions were. Victorians of all schools of thought were con-temptuous of those who would 'botanize upon their mother's grave', a procedure that Bentham's felicific calculus might have allowed.

It was, too, an earnest moralizing age. Cynicism was regarded as deeply shocking, at least until about 1880, after which it partly came back into fashion. Those who retained some tincture of the cynicism of an earlier age (Palmerston and Disraeli, for instance) needed to conceal it from the public. This helps to explain what at first sight seems a puzzling phenomenon. How is it that all parties seem to gain, and hardly any to lose? It is the age of deep Evangelical influence (especially up to about 1850 or 1860). It is the age of the burgeoning of the Oxford Movement, of the Catholic Revival, of the Broad Church, but also of the development of Utilitarian influence, of Biblical criticism and of unbelief in several new forms. One is inclined to feel that there must be something wrong. The sums do not add up. But this overlooks the decline in mere conventional, passive acceptance of the customs and standards of society. Strong conviction and party spirit con-quered much of the territory previously occupied by Laodicean indifference. The general breeze of reforming zeal affected the religious and the secular alike.

Earnest reformers are always strongly aware of time, and especially of the difference between the present and some imagined future. And this, in turn, gave the sense of the past a specially poignant flavour. While they talked of progress and hoped for the future general triumph of their own principles, many were seeking an image of the desired future in the past. The many controversies about medieval society, dismissed as barbarous by Dickens, sentimentally recreated by Disraeli in *Sybil*, seriously advocated as a model for the nineteenth century by Pugin, and to some extent by Cobbett – all testify to a deep anxiety about modern civilization. This anxiety was most acute in the 1840s, and least felt perhaps in the 1870s. The sense of crisis declined, and with it something of the characteristic early Victorian earnestness.

The Evangelical Revival had been in full swing for a whole generation before the Queen's accession, but ideas take time to filter down to ordinary people; and we may guess that it was at the height of its general influence on all classes in the first twenty years of her reign. George Eliot brilliantly catches its effect on the simplest in *Amos Barton* (1857), set about 1832.

> 'Eh, dear,' said Mrs Patten ... 'I don't understand these new sort of doctrines. When Mr Barton comes to see me, he talks about nothing but my sins and my need o' mercy. Now, Mr Hackit, I've never been a sinner. From the fust beginning, when I went into service, I al'ys did my duty by my employers. I was a good wife as any in the county...'
>
> (ch. 5)

Mrs Patten, without in the least understanding her words, is pointing to a great gulf in religious history. To her, as to so many people in the previous century, sin meant conduct that is criminal or grossly immoral or obviously antisocial. But Amos Barton meant by sin what Bunyan had meant when he wrote *Grace Abounding*, and what both would have maintained was meant by St Paul. It was perfectly compatible with respectability; it meant that general alienation from God, conceived as the natural and inevitable condition of human nature before it has received the gift of saving faith in the power of Christ's redemptive sacrifice.

The other leading Evangelical doctrines can be simply stated. There was a complete reliance on the authority and literal truth of the Bible and a refusal to accept any other kind of authority. This helps to explain what is at first sight puzzling, that the movement was at the same time Anglican and Dissenting. There was often a considerable difference in education, social class and accent be- tween an Anglican Evangelical rector and a Dissenting minister, but very little in doctrine. There was a fierce opposition to Rome and to any groups in the Church of England that were supposed (often mistakenly) to be influenced by Rome. There was a strong distrust of all ceremony; sacraments were ignored or admitted grudgingly.

The coherence of all this was much more emotional than it was intellectual. Intellectually it was riddled with difficulties, which for a long time were seldom considered. First, the Bible, though always praised as divine, had to be read very selectively. Salvation by faith alone was flatly contradicted in the Epistle of St James. St Paul might seem to be a supporter of nineteenth-century Evangelicalism in the Epistle to Romans, but his vehement assertion of the Real Presence in the Eucharist might be ignored. The early chapters of St Luke's gospel were regrettably Marian; and the Acts of the Apostles showed an early Church acting with decisive authority before the Gospels were written. And where did the Bible come from? Who decided that it had authority? Well, again, the early Church, precisely the body the Evangelicals were rebelling against. Considerations like these would lead many who had been brought up as Evangelicals or who had adopted their tenets in youth to move on to High Church or Catholic views. The children of the so-called Clapham Sect, many of them famous Victorian figures, like Leslie and Fitzjames Stephen, Macaulay, and the Wilberforce brothers, all moved away from the parental doctrine in one direction or another.

Nevertheless the impact of the movement on the country up to about 1860 was enormous, both in public and private life. The abolition of slavery (1833) went hand in hand with family prayers, distrust of theatres and novel-reading, and a generally earnest tone. Prudery might be intertwined with purity. The taunt that the vices castigated by the Evangelicals were those that cost money, while pride, avarice and ambition were spared, might be seen to possess a grain of truth; but still, the sincerity, energy and practical effectiveness commanded and deserved respect.

Based on the Bible (or parts of it) and distrusting ceremony, it was, of course, the religion of the word, not of the sign. No doubt this is one reason for the immense superiority of Victorian literature over its visual art. To turn from Dickens or Ruskin or George Eliot to the paintings of Rossetti or Leighton is to make a catastrophic descent. Many people who read and enjoyed the best authors of the time were satisfied with ponderous and ugly ornaments. Ruskin, who unusually emerged from an Evangelical upbringing with a passionate devotion to art, might castigate his contemporaries for their visual Philistinism and be heard with respect, but only a few followed his lead.

Ruskin's own account of an Evangelical upbringing in *Praeterita* (1885–9) stresses the horrors of the Evangelical Sunday, which, he says, he began to dread by the middle of each preceding week. In *Little Dorrit* (1855–7) Dickens shows a middle-aged man returning to London after many years abroad, and musing thus, alone in a coffee-house on Ludgate Hill:

'Thank Heaven!' said Clennam, when the hour struck, and the bell stopped. But its sound had revived a long train of miserable Sundays, and the procession would not stop with the bell, but continued to march on. 'Heaven forgive me,' said he, 'and those who trained me. How I have hated this day!'
There was the dreary Sunday of his childhood, when he sat with his hands before him, scared out of his senses by a horrible tract which commenced business with the poor child by asking him in its title, why he was going to perdition? . . . There was the resentful Sunday of a little later, when he sat glowering and glooming through the tardy length of the day, with a sullen sense of injury in his heart, and no more real knowledge of the beneficent history of the New Testament, than if he had been bred among idolaters.

(ch. 3)

Dickens exaggerates, but plenty of evidence (Augustus Hare's *Story of My Life*, for instance) could be called to show that the exaggeration is not here intolerably great. We are all so used to the idea of the Puritan Sunday, that it may come as a surprise to consider how flimsy its basis was. The Christian Sunday is, of course, not the Jewish Sabbath at all, but the day of the Resurrection, the first day of the week, a day of rejoicing (which is why the forty days of Lent are counted with Sundays omitted). As Ruskin was to point out with great eloquence, the Jewish Sabbath was part of the Law, which St Paul had declared abrogated. Why then did Evangelicals wish to restore it? And why in this instance only, and not (say) in the prohibition of pork? The strange thing is how little these questions were considered, even by highly intelligent men like William Wilberforce and Sir James Stephen. It is a characteristic instance of the intellectual vulnerability of the Evangelical cause, just when it seemed to be carrying all before it.

But the Evangelical Sunday, as experienced by children like Ruskin, Hare and the fictional Clennam, points to another weakness too. There was a lack of insight into human nature. The original idea had been a fine and inspiring one, to offer God's own day to him, unsullied by frivolities. But human nature (especially in childhood) is so constituted that concentration on one object for fifteen hours on end is impossible to it. A moderate amount of recreation might have made the day both pious and happy. As no amusement whatever was allowed, it became a terrible unchartable gulf of time from which only sleep could bring deliverance.

There is a further paradox here about authority. By doing away with all religious authority except the Bible, parental authority became, in practice, absolute. It was the parents who awed the children into restraining their natural inclination to play or even read. Often meaning very well, Evangelical parents were perceived as tyrannical killjoys. The father who madly dared to say 'I stand in the place of God to you' might cause the children's resentment against him to be transferred to God Himself.

For those (perhaps the majority of readers today) who form their image of the Evangelicals from reading the novelists, a caution is necessary: Dickens, Thackeray and even the fair-minded Trollope (who gave Mr Slope an unpleasant, greasy palm) are too angry to be just. They were, in part, on the defensive against those who denounced novel-reading as at best a waste of time, and at worst morally pernicious. They were repelled by what they saw as Philistine self-righteousness. A more balanced picture is to be found in the works of Hale White ('Mark Rutherford') and George Eliot.

George Eliot's own loss of faith in the Evangelical creed, which deeply influenced her early formative years, is one of the emblematic tableaux of the age. To her father she wrote (28 February 1842):

I do not hope to convince any other member of our family and probably not yourself that I am really sincere, that my only desire is to walk in that path of rectitude which however rugged is the only path to peace, but the prospect of contempt and rejection shall not make me swerve from my determination . . .

(G. Haight, *George Eliot, A Biography*, 1968, p 42)

It is the very language of an eloquent Evangelical sermon. The agnostics and the High Church both showed the pervasive influence of the Evangelical creed. But if we turn to George Eliot's portrayal of the Evangelicals in her novels, we find a treatment at once more discerning and more sympathetic than those of Thackeray and Dickens. Two contrasted figures particularly stand out, Rufus Lyon, the minister in *Felix Holt* and Bulstrode in *Middlemarch* (1872). The first is deeply sincere, though not immune to unexpected bursts of passion, so steeped in Biblical study that even his everyday domestic language is formed in its idiom. His sympathetic, but not fully comprehending, exchanges with Felix Holt, whose views are similar to the author's, shows that for George Eliot the sense of moral continuity with the Evangelical tradition she had abandoned was at least as important as intellectual divergence. Lyon's selfless and little requited devotion to his more worldly daughter shows the author's approval of the human aspects of what many considered a narrow tradition. There is a sense of rectitude and simple dignity which contrasts favourably with the land-owning Transomes, loveless, brooding and bitter; and, though George Eliot is by no means hostile to the Anglican establishment, it appears, in this book at least, less concerned for the real life and interests of the people than Lyon's chapel.

Bulstrode is a more complex figure; through him the author raises the question of hypocrisy, often treated by others in a superficial and sneering spirit. Bulstrode is a wealthy banker with a disreputable, though not strictly criminal, past. He comforts himself with phrases like 'sacred accountableness' into believing that all his profits are being used for the glory of God. But he is less aware of being comforted also by the conviction that no one in Middlemarch will ever know about his past. When this conviction eventually proves mistaken, he is forced to perceive the gulf between a comfortable, general admission of being a sinner entirely without merit, full of phrases like 'Our righteousness is filthy rags', and specific offences which his neighbours will consider fatal to his reputation for respectability. George Eliot here is pointing with consummate art to a paradox about the Evangelicals which still has the power to puzzle and confuse. How is it that those who believed in salvation by faith alone and proclaimed the absolute impossibility of acquiring merit by good conduct were often at the same time the most strict and censorious about others, and the most touchy about their own moral reputation? One reason was that for this school conversion was supposed to be decisive and unrepeatable. It *ought* to transfer the old creature at once into the new. There was no provision for later recovery after lapses, as in the Catholic system of confession and absolution. This meant that sin after conversion took on a grim and threatening aspect; it might cast doubt on the reality of conversion itself. When the Evangelical said he was the chief of sinners, he meant that he was so by nature but that God's grace had released him from this condition into the glorious liberty of the children of God. If his conduct was not such as to render this plausible, there was a strong temptation to assume or pretend that it did because the alternative was too terrible to contemplate. So we have the paradox, perfectly illustrated in Bulstrode, that a man who proclaims himself a worthless sinner is aghast at the idea that he could actually sin. But George Eliot is more sensitive than most others in showing the inner torments which the paradox could engender. In comparison, Pecksniff is only an amusing caricature.

When we read personal accounts of an Evangelical upbringing, like those of Ruskin or Hare, we may be impressed at the same time with its formidable power, its capacity to develop and canalize energy (either into selfless or ambitious channels) and by its hard, unloving, unforgiving temper. Each aspect might be thought equally important in the formation of the early Victorian age, an age at once serious, reforming, inventive, and creative of new wealth on a vast scale.

Despite the difference of principles (to say nothing of possible dislike and distrust) between the Evangelicals and the Oxford Movement, there is a historical continuity. They share seriousness: moral in both, intellectual much more in the Oxford Movement. In some ways, the Oxford Movement may be regarded as providing the answers to some of the Evangelical intellectual dilemmas sketched above. Whether, like Keble, they had inherited a High Church family tradition, or, like Newman, had experienced an early Evangelical phase, they saw that experience, however precious, could not provide the rational foundation needed in an age of increasing scepticism, nor the organization which would be indispensable when the State's patronage was withdrawn. It was necessary to return to the foundations in the teaching of the Apostles and the Early Church. When this was done, Protestantism was at once refuted because there was no trace of its characteristic doctrines before the fourteenth century; and to deny that the people who wrote and first read the New Testament knew what it meant, and to say that this had suddenly been revealed for the first time to Luther or Calvin or Henry VIII was an absurdity which no one would have tolerated in a secular context.

In the seventeenth and eighteenth centuries a certain complacency was possible in High Church minds, because the order of

Church and State could be conceived as unalterable. There could have been no clearer signal that this age was over than the first of the *Tracts for the Times* (written by Newman, but published anonymously):

> Should the Government and Country so far forget their God as to cast off the Church, to deprive it of its temporal honours and substance, *on what* will you rest the claim of respect and attention which you make upon your flocks? Hitherto you have been upheld by your birth, your education, your wealth, your connections . . . on *what* are we to rest our authority when the State deserts us?
>
> (A. O. J. Cockshut (ed.) *Religious Controversies of the Nineteenth Century*, 1966, pp 63–4)

A little earlier the same tract had spoken of the possibility that the bishops might have to endure the spoiling of their goods and martyrdom, and called this a 'blessed termination'. This was fighting, revolutionary talk, none the less because it found its source in events and sayings eighteen centuries old.

The answer to the Tract's rhetorical question was Apostolic Succession. And here there were many ironies lurking. In the first place the orders derived from Rome, which, however, denied that they had been truly maintained in the upheavals of the sixteenth century; but in any case, the fact was unpleasing because a firm anti-Roman stance was characteristic of the first phase of the Movement, down to about 1839. Then the authors of the *Tracts* were well aware that as the introduction to the first volume of *Tracts* put it, they were preaching to the Church doctrines 'which . . . at present have become obsolete with the majority of her members.' In some ways the key figure in the Oxford Movement is the bishop, mentioned much later in Newman's *Apologia* (1864), who on reading a tract on Apostolic Succession 'could not tell whether he held the doctrine or not.' In fact, he was a bishop but had never needed to ask himself what a bishop was. Nothing could be more eloquent about the illusion of a settled order of society in which the Anglican Church would always have its privileged place. There had been no need to ask what a bishop was, any more than there is any need for a young stockbroker to ask himself why he wears a dark suit and leaves the bottom button of the waistcoat undone. He does so because it is the thing to do; and bishops had seemed as immoveable as the throne and the House of Lords.

The Oxford Movement was, above all, a protest against Erastianism, a system of subordination of Church to State, so that a Prime Minister appointed bishops, just as he gave away political offices, and expected the same obedience in one case as in the other. But the Tractarians were still claiming that the Church of England was the church of the nation. Keble's Assize sermon of July 1833 (usually regarded as the beginning of the Movement) spoke of 'national apostasy', because the Whig government proposed to tamper with the territories and revenues of bishops of the Church of Ireland. But the Church of Ireland was, in practice, a Protestant stronghold in the midst of a subject Catholic people. It was highly paradoxical for Keble to maintain that he was coming to the defence of this in the name of Catholic principles. Yet so accustomed were both Keble and his hearers to the immemorial idea of British rule in Ireland that the paradox was very slow in being noticed.

The revival of the Catholic sacramental system was a less difficult matter, because the forms and ceremonies were there, in the Prayer Book; and, though often neglected and belittled, to a certain extent in the customs of the parishes. Keble, who had a great reverence for the poetry of Wordsworth, was able to produce a synthesis of traditional sacramental doctrine and the Wordsworthian idea of natural objects as signs of a transcendent order. In this way some of the enthusiasm of the Romantic period was diverted into channels very different from those in which it had flowed at first.

The ascetic side of the Movement is easily misunderstood. It emphatically was not continuous with the old Puritan distrust of innocent amusement. The Tractarians reverted to the Catholic idea of sacrifice, of the lower to the higher or of the good to the better. Thus celibacy was honoured as the sacrifice of the great blessing of marriage, fasting as the sacrifice of part of God's bounty of the fruitful earth. The difference was much more than theoretical; it was felt in numerous nurseries and schoolrooms. There is a cheerfulness in the Tractarian family, even in its most serious form (as described by Charlotte Yonge, for instance) which is worlds away from the upbringing described by Ruskin.

Yet there was an absence of a living tradition of spiritual discipline, well seen in the case of Hurrell Froude, one of the founders of the Movement, who died less than three years after it began but whose writings were an abiding influence over the survivors. His *Remains* (1838) reveal a young man very much in earnest in his search for holiness, but lacking a spiritual guide who could moderate his zeal and calm his scruples. A review of the book by Nicholas Wiseman (later Cardinal and first Archbishop of Westminster) is of interest as giving a sympathetic critique from the point of view of a more regular tradition of Catholic spirituality:

The consequences of all this irregular and undirected austerity, into which with youthful eagerness he rushed, was, that ... his spirit ... flagged, and at length grew weary, and so fell into that despondency which failure will produce in sensitive minds.

(Cardinal Wiseman, *Essays on Various Subjects*, 1853, vol II, p 83)

Wiseman was the first Catholic to take a deep interest in the Oxford Movement; he was to influence its course a little later when an article of his in the *Dublin Review* gave Newman the first doubts he had had about the soundness of the Anglo-Catholic position. But Newman and Pusey might not have disagreed with his account of Froude. They knew they were trying to recreate something overlaid with generations of Protestant prejudice and popular neglect. These were the fears which Newman expressed when he said that while Protestantism and Popery (as he still called it) were undoubtedly real religions, Anglo-Catholicism might prove to be only a paper system. He knew, better than most, that while theology is necessary to religion, it is not itself religion, and that to take a strong hold on the public, a religious system needs traditions, habits, sentiments as well.

The first leaders of the Movement were not much interested in ritual. But it is natural that a new (or ancient revived) doctrine should gradually affect liturgy. While the assumptions of ordinary Anglicans had been Protestant, it was natural that the pulpit should dominate the altar; when a high sacramental doctrine was introduced and the Real Presence of Christ in the Eucharist once again taught, forms and ceremonies to honour it were bound to follow. Later followers of the Oxford Movement were known to their opponents as Ritualists (or sometimes Puseyites). Disraeli, whose sympathy with the Movement had very much cooled by the 1870s, made it one of his first concerns when he became Prime Minister for the second time in 1874, to introduce a Public Worship Regulation Act, directed against ritualism. The Archbishop of Canterbury, A. C. Tait, was an extreme Erastian, who eagerly concurred. Ritualist churches had begun to flourish especially in the East End of London and the poorer parts of other large cities. The clergy who worked in them often had to face not only Protestant violence but also vandalism and legal prosecution. It was an interesting commentary on the Protestant spirit of England that it was the reverent and devout Anglo-Catholics who fell foul of the law while the roughs who attacked them and desecrated their churches seldom did. Archbishop Tait laid himself open to the complaint that he preferred a dead, almost empty Protestant parish church to a ritualist one with a large and enthusiastic congregation. As ordinary people are more aware of what they see and hear than of any intellectual process, it was the ritualist issue which excited public feeling and roused the warmest controversy. But the Erastian issue was really the more fundamental; and we can appreciate the strength of the Erastian tradition in governments of all parties if we read Lord John Russell's reply to the Dean of Hereford, who had warned him that he might not be able to vote for the Government's nominee for the diocese:

> Woburn Abbey, Dec 25.
> Sir,
>   I have had the honour to receive your letter of the 22nd instant, in which you intimate to me your intention of violating the law.
>   I have the honour to be your obedient servant,
>   J. RUSSELL
>   (A. O. J. Cockshut, op. cit., p 113)

Did he, one wonders, send this contemptuous letter deliberately on Christmas Day to add to its sting or did it not occur to him that Christmas Day had anything to do with Church matters?

In the first few years of the Movement certain deep intellectual and temperamental differences went for the most part unnoticed. For Keble and Pusey allegiance to the Church of England was primary and unquestionable. They wished to reform and improve a Church which they believed could never really fail. Froude and Newman owed their allegiance first to the Universal Church; and their conviction that the Church of England was a living part of this was only provisional, a conviction strongly rooted, certainly, but capable of being shaken or eventually destroyed. This is the point (it is now easy to see with hindsight) where the cleavage between the Oxford Movement and the Catholic Revival was to appear.

Though the history of the Oxford Movement and the Catholic Revival are closely linked, it is a fallacy to suppose that the latter first began solely under the influence of the former. Dr Bramston, Vicar Apostolic of the London District after the death of Dr Poynter in 1827, was a convert who had been received into the Church as far back as 1790. Other notable conversions, such as those of Kenelm Digby and Pugin ante-dated by some years Newman's first doubts about Anglicanism. At the same time the Irish immigration was swelling the number of poor Catholics far beyond eighteenth-century levels.

Two points were, above all, important in the relation between the Oxford Movement and the Catholic Revival. First, the line of thinking which the Oxford Movement began was bound eventually to find Rome in its path. English Protestants contrived to ignore it by being extremely insular both in time and space. The Oxford leaders might be insular in their Englishness, but their studies laid them open to the full sweep of Christian history. It was impossible to evade for ever the thought expressed by W. G. Ward in 1841:

> Let us bear to think that twelve centuries and all the Church have something to say, when at odds with three centuries and a small part of it.
> (in *The British Critic*, October 1841)

It is a tribute to the power of Newman's early impression that the Pope was anti-Christ, remaining as a 'stain on the imagination' after his intellect had rejected it, that he had no doubts about Anglicanism until about 1839, and after that it took him six more years to become a Catholic. The Oxford Movement was a crucible out of which two different metals were produced; in both parties there were distinguished, learned, even saintly people. But the main difference between the Catholic converts and the mid-Victorian Puseyites was that the first were dynamic. They were the ones who had followed the argument to the end. A comparison of the poetry of Gerard Hopkins with that of Keble is emblematic. The first is bold and original, and where it makes use of old models, employs them in startlingly new ways. The second is a voice of tender recall to childhood pieties; and is redolent of the country parsonage, and the old family life described at length in the novels of Keble's pupil, Charlotte Yonge. The first confronts the industrial age, the ravages of which the author saw at close quarters in Liverpool; the second is a wistful plea to be content with the England that was passing away.

The other important point was higher education, of which Catholics, like Dissenters, had been largely deprived. A very learned cradle Catholic, like Wiseman (born in Spain and educated mainly in Rome), was most exceptional in an English context, but the converts from the Oxford Movement were often drawn from the academic élite. A new tone of intellectual respect is discernible in educated Protestant discourse about Catholicism. Thackeray was typical when he said that he had rather believe he was an ass than that Newman could believe anything impossible. Or rather, he was typical of the more perceptive and aware. The alarming popular clamour (regrettably fanned by some Anglican prelates who should have known better) about 'Papal Aggression' in 1850 was evidence of that low prejudice which Newman so brilliantly satirized in *The Present Position of Catholics*. And what was 'Papal Aggression'? It was merely an administrative change from the organization of the Catholic episcopacy in England, about which the British Government had been consulted beforehand. The outcry proved to be almost the last outbreak of popular Protestant violence on the mainland. Later in the century Lord Ripon could become Viceroy of India and Cardinal Manning could sit on Government Commissions with Royal Dukes. Both were converts.

So the Catholic body increased in education and confidence at the same time as it rapidly advanced in numbers. There was a marked change after the 1840s from the *gens lucifuga* (people that shun the light) whose history can be studied, for instance in Bernard Ward's *Eve of Catholic Emancipation*.

The new confidence could even be strident, as it was in men like F. W. Faber and Coventry Patmore. But for all the intellectual gains, the bulk of Catholics in England were still poor and ignorant and emphatically urban. The Catholic priest, whether a man of deep education or not, was constantly confronted with the advancing nineteenth century in its rawest and most rapidly-changing guise. He might be appalled, but he was in no danger of being out of date or out of touch. The Barchester image of the Anglican Church was not the whole story; but it was true enough in part to make a strong contrast here.

The Catholic body was, however, (rather oddly) like the Anglican in being the prey of party spirit. In Rome, it was said, a whimsical theory prevailed that the English were naturally quarrelsome. It was not, in the main, a quarrel between cradle Catholics and converts; though some of the old Catholics, who had once been content to refer to Mass as 'Prayers' may have been affronted at the new Italianate devotions at the Brompton Oratory. The mutual distrust of Newman and Manning had its ironical as well as its poignant side. Manning as Archdeacon of Chichester had still been preaching Protestant sermons on Guy Fawkes Day while Newman was on his Anglican death-bed at Littlemore. Yet in 1865 Manning was Archbishop of Westminster, the supreme Catholic authority in England under the Pope, while Father Newman was still a simple priest at the Oratory at Birmingham. The great gifts of each were perhaps really, though neither could feel this, complementary. Newman was the thinker, probing for ideas which were to come to fruition in the general body of the Church at the Second Vatican Council in the 1960s – Manning the great organizer, who faced and executed the stupendous task of providing pastoral care for a million new Catholics, most of whom had hardly a penny to spare.

One of their most significant differences was on the subject of higher education. Manning's attempt to form a Catholic University at Kensington failed; might it have succeeded if he had asked Newman's help, as he pointedly refrained from doing? Newman wanted Catholics to have their share of the traditional education which had formed himself and Manning; and he said he could not see why Oxford, which had made him and so many others Catholics when they didn't know any cradle Catholics, was more dangerous to faith than the Army, the bank or the city. It was not till after both men were dead in the 1890s that Newman's policy prevailed in Rome. Manning's influence in Rome was paramount on English affairs until the death of Pius IX in 1878, and still strong thereafter, though Leo XIII overrode his doubts about Newman's fitness for the cardinalate in 1879. In the previous year Newman's first reappearance in Oxford as Honorary Fellow of Trinity, where he had been an undergraduate sixty years before, was a kind of signal that England and Catholicism had made peace. Paradoxically, but most plausibly, Newman attributed much of the party spirit to early memories among the converts of hostility between High and Low Church in the Church of England. Certainly, as the Oxford Movement receded into history, it declined.

The Broad Church is in some ways the most elusive of all the Victorian parties; and this should not surprise us. Much more than the others it found its centre, not in doctrines, but in feelings and attitudes. Its adherents were, usually, active, enthusiastic men of the world, especially those concerned with education. Thomas Arnold, who may serve as a type of the Movement, was just as strongly aware as the Tractarians that deep social changes would accompany and follow the Reform Bill of 1832, but the conclusions he drew from this were entirely different. He wished to fill the gap left by declining social deference with an increase of state control. He was unlike most Erastians, and very unlike his eighteenth-century latitudinarian predecessors, in being an Erastian on principle, not in the least through worldly slackness. He believed that the *raison d'être* of the schisms which had led to the formation of the Dissenting sects had passed away, and that all good Protestants could be reunited on the basis of simple creed, national feeling and the Royal Supremacy. This simple creed was by no means vague or woolly, for it included the Divinity of Christ, and thus excluded the Unitarians. Catholics were a problem to him, but he wondered rather wistfully whether they might not eventually prefer the Church of England to the Church of central Italy. This sentiment (which could only make a Catholic smile) reveals the intensely political and territorial nature of his vision; also perhaps his inability to enter imaginatively into views different from his own. His scorn and anger were reserved for the Tractarians, who, he thought, were trying to go against the real genius of the Church of England by making it a matter of creeds and sacraments and ritualistic trivialities and by denying its traditional Protestant basis.

The thinker of the Movement was A. P. Stanley, Dean of Westminster and pupil and biographer of Arnold. His life of Arnold conveys in high intellectual form what Thomas Hughes's *Tom Brown's Schooldays* showed at a popular level, the extraordinary force of Arnold's personality and the depth of his influence both on the intellectual élite and on the ordinary Philistine English boy. Arnold's pupils included many successful headmasters as well as his son Matthew and A. H. Clough. The shock felt at Arnold's early death in 1842 is well conveyed both in Stanley's book, and in his son's poem *Rugby Chapel*, written some fifteen years later.

The driving-force of the Broad Church was a genuine and infectious moral enthusiasm, which for a time, in Rugby and some other places carried all before it and seemed not to need any justification. Its strength was that it was both inward and outward. It laid stress on the disposition of the heart equally with practical social duties. At the same time it had three weaknesses, largely unperceived in Arnold's time, but becoming increasingly obvious later. First, the enormous stress on personality and personal influence meant that it could not easily be transmitted from one generation to another. Second, its moral enthusiasm, though broad and generous enough in intention, was very much the product of one class and one type of education in one country. It could perhaps only have developed in a country, like early- and mid-Victorian England, which possessed an instinctive sense of superiority. The 'English gentleman' (which did not mean quite what it had meant thirty years earlier, for it referred now as much to moral excellence and education as to birth) was assumed to be the type to which all nations and all classes must and inevitably would aspire. The French and the Italians no less than the Hottentots and the aborigines could only be judged by their success or failure in conforming to the type. It was not sufficiently understood that there were other types, other spiritual ideals in the world, some of them more persistent, more deeply-rooted than this; some people, the disciples of St Ignatius or of Rousseau, for instance, actually might not want to become more like clean English schoolboys.

Third, and most important of all – being in the main, and increasingly as time went on and the age of Jowett succeeded that of Arnold, an ideal of secular excellence and practical action – its original religious impulse was liable to be blunted and to become eventually (to change the metaphor) as indistinct 'as water is in water'. Here the 'religious' works of Arnold's son are perfectly emblematic. Books like *God and the Bible* and *St Paul and Protestantism* retain the father's strong preference for the Church of England over the sects and show a delicate appreciation of the beauties of the Elizabethan liturgy, and they leave the reader unpersuaded that the author really believes in God, Creator and Redeemer, rather than as a mere figment of an idealist philosopher's dream.

Von Hügel's words are applicable to all such dreams:

Nothing would be more alarming in reality than to find that religion, when pressed, could give us nothing but just what we want; we, you and I, at any one date within our human lives, so incomplete, so very little, so very short.

(The Reality of God, 1931, p 15)

On the whole, this fits the most celebrated Broad Church productions, such as *Essays and Reviews* (1860), a symposium to which Jowett and Mark Pattison contributed, and Seeley's *Ecce Homo* (1865). It is not perhaps quite fortuitous that Seeley was later to become one of the leading academic proponents of imperialism; it would hardly have occurred to him that the whole world might not want to be English.

Gradually, to many perhaps imperceptibly, the Broad Church movement lost something which Thomas Arnold had partly retained, the sense of the scandal of the Cross, 'foolishness to the Greeks', without which the drive and meaning of the Gospel is lost. This was a real (though often little remembered) link between Catholics, Tractarians and Evangelicals. None of them thought that a Christian ought to be or could be wholly comfortable in this world. Jowett's Balliol, by implication, proclaimed the opposite; and as usual, what was only implied was more powerful than if it had been stated. For many earnest, able and ambitious late Victorians, Broad Church pieties, plain living, high thinking, and a sincere devotion to what Ruskin called the 'great goddess of getting-on' and Lawrence was later to call the 'Bitch goddess' – all this was for many an easy bridge of transition to agnosticism.

*

Unbelief was as varied and confusing in its manifestations as belief. We may begin with what was perhaps the smallest and least influential group, those who reject all religion as a monstrous error or fraud. This might be combined with a romantic pagan longing, as in Swinburne, who wrote, adapting the words attributed to the dying emperor Julian in the fourth century:

Thou hast conquered, O pale Galilean; the world has grown grey from Thy
breath; . . .
Though before thee the throned Cytherean be fallen, and hidden her head,
Yet thy kingdom shall pass, Galilean, thy dead shall go down to thee dead.
('Hymn of Proserpine')

Blasphemy could express either an extreme optimism or an extreme pessimism. Thus Swinburne writes:

Glory to Man in the highest! for Man is the master of things.
('Hymn of Man')

In utter contrast is James Thomson's bitter cry:

Who is most wretched in this dolorous place?
I think myself; yet I would rather be
My miserable self than He, than He
Who formed such creatures to His own disgrace

As if a Being, God or Fiend, could reign,
At once so wicked, foolish, and insane,
As to produce men when He might refrain.
(*The City of Dreadful Night*, Section VIII)

And yet the contrast is perhaps not really as great as it appears. Swinburne's optimism lacks any rational basis and is belied by the romantic pessimism and sad, perverse delight which pervades both his poems and his letters. Thomson's despair conceals a self-congratulatory enjoyment in his supposed boldness and frankness. Both poets are essentially making gestures; neither is making a serious attempt to see life steadily and whole.

The brilliant and short-lived mathematician, W. K. Clifford, while just as emotional as Swinburne and Thomson, is very different because he conceives himself to be in the vanguard of a great forward movement of humanity, which, guided by reason and science, will eventually transcend all previous incomplete achievements of civilization. Religion, like magic, superstition, poverty, bad hygiene and other evils and delusions, will fade away:

The dim and shadowy outlines of the superhuman deity fade slowly away from us; and as the mist of his presence floats aside, we perceive with greater and greater clearness the shape of a yet grander and nobler figure – of Him who made all Gods and shall unmake them. From the dim dawn of history, and from the inmost depth of every soul, the face of our father Man looks out upon us with the fire of eternal youth in his eyes, and says, 'Before Jehovah was, I am'.

(*Lectures and Essays*, 1875, vol II, p 245)

It is notable that in this passage 'Man' is an entirely abstract idea; it does not require (or perhaps permit) any comparison with human beings as actually existing or experienced. Clifford might have maintained that humanity was to be transformed, but he simply refuses to allow the raising of the question, 'How is this to come about?' Yet the hopefulness is genuine, even though he himself could perhaps not have analysed its sources. There is an uncritical mingling of the social optimism of Macaulay, based on a particular view of political and economic history, with a one-sided reading of biological evolution, which would probably have been rejected by Darwin, and most certainly by T. H. Huxley. There is an absence of English moderation and commonsense, which would ensure that few of his contemporaries would be his followers. Nevertheless, Swinburne, Thomson and Clifford all testify in their different ways to the bewildering variety of an open and rapidly changing society.

Clifford would probably have said that his optimism was based mainly on the manifest progress of science. But T. H. Huxley, the most thoughtful popularizer of the new biological ideas, wrote:

The theory of evolution encourages no millennial anticipations. If, for millions of years, our globe has taken the upward road, yet, some time the summit will be reached and the downward route will be commenced.

(*Evolution and Ethics*, 1894, p 85)

He was speaking, no doubt, of very long spans of time, and the ordinary man has little concern for any period beyond that of his own grandchildren; but the salient point is that, unlike Clifford, he assumes the undeniable truth that we did not make the world or determine our place in it. Whether as a race or as individuals, we are in the grip of forces far stronger than ourselves. Denying the existence of God will fundamentally change the way in which these forces are perceived, but it cannot alter the plain facts of the case. Whether one finds the idea of being (as a race) alone in the universe, with no superiors, exhilarating or alarming is perhaps mainly a matter of temperament. Clifford was not the only Victorian

scientist to ascribe to conclusions reached through his own temperamental constitution the status of facts discovered by science.

If we turn to literature, we shall find equally strong contrasts in
the way evolutionary ideas affected the imagination. George Eliot
(*The Mill on the Floss*, ch. 9) proleptically satirizes all future social
Darwinians and all who dream that science somehow gives the
strong a moral licence to oppress the weak, when she says that
'Nature' impelled Tom Tulliver to attack a superannuated
bluebottle. George Meredith takes evolution in an optimistic
sense, Thomas Hardy in a pessimistic, and Tennyson toys with
both views.

Many thoughtful agnostics were exercised by the fear of an
imaginative and emotional void in the hearts of those who had
abandoned or had never held Christian faith. The many different
attempts to cope with this difficulty can be divided into two main
types. The first wished to substitute a coherent system of ideas,
which would propose an explanation of the general meaning and
purpose of life and offer a set of moral precepts to guide individual
choices. The most notable of these were the Utilitarians, discussed
in the previous chapter, and the followers of the French thinker
Auguste Comte.

According to Comte's positivist system, all human conceptions
pass through three stages, the theological, the metaphysical and
the positivist. In the last (Comte was one of many thinkers who
suffered from the delusion that his particular system was history's
last word) the search for causes is abandoned, and in its place
there is a system of relations, governed by fixed and invariable
laws. Positivism takes all knowledge and discovery for its province
and undertakes to show how every science is related to every
other. Ethics, too, is a science. Positivism was once described as
Catholicism minus Christianity. From a religious point of view
Comte's most original idea was that the cult of the saints could be
detached from what in the Catholic system gave it its only *raison
d'être*, the worship of God. Saints of positivism would be chosen
for intellectual or political eminence just as much as for sanctity.
The greatest saint, naturally, was Comte himself who was
addressed thus:

> Great Teacher and Master, Auguste Comte, Revealer of Humanity to
> all her children, Interpreter of her Past, Prophet of her Future, Founder
> of her Religion, the one, the Universal Religion, to which all other
> Religions bear witness.
>
> (T. R. Wright, *The Religion of Humanity*, 1986, p 84)

It is interesting that these people who did not believe in God, were eager to claim the word 'religion' as their own. A recent historian of the movement in England writes:

> Death is perhaps the most obvious way in which the objective world fails to satisfy man's subjective requirements and Positivism accordingly provides him with an 'ideal resurrection' through the power of the imagination, a 'subjective immortality' in which the dead live on in the memory of the living.
>
> (ibid., p 21)

This idea had considerable influence, and echoes of it can be found in writers as diverse as George Eliot and Samuel Butler. Yet there is a core of realism even in the most dreamy and enthusiastic temperament. It may be that one reason why so many leading Positivists, including Comte himself, were depressive, was that they could not really persuade themselves that leaving behind a good name and a good influence was in the least the same thing as the Resurrection of the Dead.

The second type of response to this insistent fear of an emotional void is instanced by Carlyle (see previous chapter) and George Eliot. It was to separate the feelings, attitudes and duties which religion had fostered from the doctrines which it preached. It might even be maintained, as by George Eliot, following Feuerbach, that the feelings were the original stuff of religious experience, and the doctrines, including belief in God, had followed from the feelings. In this way Christianity was as completely true in one sense as it was untrue in another. This way of viewing the question had great advantages over some minimizing and modernizing versions of Christianity, such as that proposed in *Essays and Reviews*. For instead of tearing away inconvenient parts of the structure, a procedure as risky in thought as it is in house repairs, the structure was maintained intact, but explained in a different way and given over to a new purpose.

A powerful critique of this whole movement, which had considerable literary influence, was made by Fitzjames Stephen, who wrote:

> Whether Christianity is true or false, and whether European morality is good or bad, European morality is in fact founded upon religion, and the destruction of the one must of necessity involve the reconstruction of the other. Many persons in these days wish to retain the morality which they like, after getting rid of the religion which they disbelieve. Whether they are

right or wrong in disturbing the foundation, they are inconsistent in wishing
to save the superstructure.
(J. F. Stephen, *Liberty, Equality, Fraternity* (1873) ed. R. J. White, 1967, p 99)

There can be little doubt that George Eliot, Matthew Arnold, Mrs
Humphrey Ward and others owed their absolute certainty of the
authority of conscience to their early religious training. This implied
that they would be in difficulties when attempting to pass on their
deeply-felt moral intuitions to their successors. In particular this
would prove to be true of their high-toned moral enthusiasm, which
must have had a religious source. Interesting literary versions of the
attempt to create religious enthusiasm without dogma are to be found
in Mrs Ward's *Robert Elsmere* (1888) and, in an earlier and more
sketchy form, at the end of Hardy's *The Return of the Native*.

A key question here was, does the moral sense depend on the
beliefs held (both by society and the individual person), or is
conscience a primary human attribute, which can indeed be rightly
nurtured by true teaching and warped or distorted by bad, but which
exists in principle before any teaching is given? Fitzjames Stephen
would have chosen the first alternative; Newman and (probably)
George Eliot the second. A subtle contribution to this debate was
made by Walter Pater, a man deeply influenced both by the Oxford
Movement and by the agnostic currents of his time. In his novel of the
second century *Marius the Epicurean* (1885) he shows the most
selfless and philosophical of Emperors, Marcus Aurelius, quietly
getting on with his administrative work in the royal box of the Roman
arena while gladiators are being slaughtered below to the delight of
the crowds. Pater's point is that while the pagan philosopher would
consider such spectacles vulgar and tasteless, he would not feel any
burning sympathy with the victims. His ideal of detachment is
inhuman both by Christian standards and in the view of
nineteenth-century agnostics living in a culture nurtured by the
Christian centuries. The implication then is that Christianity
brought the new element of charity to the suffering and wretched.

In all these varying agnostic groups there is one conspicuous
absentee, or, at most, very rare visitor. That is the cool, superior,
sneering scepticism of some eighteenth-century intellectuals, such
as Voltaire and Gibbon. In faith, in doubt, in denial, the early and
mid-Victorians were passionate and emotional; and if we wish to find
anything even faintly reminiscent of this earlier spirit, we must go
right to the end of the century and the beginning of the next, to
people like A. E. Housman and Lytton Strachey.

The reader will have noticed that I have so far said nothing about the causes of religious doubt. This is because I think that most of the usual accounts are at best, simplistic, and, at worst, simply untrue. In particular, the destructive influence of Darwin is largely mythical. If we look, for instance, at a very interesting book often quoted in this connection, Gosse's *Father and Son* (1907), we shall find that it does not show what it is commonly supposed to show. In the first place, Philip Gosse, the father, belonged to a tiny sect, a splinter group from a sect already very small and unrepresentative. His reading of *Genesis* as a divinely inspired scientific tract was open to overwhelming objections, both theological and commonsensical, quite apart from any others that might arise from geology. Finally, the elder Gosse did not lose his faith; the younger did, but would have done so anyway, because of his rebellion against the sectarian exclusiveness, imaginative narrowness and moral strictness of the father. The incident in which a Christmas pudding prepared for the boy by the servants is called 'an accursed thing' was far more important in the formation of the son's views than any controversy about evolution. For some, certainly, the new evidence that the earth and the human race were both unimaginably older than had previously been supposed was disturbing, but it was a disturbance more of the feelings than of the intellect. Moreover, the imagination had always had to cope with apparently unlimited space; and some, like Pascal, had found this idea deeply disturbing long before the new science had been heard of.

For some, George Eliot in particular, German Biblical criticism was a crucial factor. And there is no doubt that the traditional Protestant way of reading the Bible literally, and without regard to human authorship or historical circumstance, made this seem much more threatening than it really was. There were others who were repelled by what they took to be the barbarism of the Old Testament war narratives. It is an odd and revealing fact that most controversy centred on the Old Testament, rather than the New, reflecting in this the characteristic bias of English Protestant religion. Others were so impressed by the apparent uniformity of nature, as revealed in the 'immutable' laws of Newton, that they said, with Matthew Arnold and the fictional Robert Elsmere, 'Miracles don't happen'. What is clear, however, and very often overlooked is this: every piece of evidence used in religious controversy was available equally to Catholics, Protestants and agnostics of good education and ability. They were all capable of being interpreted in good faith and with fair plausibility to fit all these views.

More important from the literary point of view than any new secular system, was a pervasive unease, a sense that the rapidity of change, both intellectual and social, left uncertainty everywhere. A pervasive image in many different kinds of Victorian literature is what Tennyson calls 'a haunt of ancient peace', a country house or vicarage, where the nineteenth century has hardly impinged. This takes its point from the fact that the writer dreads the coming moment when it will be swept away, or altered out of recognition by inexorable forces. The sense of an inevitable onward movement, its purpose unknown and direction obscure, was painful to thoughtful and sensitive people. Sometimes people who had, intellectually speaking, travelled very far from traditional orthodoxies, were the most obviously nostalgic, like Hardy when he wrote:

> Christmas Eve, and twelve of the clock.
>   'Now they are all on their knees',
> An elder said as we sat in a flock
>   By the embers in hearthside ease.
>
> We pictured the meek mild creatures where
>   They dwelt in their strawy pen,
> Nor did it occur to one of us there
>   To doubt they were kneeling then.
>
> ('The Oxen')

3

MATTHEW ARNOLD (and A. H. CLOUGH)

Kenneth Allott

The recognition of Matthew Arnold's distinction as a representative Victorian man-of-letters – and even T. S. Eliot, who found many of his ideas deeply antipathetic, has admitted that he was 'in some respects the most satisfactory man-of-letters of his age' (*The Use of Poetry and the Use of Criticism*, 1933, p 104) – depends on an adequate response to both his poetry and his prose. For some students it is the critical prose that counts and the poetry is of less interest. Quite possibly Arnold might have agreed with them. Of Sainte-Beuve, his master in criticism, he wrote in 1869 with an unmistakable autobiographical reference:

Like so many who have tried their hands at *oeuvres de poésie et d'art*, his preference, his dream, his ideal was there; the rest was comparatively journeyman-work, to be done well and estimably rather than ill and discreditably, and with precious rewards of its own, besides, in exercising the faculties and in keeping off ennui; but still work of an inferior order.

('Sainte Beuve' (1869), *Complete Prose Works*, ed. R. H. Super, 1960–1977, vol V, p 305)

Yet while sympathizing with the French critic's predilection, he decided judicially that the criticism was first-rate, the poetry second-rate. He might have accepted amiably a similar assessment of the value of his own mixed productions, although he must have known that his poetry was much superior to Sainte-Beuve's. Arnold's example forbids us to make exaggerated claims on his behalf. The poetry has 'some want of flame, of breath, of opinion' ('Sainte Beuve', *Five Uncollected Essays of Matthew Arnold*, ed. K. Allott, 1953, p 72); the prose moves without constraint. In both verse and prose he was predominantly an intellectual, whose detachment seemed to cruder spirits supercilious. He was never in his own day a popular writer like Tennyson or Dickens appealing to a broad cross-section of the reading public. If towards the end of his life his poems were known to 'all lovers of poetry' and his prose was read by 'all who care for letters', the number of people in these categories was not large; and only one of his books, *Literature and Dogma* (1873), achieved the circulation of a bestseller. He spoke from the beginning to thoughtful and serious-minded people of some education, a group that remained faithful to him and grew in a modest way more numerous with the years. His success in catching the ear of the general public with phrases that epitomized his ideas – 'Barbarians, Philistines and Populace', 'to see the object as in itself it really is', 'the grand name without the grand thing', 'the remnant', 'that great rope, with a Philistine at each end of it talking inutilities' (of the Atlantic telegraph) – meant that some notion of what he stood for became familiar far beyond the circle of his actual readers.

Matthew Arnold (1822–88) began by being a poet and his literary career has two distinct phases, most of his poetry being written before 1857, the year in which he was elected Professor of Poetry at Oxford, and most of his critical prose after that date. As a Victorian poet he is usually ranked after Tennyson and Browning, but it is clear that Arnold did not think that his poetic achievement was of a radically inferior order to theirs, although he wrote fewer poems and was aware that he was master in them of a far narrower range of invention. Two years after his last original collection of poems, *New Poems* (1867), when Tennyson was still building up his Arthurian cycle of poems and Browning was enjoying his first great popular success with *The Ring and the Book*, Arnold wrote to his mother:

My poems represent, on the whole, the main movement of mind of the last quarter of a century . . . It might be fairly urged that I have less poetical sentiment than Tennyson; and less intellectual vigour and abundance than Browning; yet because I have perhaps more of a fusion of the two than either of them, and have more regularly applied that fusion to the main line of modern development, I am likely enough to have my turn, as they have had theirs.

(Letters of Matthew Arnold, 1848–1888, ed. G. W. E.
Russell, vol II, p 9. Cited below as Letters)

His expectation that his turn would come has had a kind of fulfilment in the twentieth century. In his poems he speaks to us more directly and intimately than Tennyson or Browning, and his outlook is nearer to our own and therefore more congenial. His best poems are truthful, sometimes bleak, reports on experience, suggesting that he understood himself and the world he lived in and was not tempted to soften and blur the intimidating outlines of his vision. Although the poetry is suffused with melancholy and the prose is either high-spirited or more soberly cheerful, an impartial observer will recognize that the same wish 'to get breast to breast with reality' (*Letters of Matthew Arnold to Arthur Hugh Clough*, ed. H. F. Lowry, 1932, p 86) is active in both and that both are aspects of a single 'criticism of life'.

As a writer of expository and critical prose Arnold's eminence depends most visibly on the variety of his interests and the intelligence and literary tact he brought to bear with such single-mindedness on the discussion of literary, social, educational and religious issues. He touched his age at more points than almost any other Victorian writer and is saved from the reproach of a mere miscellaneousness in his prose works, many of them made up of occasional lectures and contributions to periodicals, by the concern that runs through them all for the quality of the civilization around him – that is, both for the quality of the thought and feeling exhibited in the literature and public life of Victorian England, and for the quality of the lives Englishmen were able to lead when the material conditions of their existence were being rapidly altered and most of the values by which an earlier generation had lived were being disconcertingly questioned. He was a major literary critic – the only major critic between Coleridge and T. S. Eliot – partly because, like his predecessor and his successor, he could not be simply a literary critic: the seriousness with which he attended to literature compelled him to stray beyond literature for the real answers to literary questions and drove him to make up his mind about matters that divided theologians or the politicians framing social policies. But it was not only the tendency of literary questions to widen uncomfortably in a period of social transformation that led Arnold in the 1860s and 1870s to write on social and religious issues. He had been brought up by his father Thomas Arnold (1795–1842), the famous 'reforming' headmaster of Rugby School whose radicalism several times lost him the chance of a bishopric, to believe that a man was uneducated if he was uninformed about politics and religion. This bent was confirmed when, in order to be able to marry, Matthew accepted appointment in 1851 as a Government inspector of schools, a post he owed to the favour of the old Whig statesman, Lord Lansdowne, whose private secretary he had been since leaving Oxford, and came to have first-hand experience of the narrowness, unloveliness and self-satisfaction of Dissent in the manufacturing Midlands and North. As a layman, he was at first restricted to inspecting Nonconformist schools –

Church of England and Roman Catholic schools were inspected by clergymen. What these schools taught him about the life of a large section of the population ensured that a critical habit of mind would not be exercised solely upon literature. Yet when this has been said and *Culture and Anarchy* (1869) has been recognized as a classic, it is Arnold's literary criticism that we read and reread for instruction and refreshment. 'From time to time, every hundred years or so,' writes T. S. Eliot, 'it is desirable that some critic shall appear to review the past of our literature and set the poets and the poems in a new order . . . Dryden, Johnson and Arnold have each performed the task as well as human frailty will allow' (op. cit., pp 108–9). To which we may add, since this handsome judgment stresses the historical importance of the critic, that Arnold's presence and authority make themselves felt in contemporary critical discussion as frequently and almost as strongly as if he were still our contemporary.

This summary sketch of the nature of Matthew Arnold's critical activity would be incomplete without some notice of the manner in which he presents his views. Dr Arnold had been a vehement controversialist on the liberal side in religion and politics – he was addicted, for example, to the use of such words as 'detestation' and 'abhorrence' in speaking of the opinions of his Tory or Tractarian opponents – and his son Matthew seems to have decided at an early age that vehemence was a less effective weapon in controversy than moderation if you wished to win over the opposition or to attract the uncommitted to adhere to your opinions. In 1863 he wrote:

Partly nature, partly time and study, have also by this time taught me thoroughly the precious truth that everything turns upon one's exercising the power of *persuasion*, of *charm*: that without this all fury, energy, reasoning power, acquirement, are thrown away . . . Even in one's ridicule one must preserve a sweetness and good-humour.

(*Letters*, vol I p 201)

The adoption of an urbane manner prevented controversy on subjects about which men felt violently from degenerating into the printed equivalent of rowdyism and brawling.

The dominant impression likely to be left on most readers by a study of Arnold's prose writings is of a native good sense and balance, a combination of shrewdness, wholesomeness and fastidiousness. He urges his opinions positively but not as if they are his personal possessions, so that we are convinced that he will not consciously push an argument in favour of his case or play down one that tells against him (unconsciously he does both of these things occasionally in the social and theological essays); he does not parade his learning, but his reading is obviously wide; his prose style is sinuous rather than powerful, unheated (though there are traces of an uncharacteristic warmth in the first edition of *Culture and Anarchy*), and laced with wit and irony; and he is capable of the return on himself and his ideas that he so much admired in Edmund Burke. In his literary criticism he is customarily flexible and subtle in his response to the object of scrutiny, and in such early essays as *On Translating Homer* (1861) and 'Maurice de Guérin' (*Essays in Criticism*, 1865) there is something more: the exhilaration of a man who has come into his rightful inheritance. If in his social and theological writings 'the moral and social passion for doing good' is sometimes at war with disinterestedness and there is less sparkle in the prose, we do not usually feel that we are being browbeaten or unfairly got at, as we often feel in reading Carlyle or Ruskin. Arnold's techniques of persuasion are less flamboyant, they coax rather than overwhelm. His rhetoric is of the cooler, more equable sort that we find with individual variations in John Stuart Mill, George Eliot and John Henry Newman. What such different writers have in common with each other and with Arnold is the intellectual scrupulousness that is a distinctive moral resource.

The bulk of the poetry for which Matthew Arnold is now remembered belongs to the single decade 1847–57 and, within that span, is most thickly concentrated in the five years centred on 1850. From childhood his was clearly a divided nature, with on one side his father's seriousness and active itch to improve things and on the other the 'mobile, inconstant, eager' but passive temperament of the Romantic poet with its tendency to surrender to 'depression and *ennui*' (Arnold's own phrases). It was because the moral, energetic half of his divided nature so strongly disapproved of the 'dark disordered city' of his poetic self (the expression is from W. H. Auden's sonnet on Arnold) that his genuine poetic life was so short. Something in his make-up responded only too distinctly to his father's earnestness. For a while he was able to inhibit this response and evade care and responsibility. His remedy as a schoolboy and Oxford undergraduate, and during his bachelor years in London before his marriage, was to disappear behind a pose of insouciance and apparent frivolity. He hid himself so successfully that Dr Arnold, who died in June 1842 when Matthew was completing his first year at Balliol, too gravely regarded him as an unregenerate spirit, and his family and friends were surprised by the seriousness and melancholy of his first collection of poems in 1849. He was then twenty-six.

At the risk of over-simplification it may be said that temperament speaks in much of the poetry and in the imaginative insights of the literary criticism, character and morality in some of the poems (usually the inferior ones), in the missionary impulses of the literary criticism, and more and more plainly in the social and theological essays. Arnold always insisted that his father, despite his many virtues, was not a poet. When he boasted in the 1860s and 1870s of being 'papa's continuator' in his criticism, he was really confessing that the once recessive moral fraction of his nature was now dominant. It began to take charge when he married in 1851 and, as the phrase goes, settled down. He often grieved over the loss of poetry, complaining pathetically in letters to his friend Arthur Hugh Clough, another divided nature, and to his favourite sister 'K' of the difficulty of composing poetry while earning his living at the perpetual drudgery of school-inspection. The difficulty was not exaggerated, but in his heart of hearts he must have known that broken leisure was not the real problem and that he had betrayed his muse. It has become a commonplace in critical studies of Arnold's poetry to observe that the death of the son Sohrab at the hands of the mighty warrior Rustum in 'Sohrab and Rustum' is a symbolic representation of the poet's sacrificial willingness to reject his poetic self in order to identify himself with Dr Arnold's missionary vigour. To employ another phrase from Auden's sonnet, he 'thrust his gift in prison till it died' (*Another Time*, 1940, p 58).

Inevitably Arnold's sense of what he could accomplish in prose with much less wear and tear to the personality than was demanded by poetic composition grew after 1857 when he was elected Professor of Poetry at Oxford and began to lecture. (He was the first holder of the Chair to lecture in English.) Between 1857 and 1867, the period of his professorship, few poems were written, although one or two of them, such as 'Thyrsis', his elegy on Clough, and 'Obermann Once More', have an important place in the canon. Arnold's first two volumes, *The Strayed Reveller, and Other Poems* (1849) and *Empedocles on Etna, and Other Poems* (1852), were published pseudonymously – probably so that he might not benefit from his father's fame – and sold comparatively few copies. Already with *Poems* (1853), his third collection and the first to which he appended his name, the conflict in his nature was compelling him to censor and edit his work: the book contains pieces chosen from his two pseudonymous volumes, together with such new poems as 'Sohrab and Rustum' and 'The Scholar-Gipsy', and a remarkable preface, his first published essay in literary criticism, in which he defended his refusal to reprint 'Empedocles on Etna', attacked the subjectivity and the lack of concern for structural unity in the verse of the day (the real enemy being his own melancholy), and came out strongly against modern subjects in poetry. In *Poems, Second Series* (1855) Arnold rescued more pieces from his two early volumes, but there were only two new poems. One was 'Balder Dead', based on Scandinavian mythology, a companion epic fragment to the Persian 'Sohrab and Rustum' and, like it, an attempt to escape from a subjectivity Arnold felt to be dangerous because it gave expression to a sense of futility that he was determined to master. In the 1853 volume Clough had preferred 'The Scholar-Gipsy' to 'Sohrab and Rustum', but Arnold at once rebuked him for his preference.

Homer *animates* – Shakespeare *animates* – in its poor way I think Sohrab and Rustum *animates* – The Gipsy Scholar at best awakens a pleasing melancholy. But this is not what we want.

(*Letters to Clough*, p 146)

The relegation to an inferior status of 'The Scholar-Gipsy', now recognized to be a masterpiece, and the suppression of 'Empedocles on Etna', which is certainly Arnold's most ambitious poem, are indications of the struggle to force his inspiration in a prescribed direction. Between 1855 and 1867 there was only *Merope* (1858), a tragedy on the classical Greek model. It illustrated very clearly the feebleness of the poetry Arnold was capable of writing with 'character' rather than 'temperament' in the saddle, and his voluble defence of it against the criticisms of his friends reveals that he was less satisfied with it than he claimed to be. *New Poems* (1867) was Arnold's last new collection of verse. It was blown up to a respectable size by the revival of 'Empedocles on Etna', but much else in the volume was not new at all – for example, half-a-dozen pieces were further salvaged from 1849 and 1852, and of two apparently new poems, 'Calais Sands' and 'Dover Beach', the first belongs to 1850 and Arnold's courtship of Frances Lucy Wightman, the second probably to 1851 in the months following their marriage. A group of religiose sonnets, which are with *Merope* the most depressing of all Arnold's poetic performances, begs us to accept good intentions as a substitute for creative imagination. The sonnets show up all the more badly in their awkward contrivance because they appear beside Arnold's bitterly truthful exploration of his feelings in 'Growing Old', a powerful short lyric probably provoked by impatience with the smugness of Browning's 'Rabbi ben Ezra.'

Even in *The Strayed Reveller* (1849) explicit moral intention intrudes and disfigures some of the poems. The most interesting poems in the book, apart from the lyrics 'To a Gipsy Child by the Sea-Shore' and 'In Utrumque Paratus', and the much longer 'Resignation', which by its final position gains authority as a personal statement, are the narratives 'Mycerinus', 'The Sick King in Bokhara' and 'The Forsaken Merman' and the tableau pieces 'The Strayed Reveller' and 'The New Sirens'. 'The Strayed Reveller' describes in free verse that recalls Goethe's poems loosely modelled on Greek lyric measures the burden of vicarious suffering the poet has to bear as

> . . . the wild, thronging train,
> The bright procession
> Of eddying forms . . .

sweeps before his mind: he is condemned to feel as a man and to see as a god. By contrast, 'Resignation', in which Arnold seems to have remembered some of Wordsworth's ideas in 'Tintern Abbey' for the purpose of disagreeing with them, sees the poet's role as simply that of a spectator. Nature seems to 'bear' rather than 'rejoice' and is quite indifferent to man. The poet

> Whose natural insight can discern
> What through experience others learn;
> Who needs not love and power, to know
> Love transient, power an unreal show;
> Who treads at ease life's uncheer'd ways . . .

should not be blamed for his detachment. Fate's ear is 'impenetrable', and it is only through our failure to see things as they are that we forget

> In action's dizzying eddy whirl'd,
> The something that infects the world.

In this first volume Arnold's selection of subjects and themes is less a matter of simple aesthetic choice than of a balance between this and the wish 'to get breast to breast with reality'. The second collection of poems in 1852 was inspired by a similar purpose. It contains the love-lyrics later to be distinguished as the two sequences 'Switzerland' and 'Faded Leaves', the narrative poem 'Tristram and Iseult', 'Memorial Verses' (an elegy on Wordsworth), and 'Stanzas in Memory of the Author of "Obermann"', as well as a number of unrhymed lyrics, namely 'The Youth of Nature', 'The Youth of Man' and 'The Future', which Arnold seems to have thought of as 'pindarics'. Although all these poems are in varying degrees meritorious and worth detailed study, attention will have to be given here at their expense to the 'dramatic poem' which supplied Arnold with his volume's title.

'Empedocles on Etna' resembles Byron's *Manfred* superficially in form, but it is a better organized and more coherent work. The poem is seen in a proper perspective as Arnold's most serious attempt in poetry to gain the 'intellectual deliverance' which is 'the peculiar demand of those ages which are called modern' ('On the Modern Element in Literature', *Complete Prose Works*, vol I p 19). The attempt was a failure, but by a paradox it is the expression of this failure that is responsible for the poem's artistic success. Intellectual deliverance begins, Arnold says, when we grasp the general ideas which give the law to the multitudinousness of past and present fact, but it is not perfect until

. . . we have acquired that harmonious acquiescence of mind which we feel in contemplating a grand spectacle that is intelligible to us.

(ibid., p 20)

There is an assumption here that intelligibility will issue in acquiescence, but what 'Empedocles on Etna' actually teaches is that acquiescence may be willed, but that it cannot be felt wholeheartedly.

The dramatic poem has only three characters, two of whom Callicles and Pausanias, are there as foils to Empedocles, the mature poet and philosopher who commits suicide at the poem's climax by throwing himself into the crater of Etna. Callicles is a young poet whose happiness and ability to sing are as yet unshadowed by 'l'excès de douleur produit par l'abus de la pensée'. He represents what Empedocles was in his own youth and is seen only in the moist, fertile 'forest region' at the foot of Etna, as Empedocles, the man in whom the habit of analysis has destroyed the power to feel and the wish to live, is associated with and seen alone only at the 'charr'd, blacken'd, melancholy waste' of the volcano's summit. The Stoic preachment which Empedocles bestows on his friend Pausanias, telling him that the destruction of illusion and the contemplation of naked reality need not lead to despair if he moderates his expectations of life ('Because thou must not dream, thou need'st not then despair'), takes place exactly half-way up Etna at the point where the climbers come out of the shade of the forest into the burning sunlight of the upper slopes. This scene is set at noon; the earlier scene at the foot of the volcano (in which only Callicles and Pausanias appear) occurs shortly after sun-rise; the last scene at the summit, which contains Empedocles' long soliloquy punctuated by the songs of Callicles from below, is timed at midnight. This association of particular characters and attitudes to experience with particular times and places is one means by which we are led to see that the ascent of the volcano depicts the passage from innocence to experience. Empedocles cannot live by the resignation he has preached to Pausanias. Despondency is more real to him than the sentiment that 'Life still leaves human effort scope'. With his move from comforting illusion into what Yeats called 'the desolation of reality' the spring of his life has snapped.

Arnold, like Empedocles, needed truth and joy, but as a poet found them to be incompatible.

> And yet men have such need of joy!
> But joy whose grounds are true . . .
> ('Obermann Once More')

Because the service of reason chilled 'feeling and the religious mood', because following 'the pale cold star of Truth' ('Stanzas from the Grande Chartreuse') destroyed the joy necessary for the fullest artistic creation, because he could bear no longer to juggle with the equal claims of two necessities, Arnold suppressed 'Empedocles on Etna'. Everyone has admired the songs and lyric interludes of Callicles, which break up and relieve the speeches of Empedocles, but a valid critical judgment of the poem must acknowledge the high poetic level on which the whole of the second act is sustained. Except in the magnificent *coda* of 'Sohrab and Rustum' and in a few lyrics, which have to include 'Dover Beach' and 'Yes! in the sea of life enisled', Arnold never wrote with such intensity or poignancy again.

Poems (1853), often described as the poet's most important single volume of poems, included 'Sohrab and Rustum' and 'The Scholar-Gipsy'. While 'The Scholar-Gipsy' celebrated what Arnold later admitted to be 'the *freest* and most delightful part, perhaps, of my life' in its recollections of undergraduate wanderings in 'that unforgotten Oxfordshire and Berkshire country' (Letter quoted in Mrs H. Ward, *A Writer's Recollections*, 1918, p 54), 'Sohrab and Rustum' had nevertheless to be preferred because it had been written to illustrate, in the words of the critical creed of the 1853 Preface, 'the all-importance of the choice of a subject; the necessity of accurate construction; and the subordinate character of expression' (*Complete Prose Works*, vol I p 12). After 'Empedocles on Etna' it represents a diminished ambition. In his defence of *Merope* (1858) Arnold spoke of a kind of poetry in which 'perfection' might be approached without 'an actual tearing of oneself to pieces', a perfection of form without 'perfection in the region of thought and feeling' (*Letters*, vol I p 63); and 'Sohrab and Rustum', although charged with feeling by the personal significance the story developed for Arnold, is the first stage on the downward journey that leads through 'Balder Dead' to the nearly lifeless *Merope*. From the critical viewpoint which Arnold had reached in 1853 his satisfaction with 'Sohrab and Rustum' is understandable, but it is still surprising that he did not see that in its emotional tone and final effect on the reader it is close to 'The Scholar-Gipsy'. It is the influence of Keats that gives this pastoral lament for youth with its hopefulness and *brio*, which are sapped by living in the world, a sensuous richness unusual in Arnold's poetry. F. R. Leavis has urged the intellectual weakness of the elegy while admitting its charm, but this judgment seems to me too severe. The scholar gipsy, a Callicles magically preserved from becoming an Empedocles, is a figure borrowed from Glanvill to allow Arnold to criticize Victorian civilization by opposing an ideal world to the acutal. 'Yes', he writes to Clough in 1853, '– *congestion of the brain* is what we suffer from – I always feel it and say it – and cry for air like my own Empedocles' (*Letters to Clough*, p 130). It is not to the point to ask when

> . . . wits were fresh and clear
> And life ran gaily as the sparkling Thames . . .

if by juxtaposing two kinds of existence, 'the infection of our mental strife', which destroys the possibility of spontaneity and happiness, can be brought home. In 'Memorial Verses' Arnold had named Goethe 'Physician of the iron age', and here the imagery is all of sickness:

> . . . this strange disease of modern life
> With its sick hurry, its divided aims
> Its heads o'ertax'd, its palsied hearts . . .

> But fly our paths, our feverish contact fly!

I do not think it is true to say that 'What it was that the Scholar Gipsy had that we had not, Arnold doesn't, except in the most general terms, know' (F. R. Leavis, *Revaluation*, 1936, p 191). He tells us in a succession of stanzas – with as much concreteness as we have a right to expect – what constitutes the scholar gipsy's health.

Nothing new in *New Poems* (1867) quite reaches the level of the best writing in Arnold's 1852 and 1853 collections. 'Thyrsis', the elegy on Clough, leans heavily on its predecessor 'The Scholar-Gipsy', with which it shares the stanza Arnold adapted from Keats, and its classical embroidery has a slightly self-conscious air. The sixth stanza is a good instance of the colour and fluency of the best descriptive writing:

> So, some tempestuous morn in early June,
>   When the year's primal burst of bloom is o'er,
>   Before the roses and the longest day –
> When garden-walks and all the grassy floor
>   With blossoms red and white of fallen May
>   And chestnut-flowers are strewn –
> So have I heard the cuckoo's parting cry,
>   From the wet field, through the vext garden-trees,
>   Come with the volleying rain and tossing breeze:
> *The bloom is gone, and with the bloom go I!*

It is significant that the stanza is about something lost. 'Bloom' is a favourite word with Arnold; it signifies what is too easily destroyed. Arnold's recognition of the world's beauty and delight is heartfelt, but it cannot be for him a simple, unmixed feeling. The beauty traps us into falsity unless we also recognize, as he says in 'Dover Beach', that

> . . . the world, which seems
> To lie before us like a land of dreams,
> So various, so beautiful, so new,
> Hath really neither joy, nor love, nor light,
> Nor certitude, nor peace, nor help for pain . . .

'Obermann Once More' is another poem that must be adjudged inferior to its predecessor. 'Stanzas in Memory of the Author of "Obermann"' belongs in its inception to 1849 and was 'conceived, and partly composed, in the valley going down from the foot of the Gemmi Pass towards the Rhone' (Arnold's 1869 note). This was towards the end of Arnold's relationship with the Marguerite of the 'Switzerland' poems, and the farewell addressed to the spirit of Senancour is also a farewell to her and to youth, irresponsibility and, ultimately, the writing of poetry. In 'Obermann Once More', which was written between 1865 and 1867, Senancour is constrained, in accordance with Arnold's sanguine hopes for the success of liberal ideas in the 1860s, to preach that the poet has a duty to fulfil to men in helping them to secure

> One common wave of thought and joy
> Lifting mankind again!

Here we note that thought and joy, once sadly judged to be incompatible, are forcibly coupled in an energy of inspiration. Sainte-Beuve's comment, 'C'est un Obermann transfiguré', seems just (quoted in C. B. Tinker and H. F. Lowry, *The Poetry of Matthew Arnold: A Commentary*, 1940, p 271). He has come to have something of Dr Arnold's bearing. The symbolic dawn at the end of the poem, which is intended to herald a new age of hope by recalling the earlier dawn that broke on the exhausted Roman world with the advent of Christianity, is poetically quite unconvincing.

How are we to sum up? Although he objected aristocratically to any Byronic parade of his restlessness, and there is therefore always a discretion and an economy about the expression of the distinctive Arnoldian pathos, Matthew Arnold is, as T. S. Eliot says, 'more intimate with us than Browning, more intimate than Tennyson ever is except at moments, as in the passionate flights of *In Memoriam*' (*The Use of Poetry and the Use of Criticism*, p 105). It is with fatigue, disenchantment and regret that essentially the poems have to do, and it is the resistance that Arnold offers to these feelings that prevents the poetry from being enervating. In this resistance the 'moral' Arnold is present, and yet the sense of futility is barely kept at bay by the struggle to practise Stoic composure. 'He had no real serenity', writes T. S. Eliot with an insight furnished, I think, by self-knowledge, 'only an impeccable demeanour' (ibid., p 119). This is exact. The poems such as 'Rugby Chapel' or 'The Second Best' in which Arnold praises courage and perseverance or tries to promulgate hope are comparatively few in number. They are also usually inferior poems, being too obviously written with gritted teeth, metaphorically speaking, to suspend our disbelief. Arnold's deepest feeling in his poetry is that he has been born into an

> . . . iron time
> Of doubts, disputes, distractions, fears . . .,
>   ('Memorial Verses')

that he is a wanderer between two worlds, 'one dead/The other powerless to be born' ('Stanzas from the Grande Chartreuse'), that his age in its 'true *blankness* and *barrenness* and *unpoetrylessness*' (*Letters to Clough*, p 126) has made it virtually impossible for him not to be divided against himself. Therefore men must

> . . . waive all claim to bliss, and try to bear;
> With close-lipp'd patience for [their] only friend . . .
> ('The Scholar-Gypsy')

He wrestles with discouragement because he is the son of Dr Arnold and will not yield to despair. He believes that it should be possible to embrace the truth not only with an appearance of composure, but with real joy; he cannot feel this joy, however hard he tries; and he is unsure whether the fault belongs to his time or is partly due to some inadequacy in his own nature.

When Arnold fully understood the sombreness of his poetic nature, he stopped writing poetry, but by then he had produced a body of poetic work which, in spite of its restriction to a few themes and its lack of ease in execution, has permanent value. Sometimes lack of ease becomes clumsiness. He is undramatic – it is the elegiac rather than the dramatic note that is uppermost in the narrative poems 'Tristram and Iseult', 'Sohrab and Rustum' and 'Balder Dead', and it must be conceded that this makes for monotony. Poems of the type represented by 'A Summer Night' and 'The Buried Life' develop too haphazardly and are perilously close to the 'thinking aloud' condemned in Wordsworth. Yet Arnold is Wordsworthian rather than Keatsian (except in 'The Scholar-Gipsy', 'Thyrsis' and the third part of 'The Church of Brou'), and it is the Wordsworthian example supporting a personal voice that we find in the Cadmus and Harmonia interlude in 'Empedocles on Etna', for example, or in such a subdued 'average' passage of Arnold's verse as the following from 'Bacchanalia':

> The evening comes, the fields are still.
> The tinkle of the thirsty rill,
> Unheard all day, ascends again;
> Deserted is the half-mown plain,
> Silent the swaths! the ringing wain,
> The mower's cry, the dog's alarms,
> All housed within the sleeping farms!
> The business of the day is done,
> The last-left haymaker is gone.
> And from the thyme upon the height,

And from the elder-blossom white
And pale dog-roses in the hedge,
And from the mint-plant in the sedge,
In puffs of balm the night-air blows
The perfume which the day forgoes.

There is nothing extraordinary here – the language, the rhythms, the structure of the syntax are all simple – but it is writing that should win respect.

It is only in their poetry, since Clough's prose apart from the Epilogue to 'Dipsychus' is of little account, that the achievements of Arnold and Clough are in any way commensurable, and even this statement would probably have been regarded as dubious if not manifestly absurd a generation ago. But literary reputations are not stationary and Clough has deservedly enjoyed some revival. Swinburne once wrote a limerick beginning 'There was a bad poet named Clough,/Whom his friends found it useless to puff', but the sneer has boomeranged. It is the Swinburnian logorrhoea that is now found tedious. It is no longer enough to think of Clough as the author of a single anthology-piece, 'Say not the struggle nought availeth'. Many modern readers of *Amours de Voyage*, 'Dipsychus', 'Easter Day', 'The Latest Decalogue' and 'Natura Naturans' would be willing to agree with the character in Graham Greene's *The Quiet American* (1955) that 'He was an adult poet in the nineteenth century. There weren't so many of them'. Clough is too unequal a poet and left behind him too much unfinished and unrevised work for him to stand appropriately at the side of Arnold, but in some respects he is a more original poet. His poetry deserves less cursory treatment than I am here able to give it.

Arthur Hugh Clough (1819–61) and Matthew Arnold were friends from their Oxford days, and there is a reasonable justification for classifying them both as Victorian 'poets of doubt' and dealing with them together in the same chapter. Arnold wrote to Clough in America in 1853, 'I really have clung to you in spirit more than to any other man . . . I am for ever linked with you by intellectual bonds – the strongest of all' (*Letters to Clough*, pp 129, 130), and later in the same year on his return to England Clough acknowledged the nature of the tie between them in a letter to his fiancée complaining of some of his other friends:

They all got so *churchy*; there is no possibility of getting on thoroughly –
Matt Arnold is not churchy . . . I am very glad I have not conformed *more*
than I have – I shall pick up some misbelieving friends in London I dare
say.

(*The Correspondence of A. H. Clough*, ed. F. L. Mulhauser,
1957, vol II, pp 460–1)

The sense of desolate loss experienced by the generation of those
who were young in the 1840s when their religious certainties
crumbled has never been more plangently expressed than by
Clough in 'Easter Day' which is subscribed 'Naples, 1849'.
Arnold's treatment of the same theme in 'Stanzas from the Grande
Chartreuse' is more reflective. For full appreciation Clough's poem
needs to be read at length since so much of its effect depends on the
use of brooding, grief-stricken repetition, but the urgency of the
feeling and the directness of its rendering can be sampled in the
following extract:

> Eat, drink, and play, and think that this is bliss!
> There is no Heaven but this!
> There is no Hell; –
> Save Earth, which serves the purpose doubly well,
> Seeing it visits still
> With equallest apportionments of ill
> Both good and bad alike, and brings to one same dust
> The unjust and the just
> With Christ, who is not risen.
>
> Eat, drink, and die, for we are souls bereaved:
> Of all the creatures under this broad sky
> We are most helpless, that had hoped most high,
> And most beliefless, that had most believed.
> Ashes to ashes, dust to dust;
> As of the unjust, also of the just –
> Yea, of that Just One too.
> It is the one sad Gospel that is true,
> Christ is not risen.

It is, in my opinion, one of the great 'religious' lyrics of the Victorian
period.

Clough's terror of intellectual dishonesty, which grew at times so
neurotic that he found it almost impossible to choose between two
or several courses of action open to him, was the result of his total
commitment to Dr Arnold's beliefs and attitudes at Rugby and his
inability to sustain those beliefs when he met the Tractarian

doctrines at Oxford and faced the probing questions of W. G. Ward, his Balliol tutor, who was then on the path that was to take him before Newman into the Roman Catholic Church. Liberal theological opinion, to which Newman was bitterly hostile, was nevertheless admitted by him to have been 'invested with an elevation of character which claimed the respect even of its opponents' (Note A: Liberalism, *Apologia pro Vita Sua*, 1874 edn, p 292) when Dr Arnold's Rugby pupils went up to Oxford. Clough was one of these pupils. Although he was four years older than Matthew Arnold, he was in many ways less mature and less nimble of mind. His Rugby and Oxford experiences left him not only uncertain what he believed, but paralysed by the suspicion that if he made up his mind to believe or do anything it might be for 'factitious' reasons:

> I do not like being moved: for the will is excited: and
>   action
> Is a most dangerous thing; I tremble for something
>   factitious,
> Some malpractice of heart and illegitimate process;
> We are so prone to these things with our terrible notions
>   of duty.

This is Claude, the hero or anti-hero of Clough's epistolary verse-novel in free accentual hexameters, *Amours de Voyage* (written 1849, but not published till 1858), but the fact that Clough could analyse Claude's disposition so dispassionately does not mean that he does not share this disposition (as one or two American critics have tried to argue). *Amours de Voyage* is the story of a man whose scruples about his sincerity cause him to hesitate, palter and delay until he has lost the girl whom he met in Rome during the siege of the city by the French. At first he is doubtful whether he is really in love. When she leaves Rome with her family and disappears, he becomes certain that he is in love and is stirred to action. He pursues her through Italy to the frontiers of Switzerland, but all his inquiries fail. Finally, he surrenders the chase and again wonders:

> After all, do I know that I really cared so about her?
> Do whatever I will, I cannot call up her image . . .

Earlier in a state of deep depression at his lack of success in his search he hears a barrel-organ playing 'an English psalm-tune' in the streets of Florence, is sentimentally comforted by it, and thinks for a moment that he has gained 'a religious assurance'. But immediately in revulsion he brands this comfort as a temptation:

> I refuse, reject, and put it utterly from me;
> I will look straight out, see things, not try to evade them;
> Fact shall be fact for me, and Truth the Truth as ever,
> Flexible, changeable, vague, and multiform, and
>   doubtful –
> Off and depart to the void, thou subtle, fanatical tempter!

The 'subtle, fanatical tempter' is externalized as the Spirit in 'Dipsychus', a dramatic poem which was published fragmentarily by Mrs Clough after her husband's death at Florence in 1861 and has been known in as complete a form as its unfinished state allows only since the modern collected edition of Clough's poems in 1951. 'Dipsychus', set in Venice on a summer holiday, is a dialogue between moony, anxious idealism and cynically shrewd, worldly commonsense. From the names of Dipsychus (Faustulus) and the Spirit (Mephisto) in early drafts of the poem it is evident that Clough took a hint from Goethe, but his treatment of the subject is entirely independent. Many of Clough's poems deal with love and marriage, and in 'Dipsychus' he writes with a degree of sexual frankness that would have offended many Victorians. The Spirit's lively songs – '"There is no God", the wicked saith', 'How pleasant it is to have money' – have often been printed out of context, but, like the songs of Callicles in 'Empedocles on Etna', they lose by being separated from the speeches on which they are intended to comment. The Spirit stands for conformity to the ways of the world: Dipsychus should go into society, accept its conventions while seeing through them, build a career and make a good match. His scruples about such matters are as absurd as his Puritan ditherings when eyed by Venetian girls, sexual experience being to the Spirit

> But heavens! as innocent a thing
> As picking strawberries in spring.

The centre of the debate in a poem that develops slackly and lacks a firm shape is to be found in scenes ix and x. In scene ix Dipsychus, grumbling that God's 'newer will' is that

> We should not think of Him at all, but trudge it,
> And of the world He has assigned us make
> What best we can . . .,

twists between the alternatives of 'waiting for the spark from heaven to fall' like the Scholar-Gipsy and what seems to him abject surrender. The Spirit warns:

> Devotion, and ideas, and love,
> And beauty claim their place above;
> But saint and sage and poet's dreams
> Divide the light in coloured streams,
> Which this alone gives all combined,
> The *siccum lumen* of the mind
> Called common sense: and no high wit
> Gives better counsel than does it.
> Submit, submit!

In scene x the Spirit is given the dignity of blank verse for the first time for his savage portrait of the poetic idealist's inadequacies. His attitude to Dipsychus is very much that of the worldly uncle in the prose Epilogue. The young men of his nephew's generation, the latter says:

... seem to me a sort of hobbadi-hoy cherub, too big to be innocent, and too simple for anything else. They're full of the notion of the world being so wicked, and of their taking a higher line, as they call it. I only fear they'll never take any at all.

Dr Arnold is responsible for making young men so highminded and helpless – 'It's all Arnold's doing; he spoilt the public schools' – but the nephew, although ready to admit that the young men may have been spoilt, objects to the attack on Dr Arnold and attributes the trouble to the 'over-excitation of the religious sense' caused by 'the religious movement of the last century, beginning with Wesleyanism, and culminating at last in Puseyism'.

Clough's abandonment of 'Dipsychus' after his marriage has been paralleled with Arnold's suppression of 'Empedocles on Etna', but in fact after 1853 Clough wrote virtually no verse until his final break-down in health. On sick-leave from the Education Office in 1861 he produced '*Mari Magno* or Tales on Board', which, owing its framework to Chaucer, its manner more to Patmore than to Crabbe (the latter being one of Clough's admirations), picks dispiritedly at old themes and is a sad declension from *Amours de Voyage* and 'Dipsychus'. It is in Clough's poetic career what *Merope* is in Arnold's. But these comparisons between Clough and Arnold may be misleading. Their poetic ideals were in many respects opposed. Clough favoured the subjects from modern life that Arnold impatiently dismissed in his 1853 Preface. Arnold discovered a want of concern for the beautiful in Clough's lyrics and never did justice to the intelligence or raciness of the verse-novels and satirical poems, although he did prefer *Amours de Voyage* to Tennyson's *Maud*. He would have found 'Dipsychus' unsettling and objectionable. Some of Clough's shorter poems are properly described as drab, dully surfaced and ramshackle, but there are others – for example, the charming and original 'Natura Naturans' and the unexpectedly elegant 'Epithalamium' – which are free from these faults. In part of his censure at least, one suspects, Arnold was denying himself an individual response to his friend's poetry out of deference to Victorian notions of the poetical in subject and treatment. 'Thyrsis', though a poem of affection, has contributed to a false view of Clough's achievement. There is a tragi-comedy of imperfect sympathies. Neither Arnold nor Clough really understood or sympathized with what the other was doing in poetry, and each censured in the other weaknesses he feared in himself. It is curious that Arnold's wit and sociability were expressed exclusively in his life and in his prose, the poetry being the vehicle of seriousness and melancholy, whereas Clough, who after his Oxford days was often glum and taciturn in company, in his poems gives us the fun and high spirits of the reading-party in the Scottish Highlands in *The Bothie of Toperna-Vuolich* and the wit of 'The Latest Decalogue'. Arnold has had his critical due as a poet. Clough's own neglect of his poetry explains in some measure the critical neglect of it in the twentieth century. With the modern editions of the poems and letters and the biographical and critical studies of Clough now available we are in a position to see him steadily and see him whole. His reputation is bound to grow as his position as one of the most interesting and attractive minor poets of the Victorian period is more widely recognized.

To Arnold his prose writings formed a single web. 'Whoever seriously occupies himself with literature will soon perceive its vital connection with other agencies,' he wrote in the preface to *Mixed Essays* (1879), adding pertinently '. . . literature is a part of civilization; it is not the whole.' (*Complete Prose Works*, vol VIII, p 370). It is with civilization or 'the humanization of man in society' that the serious critic has to do, Arnold asserts, and in 'Heinrich Heine' he sets out his special task in Victorian times.

Modern times find themselves with an immense system of institutions, established facts, accredited dogmas, customs, rules which have come to them from times not modern. In this system their life has to be carried forward; yet they have a sense that this system is not of their own creation, that it by no means corresponds exactly with the wants of their actual life, that, for them, it is customary, not rational. The awakening of this sense is the awakening of the modern spirit. The modern spirit is now awake almost everywhere; the sense of want of correspondence between the forms of modern Europe and its spirit, between the new wine of the eighteenth and nineteenth centuries, and the old bottles of the eleventh and twelfth centuries, or even of the sixteenth and seventeenth, almost every one now perceives; it is no longer dangerous to affirm that this want of correspondence exists ... To remove this want of correspondence is beginning to be the settled endeavour of most persons of good sense. Dissolvents of the old European system of dominant ideas and facts we must all be ... what we have to study is that we may not be acrid dissolvents of it.

(Essays in Criticism (1865), ibid., vol III, pp 109–10)

This preaches the gospel of an inevitable transformation, but we should note that in his dislike of acridity Arnold implies that the genuine reformer is also the true conservative, and that without an imaginative appreciation of how well 'the old European system of dominant ideas and facts' once served civilization we are likely to fall into doctrinaire Jacobinism, namely 'Violent indignation with the past, abstract systems of renovation applied wholesale' (*Culture and Anarchy* (1869), ibid., vol V, p 109). The same belief that a willingness to accept necessary change is in practice conservative – since it is a force making for social cohesion – inspired Dr Arnold's liberalism.

If the prose writings were a single web to Arnold, to us some parts of the web are more valuable than others. The theological essays, in which the instinct to conserve fights for its existence and survives only by a slippery piece of mental legerdemain that deceived its author, were important to Arnold but are less important to us. 'At the present moment,' we find him saying in 1875, 'two things about the Christian religion must surely be clear to anybody with eyes in his head. One is, that men cannot do without it; the other, that they cannot do with it as it is' (*God and the Bible* (1875), ibid., vol VII, p 378). On the one hand, the *Zeitgeist* had shown theology to be a pseudo-science. It is convenient to retain the word God as a shorthand sign for '*that stream of tendency by which all things seek to fulfil the law of their being' (St. Paul and Protestantism* (1870), ibid., vol VI, p 10), but Christianity must be demythologized. On the other hand, conduct is three-fourths of life and, since religion is essentially 'morality touched by emotion' (*Literature and Dogma*, ibid., vol VI, p 176), it is only religious feeling that is capable of converting unappetizing ethical precept into an inspiration acting on men's lives. Arnold's analysis of the way in which theologians have distorted the language of the Bible is acute, but his belief that men will still be fired to action and heroic self-sacrifice by his watered-down version of Christianity is optimistic. He wishes honestly and valiantly to assert nothing that is not verifiable, but when from the unenlightened but unobjectionable 'stream of tendency by which all things seek to fulfil the law of their being' God becomes 'the enduring power, not ourselves, which makes for righteousness' (*Literature and Dogma*, ibid., vol VI, p 200), Arnold is already reading history with a squint and creating a new unpicturesque myth in place of the old picturesque one. As Lionel Trilling points out, the author of *Literature and Dogma* is not at ease in his position – 'That Christianity is true: that is, after all, the one thing that Arnold cannot really say' (*Matthew Arnold*, 1939, p 364).

What made Arnold so anxious to 'save' Christianity from its orthodox apologists was his sense of the immense part religion had played historically in the 'humanization of man in society'. The religious tendency to reverence an 'Eternal not ourselves' was a permanent one, and 'All tendencies of human nature are in themselves vital and profitable' (*On the Study of Celtic Literature* (1867), *Complete Prose Works*, vol III, p 348). The notion that man's development must be many-sided is repeated again and again in Arnold's literary criticism and social writings – it is at the centre of *Culture and Anarchy* (1869) – and is forcibly expressed in the late 'A Liverpool Address':

Money-making is not enough by itself. Industry is not enough by itself. Seriousness is not enough by itself. I speak now of the kinds of stimulus most in use with people of our race, and above all in business communities . . . Respectable these kinds of stimulus may be, useful they may be, but they are not by themselves sufficient. The need in man for intellect and knowledge, his desire for beauty, his instinct for society, and for pleasurable and graceful forms of society, require to have their stimulus felt also, felt and satisfied.

(*Five Uncollected Essays*, 1953, p 88)

Political power was passing to the Philistine middle-class, and Arnold's professional experience as an inspector of schools had made him exceptionally aware of the unfitness of members of this class to govern. They had 'a defective type of religion, a narrow range of intellect and knowledge, a stunted sense of beauty, a low standard of manners' (*Mixed Essays* (1879),[1] *Complete Prose Works*,

---

[1] The introduction to this book is reprinted as 'Democracy' alongside the later essay 'Equality' in *Mixed Essays* (1879). The two essays are Arnold's most interesting contributions to social thinking apart from *Culture and Anarchy*.

vol VIII, p 369). Carlyle spoke of the Second Reform Act (1867) as 'the calling in of new supplies of blockheadism', but Arnold knew with whom the future lay. His concern was not narrowly political. As he puts it in 'The Future of Liberalism' (1880), 'the master-thought by which my politics are governed is . . . the thought of the bad civilization of the English middle class' (*Irish Essays* (1882), ibid., vol IX, p 137).

This master-thought which inspired Arnold's campaigning for a proper national system of secondary education from the time of his *The Popular Education of France* (1861) until the end of his life, is kept steadily before us in *Culture and Anarchy* (1869) and is satirically illustrated in *Friendship's Garland* (1871). *Culture and Anarchy*, Arnold's most sustained essay in social criticism, examines the 'bad civilization of the English middle class' in a framework provided by an analysis of the three classes of English society (the famous division into Barbarians, Philistines and Populace), a discussion of the English love of 'doing as one likes' (a phrase which glances critically at John Stuart Mill's *On Liberty*), and the prescription of culture as 'the great help out of our present difficulties' (*Complete Prose Works*, vol V, p 233). In *Friendship's Garland*, a light-hearted work that Arnold obviously enjoyed writing, the mouthpiece of the author's ideas is an irascible Prussian savant, Arminius Von Thunder-ten-Tronckh, a descendant of the character in Voltaire's *Candide*, and Arnold himself appears ironically as a feeble and harassed but patriotic defender of English institutions and customs living penuriously in a garret in Grub Street. Mr Bottles, the complacent Philistine manufacturer with the villa at Reigate, is set three-dimensionally before us with all his want of 'sweetness and light', and Arminius barks 'Get Geist' at the English people. The expression 'the two noblest of things, which are sweetness and light' is taken by Arnold for *Culture and Anarchy* from Swift's 'Battle of the Books', as the terms 'Hebraism' and 'Hellenism' are borrowed from the German poet Heine. Sweetness and light are both connected with Hellenism. All classes in English society lack light, i.e., are inaccessible to ideas, but the Philistines, who are also wanting in sweetness, stand in particular need of hellenization. Hellenism is needed to balance the Hebraism that characterizes the narrow life of that typical Philistine, the strict earnest Dissenter whose horizon is bounded by his home, his office or factory, and his chapel. The Philistines of the middle-class, the inheritors of the Puritan tradition, are 'the best stuff in the nation', Arnold believes, but they must be radically transformed.

Look at the life imagined in such a newspaper as the Non-conformist, – a life of jealousy of the Establishment, disputes, tea-meetings, openings of chapels, sermons; and then think of it as an ideal of a human life completing itself on all sides and aspiring with all its organs after sweetness, light and perfection.

(ibid., vol V, p 103)

'Culture' in *Culture and Anarchy* strongly recalls 'criticism' in 'The Function of Criticism at the Present Time', the key essay of *Essays in Criticism* (1865). It is not 'a smattering of the two dead languages of Greek and Latin', as was supposed by John Bright, whose politics Arnold distrusted. It is

. . . a pursuit of our total perfection by means of getting to know, on all the matters which most concern us, the best which has been thought and said in the world; and through this knowledge, turning a stream of fresh and free thought upon our stock notions and habits.

(ibid., vol V, p 233)

(Cf. 'The Function of Criticism at the Present Time' (1864). 'Its business is . . . simply to know the best that is known and thought in the world, and by in its turn making this known, to create a current of true and fresh ideas' (ibid., vol III, p 270)). Culture, that is to say, acts as a dissolvent. To Arnold human perfection means both 'a *harmonious* perfection, developing all sides of our humanity' and 'a *general* perfection, developing all parts of our society' (ibid., vol V, p 235). The Philistines, who suppose energy and strictness of conduct enough for perfection, are 'incomplete and mutilated men' (ibid., vol V, p 236). What Arnold fears with the decline in aristocratic prestige which must follow the transfer of political power to the middle-class is the Americanization of English society. The aristocratic Barbarians have supported some respect for intellect, have exemplified some amenity in their mode of living. 'America', he writes, 'is just ourselves, with the Barbarians quite left out and the Populace nearly . . . From Maine to Florida and back again, all America Hebraises' (ibid., vol V, p 243).

The nation once Americanized will be in danger of forgetting that there are standards in matters of taste as well as in morals, and that popularity is not commonly a mark of excellence; and Arnold instances the 'unutterable external hideousness' of London (ibid., vol V, p 103) as an example of the depth of English failure already existing. Most Englishmen now believe, he thinks, that 'our greatness and welfare are proved by our being so very rich' and put their faith in machinery, but 'Greatness is a spiritual condition worthy to excite love, interest, and admiration' (ibid., vol V, pp 96, 97), the England of Victoria excites these less in mankind at large than the England of Elizabeth I, and private opulence with us exists beside public need. The Englishman's failure to rise above personal and class interests to an idea of the State as a 'centre of light and authority' is due to his infatuation with a false idea of liberty ('Doing as One Likes'), the fruit of which is the anarchy Arnold discovered in the England of the 1860s. Yet every man has in himself a 'possible Socrates' (ibid., vol V, p 228), a disinterested and classless 'best self', of which the State should be the collective representation. This is, of course, the State conceived as an ideal, and Arnold is aware that the actual number of '*aliens*', as he calls those in each class led, not by their class spirit, but by a general '*humane* spirit' (ibid., vol V, p 156), is small. In spite of this he argues that it is only by growth in respect for the idea of the State as a civilized agent that a divided society will ever attain a 'strict standard of excellence' and a belief in the 'paramount authority of right reason' (ibid., vol V, p 147). Some critics have cocked an ear for Hegelian overtones when Arnold writes about the State, but J. Dover Wilson has replied – rightly, in my opinion – that 'Arnold had no leanings whatever towards the absolute State. His ideal was the service State in a democratical society' (*The Social and Political Ideas of Some Representative Thinkers of the Victorian Age*, ed. F. J. C. Hearnshaw, 1933, p 186).

Culture speaks 'through *all* the voices of human experience which have been heard upon it, of art, science, poetry, philosophy, history, as well as of religion' (*Culture and Anarchy, Complete Prose Works*, vol V, p 93), but there can hardly be any question that for Arnold it spoke most intimately and persuasively through great literature. His enjoyment of it from a very early stage was accompanied by an active critical play of mind. For example, in his remarkable correspondence with Clough we find him at one time toying with the notion of propriety of form as 'the sole *necessary* of poetry as such' and talking of 'the grand moral effects produced by *style*', at another maintaining that 'modern poetry can only subsist by its *contents*' (*Letters to Clough*, pp 98, 101, 124). Critical ideas develop. With Arnold we can see them developing from one work to the next. Scholars with a peculiar conception of the kind of consistency to be expected of a serious critic can therefore point to 'inconsistencies', which are sometimes real but more often are, properly speaking, changes of emphasis, related either to the differing objects of the critic's attention or to his judgment of what

needs especially to be said at one moment of time. In the preface of
Essays in Criticism (1865), his first miscellaneous collection of critical
essays, Arnold proposes as his aim 'to pull out a few more stops in that
powerful but at present somewhat narrow-toned organ, the modern
Englishman' (*Complete Prose Works*, vol III, p 287). For this purpose,
he tells us in 'The Function of Criticism at the Present Time', which I
have already described as the key-essay of the collection, the critic
must be 'disinterested' and must see Europe

. . . as being, for intellectual and spiritual purposes, one great confederation, bound to a joint action and working to a common result; and
whose members have, for their proper outfit, a knowledge of Greek,
Roman, and Eastern antiquity, and of one another.
                                                    (ibid., vol III, p 284)

There is little comfort here for Dickens's Mr Podsnap, who, it will
be remembered, thought other countries than England 'a mistake'
except for purposes of trade. 'The English critic of literature,'
Arnold replies, 'must dwell much on foreign thought . . .' (ibid., vol
III, pp 282–3). In the eight essays that follow 'The Function of
Criticism at the Present Time' he illustrates this necessity: he writes
on 'The Literary Influence of Academies', on French and German
authors (Maurice and Eugénie de Guérin, Joubert, Heine), on the
philosopher Spinoza's interpretation of the Bible, on 'Pagan and
Mediaevel Religious Sentiment', on the Stoic emperor Marcus
Aurelius. Not one essay is devoted to an English subject. Arnold
brushes aside chauvinistic murmurings blandly with the observation
that the critic's duty is to familiarize us with 'the best that is known
and thought in the world' and 'much of the best . . . cannot be of
English growth, must be foreign; by the nature of things, again, it is
just this we are least likely to know' (ibid., vol III, pp 270, 282).
    More important than Arnold's assault on English insularity in
Essays in Criticism (1865) is his explanation of the dignity of the
critical vocation. In 'The Function of Criticism at the Present
Time' he remarks that modern poetry needs 'a great critical effort
behind it; else it must be a comparatively poor, barren, and short-
lived affair' (ibid., vol III, pp 261–2). For a creative epoch of
literature 'two powers must concur, the power of the man and the
power of the moment', an idea Arnold developed from his concept
of 'adequacy' in an age's literature in 'On the Modern Element in
Literature', his inaugural lecture at Oxford in 1857. The artist's real
job is one of 'synthesis and exposition, not of analysis and discovery'. The discovery of ideas is the business of the philosopher;

the critic makes ideas current; the artist's gift lies in 'the faculty of being happily inspired by a certain intellectual and spiritual atmosphere' (ibid., vol III, p 261). The critic, then, is much more than a judge. Not only does he interpret the original artist to his age, but he prepares the way for the artist of the next generation by furnishing him with an atmosphere of 'true and fresh ideas'. Literature cannot be in a healthy state without the critic. Arnold's awareness of how subtly literary judgments are formed is impressive and indicates in what respects his mind was more like John Henry Newman's than Dr Arnold's. He writes:

. . . judging is often spoken of as the critic's one business, and so in some sense it is; but the judgment which almost insensibly forms itself in a fair and clear mind, along with fresh knowledge, is the valuable one; and thus knowledge, and ever fresh knowledge, must be the critic's great concern for himself. And it is by communicating fresh knowledge, and letting his own judgment pass along with it, – but insensibly, and in the second place, not the first, as a sort of companion and clue, not as an abstract lawgiver, – that the critic will generally do most good to his readers. Sometimes, no doubt, for the sake of establishing an author's place in literature, and his relation to a central standard (and if this is not done, how are we to get at our *best in the world?*) criticism may have to deal with a subject matter so familiar that fresh knowledge is out of the question, and then it must be all judgment . . . Here the great safeguard is never to let oneself become abstract, always to retain an intimate and lively consciousness of the truth of what one is saying, and, the moment this fails us, to be sure that something is wrong. Still, under all circumstances, this mere judgement and application of principles is, in itself, not the most satisfactory work to the critic; like mathematics, it is tautological, and cannot well give us, like fresh learning, the sense of creative activity.

(ibid., vol III, p 283)

This passage should be placed beside an equally impressive passage in *On Translating Homer: Last Words* (1862) on the difficulty and delicacy of the criticism of poetry:

To handle these matters properly there is needed a poise so perfect that the least overweight in any direction tends to destroy the balance. Temper destroys it, a crotchet destroys it, even erudition may destroy it. To press to the sense of the thing itself with which one is dealing, not to go off on some collateral issue about the thing, is the hardest matter in the world. The 'thing itself' with which one is here dealing, – the critical perception of poetic truth, – is of all things the most volatile, elusive, and evanescent; by even pressing too impetuously after it, one runs the risk of losing it. The critic of poetry should have the finest tact, the nicest moderation, the most free, flexible, and elastic spirit imaginable; he should be indeed the 'ondoyant et divers', the *undulating and diverse* being of Montaigne. The less he can deal with his object simply and freely, the more things he has to take into account in dealing with it, – the more, in short, he has to encumber himself, – so much the greater force of spirit he needs to retain his elasticity.

(ibid., vol I, p 174)

In this and the previous long passage quoted Arnold is functioning at the top of his critical powers in looking at the critical act itself. By the extreme care he takes to preserve his balance in walking the critical tightrope (for example, both 'fresh learning' and the need not to be encumbered by it, both absorption in the work under review and simultaneously a withdrawal of one part of the mind to ensure that a self-regarding delight in one's own ingenuity is not taking over) the reader is pre-disposed in favour of the actual judgments on literature that Arnold makes when he discusses translators of Homer or the defects of English Romantic poetry.

To see Arnold at work in practical criticism, as we see T. S. Eliot at it in his analysis of the opening scene of *Hamlet* in *Poetry and Drama* (1951), we must ignore the two series of *Essays in Criticism* to read *On Translating Homer* (1861), in which he offers advice to future translators of the *Iliad* by examining in detail how the translations of Chapman, Pope, Cowper and F. W. Newman have fallen short, or to look at the pages in *On the Study of Celtic Literature* in which by a nice use of quotations he distinguishes the different poetic 'ways of handling nature', and, in doing so, incidentally refines on the meaning given to 'natural magic' in the earlier essay on Maurice de Guérin. Arnold sensibly refuses to define such critical terms, which were to him no more than rough scaffolding found useful in organizing his critical response to particular poets or poems. 'The grand style', he says, 'is the last matter in the world for verbal definition to deal with adequately' (*On Translating Homer: Last Words* (1862), *Complete Prose Works*, vol I, p 188). Instead of defining his terms he offers selected quotations to make their intended meaning plain. 'To be able to quote as Arnold could,' comments T. S. Eliot, 'is the best evidence of taste' (*The Use of Poetry and the Use of Criticism*, p 118).

Essays in Criticism, Second Series (1888), contains Arnold's most important essays on English literature. 'The Study of Poetry', which opens the volume, was originally written as a general introduction to T. H. Ward's *The English Poets* (1880). It is in this essay that Arnold speaks of poetry as 'a criticism of life under the conditions fixed for such a criticism by the laws of poetic truth and poetic beauty'

(*Complete Prose Works*, vol IX, p 163), describes the dangers of the 'personal' and 'historic' estimates of poetry to the real estimate that we need, recommends having 'always in one's mind lines and expressions of the great masters . . . as a touchstone to other poetry' (ibid., vol IX, p 163), and sketches a highly selective survey of the history of English poetry from Chaucer to Burns. From this survey everybody remembers that 'high seriousness' is refused to Chaucer and that Dryden and Pope are dismissed as 'classics of our prose', but when the whole essay is read these judgments appear less eccentric than when thus isolated: there is a sense in which Chaucer is less serious than Villon (yet one wonders if Arnold thought that *any* comedy could have 'high seriousness', or if he had read 'Troilus and Criseyde'); and, although Dryden and Pope are certainly classics of our poetry, Arnold's epigram expresses the sharp drop in the imaginative temperature that is felt as we move from Elizabethan, Jacobean and Caroline poetry at its best to the poetry of the late seventeenth and early eighteenth centuries.

Other essays in *Essays in Criticism* (1888) deal with four of the Romantic poets (Wordsworth, Byron, Keats, Shelley) and with Gray. For Gray Arnold had a fondness founded on a temperamental affinity. 'He is the scantiest and frailest of classics in our poetry, but he is a classic' (ibid., vol IX, p 181). The valuation of Wordsworth as indisputably the greatest of the Romantic poets and the recognition of a Shakespearean felicity in Keats are judgements that modern taste endorses. The essay on Keats, in particular, is full of sound things excellently said, as, for example, the remark that 'Even in his pursuit of "the pleasures of song", however, there is that stamp of high work which is akin to character, which is character passing into intellectual production' (ibid., vol IX, p 181). The essay on Shelley was a review of Dowden's biography of the poet and exhibits Arnold's impatience with the professorial flow of whitewashing sentiment. He intended to supplement this essay with another on Shelley's poetry, but there is no reason to think that, had he lived to write it, he would have changed his view that 'a want of humour and a self-delusion such as Shelley's' (ibid., vol IX, p 181) must have seriously debilitating effects on a man's poetry. Arnold's judgment of Shelley is disliked by the poet's admirers, but it has legs to stand on.

From this brief account some idea of the range and quality of Arnold's literary perceptions should have emerged. It should not be necessary to say that our valuation of him as a literary critic does not depend on our sharing all his literary tastes, just as it would be very odd if our judgment of him as a social thinker were made to hang on our agreement or disagreement with him over specific social and educational questions. Arnold had a discriminating taste in literature, but we suspect that he was too inclined to identify the serious with the solemn (like other Victorians). He saw clearly much that was wrong in Victorian England, but perhaps he had too much simple faith in the power of education to put things right. What is finally important is the example he sets us of critical integrity by his devotion to the discovery of the truth about any matter in hand, and his candour in avowing the truth – but temperately and with discretion – when he thinks that he has discovered it. There are in Arnold as an older man occasional signs of a stiffening sensibility – for example, in the testiness of a large group of political essays, which are fed by his dislike of Gladstone, and in his unease in his sixties at any freer treatment of sex in French novels and plays than he had been accustomed to as a young man reading the then rather shocking novels of George Sand. It would be inappropriate to lay much stress on these signs. There are fewer of them in Arnold than in most of his great literary contemporaries. To an unusual degree he preserved his flexibility of mind and remained open to new impressions to the end of his life. As a man he conquered 'the haunting, the irresistible self-dissatisfaction of his heart' ('On the Modern Element in Literature', *Complete Prose Works*, vol I, p 35), made the best of an arduous and not very rewarding professional life, and worked industriously at his books. They are still profitable to read as the productions of a civilized man who cared deeply and intelligently about literature and society.

4

DICKENS

Alan Shelston

Dickens has always presented problems for literary criticism. For theorists whose critical presuppositions emphasise intelligence, sensitivity and an author in complete control of his work the cruder aspects of his popular art have often proved an unsurmountable obstacle, while for the formulators of traditions his gigantic idiosyncrasies can never be made to conform. And if difficulties such as these have been overcome by the awareness that Dickens sets his own standards, or rather that the standards that he sets, far from being inimical to great art, are his own expression of it, there remains a further problem: since his own lifetime Dickens has invariably seemed as much an institution as an individual. The institution of the 'Dickens of Christmas', celebrated by Chesterton, but derided by more sophisticated critics ever since, has given way to the Dickens of the academic thesis. The change may perhaps be defined by suggesting that, whereas it was once necessary when advancing the claims of Dickens to insist that he was not an entertainer, it is now becoming increasingly necessary to insist that he was. The invaluable reassessment of the later novels which has taken place in recent years, emphasizing in particular the social and psychological aspects of their symbolism and structure, has sometimes gone close to producing a Dickens that his contemporaries would have recognized as, at most, only part of the picture. Dickens's art was at once varied and constant; if themes, emphases and preoccupations develop towards the ultimate pessimism of *Little Dorrit* and *Our Mutual Friend*, it is important to remember that Flora Finching and her aunt are cousins, not far removed, of Mrs Bardell and Mrs Gamp, that Pecksniff and Podsnap have much in common, and that the atmosphere of nightmare that is felt so intensely in *Edwin Drood* has been lived through before in Jonas Chuzzlewit's solitary return from the murder of Mr Montague Tigg. Dickens's early success with his public gave him an assurance that led to increased powers of poetic expression and narrative technique, and it gave him also the confidence to assert his thematic priorities to a point where they contradicted the social assumptions of many of his readers, but he never rejected the basic methods which had brought him his initial success. When he collapsed in 1870, having almost completed the sixth instalment of *Edwin Drood*, the manner of his death was peculiarly appropriate: his audience were left in the state of anticipation to which he had accustomed them, but this time there was to be no resolution.

In the nineteenth century the writing of novels emerged from a permitted indulgence to an acceptable career. Fielding and Smollett, Dickens's heroes, did not depend on their novels for a living any more than did Richardson and Jane Austen, whereas for Dickens, Thackeray, Trollope and Henry James, their art ensured not only a means of subsistence but social prestige as well. It is customary to think of Dickens as a critic of much of the Victorian ethos, but whatever reservations the novels may express about self-aggrandizement, no career could demonstrate the ideal of the self-made man more effectively than his own. The boy whose formal education was so abruptly interrupted by his father's financial disasters sent his own eldest son to Eton; the child who had visited his father in the Marshalsea prison was listened to as an adult on the subject of penal reform. The facts of Dickens's early life have been rehearsed frequently enough and there is little need to recount them here other than to emphasize the extent to which Dickens, the chronicler of afflicted children, saw in his own childhood the archetypal experience of the child frustrated by the pressures of an urban and commercialized environment. The account of his childhood employment in the blacking-shop which he gave to his biographer Forster has often been quoted:

> The deep remembrance of the sense I had of being utterly neglected and hopeless; of the shame I felt in my position; of the misery it was to my young heart to believe that, day by day, what I had learned, and thought, and delighted in, and raised my fancy and my emulation up by, was passing away from me, never to be brought back any more, cannot be written. My whole nature was so penetrated with the grief and humiliation of such considerations, that even now, famous and caressed and happy, I often forget in my dreams that I have a dear wife and children; even that I am a man; and wander desolately back to that time of my life.
>
> (John Forster, *The Life of Charles Dickens*, Bk I, ch. 2)

Dickens is notoriously self-indulgent in this reflective mood, but the complaint is supported by the facts, and the tone of the passage, especially of its conclusion, was to be transmuted to the tone of *David Copperfield* and *Great Expectations*.

The extent to which the career of Dickens the novelist was the life of Dickens the man is best indicated simply by listing his full-length novels with the dates when they appeared. His first publications of any consequence were the *Sketches by Boz* which began to come out in 1834. From that date his novels appeared as follows (the dates are those of their first appearance, in instalment or serial form):

Pickwick Papers (1836–37); *Oliver Twist* (1837–39); *Nicholas Nickleby* (1838–39); *The Old Curiosity Shop* (1840–41); *Barnaby Rudge* (1841); *Martin Chuzzlewit* (1843–44); *Dombey and Son* (1846–48); *David Copperfield* (1849–50); *Bleak House* (1852–53); *Hard Times* (1854); *Little Dorrit* (1855–57); *A Tale of Two Cities* (1859); *Great Expectations* (1860–61); *Our Mutual Friend* (1864–65); *Edwin Drood* (unfinished) (1870).

A man of phenomenal energy, Dickens combined his literary career with a variety of social and theatrical interests. Some of the social concerns are interestingly documented in Philip Collins's two studies, *Dickens and Crime* (1962) and *Dickens and Education* (1963), while the theatrical involvement embraced writing, acting and producing for the stage, and culminated in the famous public readings from his own works. But a glance through the list of the novels shows the extent to which Dickens's life was dominated by the demands of authorship, for apart from the gaps between the last three items there is scarcely an unproductive year. When one considers how each of the novels appeared in either weekly or monthly instalments, and that they were supplemented by short stories and occasional journalism, as well as, from time to time, the duties of an editor, it can fairly be said that Dickens's literary activity over a period of more than thirty years was uninterrupted. (For reasons of space I have confined myself in this study to the novels alone. A full study of Dickens would, of course, pay proper attention to the other aspects of his literary career and in particular to the short stories, some of which throw interesting light on his development.)

The practice of serial publication, a publisher's device to facilitate sales which became an important factor in the development of nineteenth-century fiction, had consequences for Dickens's novels which it is difficult for the modern reader confronted by a set of eight-hundred page volumes to appreciate. Of the novels listed above, nine were originally published in illustrated monthly parts, each consisting of three or four chapters. Of the remaining six, one, *Oliver Twist*, appeared as a monthly serial in the magazine *Bentley's Miscellany*, while the other five, all of them rather shorter, were published in serial form in weekly papers. The effect of such a method of publication on the tone and content of the novels concerned was considerable. In the first place the need to maintain interest by the deployment of an easily identifiable narrative was paramount. Much has been made of the complexity of Dickens's plots but fundamentally a Dickens novel is based on a simple narrative concept like Pickwick's journey, the lives of Oliver Twist, David Copperfield, or Pip, or the hidden secrets of *Bleak House, Little Dorrit* or *Our Mutual Friend*. On the other hand, with a basic story established, there is ample opportunity for the multiplicity of character and event for which Dickens is famous; the dual nature of the process is revealed clearly by Dickens's device of two separate narratives in *Bleak House*. The wealth of apparently extraneous detail that is a feature of the novels has sometimes led to the supposition that Dickens wrote without plan, but the information that he gave to Forster, together with his own notes for individual novels, shows very clearly the extent to which, particularly in his later novels, he formulated a basic narrative concept to which he could keep firm hold as his novel progressed.

Serial publication thus posed its own technical problems and to a large extent dictated their solution. It also had the effect of intensifying the relationship between the author and his audience to a degree that can perhaps be compared with the oral narrative poem or the Elizabethan stage. To some novelists, conscious of what they saw as more important obligations, the need to tailor their novels to popular demand was a source of irritation: Mrs Gaskell, for example, had disagreements with Dickens himself over the serialization of her industrial novel *North and South* in his magazine *Household Words*. More than technical issues were at stake, however. In two vital areas audience-demand was a controlling factor over the content of Victorian fiction: the taboo on explicitness in the examination of sexual relationships, and the exploitation of sentiment, which in many ways can be seen as a substitute for a more realistic examination of human emotion.

It should be said straight away that very few major Victorian authors felt these aspects of public taste to be unduly crippling. As Kathleen Tillotson has pointed out, 'With very few exceptions, novelists were contented with such limitations as existed, and moved freely within them, or figure-skated along the edge' (*Novels of the Eighteen-Forties*, 1954, p 64). Dickens, however, seems not merely to have accepted these conditions but to have positively endorsed them. Conscious that his instalments were read, as they appeared, at family gatherings, he ensured that they contained nothing that a Victorian family would blush to hear. Furthermore, his manipulation of pathos, evidenced not only by individual incidents like the death of Little Nell and Paul Dombey, but by the total concept of characters like Esther Summerson in *Bleak House* and Amy Dorrit, provides a feature of the novels that to a modern reader can require considerable explanatory apology.

Obviously the emphasis on the pathetic can be attributed to some extent to popular demand: it is well known that at the time of writing *The Old Curiosity Shop* Dickens received numerous letters on the fate of his heroine. What must also be stressed are the powerful elements of sentimentality and morbidity in Dickens's own character which enabled him to respond to this aspect of popular taste. Little Nell was the fictional parallel of Dickens's sister-in-law Mary Hogarth, over whose early death he had grieved inconsolably. She became more than a figure of fiction to her creator, however: approaching the climax of *The Old Curiosity Shop* Dickens told Forster, 'All night I have been pursued by the child; and this morning I am unrefreshed and miserable.' (Forster, op. cit., Bk II p 7). To self-indulgence in the pathetic was added an impulse towards the violent and the macabre. Dickens's readings from his own works show clearly the way in which he wished not only to gratify his own emotional needs in his fiction but also to witness its effect on his audience at first hand. Along with the comic scenes, he liked to include in his programmes the most affecting or disturbing passages from the novels – the death of Paul Dombey, the Bob Cratchit scenes from *A Christmas Carol*, the Smike scenes from *Nicholas Nickleby* and, most dramatic of all, the murder of Nancy from *Oliver Twist* – and he measured his success by the degree of emotional response that he could exact from an often weeping audience. In a revealing letter to his wife, describing a private reading, he wrote: 'If you had seen Macready last night, undisguisedly sobbing and crying on the sofa as I read, you would have felt, as I did, what a thing it is to have power.' (Quoted in E. Johnson, *Charles Dickens: His Tragedy and Triumph*, 1953, p 532.) The enjoyment of this sense of power over his audience gives us a clue to much that we find disturbing in Dickens's novels: more than any other novelist he needed not merely the applause of his audience but their submission. At the end of his career Dickens wrote in the last pages of *Our Mutual Friend*:

> . . . that I hold the advantages of the mode of publication (i.e. in serial form) to outweigh its disadvantages, may be easily believed of one who revived it in the Pickwick Papers after long disuse, and has pursued it ever since.'
>
> (Postscript)

Even he, however, can hardly have been aware of the full implications of the form for the development of his art.

If the more startling aspects of Dickens's fiction can be traced to traits in his own temperament it must be recorded that his comedy also has its origins in the man himself. Much has been written of his comic technique, but his letters reveal very clearly that the source of his comedy was not a conscious technique, in the literary sense, but a combination of vision and expression that was habitual to him. Writing, for example, of the domestic upheaval caused by some house alterations which he had set in progress he builds up a scene and an atmosphere in much the same way as he does in the novels:

> I am perpetually wandering (in fancy) up and down the house and tumbling over the workmen. When I feel that they are gone to dinner I become low. When I look forward to their total abstinence on Sunday I become wretched. The gravy at dinner has a taste of glue in it. I smell paint in the sea. Phantom lime attends me all the day long. I dream that I am a carpenter and can't partition off the hall.
>
> (Quoted in Johnson, op. cit., p 748)

In a similar letter, describing the same events, Catherine, his wife, is 'all over paint, and seems to think it is somehow being immensely useful to get into that condition'. Here we have not only the elaboration of detail in the accumulation of comic disaster that we know so well from the novels, but also that spontaneous inter-relationship of perception and articulation that is the hallmark of Dickens's mode of comic expression. The sentence about his wife, for example, inconsequential though it is, could not have been rendered in any other way and it is typical of countless such observations that appear in the novels, giving to their comedy its inimitable flavour. Character and incident proliferate in Dickens so naturally because they are the product of an imagination that was never still, and of an impulse towards the dramatic evidenced not only by his theatrical activities but by the details of his day-to-day existence. Dickens would never have understood a theory of fiction based on the detachment of the author; the novels, as they stand, are the expression of the man who wrote them.

The origins of Dickens's literary career can be traced to his early employment as a journalist. This work took him first to the Law Courts, including the Court of Chancery, and then to Parliament, and his contempt for these institutions, evinced most powerfully in *Bleak House* but reappearing consistently throughout his work, is based on the first-hand knowledge of them that he gained at the outset of his career. From reporting he moved on to descriptive journalism of a more imaginative kind and from 1834 to 1835 he wrote a series of sketches which appeared first in the *Monthly Magazine* and then in the *Evening Chronicle*. Some of these, together with some additional sketches written for the occasion, were collected and published in two illustrated volumes under the title *Sketches by Boz* in February 1836. Forster remarks that 'The Sketches were more talked about than the first two or three numbers of *Pickwick*' (op. cit., Bk I p 5), and certainly they were well received at the time. Their appearance in the *Evening Chronicle* had already attracted the attention of the publishers Edward Chapman and William Hall who invited Dickens to write a series of similar pieces to accompany a set of illustrations that they intended to bring out on sporting themes. From the start the text became more important than the illustrations and *The Posthumous Papers of the Pickwick Club* was born. The work appeared in monthly numbers, running from April 1836 to November in the following year.

Initially the venture seemed to be a failure. The opening numbers sold only four hundred copies and were dismissed by such reviewers as noticed them, but with the fourth number sales began to improve and *Pickwick Papers* suddenly became a triumph, selling 40,000 copies at the height of its success. Readers of Mrs Gaskell's *Cranford* will remember how Captain Brown was run over by a railway train while engrossed in the latest number of *Pickwick Papers*; his enthusiasm was paralleled with less disastrous consequences throughout the country and at all levels of literate society. Once it had caught on, the book was not just another literary success but a phenomenon and its boisterous and inconsequential spirit came to represent – and indeed to misrepresent – its author for generations to come.

The form that *Pickwick Papers* took was not original. R. S. Surtees had already established himself as a humorous celebrant of sporting life and the sketches which he wrote for *The New Sporting Magazine*,

and which were later re-published as *Jorrocks' Jaunts and Jollities*
(1838), were the direct source of Dickens's material, most notably
of the trial of Bardell vs Pickwick. There was indeed a vogue for
this kind of comic realism on familiar topics which had probably
attracted the publishers in the first place. But Dickens brought to
the form not simply a wish to emulate a successful predecessor but
also a comic imagination nurtured on the classics of the picaresque
novel. In *David Copperfield* Dickens tells us that his hero had 'a little
room upstairs. . . . From that blessed little room, *Roderick Random,
Peregrine Pickle, Humphry Clinker, Tom Jones, The Vicar of Wakefield,
Don Quixote, Gil Blas* and *Robinson Crusoe* came out, a glorious host,
to keep me company' (Forster, op. cit., Bk I p 1). *Pickwick Papers* is
in direct line of descent from such a tradition, with Mr Pickwick
and Sam Weller as anglicized Quixote and Sancho Panza,
journeying in the last days of the stage-coach through pre-industrial
England. The story, based on the unpredictable adventures of a
journey, exploited so successfully by Fielding and Smollett, was
rendered obsolete by the coming of the railways, and it is worth
remarking that *Pickwick Papers*, the first novel of the greatest urban
novelist, was also, in a very real sense, the last major novel of the
pre-railway age.

The narrative devices of *Pickwick Papers*, its loosely-connected
sequence of events, its interpolated stories and its mildly mock-
heroic set-pieces, are techniques that Dickens had learnt from his
eighteenth-century predecessors; from them also he inherited the
comic amplitude and boisterous humour that is typical of much of
the book. Pickwick drinks himself to sleep in Mr Wardle's
wheelbarrow and is deposited as a vagabond in the village pound,
there to be pelted with rubbish; when Mr Winkle goes shooting, Mr
Tupman 'saved the lives of innumerable small birds by receiving a
portion of the charge in his left arm.' Pickwick himself comments
on the source of much of the comedy:

'Does it not, I ask, bespeak the indiscretion . . . of my followers, that,
beneath whatever roof they locate, they disturb the peace of mind and
happiness of some confiding female?'

(ch. 18)

Such scenes, however, are always more decorously comic than their
counterparts in Fielding and Smollett, and the predominant tone of
Pickwick Papers is one of benevolence and well-being. Good food, so
often a source of comfort in Dickens, is never so effective in
resolving disaster as it is in his first novel. The interpolated stories,

in which can be seen hints of the violence that was sometimes to predominate in the later novels, are too crude to affect the basic atmosphere more than marginally and even the social realism of the Eatanswill election is presented in such a way that its less pleasant aspects are tempered by the overall sense of inconsequence.

The world of *Pickwick Papers*, however, is not simply the world of Dingley Dell and Eatanswill, neither is its total effect as disjointed as its loosely-constructed technique would perhaps imply. The novel is given shape both by a subtle development in the character of Pickwick himself and by the way in which its thematic concerns, most notably in the sequence of events involving Pickwick and the law, have the common element of an attack on inhumanity and selfishness. The affair with Mrs Bardell begins as a typically Pickwickian episode, but as Pickwick becomes more deeply involved with the legal process, described as an instrument for 'the torture and torment of his majesty's liege subjects' and 'the comfort and emolument' of its practitioners, there is an increasingly serious edge to the comedy. Ultimately, in the Fleet prison, Pickwick is brought face to face with misery and the effect is not compromised in any way. When the 'Chancery prisoner' dies of consumption, a note is introduced into the novel that its readers have been prepared for over a series of scenes but which its earliest numbers hardly anticipated. In his solicitor's office Pickwick reflects that 'When a man bleeds inwardly it is a dangerous thing for himself; but when he laughs inwardly, it bodes no good to other people' (ch. 31); the thought has an intensity that indicates the development of Pickwick himself from a myopic comic butt to a figure of wisdom and sensitivity. He himself may not be aware of the development, which was perhaps to some extent subconscious on the part of his creator, but it is consistent with a gradual process of unification that is apparent in *Pickwick Papers* as a whole. If we still remember the novel primarily in terms of its superb range of comic incident and character we cannot re-read it and remain unaffected by its social concern and above all by its ultimate affirmation of the pre-eminence of human charity.

Such concerns, of course, are the preoccupations of the novels that followed *Pickwick Papers*, *Oliver Twist* and *Nicholas Nickleby*, both of which take as their central situation the plight of children in the face of institutional cruelty. Undoubtedly Dickens's success with *Pickwick Papers* had given him the confidence to put his own interests at the centre of his fiction, and in practical terms the financial security which it had brought him made it possible to experiment with themes of his own choosing. The change surprised some of the readers of *Pickwick Papers* who, seeing in *Oliver Twist* simply another example of the 'Newgate Novel', objected to its preoccupation with low life. Such reservations were a minority judgment however, and, after all, both *Oliver Twist* and *Nicholas Nickleby* continue to show the imaginative fertility that had brought about Dickens's early triumph.

Of the two novels *Oliver Twist* is the most consistently effective as an attack on social injustice. Far more successfully than *Nicholas Nickleby*, it creates within its comedy the element of evil by which its child-hero is threatened, and the malignancy is rendered more complex by the way in which it is embodied not only in the dramatically criminal figures of Fagin and Bill Sikes but also in the representatives of established authority like the Board of Guardians and the police magistrate Mr Fang. Here Dickens emphasizes for the first time a quality that was to become a theme of his later work: the innocent are caught between the Scylla of crime and the Charybdis of legalized repression. 'Mrs Sowerberry, the under-taker's wife, who had a good deal of taste in the undertaking way', emphasizes the point; the repressive mentality has invaded the family hearth. Compared with this enveloping atmosphere of in-humanity, the cruelties of *Nicholas Nickleby*, for all their vividness, seem parochial; Dotheboys Hall exists not at the centre of the novel but at its perimeter, and once it has been destroyed the novel is given over to issues of romance and to a series of comic portraits which, splendid in themselves, tend to dissipate its thematic inter-est. Despite the death of Smike, Wackford Squeers is more a figure of fun than the embodiment of inhumanity that Dickens intended, while the wicked Uncle Ralph and the decadent Sir Mulberry Hawk are scarcely more substantial than those intolerable mani-festations of goodness, the Cheeryble twins.

Dickens's next two novels, *The Old Curiosity Shop* and *Barnaby Rudge*, can also usefully be considered as a pair in that they appeared in quick succession in a periodical of his own devising, *Master Humphrey's Clock*. Furthermore, as distinct from the other early novels, they involved a more hectic process of composition, appearing in weekly instead of monthly instalments. The very factor which was responsible for *The Old Curiosity Shop's* compulsive effect on Dickens's contemporaries, his treatment of the life and death of the heroine Little Nell, has led to its notoriety with succeeding generations. Edward FitzGerald copied out all the parts of the book which involved Little Nell herself: modern opinion would go to the opposite extreme and delete them, leaving an interesting range of incidental characters and some social commentary on industrial England of considerable force. In fact, *The Old Curiosity Shop* deserves more generous consideration than this. Professor K. J. Fielding has commented effectively on its resemblance to allegory (*Charles Dickens*, 1958, pp 52–4), and, like other Dickens children, Little Nell herself assumes symbolic significance when set against the avarice of her persecutors, Quilp and Sampson Brass. *Barnaby Rudge* is a novel of a different kind. Based on the Gordon riots, it is in many ways a more stimulating novel on the theme of revolution than the more famous – and more sentimental – *A Tale of Two Cities*. For Dickens, the revolutionary, like the criminal, was a figure of compelling interest; while the behaviour of such characters might be rendered explicable, even sympathetic, by the circumstances in which they found themselves, ultimately they figured as expressions of evil far beyond the powers of rational analysis.

In the five years from 1836 to 1841 Dickens had thus produced five long novels, all of them, to a greater or lesser degree, bestsellers. Unknown seven years earlier, in 1842 he visited America as a literary celebrity. The visit began auspiciously enough, but despite his appreciation of the lavish hospitality of his hosts Dickens could not resist the opportunity to refer repeatedly in his public pronouncements to the vexed issue of international copyright, and in particular to the pirating of English works by American publishers. While undoubtedly in the right, as ever he lacked discretion, and the result was a series of attacks on him in American newspapers for which he, in return, exacted revenge, at first mildly in his *American Notes*, published in 1842, and then more vehemently in the American sections of his next novel, *Martin Chuzzlewit*.

Martin Chuzzlewit, to Dickens's alarm, met with a very lukewarm reception. For Dickens, with his emotional need for the support of his audience, this was particularly distressing, all the more so since he thought the book 'in a hundred points immeasurably the best of my stories.' It has been cogently argued that its comparative failure was due not so much to its own weakness as to the limitations of its predecessor, *American Notes*; whatever the reason, it caused its author intolerable anxiety.

Martin Chuzzlewit's lack of contemporary success is particularly surprising when one considers that in some ways it re-invokes the spirit of *Pickwick Papers*. There is, of course, no Mr Pickwick, but Mark Tapley, the pot-boy who becomes the hero's inseparable man-servant, is in the vein of Sam Weller, and the recourse to the familiar aspects of the coaching-inn and the feast are reminiscent of Dickens's first success. *Martin Chuzzlewit*, however, was written to a definitely preconceived thematic plan. It has a story devised to demonstrate the eventual triumph of goodness, and the characters also were intended to emphasize the novel's thematic concerns. According to Forster, 'the notion of taking Pecksniff for a type of character was really the origin of the book; the design being to show, more or less by every person introduced, the number and variety of humours that have their root in selfishness' (op. cit., Bk III p 8). *Martin Chuzzlewit* is thus both a return to the spirit of *Pickwick Papers* and, in technique, a development from it. In that it can perhaps be seen as the culmination of Dickens's early novels it is worth considering in some detail.

Certainly Forster's emphasis on character is borne out by the book itself. Its plot is an amalgam of the improbable and the sentimental, but for what Forster referred to as 'the exuberance of comic invention' its characters are unequalled elsewhere in Dickens. Pecksniff, the hypocritical architect whose moral enunciation – '"Charity, my dear . . . when I take my chamber-candlestick tonight, remind me to be more than usually particular in praying for Mr Anthony Chuzzlewit, who has done me an injustice"' (ch. 4) – is superbly parodied by his own drunken declamation at Todgers's boarding-house. Mrs Gamp, the bibulous sick-nurse and layer-out of the dead who regards her clients in the former function in terms of their potential for the latter, and Mrs Harris, a creature not only of Dickens's imagination but Mrs Gamp's as well, are only the more prominent members of the cast of a comedy as expansive as any that Dickens wrote. The inventiveness of the comedy in fact defeats Dickens's moralistic intentions: in a world in which the eventual happiness of the good is scarcely in doubt Pecksniff himself becomes a self-sustaining figure of delight.

Martin Chuzzlewit is not only memorable for its comedy, however. In its variety of scene it achieves considerable atmospheric complexity and in its London scenes in particular it suggests that sense of the density of urban experience that was to become the hallmark of the later novels. When Pecksniff brings his daughters, Mercy and Charity, up to town he brings them to an exciting new world of

. . . steeples, towers, belfries, shining vanes, and masts of ships: a very forest. Gables, house-tops, garret-windows, wilderness upon wilderness. Smoke and noise enough for all the world at once.

To the onlooker, however, the scene becomes one of menace:

The tumult, swelled into a roar; the hosts of objects seemed to thicken and expand a hundredfold; and after gazing round him, quite scared, he turned into Todgers's again, much more rapidly than he came out . . .
(ch. 9)

and when Mercy Pecksniff is inveigled into marriage with Jonas Chuzzlewit, who during the course of the novel becomes wifebeater, murderer and suicide, the threat becomes reality. If London is the site of Mrs Todgers's boarding-house, it is also the site of the dwelling-place of Jonas, incarcerated with his aged father and the senile and terrified servant, Chuffey. While the outcome of *Martin Chuzzlewit* confirms its benevolent ethos, Dickens extracts from the sub-plot of Jonas's career a disturbing atmosphere of the macabre. *Martin Chuzzlewit* has its imperfections – amongst them the extended American journey of its hero which Dickens introduced unashamedly in an attempt to stimulate sales, and which, though a sustained *tour-de-force*, can never overcome its digressive effect – but they are the faults of an imagination on the rampage. Dickens may have set out with an end in view, but he found, as he wrote the novel, that, as Forster records, 'it seized him for itself . . . he wept over it, and laughed, and wept again, and excited himself to an extraordinary degree . . . and walked thinking of it fifteen and twenty miles about the black streets of London, many and many a night after all sober folks had gone to bed' (Bk IV p 4) Such self-absorption was indeed not uncommon to Dickens, but it did not always achieve such fortunate results as it did in this case. From this point his novels were to achieve an often overpowering symbolic and thematic intensity, but they did so to some extent at the cost of the unrestrained comic invention that proliferates in the earlier novels, and to such potent effect in the best scenes of *Martin Chuzzlewit*.

In the novels discussed so far the techniques, both of the fiction itself and the social criticism embodied within it, are relatively straightforward. The institutions which Dickens attacks, the workhouses in *Oliver Twist* or the Yorkshire schools in *Nicholas Nickleby*, are easily recognizable, and once the abuse has been overcome, the way is open to a happy conclusion. Dickens's conception of character in these novels is similarly uncomplicated: hence the optimism which they imply, which in itself is made more acceptable by the way in which they are distanced in time from the late 1830s and early 1840s when they were written. The stagecoach world of *Pickwick Papers*, *Nicholas Nickleby* and *Martin Chuzzlewit* is fundamentally stable and comforting, and it is only parenthetically that the violence of the changes implicit in the industrialization of society breaks in – as with the London sections of *Oliver Twist* or, more specifically, Little Nell's journey through the Midlands in *The Old Curiosity Shop*. In *Dombey and Son*, however, and in most of the novels which follow it, Dickens locates his action, at least in spirit, in the immediately contemporary world, most emphatically perhaps in *Dombey and Son* itself, with its constant reference to the railway, a symbol of social change of perhaps uncontrollable potential, but also in novels like *Bleak House*, with its descriptions of the squalor of living conditions in the overcrowded city, *Little Dorrit*, like *Dombey and Son*, emphasizing the destructive inter-relationship of economic and moral attitudes, and finally, *Our Mutual Friend*, where the forces of business speculation are seen at work on the raw material of rotting corpses, dunghills – and marriage. As Humphry House has pointed out, the specific abuses attacked in these novels are often things of the past – most obviously so in the case of the Marshalsea prison in *Little Dorrit* – and the physical settings are sometimes a mixture of the con-temporary and the recollected past, but the institutions are im-portant not in themselves but as metaphors for a repressive social psychology, in itself the consequence of a predominantly selfish economic ethos, that in its pressure on the helpless individual is identifiably Victorian. The opening of *Little Dorrit* gives the date of the action as the eighteen-twenties, but when Arthur Clennam, its hero, returns to his inheritance the description of the city that greets him in no way evokes the sense of the past:

> It was a Sunday evening in London, gloomy, close, and stale. Maddening church bells of all degrees of dissonance, sharp and flat, cracked and clear, fast and slow, made the brick-and-mortar echoes hideous. Melancholy streets, in a penitential garb of soot, steeped the souls of the people who were condemned to look at them out of windows, in dire despondency... Nothing to see but streets, streets, streets. Nothing to breathe but streets, streets, streets. Nothing to change the brooding mind, or raise it up. Nothing for the spent toiler to do, but to compare the monotony of his seventh day with the monotony of his six days, think what a weary life he led, and make the best of it – or the worst, according to the probabilities.
>
> (Bk I, ch. 3)

Here we are reminded not of anything in fiction but of Blake's *London* in the *Songs of Experience*:

I wander thro' each charter'd street,
Near where the charter'd Thames does flow,
And mark in every face I meet
Marks of weakness, marks of woe.

The resemblance, of course, is far from coincidental: both Blake and Dickens have at the heart of their work a sense of the threat to the human spirit from the forces of repression, and they locate that threat symbolically in the rapidly developing urban and industrial world around them. The London of *Little Dorrit* though, however specific the dating of the novel, is the London of the tangible present, just as it is in the other later novels (even, in a very special way, in *A Tale of Two Cities*). From the time of *Dombey and Son* Dickens becomes, in the fullest sense, a Victorian novelist.

In the space available here it is scarcely possible to discuss each of the later novels in detail and it must be emphasized that generalizations about them must be qualified, not only by the way in which Dickens presents different aspects of his analysis of society in the novels already mentioned, but also by the diversifying effect of the other novels of this later period, most notably *David Copperfield* and *Great Expectations* with their strongly autobiographical overtones, and *Hard Times* and *A Tale of Two Cities* with their concentration on specific issues. The generalization that I have outlined in the preceding paragraph, however, will, I hope, serve as a context within which discussion of individual novels can take place. For the purposes of this essay I intend to concentrate in some detail on *Dombey and Son* before going on to suggest resemblances and qualifications that may arise from the novels which followed it.

Just as *Martin Chuzzlewit* was written with a preconceived moral end in view, so *Dombey and Son* was intended to convey a similar message. Forster records that Dickens told him that the intention in the case of *Dombey and Son* was 'to do with Pride what its predecessor had done with Selfishness' and he goes on to quote a long letter from Dickens outlining the proposed plot in some detail: 'This is what cooks call "the stock of the soup". All kinds of things will be added to it of course.' Dickens's letter emphasizes the central issue of Dombey's pride, expressed in his preoccupation with his son, Paul, and the consequent alienation, on Paul's death, from his daughter, Florence, leading up to 'the decay and downfall of the house, and the bankruptcy of Dombey, and all the rest of it' (Forster, Bk VI p 2) It makes no mention of Dombey's second marriage, and thus of the way in which the climax of the novel is intensified by Edith Dombey's desertion of her husband, but the novel as it stands is a remarkably consistent development of Dickens's original idea. In particular, his conception of Dombey's character is far more complex than anything he had attempted so far and the relationship of every aspect of the novel to the psychology of its central character is consistently and convincingly handled.

What Dickens's communications with Forster do not stress so emphatically is the way in which Dombey's ruling passion is conceived specifically in economic terms. This is implied, of course, in the ambiguity of the novel's title: 'Dombey and Son' is both a paternal relationship and a commercial concern, and Dombey's tragedy is the result of his inability to distinguish between the two. The point is underlined in the opening chapter of the novel – in contrast with that of *Martin Chuzzlewit*, perhaps the most effective that Dickens ever wrote:

'The house will once again, Mrs Dombey,' said Mr Dombey, 'be not only in name but in fact Dombey and Son; Dom-bey and Son!' . . .
. . . These three words conveyed the one idea in Mr Dombey's life. The earth was made for Dombey and Son to trade in, and the sun and moon were made to give them light. Rivers and seas were formed to float their ships; rainbows gave them promise of fair weather; winds blew for or against their enterprises; stars and planets circled in their orbits, to preserve inviolate a system of which they were the centre. Common abbreviations took new meanings in his eyes, and had sole reference to them: A.D. had no concern with anno Domini, but stood for anno Dombei – and Son.

(ch. 1)

The first part of the novel is devoted to the stultifying effect of Dombey's inability to see the world except in terms of his own commercial pride: the Dombey children, Paul and Florence, are isolated in a world which denies their natural impulses and affections. Paul, doomed with a precocious world-weariness almost before the novel has begun, dies, and 'Dombey and Son is a Daughter after all'.

The pathetic death of Paul Dombey, more intensely rendered in its way than that of Little Nell, is a reminder that Dickens's new control over his material does not involve any change in his basic fictional techniques. In the confrontation between authority and the child Dickens presents the conflict in much the same way as in the earlier novels, exploiting, for example, the combination of comedy and pathos familiar from *Oliver Twist*. For his education Paul is sent first to Mrs Pipchin, who runs 'an infantine Boarding-House of a very select description' with all the selfish asperity common to Dickensian widows, and then to Dr Blimber's boarding school:

> 'Ha!' said Dr Blimber. 'Shall we make a man of him?'
> 'Do you hear, Paul?' added Mr Dombey, Paul being silent.
> 'Shall we make a man of him?' repeated the Doctor.
> 'I had rather be a child,' replied Paul.
> 'Indeed!' said the Doctor. 'Why?'

(ch. 11)

The comic juxtaposition of uncomprehending adult and un-sophisticated child is reminiscent of Oliver's asking for more, but in *Dombey and Son* scenes like this are integrated into the presentation of Paul Dombey's childhood in a way which qualifies their comedy and emphasizes, by contrast, the completely enveloping nature of the ethos that destroys him.

Dombey's obsession with the power of money lies at the heart of the novel and its repressive consequences are emphasized not only in terms of plot but by the way in which character and location are organized towards a total symbolic effect. It is a common Dickensian technique to identify characters by the life-style of their establishments and he employs it perhaps more purposefully in *Dombey and Son* than in any other of his novels. The business house of Dombey, where fortunes are made and life is destroyed, is contrasted with Sol Gills's shop, where business fails and humanity flourishes; the suffocating institutions presided over by Mrs Pipchin and Dr Blimber can be set against Staggs's Gardens, the home of Paul Dombey's first nurse, and Mrs MacStinger's lodging-house, where if children run wild they at least run naturally. Minor charac-ters, like Miss Tox, Major Bagstock and John and Harriet Carker, are all presented in the homes which they have made for themselves and which express their personalities so precisely. At the centre of the novel Dombey's own house, with its cheerless rooms and staircases, is no home at all: from its windows Florence looks across the street to where she sees a very different household, with a very different head:

When he had dined, she could see them, through the open windows, go down with their governess or nurse, and cluster round the table; and in the still summer weather the sound of their childish voices and clear laughter would come ringing across the street into the drooping air of the room in which she sat. Then they would climb and clamber upstairs with him, and romp about him on the sofa, or group themselves at his knee, a very nosegay of little faces, while he seemed to tell them some story. Or they would come running out into the balcony; and then Florence would hide herself quickly, lest it should check them in their joy, to see her in her black dress, sitting there alone.

(ch. 18)

For all its considerable qualities of plot it is through effects and contrasts such as these that *Dombey and Son* makes its most telling effect. At the climax of the novel we are again brought back to the Dombey mansion:

It is a great house still, proof against wind and weather, without breaches in the roof, or shattered windows, or dilapidated walls; but it is a ruin none the less, and the rats fly from it.

(ch. 59)

Alone, the ruined Dombey wanders its corridors at night. He contemplates suicide and is melodramatically saved by the daughter he had spurned, but far more instrumental in the assertion of Dombey's downfall than the events is their setting. The great empty house, which has seen the birth and death of Paul, Florence's solitary growth to womanhood and the hollow triumph of Dombey's remarriage, is an expression of nemesis far more potent than the events of his career can possibly be.

Running parallel with Dombey's career is that of his unloved daughter: as he moves obdurately towards disaster, she leads a life of emotional starvation from which she is ultimately rescued by her marriage to Dombey's clerk, Walter Gay. Here again the atmospheric contrasts are as important as the narrative events; against the sterility of Florence's environment is set the vitality of the influences which surround Walter Gay. It is worth emphasizing, however, that, just as Dickens's firm hold on the character of Dombey at the centre of the novel gives it coherence and power, so the character of Florence is handled with a sensitivity that gives particular force to her part in the novel. Unlike Esther Summerson in *Bleak House* and Amy Dorrit, Florence Dombey draws from the reader a sympathy consistent with the facts of her situation, largely perhaps because the importance of her role is not specifically emphasized but develops as a consequence of the novel's central theme. This is not to suggest that Dickens deliberately adopted a more naturalistic approach in *Dombey and Son*, which as much as any other Dickens novel, has its high points of melodrama, comedy and pathos. What can be said is that these effects are skilfully controlled towards a unified expression of its central concerns in a way which was new to Dickens, and which was to open up new possibilities for the development of his art. (For a fuller discussion of points mentioned here and of many others see Kathleen Tillotson's excellent chapter on this novel in her *Novels of the Eighteen-Forties*.)

While working on *Dombey and Son* Dickens had confessed to the need he felt to control some aspects of his imagination:

> Invention, thank God, seems the easiest thing in the world; and I seem to have such a preposterous sense of the ridiculous ... as to be constantly requiring to restrain myself from launching into extravagances in the height of my enjoyment.
>
> (Forster, op. cit., Bk V, p 5)

The admission is an interesting testimony to the way in which Dickens regarded his creative impulse, and in *David Copperfield* he seems to have been able to relax the restraint which he had imposed upon its predecessor. *David Copperfield's* traditional popularity has always depended to some extent on the 'preposterous sense of the ridiculous' manifested in characters like Micawber and Betsy Trotwood, while the extent of Dickens's 'enjoyment' in the novel is communicated by the particular quality of its reflective tone:

> I never hear the name, or read the name, of Yarmouth, but I am reminded of a certain Sunday morning on the beach, the bells ringing for church, little Em'ly leaning on my shoulder, Ham lazily dropping stones in the water, and the sun, away at sea, just breaking through the heavy mist, and showing us the ships, like their own shadows.
>
> (ch. 3)

The beautifully realized sense of place, achieved again later in the descriptions of the marsh country in *Great Expectations*, is typical of the best of *David Copperfield*; nostalgia is far too crude a term to define its evocative sensitivity. The attention paid to the other major novels of Dickens's later period by modern critics has led to some neglect of what was once regarded as the representative Dickens novel and it is a neglect that amounts to self-deprivation. But when this is said, it has to be admitted that there is much that is unsatisfactory in *David Copperfield*. In his Introduction to the Everyman edition, written in 1907, Chesterton commented that 'although this is the best of all Dickens's books, it constantly disappoints the critical and intelligent reader.' So much the worse for him, one is tempted to respond, but Chesterton defines the more worrying aspects of *David Copperfield* when he discusses the novel's conclusion: 'I do not like the notion of David Copperfield sitting down comfortably to his tea-table with Agnes, having got rid of all the inconvenient or distressing characters of the story by sending them to Australia.' Dickens was not above getting rid of his more inconvenient or distressing children by sending them to Australia in real life, but the fictional experience is somehow less excusable. The combination of fiction and selective autobiography makes *David Copperfield* a disturbingly self-centred book: its hero is embarrassingly prone to a tendency to self-pity and wishful thinking which he never really outgrows and which is hardly improved by the smugness with which he regards himself at the conclusion of the novel:

> I had advanced in fame and fortune, my domestic joy was perfect, I had been married ten happy years.
>
> (ch. 63)

The unity which Dickens had had to create in *Dombey and Son* is embodied in *David Copperfield* in its first-person narrative but, in spite of the special circumstances surrounding it, it has important factors in common with the other later novels. Like Florence Dombey, David Copperfield suffers a loveless childhood, emphasized in this case by the physical and psychological violence of his stepfather's oppression. In a variety of ways, most obviously in the story of Little Em'ly, this is a Dickensian Song of Experience: the novel has no clearer message than its demonstration of the fragility of childhood innocence. Coupled with this is the sense of isolation, amounting on occasions to desolation, which surrounds David himself as the people to whom he commits himself in his search for security – Steerforth, Dora, even, though through no fault of his own, Peggotty – prove fallible. Given such a demonstration of the instability of existence, how can the marriage to Agnes seem other than a sham? Marriage, in fact, is to seem increasingly a mockery as a means of conclusion in the later novels: what in *Martin Chuzzlewit* is an acceptable convention of comedy becomes in *Little Dorrit, Great Expectations* and *Our Mutual Friend* almost a matter for apology.

David Copperfield, for all its variety of character and situation, is, of course, a deeply introspective novel. In the two great novels of the eighteen-fifties which followed it, *Bleak House* and *Little Dorrit*, Dickens turned, more completely than ever before, to an analysis of society. These two novels have attracted so much attention in recent years that it would serve little purpose to attempt a comprehensive account of them here, even were it possible, and instead I intend only to refer to specific issues arising from them: in the case of *Bleak*

House the unusual narrative method that Dickens adopted, and its implications for the view of society presented in the novel, and in the case of *Little Dorrit* the organization of the novel towards the expression of an unrelenting social pessimism. (On *Bleak House* see in particular M. D. Zabel's essay in *The Dickens Critics*, ed. Ford and Lane. Edgar Johnson's chapter on *Little Dorrit* in his *Charles Dickens* is one of his finest and should be consulted.)

Dickens began work on *Bleak House* at the end of 1851, a year which has often been taken to mark a turning-point in Victorian social history. The Great Exhibition of that year affirmed a commercial and nationalistic pride that could hardly have been predicted from the social unease of the eighteen-thirties and forties: the fifties were the first decade of Victorian self-confidence. The limitations of such an over-simplification have been expertly demonstrated by Professor Asa Briggs (*Victorian People*, ch. 2), and Dickens himself, no admirer of the Exhibition, was in fact probably more concerned with a speech which he made in the same year on behalf of the Metropolitan Sanitary Association, during the course of which he proclaimed:

That no man can estimate the amount of mischief grown in dirt, – that no man can say the evil stops here or stops there, either in its moral or physical effects, or can deny that it begins in the cradle and is not at rest in the miserable grave, is as certain as it is that the air from Gin Lane will be carried by an easterly wind into Mayfair, or that the furious pestilence raging in St Giles's no mortal list of Lady patronesses can keep out of Almack's.
(Quoted in Butt and Tillotson, *Dickens at Work*, 1957, p 191)

In *Bleak House* Esther Summerson catches smallpox from the crossing-sweeper, Jo; her aristocratic mother dies at the gate of the poison-infested burying-ground close by Tom All-Alone's. The all-embracing nature of social evil in *Bleak House* is thus made explicit through a symbolism born of Dickens's immediate social concerns. Richard Carstone, the doomed ward of the Court of Chancery, says of that court's operations:

'My head ached with wondering how it happened, if men were neither fools nor rascals and my heart ached to think that they could possibly be either. . . .'
(ch. 5)

The comment applies not just to Chancery itself, but by extension to the social system of which it is presented as the representative institution in the novel.

To emphasize the extent of his social preoccupations in *Bleak House* Dickens deliberately contrived a dual-narrative in which the life-story of his heroine, Esther Summerson, related as a first-person narrative, is interwoven with an extensive range of imaginative social documentation provided by the author himself. The effect is a subtle one – the novel gains stability from the progressive unravelling of Esther's story, while leaving Dickens free to expatiate on various examples of social abuse in the manner of his earlier picaresque method. The evils which he attacks, ranging from slum-dwelling to misguided philanthropy and including every form of exploitation, are indeed related to the main plot, but the fact that the novel is deliberately compartmentalized in this way allows Dickens to extend his social criticism without limitation.

There is, however, a further effect of the narrative method that is vital to an understanding of *Bleak House*. If Dickens supplies his analysis in what might loosely be called the picaresque section of the novel, his remedy is contained in the 'linear' narrative of Esther's life-story, and in particular in its account of her relationship with Jarndyce, the father-figure of the novel, who knows the ways of Chancery and constantly asserts the futility of opposition. Jarndyce's method of alleviation is a simple one springing from his inexhaustible bank-account, and, in fact, all that Dickens can offer against the realistic depredations of the social system is charity of improbably mythic proportions. The inadequacy of such a solution is best demonstrated by the way in which Jarndyce, a descendant of the Cheerybles of *Nicholas Nickleby* and Mr Brownlow in *Oliver Twist*, is presented as a figure of semi-divine potential. At the climax of *Bleak House*, when he has made Esther a present of not only her home but also her husband, she describes her reaction:

I was cold, and I trembled violently; but not a word he uttered was lost. As I sat looking fixedly at him, and the sun's rays descended, softly shining through the leaves upon his bare head, I felt as if the brightness on him must be like the brightness of the Angels.

(ch. 64)

The unrealistic nature of Jarndyce's role in *Bleak House*, far from providing an answer to the social evil documented in the novel, is, in fact, an expression of pessimism about the prospects of social change as intense as any expressed by the social analysis itself; in that Esther's narrative is ostensibly optimistic, the dual-narrative method can be seen as enabling Dickens to put forward a solution to the problems outlined in the novel which he could scarcely have endorsed in rational terms.

The pessimism implicit in *Bleak House* finds overt expression in *Little Dorrit*, written some five years later. Here Dickens reverts to the world of *Dombey and Son* in that the novel is given a specifically commercial setting: the inter-relationship between financial preoccupations and selfishness is emphasized not only by the thwarted life of the hero Arthur Clennam, a Paul Dombey who managed to survive, but also, in parody, through the social pretensions of William Dorrit, the Father of the Marshalsea, existing in fantasy when he is imprisoned and in fact after his release. The theme is given a fuller social perspective by the career of the financier, Merdle, surrounded by pillars of the establishment until he is exposed as 'the greatest Forger and the greatest Thief that ever cheated the gallows' (Bk II, ch. 25). The structure of *Little Dorrit* is a simple one compared with the ingenuity of *Bleak House*; the real issue is not, as Dickens himself was forced to enquire in a memorandum, how the Clennams are related to the Dorrits, but how the course of their lives demonstrates the hopelessness of existence in the prison-world that the novel portrays. The prison-symbolism of *Little Dorrit* has received ample comment: one need only remark here on the way in which the actual prisons of the novel and life itself as it is portrayed there become interchangeable. Dorrit released is Dorrit enchained: Clennam imprisoned is Clennam liberated, at least temporarily, from the pressures of the outside world. *Little Dorrit* ends with the marriage of Clennam to the heroine, Amy Dorrit, but the sense of release that this convention had given in the earlier novels is never attempted. The marriage takes place in an atmosphere devoid of festivity and the concluding sentence of the novel describes how, after it,

> They went quietly down into the roaring streets, inseparable and blessed; and as they passed in sunshine and shade, the noisy and the eager, and the arrogant and the froward and the vain, fretted and chafed, and made their usual uproar.
>
> (Bk II, ch. 34)

Little Dorrit has its 'good' characters – Amy herself, the Meagleses, Doyce the engineer, and in their own way, the rent-collector Panks and Flora Finching, nursing her senile aunt – but they are all cast in a minor key and their capacity for happiness seems constantly overshadowed by the predominant atmosphere of defeat that the novel suggests. Here the representative institution is the

Circumlocution Office, a government department devoted to the frustration of the individual; in *Little Dorrit* Dickens seems to abandon the idea that the individual can assert himself with any hope of success against the pressures of society.

The other novels of the eighteen-fifties, *Hard Times* and *A Tale of Two Cities*, were both written in weekly instalments for Dickens's own periodicals, *Household Words* and *All the Year Round*. Of the novels written in this way only *Great Expectations* really achieves the stature of the major novels although, since its championship by F. R. Leavis in *The Great Tradition*, *Hard Times* has come to occupy a special place in Dickens studies. Written soon after the completion of *Bleak House* and after a visit by Dickens to the industrial North, it is, in fact, far more successful as an attack on Utilitarianism than as a discussion of specifically industrial issues. The economy of its form has certain advantages in this respect; *Hard Times* makes its point about its chosen target lucidly and forcefully, and certainly Humphry House's assertion that it is 'a sport and an anomaly' (*The Dickens World*, 1941, p 34) gives a misleading impression. These qualities, however, cannot disguise the fact that its characterization is often unsubtle and its irony often laboured. Amplitude is fundamental to Dickens's art, and the restrictions imposed upon him by the comparative brevity of *Hard Times* are not always successfully overcome.

A Tale of Two Cities is more of an anomaly than *Hard Times*, and some critics have related its singular emotional tone to aspects of Dickens's private life, and particularly to his involvement with the young actress, Ellen Ternan. It is probably more to the point to see this novel as an expression of the subconscious fear of revolutionary violence which Dickens had revealed earlier in *Barnaby Rudge* and which he shared with so many of his contemporaries. In the Preface Dickens refers to 'the philosophy of Mr Carlyle's wonderful book'. Carlyle's *French Revolution* had been published in 1837, at a time when it was easy to see the significance of its theme for contemporary England, but *A Tale of Two Cities*, appearing more than twenty years later, is an interesting reminder that anxiety on the subject of revolution was not confined to the first half of the century. The 'two cities' of the title are, of course, London and Paris, and if the opening chapters express a modernist's contempt for the London of an earlier age, it is not implausible to relate Dickens's account of the fall of the French aristocracy, with its hallmark of gratuitous indifference, to his comments on society in his other late novels. Indeed, some such comparison is suggested in the opening paragraph:

... in short the period was so like the present period, that some of its noisiest authorities insisted on its being received, for good or evil, in the superlative degree of comparison only.

(ch. 1)

but it is never consistently developed. Inspired by Carlyle, *A Tale of Two Cities* matches Carlyle in its rhetoric and in the vagueness with which its social and emotional themes are explored. For the complexity of tone and analysis that characterizes Dickens's other work of the period are substituted shrillness and a pervasive sentimentality epitomized by Sidney Carton's famous last words.

The pessimistic turn taken by Dickens's novels from *Dombey and Son* onwards could scarcely have passed unnoticed by contemporary reviewers. In a long review of *Little Dorrit*, for example, in *Blackwood's Magazine*, entitled 'Remonstrance with Dickens', the writer lamented what he regarded as a distortion of Dickens's natural propensities:

... we can't wait for the end of the wilderness of *Little Dorrit* before recording our earnest protest and deep lament; for in that wilderness we sit down and weep when we remember thee, O Pickwick!

(*Blackwood's Magazine*, April 1857)

The review concludes by begging Dickens not to go on 'building streets of *Bleak Houses*, and creating crowds of *Little Dorrits*'. Pleas for a return to the spirit of the earlier novels were often a way of expressing disapproval of what were felt to be dangerously radical social attitudes: Lord Macaulay's famous comment that *Hard Times* was 'sullen socialism' was not an isolated example. There were other causes for anxiety amongst Dickens's admirers. Aware of his unhappiness in his marriage, which came to a climax with his separation from his wife in 1858, and his removal to his new house at Gad's Hill near Rochester, his friend, Angela Burdett-Coutts, was afraid that his domestic difficulties had affected his writing. Certainly *Little Dorrit*, in particular, of the later novels seems in many ways to suggest an impasse: the constant atmosphere of failure surrounding its middle-aged hero has psychological as well as social implications.

Settled at Gad's Hill, however, Dickens seems to have found new resources of creative energy. His last completed novels, *Great Expectations* and *Our Mutual Friend*, together with the unfinished *Edwin Drood*, are certainly no more optimistic than the novels which preceded them – *Our Mutual Friend* especially, suggests a society more positively predatory than anything in *Bleak House* or *Little Dorrit* – but they are marked by new reserves of that fictive inventiveness which is characteristic of Dickens at his greatest, reinforced now by an increasing fascination with the macabre themes of crime and death.

Great Expectations was Dickens's second 'autobiographical' novel – 'autobiographical' in the very general sense that it presents in a first-person narrative the career, and more importantly the psychological development, of its hero. As in *David Copperfield*, Dickens makes skilful use of the narrator's recollected sense of place. From the opening chapter we are presented through the eyes of the child, Pip, with an evocative picture of the marsh country amongst which he grew up, and to which he is to return, at moments of emotional crisis, throughout the course of the novel:

> Ours was the marsh country, down by the river, within, as the river wound, twenty miles of the sea. My first most vivid and broad impression of the identity of things, seems to me to have been gained on a memorable raw afternoon towards evening. At such a time I found out for certain, that this bleak place overgrown with nettles was the churchyard . . . and that the dark flat wilderness beyond the churchyard, intersected with dykes and mounds and gates, with scattered cattle feeding on it, was the marshes; and that the low leaden line beyond was the river; and that the distant savage lair from which the wind was rushing was the sea. . . .
>
> (ch. 1)

This kind of atmospheric precision achieves symbolic force and recurs, for example, in Pip's references to the great furnace at the forge where he works with the blacksmith Joe Gargery, and in the descriptions of the decayed sterility of Satis House, the mansion of his supposed benefactress, Miss Havisham.

The theme of *Great Expectations* is that of false pride and again, as in *Dombey and Son*, it is given a specifically monetary perspective: Pip's ambitions to be a gentleman, based on the belief that he is the chosen protégé of Miss Havisham, are shattered when he learns that his sponsor is the convict Magwitch. But *Great Expectations* is, in fact, equivocal about money-values and its real strength lies in the quality of its psychological penetration, revealed not only in its account of Pip's reactions to his situation, but also in features like the mysterious split personality of the criminal lawyer Jaggers and the self-imposed death-in-life of Miss Havisham, the consequence of her having been jilted many years before. Related to, and indeed reinforcing, these psychological concerns is a fascination with crime, emphasized by the role of Magwitch and his involvement in the lives of both Pip and the unattainable heroine, Estella. In his notes for the novel Dickens wrote:

> Magwitch tried, found guilty, & left for
> DEATH
> (Butt and Tillotson, op. cit., p 30)

and at the climax of the novel he includes a highly dramatized account of the death sentence passed on Magwitch at his trial. Preoccupations which had revealed themselves in the early part of Dickens's career, in episodes like Fagin's last night alive, the suicide of Ralph Nickleby and the murder in Martin Chuzzlewit, thus recur in these final novels.

Violence and the mentality of the criminal are even more intensely represented in *Our Mutual Friend* and *Edwin Drood*, and in the latter, with the prominence given to the character of Jasper Drood, choirmaster, opium addict and presumably murderer, Dickens would seem to have intended to concentrate specifically on these issues. Dickens had published Wilkie Collins's *The Moonstone* in *All the Year Round* in 1868 and this may have induced him to write his own detective story, although *Edwin Drood* is a work of potentially far greater power than Collins's novel. Speculation on the subject of Dickens's unfinished novel, however, while fascinating, is not always productive, and I therefore intend to conclude this survey of Dickens's work with a discussion of *Our Mutual Friend*, his last, and arguably his greatest, completed novel.

Our Mutual Friend has had a chequered critical career. Its opening numbers were not altogether well received and Dickens endured considerable anxiety about its progress. The young Henry James attacked it violently for its lack of discipline and 'humanity':

> What a world were this world if the world of *Our Mutual Friend* were honest reflection of it! But a community of eccentrics is impossible. . . . Where in these pages are the depositories of that intelligence without which the movement of life would cease? Who represents nature?
> (*The Nation*, I (1865), reprinted in Ford and Lane,
> *The Dickens Critics*, 1961)

and of the early critics only Shaw seems to have anticipated such modern views as those of Edmund Wilson and Edgar Johnson, who rank it with Dickens's greatest achievements rather than considering it as evidence of decline.

The first thing that has to be said about *Our Mutual Friend* is that it is a novel in which Dickens, in a way curiously comparable to Henry James himself in his last novels, takes his fictional techniques to the point of self-parody. The convoluted plot, involving its central character in not two, but three, separate identities, all involving disguise, outdoes anything its author had contrived before; we are asked to accept concealed evidence, simulated behaviour and hidden secrets as part of the day-to-day processes of existence. The characterization offers a range of grotesques like the one-legged Silas Wegg, hired to read the 'Decline-and-Fall-Off-The-Rooshan-Empire' to the equally improbable Golden Dustman Noddy Boffin, Mr Venus, taxidermist and dealer in 'human warious', and Jenny Wren, the deformed dolls' dressmaker, whose love for the good Lizzie Hexam alternates with sadistic fantasies about the fate of her enemies. *Our Mutual Friend* seems at times like a vast and somewhat decaying baroque structure, threatening at any moment to collapse.

The effect of this exaggeration of technique, like that of James's prose in *The Ambassadors*, is one of challenge to the reader, and it is a challenge which, if accepted, intensifies the thematic concerns of the novel. These, crudely, are two-fold and combine the preoccupations which I have outlined in the earlier novels – social constriction, based on obsession with money, and psychological stress, particularly of a violent kind.

Our Mutual Friend is set very firmly in the present: 'In these times of ours, though concerning the exact year there is no need to be precise' (Bk I, ch. 1). The history of the Harmon inheritance, which consists of a series of dust-heaps containing untold wealth, is introduced at a society dinner, whose members are presented as typical of the Victorian ruling-class: Veneering, the spectator, who is to become an M.P., Podsnap, the successful businessman, confident in his own incontrovertible and jingoistic morality, and a group of upper-class decadents to whom life is simply a bore. These characters survive at the end of the novel – if Veneering's fraudulent career is about to be exposed, this is mentioned only casually and he will easily be replaced – to conclude the narration of the Harmon story. The implications are obvious: social status may be based on shaky foundations –

. . . traffic in Shares is the one thing to have to do with in this world. Have no antecedents, no established character, no cultivation, no ideas, no manners; have Shares.

(Bk I, ch. 10)

– but the system is immovable. The imagery of speculation is repeated throughout the novel; when the humble Boffins, temporarily enriched by the inheritance, decide to adopt an orphan,

> The suddenness of an orphan's rise in the market was not to be paralleled by the maddest records of the Stock Exchange. He would be at five thousand per cent. discount . . . at nine in the morning, and (being enquired for) would go up at five thousand per cent. premium before noon.
>
> (Bk I, ch. 16)

Silas Wegg speculates in ingratiation (Bk I, ch. 5), while a pair of confidence-tricksters, the Lammles, speculate in each other in marriage and, disappointed, attempt to entrap another acquaintance, 'Fascination' Fledgeby, the child of a similar mercenary marriage. They

> . . . all had a touch of the outlaw, as to their rovings in the merry greenwood of Jobbery Forest, lying in the outskirts of the Share Market and the Stock Exchange.
>
> (Bk II, ch. 5)

In *Bleak House* and *Little Dorrit* Dickens took institutions as metaphors for social malaise: in *Our Mutual Friend* he attacked an economic system, engaging it not on the grounds of theory, but in terms of its effects on human behaviour.

This theme is emphasized by the magnetizing effect of the Harmon inheritance on those who come into contact with it and *Our Mutual Friend* can justly be said to be a fitting culmination to the vein of social criticism which Dickens embarked upon in *Dombey and Son* and pursued through the novels which followed it. Bound into its story also is the interest in the more dramatic aspects of human psychology, which had been hinted at in the early novels and which re-emerged more powerfully towards the end of Dickens's career. The world of *Our Mutual Friend* is a Waste Land in which boredom and criminality flourish. Boredom is seen in the behaviour of the enervated young lawyer, Eugene Wrayburn, who is eventually rescued from his affected nihilism, after a ritualistic immersion in the Thames, by the love of Lizzie Hexam, the waterman's daughter; criminality is revealed through the underworld behaviour of the river-scavengers; and, more specifically, the uncontrollable passion of Wrayburn's rival, the schoolmaster Bradley Headstone, is an extended study in violence on a level which Dickens had scarcely attempted before; inevitably melodramatic, he nevertheless conveys a power born of Dickens's own propensities towards the extremes of emotion.

An account as brief as this can only hint at, and over-simplify, the complexity of a novel like *Our Mutual Friend*. If this novel lacks the thematic coherence of *Dombey and Son*, the range of *Bleak House* or the atmospheric consistency of *Little Dorrit*, it more than compensates for these omissions by the intensity of its satire and by the power of its insights and implications. The eccentricity of its characterization has been cited as evidence of its author's tiredness in the last stages of his demanding career; in fact, *Our Mutual Friend* is an astonishingly inventive, if at times morbid, novel, and far from indicating exhaustion it developed new areas of interest, some of which obviously were to have been explored in *Edwin Drood*.

The reservations expressed by some of the reviewers about the social stance adopted by Dickens in his later novels seem not to have been reflected in his general popularity. He was elated to be able to claim that *Edwin Drood* was meeting with more success than any of its predecessors. His death, like that of Tennyson, the other great Victorian writer to become an institution in his own time, was an occasion for national mourning; a special train conveyed his coffin from Gad's Hill to London for its interment in Westminster Abbey. Like Shakespeare, Dickens worked in a popular medium at a time when it was becoming the predominant literary form and, like Shakespeare, he enriched it through the fertility of his imagination and the extent of his vision. In that that vision, in even the darkest of the novels, remained fundamentally comic, I suspect that, where criticism has found him wanting, it is often because comedy, of its nature, presents particular problems for the moral certitude which criticism tends to embody. This in itself is a measure of Dickens's greatness: like all great artists he forces us to reconsider the attitudes which we bring to art.

5

SURTEES, THACKERAY AND TROLLOPE

Arthur Pollard

Surtees, Thackeray and Trollope, though by pairs having obvious affinities, may at first sight seem an ill-assorted trio. Surtees is little known, but perhaps becoming better so; Thackeray was regarded by many as the greatest novelist of his generation; and Trollope made his mark, by other things as well, but certainly by his prolixity and competence. The three of them share, however, at least one quality. They each possess a thorough, reliable, informed and well-defined knowledge of their world; and to that each brings his own critical view. It may be an over-simplification, but it is true enough to classify all three broadly as satirical realists.

Robert Smith Surtees (1805–64), of Durham Tory squirearchical stock, tried the law and did not like it. What he did like was hunting and writing, and he combined the two, first in his journalism for the *New Sporting Magazine* where the immortal Jorrocks made his initial appearance and later in the seven completed and one discarded novel (*Young Tom Hall*) which followed his first book, *Jorrocks' Jaunts and Jollities* (1838). This latter is a collection of sketches, presenting the fat, rough, irrepressible, generous-minded grocer of Great Coram Street in a variety of situations, a man for whom 'Fox-'unting is indeed the prince of sports. The image of war without its guilt, and only half its danger' ('The Turf: Mr. Jorrocks at Newmarket'). Jorrocks is a bit of an egotist, he has a lot to say for himself, he is even loud in saying it, but, somewhat like Falstaff, there is a largeness more than physical about him by which he never loses our sympathy.

It was in Surtees's next work, *Handley Cross* (1843), that Jorrocks reached his full development. This novel is picaresque and formless, a reminder, as also by the robust activity and vigorous and sometimes shady characters within it, of how much Surtees belongs to the Fielding and Smollett tradition of the preceding century. Handley Cross (possibly based on Leamington Spa) is the place to which Jorrocks is invited to be Master of Foxhounds ('Talk of a M.P.! vot's an M.P. compared to an M.F.H.?' – ch. 11). In the process of his elevation this Don Quixote acquires his own Sancho Panza in the person of James Pigg, his candid and not over-scrupulous huntsman, another of Surtees' unforgettable creations. The first meeting of master and man makes clear why comparisons are often made between Surtees and Dickens. There is the sharp, concise, unforgettable detail whether of description of appearance or of speech:

> He was a tall, spindle-shanked man, inclining to be bald . . . A drop hung at his nose, and tobacco juice simmered down the deeply indented furrows of his chin. His dress was a strange mixture of smart-coloured misfitting clothes . . .
> 'Humph!' grunted Mr Jorrocks, as he eyed him, observing aloud to himself, 'Vot a long-legged beggar it is,' inwardly resolving that he wouldn't do.
>
> (ch. 20)

But Pigg did. The conversation that follows has Jorrocks with Southern ignorance hazarding of Pigg's birthplace that 'Cannynewcassel' might be 'near Dundee'. The rest of their acquaintance, as of so much Surtees, is a mixture of the energetic and the unexpected. Hunting is intermingled with social events – dinners, visits and the like, but not least with Jorrocks's own lectures on ''unting', a down-to-earth activity or, as Jorrocks puts it, 'Gentlemen wot take their ideas of 'unting from Mr. Hackermann's pictor-shop in Regent's Street must have rum notions of the sport. There you see red legs flyin' out in all directions, and 'osses apparently to be had for nothing.' Besides rejecting such unrealism, Surtees took the opportunity also of savaging his famous and by him little-loved fellow-hunting writer, 'Nimrod' (C. J. Apperley), in the guise of Pomponius Ego. Much of the latter part of the novel is taken up with Surtees's exploiting his early apprenticeship to the law in his account of the suit of Doleful vs Jorrocks and the incredible insertion of the trial of Jorrocks under the Lunacy Commission. We are in a different and decidedly less interesting world than that which preceded it.

Neither of Surtees's first two books had been much of a success and *Hillingdon Hall* (1845) which completed the Jorrocks trilogy did no better. The Cockney grocer has now given up hunting and set up as country squire and enlightened agriculturist, advocating fertilizers, drainage and the like. The novel was, in fact, inscribed to the Royal Agricultural Society. The story leaves us with little to remember beyond the matrimonial intrigues of Mrs and Miss Flather (worthy indeed of Trollope!) and the hostilities of Jorrocks with the Duke of Donkeyton and his son, the Marquis of Bray, whom Jorrocks defeats in the election so that our ertswhile M.F.H is now become M.P.! We never, however, see him in that role. The next novel, *Hawbuck Grange* (1847), was shorter, returned to hunting and did no better than its predecessors. It is really back to the *Jaunts and Jollities* model, a series of sporting sketches with only the most tenuous continuity in the person of Tom Scott, who is amongst Surtees's most genial but not most memorable characters. The presence of a genuine love-affair – between Tom and Lydia Clifton – is unusual in Surtees, but it is also half-hearted and abortive.

The later books contain some shady characters, Kipling's Midmore finding Surtees' world initially to be 'a heavy-eating, hard-drinking hell of horse-copers, swindlers, matchmaking mothers, economically dependent virgins selling themselves unblushingly for cash and lands: Jews, tradesmen, and an ill-considered spawn of Dickens-and-horsedung characters' ('My Son's Wife' in *A Diversity of Creatures*, 1917, p 333). They are all there in *Mr. Sponge's Sporting Tour* (1853). Once again, as the title itself makes clear, we have the picaresque pattern; and, though very different, once again we have a central character of Jorrocksian proportions – indeed, more interesting because more complicated than Jorrocks. Sponge is 'a good, pushing, free-and-easy sort of man, wishing to be a gentleman without knowing how.' His is a world of fools and rogues or would-be rogues. He fleeces the former and is a match for the latter. There is a whole gallery of characters – the innocently eccentric Jogglebury Crowdey with his passion for making gibbey-sticks; Puffington the cit turned squire, a 'man of p-r-o-r-perty'; the pretentious snob Jawleyford and his designing daughters; the sufficiently named Sir Harry Scattercash; and, for the first time encountered, a rogue to match Sponge himself, Facey Romford, and 'the beautiful and tolerably virtuous Miss Glitters of the Astley's Royal Amphitheatre' (ch. 71) spending a few days with her old friend, Lady Scattercash – of similar origins. Most striking of all, however, are Lord Scamperdale and his hanger-on, Jack Spraggon, of the Flat-Hat Hunt, living in the servants' quarters of the family mansion and living on gin and tripe. Their invective matches the meanness of their existence. Thus to Sponge on one hunting occasion:

'Oh, you scandalous, hypocritical, rusty-booted, numb-handed son of a puffing corn-cutter. . . .'

'Oh, you unsightly, santicified, idolatrous, Bagnigge-Wells coppersmith, you think because I'm a lord and can't swear or use coarse language that you may do as you like . . .'

(ch. 23)

But how amongst all this vigorous portrayal of hard-riding, hard-drinking sportsmen Surtees manages also to castigate social climbing, the marriage-market, wild young men with no sense of values, the decadence of the aristocracy and the like! No wonder Thackeray thought the characters of this novel 'capital, and the Flat Hats delightful . . . Scamperdale's character perfectly odious and admirable.' The linkage of those two adjectives exactly fits what Thackeray made of some of his own creations in *Vanity Fair*.

Putting aside *Young Tom Hall*, unfinished because of a quarrel with his publisher Harrison Ainsworth, the next two novels are *Ask Mamma* (1858) and *Plain or Ringlets* (1860). In the former the comic verve of earlier work gives way to more savage satire. The Earl of Ladythorne is too simply the obvious *roué*; the devious devices of the Jew-landlord and hunt-master Sir Moses Mainchance, are exposed; the chase after Billy Pringle 'the Richest Commoner in England' by every eligible (and even ineligible) female in sight is a sordid business – and, to complete matters, we are told right at the outset that Billy 'was only an underbred chap . . . as good an imitation of a Swell as ever we saw . . . Fine shirts, fine ties, fine talk, fine trinkets . . . Billy was liberal, not to say prodigal in all these. The only infallible rule we know is, that the man who is always talking about being a gentleman never is one.' *There* is a theme that would occupy Thackeray and Trollope also. *Plain or Ringlets* is even less interesting with an unattractive and forgettable hero Bunting (Admiration Jack), whole areas of the novel adapted from *Young Tom Hall*, and not really taking off until a quarter of the way through when Jock Haggish and his hounds appear. The Duke of Tergiversation is amongst Surtees's better creations and the ball at Tergiversation Castle one of his great scenes, but John Welcome was surely right in believing that the book's principal value is not as a novel but as a panorama of 'a Victorian watering-place, its picnics, race-meetings and mild diversions, its reflections on the dangers of high play and *louche* society, discounting bills, railways [and] London clubs . . .' (*The Sporting World of R. S. Surtees*, 1982, p 173).

So we come to the last, and what Surtees intended to be his last novel, *Mr. Facey Romford's Hounds* (1865). We are back to the manner and quality of *Mr. Sponge's Sporting Tour*, and both title-characters are back with Lucy Glitters (Mrs Sponge) who will go to Australia at the end with Romford, the latter to join Sponge in setting up a bank in Melbourne! Though Surtees always believed that his rogues would be exposed, the emphasis of much that he writes is Jonsonian with those capable rogues preying upon pretentious incompetents. In particular, he directs his satire against the new rich, the Watkins and the Hazeys, commerce trying to set up as gentry. But in the end, as with Jonson, the house of cards collapses, the confidence-trick is exposed, Facey and Lucy are sent on their way.

Surtees's world is hard, unremitting, unforgiving. V. S. Pritchett called him the novelist of 'violent sport' (*The Working Novelist*, 1965, p 91), and there is no doubt of his celebration of the energetic physical side of human nature. His glorification of 'the flesh' gives to his work a vivacity and at the same time a seaminess that makes us both enjoy and deplore his most memorable characters. The heartiness of Jorrocks gives way to the ambivalences of Soapey Sponge and Facey Romford. It is a world that, as we have seen, Thackeray understood and appreciated.

In his own generation Thackeray was often compared with Dickens. Subsequently he has more usually been placed alongside Trollope, sometimes to the discredit of the latter. There are marked resemblances, but the differences are more obvious. Both are concerned with the life of middle-class and aristocratic society, but Trollope seems nearer both in time and place to his world than Thackeray does to his. Thackeray is much more a storyteller and less of a reporter. He sets up his tales as the showman. There is also a world-weary, mildly sardonic note about his observations, as of a man who has seen and known all and retired from it, a man with the wisdom and experience of age. On the whole, Trollope is not so disillusioned.

William Makepeace Thackeray (1811–63) was born in Calcutta, the son of an East India Company official who died when the boy was barely five. The child returned to England and was eventually sent to school at the Charterhouse (1822–6). His mother married as her second husband a former lover, Major Carmichael Smythe, whose earlier advances had been frustrated by her parents. Thackeray got on well with his stepfather who even helped him to buy a journal after periods at Cambridge and in the study of art and the law had proved vain. The journalistic adventure was no more successful and this together with gambling and investing in an Indian bank dissipated the legacy which Thackeray inherited on attaining his majority. Meanwhile, he met and married Isabella Shawe, who, however, after a brief period of happiness fell ill and became insane. He subsequently derived some comfort from his friendship with Mrs Brookfield, though this was not without cost to his relations with her husband, William Brookfield.

Although his own attempts at running a journal proved such a failure, Thackeray had at last found a career. He began to contribute to *Fraser's Magazine*, in which he was eventually to publish among others his *Yellowplush Papers* (1837–8; collected 1856), *Catherine* (1839–40), *The Great Hoggarty Diamond* (1841) and *The Luck of Barry Lyndon* (1844; revised as *The Memoirs of Barry Lyndon*, 1856). His work also appeared regularly in *Punch*, to which his most notable contribution was *The Book of Snobs* (1846–7; in book-form 1848; complete, New York, 1852). It was not, however, until the writing of *Vanity Fair* (1848) that the world recognized the appearance of a new novelist of the first rank. By that date Dickens was bringing out his eighth major work, *Dombey and Son*. There followed seven rich years with *Pendennis* (1849–50), *Henry Esmond* (1852), *English Humourists of the Eighteenth Century* (1853) and *The Newcomes* (1854–5). Though he was by no means worked out, Thackeray never again attained the achievement of these years. *The Virginians* (1858–9), the sequel to *Esmond*, cannot really abide comparison with its predecessor, whilst *Lovel the Widower* (1861), *Philip* (1862) and *Dennis Duval* (1864) are sadly repetitive indications of a great talent in decline. All these, together with the charming *Roundabout Papers* (1863), appeared in *The Cornhill Magazine*, of which Thackeray was first editor. He died suddenly on 23 December 1863, a victim of the heart-trouble that had afflicted him for some years and was no doubt largely responsible for the loss of his creative energy.

Thackeray did not possess an inventive imagination. Hence his stories tend to be histories, chronological tales, rather than complex relationships of events and people. Hence also his reliance on areas of life and types of people he himself had known. His own false starts – university, law, art – were useful to him, especially in *Pendennis*, which is often regarded as an 'autobiographical' novel. Many of his characters and places are easily traceable to actual counterparts – Colonel Newcome to Major Carmichael Smythe,

Major Pendennis to his father-in-law General Shawe, Greyfriars to Charterhouse, to mention but a few. (On this subject *in extenso* see G. N. Ray, *The Buried Life*, 1952.) Next to his own experience is that of history, and especially his beloved eighteenth century, which provided material both for lectures (*The English Humourists* and *The Four Georges* (1860)) and for novels (*Esmond* and *The Virginians*).

With the notable exception of Swift, Thackeray was at home with the writers of that era. 'Addison's honoured name' could hardly attract a superlative too extravagant. The whole style of *Esmond*, a measured imitation but in no sense a parody, is a tribute to Addison. Both men enjoyed being spectators and each was a 'preacher without orders' ('Addison and Congreve', *English Humourists*). Thackeray's discursive manner also owes something to Fielding, whose candid portrait of life, and especially of sexual relations, he admired whilst at the same time he regretted that the *mores* of his time forbade him to imitate it. But there were important differences, differences which Bagehot has isolated in his contrast of Fielding's 'bold spirit of bounding happiness' with his successor's more 'anxious temperament'. Bagehot went on to press the sentimental or, rather, 'sensibilitous' comparison with Sterne. Certainly Thackeray shares the faculty of seeing things 'from a *sensitive* aspect', but Sterne's sentimentality seems much more integrated, more essentially part of the man and the work, than does Thackeray's.

By comparison with the great names of the preceding century Thackeray considered most of his contemporaries insignificant. In 'Novels by Eminent Hands' (originally 'Punch's Prize Novelists', 1847) he satirized Disraeli, Lever, G. P. R. James and Lytton among others. The parody of James begins with the ubiquitous horseman of that author's tales, whilst that of Lever ('Phil Fogarty, a Tale of the Fighting Onety-Oneth') catches this writer's rollicking Irish military narrative brilliantly. The main target, however, was Lytton, who was castigated both as a writer about fashionable life (*Pelham* (1828), for example) and of 'Newgate novels' (*Paul Clifford* (1830), *Eugene Aram* (1833)). Thackeray considered this type of novel dangerous and even Dickens came under his strictures. Both *Catherine* and *Barry Lyndon* were intended as partly ironic, partly direct condemnations of such writings, and in the former we read:

And here, though we are only in the third chapter of this history, we feel almost sick of the characters who appear in it . . . But how can we help ourselves? The public will hear of nothing but rogues; and the only way in which poor authors, who must live, can act honestly by the public and themselves, is to paint such thieves as they are: not dandy, poetical rose-water thieves . . . They don't quote Plato, like Eugene Aram . . . or die white-washed saints like poor 'Biss Dadsy' in 'Oliver Twist'. No, my dear madam, you and your daughters have no right to admire and sympathize with any such person, fictitious or real.

Neither *Catherine* nor *Barry Lyndon* is so superb a piece of irony as that of Thackeray's master, Fielding, in *Jonathan Wild*, but *Barry Lyndon* possesses a greater degree of the necessary detachment. These confessions of an Irish rogue have indeed something of an advantage over *Jonathan Wild* in that the autobiographical standpoint gives an added level of condemnation through the blatant candour of the narrator ('It was her estate I made love to' – ch. 10). Yet Thackeray has not entirely avoided the error of his contemporaries. Despite all Lyndon's deeds and all the sufferings of others through those deeds, in the death of his son, the father's grief and the dying child's plea for his parents' reconciliation, Thackeray draws our attention to the misdirected worth of his hero and provides one of those scenes of controlled sentimentality in which he is unsurpassed.

Barry Lyndon was an eighteenth-century adventurer; his nineteenth-century successors, climbing the social ladder, had less spirit and less nobility. They were snobs. Others wrote about them; there were Lytton's 'vulgarly genteel' (*England and the English* (1833)) and Dickens's succession of them from Mr Wititterly (*Nicholas Nickleby*) to the Veneerings (*Our Mutual Friend*). It was left to Thackeray to give us a whole Theophrastan gallery of snobs. The species was more easily recognized than defined. Thackeray has snobs by birth, breeding, profession and environment. There are snobs superior (even the 'Snob Royal') and snobs inferior (or sycophants). 'He who meanly admires mean things' was Thackeray's inadequate attempt at a definition. He shows the condition as consisting of excessive admiration of rank, irrespective of worth. Persons of rank despise others, persons with wealth seek to obtain rank, and persons with neither try to attain both or to secure the patronage of someone who possesses them. In this nineteenth-century equivalent of the 'rat-race' social relationships form a labyrinth of greed, hate, flattery and hypocrisy.

Bunyan's Vanity Fair 'where all such merchandise is sold, as houses, lands, trades, places, honours, preferments, titles, . . . [where is] to be seen juggling, cheats, games, plays, fools, apes, knaves and rogues', comprehensively futile and corrupt, was a perfect symbolic setting for the characters of Thackeray's world. Even more than Surtees's, Thackeray's is a world that reminds one of Ben Jonson where lesser would-be rogues are swallowed up by greater actual rogues. In particular, in Becky Sharp we have a female version of the criminal adventurers Thackeray had condemned. But we admire Becky. We admire her as we admire Volpone – for her sheer resource and success. In a series of episodes she progresses from poor governess to belle of the Waterloo ball. She goes on to even greater triumphs, but after Waterloo there is less luck and more scheming. Her association with the dissolute Lord Steyne and her neglect of her husband and child make her less and less attractive. Her treatment of husband and child offended against the domestic pieties of Victorian England. The book, as a whole, no doubt derived some of its power from the contrast between the raffishness of its Regency setting and the changed manners of three decades later. Thackeray had no love for Evangelicals (what Victorian novelist had?), but they won the day (see, for example, F. K. Brown, *Father of the Victorians*, 1961); it is one of them, Lady Jane Sheepshanks, that he uses to bring about Becky's undoing.

Thackeray sub-titled the work 'A Novel Without A Hero'. It should not be thought that he chose a heroine instead. Becky is not; she is deceived like everyone else. Nor is Amelia Sedley with whom she is so deliberately and extensively contrasted, despite the fact that Amelia is called 'the heroine of this work' with her 'thousand kind words and offices'. These latter are just so much insipidity, like the rest of her character. As Becky increases, Amelia decreases, accepting her lot with a passivity that the Victorians may have thought more noble than later readers have done. She is apparently good, a doll of a character, naïve, trusting – and imperceptive. Dobbin with the nobility of an equally imperceptive character bullies the worthless George Osborne into marrying her; and after his death at Waterloo she rebuffs Dobbin's willingness to marry her by her obstinate, irrational and thoroughly unwarranted fidelity to Osborne's memory. Her sufferings do not dignify her; they serve a better purpose in exposing the various oppressions of husband, father and father-in-law. Dobbin is little better, so properly upright as to be a bore. Was his name indicative of what Thackeray thought about him? The novel loses some of its power in the latter stages, partly because of the change in Becky, partly because the reader is waiting for, but not very interested in, the eventual reunion of Dobbin and Amelia. To Mrs Liddell's request for such an ending,

Thackeray replied, 'Well, he shall [have her], and when he has got her, he will find her not worth having' (L. Stevenson, *The Showman of Vanity Fair*, 1947, p 172). So much irony for the conventional happy ending! The bad, like Becky, reap a sour harvest, and the good, like Dobbin, do little better.

Vanity Fair is satire in depth, at every level of participation in the novel. In Becky's picaresque progress through the ranks of society, embracing as it does the impoverished gentility of the Miss Pinkertons' school, the houses of the merchants Osborne and Sedley, the country-seat at Queen's Crawley and the acquaintance of aristocracy in Brussels and London, we see the vices Thackeray had condemned among his snobs. We see what money can do and what it makes men do, but at the same time Becky and Rawdon show 'How to Live Well on Nothing A Year' (title of ch. 36). We see, too, how Becky's beauty and sexual attractiveness make the men fools and the women jealous. The book is a comprehensive satire, and this being so, the characters are restricted in the directions along which they may develop. Like Jonson's, Thackeray's characters are 'flat', but they are also various in mode of creation and extent of development. It is necessary to mention only the different extraordinarinesses of a Sir Pitt Crawley, come almost straight out of Fielding, or a Jos Sedley, who might have migrated to Dickens.

But Lord Steyne was faithful enough to be recognizable as a version of the Marquis of Hertford, and the setting of the novel is historical. Yet it is also Vanity Fair, in which the puppets move to the master's bidding. The historical circumstances remind us that here is a version of our world; but the 'showman' warns us that there is manipulation to a predetermined end, that *Vanity Fair* is a moral tale. We are also to remember that the 'showman' both is and is not Thackeray. There is a self-authenticating logic about the events. They are what the characters make them, but the characters are also puppets in that they are in the grip of some sort of predestination, usually to wrong-doing. We are not surprised by what happens; our interest is held by anticipation, a waiting for what we feel will eventually happen. The moral therefore does not seem forced; the moralist does not have to coerce his material. The weariness behind the final exclamation is all the stronger: 'Ah! Vanitas Vanitatum! which of us is happy in this world? Which of us has his desire? or, having it, is satisfied?' Here is the disillusion and resignation that springs from the wisdom of experience. These words are a fitting epitaph to *Vanity Fair*, for in this great sad satire the view Thackeray presents is enough to persuade us that life is like that.

The profundity and sublimity of this novel were never again to be recaptured. The next work, *Pendennis*, was nearly as auto-biographical as Dickens' *David Copperfield* which was appearing at the same time. Its central character is an 'irresolute, half-ashamed, sceptical hero, conscious of his own weakness, conscious of his own ignorance ... governed by tastes and circumstances instead of principles, but clinging firm to old habits, to traditional lessons of truth and honour ... not very bad, nor very good, nor very anything' (J. Fitzjames Stephen in *Cambridge Essays*, 1855, p 184). It is a rambling tale, a cumulative characterization, built up from accounts of action and attitude rather than an interpretation developing from the experience of the character himself. It is intimate history with a multifarious background. Thackeray limits his omniscience as narrator and thereby endows Pendennis with a sense of unusual independence. The freedom of the story might almost be a reaction to the control and arrangement in *Vanity Fair*. It also reinforces the sense of Pendennis's own weakness, his tendency to drift at the mercy of events. This appears particularly in his relations with the various women of the novel, one affair after another emphasizing his vacillation and lack of principle, whilst all the time the faithful Laura Bell remains loving, but neglected.

But though Thackeray is less the puppet-master, he is more the preacher. His moralizing commentary is more intrusive, more frequent and usually less piquant than in *Vanity Fair*. The world of *Pendennis* is vicious like that of its predecessors (people like Sir Francis Clavering and Colonel Altamont are nastier than practically anything in *Vanity Fair*), but contrasted with these are Helen Pendennis and Laura Bell in the home from which Pendennis's career begins. They represent a firm moral basis for judging all else. At the same time they are not simple perfection. They seem super-ior, 'cruel critics' to poor Fanny Bolton, 'a sexual jealousy on the mother's part' towards Blanche Amory. In this way Thackeray tried to meet the perennial difficulty of creating convincingly virtuous characters. He succeeds better with Laura than with Pen's mother, for of her (Laura) he tells mainly what she does and confines comment to a minimum.

It was in the preface to *Pendennis* that Thackeray made his famous complaint about Victorian prudery by contrast with the full-blooded era of Tom Jones. He all but refers to sexual attraction in plain terms ('This point has been argued ...' – ch. 54) and in *The*

Virginians he archly claimed: 'I shall not have the least idea of what they have been doing. Have you, madam? Have you any remembrance of what used to happen when Mr. Grundy came a-courting?' (ch. 69; cf chs 20 and 41). (For an opposite view see the criticism of *Tom Jones* in *The English Humourists*.) The exclusion of, or confinement to veiled references to, sexual relations gave the Victorians plenty of difficulties, especially with their promiscuous weak young men. Thackeray chose to meet this problem in his novel in part by the use of Pen's uncle, Major Pendennis, the man of the world, a left-over from a more complaisant age, who knows what young men are made of and what adventures they get involved in better than their mothers do. His view of the world and that of Helen Pendennis provide yet another instance of that recurring conflict in Thackeray, which was worked out most crucially in just those areas of Victorian society from which the novelist himself came. Triumphant Evangelicalism, bringing a new puritanism with it – especially among the women, was ousting the laxer, but in many ways more realistic, morals of the Georgian era. Placed in this situation, Major Pendennis is like Amelia, an ambiguous character – but with this difference that Thackeray seems to have thought better of him and worse of her than he suspected some of his readers might.

Like *Pendennis*, *The Newcomes* is 'about all the world and a respectable family dwelling in it' (ch. 38). It also draws extensively on Thackeray's own experience – India, Charterhouse, art studies, even the domineering mother-in-law. The moral pattern is more obvious than in *Pendennis*: 'It is not a sermon, except where it cannot help itself . . . O friend, in your life and mine don't we light upon such sermons daily? Here on one side is Self and Ambition and Advancement, and Right and Love on the other.' (ibid.) Again we have in Clive Newcome, a weak young man as the central character. His love for Ethel Newcome, his cousin, is frustrated by her family. It is her resistance to domestic pressures that puts her amongst the most interesting characters of the book. Thackeray was deeply engaged by her situation, in which she was steered by her grandmother, Lady Kew, especially, first in the direction of one advantageous marriage and then of another. We recall that part of Becky's appeal comes from the manner in which she puts rank and money to confusion. In *The Newcomes* Thackeray fiercely compared the marriage-market to the Indian *suttee* sacrifice:

The parents in that fine house are getting ready their daughter for sale, and frightening away her tears with threats, and stupefying her grief with narcotics, praying her and imploring her, and dramming her and coaxing her, and blessing her, and cursing her perhaps, till they have brought her into such a state as shall fit the poor young thing for that deadly couch upon which they are about to thrust her . . . His Grace the Arch-Brahmin will make a highly appropriate speech, just with a faint scent of incense about it as such a speech ought to have, and the young person will slip away unperceived, and take off her veils, wreaths, orange flowers, bangles and finery, and will put on a plain dress more suited for the occasion, and the house-door will open – and there comes the SUTTEE in company of the body.

(ch. 28)

Refusing to 'believe in elder sons, and a house in town, and a house in the country' (ch. 45), Ethel shows spirit against the persuasions and cajoleries of her oppressors.

Ethel's brother, Barnes, is the villain of the book – in some ways too much so, for his evil verges at times on the melodramatic. He is snobbish, hypocritical, tyrannical and immoral – and he becomes progressively worse over the novel's history. He exemplifies the novelist's own close moral participation in this book as compared with its predecessor. Thackeray (admittedly through Pendennis, the narrator) acknowledged his danger: 'A constant desire to throttle Mr. Barnes, to beat him on the nose, and send him flying out of the window, was a sentiment with which this singular young man inspired many persons whom he accosted. A biographer ought to be impartial, yet I own, in a modified degree, to have partaken of this sentiment.' (ch. 30) And if Barnes is too bad, Clive's father, Colonel Newcome, is in danger of being too good. Set against his half-brothers and their wives (and not least by his spontaneous generosity against the sterile religiosity of the Evangelical Maria), he is too good for the world he lives in and it is obvious, as Thackeray acknowledges, that his trust in the financial security of the Bundelcund Bank will eventually prove misplaced. Adversity does not sour him, and altogether he is Thackeray's most sustained declaration of faith in human nature. In his last words about him Thackeray reminds us that the Colonel retained the goodness and innocence of a child. These words came in the impressive death-scene at Greyfriars where Newcome is now a pensioner in the place where once he had been a schoolboy. Imbued with the pathos of simple statement, the passage is free of censurable sentimentality; the emotion called forth is in no way excessive or factitious:

At the usual evening hour the chapel bell began to toll, and Thomas Newcome's hands outside the bed feebly beat time. And just as the last bell struck, a peculiar sweet smile shone over his face, and he lifted up his head a little and quickly said, 'Adsum!' and fell back. It was the word we used at school when names were called; and lo, he whose heart was that of a little child, had answered to his name, and stood in the presence of The Master.

(ch. 80)

Between the composition of these two domestic novels Thackeray had written the first of his two historical novels, *Esmond*. Despite his admiration for Scott he did not have his predecessor's sense of the colour and adventure of history. Even a fugitive Jesuit like Father Holt does not convey any of that sense of mystery or danger which one associates with Scott's novels. Thackeray's men of history are men of contemplation rather than of action, and in *The Virginians* he takes an early opportunity of moving from the wars of the American frontier to the world of Johnson's London and Tunbridge Wells. In *Esmond* Addison epitomizes all that Thackeray admired in the Augustan age (Bk II, ch. 11), whilst at the same time we get a balanced picture of the man, not only sensible and civilized but also self-important and given to somewhat pompous moralizing. In fact, Thackeray sets up a fine contrast between him and Steele with his sentimentality, kindliness and *carpe diem* spirit. I say 'sets up', for Thackeray is arranging his history. Setting of time, place, event and character is more than background, it is the very staple of the novel, but it remains a version of 'facts seen subjectively through the temperament of the writer' (Lord David Cecil, *Early Victorian Novelists*, 1934, p 88).

The novel is primarily *The History of Henry Esmond . . . Written by Himself*. But though it is written by himself, it is written in the third person. Moreover, it is the memoirs of an old man looking back on a period covering the formative years of childhood, adolescence and early manhood. Here again we have the novelist of memory. The third-person stance gives detachment and perspective, but it loses something in intimacy and vividness. Indeed, given the crises through which he passes, the misunderstanding, suffering and estrangements, Esmond seems all too often all too calm. Impossibly romantic both in politics and in love, he somehow falls short in self-revelation. What Thackeray does achieve is a sense of the child Esmond's loneliness and isolation and something of his helpless attraction towards and ultimate alienation from Beatrix. Even when Esmond discovers that he is the true heir of Castlewood we have an assessment rather than a dramatic realization:

Should he bring down shame and perplexity upon all those beings to whom he was attached by so many tender ties of affection and gratitude? degrade his father's widow? impeach and sully his father's and kinsman's honour? and for what? For a barren title, to be worn at the expense of an innocent boy, the son of his dearest benefactress. He had debated this matter in his conscience, whilst his poor Lord was making his dying confession. On the one side were ambition, temptation, justice even; but love, gratitude, and fidelity pleaded on the other. And when the struggle was over in Harry's mind, a glow of righteous happiness filled it.

(Bk II, ch. 1)

Only the novel's sure uniformity of tone saves the hero and the author from seeming insufferably priggish. Esmond, indeed, is priggish when the time comes for him to reveal his altruism to Lady Castlewood (Bk III, ch. 2).

She and her daughter Beatrix, the two main female characters, are realized far better. In Lady Castlewood Thackeray portrays a woman of quick and warm emotions, pious, tender, jealous and possessive, 'never sinning and never forgiving'. Esmond's reactions to her at the various stages of his growing-up are one of the book's triumphs. After estrangement, 'as a brother folds a sister to his heart; and as a mother cleaves to her son's breast – so for a few moments Esmond's beloved mistress came to him and blessed him' (Bk II, ch. 6). Some readers have considered Esmond's son-and-lover role as a kind of 'spiritual incest'; though not really surprising, it is difficult to accept. We should not fail, however, to see that this is part of a triangular relationship to which Beatrix contributes. Esmond's infatuation with 'this siren', the delight and despair of numberless suitors, is more readily understandable. We need to note the warnings that Lady Castlewood gives him; they are not disinterested (e.g. Bk II, ch. 8). The degree of Esmond's involvement is to be found in the asperity of some of his comments. Selfish, cruel, ambitious Beatrix may have been, but Esmond does nothing to tone down her faults.

Together these two women represent a masterly portrayal of the feminine heart and mind. A single passage will illustrate in more detail. Beatrix is speaking to Esmond:

'Hear a last word. I do love you . . . But I think I have no heart; at least, I have never seen the man that could touch it; and, had I found him, I would have followed him in rags had he been a private soldier . . . I am not good, Harry: my mother is gentle and good like an angel . . . Farewell, Cousin: mamma is pacing the next room, racking her little head to know what we have been saying. She is jealous: all women are . . .

'Farewell. Farewell, brother.' She gave him her cheek as a brotherly privilege. The cheek was as cold as marble.

Esmond's mistress showed no signs of jealousy when he returned to the room where she was. She had schooled herself so as to look quite inscrutably, when she had a mind. Amongst her other feminine qualities she had that of being a perfect dissembler.

(Bk III, ch. 8)

There is a pathos about Beatrix's compulsive frigidity which makes Charlotte Brontë's comment that she had 'eventually no heart to touch' seem wide of the mark. The 'brotherly privilege' is also a charged phrase, making the kiss so much less than Esmond wanted and reminding us that the fraternal relationship has meant other things elsewhere (see the quotation in the preceding paragraph). Finally, Thackeray is candid about Lady Castlewood: 'She is jealous,' said Beatrix – she 'showed no signs of jealousy' – she was 'a perfect dissembler'.

The Virginians is the story of Esmond's two American grandsons, George and Harry Warrington, contrasted brothers with a domineering mother. The background is first that of New England with all the grace of colonial life on the eve of the outbreak of the War of Independence, and then of England itself. It is a spacious novel, not much concerned with a coherent plot but rather with pen-portraits of places and people. There are Washington and Wolfe at length; there is the *ménage* of Colonel Lambert (another Thackerayan character virtuous to the point of stuffiness), set in its upright and kindly goodness against the rascality of Castlewood and the selfish respectability of the English Warringtons; there is the ageing and dissolute Madame Bernstein (Beatrix of the earlier novel), now more leniently handled, a somewhat affectionately labelled 'old Dragon' (ch. 31) who protects young Harry from scrapes and schemers. There are some effective contrasts, for example, between the rather wild and careless but also warm-hearted Harry and his steadier, more serious brother and between the designing Maria Esmond and the tender, faithful Theo Lambert in their relationships with Harry. *The Virginians* provides a more varied world than that of *Esmond*, but it rambles. It lacks its predecessor's well-defined story (the most clear-cut in Thackeray) and the grace and clarity of that novel's style. The narrator's alternation between third- and first-person is also irritating, whilst commentary-intrusions have become yet more frequent than in earlier works. The book as a whole shows a slackening of grip that was ever more confirmed with each remaining novel of the final years.

Thackeray's major novels were long ones – *Vanity Fair* ran to twenty monthly parts and *Pendennis*, *The Newcomes* and *The Virginians* to twenty-four. Only *Esmond* has a tightly-knit structure. The rest are 'large, loose baggy monsters'. 'A novel without a plan', one critic complained of *Vanity Fair* (Robert Bell, quoted in G. Tillotson and G. Hawes, *Thackeray, the Critical Heritage*, 1968, p 66), whilst another, R. S. Rintoul, reviewing *Pendennis*, declared 'Mr. Thackeray either cannot or will not frame a coherent story, of which all the incidents flow naturally one from another, and are so necessarily connected with each other as to form a whole' (ibid., p 98). Writing by parts may have intensified this lack of coherence, but basically it derives from Thackeray's essentially discursive method. Even then, this general criticism needs to be modified. The unity of *Barry Lyndon* is secured by the simple central idea and the concentration upon the main character, whilst in *Vanity Fair*, *pace* Bell, there is a plan which counterpoints Amelia against Becky, Dobbin against Osborne, the Sedleys against the Osbornes, the various Crawleys against each other, Rawdon against Steyne and so on – in fact, a panorama, a rich fictional world, full to overflowing with scene, incident and character.

Thackeray's discursive method, however, sometimes obscures the inner logic of his dispositions. There seems to be too much sequence and too little consequence. Sometimes the sequence, even, gets blurred in the multiplicity of activity, or the story moves too slowly, or one line of the plot is neglected at the expense of another. This happens to some extent in the later sections of *Vanity Fair*, and even more so in *The Virginians* where our attention is directed to the one brother to the total exclusion of the other for a considerable part of the novel. *Esmond*, as a tale of one man, gained in this regard, but even here there are the lengthy digressions on the age of its characters. *Pendennis* is also basically the tale of one man, but its plot is very lax by comparison with *Esmond* and there are more characters with fuller lives, even to the insertion of a whole additional story in the exploits of the Claverings and Colonel Altamont. The nature of the story in *Esmond* also presumes a definite conclusion, whereas it is no surprise in *Pendennis* to find one of those 'bufferless endings' which occur elsewhere in Thackeray. The phrase is Professor Geoffrey Tillotson's, and it is he who in his indispensable study best sums the matter up when he says: 'Instead of design Thackeray's novels give us continuity' (*Thackeray the Novelist*, 1963 edn, p 20).

This continuity is expressed, for instance, in the recurrence of characters and the treatment of successive generations in different novels. The Castlewoods of *The Virginians* resemble in character as well as blood their predecessors in *Esmond* and Madame Bernstein of the later novel is an exactly right development of Beatrix in the earlier. Thackeray believed that 'We alter very little . . . Circumstance only brings out the latent defect or quality'

(*Pendennis*, ch. 59). But critics have complained as Roscoe did in the author's own time that the latent often remains latent in Thackeray's characterization: 'Even of shallow and worldly Pendennis, how partial and limited, how merely external is our conception' (Tillotson and Hawes, op. cit., p 269). Thackeray himself could write at different times: 'I know the people utterly' (*Roundabout Papers*) and 'I declare we know nothing of anybody' (*The Virginians*, ch. 26). This is not a contradiction. Thackeray is saying that we can know people utterly in social intercourse; we cannot know them at all in their inner beings. There we have to guess. As Roscoe himself put it, 'We don't know our nearest friends; we are always dependent on our imagination.' (op. cit., p 268) Thackeray did not write the sort of novel that required this sort of imagination. Even in *Esmond* he avoided the direct first-person narration and thus secured a sense of detachment. Pendennis (and his author) are only half-joking in the question 'How can I tell the feelings in a young lady's mind, the thoughts in a young gentleman's bosom?' (*The Newcomes*, ch. 47). This may be one reason for his preference for narrator *alter ego*s; at least they could excuse an absence of omnipresence. They are also able to write as historians, relying on experience, that quality in which Thackeray was so strong that G. K. Chesterton could claim, 'He is everybody's past.' He is the novelist of memory and he evokes the emotion of experience. He looks back over lives and this too gives the sense of continuity and succession. His stories read like reliable and mature reminiscence.

But where does the narrator stand in relation to the novel? In fact, we do not take much notice of him except when he becomes actor, as Pendennis does in *The Newcomes*, and then in his dual role he becomes rather irksome. Certainly in the plentiful commentary, whatever may be the pretence, the reader assumes that the voice is the voice of the novelist himself. 'Conceive *The Newcomes* without the presence of Thackeray upon the stage – minus the view it gives us of the working of its author's mind, the glimpses of his philosophy, the touches of his feeling' (W. C. Brownell, *Victorian Prose Matters*, 1902, p 17).

What then of the author's mind? Was there a division between sceptic and idealist along the lines of the Pendennis-Warrington argument (*Pendennis*, ch. 62)? Or was there, as some have claimed, a division that made him a sentimental cynic? First, was he sentimental? Consider from areas where this might show – his treatment of women, children, death and the past. In one succession of his women there are Becky, Blanche Amory and Beatrix, in another Amelia, Laura Bell, Lady Castlewood and Ethel Newcome. Their very variety is one measure of Thackeray's judicious assessment of women. None is immaturely or impossibly idealized. Goodness indeed there is, but even of one of the most admirable, Lady Castlewood, he was led to observe: 'Even the tenderest women are cruel.' Not many children are portrayed in the novels, but of those that are Esmond is shown with deep understanding and in the relationship of Colonel Newcome and his son Thackeray deliberately eschews a fine opportunity for the sentimental: 'We forbear to describe the reunion of the Colonel and his son.' He did, however, recall the parting seven years before, the small boy's careless and speedy adjustment to the separation and his parents' different response:

How their hearts followed the careless young ones home across the great ocean! Mothers' prayers go with them. Strong men, alone on their knees, with streaming eyes and broken accents, implore Heaven for those little ones, who were prattling at their sides but a few hours since. Long after they are gone, careless and happy, recollections of the sweet past rise up and smite those who remain – the flowers . . . the toys . . . the little vacant cribs they slept in.

(*The Newcomes*, ch. 5)

This may seem sentimental to us, but the weeping father would not appear so to the Victorians. What is more important is that this account is essentially true to human experience. The passage reminds us of yet another possible area of the sentimental with 'its recollections of the sweet past'. Thackeray continued: 'Most of us who have passed a couple of score years in the world have had such sights as these to move us.' Again the appeal to the emotion of experience, the nostalgia of happy memory. The difference between Thackeray and some other writers is in his insistence. He does not leave words unspoken.

The nostalgia is a necessary concomitant of *vanitas vanitatum*. We need the happy recollections of the past to face the present and the future, for whatever else there may be, there will be the inevitable sadness of age: 'That which is snow-white now was glossy black once; . . . that calm weariness, benevolent, resigned, and disappointed, was ambition, fierce and violent, but a few years since.' Age changes a man, but yet he remains the same: 'Are you not awe-stricken – you, friendly reader . . . to think how you are the same *You*, whom in childhood you remember, before the voyage of life began!' (*Pendennis*, ch. 60). But this unchanging identity will be changed: the sadness of death will succeed the sadness of life. Whether it be the good making a good end (Colonel Newcome or Helen Pendennis) or the careless coming to a premature dissolution (Lord Castlewood or George Osborne), Thackeray imbues his death-scenes with a more than individual significance. When he tells us that Helen's 'last throb was love and last breath was a benediction' (*Pendennis*, ch. 58) or that 'Amelia was praying for George, who was lying on his face, dead, with a bullet through his heart' (*Vanity Fair*, ch. 32), we move beyond the local and particular into an awareness of the shadow of death brooding over all human relationships, an awareness that *vanitas vanitatum* is not unconnected with *memento mori*.

So much for the sentimental. Is Thackeray then a cynic? Is this inevitable in one believing so strongly in *vanitas vanitatum*? The ways of the wicked (a Barnes Newcome or a Becky Sharp) do prosper, but there is no happiness in them, nor ultimate security. The righteous man does suffer and in a wicked world he must inevitably suffer. And mistakes have a habit of exacting long and bitter payment. All this is true, but yet it would be wrong to claim, as Roscoe did, that '*Vanity Fair* is the name, not of one, but of all Mr Thackeray's works' (op. cit., p 276). We need to remember the integrity of Henry Esmond, the goodness of Helen Pendennis and Colonel Newcome, the uprightness and kindliness of the Lamberts, the courage of Ethel Newcome, even the faithfulness of Dobbin. As early as the time of *Vanity Fair* he wrote:

What I mean applies to my own case and that of all of us – who set up as Satirical-Moralists . . . that we may never forget truth and Justice and kindness as the great ends of our profession [which] seems to me as serious as the Parson's own.

(To Mark Lemon, *Letters*, ed. G. N. Ray, 1946, vol II p 282)

We remember that the preacher of Ecclesiastes, who propounded *vanitas vanitatum* as the doctrine of *taedium vitae*, nevertheless concluded positively with the advice to fear God and keep His commandments. When Thackeray looked around him he saw cause enough for *taedium vitae*:

Virtue is very often shameful according to the English social constitution, and shame honourable. Truth, if yours happens to differ from your neighbour's, provokes your friend's coldness, your mother's tears, the world's persecution. Love is not to be dealt in, save in restrictions which kill its sweet, healthy, free commerce.

(*The Newcomes*, ch. 28)

He would not therefore force an ending that contradicted the tenor of his tale. The original conclusion to *Barry Lyndon* is almost violent:

Justice, forsooth? Does human life exhibit justice after this fashion? Is it the good always who ride in gold coaches, and the wicked who go to the workhouse? . . . Sometimes the contrary occurs, so that fools and wise, bad men and good, are more or less lucky in their turn.

But none of this is cynicism. It is a moral from unflinching realism. There is a lot of evil and some good. Thackeray saw both and it is best to leave him with the description he gave himself – a 'Satirical-Moralist'.

Anthony Trollope (1815–83) shares Thackeray's satirical-moral view of life, his realism, his interest in man in society (especially in the aristocracy and upper middle-classes), his delight in following characters from novel to novel and his indifference to an extensively developed plot. When his *Autobiography* (1883) appeared just after his death, it shocked readers by the candour with which it revealed its author's down-to-earth approach to what he regarded as the business of novel-writing. Trollope was a most prolific writer, producing not only novels but also short stories, biographies, trans-lations and travel books in an unending stream. In the last pages of the *Autobiography* he counselled literary aspirants thus: '*Nulla dies sine linea* . . . Let their work be to them as is his common work to the commoner labourer.' Trollope's reward was 'something near £70,000' over twenty years of writing.

Yet he was nearly forty before he achieved much success. After school at Harrow and Winchester and Post Office experience in London, which provided material not only for the creation of such young civil servants as Charley Tudor (*The Three Clerks*) and Johnny Eames (*The Small House at Allington*) but also acquaintance with the clubs, duns and other aspects of metropolitan life which occur in the novels, Trollope spent nearly two decades (1841–59) as a postal surveyor in Ireland, broken only by a short period on similar work in the West of England (1851–53). His first two novels, *The Macdermots of Ballycloran* (1847) and *The Kellys and the O'Kellys*

(1848), were set in Ireland. Neither was successful, but this did not prevent him from using the same setting later in *Castle Richmond* (1860) and the unfinished *The Landleaguers* (1883). Both these were concerned with political and social problems, the former with the famines of the 1840s (see Cecil Woodham Smith's *The Great Hunger*, 1962) and the latter with the peasantry's rent revolt (the 'boycott') of the late 1870s. In addition, *Phineas Finn* (1869), the story of a young Irish M.P., draws on Trollope's recollections of his residence in Ireland.

But the two years spent in the West Country were more important for Trollope and for the English novel. There in Salisbury, wandering 'one mid-summer evening round the purlieus of the cathedral [he] conceived the idea of *The Warden*, – from whence came that series of novels of which Barchester, with its bishops, deans, and archdeacon, was the central site' (*Autobiography*, ch. 5). This work established Trollope's name as a novelist, and over the years there followed its successors in the Barsetshire series – *Barchester Towers* (1857), *Doctor Thorne* (1858), *Framley Parsonage* (1860), *The Small House at Allington* (1864) and *The Last Chronicle of Barset* (1867). So well did he create the place and the people that there were those in 1867 who had had enough of Barsetshire. Such were the two parsons whose particular aversion to Mrs Proudie drove Trollope to 'kill her before the week [was] over' (ibid., ch. 15). He regretted the deed, but a few lines later he writes, 'Since her time others have grown up equally dear to me, – Lady Glencora and her husband [Plantagenet Palliser], for instance.' The choice is not surprising, but it serves to remind us that the novelist's next main effort went into the Palliser or political series. These two characters were seen first in *The Small House at Allington* and *Can You Forgive Her?* (1864), but they were to appear again in *Phineas Finn* (1869), *The Eustace Diamonds* (1873), *Phineas Redux* (1876), *The Prime Minister* (1876) and Palliser, Duke of Omnium, alone in *The Duke's Children* (1880). Not all of these novels are predominantly occupied with politics (*The Eustace Diamonds* with its 'thriller' element owes something to the vogue for Wilkie Collins), nor are these the only novels about politics – a notable addition is *Ralph the Heir* (1871), drawing much from Trollope's own experience as unsuccessful Liberal candidate at Beverley in 1868. Together, however, they constitute their author's considered reflection on the political life of the period (see also *Autobiography*, ch. 16). During the quarter-century which spans the composition of these two main series Trollope also wrote some twenty other novels, prominent amongst which were *Orley Farm* (1862), *The Claverings* (1867), and that mordant magnificent satire of his times, *The Way We Live Now* (1875). From *The Warden* to this last novel marks the breadth of the spectrum through which he viewed life.

The Warden is not the novel Trollope meant to have written; it is all the better for that. He meant it to be satirical, an exposure at once of clerical abuses and of the immoderate newspaper criticism of such abuses (see *Autobiography*, ch. 5). Some of the attack against the latter remains and there are also the satirical portraits of Carlyle (Dr Pessimist Anticant) and Dickens (Mr Sentiment) as well as indirectly through the Grantly sons of the three bishops Charles James (Blomfield of London), Henry (Phillpotts of Exeter) and Samuel, 'dear little Soapy' (Wilberforce of Oxford). But the work outgrew satire in the characterization of the saintly Mr Harding, the gentle figure exposed to the glare of publicity so uncomfortably and so inculpably. Harding as the suffering centre of the novel concentrates sympathy upon himself and acts as a measure for the criticism of all the other characters.

Another triumph of this novel was the delineation of Harding's son-in-law, the hectoring authoritative archdeacon Grantly. At the end Trollope seems to admit that he is worth better than he has been able to show him, pleading that he 'lacked the opportunity of bringing him forward on his strong ground. That he is a man somewhat too fond of his own way, and not sufficiently scrupulous in his manner of achieving it, his best friends cannot deny ... Nevertheless, the archdeacon is a gentleman and a man of conscience' (ch. 20). In his next novel, *Barchester Towers*, Trollope developed this view of Grantly. This work also marks a great advance in his conception of Barsetshire. The cathedral city is fully delineated. We get a panoramic view from the cathedral close. *The Warden* had chosen a topical ecclesiastical scandal as its subject (see R. Arnold, *The Whiston Affair*, 1961). Now Trollope introduces in Proudie one of the new Low-Church bishops of the Palmerston-Shaftesbury epoch after 1855. Ecclesiastical animosities give the book flavour, but the antagonisms of Grantly (aided by Arabin, a Tractarian imported from Oriel) against the Bishop's party, which means Mrs Proudie and the chaplain Slope, are basic human conflicts, seen for the most part from a wry comic angle. This is especially evident in the discomfitures of Archdeacon Grantly, now a much more sympathetic figure. He is baffled and angered by the 'Bishopess' and Slope; we enjoy this. But they are unscrupulous, and so we sympathize with him, and our sympathy adds to our delight when these two are routed. The agent of their distress is one of Trollope's strokes of genius, Signora Vesey-Neroni, daughter of an absentee prebendary, mysteriously married, mysteriously crippled, irresistibly attractive. Trollope also employs her in an unobtrusive way as a shrewd commentator on and stimulator of the action of the novel. Above and beyond his success with individuals, however, is his evocation of the ethos of Barchester, with its sense of a confined society, magnifying small issues as such a community does, suggesting the discrepancies between the ideal (which a cathedral-close in particular should suggest) and the reality, yet despairing of nobody. (Trollope admits that even Slope acted according to his lights.) In this novel, once and for all, Trollope revealed what is perhaps his greatest quality – his unwavering understanding of the behaviour of ordinary men and women.

In the next Barsetshire novel, *Doctor Thorne*, money matters for the first but not by any means the last time in Trollope. Here too, to use the words of Henry James, he 'settled down steadily to the English girl' (*Partial Portraits*, 1888, reprinted in D. Smalley, *Trollope, The Critical Heritage*, 1969, pp 525–45). The main character is Dr Thorne, but the novel is about love and money as they affect his niece and ward, Mary Thorne. No less than in Jane Austen's works Trollope's heroines' fates usually depend on finding a 'nice man' and a competence, and these two do not always go together. Trollope was not so bitter as Thackeray about the marriage-market, but he explored with unsurpassed precision that love-hate relationship which subsisted between rank and wealth in his time. The Gresham squirearchy's 'fine old English fortune' has been ruined by a marriage into the aristocracy (Lady Arabella de Courcy), and now, sublimely ignoring the cause of the trouble, she and her family insist that her eldest son, Frank, 'must marry money'. But Frank is in love with Mary who is not only penniless but has no pretensions to birth either. Not that this matters if the money is there, but the de Courcys claim that it does. They ruin Gresham, persecute Frank, scorn the rough-hewn but successful railway-contractor Scatcherd on whose loans the Greshams survive, and despise Dr Thorne who is the intermediary for the loans. Thorne and Mary are the links in the story. They are also the moral constants, placing everything and everybody in proper perspective. The doctor's moral probity presents the book's central dilemma, for he alone knows that Mary is Scatcherd's niece (as the illegitimate daughter of the latter's sister and his own brother) and as such his likely heiress. She is a proper match for Frank by de Courcy standards. His secret knowledge is the book's central irony, but there is more than Mary's financial eligibility. Nothing can erase her illegitimacy, and both Squire Gresham and Thorne himself are proud of their birth. When Thorne tells Gresham of her fortune, he has to add the wish 'that her birth were equal to her fortune', but he adds also 'as her worth is superior to both' (ch. 46). It is that which makes the happy ending acceptable. It may seem too good to be true, but it is morally appropriate as a vindication of integrity and constancy.

Trollope's own favourite 'English girl' was Lily Dale in *The Small House at Allington*. Hers is the history of a mistaken choice, the preference of the handsome but superficial and self-seeking Adolphus Crosbie over the devoted Johnny Eames; but when Crosbie deserts her, Trollope does not succumb to the facile solution of marrying Lily to Johnny Eames. Elsewhere he is not so rigorous: Emily Wharton in *The Prime Minister* is permitted after her degrading experience with Lopez to marry Arthur Fletcher and Alice Vavasor in *Can You Forgive Her?*, after hovering between her worthless cousin George Vavasor and the much steadier John Grey, eventually accepts the latter. In this novel also we have the wrong result for Lady Glencora, for choice it can hardly be called in that she had been coerced into a loveless marriage with Plantagenet Palliser, heir to the Duke of Omnium. His dry austerity and commitment to politics contrast with the charm of her former lover, the worthless Burgo Fitzgerald. Only at the last minute is Fitzgerald prevented from eloping with her. There follows a scene unusually strong for Trollope, in which Lady Glencora declares her love for Fitzgerald and asks her husband to let her go. Her passion contrasts violently with his detachment – 'If you cannot love me, it is a great misfortune to us both. But we need not therefore be disgraced' (ch. 48).

The dilemma of choice also informs the action of *The Belton Estate* (1866) where Clara Amedroz has to decide between the somewhat uncouth farmer Will Belton and the polished but self-seeking Aylmer. Money again enters into the story with the Belton Estate's having gone by the death of Clara's brother to Will and her own expected fortune from her aunt Mrs Winterfield being bequeathed to Aylmer after he had promised to marry Clara. E. A. Baker is right when he says that '*The Claverings* is a variation on the Belton theme with the sex of the rival lovers reversed' (*History of the English Novel*, vol VIII, 1937, p 151). Harry Clavering is immature. This is one reason why Julia Brabazon rejects him ('She had grown old earlier in life than he had done . . .'); Lord Ongar's money was another ('. . . and had taught herself that romance could not be allowed to a woman in her position.') (ch. 3) After Ongar's early death the book is taken up with Harry's vacillation between his troth to the good-hearted but quite ordinary Florence Burton and the attractions of Julia, wealthy, beautiful and in love with him. Victorian respectability triumphs, above all through Harry's mother, who insists on the marriage to Florence. More than any of Trollope's novels, this one with its story of moral cowardice would seem most likely to provoke the most widely different reactions now as compared with a century ago when it was written.

Inheritance is one of Trollope's favourite devices. One inheritance creates one problem in *The Claverings* and the prospect of another solves another problem. *The Eustace Diamonds* indicates the inheritance in its title, and this novel also presents Frank Greystock with a dilemma of choice not unlike Harry Clavering's. *Lady Anne*, with its tale of the true love of a lady of high rank and a tailor, in some ways resembles *Doctor Thorne*, and as with that novel there is an inheritance at the end to bless the true love. Inheritance has more sombre implications in *Orley Farm*, the plot of which, said Trollope, was 'probably the best I ever made . . . I do not know that there is a dull page in the book' (*Autobiography*, ch. 9). Like Lady Lovel, the heroine's mother in *Lady Anna*, Lady Mason in *Orley Farm* is a guilt-ridden, ambitious woman. Hers is a tragedy of misdirected maternal love. Her whole position is at risk as a result of a forged codicil to her husband's will, by which she had tried to secure for her own son a small portion of the estate which otherwise would have gone in its entirety to the son of an earlier marriage. The arrangement of characters and their ways of life is such that our whole sympathy rests with Lady Mason. In her and her staunch friend Sir Peregrine Orme Trollope works out the conflicts between personal moral choices and rigid social codes. He shows, too, the divergence between justice and law. Above all, he portrays Lady Mason with all her nobility as she faces her accusers and her apparently inevitable disgrace.

Orley Farm has an intensity rare in Trollope. It is, however, found again in *The Last Chronicle of Barset*, and again he takes a character under the cloud of accusation, this time unjust accusation. Mr Crawley, the parson of Hogglestock, is a more striking individual than Lady Mason – a man of considerable ability, deeply frustrated, fiercely independent, pathologically gloomy, a character reminiscent of Dostoievsky. But he is without the Dostoievskian proportions: he remains the sort of man we think we might meet. *The Last Chronicle* is extensive in its reference and not always as relevant as it might be. The Johnny Eames episodes in London are something of an excrescence, and so is the death of Mr Harding. We would willingly lose the first, but not the second. Some of this extraneous narrative was no doubt part of the tidying-up operations as Trollope closed the Barsetshire series. It also serves another purpose. All that is happening makes the reader realize that the world passes by whilst an individual suffers. This helps to intensify the effect of the sympathy of Crawley's friends. His daughter Grace, in particular, emerges in all her self-sacrificing nobility, worthy of the hand of Major Grantly whose suit has been jeopardized by her father's possible disgrace and his father's opposition. The meeting of these two, rich archdeacon and poor curate, at the end deserves quotation, for in it is embodied the supreme Trollopian recognition: 'We stand on the only perfect level on which such men meet each other. We are both gentlemen' (ch. 83).

That remark belongs to a world of birth, breeding and status. It was the supersession of this world by one of wealth, power and position which provoked Trollope's ire in the darkest of his novels, *The Way We Live Now*. At its centre is the foreign financier, Melmotte (most of Trollope's foreigners are of either dubious or only too obvious morality). Around him is a group of effete aristocrats. Bogus shares in an American railway and gaming at the Beargarden (note the name) comprise much of the book's concern. Over against these characters is the Norfolk squire, Roger Carbury, representative of the old order, Trollope's mouthpiece in condemning the new, but ineffectual in doing so. The world is a beargarden, and all the individuals in it are utterly isolated. Even the less repulsive characters like Lady Carbury indulge in some not very praiseworthy practices. In its wide-ranging condemnation of society – politics, religion, family life, law, finance, the squirearchy, London clubs, the rural poor, even the Americans – this novel is Trollope's *Vanity Fair*. At times it is even more sombre than Thackeray's novel, but its very concern to hit out in so many directions is one means by which it fails in the sustained intensity that marks its predecessor.

The disillusion that is concentrated in *The Way We Live Now* is to be found also in the political novels. The personal and political idealism of Phineas Finn endures many a buffeting in the two novels about him. Likewise, the world of *The Prime Minister* and *The*

Duke's Children is a place where standards of behaviour are very relative indeed. Finn, and even more Sir Thomas Underwood in *Ralph the Heir*, see the chicanery of electioneering. Finn and Palliser know the nature of political intrigue, the compromise and worse that politics involves. The central question for both of them is that which Finn asks: 'Could a man be honest in Parliament, and yet abandon all idea of independence?' (*Phineas Finn*, ch. 58). With both the clerical characters of the Barsetshire series and with his political characters Trollope, as he said at the end of *The Last Chronicle of Barset*, concentrated upon 'the social and not the professional lives'. In fact, he refers to his 'series of semi-political tales' (*Autobiography*, ch. 17). In the same passage he wrote: 'If I write politics for my own sake, I must put in love and intrigue, social incidents, with perhaps a dash of sport, for the sake of my readers.' For the most part, this is only too evident, especially in a comparatively unsuccessful work like *Ralph the Heir*. Elsewhere, however, despite the occasional touch of sensationalism (e.g., the Bonteen murder in *Phineas Redux*) there is some powerful 'social' fiction, not least in the Lady Laura Standish sections of *Phineas Finn*. Her husband, the Scottish millionaire, Kennedy, morose to the point of insanity, has all the makings of a Mr Crawley. Compared with the Finn novels, the later pair based on Palliser (*The Prime Minister* and *The Duke's Children*) show some decline in intensity and concentration.

In all, Trollope wrote some forty-seven novels. Good as they are, the Barsetshire series have attracted a disproportionate amount of praise. The summary of some of the novels given above should show that Trollope's achievement is more various, and sometimes more sombre, than the Barsetshire novels would suggest. And his popularity in his own time took in far more than these. Judged by sales and contract figures, Trollope reached his peak about 1869, whilst his last years from 1876 marked a steep decline. Immediately after his death it plummeted almost into oblivion. (On this subject see M. Sadleir, *Trollope, A Commentary*, rev. edn, 1945, ch. 10.)

In Trollope's world of the upper middle-class and the aristocracy he is concerned for the ideas of the 'gentleman' and of decorum. It is a world where established and accepted ideas and attitudes count for much. Birth, class, rank, property and primogeniture are the several foundations on which the social edifice stands. They need to be secure. Trollope's concern for social wholeness makes him a conservative, and in the rapidly changing ethos of the Victorian age he was almost inevitably something of a sentimental conservative.

Without necessarily agreeing entirely with Ronald Knox one can see that he is pointing in the right direction when he says that Trollope 'could not save the old order of things, the world of privilege he so intimately loved, but his sympathies have embalmed the unavailing conflict' (Introduction to the Oxford edition of *The Warden*, 1952, p xviii). To do this he needed to catch, as he has done, the 'manners' of his society in the sense that Lionel Trilling has so accurately defined these, 'a culture's hum and buzz of implication . . . the whole evanescent context in which its explicit statements are made . . . that part of a culture which is made up of half-uttered or unuttered or unutterable expressions of value' (*The Liberal Imagination*, 1955, p 206). In this Trollope has matched Jane Austen, and over a broader canvas. In the society he portrays, 'highly organized, if not complex' (Joseph Conrad – letter to A. N. Monkhouse, 8 February 1924, in Manchester University Library), Trollope suggests the nice gradations between delicacy and coarseness that flourish in a period of flux, but he is especially interested in 'the old order of things' where delicacy is at once the measure and the product of social behaviour. It is sometimes necessary for a character to pit himself against the accepted code, especially in affairs of the heart; personal integrity and loyalty requires it, for example, of a Frank Gresham. Nevertheless, Trollope does not allow us to forget that in Frank's nobility there is more than a touch of the quixotic. Within a society subscribing to a firm set of *mores* there is also plenty of opportunity for tracing the irrevocable nature of the one mistake. Consequences may vary but they are inevitable, whether it be in the history of a Harry Clavering, a Mark Robarts (*Framley Parsonage*) or a Lady Mason.

This reminds us that Trollope's was a moral criticism of life. In the famous twelfth chapter of the *Autobiography* he is emphatic about this. He sees his task under the same image as Thackeray used: 'The novelist, if he have a conscience, must preach his sermons with the same purpose as the clergyman, and must have his own system of ethics.' Social observation becomes the preliminary to anticipated moral improvement. We should be 'taught to see the men and women among whom we really live, – men and women such as we see ourselves, – in order that we should know what are the exact failings which oppress ourselves, and then to hate, and if possible to avoid in life, the faults of character which in life are hardly visible, but which in portraiture of life can be made to be so transparent' (*Ralph the Heir*, ch. 56). Trollope was rarely so didactic in statement and almost never so in practice. We do not have the commentaries which Thackeray gives us. In another statement (*The Eustace Diamonds*, ch. 35) he expresses himself content if a novel's moral impressions produce a limited improvement.

In this relationship of author and reader we need to recognize the importance for Trollope of the ordinary man or woman, 'men and women such as we see ourselves'. In that phrase Trollope links not only author and reader but also the characters of his novels. I can best illustrate the point by quotation from the critics. Trollope, says Michael Sadleir, 'believed that the ordinary man or woman is at heart an honourable, kindly creature' (op. cit., p 153). He takes persons of this kind or, in Sir Walter Raleigh's words, 'starts off with ordinary people that bore you in life and books and makes an epic of them because he understands affection which the others take for granted or are superior about' (*Letters*, 1926, p 272). The same regard for the individuality of people inspires both his creation of character and his attitude to his reader. He has what Conrad elsewhere in the letter quoted above called 'his gift of intimate communion with the reader.' Sane, sympathetic, with a confident belief in human nature, these are the qualities that make up his quiet and deep view of life.

Interest and affection produce what James called 'his great, his inestimable merit . . . a complete appreciation of the usual . . . He felt all daily and immediate things' (op. cit., p 527). With typical acuteness James showed how this centred upon character: 'We care what happens to people only in proportion as we know what people are' (ibid., p 530). Or, in Trollope's own words:

[The author] desires to make his readers so intimately acquainted with his characters that the creatures of his brain should be to them speaking, moving, living, human creatures . . . He must know of them whether they be cold-blooded or passionate, whether true or false, and how far true, and how far false . . . I have lived with my characters, and thence has come whatever success I have obtained.

(*Autobiography*, ch. 12)

With ordinary people in fairly ordinary situations ('family feuds, . . . household discomforts and household pleasures . . . small malignities and daily kindnesses' – *The North British Review* XL (May 1864)) he reveals a range of emotions – love and hate, pride and arrogance and envy, ambition, courage and kindness, to name but a few – at work, in his characters. He presents these characters fully formed; he does not show them in course of development. He shows them in action; he demonstrates rather than analyses. This is not to say that his characters are either static or predictable. He shows them against a background of changing circumstances which modify their behaviour. He does not seek surprise, but he exploits what a writer in *The North American Review* (XC (1864)) called 'his power of tracing the moral effects of minute circumstances and minute actions'. This can be seen, for instance, in all the consequences that follow upon the inciting of Dockwrath to enquire into the Mason will. Lady Mason has committed the forgery, but Trollope is not mainly interested in what will happen to her or even to her own feelings. What does matter to him is her behaviour, the way in which a woman of her background and character acts (rather than feels) under the different stages of such an accusation. To take a single example:

A second bed had been prepared in Lady Mason's room, and into this chamber they both went at once. Mrs Orme as soon as she had entered, turned round and held out both her hands in order that she might comfort Lady Mason by taking hers; but Lady Mason, when she had closed the door, stood for a moment with her face towards the wall, not knowing how to bear herself. It was but for a moment and then slowly moving round, with her two hands clasped together, she sank on her knees at Mrs. Orme's feet, and hid her face in the skirt of Mrs. Orme's dress.

(*Orley Farm*, ch. 70)

The scene as a whole moves up to the exclamatory question which is the chapter's title, 'How am I to bear it?' This question has been preceded by the sentence: 'To Mrs. Orme it was marvellous that the woman should even be alive – let alone that she should speak and perform the ordinary functions of her daily life.' Mrs Orme is the expression of the reader's feelings, his presence in the novel. He wonders, like Mrs Orme, and yet he feels that Trollope is right. People of Lady Mason's position do in her circumstances go on. He is supremely the novelist of outward behaviour, of characters facing the world.

Given this mode of treatment, familiarity is a great asset to him, as can be seen from such extended and developed characters as Grantly, Palliser and Finn. Trollope's own attitude changed towards the first two; the character does not alter, but he himself becomes less critical. Grantly never loses his impetuous and assertive manner, but he is placed in situations where he appears more sympathetic, either because his opponents are unpleasant or because he is the comic victim, humiliated by them, or because he has scope for generosity. Something of the same development takes place with Palliser. On his first appearance in *The Small House at Allington* one reviewer considered him a 'caricature [of] a mathematical formula', and in *Can You Forgive Her?* his most notable quality is frigidity. Later, especially in *The Prime Minister*, we see a concomitant in his unsparing dedication to his work, and by the end of *The Duke's Children* we have completed the sad picture of an essentially austere and lonely man, sad because constitutionally he could be no other than he had been, a man in many ways admirable but incapable of inspiring love.

Love between young people Trollope considered an indispensable element in his stories: 'A novel can hardly be made interesting or successful without love' (*Autobiography*, ch. 12). 'Trollope's heroines,' says James, 'have a strong family likeness, . . . it is a wonder how finely he discriminates between them' (op. cit., p 542). He does, in fact, distinguish neatly in such qualities as scruple, grace, vivacity and beauty. Some of the heroines disappoint somewhat by their lack of positive qualities (Lucy Morris and Florence Burton, for example), but others are strong in the face of unfavourable odds (Mary Thorne, Lily Dale, Lucy Robarts), and there is even a Madeline Staveley to prefer 'mind to matter, which is a great deal to say for a young lady' (*Orley Farm*, ch. 52). Some of Trollope's older women are even better delineated than his younger ones, perhaps because he can deal in these cases with more firmly defined characters – the dignity, for instance, of Lady Mason or the resource of Lady Carbury, the assertiveness of Mrs Proudie or the unillusioned but not in the least cynical candour of Miss Dunstable.

Trollope was a realist and most of his characters represent quite ordinary people, but the last two mentioned above remind us that he could operate on different levels. We can accept the occasional saint like Mr Harding or the occasional villain like Melmotte (Lopez in *The Prime Minister* is more doubtful, perhaps because his villainy is not so deeply motivated; he is altogether more shallow), but a Mrs Proudie shows Trollope moving on the frontiers of caricature, as he does elsewhere in *Barchester Towers*, with Slope and in the Barsetshire series generally with more peripheral characters like Fillgrave, the rival doctor to Thorne. There are a number of minimal characters whose names alone are sufficient to characterize them – Neversayedie, Nearthewinde and Closerstil or even the Reverend Mr Quiverful (with his fourteen children). These names have been criticized as introducing a note inconsistent with the predominant realism. In fact, however, the ordinary view of life includes in its background characters so little known as to be identified only by a single noticeable trait and perhaps even nicknamed by it. And this view of life includes those who look more like caricatures than average beings, 'characters' we often call them. Trollope has some of these; *Orley Farm* is an outstanding example with the lawyer Chaffanbrass (see also *The Three Clerks* and *Phineas Redux* – an interesting example of Trollope's continuity even with a lesser character), Moulder and Kantwise. This trio is reminiscent of Dickens.

Trollope does not rely very much on events. 'The novelist has other aims than the elucidation of his plot' (*Autobiography*, ch. 12). The 'ravages of love' (to quote James again) served him well – marrying and failing to marry and marrying unhappily. So did everyday affairs of business – signing a bill, filling a place, casting a vote, talk in a club. All contributed to that 'picture of common life enlivened by humour and sweetened by pathos' (*Autobiography*, ch. 7) which constituted his definition of the novel. Yet, realist though he is, Trollope has provided, in Hugh Sykes Davies's phrase, 'the common reader's most common weakness in his choice of fiction, his liking for some more or less adult fairyland' (*Trollope*, 1960, p 21). (Likewise, the happy endings may seem too much and too often to be the 'sweetmeats and sugarplums' that *Barchester Towers* said the novel should close with.) This criticism can be levelled against Barsetshire itself; it is an idyllic addition to England, but we have to remember that the real England is still there, especially London with its troubles. It is more difficult to level it against the later work, and even in Barsetshire it is not escapism. The idyllic emphasizes the realistic; the background is often pleasanter than the characters in front of it. Even the better among them can provoke their creator to acerbity: 'In her heart of hearts Mrs. Grantly hated Mrs. Proudie – that is, with that sort of hatred one Christian lady allows herself to feel towards another' (*Framley Parsonage*, ch. 17). Here is another example of Trollope's 'gift of intimate communion with the reader'; he hits exactly the note that his reader would. He thinks and feels plainly and 'with a considerable tone for satire . . . he had as little as possible of the quality of irony' (James, op. cit., pp 528–9). Trollope's directness and lack of subtlety stimulates the reader's confidence in him.

His style matches his manner. In his own study of *Thackeray* (1879) he required style to be 'easy, lucid and grammatical'. Trollope's is. It is relaxed, too much so at times. 'Every sentence and every word used must tend to the telling of the story' (*Autobiography*, ch. 12), but sometimes they don't. It is unpretentious and usually efficient; he rarely seeks rhetorical effect. In a characteristic English way he prefers the unadorned and the understatement to the decorative and the dramatic. His tone is that of civilized middle-class conversation, and, as James observed, 'by no means destitute of a certain saving grace of coarseness' (op. cit., p 528). His particular regard for what dialogue should be (see *Autobiography*, ch. 12) and his success in making it so has much to do with the establishment of tone. Some of the colloquies are, if anything, too realistic in their laggard pace and even their inadequate significance. Both his stylistic laxity and his verbosity in dialogue may well be attributable to the situation that evoked such feeling in the words: 'In writing a novel the author soon becomes aware that the burden of many pages is before him' (ibid.).

When he feels the burden most, Trollope is only the 'first-rate plodder' which *The Dublin Review* (LXXI) called him in 1872. More often, however, with his straightforward style and balanced view of life, detached, tolerant, good-humoured, he makes us look afresh at people and events much like those we know. In this sense he gratifies what James, who is still the most perceptive of his critics, called 'the taste for emotions of recognition'. Thereby 'Trollope will remain one of the most trustworthy, though not one of the most eloquent, of the writers who have helped the heart of man to know itself' (op. cit., p 545).

6

THE BRONTËS

Wendy A. Craik

Although Dr Leavis found it 'tempting to retort that there is only one Brontë' (*The Great Tradition*, 1948, p 41), meaning that Emily Brontë was the only genius of the three, most general readers succumb to the same temptation in quite another sense. They assume unconsciously that all three, Emily, Charlotte, and Anne, write novels of the same kind, but in descending order of success. The assumption is a natural and reasonable one, because life offered, or rather, thrust upon them, the same material from which to create, while they themselves, as sisters deeply attached to each other, their home, and the rest of their family, welcomed their fate. For the student and critic the temptation increases, because life rarely offers him the gift of three talents, all major in some degree, all of one blood, and of the same generation, using not only the same form, the novel, but using it in a way that makes the fullest possible use of personal experience. Moreover the experience is not only that of events, people and society encountered together, but also a private spiritual and imaginative life lived for the most formative years in common. In childhood their private fantasy-world belonged to all the children, including Branwell, and although Branwell of necessity, and Charlotte from independence of spirit, fell away, Emily and Anne continued theirs to their lives' end.

While the study of their common ground and the literary uses they found for it is a legitimate and fascinating study, the danger rises when such a study interferes with a just and proper estimate of the quality of what they created from it, when, as is all too easy, one becomes unable to see the literary wood for the biographical trees. Enough valuable and scholarly research has been done on the springs of the Brontë genius and the experience which fed it to render it unnecessary, as well as a practical impossibility, to continue it here. Mrs Gaskell's excellent *Life of Charlotte Brontë*, written and published only two years after its subject's death in 1855,

remains the most valuable single source of biographical information, while Fanny Ratchford's *The Brontës' Web of Childhood* is
the authoritative study of the evidence of their inner development.

Only four years separated Charlotte (1816–55), the eldest
surviving member of the children of Patrick Brontë and his wife
Maria Branwell, from Anne (1820–49), the youngest. Although
all three of the novelists are vigorously and outspokenly devoted to
their Yorkshire West Riding home, they all betray the influence of
their parents' origins elsewhere. Their father was an Irishman, born
Patrick Prunty, who changed his name by analogy with that of
Nelson's title as Duke of Brontë, in the same way as Charlotte wove
into her childhood fantasies endless variations on the names and
titles of her own hero, the Duke of Wellington. Although spending
the greater part of his life as the Anglican incumbent of Haworth,
Patrick Brontë had, at Cambridge and after, been under the influence of Wesley and his followers, as had his wife, Maria
Branwell. She was a Cornishwoman from Penzance, and on her
death in 1821, after nine years of marriage and six children, when
Charlotte was five, Emily three, and Anne a year old, the Brontë
children were cared for by her unmarried sister Elizabeth, who
remained at Haworth until her death over twenty years later. The
children of the family were thus turned in upon themselves for
society and comfort by an eccentric and solitary father, a strict aunt,
the isolation imposed upon them by their own status in Haworth,
and the position of the village itself. Their likeness to their parent
intensified the effects of his treating them quite unlike children,
forcing their unusual intelligence and sensibility into unusually
early growth and abnormally developing their intellectual and moral
powers. The room which the children occupied during the day was
significantly termed, not the nursery, or even the school-room, but
the study. From this early stage began the habit of imaginative
playing-out of fantasies which is natural to all young children, and
the very individual one of blending into it adult matters from real
life. They draw constantly upon the politics and political figures of
the day, such as Wellington, Napoleon, Wilberforce; upon very
adult settings and events – wars, national upheavals and all the
internal politics of quite imaginary countries – and upon, in a sense,
very adult passions, resulting in rivalry and hatred between kinsfolk,
murder, treachery, jealousy and adultery. The consequences of
knowing theoretically the outside world, while having personal contact with very few people, together with the consequences of intensely heightening their own imaginations and passions, while

having virtually no first-hand knowledge of those of others, are manifest in the novels of all three sisters, and most powerfully used by Emily, the most self-contained of the three. The imaginative epics created by the brother and his three sisters sprang from the personalities they originally assigned to some wooden toy soldiers, but over the years grew into a full-blown fantasy country off the coast of Africa and (later) in the Pacific, whose annals they wrote, whose newspapers they created and whose history they decreed, where necessary by the intervention of supernatural forces (provided by themselves in person). Probably the most significant qualities, besides the remarkable mixture of the real outside world with the personal imagined one, are the force of the passions displayed and the complete acceptance of all kinds of wickedness, provided that the act is the manifestation of passion. The joint world in due course split into Angria, controlled by Charlotte and Branwell, and Gondal, controlled by Emily and Anne; but the surviving evidence of both reveals that in them the moral standards of everyday life are not so much violated, as merely irrelevant, and thus that Emily's novel *Wuthering Heights* is closer to her inner imaginative being than are Charlotte's or Anne's, even though theirs are on the face of it more autobiographical.

Circumstances conspired to force the child Charlotte into facing social and moral responsibility. In 1824 the four eldest girls, Maria, Elizabeth, Charlotte, and Emily were sent away to Cowan Bridge to a school run by the Rev. Carus Wilson for the daughters of poor clergymen. Here Maria and Elizabeth died, leaving Charlotte the eldest in the family. She immortalized her experiences and the school in Jane Eyre's at Lowood Institution, out of Maria's death found wherewith to create Helen Burns's, and exposed her child's-eye view of Carus Wilson in Mr Brocklehurst. One might well estimate that it was from this period that Charlotte, naturally religious, developed the strong sense of duty to herself and to others and of personal responsibility, which she showed throughout her life. To examine how these conflict with the inner life of the imagination and the passions is the great preoccupation of all her novels; to reconcile them her great achievement.[1]

---

[1] Like her father she was Tory in politics and had affinities with Evangelicalism in faith. His example may have inspired his family also in their literary composition – he had himself published both prose and verse – although the private nature of their writings, and the form in which they produced them – miniature imitations of books and newspapers, not in long-hand but in a kind of print – suggest inner compulsion, rather than any desire for fame.

The Brontë children remained at Haworth for the next five years in a process of self-education, during which most of the surviving juvenilia were produced. In 1831 Charlotte was sent to her second school, run by a Miss Wooler at Roe Head near Halifax. Here she met her three closest lifelong friends, Mary Taylor, Ellen Nussey and Miss Wooler herself, and acquired much of the knowledge and experience out of which she was to create *Shirley* – the West Riding setting, the oral accounts of mill-breakings and the troubles of mill-owners and workers in the Industrial Revolution. She also got to know Mary Taylor's family, whom she recreates as the Yorkes. Ellen Nussey contributes something to the second heroine Caroline Helstone, but her chief importance to posterity is as the recipient and preserver of the most intimate and personal of Charlotte Brontë's letters. In 1835 Charlotte returned to Roe Head as a teacher, and Emily went as a pupil. Charlotte was a success; but Emily was so unhappy that she went home within three months, and Anne replaced her. A number of Emily's poems date from this absence from home, most of them superficially expressing the longing for the moors which makes it possible, though unenlightening, to diagnose Emily's agony simply as home-sickness.

From 1837 to 1842 the family was broken up, with Anne and Charlotte taking various posts as governesses, while Emily taught for six months in a school at Southowram near Halifax. The spiritual difference between Emily and the others is clear in the use to which they put their experiences and the way they bore them. Charlotte and Anne drew freely upon the places they lived in and the people they met, in *Jane Eyre* and *Agnes Grey*: Emily used only the scenery, for some of the settings in *Wuthering Heights*. Charlotte and Anne, unsuited to teaching small children though they were, survived. Emily succumbed (in Charlotte's words) to 'hard labour from six in the morning to near eleven at night, with only one half-hour of exercise between' (Letter to Ellen Nussey, October 1837). It has been suggested with great probability that Emily was beaten, not by the physical labour, but by having no chance to live the private spiritual life which was vital to her, which found expression in the Gondal stories and her poems, and which made her, as she herself says, 'comfortable and undesponding' (Birthday Note, 31 July 1845) and wholly self-sufficient in her routine, domesticated and utterly humdrum life at Haworth. She left home only once more, to stay in Brussels in 1842 with Charlotte, and learn French and German so as to be better qualified to set up a school of their own. She was recalled by their aunt's death, while Charlotte remained as both pupil and teacher.

Brussels, which had no artistic influence on Emily, had a shattering one on Charlotte (then aged 26), out of which came first *The Professor* and later *Villette*. Whether or not one believes, on the evidence of several (certainly impassioned) letters from Charlotte to M. Héger, the teacher-husband of the Belgian *pension's* proprietress, that Charlotte fell in love, there can be no doubt that out of him, his wife, their school and its pupils, and Brussels itself, she was able to create first the setting and some of the characters of *The Professor*, and later to realize Lucy Snowe's vision of the city of Villette, the *pensionnat* and its inmates, and Mme Beck and Paul Emmanuel.

The other member of the family, Branwell, also had literary aspirations. Although he has received critical attention,[1] his only real interest is as an influence on his sisters and as a contrast to them. His own prose and poetic outpourings demonstrate that the atmosphere of the parsonage, without the personality and the power to transmute, produced only trash. His career was one of continuous failure, as a would-be London art student, as a practising painter in Bradford, as a tutor, and even a railway clerk on the Leeds and Manchester Railway. He degenerated into a dipsomaniac and drug-addict, making life for all at Haworth parsonage a dangerous and harrowing agony until his death in 1848. His contribution to the novels was partly simply to provide material – all three sisters unhesitatingly depicted drunkenness and degradation – but much more to confirm them in what their private imaginings had begun, in treating the material of melodrama and of baroque and Gothic horror as inevitable and essential elements of real life. Anne alone consciously and deliberately, and very painfully to herself, used Branwell and his fate with a social as well as literary purpose, when writing *The Tenant of Wildfell Hall*.[1]

The rest of Charlotte's life, from the return from Brussels in 1844 at the age of 28 to her death in 1855, is a sad record of deaths and private agonies, little compensated by the sisters' gradual professional success as novelists. First there was Branwell's decline and death in September 1848. Emily died only three months later,

---

[1] Notably from a few earnest defenders: Francis H. Grundy (*Pictures of the Past*, 1897), and Francis A. Leyland (*The Brontë Family: with Special Reference to Patrick Branwell Brontë*, 1886). The myth begun by the latter that Branwell conceived the whole of *Wuthering Heights* and wrote the opening chapters dies hard.

causing almost as much suffering to her family by her rigid and self-contained refusal even to acknowledge her illness as her brother had by his self-indulgence. Anne died of a pulmonary complaint, like her sister, in the following May. The effect of facing these sorrows, with no support, but only the necessity for giving it to an eccentric and self-absorbed father, darkened Charlotte's already austere view of life, shaded the latter part of *Shirley* – whose composition was interrupted by Emily's death – and coloured the whole of her last novel, *Villette*. Charlotte's marriage to her father's curate Arthur Bell Nicholls in June 1854 can hardly be seen as the blessing Mrs Gaskell suggests; as Charlotte's letters reveal, it caused her considerable anxiety for a long time, as a prospect disagreeable to her father and of doubtful attraction to herself; the pregnancy in which it resulted undoubtedly hastened her death.

The literary progress of the sisters began in 1845, when Charlotte, discovering some poems written by Emily, initiated the project of a joint volume of poems, published under their pseudonyms in 1846 as *Poems by Currer, Ellis, and Acton Bell*. The private publication cost £31, the *Athenaeum* reviewed it, and two copies were actually sold. However, a start had been made and as a result Charlotte wrote *The Professor*, Emily *Wuthering Heights*, and Anne *Agnes Grey*. The last two came out together, in three volumes in December 1847, virtually unnoticed. *The Professor* was continuously rejected but, on the encouragement of the publishing house of Smith and Elder, Charlotte offered them her second attempt, *Jane Eyre*, which appeared in October 1847. It was an immediate success. *The Tenant of Wildfell Hall* came out in 1848, to reviews disapproving its subject. *Shirley* appeared in 1849 and marked the virtual end of Charlotte's anonymity: the setting and some of the characters were promptly identified locally, while the attempts of Emily's and Anne's publisher to pass off their work as 'Currer Bell's' forced her into justifying herself to her publishers for what looked like breach of contract. In 1853 came *Villette*.

---

[1] Branwell's passion for Mrs Robinson, the mother of the family at Thorp Green, where he and Anne worked as tutor and governess, has wasted far too much time and attention. Whatever the facts (which are demonstrably fewer than his family and Mrs Gaskell believed, being mainly Branwell's own invention, whether through drug-induced illusion, or as guilty self-exculpating lies to raise him in the eyes of his family), they had few literary uses for the novelists and produced no more than a passing allusion by Charlotte in *The Professor* to the degrading nature of illicit passion.

Charlotte alone made any contact with the literary world of her day, and that scanty. She met Thackeray and made friends, mainly by correspondence, with Mrs Gaskell, Harriet Martineau and the novelist and critic G. H. Lewes. She read widely among her contemporaries, in volumes sent by her publishers, but the only reading which leaves a mark on her own work is that which can be seen in all three sisters, the reading of their youth: the Bible, Shakespeare, Bunyan, the eighteenth-century essayists, Scott, Byron and the political periodicals of the early nineteenth century. The only contemporaries to leave their mark are Thackeray and occasionally Tennyson.

Charlotte Brontë, judged by the esteem of her contemporaries, makes claim to be the major figure of her family; by bulk and variety she is the professional. Whatever the final estimate, her work must be judged by the highest standards, in its own right, and not merely, as Dr Leavis suggests, as 'a remarkable talent that enabled her to do something first-hand, and new in the rendering of personal experience, above all in *Villette*' – a talent that he judges to be 'of a minor kind' (*The Great Tradition*, p 41).

However, her first attempt, in a public, professional sense, at the novel (putting aside, that is, the private family narratives never intended for outside readers) is undoubtedly minor. *The Professor* is not, within its limits, a failure; it has striking originalities and a few great scenes and passages, but it always remains on a lower level than her other three works. Smith and Elder were wise to reject it, and, since it drove Charlotte Brontë to write *Jane Eyre*, and since, had it been published, she could never have felt free to re-work and transmute its Belgian material and characters in *Villette*, readers must be grateful to them for doing so. *The Professor* must always remain the last read, as it was the last published, of the Brontë novels. Its main importance for the critic, as for its author, is that it enables one to explore what Charlotte Brontë required of a novel, what are its legitimate constituents, and how these constituents are to be used to valid artistic ends. Since the novel is plainly not wholly successful, it is easier to see the originality of its author's starting-point and methods, and the nature of the power that vivifies them, than it is either in a fully achieved masterpiece like *Jane Eyre*, or in a misconceived variant like *Shirley*.

Her own professional aims are surprisingly at odds with the effect she always produces, at her greatest, upon her readers. In her preface to *The Professor* (written when she was hoping, after the success of *Jane Eyre* and *Shirley*, to get it into print) she says:

I had got over any such taste as I might once have had for ornamented and redundant composition, and come to prefer what was plain and homely. At the same time I had adopted a set of principles on the subject of incident, etc., such as would be generally approved in theory, but the result of which, when carried into practice, often procures for an author more surprise than pleasure.

I said to myself that my hero should work his way through life as I had seen real living men work theirs – that he should never get a shilling he had not earned – that no sudden turns should lift him in a moment to wealth and high station; that whatever small competency he might gain, should be won by the sweat of his brow; that before he could find so much as an arbour to sit down in, he should master at least half the ascent of 'the Hill of Difficulty'; that he should not even marry a beautiful girl or a lady of rank. As Adam's son he should share Adam's doom, and drain through life a mixed and moderate cup of enjoyment.

Her work, therefore, is to be wholly about real life, drawing on the material of life, with no concessions to fantasy, romance or wish-fulfilment, and, above all, no dependence on previous literary conventions or models. In *The Professor* she keeps almost too rigidly within her self-imposed limits. The career of William Crimsworth begins as a clerk in his manufacturer brother's West Riding factory, continues as a tutor in a Belgian school, is enlivened only by his soon successful love for a fellow-teacher and pupil, and by his employer's unreturned passion for himself, and culminates only in a happy retirement to England again, on the income of several years of successful school-keeping; such a career is inadequate to the power with which Charlotte Brontë endows him of feeling deeply and powerfully and thinking originally, and inadequate also to Charlotte Brontë's own patent power to utilize such thought and feeling in the medium of the novel. But *The Professor* is full of the flavour of things to come. It reveals that its author is developing the autobiographical form in a new way, enabling her to use personal experience to valid artistic ends. (It is significant that her first- person narrator is a means of involvement with the material, but of detachment from the author, since he is, unlike herself, a man.) It possesses the vivid and powerful creation of secondary and unattractive characters done with both scrupulous fairness and with great vigour: Mlle Reuter here, with the charms of intelligence and health, counteracted by cold-heartedness and deceit, looks forward to Mme Beck; the vigorously realized Belgian schoolmaster Pelet, and the Englishman Yorke Hunsden, a compound of conscious Yorkshire bluntness and eccentricity with culture and social polish, point the way to *Shirley* and to *Villette*. Her power to recreate all the moods and passions, transient and cumulative, which attend loneliness, her power to convey their associations with place, time and weather, and to develop her own highly idiosyncratic style in which the heightened, ornate and rhetorical, and the simple and homely co-exist without bathos and may be used with conscious humour as well as for intense drama – all these reveal a writer who knows what she intends, and has the means at her disposal. Her next novel showed her superbly able to use the one and achieve the other.

Though *Shirley* has a wider canvas, and *Villette* a deeper and stranger exploration of the human spirit, both have fallings-off and flaws. *Jane Eyre* is Charlotte Brontë's nearest claim to perfection.

Its achievement rests mainly upon its heroine. More than most first-person narrators, she is the Prince of Denmark of her *Hamlet*, in that everything in the novel bears in some way upon the emotional and spiritual progress which is the essence of the work. Charlotte Brontë's most obvious success is her conscious one, of taking a heroine who is plain, socially insignificant (not even romantically destitute like Oliver Twist), prim to puritanism in her manners, yet utterly unconventional and highly idiosyncratic; she then ensures with never-failing skill that the reader shall care as passionately for her as she herself does about the crises with which life faces her. But Jane Eyre is the means whereby her author achieves greater ends, becoming able to handle material and spiritual states, and to evolve techniques, not hitherto accessible in the novel. Through her heroine Charlotte Brontë embarks for the first time upon the problem of how the vital needs of the individual soul may be reconciled with those private moral standards, and of the claims of the social world in which the individual must occupy a place. The spiritual needs of Jane Eyre are all too easily summarized as 'love', but the terms in which she declares her passion to Mr Rochester comprise more than himself:

'I grieve to leave Thornfield: I love Thornfield: – I love it, because I have lived in it a full and delightful life, – momentarily at least. I have not been trampled on. I have not been petrified. I have not been buried with inferior minds, and excluded from every glimpse of communion with what

is bright, and energetic, and high. I have talked, face to face, with what I
reverence; with what I delight in, – with an original, a vigorous, an
expanded mind.'

(ch. 23)

The adjectives here are astonishing ones to apply to the man one
loves, even for so idiosyncratic a stylist as Charlotte Brontë. Their
use reveals deeper issues and demonstrates the vitality of all those
sections of the novels which do not concern the 'love-story'. The
events at Gateshead when Jane is a child persecuted and neglected
by her aunt and cousins, at Lowood Institution where she is a
schoolgirl starved in body, and at Morton where she is a school-
teacher tormented in mind and starved in soul, are all part of this
deeper examination which is made through Jane. The early
episodes, at Gateshead and Lowood, are essential if the reader is to
see the sources of the strength whereby Jane rejects Mr Rochester,
and to acknowledge the validity of the principles which compel her
to do so. Courage and strength of feeling are what Charlotte Brontë
bestows on Jane as given by nature: they enable her to defy her
bullying cousins and her harsh aunt. But they are instinctive and
amoral. The eleven-year-old Jane who routs her aunt discovers
that, unsupported and undirected, they lead to no end:

Something of vengeance I had tasted for the first time; as aromatic wine it
seemed, on swallowing, warm and racy: its after-flavour, metallic and
corroding, gave me a sensation as if I had been poisoned.

(ch. 4)

At Lowood she learns of other means of facing life's challenges –
those embodied in Helen Burns, who meets hers with a fortitude
that takes the form of Christian resignation and meekness under
suffering. Although this can never be Jane's way, it enables her to
move from her own non-Christian stand:

'You are good to those who are good to you. It is all I ever desire to be . . .
When we are struck at without a reason, we should strike back again very
hard; I am sure we should – so hard as to teach the person who struck us
never to do it again.'

(ch. 6)

Jane sees the force of what Helen says, but sees also, in her reply to
Helen's supposition below, a consideration that does not bear on
the solitary Helen:

'If all the world hated you, and believed you wicked, while your own
conscience approved you, and absolved you from guilt, you would not be
without friends.'

'No; I know I should think well of myself; but that is not enough: if others don't love me, I would rather die than live – I cannot bear to be solitary and hated.'

(ch. 8)

By the climax of her testing at Thornfield, Charlotte Brontë makes us recognize the validity of Jane's position when she is tempted within herself by the ideas that equally tempt the reader:

'Who in the world cares for *you*? or who will be injured by what you do?' Still indomitable was the reply – '*I* care for myself. The more solitary, the more friendless, the more unsustained I am, the more I will respect myself. I will keep the law given by God; sanctioned by man. I will hold to the principles received by me when I was sane, and not mad – as I am now.'

(ch. 27)

Her further test at Morton is made by St John Rivers, who offers her a life devoted to a noble cause, but at the price of complete self-suppression, and what amounts to the killing of her personality. Finally, at Ferndean, enriched by her new knowledge of family life with her three new-found cousins, wiser by her struggle against sterile self-denial, Jane finds, reunited at last with Mr Rochester, what suits her (in her own words) 'to the finest fibre of [her] nature' (ch. 37).

Charlotte Brontë's triumph in creating Jane is so complete that it is easy to respond to the careful structure and to overlook it, easy to feel that Jane's character is so complete that it must be her author's. The autobiographical method works so well that the many shifts of narrative viewpoint, which make it succeed, go unnoticed. The great innovation of the method lies in the subtle use of retrospect. Jane is purportedly writing ten years after the final chapter, but within the progress of the action the Jane who experiences constantly pauses to assess her position, to steady herself, whether it is to reverberate mindlessly to Mr Rochester's near-protestation of love after the fire (ch. 15), or coldly balance her plain self with the flashing Miss Ingram (ch. 17). The long chapter in which she goes back to Gateshead for Mrs Reed's death (ch. 21) involves reassessments at a greater distance in time, of her childhood eight years before.

The method, of purported autobiography, and this structure, of scenes of passionate involvement controlled and curbed by intervals of constant intellectual reassessment in retrospect, is taken further in *Villette*. Here also the success is so complete that Lucy Snowe has been discussed as if she were her own author, different though she is from Jane Eyre. Lucy is much further than Jane from what most readers think of as a 'normal' personality; the furthest retrospect of herself is greater – she is writing in her old age, when her hair 'lies now, at last white, under a white cap, like snow beneath snow' (ch. 5) – yet her sufferings, coming from far stranger depths of personality, are as painfully realized as Jane's. The agonies of loneliness, hypersensitivity, melancholy, and introspection, though they cause Lucy moral *problems*, are not shaped by moral *considerations* as Jane's are. Lucy has a harder struggle than Jane, not merely to reconcile the needs of her personality with the rules of society, but to survive as a person at all, in a society whose pressures not only threaten to annihilate her, but actually intensify the conflicts within her own nature. Charlotte Brontë is approaching (from a very different direction) the world of Henry James, in which the standards of judgment must be termed, inadequately, aesthetic. The novel's failures are not because of its strange heroine, nor of her stranger situation (being, like Catherine Earnshaw, in love with two men at once), but because of its divided aims. Lucy, the child of misfortune, is contrasted with Paulina de Bassompierre, in whom Charlotte Brontë intends to portray a nature equally finely balanced, whose destiny is fulfilment and happiness. Unfortunately Charlotte Brontë's powers of characterization are of a kind that catch fire only through a central consciousness. The detachment necessary to such an end cuts her off from her strength; Paulina, and those who concern her, seem unrealized and mechanical as soon as they cease to be of vital concern to Lucy. Charlotte Brontë herself acknowledged the fault, diagnosing that Paulina lacked 'the germ of the real' (Letter to George Smith, December 6, 1852).

Charlotte Brontë's characters other than her heroine have always presented the paradox of seeming to have intense life, yet, when considered separately, of seeming often incredible. After Lucy, one recalls Mme Beck and Paul Emmanuel as two of the author's finest achievements. Yet of Paul Emmanuel it can be said, as David Cecil said of Mr Rochester, that no flesh-and-blood man could be so exclusively composed of violence and virility and masculine vanity (*Early Victorian Novelists*, 1934). The life the reader responds to in them is not so much their own, but what they have for the heroine through whose eyes, nerves and heart we perceive them. The reader judges them for the way they impress *her* rather than himself. The method explains the power of such unobtrusive triumphs as Bessie Leaven and Mrs Fairfax in *Jane Eyre* and Mrs Bretton in *Villette*, as well as of such evident and original triumphs as Mrs

Reed, St John Rivers and Mr Rochester in *Jane Eyre*, or Mme Beck and Paul Emmanuel in *Villette*; it explains also the vigour of what have been thought her failures – *Jane Eyre's* Blanche Ingram and her astonishing mother, or *Villette's* Ginevra Fanshawe, Père Silas and Mme Walravens. The reader, sharing the narrator's experience, feels as she does. However, such feeling never warps judgment. Indeed, Charlotte Brontë constantly forces her reader to make his own assessments of her characters, to check the heroine's conclusions against the facts she provides. One can see how Mr Rochester both understands Jane and misjudges her during their courtship, how he can be the man who realizes that

'If I bid you do what you thought wrong, there would be no light-footed running, no neat-handed alacrity, no lively glance and animated complexion.'

(ch. 20)

and equally the man who, after she has agreed to marry him, attempts to treat her as a sultan treats a favourite: and how both aspects look forward to his greatest offence against her, in trying to cheat her into wrong-doing and a bigamous marriage. Mme Beck in *Villette* is an even more complex case, since the narrator's attitude to her changes with time. The qualities which make Mme Beck morally indefensible but amusing, attractive and in some degree estimable – her coldhearted composure, the tidiness and desire for propriety which lead her to search, with exquisite neatness and efficiency, the belongings and letters of her employees, the quietly inflexible will, which manipulates (by lying if necessary) any chance event that will give her her own way – all these can seem, to the reader as to Lucy, reprehensible but amusing, when Lucy herself is secure in having no secrets to hide and no desires which cross Mme Beck's. However, when Lucy, in love with Paul Emmanuel, becomes a threat to Mme Beck's plans to keep him for herself and her school, Mme Beck becomes a powerful danger, the more effective in that the reader is never allowed to relax into simple hatred. The virtues of her defects remain unchanged.

When the central narrator is removed, the shaping power it imposes is removed also. Henry James's condemnation of autobiographical novels as 'loose baggy monsters' applies much more to *Shirley*, Charlotte Brontë's only non-autobiographical one, than to the rest. Though her motives in making her second novel quite different from her first are excellent, her intentions were beyond her equipment. A panorama of the West Riding during the Industrial

Revolution, to be revealed through the spiritual progress of two young women, one rich, brilliant and fortunate, the other dependent, subdued, and unhappy, who are in their turn to be presented by a detached, Thackerayan, ironic, moralizing narrator – such a project called for too many qualities Charlotte Brontë did not possess and rendered useless some of the best that she did.

The two greatest deficiencies in *Shirley* are an uncertain sense of direction and an unsatisfactory narrative method. The novel has two quite different kinds of theme, interrelated by the action, but demanding, to succeed, two different kinds of narrative. The first centres upon the hero (if the novel can be said to have one), Robert Moore. This theme examines the force of personality and circumstances in shaping a man's fate, as the combined pressures of lack of money, the perils besetting Yorkshire millowners and the clothing industry and the political state of England or Europe and indeed of America all work upon his character to change it and, with it, determine how his life shall go. The other theme is worked out in the eponymous heroine Shirley and in the novel's central perception, Caroline Helstone. Through them the novel explores the dilemma of woman in nineteenth-century middle-class society, forced to find a life for herself, yet deprived (if she does not marry) of the means, not only of fulfilling her emotional needs, but of keeping any sense at all of a purpose in life. The novel aches with the pain of Caroline's question when, knowing that she will not marry Robert and that she is prevented from finding a career for herself, she asks:

'What am I to do to fill the interval of time which spreads between me and the grave?'

(ch. 10)

The first theme is the one embodied in the plot; but a résumé of that plot would not even suggest the existence of the second. The first is done dramatically, with vigorous action and racy dialogue; the second by long revelations of Caroline's spiritual sufferings, by curious duologues beween her and Shirley in strangely heightened language, by curious non-novelistic devices – like Shirley's remarkable 'devoir' on 'La Première Femme Savante' – and finally by a brutal change of narrative method in Louis Moore's journal. Both themes are more successful than such analysis suggests and are interrelated, often enmeshed. Their material often overlaps, particularly as regards the characters taking part. Shirley and Caroline are part of Robert's story, he an important element in theirs; Mr

Yorke the mill owner, Caroline's despotic uncle the Rev. Mr Helstone, and Robert's sister Hortense concern both stories. The same scenes may advance both.

Even more vitally, both themes are coloured by what almost amounts to a third – Charlotte Brontë's potent and original apprehension of what time passing does to the lives of men. She first learned the use of recent history from Scott, but she adapted it to something quite other than his romantic nostalgia in *Waverley* or even his more serious aims in *Heart of Midlothian*. For probably the first time in the English novel, characters not only feel themselves to be mortal, but feel themselves hemmed in by the pressures on their own fates, not only of the chances of history, but also of precious life slipping away. Whether Robert goes bankrupt or not and whether he can marry Caroline depends upon the movements of nations: the repeal of the Orders in Council, allowing American trade, only barely saves him from financial ruin; while Caroline's question above reverberates through the novel, with its plangent periphrasis for 'life' – 'the interval of time which spreads between me and the grave'.

Unfortunately, the narrative method chosen by Charlotte Brontë impedes her. Her Thackerayan stance often suits the first theme, but it is fatal to the second. To be detached, humorous, ironic, would-be urbane (though urbanity does not suit so uncosmopolitan a writer) may suit the delineation of Robert the latter-day Coriolanus, or the trenchant Yorkshire types, or the comic curates; it is fatal to the interior stresses of a Shirley and still more of a Caroline Helstone. Charlotte Brontë's intentions in *Shirley* were excellent – to avoid writing a second *Jane Eyre*, to extend both her own range and that of her form, to examine both society and new and deeper recesses of individual consciousness. But what she produced must be considered, in the final judgment, a noble failure. Her claim to greatness must rest upon *Jane Eyre* and *Villette*.[1]

*

[1] A few fragments exist of unfinished novels, notably a fragment concerning two brothers called *The Moores* (printed in W. R. Nicoll's edition of *Jane Eyre*, 1902) recalling *Shirley* only by the name; and the opening chapters of a work stopped by marriage and death, called *Emma* (first printed in the *Cornhill Magazine*, April 1860), which treats the sufferings of an unattractive small girl, thought to be rich and found to be poor, whose stay in a small school is chronicled by a dispassionate male observer. Neither is of artistic interest. They are merely outlines too rough to help much in a study of their author's processes of creation.

Anne Brontë dwells in the shadow of her two sisters. Though undeniably less than they, she is no mere pale copy of either. She is of interest to the student of all three for her original use of their common material; she is of interest in her own right for being, apparently quite unwittingly, a startling innovator, not, like Emily, in structure and theme, or like Charlotte, in intention and apprehension, but in materials and morals.

It is impossible to miss the originality of her subject in *The Tenant of Wildfell Hall*, a controlled, unsparing study of drunkenness, debauchery and degeneration which proceeds inexorably to its conclusion in death, examining on the way the consequences of sin to the sinner himself, to those in his private life, and to the society around him. Although the title suggests Helen Huntingdon (the 'tenant') as the central interest and although the first quarter of the novel is the autobiography of Gilbert Markham, a young North-country farmer who connects himself with the main story only by falling in love with the mysterious Helen, nevertheless the novel's prime mover, the reason for its existence, the source of its power, is Arthur Huntingdon, Helen's husband. His career, from marriage to death, is chronicled in the bulk of the novel.

Anne's own statement of her purpose in writing, in her preface to the second edition, is a naïve one:

I could not be understood to suppose, that the proceedings of the unhappy scapegrace, with his few profligate companions I have introduced, are a specimen of the common practices of society: the case is an extreme one, as I trusted none would fail to perceive; but I knew that such characters do exist, and if I have warned one rash youth from following in their steps, or prevented one thoughtless girl from falling into the very natural error of my heroine, the book has not been written in vain.

Anne Brontë as a novelist is not so naïve. Aware of her moral purpose and competent with the usual tools of the novelist, she is, rather, innocent and candid, unaware only of the starting novelty of her material and the unconventionality of her moral conclusions. Using the unfortunate Branwell (as Emily had used him in *Wuthering Heights*) she chronicles how self-indulgence degrades and ruins Arthur Huntingdon and how Helen Huntingdon, attempting again and again to save him, her love for him, their marriage and the upbringing of their son, finds that such suffering, far from ennobling her, tempts her in desperation to accept a lover as a means of escape:

then I hate [Huntingdon] tenfold more for having brought me to this! – God pardon me for it – and all my sinful thoughts! Instead of being humbled and purified by my afflictions I feel that they are changing my nature into gall.

(ch. 35)

Anne Brontë faces all the practical realities of the situation, not least the power of the law, which makes Helen the guilty party if she leaves her husband, and so deprives her of the right to the custody of the son for whose sake she wants to go. Her scenes are fully realized by nicely chosen details; she delineates the full horror of life with drunkards, revealed by a man who scoops out half-dissolved sugar-lumps from his oversweetened coffee and dumps them back in the sugar-bowl, or by a sober man who has to use a drawing-room candle to burn the hands of a drunkard restraining him (ch. 31); she faces also the horror of nursing a man dying of alcoholism and gangrene; she may not turn the reader's stomach, she certainly chills his nerves.

Like *Wuthering Heights, The Tenant of Wildfell Hall* begins almost at the end, a well-chosen device with some of the same effects. Anne Brontë, working on a subject which threatens both sentimentality and melodrama, avoids both. To do so, she does away with suspense. By knowing the conclusion, the reader is enabled to concentrate on what is being put before him, without anxiety as to the eventual consequences, which he already knows. Also like *Wuthering Heights*, the novel's ending is a diminuendo; Helen's final, happy marriage to Gilbert Markham, though less interesting than what has gone before, is a necessary part of the novel's themes as well as plot, to show that her sufferings have not wholly dehumanized her: Anne consciously rejected her sister's conclusion in *Shirley*, that

Sweet wild force following acute suffering, you will find nowhere: to talk of it is delusion. There may be apathetic exhaustion after the rack; if energy remains, it will be rather a dangerous energy – deadly when confronted with injustice.

(ch. 7)

Agnes Grey is less startling, yet almost equally uncompromising. As a heroine, Agnes herself is colourless, but she is the heroine in only a limited sense. She is Anne Brontë's Fanny Price. The novel concentrates upon the kind of society and standards Agnes encounters during her career as a governess with two provincial middle-class country families, the Bloomfields and the Murrays.

Her main role in the novel is as the reader's means of seeing this society and judging it. Faulty standards of education and upbringing are the author's theme here, bodied forth pre-eminently in the brilliant coquette Rosalie Murray, who fulfils her destiny under Agnes's anxious, disapproving, partly affectionate, wholly ineffectual observation. The author follows Rosalie inexorably through the last phases of education, through her coming out into society, flirtations with the local clergy, arranged courtship, marriage for money and rank, to the end of her first year of married life, looking ahead to the prospect of a barren existence whose only bitter comfort is to watch a daughter 'grow up to eclipse me, and enjoy those pleasures I am forever debarred from' (ch. 23), all without realizing that she is condemning that same daughter to the same dreadful upbringing, frivolous and arid, as has ruined herself.

Agnes Grey, less sombre than the later novel, gives its author opportunities both for humorous irony and delicate description. The irony, far from being kept away from Agnes the narrator, often works at her expense. Naïvely enthusiastic over the charms and satisfactions of teaching small children, deciding that

the clear remembrance of my own thoughts in early childhood would be a surer guide than the instructions of the most mature adviser.

(ch. 1)

she reinforces her case by quoting Thomson:

Delightful task!
To teach the young idea how to shoot!

a sentiment (and an expression of it) trite even when Jane Austen bestowed it upon Catherine Morland in *Northanger Abbey*, whence, in fact, Anne Brontë may have borrowed it (and its ironic intent) since this, though identical with Jane Austen's version, is actually a misquotation of the original lines from Thomson's *Seasons* ('Spring', 1149). If the clue here is missed, the reader soon sees Agnes's ignorance promptly done away with by the atrocious Bloomfield children. Anne Brontë, like her sisters, takes a robust delight in the grotesquely, even horrifyingly, comic, as the behaviour of this same Bloomfield family demonstrates. That she intends them to be comic as well as horrifying, her own descriptions prove: Mr Bloomfield, for instance, 'had a large mouth, pale, dingy complexion, milky blue eyes and hair *the colour of a hempen cord*' (ch. 3: my italics). When occasion offers, descriptions are both delicate and lyrical, as when Agnes, on a visit to her former pupil Rosalie, now Lady Ashby, sits neglected in her room:

As I was not rich enough to possess a watch, I could not tell how time was passing, except by observing the slowly lengthening shadows from the window; which presented a side view, including a corner of the park, a clump of trees, whose topmost branches had been colonized by an innumerable company of noisy rooks, and a high wall with a massive wooden gate: no doubt communicating with the stableyard, as a broad carriage-road swept up to it from the park. The shadow of this wall soon took possession of the whole of the ground as far as I could see, forcing the golden sunlight to retreat inch by inch, and at last take refuge in the very tops of the trees. Ere long, even they were left in shadow – the shadow of the distant hills, or of the earth itself; and, in sympathy for the busy citizens of the rookery, I regretted to see their habitation, so lately bathed in glorious light, reduced to the sombre, work-a-day hue of the lower world or of my own within. For a moment, such birds as soared above the rest might still receive the lustre of their wings, which imparted to their sable plumage the hue and brilliance of deep red gold; at last that too departed. Twilight came stealing on; the rooks became more quiet; I became more weary, and wished I were going home tomorrow.

(ch. 20)

Undoubtedly a minor talent, Anne Brontë's is indubitably a considerable one, worth more than the scant attention usually spared from her sisters. The great differences of material, structure, tone and treatment, the extra depth and complexity of her second work, suggest that she had more to say than fate allowed her, and more, and growing, powers as a writer.

The same claims for a great and enlarging future cannot be made for Anne's far greater sister, Emily. *Wuthering Heights* is generally accepted as the Brontë masterpiece; but it stands alone, not only apart from the work of the other members of the family, but from any other novel. It had no precursors and has had no successors worth considering. The only literature close to it is Emily Brontë's own poems, which, great though some of them are, are chiefly valuable for revealing what has gone into the making of the novel. Neither they nor *Wuthering Heights* itself give any hint that anything more could have come out of it. On a literary level, Emily Brontë died fulfilled.

While the greatness of the novel has been owned in steadily increasing enthusiasm ever since its very unsensational publication, opinions vary widely over what constitutes that greatness. The reader who responds to the force of the whole often has reservations about its parts – about the characters of the leading figures, Heathcliff and the elder Catherine, about the remarkable narrative method (by means of two main fictional narrators and several minor ones), about the attitudes to religion which lie behind the events, even about the quality and amount of the supernatural forces introduced.

Emily Brontë is the most self-effacing of writers, but she gives her readers clearer leads than she seems to do. One of the clearest is about her topic. The first chapter introduces the chief character, Heathcliff, whose doings occupy the bulk of the narrator Lockwood's attention for the next three; in the fourth, asking the housekeeper Ellen Dean for 'something of my neighbours,' he goes on to request, specifically, Heathcliff's history; in Ellen's story (the bulk of the novel) he gets precisely what he asked for. The known span and compass of Heathcliff's life at Wuthering Heights is the span and compass of the novel. When he is not there there is no story – as is demonstrated most strikingly by the way Ellen Dean passes over in a few sentences the three years of his absence, even though during them Catherine has her first major illness and experiences the first part of her married life with Edgar Linton. Heathcliff is, therefore, the structure of the novel.

Powerful though Heathcliff is, another is more. There can be few novels in which the heroine dies less than half-way through; there can be few heroines whose passion so permeates all its pages. She is Heathcliff's motive, his hold on life, just as she declares he is hers. Her confession that

'my great thought in living is himself. If all else perished, and *he* remained, *I* should still continue to be, and if all else remained and he were annihilated the universe would turn to a mighty stranger.'

(ch. 9)

is partnered by his prayer to her at her death:

'Be with me always – take any form – drive me mad! only *do* not leave me in this abyss where I cannot find you! Oh God! it is unutterable! I *cannot* live without my life! *I cannot* live without my soul!'

(ch. 16)

Through him she lives on for another eighteen years, until he has unconsciously completed his task of restoring the equilibrium of society at the Heights and Thrushcross, which was disrupted by his arrival as a dirty, ragged, black-haired foundling, the cuckoo in the Earnshaw nest, and next by Catherine's self-destroying act when, spiritually bound to him, she gave herself to Linton, thereby splitting her very nature in two.

These two are the life of the novel, its *raison d'être*. The social, spiritual, even supernatural, disturbances are but repercussions of the disturbances in them; the other characters (barring the narrators) exist only in relation to them and are seen by their light. The novel opens with them. Lockwood meets Heathcliff first, at the point in his career when his task of vengeance is virtually completed. Nothing stands in the way of a union between the younger Catherine, the Linton heir (herself half Earnshaw), and Hareton, inheritor of Wuthering Heights. Nothing now therefore prevents Heathcliff from his union with Catherine, as he himself dimly perceives in his later confession to Ellen Dean:

'I get levers and mattocks to demolish the two houses, and train myself to be capable of working like Hercules, and when everything is ready and in my power, I find the will to lift a slate off either roof has vanished. My old enemies have not beaten me; now would be the precise time to revenge myself on their representatives: I could do it; and none could hinder me. But where is the use? I don't care for striking; I can't take the trouble to raise my hand.'

(ch. 33)

Almost immediately after Lockwood meets Heathcliff in the flesh, he meets Catherine also, in the spirit. In the brilliantly-conceived nightmare she is not the woman who died, but a child, who wails that she has been 'a waif for twenty years' (ch. 3). Lockwood sees, in fact, the only complete Catherine, the child who has not yet separated herself from her more essential self, Heathcliff. When death reunites them, social order returns, the younger generation are free to be happy at Thrushcross, and Joseph to behave with his old curmudgeonly gusto at the Heights; Ellen, the barometer of disturbance in both places, is happy in the union of her two charges. We are able to accept both Lockwood's faith that no one could 'imagine unquiet slumbers for the sleepers in that quiet earth' (ch. 34); and to accept equally that 'they *walk*', that the boy with the sheep has seen 'Heathcliff and a woman, yonder, under t' nab' and that Joseph has seen 'two on 'em, looking out of his [Heathcliff's] chamber window, every night since his death' (ibid.); the whole novel has gone to prove that such indeed is their heaven; to be thus is to be at peace, reunited with each other and with the Heights.

While it is underestimating Emily Brontë to suggest that the other characters are mere shadows, yet it is safe to say that their personalities are limited to what they share with those of the protagonists. The range of emotions and responses in *Wuthering Heights* is limited, though the depth of the emotions is far from being so. All characters exhibit courage, meet adversity with defiance, and counter wrong with the urge to vengeance. Isabella, her love for Heathcliff turned to hate, taunts, goads and defies him; Hindley Earnshaw, drunken and bankrupt, protests that he will have pleasure in sending his own soul 'to perdition, to punish its maker' (ch. 9). They never feel that resignation is a virtue, or that they should exercise self-control: all that is required of them is that they accept the full consequences of their acts. Even Edgar Linton, the nearest to a type of Christian virtue, is more willing to die to be with Catherine than to live and take care of his daughter.

Such positions necessarily result in violence, and violence in cruelty. Even so, the novel is neither as violent nor as cruel as it seems. Much of the violence is of expression and interpretation, not action; most of the cruelty is not gratuitous or sadistic, but the inevitable breaking out of overwhelming passions. Emily Brontë takes care that the outward surface of life shall not heave or break too often with all the turbulence beneath: Kenneth the doctor visits the Heights and sees nothing much amiss; the housekeeper Zillah sees little to disturb her even while young Linton Heathcliff is dying. The great scenes of violence are not as memorable as the great scenes of passion: one remembers Catherine's self-revealing delirium (ch. 12), her last scene with Heathcliff (ch. 15) or those just before his death (chs 33 and 34) more vividly than that in which he almost kills Hindley and Isabella on the night of Catherine's funeral (ch. 17). Significantly, this last – containing perhaps the most brutal acts Heathcliff, the most brutal character, commits – is not simply an outburst of self-indulgent spite against those who have injured him. He has been goaded past bearing by Isabella's taunting his most vital feelings:

'Heathcliff, if I were you, I'd go stretch myself over her grave and die like a faithful dog. The world is surely not worth living in now, is it? You had distinctly impressed on me the idea that Catherine was the whole joy of your life: I can't imagine how you think of surviving her loss.'

(ch. 17)

She has hit on the truth; he has indeed meant to die to be with her; but, as he tells Ellen later, he has come up again to the Heights in the firm faith that the spirit of Catherine is accompanying him home and that he will see her there:

'Having reached the Heights, I rushed eagerly to the door. It was fastened; and, I remember that accursed Earnshaw and my wife opposed my entrance. I remember stopping to kick the breath out of them, and then hurrying upstairs, to my room and hers.'

(ch. 29)

He is cruel, not for sadistic self-satisfaction, but out of an overriding passion; so even is Lockwood when, unable to free himself from the child-phantom,

I pulled its wrist on to the broken pane, and rubbed it to and fro till the blood ran down and soaked the bed-clothes.

(ch. 3)

Again the action is not deliberate cruelty; the doer feels no satisfaction, still less pleasure: indeed he emphasizes that 'the intense horror of nightmare' was upon him and that '*terror* made [him] cruel.'

Paradoxically, speech is often more violent than action, and often negates what it seems to suggest. Heathcliff as a boy talks of 'painting the house-front with Hindley's blood' (ch. 6), but, secure in his union with Catherine, does nothing. When his actual revenge comes, it consists in simply letting Hindley ruin himself, while the details are not discussed at all. Even more striking are the abounding allusions, in imagery and speech, to heaven, hell, God, the devil, damnation, the supernatural and the more fearsome figures of folklore. It is constantly suggested that Heathcliff may be a fiend, a hobgoblin, or a devil. He and Catherine, and the other characters, talk of their own future life beyond death with the most startling misuse of the conventional Christian terms. The result is to make the reader take nothing on trust, to reject not only the usual connotations of the concepts but the concepts themselves, and so draw gradually to Emily Brontë's own strange non-Christian sense of the universe.

In this novel with no authorial voice, told wholly by characters, their viewpoints and reliability are structurally and thematically all-important. Almost all characters are narrators at some point. They divide into three groups. The brief incidental tellers of events – the doctor Kenneth or the maid Zillah – are a familiar feature of the novel form, like the 'messengers' of drama: purveyors of information when the main action cannot focus on it. Secondly, characters important to the main action – like Heathcliff, Catherine, Isabella, the younger Catherine – can all be depended on in the traditional way, to be truthful about events, and open about their own feelings, but not necessarily to be adequate or reliable in their interpretations of them.

Separate from all these are what all readers see as the two main narrators, Lockwood and Ellen Dean. Lockwood is unusual in the nineteenth-century novel for being peripheral and (a pseudo-romantic Byronic poseur) not sympathetic to the reader. He is therefore patently unsafe and inadequate as interpreter of character and motives. He too, though, is wholly reliable when telling of facts, the actions and speech of others, and of what happens to himself. The reader must trust him, since for the first three vital chapters he is the only informant there is, and what he tells there is in any case largely corroborated by Ellen later.

Ellen, the main narrator, is central, the only one (barring the comic choric Joseph) who lives through and in the whole action. She is designed to be trustworthy: she tells her tale for no personal reason, but because Lockwood asks her; she contrasts with him in her practical good sense; she expresses natural if not always rational reactions; and she has no *parti pris* except an affection for Hindley, her coeval, and for her two nurslings the younger Catherine and Hareton Earnshaw: all these qualities make her dispassionate and factually truthful about Heathcliff and Catherine. She, too, is in-adequate in her interpretation. She satisfies the reader's urge for normal explanation at the same time as she conveys that no normal or conventional one is adequate, and like the rest of the characters falls short of or beside the mark. A Christian cosmology fails her, and its vocabulary – heaven, hell, damnation, salvation, evil and good, and even human kindness – seem beside the point in the conflict, gradually evolving and finally reconciling over two generations, of dwellers at the Heights and the Grange. Equally in-secure are her alternative impulses to see it in terms of folklore, involving demons, goblins, witches or fairies. However, Ellen has the reader's trust, even though knowing that to ask as she does whether Heathcliff is a 'goblin' (and still more to ask, as Isabella does, 'is he a devil?') is unanswerable because it is the wrong question. She is much more pertinent – and sharply foregrounded – when she breaks off her tale after Catherine's death, to ask Lockwood 'Do you think such people *are* happy in the other world, sir? I'd give a great deal to know' (ch. 16). As he says, the question is 'somewhat heterodox'; it is at the core of the novel. Its answer anticipates Lockwood's position in the novel's last sentence when he 'cannot imagine unquiet slumbers for the sleepers in that quiet earth'. Ellen sees that the just-dead Catherine's corpse 'asserted its own tranquillity, which seemed a pledge of equal quiet for its former inhabitant' (ibid.). Yet Catherine is in some sense far from 'quiet' as long as Heathcliff lives – she can even invade Lockwood's dreams – and even after both are dead Joseph and the boy with the sheep are witness that 'they *walk*'. By such series of hesitant speculations, partial contradictions and reserved judgments, the reader, guided but not decided by the text, becomes the interpreter. No one character has the reader's full vision or the same quantity of evidence. The last word on the topic, wryly, is Ellen's to Lockwood (it could well be Emily Brontë's to the reader): 'You'll judge as well as I can, all these things: at least, you'll think you will, and that's the same' (ch. 17).

Within her only novel Emily Brontë has created the world in her own image, and peopled it with the powerful impulses of her own nature. Much is omitted; but the power of what it contains is unique.

> The earth that wakes one human heart to feeling
> Can centre both the worlds of heaven and hell.

The difficulties that face the reader of *Wuthering Heights* face even more forbiddingly the reader of her poems. While it is possible to approach the novel without any knowledge of whence it sprang, many of the poems are almost unintelligible if their provenance is unknown. While some few are unmistakably great lyrics, many are interesting mainly as evidence of the mind and private world from which the novel sprang. Thirdly, while it has been proved that most, if not all, of them are dramatic monologues – the outbursts of invented characters in imagined situations – several of them draw upon states of apprehension known only to the mystic.

The poems have the same limitations as the novel; they are most at home with elemental and extreme emotions – the intensest love, extreme hate, suffering, fortitude or grief. They work by suggestion rather than reason, and depend upon a close union between man and nature; they express themselves in a highly personal mixture of the almost casually idiomatic and the highly rhetorical, through a limited range of powerful images; they are poems of mood, more often preoccupied with coming death and a lost past than with a living and absorbing present; when they do deal with the present, the tone is most often melancholy or brooding. What are perhaps

Emily Brontë's two best-known lyrics embody many of her most striking qualities – the lines beginning 'No coward soul is mine' and those beginning 'Cold in the earth'.

The first has been taken as her own creed, especially since Charlotte Brontë erroneously stated that they were 'the last lines my sister Emily ever wrote'. (They exist, however, in a manuscript dated January 2, 1846 – nearly three years before her death, differing but little from Charlotte's text.) They would, if so, be remarkable for the daughter of a Low-Church vicar of the Church of England. There is no theology in them: the deity is defined no more than as the

> God within my breast
> Almighty ever-present Deity!
> Life, that in me has rest
> As I, undying Life, have power in Thee!

The final stanzas assert that death shall have no dominion, in a way that shows the same sense of man's relation to the universe as that postulated in the novel, though the terms in which it is expressed here are the converse:

> Though earth and moon were gone,
> And suns and universes ceased to be,
> And thou wert left alone,
> Every existence would exist in Thee.
>
> There is not room for Death,
> Nor atom that this might could render void,
> Thou – THOU art Being and Breath,
> And what THOU art may never be destroyed.

This conclusion is the positive expression of Catherine's negative, her cry that 'if all else remained, and [Heathcliff] were annihilated, the universe would turn to a mighty stranger' (ch. 9).

Although many of Emily Brontë's poems, like 'Cold in the earth',[1] might fairly be termed dramatic monologues, they are far removed from those of that most notable practitioner, Browning. The stance and tone are unusual. There is no place for an auditor and one has no sense that any reader of the poem is being taken into

---

[1] Emily Brontë's own heading to this lyric is *R. Alcona to J. Brenzaida*, alluding to two great figures of the Gondal epic. J. Brenzaida is the Emperor Julius, who was treacherously slain at his own coronation. Rosina Alcona was his wife, with a spirit as fiery as his own, who had disposed of one husband to marry him, who ruled, and had many lovers, afer him. She is the Cleopatra of Emily's epic and has much in common with Catherine Earnshaw.

account: the speaker of this one, the woman wailing for her lover dead for 'fifteen wild Decembers', is speaking to the dead alone. Nor does the poem express any trace of the nostalgia or gentle melancholy that would be natural after so long: she 'forgets' him because she dare not remember a still passionate grief it would kill her to indulge; she

> Dare not indulge in memory's rapturous pain,
> Once drinking deep of that divinest anguish
> How could I seek the empty world again?

The passion is the more fierce for being held in check, for being indeed never indulged. The poem is not an indulgence, but an explanation: as in the novel, still waters run deep and strong, but absence of action is not absence of passion.

Emily Brontë's poetic techniques work upon the mind through the senses and by associations. She keeps to essentials:

> Cold in the earth, and deep snow piled above thee!
> Far, far removed, cold in the dreary grave!
> Have I forgot, my only love, to love thee,
> Severed at last by time's all-severing wave?

This is the germ of the whole. The cold and the vicious 'severance' are spiritual and metaphorical, as well as actual, suffered by the speaker as well as the dead. Cold, distance and time are taken up and explored as the poem progresses, and produce a mass of tensions, for while cold suggests rigidity, the vocabulary and imagery are all of movement and violence – thoughts *hover* and *rest their wings*, wild Decembers *melt* into Spring. Again as in *Wuthering Heights* there comes a point at which the image, impossible in literal terms, comes to be the 'real' truth, with the speaker's

> burning wish to hasten
> Down to that tomb *already more than mine.*
>
>   [my italics]

Although passion is what the reader notices most, a real poetic, controlling intellect is at work without which the passion would be of little worth.

Emily Brontë, on the evidence of the poems, has been termed a mystic. It is true that some of her poems call upon experiences that it is difficult to define in any other way; it is equally true that they too are the utterances of imaginary characters in invented situations. Best known among them are perhaps the lines beginning

'He comes with western winds',[1] probably one of the most remarkable attempts to define and realize the indefinable and unrealistic that has ever been made.

The poems of Charlotte and Anne, though they achieve competence, though Anne wrote one or two hymns that are still used, and though Charlotte was consciously competent in rhythm and metre where Emily often faltered, are nevertheless the words of Mercury after the songs of Apollo. Had their authors not been novelists, they would never have been considered as poets. But apologies are unnecessary. The Brontës stand secure. It is few families that can claim one good novelist, one great one, and one woman of genius who produced a unique novel and a handful of immortal verse.

---

[1] This poem begins two lines earlier in some editions, with the words 'A messenger of hope comes every night to me'; the reason is that the lyric is an extract from a longer, narrative, Gondal poem and that this monologue begins, properly, in the middle of a stanza.

7

MRS GASKELL AND GEORGE ELIOT

Barbara Hardy

Although there are two places – Knutsford in Cheshire, and Manchester – which provided sources and images for much of Elizabeth Gaskell's writing, hers was not a life which can be very obviously mined for constructive criticism. We have to observe the background of Unitarianism, on her father's side and her husband's, her domesticity, her social contacts with the industrial world and the literary world, in the North, in London and in Europe. We need to insist on her close and sympathetic knowledge of the lives of the poor. Her letters show how she and her daughters were exhausted and appalled by their relief work in Manchester during the cotton famine of the early sixties, for instance. And there are many points of detail in the novels that can be traced back to a direct or indirect biographical source, like the change of faith of Mr Hale in *North and South*, which transforms but uses her own father's conscientious resignation from the Unitarian ministry, or the celebrated anecdotes about the cow's flannel coat and the cat who swallowed the lace in *Cranford*. But if there were crises in her emotional and intellectual life, like the crises which mark the lives of the art of Dickens, Thackeray, and George Eliot, they remain invisible. Hers is a remarkable and various body of novels and stories which have to be looked at in and for themselves.

This is of course not to deny that her most important works are very potent social expressions both in their steady and complete presentation of a society in whole and parts, as in *Cranford* and *Wives and Daughters*, and as criticisms and appeals, showing a view of contemporary society, its suffering, irrationality and injustice, in that clear but never impersonal mirror which she holds up to her time. Critics of the late fifties and sixties, rightly reacting against an older and pretty persistent view of her art as the product of a minor, charming, but slender talent, emphasized the eloquence of her sociological thinking and feeling, and both Kathleen Tillotson, in

Novels of the 1840s, and Edgar Wright examined her didacticism and handling of social facts. Wright, and Arthur Pollard also, stressed her importance as a psychological novelist, whose social analysis depends very markedly on a realistic handling of the language, manners and passions of human beings. Looking at her in the large context of the Victorian novel, I am impressed anew by her freedom from simplification and caricature. The great social critics in nineteenth-century English fiction are, I suppose, Jane Austen, Dickens and Thackeray. Theirs is basically an art of fable, of bold and telling outline, of the conspicuous and critical embodiment of ideas in satiric forms. Mrs Gaskell is unusual as a social novelist in her avoidance of satire. Not that this avoidance is always a merit in her novels: at times she too is writing a kind of fable, most notably in her first novel, *Mary Barton*. Here the portrait of the manufacturing class and of trade unionism is the worst kind of caricature, crude, very simplified, stereotyped and lacking both the bite of humour and its frank admission of bias and exaggeration. But strengths and weaknesses are often very intimately associated and if we pay for this absence of satire by such embarrassing and implausible crudities, we also gain the particularly intimate, alert and live creations of her sympathy, which manage, almost miraculously, to stay well on this side of sentimentality.

Pollard has truly said that Mrs Gaskell 'is never a propagandist; or if she is, she is only a propagandist for sympathy'. This seems to point to the heart of her individuality as a novelist, as well as showing the way to reconcile the praise of her sociological imagination with that of her psychological powers. If I had to fix a label to her special contribution to what we conveniently call 'The English novel', I would describe her as essentially a novelist of sensibility. It is a phrase which describes her changing powers throughout her career. Although she wrote only six important novels, one fine *nouvelle, Cousin Phillis*, and one of the best Victorian biographies, *The Life of Charlotte Brontë* (as well as many stories and sketches, some good but many really very undistinguished), her talent is a various one.

Mrs Gaskell did not say a great deal about her art but what she did say provides an excellent entry into the imagined world of her novels. That very phrase, 'imagined world', is a commonplace but generally useful critical formula, expressing the novel's inventiveness, unity, and double concern with the individual life and the portrayal of environment. But it seems rather inappropriately used of Mrs Gaskell. When she talks about her novels, she insists, rather as D. H. Lawrence did, on her own therapeutic relation to her creations. This comes out very noticeably, for instance, when she compares her own writing with that of Charlotte Brontë, whom she knew and responded to sympathetically. She says this, in a letter of April, 1853:

The difference between Miss Brontë and me is that she puts all her naughtiness into her books, and I put all my goodness. I am sure that she works off a great deal that is morbid *into* her writing, and *out* of her life; and my books are so far better than I am that I often feel ashamed of having written them as if I were a hypocrite.

In no way at odds with this comparison, I think, is her suggestion that *Mary Barton* was a novel which perhaps suffered from working off too much that was morbid into the novel out of her life. It is well known that she undertook the novel, at her husband's suggestion, after the death of her ten-month-old son from scarlet fever, and she talks revealingly about its darkness and its origin in what she thinks might be 'a wrong motive for writing . . . sure only to produce a failure'. She saw the novel as an especially effective refuge and calm refreshment for women, but concluded, after a good deal of wounding criticism, not entirely of an aesthetic kind, that she was perhaps in error when she used the composition of the novel as a 'refuge to exclude the memory of painful scenes which would force themselves upon my remembrance'.

To begin then, with *Mary Barton*. Seeing it as a novel of sensibility is essential when we look at its origin in personal suffering, and when we look at her reactions to the criticism of the novel, so different from the confident resentment of insensitivity, which can be found, for instance, in George Eliot. In Mrs Gaskell's self-doubting, honestly explanatory and searching comments on the response (not so much of literary critics as of people in Manchester of whom she knew) can be found the sense of a wounded nerve of feeling disappointed or frustrated in the very act of heartfelt appeal. She has this to say in a letter about the possible imbalance or injustice which certain readers felt about the novel:

I can remember now that the prevailing thought in my mind at the time when the tale was silently forming itself and impressing me with the force of a reality, was the seeming injustice of the inequalities of Fortune. Now, if they occasionally appeared unjust to the more fortunate, they must be-wilder an ignorant man full of rude, illogical thought, and full also of sympathy for suffering which appealed to him through his senses. I fancied I saw how all this might lead to a course of action which might appear right for a time to the bewildered mind of such a one, but that this course of action, violating the eternal laws of God, would bring with it its own punishment of an avenging conscience far more difficult to bear than any worldly privation. Such thoughts I now believe, on looking back, to have been the origin of the book. 'John Barton' was the original title of the book.

Mary Barton, as it was eventually called, is a novel which cuts a deep channel both for the personal bereavement and her sympathy for the sufferings of the industrial poor. Those feelings are so merged in their profound and fierce flow that I would make no attempt to speculate about their causal relation: feelings for children are conspicuous, and highly relevant in the book, but coming invariably out of all such feelings, from every aspect of this story of family unity, disintegration and pain, is a bewildered and frustrated social questioning. Arthur Pollard quotes her attempt to reason with a poor man about his bitter hostility to the rich, and his answer, reasoned in tears, 'Aye, ma'am but have ye ever seen a child clemmed to death?' *Mary Barton* begins with a revised version of this question when John Barton asks what the 'gentlefolk' have ever done for him:

If my child lies dying (as poor Tom lay, with his white lips quivering, for want of better food than I could give him), does the rich man bring the wine or broth that will save his life?

The novel is punctuated by comments on child-death. Some are very muted, and no less touching for that, as in the words 'the aged, the feeble, the children, when they die, are scarcely noted by the world'. Some are more strikingly personal. Moreover, the novel insistently takes us back to the childhood even of the adult characters, and certainly two of the long digressions (sometimes criticized as instances of imperfect grasp of construction) seem to be justified by this insistence. Job Legh's story of how he and his friend brought their grand-daughter Margaret, as a small and very helpless baby, from London to Manchester, and Alice Wilson's tales of her childhood (to which she reverts in her happy deathbed) both give new colour to the primary feeling for children. Job's story has a comic, even grotesque, way of loving and pathetic appeal, Alice's has a radiant, innocent, pastoral joy. Not only is there this variety of emotional colour, and the much-needed relief from the horrors and desolations of the child-deaths, but also there is always Mrs Gaskell's characteristic social and psychological particularity. I would claim that it is this particularity that distinguishes her 'morbidity' from the strong general demands, sentimental and distastefully morbid, of Dickens's Nell and Tiny Tim. Her morbidity is excessive, in a strict aesthetic sense, taking us out of the novel in a way which is both painful and under-distanced, but which also makes it appropriately painful propaganda for the sympathies. It is revelatory fiction such as George Eliot was trying to write in *Scenes of Clerical Life*, but its materials have a horror, pity and passionate hysteria, which find no place in George Eliot.

This hysteria is in the materials. Mrs Gaskell dramatizes the passions, but controls them and keeps them individual. At times she steps outside the story to reason and explain, to placate her gentle reader and beg a tolerance for the violence of these agitators and assassins, but then she says, 'Let us now return to individuals'. Her sensibility takes in and shows the full range of experience, to take us, as Zola does, from comfort to bleakness, from nourishment to starvation, from some small colour and ornament to bareness and squalor. The interestingness of the novel and its emotional appeal go together. She wants to show the fall from one state to a worse, like any tragedian. She wants also to show, in a sharply argumentative way, the working-class culture, its ceremony, sociability, hospitality, song and science. Thus she creates not only a realistic picture of the culture (in a way that Gissing, when he takes us inside the houses and habits of the poor, usually fails to do), but gives animation and richness to what is not just a fable, and shows not the being of two nations, but their becoming. If she simply contrasted the starvation and disease in the poor home with the breakfasting of the rich (as she does at one point in the novel) we would have an effective simplification but a less complete picture, and, ultimately, a less potent appeal to the heart. Hers is, like George Eliot's, a very conservative imagination, and these novels combine a realistic report with a very modest demand, not for a radical redistribution, but for a minimal nourishment for body and soul.

A similar truthfulness comes out of her knowledge that her two nations are not all that separate in origins: she knows Mrs Carson, who was working-class, is particularly isolated and barren because she has no resources, and we appreciate also the importance of goods and money, in a novel about the material, not the hereditary, basis of class, about labour and capital, not about blood and rank. I stress this truthfulness because the novel's plotting, as too often in Mrs Gaskell, is strained and even implausible. She said that John Barton was her hero, the character round whom 'all the others formed themselves ... the person with whom all my sympathies went, with whom I tried to identify myself at the time, because I believed from personal observation that such men were not uncommon', and his displacement is the novel's great failing. Her publishers apparently persuaded her to call the novel *Mary Barton*, but the chief cause for the change must be the shift in the emotional centre. With John's guilt comes his inevitable absence from the scene, and our lack of access to his inner life. Though the thread of Mary's feelings has from the beginning been woven in with his, it too rather thins out in the more heavily plotted final episodes, where the novel turns from sensitive social appeal and psychology to the sensational, highly active, and rather over-optimistic conclusion. It is perhaps because of the powers of feeling in the main body of the novel that the last third is so disappointing.

Like *Mary Barton*, the other novels, whatever their material and themes, have this potency and variety of feeling. Even the stagey villain, Harry Carson, his father, and Esther, the prostitute, lose a little of their staginess in being brought into the mainstream of feeling: we see them too as children or parents, not as divided from the rest of the action in melodramatic stereotype throughout. The only other novel which shares the partial staginess and the over-optimistic ending is *Ruth*, another social novel, separated from *Mary Barton* by *Cranford*, and thus making it impossible for us to talk about Mrs Gaskell's 'sociological period'.

Mary Barton's powerful topicality (as a novel about Chartism appearing less than ten years after the Charter had been rejected, and at a time of depression, insecurity, and great want) made it a successful and much-discussed novel. *Ruth* had a similar success. It was very widely reviewed, receiving high praise for its truth and moral beauty, as well as hostility and disapproval. Mrs Gaskell was deeply hurt by the disapproval, but even though the book was banned by fathers of families and even burnt, she believed in its seriousness and fervour. There are perhaps two chief reasons for the antagonism it aroused: its subject, which was seduction and illegitimacy, and its theme, that of Hardy's *Tess*, the moral innocence of the seduced girl.

It is in fact a very narrowly didactic book, which deals with a much more simply saintly woman than Tess, and which is a fable of atonement, by love and death. One might say that Ruth's nobility almost puts her beyond the typical social problem which she is intended to represent. The book has certain flaws: it begins by showing the seduction of a very simple little girl, and eventually shows her as a much more intelligent and complex woman, rather startlingly enlarging her character and creating a resolution which to my mind makes for disunity and implausibility. We may very well understand how the flaw came about. Mrs Gaskell shows the inner life of Ruth sporadically, so that some of her reactions are available, some rather arbitrarily absent. The necessary sexual reticence of the Victorian novel, even in the forties, meant that our knowledge of Ruth is really very incomplete, and though some aspects of her sensibility are very finely presented – like her reactions to the natural scene and to people in Wales – some of the portraiture is rather external. In the later parts of the novel Ruth's fears and insecurity about her child, especially when her seducer comes back into her life, are movingly and persistently shown, as are the feelings and moral life of the Bensons and the Bradshaws. Live and moving too is the more reticent but decorous treatment of the alienation and reserve of Leonard, the child, after he finds out that he is illegitimate, and the breaking of shame by eloquent pride in the moment when he finds that his mother is a beloved public heroine. But there are ellipses and dead patches in the novel, and the apotheosis by death seems at once inevitable, and unadventurous. Unlike *Mary Barton* and *North and South*, the novel fails to give a complete enough rendering of its characters. What is meant to be another typical plea on behalf of social suffering becomes inappropriately idealized – why plead for saints like Ruth? – and over-simplified – how about the sympathy needed by more ordinary victims of the social traps? But it must be admitted that the idealized portrait has considerable beauty and if the novel is read as a study in saintliness rather than in sin, its humanity and drama will be more impressive.

Mrs Gaskell's novels always have the interest of particularity. Ruth's idealization never takes off from the solid earth to become stereotyped or lachrymose, like the portraits of Agnes Wickfield or Esther Summerson. In *Ruth* there is the solidity and vividness of the comic-serious relationships of the Bensons and the Bradshaws, the enacted and implied complexity of Jemima Bradshaw, and the unpatronizing beauty and humour of the characterization of the servant, Sally. In *North and South*, the best of the three social novels, there is this kind of solid and varied realism of character and a much freer treatment of the element of fable. Mrs Gaskell realizes at this stage that fictions are created by people, necessarily but falsely, and that degree of simplification and crudity which escaped her control in *Mary Barton* and *Ruth* seems, in this remarkable novel, to have been assimilated, dramatized, and finally criticized.

In *North and South* it is the characters, not only the author, who construct fables. The novel shows the dangerous inadequacy of fables, and its characters are educated out of their fictions and face the complexity of loving, working, serving, and leading. Having said this, I must add that the novel's ability to face complexity and do, as George Eliot said we must, 'without opiates', is in the end limited. Like most Victorian novels, it mends matters with authorial magic, and the problems of love and industrial failure are solved and dismissed by coincidence and that favourite device of the bourgeois novel, the unexpected legacy.

Mrs Gaskell shares these limitations with Dickens and George Eliot and Charlotte Brontë – with all the great Victorian novelists, perhaps, except the Thackeray of *Vanity Fair*'s great, sour, truthful satire. In spite of them, she writes a novel of penetrating psychology. In the previous novels we are moved by the poignancy of feeling, which makes the ever-interesting and effectively appealing narrative medium, but in *North and South* there is a new element, of surprising psychological content. We are moved and held not just by the dramatic liveliness, but by what it reveals of human nature.

This revealed depth of content is the fact of human fiction, the fabling about *North and South* which forms the central dream of the novel. It is a dream dreamt by the heroine, Margaret Hale, and like many human dreams, it is dreamt as a stabilizing reaction to instability. Intuitively or deliberately, Mrs Gaskell shows Margaret on the eve of returning to the place and parents she has known only discontinuously during her adolescence. Her return brings her not the pastoral peace and family joy she expects and needs, after the disruptions and oppressive joys of London life, but a father who is about to resign his ministry, and indeed a father and a mother who lean on her, heavily and pathetically. This is the first stage in her waking and dreaming: the pastoral dream and the childhood idyll fail. When the Hales move to the North, the dream returns again in a protective and temporarily restorative fashion. She has been teased in London for the sort of pastoral idealized picture she has of Helstone, the village of her childhood, and in the grim Darkshire where they try the new life, the pastoral dream is first needed, then tried, and, after a long, slow testing in complex experience and varied relations, found wanting.

It is not the only illusion in the novel. Matched with it, in strength, unity and partial plausibility, is Mr Thornton's unenlightened belief in autonomy, freedom and power of master over worker. This is a dream which, like Margaret's, is dreamt by someone sufficiently sensitive and intelligent to allow intransigent experience to shatter the dream. Both dreams are theoretic, and when Margaret learns what the urban North is like, and when Thornton learns the humanity and limited freedom of his workers, theory collapses before the largeness and complexity of life as it is. As Arthur Pollard is careful to point out, Thornton remains a benevolent master, putting his faith in workers' welfare and good communication. Moreover, he does not succeed in trade but fails. As in the earlier novels, what is impressive is not a confident radicalism but a tentative questioning of the present, not a grasp of economics but a grasp of the individual case. She takes a step beyond *Mary Barton* and *Ruth* in the very mutedness of *North and South*: the action is on a smaller, less heroic scale, and there is no trace of the stereotyped fable of *Mary Barton*.

The novel moves insistently from and between its two personal centres of feeling. At last her novel of sensibility is both balanced and complete. We oscillate between Margaret and Thornton, and their range of sensibility prominently includes pride, passion, anger, sensitive sympathy, and moral admiration. These passions largely make up the characters and their affinity. They also unify the action as well as the characters because they are available, most genuinely, in the intimate personal relationship of sexual and filial love, and in a series of reactions to society that cut across class divisions. This kind of emotional continuity is, in its very nature, inaccessible to illustration, especially in an essay, and I can only briefly refer to typically rich and mobile scenes like that of Thornton's first proposal of marriage to Margaret, the scene in which she first makes friends with Higgins and Bessy, and the scene where Thornton first goes to see Higgins in his home. You will notice the way Mrs Gaskell always shows or tells – usually both – what the characters are feeling, and how she pushes on the emotional development and change variously and continuously. There are no *lacunae* where you do not know (and need to know) what the character is feeling, as in *Ruth*. You will notice too how often the feelings are not specialized, not kept in separate compartments. Thornton's anger at Margaret's refusal resembles his anger at Higgins's egalitarian and rational honesty, and these strong characters can feel furious and respectful as their pride and anger fight, against each other's pride and anger, and against themselves. One of the admirably honourable qualities in the characters of Mrs Gaskell is the reasonable passion. If Jane Austen is the first English novelist to show and be aware of showing a reasonable sexual love, so Mrs Gaskell deserves some praise for showing, with depth and delicacy, a reasonable pride, a reasonable anger, a reasonable despair. The characters are animated, distinguished, and, finally, unified by their feelings.

It is this dramatized sensibility, I believe, which takes us over the weak spots of the action, like the melodramatic and coincidental business of Frederick's return, Thornton's encounter with Margaret and her brother and the consequent misunderstanding. It is the display and analysis of passions and intelligence which makes such an effective medium for what I have called the theme of dreams and fables. Margaret is forced by reason, respect and sympathy to see that North is not wrong to South's right, and Thornton is forced by reason, respect and sympathy to see that communication between master and servant is not only possible but honourable, and that violence and despair have their reasons, as well as their madness.

The novel has many complex moments of feeling that lie beyond this simple account, and such complexities are present in all the other novels, which are less conspicuous in their social criticism. To go back to *Cranford*, her second novel, we find there not only the charm, pathos, and humour for which it has always been celebrated, but a considerable complexity and subtlety in the presentation of feeling. It is a novel with a displaced personal centre, unlike the others. It is a deliberately handled, almost a Jamesian, displacement. The narrator is Mary Smith, whose sympathy and irony are both more sophisticated and more available than the sensibilities of any of the more involved characters, and with Mary we gradually accumulate a full view of the story. The true active centre is Miss Matty. We piece together, from retrospect, hint, and expressive incident, her timidity, her courage, her spinster's loneliness, her lost love, her family feeling and her suffering. Ultimately, when all is pieced together, it becomes a story of unguessed-at integrity. The bits fit together: Miss Matty's pride, consistency and real dignity when she, unlike the other dear ladies, assumes that they will not accept Mrs Jamieson's afterthought invitation; her insistence on honouring the Town and County Bank note instead of buying the new dress; and her forbearance when Martha wants to have a follower; all these illustrative incidents create the strong side of Miss Matty, whom we, like Mary, first see as a sweet, eccentric, not very bright, rather dependent old lady. We piece together the story too, first seeing the man she might have married, in the opaque humour of the visit, which allows no tremble of sentiment to get through, and later learning slowly what had happened, through odd bits of gossip, and then in the news of his death. The piecemeal method, like the indirect discovery, is natural, in this most natural-seeming chronicle where naturalness is decorous, and moving, as we accumulate impressions in a continuous process of slight shocks and revisions. Moreover, the rambling and anecdotal form picks up links in this process. What looked at first like (and was probably started as) a series of episodic sketches, turns out to have a very cunning continuity, quality, and power to move. What looked like insipidity or mere charm turns out to rebuke us for having jumped to interpret it as insipidity or mere charm. *Cranford* teaches us, by a dynamic process, not to be too easily charmed by quaintness, not to pity precipitately what we may have eventually also to admire. Without wishing to analyse its delicacy out of existence, I should like to praise it for the kind of delicacy which reveals strength. It is an apparently unassuming novel, and its apparent charm and sweetness are as profound and as deceptive as Miss Matty's. It is a novel whose form is perfectly appropriate to its content, so that the two are not separable.

Cousin Phillis, Sylvia's Lovers, and *Wives and Daughters,* coming together, in that order, at the end of Mrs Gaskell's short life, all possess the perfection and subtlety of *Cranford* and add new profundities of vision and feeling. *Cousin Phillis,* her very best piece of short fiction, also has a displaced and detached narrator. Paul Manning is rather like Nelly Dean, in *Wuthering Heights,* not all that detached from the passions he observes and narrates. Again, by a slight delicate shift of a kind usually praised in Henry James, Mrs Gaskell makes a perfect movement from expectation to surprise. We learn to read Paul as narrator, but in the precipitating event of the story, he becomes a responsible agent, and yet preserves the observer's role, which has encouraged his fault and determines the nature of his punishment. It is also, like *Wives and Daughters,* a perfect instance of control and reserve: its joys and griefs are largely inner and unspoken ones, its very action is contained in the mind and in the heart. It is also, like everything she wrote, full of psychological variety. Mrs Gaskell really has no minor characters, and both Holdsworth and Holman are as complete, complex, and surprising in their individuality as Phillis herself. The beautiful and bookish country girl, vulnerable, strong, romantic, realistic, loving and sharp, is a brilliant creation who might even, read at the wrong time, suggest a certain softness in Hardy's Tess.

Wives and Daughters, like *Cousin Phillis,* reveals almost unbearable sadness, and shows how human beings bear it. The intensity of grief and the reserve or resolve that makes heartbreak endurable or even mendable, is shown in Molly Gibson, with a patience, pride, and self-aware humour which belongs both to the presentation and to the character. The novel is most remarkably modest, quiet and genial. Molly's passionate feelings are recognized and proffered in a complexity which cannot even be named – does she feel 'anger, dislike, indignation', her author asks, and takes refuge in the intensity and open suggestiveness of an image: 'It was as if the piece of solid ground on which she stood had broken from the shore, and she was drifting out into an infinite sea alone'. Molly's loss of her happy life with her father, then later, the loss of her lover, and later still, the temporary loss of her good name, are all fairly small and fairly private griefs, compared with the deaths and pangs and shames in *Mary Barton*, *Ruth*, or even *North and South*, but they are real, important, and fully expressive of the problems of moral and social growth and adjustment.

Molly and Sylvia of *Sylvia's Lovers*, in my opinion Mrs Gaskell's greatest novel, are interesting passive characters, whose lives, like those of many women in and out of fiction, tend to be rather more manipulated than the lives of men. Their passiveness, however, is quite different. Sylvia's life is highly determined, and by social forces: her lover is carried off by the press-gang, her father hanged for violence against the gang, her mother's reason destroyed, and her marriage made by the isolation, desolation and economic dependence brought about by all these incidents. But her feelings, unlike Molly's, are not only strong but have to be expressed: and if she is acted upon, her vitality of feeling becomes an active force. It attacks and exiles her husband in its sheer ferocity. But her passions are complex, and if Philip had learnt to read them as we do, he would have seen her characteristic shift, brought about by sympathy and by reason, from rejection to forgiveness. In *Sylvia's Lovers* and *Wives and Daughters* Mrs Gaskell seems less interested in the development of sensibility, as in some of the earlier novels, than in its individual pattern, and consequences. She shows, in a way very anticipatory of Hardy, the ironic clash between individual passions. Mrs Gaskell sets out the kind of vulnerability, innocence, pride, and acceptance, which we will find typical of Molly's adult life, in the early scene where Molly is lost and neglected and let down by her future stepmother. In the varying crises of the novel, the same pattern of feeling and response is provoked, developed, and worked out. Similarly, Sylvia's passionateness, sensuousness, imaginative sympathy, and toughness are shown in the first scene when she goes to buy a cloak and stays to cheer and grieve with the crowd, and are repeated later, many times. The cycle returns most importantly when she refuses to forgive the man responsible for her father's death, but then recoils on her own hardness. This anticipates the revengeful unforgiving passion and recoil to love, with which she meets the discovery of Philip's deception. Philip's track of feeling plays against and with hers, and they are both two of the most moving, emotionally complex and morally tolerant studies of human strength and weakness in the English novel. Sylvia has a marvellous vitality and range of passions which is seldom shown in fiction apart from high intelligence. And the novel's ending, which brings us face to face with inevitable hurt, unnecessary hurt, spent life, new life, strong love, endurance, exhaustion, and the joining of reconciliation with parting, is one of the saddest experiences in the range of Mrs Gaskell's imaginative achievement.

Mrs Gaskell wrote to tell George Eliot how much she admired *Scenes of Clerical Life* and *Adam Bede*, and George Eliot replied saying that she had been aware that her attitude to Life and Art 'had some affinity with the feeling which . . . inspired "Cranford" and the earlier chapters of "Mary Barton"', and had read *Cranford* while writing *Scenes* and *Mary Barton* while writing *Adam Bede*. What she thought about the affinity is a matter for guessing. We know that she also liked *The Life of Charlotte Brontë* and *Sylvia's Lovers* but was critical of the '"dramatic effect" and "love of sharp contrasts"' which she said were obstacles to complete sympathy and typicality in *Ruth*. She rather liked such contrasts herself, though they were perhaps given subtlety and finesse by the greater degree of complexity which they generally possess. There is an affinity between her early work and Mrs Gaskell's attitude to life and art, in their sympathy, a quality of the imagination not restricted to the creativity of art. It is interesting that George Eliot speaks of the affinity as felt in the early work. In *Scenes* there is not only the deliberate attempt to show ordinariness and average sensibility, but even the convention of a spectator's *persona*. There is also the half-critical but sympathetic reaction to quaintness and humour. But such novelistic affinity was not lasting. The sympathy that showed itself in analysis of average lives and ordinary sensibility created all Mrs Gaskell's novels, but none of George Eliot's, except for the three stories in *Scenes* and *Silas Marner*, all, significantly, short pieces. She began by wanting to show ordinary life to over-stimulated palates and sensational expectations, but very soon moved from homely realism to what was truly her *métier*, the drama of intellect and sensibility in strong and unusual characters.

We should carefully distinguish the social and the psychological aims here. Both novelists genuinely succeed in showing the lower-class sensibility and suffering, after the manner of Dutch painting, as George Eliot says in *Adam Bede*. But Mrs Gaskell is very much more socially and politically didactic, despite her conservatism, than George Eliot, and one might argue too that she is more sharply sceptical and less complacent than George Eliot in her treatment of labour-relations in *Adam Bede* or of political agitation in *Felix Holt*. George Eliot is much more confident of the rightness of Adam's attitude to his more frivolous fellow-workers, and of the wrongness of the mob-violence than Mrs Gaskell's more troubled questioning ever allows her to be. George Eliot seldom goes into the psychology of the 'wrong' action as sympathetically as Mrs Gaskell. Indeed, one reason for the revival of interest in Mrs Gaskell may lie in her appealing lack of moral absolutism. George Eliot is much closer to the very unmodern Shavian character who is certain of the difference between right and wrong, both in political and personal morality. She is also more rationally in control of her moral system. When she criticized Mrs Gaskell for siding so simply with Branwell Brontë, we can perhaps see her rationality set against the more impetuous sympathies of the older novelist. The comparison is ironic though, since it was Mrs Gaskell who wrote both to admire the younger woman's novels *and* to wish that she was really Mrs Lewes. But even George Eliot's social deviation was moral and rational, perhaps a little doctrinaire.

What George Eliot swiftly moves on to do is to depict the social and personal dramas whose protagonist has considerable stature. Adam Bede, she says, is not an ordinary man. His rationality, his intelligence, and his creative competence make him the first of her line of extraordinary heroes and heroines. They are always embedded in a 'world' of Amos Bartons, Silas Marners, and Hetty Sorrels, but their mind always provides a complex and articulate stage for inner action. George Eliot's characters have a capacity for moral action and development which seems, pretty clearly, to derive from her own experience, transformed, varied, and inventively recreated though it was.

Mary Ann Evans, as she was born, had the kind of heavily plotted life of crisis that we find in her novels. Even as a young woman, she was very sensitive to periodicity, discontinuity, and development. What seems to have been a temperamental cyclical quality must have encouraged and in its turn been further provoked by larger crises. George Eliot is very like Wordsworth in the way she seems to need and perhaps to create crises which force a formulation of identity. They shared an acute sense of continuity and discontinuity: of needing and losing a feeling of temporal unity in which past, present, and even future seemed to be linked, and of needing and losing a feeling of unity of sensibility, in which reason and the passions seemed to be linked. George Eliot can see life as divided into poetry and prose, as a series of movements and losses, of moving from 'the poetry of girlhood', 'the poetry of love and marriage', 'the poetry of maternity' and 'the very poetry of duty' into the world of 'naked prose'. This kind of pattern can be very easily traced in most of her novels as a process of illusion and vision which takes us from dream to dream until we are – at times by assumption rather than fictional demonstration – 'nearer reality'. The whole process is a mid-Victorian evolutionary myth, itself an illusion persuasively grounded on an awareness of the psychological processes of deception, dream and drug.

In her personal life, however, we see a series of crises arranged, naturally enough, in a less evolutionary sequence. There was the first crisis of identity and continuity when, in 1848, she stopped going to church, in an almost sacramental disclosure of her loss of Christian faith. There followed a deeply troubling sense of dislocation, uprootedness, and subsequently an attempt to restore good relations with her father, in the realization that there was emotional continuity even if belief had been sharply broken. The second crisis, about which we know rather little, in terms of the chronicle of inner life, comes in 1854, when she went to Europe with George Henry Lewes. In her letters to some of her friends, to whom she can admit the truth about their unmarried 'marriage', and in a letter to her brother Isaac, in which she cannot tell the truth, the attempt to hang on the past, and to the personal tradition of family unity, is plain. It is this need for a temporal and personal unity which explains her gratification when, on her marriage to John Cross, Isaac wrote to break the long silence and to forgive.

Her own life was no doubt even more eroded and discontinuous than we know, but these two very conspicuous crises involved a break with the past, choice and conflict between emotional conservatism and intellectual and emotional courage, and provide the model for her art. Characteristic imagery of her novels always reminds us of the importance of a sense of unity: the image of the labyrinth, the snapped thread, the path, and the current, amongst others, all stand as emblems for the dramatic choices and conflicts to be found in her life and in her books.

It is the content as well as the structure of personal experience that creates art from life. Because she rejected Evangelicalism, which at some stages was as anti-life and narrowly puritanical as her aunt's and Dinah's Methodism, in favour of a life-devoted humanism, her novels consistently and persistently make a plea for social love, fellowship, duty to people. If the insistence on human relationship as a duty replaces the Christian ethic (in her case, as seen in some of her early gloomy letters, an especially uncreative and unattractive ethic), so the sense of collective creation took the place of the Christian immortality. The Positivist hymn, 'O let me join the choir invisible' shows this replacement, and so also does the emphasis placed in the novels on the contribution to society, like Adam Bede's and Caleb Garth's land-improvements, or – twisted ironically – Rosamond Vincy's deceptive legacy from a fine musician's dead touch.

There is the value, too, attached to moral self-determinism, as it is seen in all the novels but most plainly in the wrong moral choices of Tito Melema in *Romola*, set out as a pattern of deterioration, and the right moral choices of Maggie, set out as a rather more complex and unsteady pattern of growth. This gives to the novels something like the systematic, confident, and usually optimistic framework of the Christian Providence novels of Defoe or Charlotte Brontë. It is the kind of firm moral pattern and reference that is both typically Victorian in its humanist substitutions, and typical of George Eliot.

If this kind of pattern were the only moral interest to be found in the novels of George Eliot, the reader would do well to prefer Mrs Gaskell. But George Eliot's imagination creates characters, events and relationships that have an individual colour and complexity that light up the system, create great novels, make sense to us today, make a picture out of the diagram, *incarnate* (her word) the ideas.

Scenes of Clerical Life show how soon she could look sympathetically at the religious life, whether successful or unsuccessful, and they show too her interest, even within the span of fairly short stories (first serialized as two-part tales in *Blackwood's Edinburgh Magazine*), in the ethic of love. She dramatizes lovingly both the great demands of human intimacy and need, and Wordsworth's 'little, nameless, unremembered acts/Of kindness and of love', with their warming or restorative powers. The *Scenes* show, too, her interest in human development, though this is drawn in a very simplified pattern, and is sometimes rather said to have happened than shown to have happened. On the whole, the process of growth is not melodramatized but implied in the crucial moment, rather than set out at length. There is the awakening moment, as when Caterina strikes the piano, an incident which very effectively dramatizes and particularizes the metaphor of 'striking a chord' and plausibly restores past feeling after breakdown. There is the temporary growth, which is *not* a final transformation, when Amos Barton throws himself on his wife's grave not only in grief but in the desperate effort to retain grief. Such events show George Eliot's emphasis on the continuity of feeling.

If there are these good moments, there are also the weak ones, such as the assumption or appearance of growth and conversation or change in Janet Dempster, Tryan or Gilfil, where difficulties are passed over and the resounding triumph over the victory of love is scarcely earned. But the *Scenes* have good moments of humour, and at their best an honest, Wordsworthian gaucheness.

George Eliot's psychological powers were no doubt inhibited by the chosen materials. Unlike Mrs Gaskell, she needed a highly complex intellectual and creative centre in character. Once this is achieved, as in Adam, Maggie, Dorothea, Felix, Esther, Romola, Gwendolen, Deronda, Mordecai, she can then produce marvellously live and sympathetic small studies of the simple soul. Hetty Sorrel's narrow little fantasy-life, with scarcely room in it for more than clothes and faces, is an animated and functional mini-ature, but the central characters of Adam and Arthur give George Eliot her proper scope. In them she takes time and space to show two very different types of moral character, both changing, both clearly conditioned by position, possessions, and economic morality, both in a way self-regarding and narrow, even though one acts benevolently and the other selfishly. Perhaps we can see here why a novelist who so delighted in antithesis, both of character and event, should criticize the contrasts in Mrs Gaskell. George Eliot's formalism is always overlaid and qualified by a complex pattern of resemblance, difference, and change. Her contrasts are very mobile, so that when we think we are reading them accurately, we may be caught out, and suddenly forced to see Dinah's limitations of sympathy as well as Hetty's, or Adam's hardness as well as Arthur's.

The novels of George Eliot depend on a constant presence and

movement of feeling, like Mrs Gaskell's, but the more in-
tellectualized subject makes for a cross-hatching of feeling and
analysis. Mrs Gaskell is the kind of novelist whose inner action is
filled to the brim by the passions and reflections of the characters.
George Eliot's, despite her intellectually eloquent characters, has a
space between the life of the created world and the world of author
and reader. There was a time, not so long ago, when it was
necessary to explain and justify the insistent presence and commentary of the omniscient author in the novels of George Eliot, but
more recent criticism has shown the mobility, the varying function,
and the dramatization of the author's presence, both in language
and imagery. It would be a mistake, however, to insist too strongly
on George Eliot's dramatic merits. Henry James, happily and just-
ifiably praising his own creation in the Preface to *The Portrait of a
Lady*, said that he had tried to achieve – and believed he had
achieved – scenes of inner action which had 'the vivacity of picture
and the economy of drama'. George Eliot's own commentary has
the vivacity, but not the economy. It is an essential part of her
individuality as a novelist that there should be this uneconomical
spread, the excess of reflection.

It is this authorial centre from which the feelings of the novel are
directed, and I would wish to emphasize its sensibility, as well as its
intellectual activity. It is very rare to find the author's voice commenting in order simply to explain or analyse: even where explanation and analysis is present, it is presented in the medium of
feeling. Because George Eliot tends to have a fairly small spectrum
of feeling 'for' and 'about' her characters, the light and shade is
chiefly presented in the dramatized actions and language, and in
each novel there is a movement to and from this drama and the
personal centre. Her voice tends to speak compassionately,
sometimes satirically, sometimes in a combination of irony and
sympathy, sometimes affectionately, sometimes wryly. It speaks 'for'
and 'about' the characters but it also speaks 'for' and 'about' a
generalized human nature, using 'we' and 'you' and 'I' in a roughly
similar inclusive fashion. When it pities, it pities 'all poor mortals';
when it caresses (which it sometimes does too heavily), it caresses a
human object, which, like any human object, needs love; when it
praises, it praises the common, not the rare, virtues. For although
George Eliot puts in the centre of action characters who are
powerful, energetic, creative, and intelligent, she keeps in the highroad of human powers, and even her exceptional characters are
representative. Compared with the central characters of Mrs

Gaskell, and for that matter, Thackeray and Dickens too, her characters have considerable imagination, but in their relation to their environment, in their moral mixture and complexity, and in their passions, they are typical enough. This typicality is very important to George Eliot, in part because she wants, like Wordsworth, to write an unspecialized literature of man speaking to men, *from* and *of* what she constantly calls the 'human lot', in part because it allows her to move naturally and freely from particularity of character and action to the generalization that bridges the experience central in the novel to the unknown but assumed experience of the reader.

In *Scenes* and from time to time in other places too, she miscalculates her tone, reaches too eagerly towards us, is too arch, too intense, too solicitous, too affectionate. In a sense it seems wrong to do what we generally do, and call these artistic faults. When I use the concept of miscalculation, it suggests a control of personality which is usually impossible, for the voice of George Eliot is usually offensive, when it is offensive, not on aesthetic grounds, but as human voices are offensive, distasteful as personality. And at times particularly distasteful, no doubt, because speaking in a voice of unfashionable feeling, vibrating richly and warmly where we like our voices to be cool, expansive where we like dry contraction and laconic understatement, uninhibited where we are inhibited, either from distrust or fear.

In *The Mill on the Floss* George Eliot creates a picture of imaginative richness which has most plainly a reference back to her own experience. It is not indulgent, even in its portrayal of Maggie, in being, as Leavis suggests in *The Great Tradition*, insufficiently critical. It is, on the contrary, very carefully critical of Maggie, both in direct commentary and through the voice of Philip: it criticizes Maggie's shift from one dream to another; it criticizes her religiosity and her lack of self-knowledge. Where it is indulgent – and I think it is 'indulgent' and not 'self-indulgent' – it is in pitying while it criticizes, in pouring over Maggie, or Mr Tulliver, or Philip, in a constant flowing of love, knowing and maternal. It is also indulgent in the resolution by plot, the restoration of the dream of childhood, relationship, and total understanding in the flood.

George Eliot is a very deliberate artist who builds up the appropriate structure by imagery, casual-seeming *double entendre* – 'She'll tumble in one day' – landscape, and folk-tradition. But in spite of the aesthetic unity of the river imagery, in spite of the foreground and background of the great waters, their economic importance and their wild threat, there is no escaping the feeling that George Eliot provided Maggie and Tom with a special Providence which is more damaging than we can suggest by simply calling it unrealistic or melodramatic. It is neither: people are killed by storm and flood, and this flood is given plenty of substance. But it does go right against the grain of the novel's sensibility and argument, which concern themselves with an evolutionary movement away from dream towards waking, from poetry to naked prose. In what seems to me George Eliot's richest and most particularized piece of characterization, Maggie is presented, against her environment, family, education, and religion, as struggling to know and not to escape or to delude herself. At each stage of shedding the dream or the drugging poem, she moves into another, slightly less delusive stage of dream or poetry. We should observe, by the way, that when George Eliot uses the idea of moving from poetry to prose, she is thinking in terms of Romantic poetry. Maggie uses Scott and Byron as escape, Esther Lyon and Mrs Transome, in *Felix Holt*, use Byron and Chateaubriand. Maggie first makes childish make-believe daydreams, simply cutting out unpleasant friction and shaping the experience anew, to her liking. Later, she finds literature an effective aid to this process, when her intelligence and experience cease to tolerate the cruder forms of wish-fulfilling shape-making. Later still, when the golden gates of childhood close, and she and Tom go home to illness, loss and the frightening responsibility for the once-responsible parents, literature fails too. George Eliot is very good indeed on the desolation which fills Maggie's life between illusions, and her portrayal of ennui, bewilderment, inactivity and misery, all joined together in a feeling defying the power of naming, is painful in its sharpness and truth. But humankind cannot live long without a dream, and Maggie is ripe for religious illusion. Again, George Eliot shows Maggie's conversion with truth and sympathy, observing without harshness the element of self-indulgence and histrionics. What is perhaps even more remarkable an achievement for such a systematic moralist as George Eliot is the next stage in Maggie's process, which is not given the evolutionary treatment, but shown, very quietly and unfussily, as sliding back into the pre-religious stage of self-gratification. At this stage various dreams merge: Maggie is scarcely carrying out her self-denying intention, but she does retain something of the 'Thomas à Kempis' altruism. She reverts to Scott, and she is fed, too, by a new source of energizing illusion, the romantic companionship with Philip which is an undemanding form of relationship, a kind of loving which can be refuge and calm repose. Finally, she is forced to discard all the illusions, after a crisis of moral choice and a thoroughly miserable and motivated renunciation which seems to reverse George Eliot's own moral choice in going to live with Lewes, while bringing out plainly the nature of her personal ethic. Maggie refuses to break an unofficial engagement, George Eliot committed adultery; Maggie renounces Stephen on the grounds of feeling and duty, to people, not laws, George Eliot committed herself to Lewes for similar reasons. In the most subtle way the novel disguises, socializes, but also defends George Eliot's own social deviation. In another subtle way Maggie's extreme conversion to religious self-denial and subsequent partial return to her 'habitual self' reverses but uses George Eliot's own conversion from Christianity. The novel is a thoroughly externalized but very personal story. It is also rich, complex, and complete in its rendering of the processes of frustration, exhaustion, and desire. Not only in the figure of Maggie, but also in the characters of Tom, Mr Tulliver and Philip, George Eliot's ability to show and to analyse reveals itself in very moving and various human materials. The powerful sensibility and imagination of Maggie placed in the centre, George Eliot's ability to substantiate the more average human stuff of Mr and Mrs Tulliver is given a subordinate but adequate place. When the wife persuades the husband to work for Wakem, or when Tulliver makes Tom write the vow for vengeance in the family Bible, George Eliot writes a wonderfully individualized version of the stuff of human crisis: the ties of marriage, for instance, are seen as powerfully binding and strangling, against the background of country and family ritual and tradition and in the words of folk-saying, proverb, cliché and the Bible.

It is this kind of richness and honesty which is undermined when George Eliot answers her heroine's final prayer, to spare her further stages of pain and loss. In her other novels, which grow in scale and intellectual analysis, there is always a tension, never quite satisfactorily concluded, between a truthful rendering of people and the meliorist attempt to show at least the possibilities of love, content, harmony. It is a kind of tension not found in Mrs Gaskell or the Brontës, and it reveals, I think, the imaginative powers and ambitions of George Eliot's greater genius. She was, like Dickens, writing the kind of novel that asked all the questions, and was at least aware of a whole range of possible answers.

She asks about the environment; contemporary society, ideal

society and society localized somewhere in history – usually in the early nineteenth century, except in *Romola* and the fully contemporary *Daniel Deronda*. So she handles three periods at once, combining the carefully researched past history (of, say, a county town in the 1830s), the present time which is implied or symbolized through historical reference (as the Second Reform Bill is in the First Reform Bill), and the future, in implications for the progress of societies shown through criticism and ideals.

She handles, too, the moral questions of individual conduct: problems of earning a living, of marrying, of staying single, of finding marriage or your job good, bad, indifferent, bearable. She handles a very great range of relationships, all typical and sharply individualized: relationships between brother and sister, brother and brother, sister and sister, parents and children, husband and wife, passionate lovers, romantically sexless lovers, friends, master and servant in a very role-limited relation, master and servant in a free man-to-man relation, rivals, old people and young people, and so on, in a very long list indeed. The list's lengthiness must only be stressed at the same time as we insist on the individuality. All these relationships are dramatized so as to show the social and personal colours of, say, the Lammeter sisters in *Silas Marner*, or Fred Vincy and Rosamond, or Gwendolen Harleth and her mother, or the Princess Alcharisi and her son, but they are also all sufficiently typical, of social and psychological conditions and roles, to make their contribution to the total moral argument.

George Eliot is a very considerable artist, as we see when we shift from the human problems – the actualities and ideals which form the subject, the end of art – to the forms, methods, and style of the novelist. In the last four novels, *Romola, Felix Holt, Middlemarch*, and *Daniel Deronda*, there is a constant experimentation with language and design. Sometimes it is a colossal failure, as with the translated Italian no-language of *Romola* (see Hemingway's *For Whom the Bell Tolls* for another, equally disastrous, version of the same answer) or in the poetic style of Mordecai in *Daniel Deronda*, where the imagery and syntax are adapted from the Old Testament and the poetic style of Jehuda Halevy. Sometimes it is a very subdued triumph of impersonation, as in the characteristic languages of *Middlemarch*, where no character lacks his appropriate style. There is always a discrimination, a realism, and an ordering in language. The language belongs to the author, and its irony, movement, and unity rely on a cross-reference from image to image or from phrase to phrase. The characters in *Middlemarch*, one by one – Dorothea,

Rosamond, Fred – all ask, 'What can I do?' in an almost operatic arrangement of words, timbres, and pitch, though that effect is a very muted one. The characters in *Middlemarch* are comparatively described in imagery of water, and the characters in *Daniel Deronda* in the imagery of horses, riders, chariots, control and submission.

The experiment in form is, of course, as in all great art, an experiment in humane analysis and moral argument. The shape of the novel is the shape of the moral vision of experience. George Eliot's characteristic form, present early but fully developed and plain from *Romola* to *Daniel Deronda*, is that of the typical Victorian three-decker novel, the double or multiple action that we find in *Vanity Fair, Bleak House* and *Our Mutual Friend*. George Eliot was using a form typical of her time, shaped and conventionalized by reading habits, costs, serial publication and a demand for expansiveness. But she shapes the form for her purpose, and the form of *Felix Holt, Middlemarch* and *Daniel Deronda* is individual, each novel differing not only from a novel of multiple action by Dickens or Tolstoy, but from each other.

The double plot of *Romola* is the comparison of Romola and Savonarola, the contrast between problems and conflicts of duty and egoism, feeling and reason, in private and public life. The double plot of *Felix Holt* (a novel which is too unified to be precisely described in this way) compares two Radicals, two kinds of political commitment and action, two classes. The act of contrast and comparison creates the form, but we also have to analyse it in terms of the relationships of the parts in final unity, for the convergence comes about differently, and individually, in each novel. In *Felix Holt* the destinies and actions converge, and what has been ironically a relationship visible to the reader but not to the character, breaks the narrative irony to become junction and discovery. After the tension, the novel's final scenes dissolve the unity, and the double action is felt to diverge, startlingly converge, and diverge again. Each shift in relationship is expressive of the social and personal separations and joinings, which form the subject of the novel. In *Daniel Deronda*, which has a more distinct double action, there is a similar narrative irony, though it is much more crucial and terrifying. Once more, there is a social division, though this time roughly between Gentile and Jewish ways of life. But the hero of *each* action is Daniel Deronda and the contrast and comparison made by the structure is made the more powerfully and ironically for this very strong and unifying bond, like the bloodstream yoking Siamese twins. That conceit is an appropriate one, for Daniel has to break the bond, and Gwendolen has to bear the pain of its un-dreamt-of breaking. The reader's double vision has formed a special context for reading both ways of life, as social and personal histories, and has created the felt knowledge of the final break. George Eliot's formal comparisons in these three novels embody stories which generalize and also show the tragic differences and dissociations of the human lot.

Her greatest novel, written between *Felix Holt* and *Daniel Deronda*, is *Middlemarch*. Here the form is one of quadruple action, though once we begin to count the parts we might well feel impelled to enumerate even more divisions. The same kinds of social irony and personal isolation are pointed out as in the other three novels, but there is no special irony of ignorance and junction and separateness, only a series of small ironies, such as Lydgate's thoughts of Dorothea and the reader's silent answering superior knowledge. The multiple form of this novel is perhaps most expressive of two other ideas: the idea of equality of interest and the idea of contingency. The form is the perfect one for proving that George Eliot's 'we' is truly meant, for it creates a rotation which makes us displace each prominent character and move on to another. It creates a model of that illusion of centrality and that fact of typicality which the novel explicitly discusses. 'Why always Dorothea?' asks the novel on one famous occasion. The perfect proof of the question's sincerity is made in a form which refuses to allow central figures to engross our attention. There are a limited number of central figures, true, but the form acts as a model, not a total imitation, and its point seems to be clearly made. The theme of contingency is discovered in the form. It is a novel which sadly but imaginatively sees not the fixity of destiny, which is so limiting and also so morally terrifying in the portrayal of Tito Melema, but its flux, its selection. How free? how determined? asks the novel and shows the variety of possibilities. The very shifts of action, the transformation of minor character in one plot to major character in another, the chanciness, the permutations which come out of contrast and comparison, the generalization, the fast movement which seems at times to blur identity, all these aspects of the structure are expressive. It is a novel as astonishingly broad in social rendering as it is profound in inner analysis and drama. It impresses us passionately with the feeling that these highly differentiated people, these various moral commitments, these richly individualized styles, are made from the same humanity.

George Eliot is perhaps the greatest psychologist in the English novel, and it is important to see her departures from psychological realism. The deviations from her richly various complex norm, like Dinah, Felix, Daniel, Mordecai, are made in the interests of that passionate vision of human societies and moral action which was more important than perfected substance, than writing the good novel. All these characters have a complex enough psyche, but they have a certain fixity, a certain monolithic quality, as of reassuring monumental instances of human virtue, or landmarks needed for George Eliot's hope and faith. Adam progresses from unimaginative rectitude to the pains of loving and knowing beyond himself; Daniel Deronda finds his roots, his identity, his role. They are not characters who are existentially open, who can show new facets, who can surprise themselves, the other characters or the reader, but dramatically imperfect characters who show, like the desperately wish-fulfilling endings, the author's need to idealize, to dream, and to transform.

8

VICTORIAN WOMEN PROSE-WRITERS

Marion Shaw

What a revolting contrast exists in England between the slavery of women and the intellectual superiority of women writers.

(Flora Tristran, quoted in Moers, p 21)

When Virginia Woolf wrote in *A Room of One's Own* that 'towards the end of the eighteenth century a change came about which, if I were rewriting history, I should describe more fully and think of greater importance than the Crusades or the Wars of the Roses. The middle-class woman began to write' (p 66), she was expressing a commonly-held but not entirely accurate belief that the woman writer appeared suddenly and that she came to dominate the literary scene. In fact it is probable that at no time during the nineteenth century did the proportion of women writers to men rise beyond 20 per cent and that this differed little from the situation in the eighteenth century, at least during its second half. What Woolf's comment draws attention to is a *perception* of the woman writer, particularly the woman novelist, as having assumed a significant and perhaps rather threatening presence in nineteenth-century England, a presence which led a literary man-about-town like George Henry Lewes to claim in 1850 that:

the group of female authors is becoming every year more multitudinous and more successful. Women write the best novels, the best travels, the best reviews, the best leaders, and the best cookery-books. They write on every subject and in every style from terribly learned books on Egypt and Etruria down to *Loose Thoughts, by a Lady* . . . In fact, the women have made an invasion of our legitimate domain.

(*Leader*, 18 May, 1850, p 189)

Lewes's exaggeration of the power and extent of female authorship was a light-hearted symptom of a general anxiety concerning women's position. With a similar uneasy jocularity Tennyson's *The*

Princess (1847) had allowed that 'The woman's cause is man's: they rise or sink/Together, dwarf'd or godlike, bound or free' but had also warned that chaos would ensue if women tried too violently to overthrow the traditional order of things.

The traditional position for the Victorian woman as far as her public life was concerned had been established by the first Reform Act of 1832 which, by employing the term 'male person' for the first time in English history, expressly debarred women from exercising the franchise it created. James Mill, the architect of the Act, stated in 1823 the principle on which such legislation was based:

One thing is pretty clear, that all those individuals whose interests are indisputably included in those of other individuals may be struck off from political rights without inconvenience. In this light may be viewed all children up to a certain age . . . In this light also women may be regarded, the interests of almost all of whom is involved either in that of their fathers, or in that of their husbands.

('Government', *Encyclopaedia Britannica: Supplement*, 1823)

This meant that for almost a century women's political function was to continue as an indirect one of influence rather than participation, in parallel with their legal and economic dependency. They were, in all respects, relative creatures, particularly after marriage in which their property, earnings, liberty and conscience belonged to their husbands, as did their children.

Opposition to this state of affairs and support for it were the poles of the debate concerning women. At one extreme were writers like William Thompson whose *Appeal* of 1825 was a fully-argued case against Mill's misapplication of the principle of Utility 'to the degradation of one half the human race', or like Harriet Martineau whose more personal complaint in 1855 was that 'I have no role in elections, though I am a taxpaying housekeeper and respectable citizen; and I regard the disability as an absurdity' (*Autobiography*, vol I, p 402). In contrast were writers like Mrs Ellis, content in 1839 to leave 'the justice of [England's] laws, the extent of her commerce, and the amount of her resources' to men whilst women's concern was with 'the domestic character of England – the home-comforts and fireside virtues for which she is so justly celebrated' (p 14). This, too, although more trenchantly expressed, was the view of Mrs Oliphant writing in 1856: 'The laws which govern human intercourse are for the most part only fixed and arbitrary demonstrations of natural rights and necessities.'

Within this political context were the more localized debates concerning women's education, their role in marriage, their position if unmarried, their interaction with the working-classes (for it was, of course, primarily about middle-class women that the 'Woman Question' was raised), and their scope and responsibilities if they became writers. During the early Victorian period, partly because of the Reform Act and partly because of new ideas flowing from post-Revolutionary France, there was an awareness that women were facing changes, that, like working-class men, they had become a focus for ideological conflict between democratic notions on the rights of individuals and traditionalist views on the 'natural' spheres and orders of society. For the woman writer at the time of the accession of Queen Victoria (herself a politically anomalous member of her sex) the effect of these controversies was to be a significant widening of her activities: new fields for enquiry, new causes to espouse, new moralities to expound and, above all, a new self-consciousness about her role, particularly as a novelist. 'I longed inexpressibly for the liberty of fiction', wrote Harriet Martineau of herself in the 1830s; 'my heart and mind were deeply stirred on one or two moral subjects on which I wanted the relief of speech . . . which could be as well expressed in fiction as in any other way – and perhaps with more freedom and earnestness than under any other form.' (*Autobiography*, vol II, p 108)

The dominant legacy of women's writing which Harriet Martineau received from her eighteenth-century predecessors was a confinement within a feminine sphere. As Jane Spencer, amongst others, has pointed out, 'the increasing separation of home from workplace in the late seventeenth and the eighteenth centuries laid the foundations for a new bourgeois ideology of femininity, according to which women were very separate, special creatures . . . confined to a special feminine sphere, as guardians of the home and of moral and emotional values' (*The Rise of the Woman Novelist*, p 15). The Evangelical Revival of the period 1780–1830, as a new 'religion of the heart', intensified this movement in its stress on marriage not only as a gateway to respectability and stability and an organizing factor in the development of middle-classness, but also as a sacramental union enshrining familial intimacy and domestic virtue. This new formulation served to enhance the position of women and at the same time placed on them the important if limited responsibility of maintaining the moral and companionate nature of marriage. Within this context it was inevitable that the expected province of the eighteenth-century woman writer, particularly the novelist, should be that of romantic sentiment. Of course, women wrote Gothic novels, Maria Edgeworth's *Castle*

Rackrent (1800) and *The Absentee* (1812) can be described as 'social-protest' novels, and there were the religious and 'useful' tracts of women like Hannah More, Mrs Barbauld and Mrs Marcet, but essentially the substance of women's writing in the pre-Victorian period was the story of a young woman's courtship, as far as the novel was concerned (which in some cases, as in the novels of Susan Ferrier, Maria Edgeworth and, of course, Jane Austen, was also an apprenticeship story in which the heroine's moral growth was a principal interest), and a woman's domestic behaviour as maiden, wife or mother in respect of non-fiction.

The Victorian novelist was overwhelmingly to retain this romantic interest as at least a framework for her fiction; those who did not use a love-and-marriage story as their basic narrative structure were unusual. The significant developments from this eighteenth-century inheritance were the greater infusion into the love story of social commentary of a serious and more or less didactic nature, and a strong sense that the wider social scene was of concern to women. The skill and versatility with which women writers developed an interplay between the romantic and the socio-political interests in their novels led not only to the 'classic' social-problem novel such as *North and South* but also to the more diffused social seriousness of *Middlemarch* and Mrs Humphry Ward's *Marcella* and to the passionate polemicism of Charlotte Brontë's *Shirley* and Olive Schreiner's *The Story of an African Farm*. Essentially, the domestic comedy of manners of a Jane Austen type became enlarged, throughout the century, to include all the serious social issues of the day. In spite of their politically marginalized position, and their presumed enclosure within the home, middle-class women, and especially women writers, increasingly expected to look outwards to their industrial society, to the problems of poverty, urban overcrowding, child exploitation and prostitution. The Victorian heroine's love-life, and her expectations of marriage, became, as it were, the woof of the material of the woman's novel, of which the warp was the Condition of England, including the condition of women in England. Of course, this was also true of the male novelists; as Vineta Colby says, 'the beauty of the nineteenth-century English novel is its sensitivity to its total world' (*Yesterday's Women*, p 6). But although the male novelists often used love stories as narrative threads, none of them, not even James or Hardy, presented quite the balance betweeen the romantic and the social interests that characterizes the work of George Eliot, Elizabeth Gaskell and Mrs Oliphant. For them the education of the female heart was equally a matter of social awareness as of domestic morality. This widening sphere of women's interests was also, and not surprisingly, evident in their non-fiction writing; as we shall see, women became some of the most daring of social commentators and even when they remained content to write of the domestic sphere, or to endorse a traditionalist view of women's role, as in the case of Mrs Oliphant, this was done with a greater political awareness and sense of the potential alternatives. As Judith Lowder Newton says, 'one only has to take manuals addressed to genteel women in the late eighteenth century and lay them alongside those written for middle-class women some sixty to seventy years later to see a deepening tension over women's power begin to manifest itself like footprints in a flower garden' (*Women, Power and Subversion*, p 2).

There were many factors leading to the increased responsiveness of the woman writer to the public world during the early Victorian period. Perhaps the most basic of these was the increase in the population of the British Isles from 9 million in 1801 to nearly 27 million in 1841, a triple increase particularly noticeable in the overcrowding and poverty of the cities and in the spread of urban ways of life for both middle- and working-classes. These factors were exacerbated by the financial recession of 1836–7, beginning a depression that lasted until 1842 and which included the bad harvests of 1839–42 and a serious smallpox epidemic. In all this, there was a visible drama of life not so readily available to the eighteenth-century woman writer, an abundance of material for both women and men but perhaps of a particularly challenging nature to women to whom the familial and social problems of population growth and economic transition appeared as an appropriate responsibility.

For the woman writer who wanted to engage with the issues of her time, there was ample opportunity to do so in the phenomenal growth in periodical literature during the early years of the nineteenth century. With the founding of the *Edinburgh Review* in 1802, the great age of the serious journal, literary and political in its orientation, began, and by 1830 with the *Quarterly Review* and the *Westminster Review, Blackwood's Edinburgh Magazine*, the *Examiner*, the *Athenaeum* and the *Spectator* in existence, the reading public was feasted with facts, opinions and comments. Such an expansion offered the woman writer a serious outlet for her thoughts, paid her well (always an important consideration for women like Mrs Oliphant and Marian Evans who earned their living by writing), and provided an intellectual and psychological stimulus for women in general and perhaps particularly for novelists. As R. G. Cox remarked, the periodicals formed a 'vast nursery' for the production of literature in which women as well as men could test their opinions and their expertise and practice their writing skills.

A woman who exemplified the trends of female writing of the early Victorian period was Harriet Martineau (1802–76). She was also a powerful influence on many of her successors: 'She is a great and good woman', wrote Charlotte Brontë to Emily; 'the manner in which she combines the highest mental culture with the nicest discharge of feminine duties filled me with admiration'. Martineau's first literary publications were, significantly, 'Female Writers on Practical Divinity' and 'On Female Education' for the Unitarian *Monthly Repository* in 1822 and 1823. In the first of these she pointed to the success women had had, particularly the admired Hannah More, in promoting virtue and bringing 'the spirit of religion into company', and in the second she argued for a greater equality in the educational treatment of girls and boys. The two articles demonstrate her belief in the intellectual capabilities of women and they also declare her didactic intentions as a writer. When she came to write the highly popular *Illustrations of Political Economy* (the first number was published in February 1832 and sold 1,500 copies within ten days) she saw her duty 'to my great pupil, the public' to write 'little books', with titles such as *A Manchester Strike, Life in the Wilds* and *Ireland*, in which 'the principles of the science [of laissez-faire economics] might be advantageously conveyed . . . not by being swallowed up in a story, but by being exhibited in their natural workings in selected passages of social life.' (*Autobiography*, vol I, p 138) The blend of fact and fiction, didacticism and entertainment, the abstract notion and the homely detail, which characterizes *Illustrations* looks forward to *Deerbrook*, Harriet Martineau's only successful novel, just as *Deerbrook* itself, published in 1839 at the threshold of the new age, points to the development of women's fiction (and some men's) during the next forty years. As Vineta Colby says:

[*Deerbrook*] is bourgeois and anti-romantic. It glorifies the solid values of home and family. It recognizes that the goal of all humans is happiness and self-fulfilment, but it constantly reminds us of the Christian-evangelical imperatives of duty, submission of the individual will, self-sacrifice, and endurance . . . It is the product of many social and literary influences of the early nineteenth century – radicalism, reform, evangelicalism, and romanticism. But these influences are ideological and philosophical, while

Deerbrook and its successors in the genre of the bourgeois love story are parochial, domestic, filled with the small details of daily living.

(Yesterday's Women, p 212)

Additionally, *Deerbrook* places a particular emphasis on female character and experience both as intrinsically important and interesting and, in the case of the heroine Margaret, as a register of the social conditions and moral qualities of the community the novel describes. Thus an ordinary woman – Margaret is the orphaned daughter of an obscure Birmingham businessman – becomes the conscience of the novel in the superiority of her moral sense and in the fictional weight this is given. So many ingredients of future women's novels are present in *Deerbrook*: the two sisters, the setting in 'middle life', the idealism about social usefulness, the social crisis (in *Deerbrook* it is an outbreak of cholera), the lover who must be chastened into worthiness of the heroine; but beyond these is its most significant contribution of confidence in women's importance not just as objects of domestic affection but as an influence for good. To later feminists this 'feminine sphere' of influence came to be regarded as an obstacle to women's advancement, but at the time when Harriet Martineau wrote, the case for women's moral dignity still had to be made and was one which she felt was historically necessary to their emancipation: 'Women who would improve the condition and chances of their sex must, I am certain, be not only affectionate and devoted, but rational and dispassionate, with the devotedness of benevolence and not merely of personal love'. It was on such grounds that Martineau disagreed with Mary Wollstonecraft, whose passionate outcry against injustice she considered politically inexpedient:

Every woman who can think and speak wisely, and bring up her children soundly, in regard to the rights and duties of society, is advancing the time when the interests of women will be represented, as well as those of men . . . the better way [than personal complaint] is for us all to learn and try to the utmost what we can do, and thus win for ourselves the consideration which alone can secure us rational treatment. The Wollstonecraft order set to work at the other end, and, as I think, do infinite mischief.

(Autobiography, vol I, p 400–2)

This, written in 1855, echoes *Deerbrook*'s fictional message of the importance of influence and example:

'Oh! Margaret, men know nothing of morals till they know women . . . Happy are they who grow up beside mothers and sisters whom they can revere! But for this, almost all men would be without earnestness of heart –

without a moral purpose – without generosity . . . It was so with me before I knew you.

(ch. 22)

Charlotte Elizabeth (Mrs Tonna) (1790–1846) differed from Harriet Martineau in the extreme Evangelicalism of her religious views and in her pronounced acceptance of female inferiority: 'We repudiate all pretensions to equality with men [except in] the underlying principle of a spiritual existence . . . Let us, then, contentedly bear our impressive designation as "the weaker vessel"'. Yet being 'a weaker vessel' did not prevent her from writing the same kind of fictionalized documentary as Martineau's *Illustrations* and also producing in 1841 a pioneering and highly influential novel, *Helen Fleetwood*, aimed at improving the lot of women. *Helen Fleetwood* has none of the fictional sophistication of *Deerbrook*: indeed, Charlotte Elizabeth disclaimed that it was fiction at all:

Let no one suppose we are going to write fiction, or to conjure up phantoms of a heated imagination, to aid the cause which we avowedly embrace. Names may be altered, characters may be grouped, with some latitude of licence; but . . . vivid indeed, and fertile in devices must the fancy be that could invent a horror beyond the bare, every-day reality of the thing!

(ch. 4)

The 'cause' she embraced was the need for adequate legislation to regulate the employment of women and children in the manufacturing industry; she also attacked the Poor Law Commissioners and the practice of luring impoverished rural families into factory work and urban degradation. Her method in *Helen Fleetwood* is to follow the fortunes, or misfortunes, of a not untypical poor family, the Widow Green and her four grandchildren and adopted grandchild Helen, from the country, where they are dispossessed of their cottage by the Poor Law Commissioners, to Manchester where each of them falls victim to the factory system, the family is dispersed, and the saintly, persecuted Helen dies of consumption. Throughout the novel Charlotte Elizabeth's Evangelicalism vies with her humanitarian anger; for instance, after a scene carrying a good deal of authorial indignation in which Widow Green is denied justice by the factory owner, we are told, with equal endorsement from the author, that the Widow 'returned to her poor dwelling in a calmer frame of mind [resulting] from having been driven closer to her Almighty refuge by rebuffs painful to flesh . . . but which rendered doubly sweet to her soul the word of promise, "*I* will never leave thee, nor forsake thee"' (ch. 11). In fact, it is Charlotte

Elizabeth's deeply conservative sense of a divine order of things which fires her reformist zeal because although suffering may bring the soul of the victim to God, injustice alienates those who practise it and informs against God's purpose:

Could it be for a moment credited that those who accumulated their wealth by this species of labour were men professing a system of belief [in which] they must each and all appear before the judgment seat of Christ, to give account of the deeds done in the body, to Him whose whole volume of inspiration is one continued prohibition of injustice and wrong?

(ch. 13)

Charlotte Elizabeth's next work, a collection of moral fables called *The Wrongs of Woman* (1843–4), employed the method of Martineau's *Illustrations* in its invention of families and individuals to illustrate an employment practice or social condition. The difference is that *The Wrongs of Woman* is a work of protest, an outcry on behalf of the thousands of women, whom Charlotte Elizabeth had observed and also read about in Parliamentary re-ports, who were driven out of their homes by necessity to work as dressmakers, milliners, pin-headers and screw-makers. Compassion for their sufferings and horror at the sexual temptations to which they were subjected combine in *The Wrongs of Woman* with an outraged sense of 'the monstrous abuse of forcing the female to forsake her proper sphere'. There is, of course, no doubt in Charlotte Elizabeth's view that the 'proper sphere' for women is in the home both by divine injunction and as a necessary stabilizing influence:

There ever has been, and ever will be, a spirit of restless discontent seeking to unsettle the minds of the lower orders; but so long as the humblest of England's wives and mothers had homes where the frugal meal might be eaten in peace – so long as those women were left to make such lowly homes pleasant to the labouring man . . . so long a great but most effective opposing force was found in continual operation against the pernicious effects of political incendiarism.

(*The Wrongs of Woman*, Bk IV, pp 136–7)

That women from a different class from labourers' wives might also create social harmony, Charlotte Elizabeth likewise had no doubt. It is evidence of her faith in the power of female influence to motivate a man like the 'noble, persevering, uncompromising Ashley', that she addressed her work to women and attributed its success (it was undoubtedly instrumental in the drawing up and passing of the Mines Act (1842), the Ten Hours Act (1847) and the Health of

Towns Act (1848)) to the persuasive exertions of a reform-minded female audience. As she never ceased to point out to her readers, to be 'wilfully ignorant [of industrial abuses], or to know that they exist, and to take no decided step towards putting them away . . . is a matter between the English Lady and Him to whom she must give account'.

Frances Trollope (1780–1863) had a much greater taste for fictional extravagance than Charlotte Elizabeth. Several of Trollope's thirty-four novels have detective-story plots and are also full of comic, sensational or satiric incidents. This is true of her two social-protest novels, *Michael Armstrong, the Factory Boy* (1839) and *Jessie Phillips* (1844). *Michael Armstrong*, based on real-life sources and, like *Helen Fleetwood*, written in support of the Ten Hours Movement, makes use of a female investigator, Mary Brotherton, who uncovers the 'crime' of child exploitation whilst also acting as the middle-class conscience in the novel; *Jessie Phillips* is a protest against the new Poor Law, particularly the bastardy clauses whereby no claims could be made against the supposed father of an illegitimate child, but the novel also contains a love-story and is something of a whodunit. Mrs Trollope was not skilful enough as a novelist to blend the fictional and the documentary elements into a coherent and plausible whole, as Elizabeth Gaskell was later to do, but nevertheless both novels are powerful indictments of current abuses and, like Charlotte Elizabeth's work, are written with readable vigour with the intention of mobilizing middle-class opinion, particularly that of the women of the wealthy manu-facturing families who were guilty of an 'extraordinary degree of ignorance' concerning the working-classes.

Jessie Phillips is also interesting as the first Victorian novel to give a sympathetic account of the fallen woman and to do so with full awareness of the class and sexual politics involved. Prefiguring both Elizabeth Gaskell's *Ruth* and George Eliot's *Adam Bede*, *Jessie Phillips* tells the story of a poor, virtuous seamstress who is seduced by the unscrupulous Sir Frederic Dalton and has a child whose murder she is accused of. Apart from the quality of the writing, the differences between *Jessie Phillips* and its more famous successors lie in the amount of direct feminist protest Mrs Trollope includes and, perhaps related to this, the comparative leniency with which Jessie's fall is regarded. Unlike Hetty in *Adam Bede*, Jessie sins not through vanity but out of love for Dalton and she is guiltless of the baby's murder. On the other hand, Trollope obviously does not feel it necessary to sanctify Jessie in order to obtain her readers' forgiveness for her heroine as Gaskell does in *Ruth*. Jessie dies at the end of the novel but a more ordinary death than Ruth's; the extraordinary death is reserved for her seducer who is drowned trying to escape justice. He is not spiritually redeemed by female goodness, but, in different vein, is brought to retribution by his sister and the woman he wants to marry who, as Joseph Kestner says (*Protest and Reform*, p 108), combine with Jessie to act as Furies driving him to destruction. Trollope's novel is melodramatic in plot and stereotypical in characterization, and its polemical concern with the bastardy clause and its unusual sense of female power and vengeance lead it into improbabilities of dialogue and situation, but in spite of, or perhaps because of, all this it communicates a vigorous anger on behalf of women, particularly working-class women in a patriarchal system which oppresses them on all sides:

The first object that met his eye was the back of a female figure, in the dress of a workhouse pauper . . . 'What in the devil's name brings you here? What do you hope or expect from daring to show yourself before my father's gate in this condition?'

. . . 'It is the welfare of your child that has sent me here. For my own sake gladly would I never have seen you more, but for my child, for your child, Frederic Dalton, I demand support.'

'Demand?' returned the villain, with a sneer. 'Where did you get your law from, Jessie Phillips? There's a sovereign for you . . . Go back to the workhouse and tell them to spend it on a caudle.'

. . . Jessie felt as if she was rather strengthened than overpowered by this brutality, and, still fixing her eyes upon him, she said 'Frederic Dalton, will you maintain your child?'

(*Jessie Phillips*, ch. 39)

The scene anticipates a famous Ford Madox Brown picture of 1857, when the issue had become much more politicized, in which a defiant, working-class woman offers a naked, newly-delivered baby to the viewer with the caption 'Take Your Son, Sir!'.

With the increased prosperity of the 1850s and an amelioration of the worst abuses of industrial production, social-protest novels of the type of *Helen Fleetwood* or *Michael Armstrong* were to be replaced by novels, pre-eminently Gaskell's *North and South*, which explored the industrial question more complexly, with less vehemence of protest and more sense of the possibility of reciprocal and assimilative strategies between middle- and working-classes, employers and workers. A hopeful time, indeed, of which the historian G. M. Young has written that 'Of all decades in our history, a wise man would choose the eighteen-fifties to be young in' (p 67).

Being a wise woman in the 1850s was also a buoyant, if less richly endowed, experience because this decade marked the beginning of the Women's Movement. Feminism to that point had been a matter of individual and often oblique protest expressed in such writings as Mrs Jameson's *Characteristics of Women* (1832) and her *Athenaeum* articles of 1846, or Lady Morgan's *Woman and her Master* (1840), Mrs Hugo Reid's *A Plea for Women* (1843) and Anne Richelieu Lamb's *Can Women Regenerate Society?* (1844). Such writings were on the increase during the 1840s and their main thrust was towards the better, more practical education of women and a proper, informed use of their influence. But during the 1850s feminism began to harden from isolated discontents into, as Ray Strachey calls it, The Cause, or, more accurately, a number of Causes: female suffrage, the admission of women into higher education, the marriage and property laws, and the plight and prospects of the unmarried woman. The more aggressive tenor of the decade was epitomized in three pieces of writing: an article by Harriet Taylor (1807–58) for the *Westminster Review* in 1851, Barbara Leigh Smith's 'Brief Summary in Plain Language of the Most Important Laws Concerning Women' (1854) and her pamphlet 'Women and Work' (1857).

The basis of Harriet Taylor's article was a report in the *New York Tribune* of a Women's Rights Convention 'claiming equality in education, in industrial pursuits, and in political rights'. This American example, Taylor says, will be followed in Britain, indeed, the first step has already been taken in a women's franchise petition, drawn up at a public meeting in Sheffield and presented to the House of Lords by the Earl of Carlisle. Taylor's position is uncompromisingly stated; the notion of a 'woman's sphere' is anathema to her:

> We deny the right of any portion of the species to decide for another portion, or for another individual, what is and what is not their 'proper sphere'. The proper sphere for all human beings is the largest and highest they are able to attain.
>
> (p 301)

and so is the claim that women have special moral and spiritual qualities: 'What is wanted for women is equal rights, equal admission to all social privileges; not a position apart, a sort of sentimental priesthood' (ibid.). Her egalitarian individualism informs her trenchant comments on the prescriptive ordering of society whereby women are always defined in relation to children or men:

It is neither necessary nor just to make imperative on women that they shall be either mothers or nothing; or that if they have been mothers once, they shall be nothing else during the whole remainder of their lives. [When] we ask why the existence of one-half should be merely ancillary to that of the other . . . the only reason which can be given is that men like it. It is agreeable to them that men should live for their own sake, women for the sake of men.

(p 311)

Where Harriet Taylor expressed a whole philosophy of women's rights, Barbara Leigh Smith (1827–91) focused on two specific issues, women's legal position and their right to work. As a founding member of the Langham Place Group[1], Barbara Leigh Smith (later Barbara Bodichon) was one of the most active feminists of the mid-century. Her 'Brief Summary . . .', written to promote a Married Women's Property Bill, sold for a few pence and was widely read; it exposed the Common Law position whereby a woman's person and property belonged entirely to her husband in whom was submerged her legal identity. 'Women and Work', less cogently argued and more controversial, even among feminists, claimed for women the right to do whatever work they were competent to do. The census of 1851 had shown a 900,000 'surplus' of women for whom employment opportunities were limited and badly paid: governessing for the middle-class woman, service or the factory for the women of the working-classes, and unemployment and poverty a constant threat to both. It was in this context that Barbara Leigh Smith made her plea that the fixed sphere of appropriate work for women should be relaxed: 'The work of our ancestresses is taken away from us, we must find fresh work. Idleness, or worse than idleness, is the state of tens of thousands of young women in Britain today'. 'Women and Work' coincided with the Marriage and Divorce Act of 1857 which, although it made divorce easier, effectively legalized the double standard and

[1] Members of the Langham Place Group included, besides Barbara Leigh Smith, Bessie Raynor Parkes, Adelaide Anne Proctor, Mrs Howitt, Mrs Jameson, Isa Craig, Emily Davies (founder of Girton College) and Elizabeth Garrett (one of the first women to qualify as a doctor). The group acted as an informal employment and educational agency (launching the Society for Promoting the Employment of Women) and published the *Englishwoman's Journal* from its offices in Langham Place.

delayed, until 1870 (earnings) and 1882 (property), Married Women's Property legislation.

Although strictly not of the decade, Charlotte Brontë's *Shirley* (1849) sets the tenor of the debates Taylor and Leigh Smith were conducting and, as a fiction, anticipates their campaigns. More than any previous novel it articulates male–female antagonisms, mistrust of marriage, and yet also a fear of singleness. Although it concludes as a comedy with a brace of weddings, its residual tone is gloomy with regard to sexual relations. It also takes a more despairing view than the other novels discussed here so far on women's ability to influence the course of social, and particularly industrial, events.

The nature of the male–female antagonism breaks down largely into contempt for women on the part of men, and women's fears and half-acceptance of this contempt, their fear of men themselves and yet their need of them: 'bondswomen and slaves', Caroline calls herself and Shirley. Men's contempt for women ranges from Joe Scott's opinion that 'women are a kittle and a froward generation' through Mr Helstone's incomprehension of them as 'a different, probably a very inferior, order of existence' to Robert Moore's insensitivity and condescension towards Caroline and Louis Moore's ardent mastery over Shirley as 'younger, frailer, feebler, more ignorant than I'. As for women's fate in marriage, the novel seems to be offering vindication of Harriet Taylor's statement that 'numbers of women are wives and mothers only because there is no other occupation for their feelings or their activities'. Mrs Pryor confesses that 'if I had not been so miserable as a governess, I should never have married', and her belief is that marriage 'is never wholly happy'. Although children may be a blessing, they are also a burden to be repudiated, as Moore initially does – 'As if there was nothing to be done in life but to . . . be having a family' – or an anguish to be parted with, as Mrs Pryor parts with Caroline. The tortured nature of sexual relations in *Shirley* is captured in Shirley's image of the mermaid-siren rising from the sea:

> 'Temptress-terror! Monstrous likeness of ourselves!'
> . . . 'But, Shirley, she is not like us: we are neither temptresses, nor terrors, nor monsters.'
> 'Some of our kind, it is said, are all three. There are men who ascribe to "woman", in general, such attributes.'
>
> (ch. 13)

There are, of course, male monsters of a female making in *Shirley* too: the dried pedant Helstone, the fools of curates, the brute that

Mrs Pryor's husband is presumed to be. The difference is that these have power whilst the women, however a monstrous an image men may attribute to them, are powerless in effect.

Yet to live in the power of men is preferable to single life, especially a single life without work. It is on behalf of the 'redundant' women of England that Caroline makes her most impassioned plea:

I believe single women should have more to do – better chances of interesting and profitable occupation than they possess now ... They scheme, they plot, they dress to ensnare husbands. The gentlemen turn them into ridicule: they don't want them; they hold them very cheap: they say – I have heard them say it with sneering laughs many a time – the matrimonal market is overstocked ... Fathers! cannot you alter these things? ... You should wish to be proud of your daughters and not blush for them – then seek for them an interest and occupation which shall raise them above the flirt, the manoeuvrer, the mischief-making tale-bearer.

(ch. 22)

Caroline's painful questioning of the role of the single women in *Shirley* – 'I shall never marry. What was I created for, I wonder? Where is my place in this world?' – is answered by the semi-autobiographical *The Experience of Life* (1853) by Elizabeth Sewell (1815–1906). Sally, its plain little heroine (the echoes of *Jane Eyre* are deliberate), is devoted to religious duty, family commitments, friends, and the setting up of a small school; her life is confined within an uneventful domestic environment unrelieved by romantic incident. The sixty-year-old narrator tells us at the beginning that this is the story of one who did 'the odds and ends' of the world's work and whose life has been unmarked by any striking event: 'No one points to the history of [such] lives as containing warning or example'. But there is example, if not warning, in *The Experience of Life*: it is the austere lesson that 'a single life need not be solitary and unblest', particularly, as happens to Sally, when financial independence renders middle- and old-age dignified and secure: 'happier at forty than thirty – happier at fifty than forty – happiest of all at sixty. It is better to be travelling towards age than away from youth' (p 309). In this respect, Sewell's novel is an adumbration of Jane Austen's comment in *Emma* that 'A single woman with a narrow income must be a ridiculous old maid, the proper sport of boys and girls; but a single woman of good fortune is always respectable, and may be as sensible and pleasant as anybody else'.

There are some parallels between *The Experience of Life* and *Rachel Gray* (1856) by Julia Kavanagh (1824–77) in that both are

concerned with drab and unromantic lives, but *Rachel Gray* as a
story about a seamstress faces the social scene more squarely than
Sewell's book and it has little of her cheerful resignation.
Kavanagh's novels in general were sober reading in their focus on
'the everyday sorrows of our commonplace fellow-men . . . in that
most prosaic stratum of society, the small shopkeeping class'. *Rachel
Gray*'s subtitle, *A Tale Founded on Fact*, and its statement in the
Preface that 'truth is its chief merit, and the Author claims no other
share in it, than that of telling it to the best of her power', aligns it
with the documentary fiction of Charlotte Elizabeth, as does also
Kavanagh's desire to educate her audience into sympathy for
'lives . . . moving in the straight and gloomy paths of mediocrity'.
But unlike Charlotte Elizabeth, and Elizabeth Gaskell in *Mary
Barton* (1855), Kavanagh avoids extreme poverty as a theme in her
writing and focuses instead on the grinding monotony and narrow
relationships of lives lived at subsistence level. Yet in spite of, or
perhaps because of, their unsensational nature, Kavanagh's novels
were popular family reading and in this they indicate a Victorian
taste for the humdrum and parochial which George Eliot was to
draw on in her *Scenes from Clerical Life* (1858).

It was part of Charlotte Brontë's understanding of the powerless
and dependent plight of women that, unlike Charlotte Elizabeth or
Mrs Trollope, she addressed her plea on behalf of single women in
Shirley to men and not to women. In this she recognized, as did the
early suffrage campaigners when they enlisted the help of men like J.
S. Mill and Jacob Bright, that whatever women's influence, the actual
effecting of reform lay within male control. But Charlotte Brontë's
despair (hardly too strong a word) goes further than this in her denial
not only of the direct power of women but of their influence also.
Shirley demonstrates that women are marginal to the main interests of
a man's life; even an affectionate family-man like Mr Yorke had been
prepared to reject the passion of his youth for business interests, and
in the scene of the riot at the mill there is a graphic depiction of
women's exclusion from the industrial scene, from class conflict and
from the economic realities of employment. High on the moor out of
reach of the action, physically vulnerable and disabled because they
have 'the long hair, the tender skin, the silks and the muslins' of
femininity, Caroline and Shirley are even more handicapped by the
knowledge of their superfluity to this scene of male business:

'Men never want women near them in times of real danger.'
'I would not trouble – I would help him,' was the reply.

'How? By inspiring him with heroism? Pooh! These are not the days of chivalry: it is not a tilt at a tournament we are going to behold, but a struggle about money, and food, and life.'

'It is natural that I should be at his side.'

'As queen of his heart? His mill is his lady-love, Cary! Backed by his factory and his frames, he has all the encouragement he wants or can know. It is not for love or beauty, but for ledger and broadcloth, he is going to break a spear. Don't be sentimental; Robert is not so.'

(ch. 19)

Shirley's dismissal of Caroline's impulse to fling herself between Robert and the rioters as sentimental delusion contrasts markedly with the assumptions concerning women's influence and its effectiveness underlying Elizabeth Gaskell's treatment of a similar episode in Chapter 22 of *North and South* (1854). Elizabeth Gaskell had little of Charlotte Brontë's awe of men; in fact, in her works men are often seen as frail and erring, lacking good sense and endurance and needing to be mothered. It is in terms of mothering, both as protection and as moral tuition, that Margaret thinks of her action in flinging herself between Mr Thornton and the rioters. She admits the instinctive nature of her act – 'But what possessed me to defend that man as if he were a helpless child!' – but also rationalizes it as the behaviour of someone who holds a superior sense of justice:

[I was] anxious that there should be fair play on each side; and I could see what fair play was. It was not fair . . . that he should stand there – sheltered, awaiting the soldiers . . . – without an effort on his part to bring them to reason. And it was worse than unfair for them to set on him as they threatened. I would do it again, let who say what they like of me. If I saved one blow, one cruel, angry action that might otherwise have been committed, I did a woman's work. Let them insult my maiden pride as they will – I walk pure before God.

(ch. 22)

In Elizabeth Gaskell's scale of values 'maiden pride' is a lesser thing than 'woman's work', that is, the mother's work of arbitration over the affairs of men. Such sentiments can be seen as congruent with John Ruskin's famous statement in 'Of Queens' Gardens' on 'the woman's true place and power' as 'sweet ordering, arrangement, and decision. She sees the qualities of things, their claims and their places'. The difference is that in Elizabeth Gaskell's case, the influence of women, although generated from a familial feeling (and she is, incidentally, probably the first novelist to recognize the maternal element in a woman's sexual response to a man), is not confined within a private, domestic sphere, Ruskin's enclosed garden, but active in the wider sphere of industrial relations.

One of Harriet Taylor's complaints in her *Westminster Review* article was against 'the literary class of women' whose anxiety to please men in the world of publishing and reviewing made them unsympathetic towards the women's cause:

[They are] ostentatious in disclaiming the desire for equality or citizenship and proclaiming their complete satisfaction with the place which society assigns to them . . . they depend on men's opinion for their literary as well as their feminine successes; and such is their bad opinion of men, that they believe there is not more than one in ten thousand who does not dislike and fear strength, sincerity, or high spirits in a woman.

(p 310)

Although George Eliot does not neatly fit Harriet Taylor's description of a 'literary class of woman', her ambivalence towards the Women's Movement has frequently been remarked on. Her attack on women writers in 1856, also in the *Westminster Review*, exhibits a characteristically complex response to the question of women's sphere and capabilities. 'Silly Novels by Lady Novelists' was written by someone not yet a professional novelist who objected to the lack of professionalism in the women novelists of her time. George Eliot (or Marian Evans, as she still was, although the review was anonymous like most periodical reviewing of the period) was deliberately distancing herself from the 'busy idleness' which produced a 'trashy and rotten kind of feminine literature', and her article expresses the anxiety of someone who fears contamination from her sex and whose attitude towards her membership of it is contradictory. In a sense, Marian Evans in this article was clearing the ground for her future as George Eliot. Her statement that 'Fiction is a department of literature in which women can, after their kind, fully equal men . . . women can produce novels not only fine, but among the very finest – novels, too, that have a precious speciality, lying quite apart from masculine aptitudes and experience', while it champions women's literary difference, has a qualifying uneasiness of tone which accords with her decision to publish her own novels under a male pseudonym, a surrogacy which informs the narrational attitudes of her (first) two fictional works of the 1850s. Here, for instance, is the coyly masculine description of Hetty in *Adam Bede*:

It is of little use for me to tell you that Hetty's cheek was like a rose-petal, that dimples played about her pouting lips . . . that her curly hair, though all pushed back under her round cap while she was at work, stole back in dark delicate rings on her forehead, and about her white shell-like ears; it is of little use for me to say how lively was the contour of her pink and white neckerchief, tucked into the contour of her low plum-coloured stiff boddice . . . – of little use, unless you have seen a woman who affected you as Hetty affected her beholders.

(ch. 7)

George Eliot's portrait of this girl who murders her illegitimate baby stresses Hetty's vanity and superficiality and her animal nature – 'kitten-like, pigeon-like' – as if there were a need to prove to the reader that her 'fall' and punishment are merited. After her seduction Hetty becomes an object of loathing and the punitive authorial tone – 'that wondrous Medusa-face, with the passionate, passionless lips . . . the rounded childish face and the hard, un-loving, despairing soul looking out of it – with the narrow heart and narrow thoughts, no room in them for any sorrows but her own' – is scarcely ameliorated by a slightly unctuous authorial pity: 'My heart bleeds for her as I see her toiling along on her weary feet' (ch. 37). Beyond this point, attention is withdrawn from her and transferred to the wronged lover, Adam, and even to the upper-class seducer, Arthur, and it is in their suffering and their moral growth that the novel's concluding interests lie. Like 'silly novels' Hetty belongs to a kind of femaleness that George Eliot could not countenance, that perhaps she feared, and that she was to return to with even greater disapproval in the character of Rosamund Vincy in *Middlemarch*. Only in Gwendolen Harleth in *Daniel Deronda* (1876) did Eliot explore with sympathy and insight the psychology of that Victorian stereotype of femininity – the pretty, vain, spoilt and useless young woman. In *Adam Bede*, however, Hetty's selfishness is regarded as beyond redemption and the maternity which ennobles the heroine of *Ruth* leaves Hetty callous and unfeeling. Interestingly, it is Adam who undergoes a maternal enlargement of sympathy:

Others thought she looked as if some demon had cast a blighting glance upon her, withered up the woman's soul in her, and left only a hard despairing obstinacy. But the mother's yearning, that completest type of the life in another life which is the essence of real human love, feels the presence of the cherished child even in the debased, degraded man; and to Adam, this pale, hard-looking culprit was the Hetty who had smiled at him in the garden under the apple-tree boughs.

(ch. 43)

George Eliot pays tribute throughout her novels to the abstract notion of motherhood but, in fact, the comic excellence of Mrs Poyser notwithstanding, Eliot's mothers are remarkable for their absence or unsatisfactoriness rather than their living goodness. This sense of dislocation between ideal and practice is vividly exemplifed in the juxtaposition, in the quoted passage, of 'the withered up . . . woman's soul' of a recent mother and the 'mother's yearning' of the wronged man.

The feminized man such as Adam temporarily becomes was a feature of women's writing of this period – Edgar Linton in *Wuthering Heights*, Philip Wakem in *The Mill on the Floss*, Charlie Edmonstone in Charlotte M. Yonge's *The Heir of Redcliffe*, for example – are sensitive and delicate, even to the point of being invalids or cripples whose confined lives must have provided parallels with those of many of their female readers. The best-selling *John Halifax, Gentleman* (1857) by Dinah Mulock (Mrs Craik) (1826–87) makes interesting use of just such a weakling in its history of the ideal self-made man, John Halifax, who rises through hard work and self-control from orphaned poverty to propertied wealth, marriage with an heiress and a chance to enter Parliament. As Elaine Showalter says, 'He might just as well have been called John Bull or Dick Whittington'. The interesting addition to this story of heroic manliness is John's friendship with the crippled narrator, Phineas Fletcher, whom he protects and cherishes and who watches John's rise with loving admiration, a Jonathan to John's David. Phineas's sexual ambivalence is an obvious opportunity for identification for his author and her readers. As a man he is able to accompany John on some of his adventures and as a cripple he is treated with physical tenderness and intimacy; a male – female figure, he is free to cross the boundaries of conventional behaviour for both sexes, as this description of a late-night return from a visit to the theatre illustrates:

For some time, listening to John's talk about the stars – he had lately added astronomy to the many things he tried to learn . . . – I hardly felt my weariness.

But gradually it drew upon me; my pace lagged slower and slower . . . John wound his young arm, strong and firm as iron, round my waist, and we got on awhile in that way . . .

When I came to myself I was lying by a tiny brook at the roadside, my head resting on John's knees. He was bathing my forehead: I could not see him, but I heard his smothered moan [and] I fancied that under cover of the night he yielded to what his manhood might have been ashamed of – yet need not – a few tears.

(ch. 6)

The sexual obliqueness of *John Halifax, Gentleman*, together with George Eliot's judgmental attitude towards Hetty and her 'fall' and Gaskell's over-compensatory sanctification of her heroine in *Ruth*, were to some extent products of an increased sensitivity in the 1850s towards the problems of sexual transgression, in particular the quite sensational amount of attention paid to the question of prostitution and the 'fallen woman'. W. R. Greg's article on 'Prostitution' for the *Westminster Review* in 1850 was, as Keith Nield has suggested, a 'watershed in the public debate' in its 'thoughtful and surprisingly direct' presentation of the topic to the literate middle-classes; it was also the expression of contradictory responses towards what came to be known during this decade, amongst exaggerated claims for the number of prostitutes, as the Greatest of our Social Evils. For the next thirty years the topic was to be widely debated in the periodical press, but the terms of the debate were initiated by Greg's article and developed by William Acton in 1857 in his book on *Prostitution*. Both writers expressed pity for women who became prostitutes and pointed to poverty as a major cause. They also both suggested as contributory factors the vanity and susceptibility of women and the insatiable sexual appetites of men: 'It is impossible to exaggerate the force of [men's] sexual desire', Acton wrote. On the assumption that men's desire is a 'natural demand' and that poverty amongst women is unlikely to be immediately eradicated, both authors pondered questions concerning the regulation of prostitution and the prevention of venereal disease. Such concern led to legislation attempting to contain the problem and culminating in the three Contagious Diseases Acts of 1864, 1866 and 1869. The protest against these acts was led by Josephine Butler in the belief that it was the responsibility of women of influence such as herself to secure justice for women and to work for an improvement in their general condition so that fewer would need to resort to prostitution for a livelihood: 'Think of this, you mothers who are living at ease, in your pleasant drawing-rooms, with your tender darlings around you! . . . you surely will not be content to preserve the holy sweetness of those whom God has given you, without a practical effort to lessen the power of those sinister social forces which are at present driving whole armies of little girls to madness and early graves' (Butler, p xix).

But although Josephine Butler could abjure her readers in 1869 to make a 'practical effort' to correct the Greatest of our Social Evils, unless a woman was as rich and independent as Angela Burdett-Coutts or as morally inspired and with as supportive a husband as Butler herself, it was difficult for her to be directly concerned with the issue, as helper, investigator (that was the province of Henry Mayhew) or as polemicist in the periodical press. Through ignorance, delicacy or moral timidity most middle-class women were excluded from the debate on sexual matters. What information came to them did so in the complexly mediated form of literary works such as *Helen Fleetwood*, *Mary Barton*, *Ruth* and *Adam Bede*. The influence of such works is difficult to estimate, but evidence that it did exist is given in Josephine Butler's claim that it was her reading of *Ruth* that prompted her campaigns on behalf of fallen women.

The 1860s saw an increase in the formal organization of the Women's Suffrage Movement and, with the defeat in 1867 of J. S. Mill's amendment to the Reform Bill to extend the franchise to women, the decade also saw the first of many parliamentary disappointments that were to frustrate the progress of the suffrage campaign for the next sixty years. The 1860s were also the years when women's entry into higher education began to be realized with the founding of Girton and Newnham Colleges in Cambridge in 1870 and 1871 respectively. The issues of the vote and education came to dominate the Woman Question during this period and were to do so for the rest of the century, although always accompanied by the related issue of the fate of the single woman. It is interesting to see this network of interests, which really condense into the right of the middle-class woman to direct participation in the legislative procedures of the country and to equality of cultural and professional opportunities, being debated by women of apparently opposing sides like Frances Power Cobbe (1822–1904) and Margaret Oliphant (1828–97). In 1868 Cobbe, a tireless worker for female suffrage, wrote an article for *Fraser's Magazine* on 'Criminals, Idiots, Women and Minors' which is a trenchant plea, in the wake of J. S. Mill's parliamentary failure, for female franchise. Earlier in the decade she had argued with equal eloquence for the right of single women (30 per cent of the female population in her calculation) to enjoy respect as useful citizens and to have access to degrees and professions. 'The "old maid" of 1861 is an exceedingly cheery personage', she says, who has 'not fewer duties than other women, only more diffused ones. The "old maid's" life may be as rich, as blessed, as that of the proudest of mothers'. But how much more useful would such women be if eligible to train professionally as doctors and nurses, doing scientifically and for payment what they already do without proper knowledge and for free. But as Shirley Foster has indicated, Cobbe's brave advocacy of female independence was, nevertheless, subject to a belief that 'Marriage was manifestly the Creator's plan for humanity' and that 'the great and paramount duties of a mother and wife once adopted, every other interest sinks, by the beneficent laws of our nature, into a subordinate place in normally constituted minds'. Indeed, it is Cobbe's idealism about the potential of marriage that fuels her feminism and makes her so strong a supporter of enlightened celibacy as preferable to the debased versions of matrimony she saw around her, the unsatisfactory nature of which she attributes to the infantilization of women which men encourage: 'The right punishment for those men who denounce schemes for the "Higher Education of Women", and ordain that women should only learn to cook and sew and mind babies, should be to spend the whole term of their natural lives in such homes as are made by the female incapables formed on such principles.'

Margaret Oliphant, on the other hand, was no supporter of women's suffrage or the women's movement at all, as her articles for *Blackwood's Magazine* in the late 1850s and the 1860s testify. The most vehement of these, 'The Great Unrepresented', was written in opposition to J. S. Mill's intention to enfranchise that group of women to which she herself belonged ('not the most interesting section of womankind'); 'the class of female householders, lone women who pay their own rent and taxes, and have their own affairs to manage . . . They are either widows whose day is over, or elderly maidens whose day has never come'. Oliphant's rejection of representative equality for this group is clear enough: 'We are content with that place in the world's economy which God has given us . . . and Mr. Mill must pardon us if we decline to seek another place'. Yet her reasons for this refusal are as contradictory as Cobbe's support for celibacy; her satisfaction with things as they were arose from something very close to contempt for legislative procedure and a sense of women's certain difference from, and probable superiority to, men:

We are not men spoiled in the making, but women . . . People write about us as if we were a curious sect, or imperfectly known species [under] the curious delusion that we ought to have been men, and that it is to our unending humiliation that we are not men. But as it happens, that is not our opinion. We are used to being women . . . Girls may object, and do object, to the disabilities which are sometimes rather hard upon them; but by the time a woman has come to the mature age at which she can understand herself and her destiny, she has in most cases got to see the justice of it, and learned to identify herself distinctly in the world.

('The Great Unrepresented', p 376)

The fatigues and disillusionments of Oliphant's own arduous life, much of it spent 'propping up' inadequate men, show through in the unromantic and slightly disingenous conservatism of this article. The novel she published the same year, *Miss Marjoribanks* (1866), although one of the funniest books of the period, displays a similar rather cynical obstinacy about the need for change. It is the story of Lucilla Marjoribanks, 'a large girl' who has learnt about 'political economy and things' at Mount Pleasant School, and who has the energy, determination and organizing ability of a general or a prime minister, yet who spends her young womanhood 'being a comfort' to her father and managing the petty affairs and intrigues of the little town of Carlingford. With some of Jane Austen's talent for satiric observation and sense of the ridiculous but without her frame of moral reference, *Miss Marjoribanks* is a disappointing novel which refuses to take even its own humour seriously. Lucilla is both an amusing and a formidable character, but neither her self-delusions nor her frustrations are explored, and when she marries at the end of the novel, with unseemly fictional haste and unlikelihood, there is the sense that deliberate limitations have been placed on the depiction of this spirited and powerful woman, that she has been sacrificed to conformity, to the need to be 'content with that place in the world's economy which God has given us'. The point is exemplified in the closing pages of the novel when Lucilla looks forward to philanthropic work in a village:

It gave her the liveliest satisfaction to think of all the disorder and disarray of the Marchbank village . . . The recollection of all the wretched hovels and miserable cottages exhilarated her heart . . . Perhaps it was not the highest motive possible, and it might be more satisfactory to some people to think of Lucilla as activated by lofty sentiments of philanthropy; but to persons acquainted with Miss Marjoribank's character, her biographer would scorn to make any such pretence.

(ch. 51)

The author's coy withdrawal both from judgment and from exploration of Lucilla's motives is, of course, in marked contrast to George Eliot's treatment of the similar hopes Dorothea entertains towards the village of Lowick in the third chapter of *Middlemarch*.

Mrs Oliphant's self-appointed role as scourge of pretentious women extended to writers of fiction. In an article on 'Novels' of

1867 she attacked a new fashion in light literature which 'perhaps began at the time when Jane Eyre made what advanced critics call her "protest" against the conventionalities in which the world clothes itself'. These stories of bigamy and seduction and *'soi-disant* revelations of things that lie below the surface of life', belong to 'the school called sensational' and have now taken 'permanent possession of all the lower strata of light literature'. This was the literature which led the 'Girl of the Period', in Eliza Lynn Linton's famous phrase, into bad habits, or at least into bad reading habits:

What is held up to us as the story of the feminine soul as it really exists underneath its conventional coverings, is a very fleshy and unlovely record. Women driven wild with love for the man who leads them on to desperation . . . women who marry their grooms in fits of sexual passion; women who pray their lovers to carry them off from husbands and homes they hate; women, at the very least of it, who give and receive burning kisses and frantic embraces, and live in a voluptuous dream, either waiting for or brooding over the inevitable lover – such are the heroines who have been imported into modern fiction.

('Novels', p 258)

It would be bad enough if such writing came from men, but the peculiarity and repulsiveness of the fashion is that 'this intense appreciation of flesh and blood . . . is represented as the natural sentiment of English girls [and] that the books which contain it circulate everywhere, and are read everywhere, and are not contradicted'. And, of course, such writing paid its author very well.

The respectable drudgery of Margaret Oliphant's career was in marked contrast to the irregular life and spectacular success of a novelist whom Oliphant nominated as the head of the Sensation School, Mary E. Braddon (1835–1915). *Lady Audley's Secret* was published in 1862 and reached its eighth edition in three months. The almost equally popular *Aurora Floyd* followed in 1863 and then novels at the rate of more than one a year (nearly eighty all told) crowned her 'Queen of the Circulating Libraries'. It is easy to see why Mary Braddon's novels provided such compulsive reading, particularly, but not only, for women; rapidly-moving plots, exciting events, danger and suspense combine with a strong sense of place and of detail and an overriding awareness of the connection between sex and power. *Lady Audley's Secret* is a subversive female fantasy in which the heroine, the frailly feminine Lucy Graham (Margaret Oliphant noted her presence as the first 'fair-haired demon of modern fiction'), lives a life of concealed bigamy and violence, and by her ruthless intelligence and sexuality undermines the landed order represented by Audley Court. Of course, Becky Sharp in Thackeray's *Vanity Fair* had tried, and Jane in *Jane Eyre* had succeeded as governess in marrying the landowner, but *Lady Audley's Secret* is more thoroughgoing in its iconoclasm and more outspokenly feminist in its claim that, outrageous though she may be, Lucy Audley is nevertheless representative of the frustrated energies of women:

> If [women] can't agitate the universe and play at ball with hemispheres, they'll make mountains of warfare and vexation out of domestic molehills, and brew social storms in household teacups ... To call them the weaker sex is a hideous mockery; they are the stronger sex, the noisier, the more persevering, the more self-assertive sex. They want freedom of opinion, variety of occupation, do they? Let them have it. Let them be lawyers, doctors, preachers, teachers, soldiers, legislators – anything they like – but let them be quiet – if they can.
>
> (ch. 25)

Elaine Showalter finds in the phenomenal success of women's sensation fiction of the 1860s a challenge to the doctrine of renunciation and submission that informed earlier women's fiction. But, of course, 'conventional' women characters were still being created by women writers, and the restrained and sacrificial heroines of George Eliot's great novels, *Middlemarch* and *Daniel Deronda*, were to follow in the decade after *Lady Audley's Secret*.

A novelist who had long held the notion of women's dependent position, yet who had somewhat contradictorily been not only a prolific writer but also a successful editor of several religious magazines and an independent financier of philanthropic schemes, was Charlotte M. Yonge (1823–1901). Like all Yonge's novels, the best-selling *The Heir of Redclyffe* (1853) and *The Daisy Chain* (1856) are coloured by High Church religious feeling, by reverence for a certain type of military manhood and by a belief in women's ideal sphere as a domestic one under the protection and guidance of a sensible man. These ideas inform one of her best novels of the 1860s, *The Clever Woman of the Family* (1865), in which the 'clever', fatherless Rachel Curtis, determined to remain single, frets at the constraints of her position and, in terms which anticipate Dorothea Brooke's frustrations in *Middlemarch*, cannot content herself with 'the quiet Lady Bountiful duties that had sufficed her mother and sister [and which] were too small and easy to satisfy a soul burning at the report of the great cry going up to heaven from a world of sin and woe'. Rachel's inexperience and gullibility lead her into many humorous and also some tragic consequences and, suitably chastened, she must eventually admit to her own foolishness and need for loving supervision:

'I used to think it so poor and weak to be in love, or to want any-one to take care of one. I thought marriage such ordinary drudgery, and ordinary opinions so contemptible, and had such schemes for myself. And this – and this is such a break down, my blunders and their consequences have been so unspeakably dreadful, and now instead of suffering, dying – as I felt I ought – it has only made me just like other women, for I know I could not live without him, and then all the rest of it must come for his sake.'

'And will make you much more really useful and effective than ever you could have been alone,' said Ermine . . . 'you see we are not the strongest creatures in the world, so we must resign ourselves to our fate, and make the best of it. *They* must judge how many imperfections they choose to endure, and we can only make the said drawbacks as little troublesome as may be.'

(ch. 23)

Ermine, a good and patient women who eventually marries her faithful lover from her early years, seems to have been made a cripple to prove how noble and forbearing '*They*' can be, what a weight of imperfections they can manfully endure.

This view that women are a responsibility that men must shoulder and that to be a husband is really to be a father (and perhaps also a mother: Charlotte Yonge's good men often nurse and cosset their ailing womenfolk) is very different from the depiction of sexual relations in a novel nearly contemporary with *The Clever Woman of the Family*, Elizabeth Gaskell's *Sylvia's Lovers* (1863). In Joseph Kestner's view, *Sylvia's Lovers*, with George Eliot's *Felix Holt, the Radical* (1866), represents the summation of the social-protest novel by women. Both novels have a lesson to teach about the Condition of England, but they do so with a diffused and mediated didacticism that no longer advocates a single solution, such as the Ten Hours Bill, as earlier social-protest novels had done. Instead, by the exercise of what George Eliot called 'veracious imagination', both novels make sophisticated investigations of current social, political and sexual abuses through an 'historical picturing . . . that might help the judgment greatly with regard to present and future events . . . the working out in detail of the various steps by which a political or social change was reached . . . brief, severely conscientious reproductions in their concrete incidents, of pregnant movements in the past' (*Essays of*

George Eliot, ed. T. Pinney, pp 446–7). In *Sylvia's Lovers* the 'pregnant movement' is the transition beginning in the last years of the eighteenth century from the spontaneous life-styles depending on agriculture and seafaring to the new commercial, entrepreneurial spirit of a dawning industrial age; in *Felix Holt* the movement is the triumph of liberalism in the period around the Reform Act of 1832. The suffering and vulnerability of the female characters in each novel, Sylvia and Mrs Transome particularly, are a poignant reminder of history's failure at such vital, 'pregnant' times to secure justice and freedom for women; they also point to the parallels between past and present, to how little women's situation has changed in the intervening years. Both novels use the condition and treatment of women as an index to the general state of the nation's health. In *Sylvia's Lovers* Philip's possessive love for Sylvia, which causes him to lie to her about her former lover and marry her on the basis of that lie, is part of the commercial instinct which makes him so successful a shopkeeper; he is a self-made, 'self-help' man of the John Halifax type, but the cost of this to his personal integrity and to honest, spontaneous affection is what the novel examines. It was a moral concern of some topicality; *Sylvia's Lovers* belongs to a time of keen and often ruthless competition, of strikes and unrest, in the aftermath of the Crimean War and during the American Civil War with its disastrous effects on the cotton industry. Gaskell is concerned to show not only, as George Eliot says in *Felix Holt*, 'that there is no private life which has not been determined by a wider public life' but also that, as Virginia Woolf was to write seventy years later, 'the public and the private worlds are inseparably connected . . . the tyrannies and servilities of the one are the tyrannies and servilities of the other' (*Three Guineas,* p 162). And although *Felix Holt* is politically a conservative novel in its defence of the privileged classes as custodians of 'that treasure of knowledge, science, poetry, refinement of thought, feeling and manners, great memories and the interpretation of great records', it too makes the point that public and private integrity are intimately connected. Harold Transome's contempt for women – 'It doesn't signify what they think – they are not called upon to judge or to act', he tells his mother as he tries to soften the blow of his Radicalism with promises of 'a new carriage and a pair of bays' – is a subtle repudiation of his assumed political progressiveness, just as her 'revenge' upon him, the knowledge of his illegitimacy, undermines his plans 'to get returned for parliament, to make a figure there as a Liberal member, and to become on all grounds a personage of weight in North Loamshire.'

*

In describing her 'Choice of a Craft' Beatrice Webb (1858–1943) records her personal ambition as an advanced young woman of the later Victorian period and the direction her ambition took:

To win recognition as an intellectual worker was, even before my mother's death, my secret ambition. I longed to write a book that would be read; but I had no notion about what I wanted to write. From my diary entries I infer that, if I had followed my taste and my temperament . . . I should have become, not a worker in the field of sociology, but a descriptive psychologist; either in the novel, to which I was from time to time tempted; or (if I had been born thirty years later) in a scientific analysis of the mental make-up of individual men and women, and their behaviour under particular conditions. For there begin to appear in my diary, from 1882 onwards, realistic scenes from country and town life, descriptions of manners and morals, analytic portraits of relations and friends – written . . . nearly always [as they] concern the relation of the individual to some particular social organization: to big enterprise or to Parliament, to the profession of law, or of medicine or of the Church.

(My Apprenticeship, ch. 3)

The craft she chose, that of social investigator, represents the fulfilment of a prime motivation of the social-protest novel: the collection and dissemination of information about the working-classes with a view to legislative reform through the prompting of both individual and collective conscience. Beatrice Webb often mentions being 'tempted' or 'haunted' by the attractions of fiction and if she had lived at the time of Charlotte Elizabeth she would no doubt have written novels. But now, in the 1880s, the need is for a scientific approach to argue the case with more political direction and to transform personalized philanthropic feeling into a social programme. The reasons which made her a social investigator and not a novelist are implied in her description of herself as a 'new' woman, 'rather hard and learned . . . with a clear analytic mind', who collected statistics and studied Blue Books:

To me 'a million sick' have always seemed actually more worthy of self-sacrificing devotion than the 'child sick in a fever', preferred by Mrs Browning's *Aurora Leigh*. And why not? The medical officer of health, who, made aware by statistical investigation of the presence of malaria in his district, [devised] schemes for draining stagnant pools . . . has a compassion for human misery as deep-rooted as, and certainly more effective than that of the devoted nurse who soothes the fever-stricken patient in the last hours of life.

(ch. 6)

But what made Beatrice Webb so effective a writer on these subjects and her autobiography *My Apprenticeship* one of the most readable of the century was her novelist's sense of character and location: 'I enjoy the life of the people in the East End; the reality of their efforts and aims; the simplicity of their sorrows and joys; I feel I can realize it and see the tragic and the comic side. To some extent I can grasp the forces which are swaying to and fro, raising and depressing this vast herd of human beings'.

Much of Beatrice Webb's investigative work was done amongst the 'sweated' trades of tailoring and dressmaking in the East End of London, the workshops where a 'woman by working very hard could earn 10s. a week, with 2s. deducted for silk . . . working from eight [a.m.] to ten [p.m.] without looking round, and master working up to two o'clock, and often beginning at five the next morning'. Webb also took over the management of an East End tenement, Katharine Buildings, owned by a group of philanthropists led by Octavia Hill, to house the poor in cheap and sanitary conditions. This is the scene of one of the few social-protest novels written by women in the last part of the nineteenth century, *A City Girl: A Realistic Story* (1887) by Margaret Harkness (1854–1921), Webb's friend and cousin. Famous mainly because Engels praised it as a 'minor work of art' in the 'truthfulness of [its] presentation . . . of the old, old story of the proletarian girl seduced by a man of the middle-class', *A City Girl* recombines elements of previous 'fallen woman' fiction by causing the seamstress-heroine, Nelly Ambrose, who lives with her unsympathetic family in an East End tenement, to be seduced by a married 'Radical and gentleman' from the West End. Nelly is a good worker and can earn enough to keep herself and her family and she is also betrothed to George, the tenement caretaker. It is not destitution or isolation that is the cause of her 'fall', but a desire for what she believes is more beautiful and cultured than anything her own life can provide. It is the same longing for superiority which stirs Hardy's Tess Durbeyfield. Nelly's lover takes her to a café to eat cake and hear music, to the theatre, to Kew Gardens, and all these experiences represent to her a world of middle-class romance and beauty which is not merely a holiday but a 'Paradise', for which she is prepared to abandon her work and her respectability. Although the ending of the novel, where George rescues and forgives Nelly, is, as John Goode says, evasive and trite, Margaret Harkness's understanding of the psychological forces which cause Nelly's downfall make her treatment of this topic the least sentimental, sensational or judgmental of any in the nineteenth century with the possible exception of George Moore's *Esther Waters*. It is, of course, an indication of the greater freedom with which such a topic could be discussed at this time, particularly as far as women were concerned, that she could write about it in such a relatively untrammelled way.

At the time of writing *A City Girl* Margaret Harkness, like Beatrice Webb, was working in the East End, and both women were members of an informal grouping of socialists who were also feminists and which included Eleanor Marx (1855–98) and Olive Schreiner (1855–1920). To Eleanor Marx the problem of women was not really one to be considered apart from ideas concerning the total overhaul of economic and social relations: 'The position of women rests, as everything in our complex modern society rests, on an economic basis . . . The Woman Question is one of the organization of society as a whole'. In 1886 she and Edward Aveling were prompted to issue this warning, in an article on 'The Woman Question' for the *Westminster Review*, to feminists, mostly of the 'well-to-do' classes, whose agitation for perfectly just aims such as the suffrage and the repeal of the Contagious Diseases Acts, was falsely based, in the view of Marx and Aveling, on notions of equal property rights or on 'sentimental or professional questions. Not one of them gets down through these to the bed-rock of the economic basis'. Even if each of these aims were achieved, 'the actual position of women in respect of men would not be very vitally touched . . . women are the creatures of an organized tyranny of men, as the workers are the creatures of an organized tyranny of idlers'. Eleanor Marx saw the end of women's oppression as a corollary to the 'tremendous social change' involved in a socialist revolution. In this she went further than most socialists of the period who regarded the Woman Question as irrelevant, diversionary or the business of privileged women. Hannah Mitchell, a working-class suffragist, recalled in her autobiography, *The Hard Way Up*, how she came to realize 'that if women did not bestir themselves the Socialists would be quite content to accept Manhood Suffrage in spite of all their talk about equality . . . Strangely enough, Mrs. P[ankhurst] and her followers found some of their bitterest opponents among the Socialists' (ch 10).

Hannah Mitchell's involvement in the suffrage campaigns came about because 'I saw there were no women in Parliament, no women councillors, no women guardians or magistrates, few women doctors – indeed few women in any well paid work at all'. In this she was registering a disappointment quite general in the last years of the century that the Women's Movement seemed to have made so few gains. The 1881 census revealed that one-third of the adult labour force comprised women aged twenty to sixty-five and that their average wage was 50 per cent of the male rate. Moreover, in July 1885 the *Pall Mall Gazette* had published W. T. Stead's article on 'The Maiden Tribute of Modern Babylon' in which an extensive trade in child prostitution was exposed. As Eleanor Marx pointed out, the double standard was still flourishing vigorously whereby 42 per cent of women were unmarried and bore 'upon their brows this stamp of lost instincts [and] stifled affections' whereas for their male counterparts society 'provides, recognises, legalizes . . . the means of gratifying the sex instinct'.

In *The Story of an African Farm* (1883), a work which powerfully influenced several generations of women and men – 'the strange little novel which had become our Bible', as Vera Brittain described it – Olive Schreiner attempted to fictionalize the related oppressions of class, sex and age. Ungainly in structure, employing parable, symbolism and, as Patricia Stubbs says, 'all the narrative methods of religious teaching', *The Story of an African Farm* tells of three children – proud, clever Lyndall, long-suffering Em and persecuted, philosophical Waldo – who are reared on a remote farm on the Karoo by ignorant and sadistic adults. The novel's distinctive power comes from its evocation of a drought-ridden landscape which reflects the thirsting spirits of the children, from its sharp sense of human cruelty in the figure of Bonaparte Blenkins and from the meditations upon injustice, power and love which the children engage in. For women readers Lyndall was, and still is, a particularly compelling character; as Elaine Showalter says, she is 'the first wholly serious feminist heroine in the English novel' and her 'declaration' in Chapter 4 was as shocking and memorable in 1883 as the writings of Mary Wollstonecraft had been nearly a century earlier. In her bitter analysis of the forces which make women frustrated and devious, Lyndall (Schreiner) remained unequalled until Simone de Beauvoir in *The Second Sex* more than seventy years later; 'One is not born but rather becomes a woman', wrote de Beauvoir, and this is Schreiner's theme too:

'Look at this little chin of mine, Waldo, with the dimple in it. It is but a small part of my person; but though I had knowledge of all things under the sun, and the wisdom to use it, and the deep loving heart of an angel it would not stead me through life like this little chin. I can win money with it, I can win love; I can win power with it . . . but being denied the right to exercise [power] openly, [women] rule in the dark, covertly, and by stealth, through the men whose passions they feed on, and by whom they climb'.

(ch. 4)

Olive Schreiner's Lyndall heralds the era of the New Woman. Although the label was not applied until 1894 (by popular novelist Ouida), the New Woman was identified as a type and by a variety of other names throughout the 1880s. She was better educated than her foremothers, inclined to be rather 'fast', 'wild' and 'manly' (such women 'smoke, shoot, play golf and cricket, are business women and travellers [and are] no longer dainty', complained Eliza Lynn Linton) and above all, she was highly critical of the marriage institution. In part the New Woman was a media creation, the grotesque du Maurier figure of *Punch* who readily became transformed into the sluttish, neglectful woman of the suffragette cartoon, but there was a reality to her in the number of women who were attacking marriage and who in their life-styles were voluntarily choosing unorthodox relationships. Mona Caird's article on 'The Morality of Marriage' in the *Fortnightly Review* in 1890 was one of the first to formulate the anti-marriage principles of this new generation of feminists. Caird recommends instead of marriage a contract between two economically independent individuals; in her view, 'dependence . . . is the curse of our marriages, of our homes and of our children, who are born of women who are not free even to refuse to bear them'. If women claimed lives and incomes of their own, 'marriage, as we now understand it, would cease to exist'. Such ideas on marriage reform stimulated both women and men to produce a crop of works during this period on the position of women within marriage or otherwise dependent on men: Henry James's *The Portrait of a Lady* (1881), Ibsen's *A Doll's House* (1889), George Gissing's *The Odd Women*, Sarah Grand's *The Heavenly Twins*, George Egerton's *Keynotes* (all in 1893), Grant Allen's *The Woman Who Did* (1895). *The Heavenly Twins*, for example, which sold 20,000 copies in the first week, was a polemical exposure of the wasteful division of the individuals (the twins of the title) into conventional sexual roles and also of the iniquities of the double standard by which another set of twins, Edith and Evadne, are destroyed, through V.D. and a self-protective frigidity respectively, by the profligacy of their husbands. This increasing intolerance towards men's sexual licence became, of course, an element in the suffragette programme – 'Votes for Women and Chastity for Men' – and provided the incentive for Christabel Pankhurst's study of V.D. in *The Great Scourge* (1913).

The volumes of short stories, *Keynotes* (1893) and *Discords* (1894), by George Egerton (Mary Chavelita Dunne, 1860–1945) were altogether more oblique in their feminism. Filled with an anguished sense of female dependence and inferiority, Egerton believed that in literature there was only one area in which men were not superior, that of woman's nature, 'the *terra incognita* of herself, as she knew herself to be, not as man liked to imagine her ... Unless one is androgynous, one is bound to look at life through the eyes of one's sex'. 'Looking at life through the eyes of one's sex' is the conscious motive behind *Keynotes* and *Discords* both in their themes, which are women's love and desire, their pain and disillusionment, and also in their style which is light and fluid, obsessed with nuance and detail, the fleeting impression and heightened emotional response. Egerton's work is perhaps the first example of 'women's writing' in the special sense that fascinated women authors of the next generation – Dorothy Richardson, May Sinclair, Virginia Woolf – and stands as a forerunner of the *écriture féminine* that has preoccupied recent feminist criticism. Egerton's story 'A Cross Line', for example, records the subtle fluctuations of a flirtation between a married woman and a man who is fishing, and 'Now Spring Has Come' tells of a woman waiting so anxiously for the return of her lover that her beauty fades and he finds her no longer desirable:

I believe he was intensely sorry for me; I asked him once you know, half playfully, half maliciously, if he had meant something; something deliciously tender which I quoted out of one of his letters. He paled to the lips ... I sprang up and turned aside his answer. I remember when I was a little child I never would pick a flower. I always fancied they felt it and bled to death. I used to sneak behind and gather up all those my playmates threw down on the road or fields, and put them into the water in the ditch or brook – even now I can't wear them. I did not wish to hurt him either, he could not help his passion-flower withering. I suppose it was written that my love should turn, like fairy gold, into withered leaves in my grasp ... What, dear? a white hair! oh, I saw several lately.

('Now Spring Has Come', *Keynotes*)

This speaker, although so modern – she talks about Tolstoy, Nietzsche, Ibsen's Hedda, 'Strindberg's view of the female animal' – is trapped in women's immemorial need for men more completely and certainly more self-consciously than her mid-Victorian foremothers. What makes Egerton's writing a feminist statement nevertheless, is the raising of this need to the level of literary 'complaint', by no means a subject to repress or to be ashamed of: 'I would use situations or conflicts as I saw them with a total disregard of man's opinions, I would unlock a closed door with a key of my own fashioning'. (Quoted in Showalter, p 211.)

To those women who opposed the New Woman and her feminist and anti-marriage philosophies, unlocking the closed door onto the *terra incognita* of femininity would equally have seemed a vulgar and self-indulgent activity. Paradoxically, although they took their stand on the special sphere they believed women should occupy, writers like Mrs Humphry Ward, Eliza Lynn Linton and Margaret Oliphant defined this sphere in social terms, according to women's roles and influence as wives and mothers; to explore what Virginia Woolf called the 'crannies' of a woman's consciousness was embarrassing and perhaps also dangerous. Eliza Lynn Linton (1822–98), an old woman by this time, but still finding an outlet for her misogyny in the traditionalist *Nineteenth Century*, felt that because women 'are more extreme and more impressible than men', there was all the more reason why 'this noisy little knot of Maenads' should keep quiet about their emotions. Women's instability, deriving from their maternal functions which are nevertheless their *raison d'être*, disqualifies them, in Linton's view, from public activity of most kinds, and particularly political life: 'The cradle lies across the door of the polling-booth and bars the way to the Senate'. To have excitable women engaging in politics would not only upset the decorous rationality of existing political conduct, but would also infect the domestic realm: 'Home means peace [but] where will be the peace of home when women, like men, plunge into the troubled sea of active political life?'

This was an argument frequently adduced by anti-suffragists and one which found its way into the most coherent statement of their principles, 'An Appeal Against Female Suffrage', which had appeared in the *Nineteenth Century* in May 1889, signed by 104 either well-connected or well-known women and asking women readers who shared its views to sign an enclosed protest form. Probably drawn up by Mrs Humphry Ward (1851–1920), the Appeal set out five points of an argument which rested on the notion of the separate spheres. Women's responsibilities 'must always differ essentially from those of men . . . therefore their share in the working of the State machinery should be different from that assigned to men'. National politics, industry, commerce and shipping, finance and foreign policy are the proper sphere for men, from which women must be debarred as direct participants by disabilities of sex and custom. This leaves, of course, the question of influence, and here the belief is that women already possess an influence on political matters 'fully proportioned to the possible share of women in the political activities of England'. Women's activities outside the home should be confined to the social sphere, on School Boards, Boards of Guardians and in work with the sick and poor, areas which call upon the qualities of 'sympathy and disinterestedness' which the 'natural position and functions of women, as they are at present, tend to develop' and which would be diminished by active political life.

The vast majority of Mrs Humphry Ward's novels are love-and-marriage stories – 'The one subject which [women] have eternally at their command . . . is the subject of love', she wrote – and explore women's role and destiny according to the doctrines of the separate spheres set out in the Appeal. Such an understanding of sexual relations had, of course, remained the dominant one throughout the century and in essentials Mrs Ward's position in the 1890s differed little from Mrs Ellis's in the 1840s. But Mrs Ward was too acute a social observer and proselytizer not to realize that her novels must take account of women's changing life-styles and aspirations. Marriage must be shown as able to accommodate women's new ambitions to be socially significant whilst still maintaining its traditional pattern. *Marcella* (1894) and *Sir George Tressady* (1896) follow the career of the beautiful (in a pre-Raphaelite manner), intelligent and altruistic but irregularly brought up Marcella Boyce, who becomes a Venturist (Fabian) in her desire to rid the country of poverty and injustice. *Marcella* opens in Brookshire with a deliberate reminiscence of Dorothea's similar ardours in *Middlemarch*, but Mrs Ward takes her heroine beyond the point where *Middlemarch* ends by exposing her to urban as well as rural poverty. Marcella becomes a nurse in the East End, and in this way Mrs Ward acknowledges the new horizons of women of this period. As genuine in her protest against poverty as her mid-century predecessors in the social-protest novel, Mrs Ward is concerned to show that the problems will not be solved by women living independent lives or becoming political activists. Marcella marries Aldous Raeburn, a Conservative aristocrat of an enlightened, paternalistic tendency, and it is as his wife, the inspiration of his political career, that her future effectiveness lies. What is disconcerting, however, is the nature of the 'influence' that is properly Marcella's, which is limited to the aesthetic and emotional. With Dorothea there was the knowledge that she was Will Ladislaw's equal, if not his superior, that without her his moral and intellectual nature would not be so well developed. But Aldous Raeburn is of a fixed and moulded goodness before he meets Marcella and she makes little difference to his political opinions or moral growth other than 'to cheer him forward on the lines of his own nature'. Her role in his life is to sympathize and to adorn, to be possessed as an image of lovely womanhood rather as he carries the sketch of her in the breast pocket of his coat. Her youth and beauty are qualities which should not be spent on pursuits other than the wifely, as Raeburn indicates when he sees Marcella in a scene of East End violence and squalor: 'Was this what her new career – her en-thusiasms – meant, or might mean? Twenty-three! – in the prime of youth, of charm! Horrible, unpardonable waste . . . to bruise and exhaust her young bloom amid such scenes – such gross abominations' (ch. 10). The novel ends with Marcella's abdication – 'she had given away all rights – even the right to hate herself' – in a scene which recalls Tennyson's *The Princess* of nearly fifty years before:

> Pale was the perfect face;
> The bosom with long sighs laboured; and meek
> Seemed the full lips, and mild the luminous eyes,
> And the voice trembled and the hand.
>
> (VII. 209–12)

'Piteously, childishly, with seeking eyes', Marcella also 'mutely' asks forgiveness from Raeburn, and he and the Prince reply similarly: 'Yield thyself up: my hopes and thine are one: Accomplish thou my manhood and thyself', says the Prince, and Raeburn's final words are, 'Does a man *forgive* the hand that sets him free, the voice that re-creates him? Choose some better word – my wife!' In *Sir George Tressady*, where the Raeburns (now Lord and Lady Maxwell) stand as foil to the troubled career and matrimonial struggles of the hero, Marcella's life is completely subsumed in that of her husband's: 'She could argue better and think better; but at the bottom, if the truth were told, they were Maxwell's arguments and Maxwell's thoughts'.

The irony of Mrs Ward's position was, of course, that, although in her novels she advocated unemployed dependence for women, in life nobody worked harder than she did or was a shrewder busi-nesswoman and political activist. This dissociation of self and heroines was unusually marked in her case, more so than was true by this time of the equally hard-working Margaret Oliphant. Although in the journalism of her old age Oliphant could still attack those who undermined traditional conduct, in her fiction there is an increasing qualification of the belief that marriage is essential for a woman and that, having got it, it is all that she needs. As Q. D.

Leavis says, Margaret Oliphant's conception of a heroine was never conventional:

> Her admirable women are clever, efficient, vital, highly articulate, practical-minded, superior and managing – but magnanimous and tolerant enough at the shortcomings and failings natural to men, whom they often see mainly as means to an end. And most original of all, the Oliphant heroine *works*, a condition otherwise almost unknown in Victorian novels outside *Jane Eyre* and *Villette*.
> (*Autobiography and Letters of Margaret Oliphant*, Introduction, p 28)

Oliphant's novels reflect an opinion she expressed when comparing herself to Charlotte Brontë:

> I don't suppose my powers are equal to hers . . . but yet I have had far more experience and, I think, a fuller conception of life. I have learned to take perhaps more a man's view of mortal affairs – to feel that the love between men and women, the marrying and giving in marriage, occupy in fact so small a portion of existence or thought.
> (ibid., p 67)

In some respects her later novel *Hester* (1883) is a reworking of *Miss Marjoribanks* in being the story of a spirited young women and her relationship with an older woman. But whereas in *Miss Marjoribanks* the older woman is silly and helpless, in *Hester* she is a successful and admired banker:

> Miss Vernon's was a reign of great benevolence, of great liberality, but of great firmness too. As she got older she became almost the most important person in Redborough. The people spoke of her as they sometimes do of a very popular man, by her Christian name. Catherine Vernon did this and that, they said, Catherine was the first thought when anything was wanted . . . her name was put to everything. Catherine Street, Catherine Square, Catherine places without number.
> (ch. 2)

She is, of course, unmarried, 'an old maid, to be sure, but an old maid who was never alone', and it is in her acceptance of the 'daughter' Hester in the place of the failed 'son' Edward that the novel's major interest lies. Although it ends sadly and questioningly, with Catherine dead, Edward gone and Hester's future uncertain, the novel in general offers a more optimistic solution than many of its contemporaries to some of the issues that had troubled women writers throughout the century: the single woman is capable of a public life of dignity and power, marriage is not to be preferred above all other states, and women can look to each other for courage and affection:

'Oh, Catherine Vernon!' she cried, 'we are both in great trouble. We have not been fond of each other; but I am sorry, sorry for you – sorry to the bottom of my heart.'

Catherine made no reply. The shock was too great, too terrible and overwhelming. She could not answer nor show that she heard even, although she did hear in the extraordinary tension of her faculties. [Hester] touched Catherine's arm with her hand softly two or three times, then after a while in utter downfall and weakness dropped her forehead upon it, clasping it with both her hands, and sobbed there as upon her mother's breast. The room was perfectly still, stretching round them, large and dim: in this one corner the little steadfast light upon the group, the mother (you would have said) hiding her face from the light, hiding her anguish from both earth and Heaven, the daughter with that clinging which is the best support, giving to their mutual misery the pathetic broken utterance of tears.

(ch. 40)

In some respects *Hester* fulfils the promise of Harriet Martineau's *Deerbrook*; 'parochial, domestic, filled with the small details of daily living' (Colby, op. cit.), as a study of a small group of individuals in relation to each other and to a community which depends on them and to whom they are responsible, *Hester* has much of the substance of the Victorian bourgeois love-story. In its differences from *Deerbrook* lies the history of the development of women's consciousness of themselves and their position during the forty years which separate them. In *Hester* women remain the moral arbiters of the novel, but their influence is less assured than in Martineau's time. Hester cannot redeem Edward by her goodness or her love for him, and it is up to Catherine to save the bank and all its dependents by her own efforts, and not indirectly through the actions of men. The trust that earlier women writers placed in marriage, the 'monogamic idealism about sex' that G. M. Young believed characterized the Victorian heyday, is shown in *Hester* to be just that, an ideal, a hope, but probably an unrealizable one. In its absence women must rely not only on their traditional strengths of patience, fortitude and sympathy for others, but also on the new strengths of independence and active service in the public world which Victorian feminism had encouraged them to develop.

9

MID-VICTORIAN NOVELISTS

Sheila Smith and Peter Denman

Disraeli, Kingsley, Reade and Collins (Sheila Smith)

'"Action may not always be happiness," said the General; "but there is no happiness without action."' All Disraeli's novels are, to some extent, self-analysis. This advice, offered to Lothair (*Lothair*, ch. 79), epitomizes Disraeli's own life. He needed the excitement of action, and he soon realized that, for him, the most satisfying activity was politics. Born in 1804 into a family of Sephardim Jews, in comfortable circumstances, he was the eldest son of Isaac D'Israeli, a scholar and writer who achieved fame with his *Curiosities of Literature* (1791–1823), essays and anecdotes about literature and writers. Isaac resigned from the Synagogue in 1817 and, although he himself never became a Christian, he had his children baptized into the Anglican church, so Benjamin's Jewish origins were no hindrance to his political ambitions although many of his opponents sneered at his Jewishness. Contemporary cartoons emphasized his Jewish appearance, and Thackeray's 'Codlingsby' (1847), satirizing *Coningsby* (1844), is strongly anti-Semitic. Disraeli never forgave Thackeray and pilloried him, seventeen years after his death, as the envious social-climber St Barbe in *Endymion* (1880), a crude and unfair caricature. The powerful intelligence of Jews, such as Sidonia, who makes and breaks kings in *Coningsby*, and the Neuchatels in *Endymion*, and the inspiration of Jerusalem, as in *Tancred* (1847) or *Lothair* (1870), haunt Disraeli's novels. His visit to Jerusalem in 1831 was the climax of his Grand Tour of Spain, Greece and the Near East. These travels and his visits to Italy and Germany formed an important part of his education which was not confined to books ('Nine-tenths of existing books are nonsense, and the clever books are the refutation of that nonsense', says Mr Gaston Phoebus in *Lothair*), although he read widely in his father's large library. His only formal schooling was a short period at

Higham Hall, near Walthamstow. There was an abortive attempt to make him a lawyer, and he dabbled in journalism, in 1825 attempting unsuccessfully to launch a daily newspaper, *The Representative*. He ran up debts and his first novel, *Vivian Grey* (1826–7), published anonymously, was an attempt to make money. Its hero is an ambitious young man who tries to achieve power by political intrigue, fails, fights a fatal duel, and escapes to the Continent where he meddles in local politics and conducts fruitless love-affairs. The novel ends, abruptly, in the middle of a thunderstorm, obviously because Disraeli could not think what to do with his hero. London society read the book eagerly because so many contemporary public figures appeared in it, thinly disguised. Acclaim changed to mockery, however, when it was discovered that the author was an obscure young man, ignorant of London society or politics. The novel was a continuing embarrassment to Disraeli. Unable to suppress it, he later pruned it for republication. Even allowing for its debt to the eighteenth-century picaresque novel, it is a shapeless book, and full of absurdly romantic visions of love and princely luxury. Vivian's exaggerated postures betray Disraeli's enthusiasm for Byron and the Byronic hero:

He looked up to Heaven with a wild smile, half of despair and half of defiance. It seemed to imply that Fate had now done her worst, and that he had at last the satisfaction of knowing himself to be the most unfortunate and unhappy being that ever existed.

(Bk VIII, ch. 1)

Yet despite the flamboyance of Disraeli's uncontrolled imagination the novel is vigorous, inventive and satirical. One character, Beckendorff, is the first of Disraeli's intelligent, experienced men with the power to influence a kingdom's fate. Speaking to Vivian, he expresses Disraeli's own philosophy of life:

No conjuncture can possibly occur, however fearful, however tremendous it may appear, from which a man, by his own energy, may not extricate himself, as a mariner by the rattling of his cannon can dissipate the impending water-spout!

(Bk VI, ch. 7)

I have no evidence to prove the efficacy of this method of dealing with water-spouts, but certainly Disraeli's own energy, intelligence and self-confidence, fostered by his friends and particularly by his sister Sarah, helped him to overcome money troubles, bouts of ill-health and failures, and made possible his brilliant political career.

In the 1830s his friendship with Edward Bulwer (whose best-selling novel *Pelham* (1828) owes something to *Vivian Grey*) made him one of the group of writers, artists and politicians who frequented the receptions of Lady Blessington and Count D'Orsay. Bulwer and D'Orsay were both dandies; and Disraeli also took pains to astound London society by his dazzling appearance and wit. One of Lady Blessington's guests described him:

He was sitting in a window looking on Hyde Park, the last rays of sunlight reflected from the gorgeous gold flowers of a splendidly embroidered waistcoat. Patent leather pumps, a white stick with a black cord and tassel, and a quantity of chains about his neck and pockets, served to make him a conspicuous object. He has one of the most remarkable faces I ever saw . . . His eye is black as Erebus, and has the most mocking, lying in wait sort of expression conceivable . . . His hair is as extraordinary as his taste in waistcoats. A thick, heavy mass of jet black ringlets falls on his left cheek . . . The conversation turned on Beckford. I might as well attempt to gather up the foam of the sea as to convey an idea of the extraordinary language in which he clothed his description. He talked like a racehorse approaching the winningpost, every muscle in action.
(J. A. Froude, *The Earl of Beaconsfield*, 1905 edn, p 52)

Disraeli had ambitions to be a poet, but had to admit failure. Froude described him reciting his *Revolutionary Epic* at a party given by his admirer, Mrs Austen. His costume was dandified and Byronic – velvet coat, shirt with the collar open at the throat, embroidered waistcoat, shoes with red rosettes – but the poem was not a success (op. cit., p 48). His romantic novel, *Contarini Fleming* (1832), also describes his short-lived aspirations to be a poet. During this period he published several novels – *The Young Duke* (1831); *Alroy* (1833), a florid historical romance, with a Jewish hero; *Henrietta Temple* (1837), a semi-autobiographical love story; and *Venetia* (1837), a fictional account of the lives of Shelley and Byron. Apart from *Alroy* these novels are of the kind which Hazlitt called 'silver-fork', purporting to describe accurately the details of fashionable life. The vogue for this kind of novel had been established by Robert Plumer Ward's *Tremaine* (1825). Despite their excesses, Disraeli's early novels have their interest. He was later embarrassed by *The Young Duke*, as he was by *Vivian Grey*, but this improbable tale has a controlling theme important in his later novels – a wealthy young aristocrat's gradual acceptance of responsibility to society. Also it is obvious that Disraeli learnt more from Byron than the cut of a collar. His satirical scrutiny of qualities he had admired or described with conviction is like Byron's treatment of romantic love in, for example, 'Beppo'. Here Disraeli scrutinizes the pose of the fated hero, which he had described with enthusiasm in *Vivian Grey*:

> While he existed, he was one of those men who, because they have been imprudent, think themselves unfortunate, and mistake their diseased mind for an implacable destiny.
>
> *(The Young Duke*, Bk III, ch. 5)

This amused awareness of the motives behind a grand gesture, which nevertheless attracts him, is of a kind with Byron's insistence on the transitory nature of passion, despite its importance:

> Think you, if Laura had been Petrarch's wife,
> He would have written sonnets all his life?
>
> *(Don Juan*, Canto III, viii)

One of the characteristics of Byron's later style is also Disraeli's — the ambivalent tone of combined mockery and admiration, in which neither the mockery nor the admiration is lost or destroyed. Byron believes in love, but he can laugh at the follies of men in love. Disraeli enjoys the glamour of aristocracy, but he mocks the aristocrat's follies. Moreover, Disraeli does not simply imitate Byron, he adapts what he borrows to his own purposes. The Duke of St James comes to trust his own emotions and dares to shape his own destiny, like a true Byronic hero. But the nature of his response to life is original. By the end of the novel the Duke is using his intelligence and perception of society to counter the Utilitarians' arguments and to make a speech on Catholic Emancipation in the House of Lords. Disraeli's flights of romantic fancy were usually related to practical affairs.

His interest in politics increased. If he could not be a poet, he would be a politician and dominate the House of Commons with the power of language skilfully used. At the end of *The Young Duke* (Bk V, ch. 6) he says how much he enjoys debate and discusses debating styles. He distinguishes between the styles of the Commons and of the Lords, remarking that Byron's Don Juan 'may perhaps be our model' in the Commons. Disraeli learnt much from the satirical tone of Byron's greatest poem, and the tone of a debater's voice — insistent, witty, controlled — is an important element in his novels.

He published political writings as well as romances during the 1830s, for example, *A Vindication of the English Constitution* (1835), in which he attacked the Whigs and the Utilitarians and declared the Tory party

... the national party; it is the really democratic party of England. It supports the institutions of the country, because they have been established for the common good, and because they secure the equality of civil rights, without which, whatever may be its name, no government can be free, and based upon which principle, every government, however it may be styled, is, in fact, a Democracy.

(p 182)

This conception of Tory politics is very important to an understanding of *Coningsby* and *Sybil* (1845). At the fifth attempt he at last got a seat in the House of Commons, becoming a Tory member for Maidstone in 1837. For some years the world of practical politics left him no time for writing novels. But as he formulated his political ideas and, from being a laughing-stock in the House, came to be regarded as a formidable speaker, he began to think of publishing his political manifesto. He chose the novel to do this because there was the chance it would reach a wide audience. He was resentful when Peel gave him no office when he became Prime Minister in 1841, but it gave him the time to write.

Novels in the 1830s were beginning to reflect the growing seriousness of the time. In *Sartor Resartus* (1833–4) Carlyle mocked society's follies and false values and devastated the novel of high fashion. His satire was echoed by Dickens in *Nicholas Nickleby* (1838–9) in his extract from the novel enjoyed by Mrs Wititterly. Dickens, the most popular novelist of the time, had directed the public's attention from high society to ordinary life. 'He has made washerwomen as interesting as duchesses', as Mrs Oliphant later remarked ('Sensation Novels', *Blackwood's Magazine*, 1862, pp 564–84). Dickens's exuberant comedy was always based on a penetrating observation of his own society. Even the romantic tales of criminals and their escapades – of the kind of Ainsworth's *Rookwood* (1834), with dashing Dick Turpin as hero – could be moral or philosophical, as in Bulwer's *Eugene Aram* (1832) or *Paul Clifford* (1830), and Dickens in his preface to *Oliver Twist* (1837–8) repudiated the false glamour of the fictional criminal and claimed he was substituting the squalid, insecure life of the real criminal; while Thackeray produced his satirical version of the criminal novel in *Catherine* (1839–40).

The 1830s and 1840s were a period when writers and reformers attempted to inform the middle-class public and influence opinion concerning the social miseries brought about by the Industrial Revolution. It was the age of Royal Commissions and Blue Books examining labour conditions in factories, the health of towns, sanitation, destitution in town and country. And the literary counterparts of these enquiries were the novels written to expose and examine social problems, novels 'with a purpose'. For example, Anthony Trollope's mother, Frances, published *Michael Armstrong* (1840), a melodramatic account of child labour in the factories; and in *Jessie Phillips* (1844) she attacked the 1834 Poor Law, as did Dickens in *Oliver Twist*. In *Helen Fleetwood* (1841) Charlotte Elizabeth Tonna exposed the miseries of the rural poor who came to the industrial town to look for work.

Disraeli's *Coningsby* was also written with a purpose. In this novel he comments upon contemporary society, but from a practising politician's viewpoint. In Disraeli's words, the novel was intended 'to vindicate the just claims of the Tory party to be the popular political confederation of the country'. His purpose gives the book direction and he writes with a new power. He takes the old literary convention of the young aristocrat's education through a series of encounters and adventures and uses it to explore the contemporary situation. He expresses his increasing opposition to Peel:

The Tamworth Manifesto of 1834 was an attempt to construct a party without principles – its basis therefore was necessarily Latitudinarianism, and its inevitable consequence has been Political Infidelity ... There was indeed a considerable shouting about what they called Conservative principles; but the awkward question naturally arose, what will you conserve?

(Bk II, ch. 5)

The novel is an attempt to answer this question, to propound the principles of a Tory party responsive to the needs of contemporary society. Coningsby, thoughtful and idealistic, questions the old-style Toryism of his grandfather, Lord Monmouth (modelled on the Marquess of Hertford, who was also to be Thackeray's Lord Steyne in *Vanity Fair*). To Monmouth, the mighty aristocrat, politics are simply a matter of self-aggrandizement and place-seeking. Coningsby believes in a different kind of Toryism which has obligations to society and is based on an ideal union of Church, Monarch and People – in fact, Young England, the creed of a small group of friends, all Tory M.P.s looking to Disraeli for leadership. They appear in *Coningsby*. Coningsby himself is George Smythe, Lord Henry Sydney is Lord John Manners, Buckhurst is Alexander Baillie-Cochrane. Young England was not a political party, rather a group of friends sharing political views. They were active for a very short period from 1842 to 1846. They attacked the Utilitarians and looked back with nostalgia to an idealized feudal system in which Church and aristocracy combined to protect the rights of the people. They criticized the 1834 Poor Law, attempted to improve working-class housing conditions, emphasized the importance of holidays for the working people and supported Lord Ashley's factory reforms. They also argued that the Church had a responsibility for men's bodies as well as for their souls. (For a full account of Young England and Disraeli's part in it, see R. Blake, *Disraeli*, 1966, pp 167–89.) Like the Oxford Movement and the later Pre-Raphaelite Brotherhood, Young England was a romantic protest against the scientific, Utilitarian economics and politics of the time. They were guilty of many follies, including an uncritical adulation of the Stuarts, particularly Charles I, and their dream of uniting aristocrat and worker was sometimes expressed in cricket matches and social functions of which the embarrassment is plain even in contemporary newspaper reports. But they genuinely desired reform, and Lord John Manners's journals show his determination to fulfil the responsibilities which he felt wealth and aristocratic position bring.

Like many Victorian novels, *Coningsby* popularizes current ideas rather than expresses new ones. They are not confined to politics. Like Carlyle, who also loathed the Utilitarians and favoured a feudal hierarchy in society, Disraeli emphasizes the wonder of the Industrial Revolution, part of the 'romance of reality' to which novelists were beginning to turn for material. 'Rightly understood, Manchester is as great a human exploit as Athens' (Bk IV, ch. 1). He also stresses the importance of an intelligent, responsible and energetic leader in this new society. 'In all things we trace the irresistible influence of the individual' (Bk V, ch. 4). Sidonia is the romantic, powerful individual in *Coningsby*, and he inspires Coningsby with his ideals.

The marriage between Coningsby and Edith Millbank, daughter of the humanitarian factory-owner, symbolizes the alliance between the traditional aristocracy, invigorated by an awareness of their responsibilities, and the new aristocracy, the great industrialists. Disraeli's adaptation of the conventional romantic plot shows perception of how the centres of power in the evolving English society were to be formed; it is a good example of his use of romance to express practical political alignment.

Coningsby is a challenge to the youth of the nation expressed not so much in the hero, who is rather a pallid character, as in the persuasive tones of Disraeli's oratory, which makes a powerful effect in the book, despite his habit of holding up the action while he debates various political themes. Apart from Disraeli himself, the great character of the novel is Lord Monmouth with his princely way of life – here in his exposition of the old Toryism Disraeli finds new purpose for his scenes of high fashion. Part of Monmouth's entourage is his creature and politician Rigby, a brilliant satirical portrait. In fact, the strength of the novel is its ability to express political activity and the minutiae of politics, not least their intrigue in which Tadpole and Taper play their part. Sidonia is an exotic, incredible dream-figure; Tadpole and Taper are all too real.

In the General Preface to the collected edition of his novels (1870) Disraeli explains:

The derivation and character of political parties; the condition of the people which had been the consequence of them; the duties of the Church as a main remedial agency in our present state, were the three principal topics which I intended to treat, but I found they were too vast for the space I had allotted to myself. These were all launched in *Coningsby*; but the origin and condition of political parties, the first portion of the theme, was the only one completely handled in that work.
Next year, in *Sybil*, I considered the condition of the people.

Using his own experiences in a tour of the northern industrial cities, but also relying on Blue Book information, Disraeli in *Sybil* explores another current idea – that of the Two Nations, the Rich and the Poor, living side by side in England yet knowing nothing of each other. Egremont, the younger son of a noble family, learns something of working-class life through his friendship with Walter Gerard, the Chartist leader, Sybil, Gerard's daughter and Stephen Morley, the Chartist journalist. Disraeli crams into the novel a bewildering number of topics – Chartist mobs, the iniquity of the truck system, the appalling conditions in which women and children worked in coal-mines, the growth of trades unions, the plight of the handloom weavers, the agricultural depression, the insanitary squalor of the agricultural labourers' existence. No wonder that the novel is disorganized, and that some of the Blue Book facts are undigested. Disraeli's imagination was not like Mrs Gaskell's; he could not enter sympathetically into the actual conditions of the poor. The handloom weaver's speech is stilted and the attempts at dialect produce only bastard Cockney. But *Sybil* is not a domestic novel, but discursive, rhetorical:

Even now, in the quiet times in which we live, when public robbery is out of fashion and takes the milder title of a commission of inquiry, and when there is no treason except voting against a minister, who, though he may have changed all the policy which you have been elected to support, expects your vote and confidence all the same: even in the age of mean passions and petty risks, it is something to step aside from Palace Yard, and instead of listening to a dull debate, where facts are only a repetition of the blue books you have already read, and the fancy an ingenious appeal to the re-crimination of Hansard, to enter the old Abbey and listen to an anthem!

(Bk IV, ch. 6)

Disraeli adapts the tone of parliamentary debate to serve the purposes of his novel – it can be quietly sarcastic and abusive, as in this quotation, or fiercely attacking, or challenging, or exhilarating. By means of this rhetoric he can refer the reader from scene to scene, using them as the points in his debate, directing the reader's attention to a panoramic view of English society. The debater's voice, and the intelligence and perception implied by the voice, hold the fragments together. The plot is both improbable and impos-sible, the love-scenes melodramatic and absurd, yet the novel reveals a tough intellect. For example, Disraeli approves of Trafford's mill and the amenities he provides for his workers, but he is aware that some people would feel oppressed by such paternalistic concern for their well-being and gives the words of a mill-hand who says as much. He describes the horrors of Devilsdust's childhood, and realizes that, harsh as life in the factory is, it provides him with a refuge and a place, however humble, in society. He represents 'Bishop' Hatton, the master locksmith, as a coarse brute, but shows that Hatton's mastery of his craft gives him an authority which England's effete aristocracy have forfeited. Disraeli is one of the few English novelists concerned with maintaining a flow of ideas in a novel. He appeals to his readers' intelligence as well as to their imagination. You may not agree with his ideas, but you cannot ignore them.

Sybil is anti-democratic. It would be surprising if, written at this date and by a man in Disraeli's circumstances, it were not. His attitude to Chartism is the same as that expressed in his speeches in the House of Commons in 1839 when Attwood supported the National Petition. He voted against Attwood's motion but sympathized with the Chartists' demands for social justice. The people themselves were not to have political power, but their leaders were to improve the people's condition. Fear of revolution, violence, disorder – a fear also found in the novels of Mrs Gaskell, Kingsley and Dickens – is evident in the riot scenes at the end of *Sybil*. The nation was to entrust itself to responsible leaders who would wield their power for the people's good; and Disraeli was determined to be one of them.

Tancred does not substantiate Disraeli's claim that it is to demonstrate 'the duties of the Church as a main remedial agency in our present state'. Tancred, a young English nobleman, renounces English society and discovers that the source of spiritual power is Jerusalem. As Robert Blake remarks of Disraeli's odd ideas about race and religion at this time, 'To him the Jew is a proto-Christian and Christianity is completed Judaism' (op. cit., 1966, p 204). The best part of the novel is the early section describing contemporary aristocratic society. The improbable incidents of Tancred's spiritual odyssey recall the rhetorical excesses of *Vivian Grey* and *Contarini Fleming*. As in his first novel, Disraeli ends the book obviously because his invention fails him. After all, any descent from Mount Sinai is bound to be an anti-climax!

The little group known as Young England drifted apart. Disraeli wanted a higher position than the leadership of a rogue group in the Tory party. In 1852 he became Chancellor of the Exchequer; and in 1868 for a few months he realized his ambition to be Prime Minister. During the years 1847–69 he had no time to write novels. But when he lost office he began to write *Lothair*, which I consider his best. It was again prompted by contemporary events: Garibaldi's abortive campaign to liberate Italy in 1867 and the wealthy Marquess of Bute's conversion to Roman Catholicism in 1868.

Lothair is an aristocrat who will possess immense wealth and estates when he comes of age. His parents are dead, and one of his guardians is Cardinal Grandison (a composite portrait of Manning and Wiseman) who was appointed to his position of trust before his conversion to the Roman Catholic Church. Brought up by his other guardian, an austere Scots Earl, Lothair does not meet the Cardinal until he is nearing his majority. Supported by the wealthy Catholic family the St Jeromes, who have a beautiful niece Clare Arundel, the Cardinal attempts to convert Lothair and secure his great wealth and position for the Roman Catholic Church. At first Roman Catholicism's graciousness and ideal spirituality attract Lothair, and he dreams of building a cathedral, although he cannot make up his mind whether it is to be Anglican or Catholic. Then by chance he meets Theodora, the inspiration of the revolutionary societies of Europe, and joins her in the attempt to free Rome from Papal and French rule. They fail and Theodora is killed. Lothair is taken wounded into Rome where he is nursed by Clare Arundel. The Roman Catholics spread the news that he was fighting on the

Papal side and that the woman who rescued him was the Virgin Mary. Lothair takes part in a great thanksgiving festival commemorating this miracle but does not realize that he has condoned a lie until next day he reads an account of the thanksgiving in a Roman Catholic journal.

In the novel's central scene the Cardinal, in gentle, reasonable words, tries to persuade him that he is mistaken, that he was in fact fighting for the Papacy. It is the climax of the long subtle campaign to possess Lothair, and at last he sees it as such. It is the most masterly scene Disraeli wrote. His ability to suggest tones of voice is at its greatest here. For a comparable fictional embodiment of brainwashing techniques, particularly the brainwasher's insidious tenderness and concern for his victim forming part of the undermining attack, English readers had to wait for Arthur Koestler's *Darkness at Noon* (1940) or Orwell's *1984* (1949). To appreciate the delicacy of Disraeli's touch in handling the contemporary fear of increasing Roman Catholic power in England one has only to compare the crude melodrama of the priest who also tries to ensnare a wealthy aristocrat in Wilkie Collins's *The Black Robe* (1881). Disraeli's attitude to the Roman Catholic Church had greatly changed since *Sybil* in which he yearned for the beauty and social security of the pre-Reformation Church as he saw it. In *Lothair* its grace and apparent concern are part of its snare. Lothair escapes the Cardinal and finally marries his former sweetheart who comes of a good Anglican family, so he and his wealth remain within the Church of England. A well-written scene is Lothair's final meeting with the Cardinal in England, when Grandison, far from showing resentment or anger at his defeat, is all sweet graciousness and urbane goodwill. *Lothair* is the most controlled and best shaped of Disraeli's novels. He had at last achieved his greatest ambition and no longer needed to strain for effect or to persuade the public that he had a substantial political programme. He was still given to sudden lapses of style. He never had the great literary artist's ear for nuances of language. Queen Victoria was understandably a little amazed at his prose. 'Mr Disraeli (*alias* Dizzy) writes very curious reports to me of the House of Commons proceedings – much in the style of his books', she wrote to the King of the Belgians in 1852. In *Lothair* he occasionally produces sentences which read like excerpts from Daisy Ashford's *The Young Visiters*. This is the description of the Cardinal at a fashionable reception:

After all, the Mikado himself was not more remarkable than this Prince of
the Church in a Tyburnian drawing-room, habited in his pink cassock and
cape, and waving, as he spoke, with careless grace his pink barrette.

(ch. 8)

But, generally speaking, the style is assured and flexible, the tone
that of a confident, controlled voice enlivening civilized conversation with illuminating wit. For example, the description of the
wealthy and nonchalant Lord St Aldegonde's red republicanism:

He was opposed to all privileges, and indeed to all orders of men, except
dukes, who were a necessity. He was also strongly in favour of the equal
division of all property, except land. Liberty depended on land, and the
greater the landowners, the greater the liberty of a country.

(ch. 21)

This extract illustrates the fascinating ambivalence of Disraeli's
attitude towards the aristocracy – his pleasure in their elegance and
his mockery at their decadence; it also demonstrates his power of
self-parody.

There are also instances of Disraeli's penetrating intelligence
producing ideas which his imagination represents in scenes and
dialogues. For example, Lothair takes Theodora and her husband
to Blenheim where his friendship with the owner allows them the
privilege of walking in the private gardens. Theodora responds to
their beauty but they express for her a principle of exclusion which
she finds depressing – 'The manners of your country are founded
on exclusion'. She dislikes the 'artificial loneliness' of the great
parks surrounding aristocratic houses. She goes on:

'I admire nature, but I require the presence of humanity. Life in great cities
is too exhausting; but in my village there should be air, streams, and
beautiful trees, a picturesque scene, but enough of my fellow-creatures to
ensure constant duty.'

'But the fulfilment of duty and society founded on what you call the
principle of exclusion, are not incompatible,' said Lothair.

'No, but difficult. What should be natural becomes an art; and in every
art it is only the few who can be first-rate.'

(ch. 25)

There is acute perception in that final epigram. In these few
sentences Sir Willoughby Patterne's grace, weakness and menace
are summed up. Disraeli was not always prolix and diffuse; he could
discipline his prose to great effect.

His last complete novel, *Endymion*, was half written by 1874, the year in which he again became Prime Minister, this time for six years. It was published in 1880. It is the fairy tale of a young man, Endymion, who by dint of intelligence, hard work, and good luck rises from obscurity to become Prime Minister. The book has a nostalgic charm, and gives a retrospective if somewhat romantic survey of political events in the 1830–50 period. But the tone is tired and the flashes of wit are rare. The novel's romantic idealism can be gauged by the description of Lord Eglinton's medieval tournament in 1839. In *Endymion* the extravagant attempt to relive the triumph and excitement of a medieval joust is a miraculous pageant of splendour and beauty. In fact, the event was a fiasco, ruined by the relentless rain of Ayrshire in August. The novel is monotonously optimistic and all comes right.

When Disraeli died in 1881 he left unfinished nine chapters of a novel describing the career of Joseph Toplady Falconet who was to have been Disraeli's satirical portrait of Gladstone.

Disraeli is an exotic among English novelists. His novels, judged by the standards of 'pure literature', are hopeless. They make much more sense if seen in the context of the eighteenth-century discursive novel, Byron's satiric narratives and Thomas Love Peacock's witty conversation pieces. He did not have a solid and secure position in the middle classes, as many Victorian novelists had, nor did he so closely direct his appeal to the middle-class public or accept their *mores*. His early books were directed at the fashionable and political society of London. And, although my researches into the public's response to *Sybil* (*Mr. Disraeli's Readers*, 1966) have shown that readers from all classes of society wrote to Disraeli about the book, none of his novels claimed the great middle-class response accorded to Dickens and Trollope. *Coningsby* went through three editions in 1844, but his first great success was *Lothair*. As Robert Blake points out, it was natural that everybody should want to read a novel written by an ex-Prime Minister. There are no insipid, middle-class ladies, adoring and submissive, in his novels, but women like Theodora, who could have been melodramatic but is, in fact, impressive, or Endymion's determined and ambitious sister, Myra. Nor do Disraeli's novels express the middle-class idea of heaven – marriage, a competence and a little house. The claustrophobic refuges provided at the end of *Oliver Twist*, *Nicholas Nickleby* and *Martin Chuzzlewit* are not found in his romances. His two great themes are aristocratic life and the business of politics, and I can think of no other English novelist who can describe them so well. The middle-class Victorian writers were, generally speaking, weak on aristocrats. The reviewer of 'Recent Novels' for *Fraser's*, April 1849, remarks on the 'tawdry lies' of the novelists purporting to describe the 'fashionable world'. As for politics, when Trollope's Duke of Omnium becomes Prime Minister he does nothing, because Trollope obviously does not know what Prime Ministers do. But Disraeli did. The speech and actions of the 'gentleman in Downing Street' in *Sybil* are entirely convincing:

> 'You must summon a council for four o'clock. I have some deputations to receive, which I will throw over; but to Windsor I must go. Nothing has yet occurred to render any notice of the state of the country necessary in the speech from the Throne.'
> 'Not yet,' said his companion; 'but what will tomorrow bring forth?'
> 'After all it is only a turn-out. I cannot re-cast her Majesty's speech and bring in rebellion and closed mills, instead of loyalty and a good harvest.'
>
> (Bk VI, ch. 1)

And Disraeli's view of both aristocracy and politics is comprehensive not rigid – he loves them and yet laughs at them, and at its best his ironic style well expresses this ambivalence.

Disraeli is not a great novelist, but he is a good one. His achievement is uneven but ultimately the interest of the novels is the interest of his own colourful personality. His energy, intelligence and flamboyant imagination inform their rhetoric, their incidents, their dialogue. 'May one not lament the degradation of a promising novelist into a Prime Minister?' asked Leslie Stephen ('Mr. Disraeli's Novels', *Hours in a Library*, 1876). But in truth Disraeli the novelist and Disraeli the politician cannot be separated.

Charles Kingsley's novels are also characterized by the writer's powerful personality, evident in style and tone. His first novel was *Yeast* (1848), published anonymously. Inspired by his brother-in-law Sidney Godolphin Osborne, Rector of Durweston, who worked to improve the living conditions of the Dorset agricultural labourers, Kingsley used the novel to shatter the notion that dirt and disease existed only in industrial towns and that life in the country was healthy and idyllic. Disraeli had made the same point in his description of Marney in *Sybil*, but *Yeast* is the first novel devoted to the subject. Like so many novels of the 1840s, *Yeast* has a serious purpose and Kingsley wants to confront his readers with reality:

Of all the species of lovely scenery which England holds, none, perhaps, is more exquisite than the banks of the chalk-rivers – the perfect limpidity of the water, the gay and luxuriant vegetation of the banks and ditches, the masses of noble wood embosoming the villages, the unique beauty of the water meadows, living sheets of emerald and silver, tinkling and sparkling, cool under the fiercest sun, brilliant under the blackest clouds. – There, if anywhere, one would have expected to find Arcadia among fertility, loveliness, industry, and wealth. But, alas for the sad reality! the cool breath of those glittering water-meadows too often floats laden with poisonous miasma. Those picturesque villages are generally the perennial hot beds of fever and ague, of squalid penury, sottish profligacy, dull discontent too stale for words. There is luxury in the park, wealth in the huge farmsteadings, knowledge in the parsonage: but the poor? those by whose dull labour all that luxury and wealth, ay, even that knowledge, is made possible – what are they? We shall see, please God, ere the story's end.

(ch. 3)

Like Disraeli's, Kingsley's style depends on oratory, but it is the oratory of the pulpit, not the House of Commons. Here the appeal is to God, and the novel's concern is moral. In his preface to the 1851 edition Kingsley says that he wrote it because he was afraid that society was losing 'the living spirit of Christianity' and he felt that most people were clinging 'to the outward letter of it, whether High Church or Evangelical; unconscious, all the while, that they are sinking out of real living belief, into that dead self-deceiving belief-in-believing, which has been always heretofore, and is becoming in England now, the parent of the most blind, dishonest, and pitiless bigotry.'

Relying partly on what he had seen of Sidney Godolphin Osborne's parish in Dorset, partly on S. G. O.'s evidence included in the *Reports of Special Assistant Poor Law Commissioners on the Employment of Women and Children in Agriculture* (1843) and partly on his experience of his own Hampshire parish, Kingsley described the agricultural labourers' crowded and insanitary cottages, the typhus they bred and the squire's indifference. Alone among the social-problem novelists of his time Kingsley gives some idea of the sexual squalor of the poor. This is one of the themes of 'A Rough Rhyme on a Rough Matter', a poem supposedly written by Tregarva, the gamekeeper, for which he is dismissed the squire's service. Frederic Harrison thought Kingsley's ballads the best things he wrote and, although it is over-explicit and too long, 'A Rough Rhyme' with its direct attack and haunting rhythm, epitomizes much of what he says in the novel. I can quote only a few verses here. A poacher's widow is speaking:

'A labourer in Christian England,
Where they cant of a Saviour's name,
And yet waste men's lives like the vermin's
For a few more brace of game . . .

'You have sold the labouring man, squire,
Body and soul to shame,
To pay for your seat in the House, squire,
And to pay for the feed of your game.

'You made him a poacher yourself, squire,
When you'd give neither work nor meat;
And your barley-fed hares robbed the garden
At our starving children's feet . . .

'Our daughters with base-born babies
Have wandered away in their shame;
If your misses had slept, squire, where they did,
Your misses might do the same . . .'

It is a courageous novel; and it frightened the publisher of *Fraser's Magazine*, where it first appeared.

It is true that Kingsley wrote the book because he desperately wanted money, but he also wanted to propagate the ideas of Christian Socialism, which taught the social responsibility of the Church and agreed with Lord Ashley's insistence that improved morals among the working classes were largely dependent upon improved living conditions. Kingsley was anti-intellectual. He had no patience with philosophy or theological niceties. He felt that the Evangelicals were too concerned with the next world to pay sufficient attention to man's happiness in this, and that the Tractarians and High Church thinkers were too idealistic and preoccupied with the past rather than with the present. In *Yeast* the hero, Lancelot Smith, a rich merchant's son, is gradually awakened to the miserable existence of the agricultural labourers largely by the efforts of Tregarva who speaks very like Carlyle. Tregarva takes Lancelot to a village fair. On the way Tregarva criticizes the Young England aristocrat, Lord Vieuxbois:

'Look at that Lord Vieuxbois, sir, as sweet a gentleman as ever God made . . . He spends his whole life and time about the poor, I hear. But sir, as sure as you live he's making his people slaves and humbugs. He doesn't see, sir, that they want to be raised bodily out of this miserable hand-to-mouth state, to be brought nearer up to him, and set on a footing where they can shift for themselves. Without meaning it, sir, all his boundless charities are keeping the people down, and telling them they must stay down, and not help themselves, but wait for what he gives them. He fats prize-labourers, sir, just as Lord Minchampstead fats prize-oxen and pigs.'

Lancelot could not help thinking of that amusingly inconsistent, however well-meant, scene in *Coningsby*, in which Mr Lyle is represented as trying to restore 'the independent order of peasantry,' by making them the receivers of public alms at his own gate, as if they had been Middle-Age serfs or vagabonds, and not citizens of modern England.

'It may suit the Mr. Lyles of his age,' thought Lancelot, 'to make the people constantly and visibly comprehend that property is their protector and friend, but I question whether it will suit the people themselves, unless they can make property understand that it owes them something more definite than protection.'

(ch. 13)

A telling point. Kingsley, although often befogged with prejudice, was not without ideas; but from this extract we must not argue that he believed in democracy. In his novels, as in Disraeli's, the independence of the lower orders must be achieved within the existing class-structure. Tregarva is careful to call Lancelot 'sir'. And of his next novel, *Alton Locke* (1850), which is concerned mainly with Chartism and working-class misery in London but also touches upon agricultural distress, Kingsley wrote:

The moral of my book is, that the working man who tries to get on, to desert his class and rise above it, enters into a lie, and leaves God's path for his own – with consequences . . . I think the cry 'Rise in Life,' has been excited by the very increasing impossibility of being anything but brutes while they struggle below.

(To an unnamed country rector, 13 Jan 1851, quoted by
F. E. Kingsley, *Charles Kingsley: His Letters and Memories
of his Life*, 1877, p 247)

Kingsley was twenty-nine when *Yeast* began to appear, and Rector of Eversley (Hampshire), the living he held until his death in 1875. His father had, like so many Victorian clergymen, taken Holy Orders because this was one of the few dignified professions open to impecunious gentlemen. The family lived for several years at Barnack, in the Fens, near Stamford. Charles loved the Fen country and later described it in his historical novel, *Hereward the Wake* (1866). They also lived at Clovelly in Devonshire, where he became interested in the sea-shore and marine life. Clovelly appears as the fishing-village Penalva in *Two Years Ago* (1854) and is described at length in *Westward Ho!* (1855). Referring to his excitement at the Crimean War but his inability to write about it because he had not experienced it, Kingsley wrote to William Cox Bennett '. . . I am essentially a Pre-Raphaelite in poetry, and can only imagine what I have seen.' This is also true of his novels. One of their strengths is his description of landscapes he knew and loved; and he can hold the reader's attention with his descriptions of the wonderful creatures Tom Thurnall, the doctor in *Two Years Ago*, finds in the rock-pools. Kingsley's accurate observation and imaginative re-creation of marine life is best seen in his book for children, *Glaucus, or the Wonders of the Sea Shore* (1855). This began as a review of books by his friend Philip Gosse, Edmund Gosse's father. Unlike Gosse, Kingsley did not find contemporary scientific discoveries a challenge to his faith in God. For him the material world was a manifestation of God's love, and scientific discovery simply a further revelation of the wonder of God's universe.

In 1836 the Kingsleys came to live in Chelsea, where Kingsley's father had the living of St Luke's. The Carlyles were near neighbours. Charles became friendly with Carlyle and was greatly influenced by his writings and ideas. Kingsley's hard-hitting style echoes his, and Mackaye in *Alton Locke* and Tregarva are obviously modelled on his friend. Carlyle had the habit of claiming God's support for his dogmatic pronouncements. In 1850 John Stuart Mill queried his right to quote God's authority for his assertion that the white races are innately superior to the black. Kingsley also assumes that the Almighty shares his prejudices and lays about him with the wrath of Jehovah when he is attacking the Roman Catholics in *Yeast* and *Westward Ho!* or Evangelical preachers and the 'unmanly' poet Vavasour who lives for art in *Two Years Ago*. Gerard Manley Hopkins who, as a Jesuit, could not be expected to sympathize with Kingsley's views, once complained in a letter that Browning

. . . has got a great deal of what came in with Kingsley and the Broad Church school, a way of talking (and making his people talk) with the air and spirit of a man bouncing up from table with his mouth full of bread and cheese and saying that he meant to stand no blasted nonsense. There is a whole volume of Kingsley's essays which is all a munch and a not standing of any blasted nonsense from cover to cover.

(*Correspondence of G. M. Hopkins and R. W. Dixon*,
ed. C. C. Abbott, 1935, p 74)

There is a great deal of 'munch and not standing of any blasted nonsense' in Kingsley's novels. His moralizing lecturing can be exhausting and a sign of prejudice rather than of thought, as his sorry public debate with Newman showed. It also reflects the increasing and unattractive 'earnestness' of the period which was later to be savaged by Samuel Butler in *The Way of all Flesh* and, more flippantly, by Wilde in *The Importance of Being Earnest*. Kingsley's ideal of the practical, 'manly' Christian, the sturdy huntsman and fisherman who would help anybody and not bother about theological speculations, later dubbed 'muscular Christianity' (a phrase Kingsley hated), is exemplified also in Thomas Hughes's hero, Tom Brown, and in Thomas Arnold's ideal public school boy, who had healthy limbs and pure thoughts.

Hughes became one of the group of Christian Socialists when he heard F. D. Maurice preach in the chapel of Lincoln's Inn. Maurice had a great influence on Kingsley, who called him 'the Master'. He had read Maurice's books at Cambridge, but he did not meet him until 1844. They became close friends. Maurice owed a considerable debt to Coleridge's thought on the social ethic implicit in the Church's teaching. He was concerned with social reform, but he believed that it could come only by religious means. A moral change of heart in individuals was to bring about the social revolution. He was a shy man, but humane and compassionate, believing that the Church should be for mankind and opposed to sectarian bigotry and exclusiveness. His appointment as Professor of Theology at King's College, London, was terminated when he published his *Theological Essays* in 1853. In this book he dared to suggest that after death God did not punish sinners for eternity. This was regarded as dangerous unorthodoxy. On 14 July 1853 Kingsley wrote to Maurice about the *Essays* remarking that they have given him courage to speak more boldly and that the book's theme will frighten people,

... especially such an expression of it as that in §3. P 144. As I read it, I shuddered, to think how here was *the* truth the cardinal truth of my own heart, to preach wh [which] I wish to live and die – And yet so new a truth to me, that till I began to read your books, I never had had an inkling of it.

(British Museum MS 41,287)

The paragraph in question occurs in Essay VII 'On the Atonement' and ends describing Christ:

One who appears as the actual representative of Humanity, cannot be a formal substitute for it. We deny Him in the first character, by claiming the second for Him.

Christ as 'the actual representative of Humanity.' This was at the heart of Maurice's teaching and why he inspired the Christian Socialists. It was why Kingsley resented Young England's patronage of the poor because this denied the dignity of a human being made in God's image. As Maurice himself wrote late in the century in *Christian Socialism* (1893), 'Our Church must apply herself to the task of raising the poor into men; she cannot go on . . . treating them merely as poor.' In terms of theology Maurice was as anti-Utilitarian and as anti-Benthamite as Disraeli was in the sphere of politics, and he had considerable influence on Christian social thought in the nineteenth century, even though his assumption that working men would readily become Christians and accept the Christian teaching and ethic caused the failure of some of his practical schemes for reform. As K. S. Inglis wrote,

What was most important in Maurice, as an influence on Christian social attitudes, was not the particular method he recommended for achieving a harmonious society but the fact that he had given a theological justification for trying to replace the spirit of competition in society by the spirit of co-operation.
(*The Churches and the Working Classes in Victorian England*, 1963, p 267)

The principle of Christian brotherhood was embodied in the Christian Socialists' establishment of Working Men's Associations for Co-operative Production, for example, the Working Tailors' Association in London in 1850. This kind of association they saw as an alternative to Chartism and the hope for the betterment of the working classes after the fiasco of the Chartists' Third Petition in 1848. This is the main theme of Kingsley's *Alton Locke*.

The hard core of Christian Socialism was represented by Maurice, Kingsley and John Ludlow, who was much influenced by Buchez, who had established workers' associations in France. In May–August 1848 the group produced a penny weekly *Politics for the People*, in which Kingsley wrote under the name 'Parson Lot'. It had no practical schemes for reform, but appealed to the working classes to realize the futility of merely political reform and emphasized the need for individual moral reform and an acceptance of Christianity. The Christian Socialists appealed to the upper classes to resist the Utilitarian philosophy and to participate in brotherly co-operation with the classes below them. Kingsley got the reputation for being a fire-brand, and when in *Yeast* he attacked the Game Laws and implied that the landowners exploited both the land and the labourers, the publisher of *Fraser's Magazine*, in which the novel was appearing, insisted that the tale be brought to a close because readers were offended. The ending of the book is very confused and shows Kingsley's harassed state and mental fatigue.

Politics for the People was followed by *The Christian Socialist* (1850–1) and the *Journal of Association* (1851). The style and attack of Kingsley's social-problem novels are those of the polemic articles which he contributed to these journals. Kingsley saw them partly as extended tracts, which helps to account for their crudity. In fact, *Alton Locke* is a fictional version of Kingsley's *Cheap Clothes and Nasty*, a revelation of sweat-shop practices in the tailoring trade based on Henry Mayhew's researches. It appeared in January 1850 as one of the 'Tracts by Christian Socialists', while he was still engaged upon the novel.

Christian Socialism as an organized movement lasted from 1848 to 1854, when the Society for Promoting Working Men's Associations (founded 1850) was wound up. Its practical achievement was the sponsorship of the Industrial and Provident Societies' Act (1852), which gave Co-operative Societies recognized legal status and a reasonably satisfactory measure of protection for their funds, the impetus Ludlow in particular gave to the Co-operative movement, and the interest in working men's education which resulted in the foundation of the London Working Men's College (1853–4). Kingsley was particularly interested in education; some of the most powerful scenes in *Alton Locke* are those in which Alton denies himself food and sleep in order to read his books; his desperate struggle against poverty, squalor and bigotry and his search for the means of achieving a better life are well done. Kingsley turns to real life for his horrors, and the most compelling descriptions are those of scenes he himself had witnessed – the slums of Jacob's Island or the miserable little boys in the fields trying, with their frozen hands, to turn the turnip cutter. While he wrote he was again over-worked and ill, and the novel is hurried and disorganized, particularly at the end. Its main fault is one common to propaganda novels – the propaganda becomes more important than the novel. Kingsley is so eager to plead the cause of Christian Socialism that he virtually abandons Alton, who has told his own story in desperate, indignant, passionate words, and allows Eleanor to preach him, passive and convalescent, a series of sermons. To allow him to be convinced by Eleanor, Kingsley makes Alton's character totally inconsistent with what it has been. At the beginning Alton has a lively and enquiring mind.

At the end he accepts Eleanor's illogical statements with scarcely a murmur. Kingsley described Alton's poetry becoming poorer as he deserts his own kind and tries, for love of Lillian, to ape the upper classes. He is blind to his character's degeneration into a cipher as soon as he accepts Christian Socialism. Carlyle's panacea, emigration, takes Alton to America at the end of the novel. He dies before he can get there and put Christian Socialism into practice.

Kingsley was always given to 'spasms of sympathy' and his interest in Christian Socialism began to cool after 1852. Also his prefaces to the later editions of *Alton Locke* show that he felt that many of the abuses he had criticized had been rectified. But he always believed that moral regeneration was dependent on improved living conditions, and all his life he preached sanitary reform. The best scenes in the long-winded novel, *Two Years Ago*, are those in which Tom Thurnall tries to teach Devonshire villagers that cholera is not a visitation from God to be passively accepted, but the result of insanitary conditions which can be changed.

Yeast and *Alton Locke* are Kingsley's best novels. *Hypatia* (1852–3), describing the struggle between Christianity and paganism in fifth century Alexandria, is, as G. H. Lewes wrote, 'ambitious, but somewhat wearisome'. *Westward Ho!* (1855) was a bestseller because it expressed the patriotic enthusiasm for war aroused by the Crimean War (it can be compared with the ending of Tennyson's *Maud*), mirrored the confidence of the English nation and voiced the contemporary fear of increasing Roman Catholic power in England. Copies of the novel were sent to the soldiers fighting the Crimean War; it is to be hoped that it consoled them for the inefficiency with which the campaign was conducted. Kingsley stopped thundering against the aristocracy and began to move in exalted company. In 1859 he became Queen Victoria's Chaplain and was later Chaplain to the Prince of Wales. In 1860 he became Regius Professor of Modern History at Cambridge, where he was remarkable for his enthusiasm and his friendly attitude towards undergraduates rather than for his scholarship.

His most attractive book is *The Water-Babies* (1862–3). In this fairy-tale he describes moral evolution in physical terms, illustrating his central belief that the physical is an expression of the spiritual, but without distorting the narrative or resorting to preaching. Kingsley tells his story with humour and gaiety – qualities obvious in his letters to his children and in Edmund Gosse's memories of him, but not greatly evident in his novels.

Kingsley's imagination was not subtle or powerful, and the

moralist in him distrusted art; to the practical parson and the vigorous sportsman art was 'unmanly'. He had none of the great novelist's joy in creation. Dickens hates and fears Chadband in *Bleak House*, but the artist delights to create an entertaining fiction to express that hatred and fear. Kingsley dislikes the stupid, frivolous apothecary's daughter in *Two Years Ago*, so he turns from her with an impatient 'Bah!' and then harangues the reader on this example of middle-class stupidity. Kingsley had something of the Philistinism criticized by Arnold in *Culture and Anarchy* (1869), and also of Hebraism, the Victorian delight in activity without sufficient thought as to the purpose and significance of that activity. Yet he was an influential writer, and particularly he stirred young people's imaginations. William Morris, writing in 1883 of his time at Oxford in the 1850s, said 'I was . . . a good deal influenced by the works of Charles Kingsley, and got into my head therefrom some socio-political ideas which would have developed probably but for the attractions of art and poetry.' (*Letters of Morris to his Family and Friends*, ed. P. Henderson, 1950, p 185) 'He woke them up in all sorts of ways, about all sorts of things', wrote Frederic Harrison (*Charles Kingsley's Place in Literature*, 1895, p 561). His energy and enthusiasm were both his strength and his weakness as a writer. They tempted him to harangue the reader, but they also gave fire to his observations and to the causes for which he fought. He dared to write about urgent problems in three of his novels, and he described with passion what he had seen of the London slums and the rural hovels, creating realistic settings of considerable power. *Alton Locke* is interesting reading because of its bitter cry against the frustrations caused by class-distinctions, even though the novel's plot stifles this protest.

'The greatest benefit we owe to the artist, whether painter, poet, or novelist, is the extension of our sympathies', wrote George Eliot ('The Natural History of German Life', *Westminster Review*, 1856 pp 51–79). The novel in the Victorian period developed in style and subject-matter by extending the areas of human experience which it explored, by making its readers more aware of themselves and of society as neither drama nor poetry did. Charles Kingsley is a minor novelist, but in *Yeast*, *Alton Locke* and *Two Years Ago* he helped to extend the novel's subject matter, and to make it more serious, more concerned with reality. He saw God, Heaven and Hell in human terms. This was an asset to him as a novelist, and gave substance to his novels.

Ten years ago the world in general had come to a singular crisis in its existence. The age was lost in self-admiration . . . We were about inaugurating the reign of universal peace in a world too deeply connected by links of universal interest ever to commit the folly of war again – we had invented everything that was most unlikely, and had nothing before us but to go on perfecting our inventions . . .

So writes Mrs Oliphant, discussing 'Sensation Novels' in *Blackwood's Magazine* (May 1862). Her words help to explain the optimistic tones of Kingsley's prefaces to the later editions of *Alton Locke* when he was turning away from Christian Socialism because he felt its mission had been accomplished. But Mrs Oliphant described how this complacent mood was shattered by war (the Crimean War was fought 1854–6; the American Civil War began in 1861) – upheavals sufficiently distanced to be regarded in England as exciting. She tries to explain the popularity of the sensation drama and the sensation novel because of the public's craving for excitement:

. . . it is only natural that art and literature should, in an age which has turned to be one of events, attempt a kindred depth of effect and shock of incident. In the little reflected worlds of the novel and the drama the stimulant has acted strongly, and the result in both has been a significant and remarkable quickening of public interest. Shakespeare, even in the excitement of a new interpretation, has not crowded the waning playhouse, as has the sensation drama with its mock catastrophes; and Sir Walter himself never deprived his readers of their lawful rest to a greater extent with one novel than Mr. Wilkie Collins has succeeded in doing with his 'Woman in White'.

Wilkie Collins's *The Woman in White*, his first resounding success, was published in 1859 in Dickens's new magazine *All the Year Round* and sent the sales soaring. The book hit the popular taste and set the fashion for sensation novels. (Others were Ellen Price Wood's *East Lynne* (1861) and Mary Elizabeth Braddon's *Lady Audley's Secret* (1862).) The solemn *Edinburgh Review* might insist on the novelist's moral appeal – 'To an inquisitive youth, novels are a series of lectures upon life, in which the professor addresses his pupils as his equals and as men of the world' (July 1857) – but one of the novels reviewed in this article was Charles Reade's *It is Never Too Late to Mend* (1856), which was a popular success partly because it dealt with the recent scandal at Birmingham Gaol (where a young prisoner committed suicide; enquiry was made into the management of the prison, and the governor William Austin was tried and imprisoned for three months), but also because the book was full of exciting incident – punishments in the prison, suicide, the adventures of a ticket-of-leave man in Australia, escapades in the Australian gold fields. The public liked a strong story-line and had come to expect a moral interest. *It is Never Too Late to Mend*, which criticized the contemporary prison system, gave it both. Browning, for example, was not popular because he was obscure and given to philosophizing. When *Men and Women* appeared in 1855, the *Saturday Review* complained 'It is really high time that this sort of thing should, if possible, be stopped. Here is another book of madness and mysticism . . .' George Eliot's meditative novels, with their concern for motive and the slow shaping of character, and George Meredith's philosophical romances, were a new departure in English fiction (*Adam Bede* was published in 1856 and *The Ordeal of Richard Feverel* in 1859, the same year as *The Woman in White*). By the time Anthony Trollope wrote his autobiography (1875–6) he could survey the literary scene and conclude:

Among English novels of the present day, and among English novelists, a great division is made. There are sensational novels and anti-sensational, sensational novelists and anti-sensational; sensational readers and anti-sensational. The novelists who are considered to be anti-sensational are generally called realistic. I am realistic. My friend Wilkie Collins is generally supposed to be sensational. The readers who prefer the one are supposed to take delight in the elucidation of character. They who hold by the other are charmed by the construction and gradual development of a plot. All this is, I think, a mistake, – which mistake arises from the inability of the imperfect artist to be at the same time realistic and sensational. A good novel should be both . . .

(ch. 12)

The argument, which Trollope thought so wrong-headed, began in the fifties (Trollope's *The Warden* was published in 1855). But the kind of sensation achieved in *The Woman in White* was different from the sensation of, for example, *It is Never Too Late to Mend*. As Mrs Oliphant points out, Collins's sensation is not usually dependent upon extraordinary happenings – murders, suicides, seductions – but 'the simplest expedients of life'. Unlike Dickens, he rarely resorts to the supernatural. He can get his effect from the appearance of a woman at night on a quiet suburban road:

I . . . was strolling along the lonely highroad – idly wondering, I remember, what the Cumberland young ladies would look like – when, in one moment, every drop of blood in my body was brought to a stop by the touch of a hand laid lightly and suddenly on my shoulder from behind me. I turned on the instant, with my fingers tightening round the handle of my stick.

There, in the middle of the broad, bright highroad . . . stood the figure of a solitary Woman, dressed from head to foot in white garments . . .

(The Woman in White, The Story begun by Walter
Hartright, Section IV)

Count Fosco, the impressive villain of the piece and Collins's most successful character, is no exaggerated melodramatic Italian. He makes his effect precisely because of the contrast between the comfortable solid reality of his appearance – he is fat, fond of pastry, vain, likes to keep pets – and the malice of his intentions.

In all his novels Collins is well able to suggest the externals of mid-Victorian society, particularly its bricks and mortar. He does not make poetry of them as Dickens does – Collins's chimneys never mop and mow as do the jeering stacks near Todgers's in *Martin Chuzzlewit* – but Valentine Blyth's house among the growing suburbs in North London places his way of life exactly in *Hide and Seek* (1854); Miss Gwilt's tireless spirit has a perfect foil in the dreary lodging set in a waste of cheap new houses, some of them still unfinished, in *Armadale* (1877); and the extraordinary legless man, Dexter, in *The Law and the Lady* (1875) is made almost convincing by his setting – the big, gloomy, old house in its grounds, defying the advance of the speculative builders and remaining aloof while the cheap little villas go up all around it. The new manor house Thorpe-Ambrose, in *Armadale*, is an epitome of high Victorian civilization:

It was a purely conventional country-house – the product of the classical idea filtered judiciously through the commercial English mind. Viewed on the outer side, it presented the spectacle of a modern manufactory trying to look like an ancient temple. Viewed on the inner side, it was a marvel of luxurious comfort in every part of it, from basement to roof.

(Bk II, ch. 2)

For the period 1850–70 was not only a period of great events in which people might be supposed to respond to exciting incident in novel and drama, it was also the age of flourishing commercial venture and middle-class comfort. Harriet Beecher Stowe, visiting England in 1853, remarked 'the matter of coziness and home comfort has been so studied, and matured, and reduced to system, that they really have it in their power to effect more, towards making their guests comfortable, than perhaps any other people' *(Sunny Memories of Foreign Lands,* 1854, p 13). But such comfort could be stifling. There is an extraordinary outburst at the end of *Armadale* when the Sanatorium, where Miss Gwilt hopes to commit her murder, is thrown open to visitors. A lot of ladies arrive:

In the miserable monotony of the lives led by a large section of the middle classes of England, anything is welcome to the women which offers them any sort of harmless refuge from the established tyranny of the principle that all human happiness begins and ends at home. While the imperious needs of a commercial country limited the representatives of the male sex, among the doctor's visitors, to one feeble old man and one sleepy little boy, the women, poor souls, to the number of no less than sixteen . . . had seized the golden opportunity of a plunge into public life.

(Bk V, ch. 3)

The commercially successful mid-Victorian period was, to the middle-classes, oppressive both physically and morally. Both Reade and Collins campaigned against the deadening concept of Respectability. Their friendship really began when Collins defended Reade against the critics who described the novel *Griffith Gaunt* (1866) as immoral and indecent. (It is Reade's best novel. It is spoilt by a conventional ending, but it is Reade's subtlest study of human relationships. It was decried because Griffith is a bigamist and because Reade described happiness in an illicit sexual relationship.) It seems to me that the sensation novel and the sensation drama were popular in such a period because they offered release in excitement. Collins's particular kind of sensation was popular because he suggested the extraordinary in the context of the monotonous lives lived by ordinary people. In *Armadale* he describes the treachery of the Norfolk Broads:

Firm as it looked, the garden-ground in front of the reed-cutter's cottage was floating ground, that rose and fell and oozed into puddles under the pressure of the foot.

(Bk II, ch. 9)

Collins's best novels are powerful, because in his neutral, prosaic style, often using a variety of narrators, each adding a vital piece to the mosaic, he evokes a solid, commercial society and discloses the pressures and horrors behind the façade, 'firm as it looked'. Sir Percival Glyde commits forgery to make it appear that his parents were married so that he could claim an estate, and plans to incarcerate his wife in a lunatic asylum to enjoy her fortune; Magdalen Vanstone in *No Name* schemes for a loveless marriage so that she can possess her dead father's money; to avert financial ruin Mr Ablewhite, the eminently respectable philanthropist, steals a priceless diamond; Miss Gwilt, like a chess-player meditating her moves, plans murder to get a title and an estate. Unconventional himself – he had two mistresses and three illegitimate children – Wilkie Collins's sensation novels have worn better than Reade's, because they expose the dark places of a commercial society, realistically portrayed.

Reade also described the horrors in contemporary society – in *Hard Cash* (1863), as in *The Woman in White*, greed for money causes a sane person to be imprisoned in a lunatic asylum; in *It is Never Too Late to Mend* he exposes the cruelties inherent in well-intentioned schemes of penal reform; in *Foul Play* (1868, written with Dion Boucicault, the Irish sensation-dramatist) the practice of risking men's lives in unseaworthy ships for the sake of the insurance; in *Put Yourself in His Place* (1870) outrages committed by trades unionists. But, unlike Collins, he cannot suggest the substantial reality of that society, partly because he is too anxious to obtrude himself and his opinions upon the reader, partly because he piles incident upon incident in his narrative until the reader is dizzy and incredulous, partly because he had, surprisingly enough, an interest in the psychology of the characters involved in his startling scenes and some of his best writing describes their inner feelings rather than outward appearances – for example, Gerard's escape from the haunted tower in *The Cloister and the Hearth* (1861) is almost cinematic. His perilous climb down the rope is described from his viewpoint; the stones of the tower passing near his face, whilst below his friends look up at him and he is aware of their raised hands, their eyes, their teeth. Similarly subjective are Robinson's experiences in the punishment cell in *It is Never Too Late to Mend*, or Alfred Hardie's anguish as he realizes that all his actions will be interpreted as those of a maniac. Both Reade and Collins shared with Dickens the view that the novel should be dramatic. They both loved the theatre and Reade wanted to make his name as a dramatist but wrote novels in order to live. He wrote over thirty plays, including translations, adaptations and collaborations. He loved the immediate response of an audience and mistrusted the power of the printed word to convey to a reader the effects he wanted; so he resorted to all kinds of typographical devices to embody his dialogue and situations – capitals for shouts, small print for whispers, drawings of objects important to the plot like the knife bearing grains of gold in *It is Never Too Late to Mend*. Both novelists turned their own plays into novels, to the detriment of the novels which become stagey with the 'tableaux' of the contemporary sensation drama, its violent action, its exaggerated gestures. Reade used his play *Gold* (1853) for the Australian scenes of *It is Never Too Late to Mend*; the early play he wrote with Tom Taylor, *Masks and Faces* (1852), became the novel *Peg Woffington* (1852). Collins wrote *The Frozen Deep* (1856) for Dickens's theatricals at Tavistock House and later turned it into a novel; *Man and Wife* (1870), which marks the decline of Collins's work as a novelist, was first conceived as a play, and *The New Magdalen* (1873) was written simultaneously with the play which Collins kept just one stage ahead of the novel. In the sensation dramas which Reade wrote from many of his novels startling effects are often achieved by the use of real water or real explosives on the stage, or real objects are used to set the scene. *Free Labour*, the play he made from the novel *Put Yourself in His Place*, had a scene 'in the course of which the audience has the pleasure of seeing Mr. Neville actually forge *real* edge tools, on a *real* anvil, with a *real* hammer – and uncommonly well he does it' (*The Times*, 31 May 1870).

This belief in fact as a source of art is evident in Reade's social-problem novels. When they were adversely criticized he referred his critics to the newspapers and Blue Books from which he had got his material. Unlike Collins, he lacked invention, and because he relied so heavily on facts, he defended himself by preaching the fallacious theory that factual reality in a play or novel ensures artistic reality. Moreover, he was so accustomed to looking at life in terms of the sensation drama (as Quiller-Couch rather unkindly pointed out, Reade for years lived with a second-rate actress, Mrs Seymour) that he exaggerated his facts into melodrama. This is true of *It is Never Too Late to Mend*, *Hard Cash* and *Put Yourself in His Place*.

It is interesting to compare these novels with *Sybil* or *Yeast* or *Alton Locke*. These earlier novels are concerned with commenting upon the nature of a whole society, and they are optimistic, looking forward to the possibilities of the future. Reade comments on specific abuses which have become apparent in society – its failure to deal with criminals, for example – and he aims not so much at society's regeneration as at public opinion which will force a small specialized group of men – like prison governors and chaplains – to act more responsibly. Reade's social-problem novels, in fact, are closely related to his journalism and publicise events and personalities as newspapers do. It was through his journalism – he was a very active journalist – that he freed a sane, wealthy man from a lunatic asylum in the Fletcher vs Fletcher case, the germ of *Hard Cash*.

His 'stage eye' and his delight in startling facts and newspaper cases help to give Reade's novels the strong tones and over-emphasis which the modern reader dislikes. There was a close relationship between novelist and reader in the Victorian period, and Reade exploited it vigorously. Collins's best novels have a subtler appeal to the reader's pleasure in solving a puzzle and each stage leads him a step nearer the solution. Reade was serious and sincere in his desire for reform, but his work shows the danger of propaganda in the novel, that character and subtle human relationships are lost in the broad effects necessary to catch public attention. Also it needs a great artist to make a temporary situation universal, otherwise the novel ceases to be interesting when the reform has been accomplished. Despite a melodramatic plot, Marcus Clarke's *For the Term of his Natural Life* (1874), on the Australian penal settlements, is a more impressive book than *It is Never Too Late to Mend*, because Clarke succeeds in making the criminals' battle with the Australian bush and the sea an image of man's insignificance and heroism.

Unfortunately, Reade influenced Collins to plead for specific reform in his later novels, for example, *Man and Wife*, based on the Report of the Royal Commissioners on the Laws of Marriage, 1868, or *Heart and Science* (1883), which attacks the vivisectionists. Collins can absorb incidental social comment into his novels, but a plot controlled by a specific social abuse narrowed his vision and his indignation disturbed the calm detachment of his style.

From the 1860s he suffered increasing pain and illness, so that he was forced to take large doses of opium. He was always a careful craftsman and he worked steadily at his fiction, but undoubtedly his art became more mechanical as his health deteriorated. But although the critics commented adversely, his popularity remained immense. When in 1884 the *Pall Mall Gazette* held a ballot to determine the most popular writer, Collins topped the poll.

Reade's first love was the theatre and, when short of money, he was not above writing a worthless pot-boiler novel like *White Lies* (1857), but both he and Collins helped to make fiction a serious craft by their unremitting labour and their theorizings on the art. Reade's energy seems to us to have been largely misspent, although George Eliot took him seriously as a writer and the young Henry James praised him. The Victorians were used to broad effects in their fiction and drama and they approved of sincere moral intention; his exaggerated writing did not seem so jarring to them as it does to us. But he created his sensation from solid subject-matter, as did Collins.

Both are minor novelists, but Collins's subtler art has worn better, and his original treatment of the sensation novel produced the modern detective novel. Both are, above all, narrators. 'Everyone writes novels nowadays but nobody tells stories', Collins complained (quoted by K. Robinson, *Wilkie Collins*, 1951, p 328). It is fashionable today to despise the art of narrative but, as E. M. Forster remarks in *Aspects of the Novel*, it is the novelist's basic art and, he implies, the simplest. On the contrary, it is a very difficult art. Perhaps the best narratives in the English language are the traditional ballads, and they are effective because they are economical and implicit:

> O laith, laith were our gude Scots lords
> To wet their cork-heel'd shoon;
> But lang or a' the play was play'd
> They wat their hats aboon.

This one verse of 'Sir Patrick Spens' evokes an aristocratic society, the dramatic encounter between such fastidious elegance and the elements and its inevitable outcome. The shoes and the hats particularize the action, and the poet's wry humour emphasizes the grim disaster without exaggerating it. Just enough details are given for the listener's imagination to work upon.

Charles Reade is a lesser narrator than Wilkie Collins because he is too explicit – he directs his reader too obviously. To a lesser degree, Collins is also guilty of this:

The construction is most minute and most wonderful. But I can never lose the taste of the construction. The author seems always to be warning me to remember that something happened at exactly half-past two o'clock on Tuesday morning; or that a woman disappeared from the road just fifteen yards beyond the fourth milestone. One is constrained by mysteries and hemmed in by difficulties, knowing, however, that the mysteries will be made clear, and the difficulties overcome at the end of the third volume.
(Anthony Trollope, *Autobiography*, ch. 13)

It is a just criticism; yet there is a pleasure in tracking the mystery to its solution. A minor pleasure, perhaps, but a real one.

Bulwer-Lytton, Le Fanu and Lever (Peter Denman)

The career of Edward Bulwer Lytton (1803–73) extended from the 1820s to the 1870s. He was by turns poet, essayist, and dramatist (the last with considerable, albeit brief, success), but the novel was his favoured form. He wrote more than twenty-five books during the forty-five years, ranging from the sentimentalism of *Falkland* (1827) through the social exquisiteness of *Pelham* (1828), the Newgate escapades of *Paul Clifford* (1830), the costume melodrama of *The Last Days of Pompeii* (1834) and *Rienzi* (1835), the occultism of *Zanoni* (1842) and *A Strange Story* (1862), the dramatized history of *The Last of the Barons* (1843) and *Harold* (1848), and the quasi-political *My Novel* (1853), to the utopianism of *The Coming Race* (1871). Confronted by such variety, recent accounts of his work have sought to absolve Bulwer-Lytton from charges of 'facile opportunism' by searching for a mythic archetypal structure under-lying the fiction and giving it an overall coherency, or at least by organizing his production into clearly defined and graduated periods. He himself, in his 1848 preface to *Paul Clifford*, attempted to impose some shape on his work:

'Looking back at this distance of years, I can see as clearly as if mapped before me, the paths which led across the boundary of invention from *Paul Clifford* to *Eugene Aram*. And, that last work done, no less clearly can I see where the first gleams from a fairer fancy broke upon my way, and rested on those more ideal images which I sought with a feeble hand to transfer to the *Pilgrims of the Rhine* and the *Last Days of Pompeii*. We authors, like the Children in the Fable, track our journey through the maze by the pebbles which we strew along the path.'

But any thought of an overall unity of purpose in his fiction can be but wishful. The variety of his work is evidence not so much of opportunism as of versatility. Although the label would not have pleased the aristocratic Bulwer-Lytton, he was a successful journeyman in the craft of letters, and was recognized as such by his contemporaries: the anecdote of how Dickens altered the ending of *Great Expectations* on his advice is well-known.

While his work is not the product of a sustained personal vision, it is the expression of a personality. This also was recognized by his contemporaries, for the literary skirmishes in which Bulwer-Lytton found himself engaged focused on himself as much as on his works, especially during his dandified early years. His personal life was also marked by abrupt changes: an intensely mothered upbringing by the widowed Mrs Bulwer-Lytton was followed by a period of alienation caused by his 1827 marriage to Rosina Doyle Wheeler. This ill-starred marriage lasted only until a separation in 1836; then came a reconciliation with his mother, from whom he inherited the

Hertfordshire house of Knebworth in 1843. At this juncture he
changed his name from Bulwer to Bulwer-Lytton and embarked on
the project of transforming the Tudor brick-built mansion of
Knebworth into a Gothicized elaboration of turrets and heraldry.
The London dandy turned landowner transferred his love of display from himself to his setting. In public life too he proved
adaptable; having been a Liberal M.P. for St Ives (1831) and
Lincoln (1832–41), he was Tory M.P. for Hertford from
1852 to 1856 and for a year held office as Secretary of State for the
Colonies. Bulwer-Lytton would not have felt any way discomfited
by an accusation of fickleness, if we can judge by his lyric 'On the
Re-perusal of Letters Written in Early Youth':

> On a past self the present self amazed
>   Looks and beholds no likeness! – Canst thou see
> In the pale features of the phantom raised
>   One trace still true to thee?

It goes on to suggest that mutability is the very stuff of life renewed.

> Happy the man in whom with every year
>   New life is born, re-baptized in the past, –
> In whom each change but doth as growth appear,
>   The loveliest change the last!

Pelham has often been referred to as Bulwer-Lytton's first novel,
but it had been preceded the previous year by *Falkland* (1827), a
short work which he suppressed a few years after it had been
published to a mixed reception of indifference and disapproval. His
suppression of it is a further instance of Bulwer-Lytton's willingness to adjust even the canon of his work in response to public taste.
Falkland clearly reveals its eighteenth-century models. Although
loftily claiming an affinity with the work of Shakespeare, Voltaire
and Maturin, all of whom are mentioned in the text, the true
begetters are Richardson for the epistolary form, Mackenzie for the
sensibility of feeling, Rousseau for the confessional impulse, and
Godwin (an early and admitted influence on Bulwer-Lytton) for the
incidentals – the heroine Lady Emily Mandeville is modelled on
Lady Emily Melville in *Caleb Williams*. In the same novel there is a
prominent character called Falkland, but it was also a name with
family associations, for the sixteenth-century Rebecca Lytton had
married the fifth Viscount Falkland. Bulwer-Lytton's novel moves
beyond its eighteenth-century models and is more than a belated
exercise in the sentimental mode. There is an attempt, through its

overstated and elliptical metaphors, to find a vocabulary for individual experience. Whereas the sentimental novel functioned as a stimulus to sensibility, *Falkland* was a record of sensations – particularly the mental turmoil of adulterous love. The record is made up of various documents: letters from those involved, extracts from Lady Emily's journal, and straightforward narrative by the protagonist's confidant and book's editor, who states that his aim is 'to chronicle a history rather by thoughts and feelings than by incidents and events; and to lay open those minute and more subtle mazes and secrets of the human heart, which in modern writings have been so sparingly chronicled'.

Some of Bulwer-Lytton's subsequent work was to return to the more 'secret' and 'subtle' sides of human nature, but *Pelham* is the most deliberately superficial of all his novels, concerned as it is with the glittering externals of appearance and repartee. This was Bulwer-Lytton's first and greatest success. It was followed by *The Disowned* (1828) and *Devereux* (1829), and the 1830s' novels which he produced in rapid succession and with commercial success: *Paul Clifford* (1830), *Eugene Aram* (1832), *Godolphin* (1833), *The Last Days of Pompeii* (1834), *Rienzi* (1835), *Ernest Maltravers* (1837) and *Alice* (1838). Although *The Last Days of Pompeii*, which like *Rienzi* is a historical romance embroidered around known and notable events and characters, enjoyed considerable vogue into the twentieth century as a juvenile 'classic', it is *Paul Clifford* and *Eugene Aram* which are the most enduring of the early novels. They are contrasting studies of the criminal and his relationship to society. Clifford is a cavalier criminal, easily disguising himself, delighting in the company of his fellow highwayman, and relishing the excitement of danger. Aram on the other hand is a solitary fatalist living out an existence darkened by a secret crime in his past and seeking refuge in philosophical contemplation. 'He was one of those earnest and high-wrought enthusiasts who now are almost extinct upon earth, and whom Romance has not hitherto attempted to portray; men not uncommon in the last century, who were devoted to knowledge, yet disdainful of its fame; who lived for nothing else than to learn.'

Aram's confession after he has eventually been brought to trial closes on a note of spiritual resignation, anticipating release from the world. The progress of Bulwer-Lytton's own career was a movement away from the dandified externality of his early years, as caricatured by Maginn and Maclise in *Fraser's Magazine*. After the 1830s, which brought the turmoil of his stressful marriage, his frenetic literary activity, the involvement with parliamentary politics at the time of the Reform Bill, his excursions into journalism and essay-writing, and his travels abroad, he seems to dwindle into a rather marginalized figure. He exists in our consciousness as the friend or host of Dickens or Disraeli or Eliot, on the periphery of other people's biographies. But Bulwer-Lytton the mature novelist merits attention on his own account. After inheriting his mother's house in 1843 the pace of his writing relaxed; in the remaining thirty-eight years he published only eight novels as against thirteen in less than half that time previously. Knebworth became his passion and he reshaped it around himself lovingly; it was his Fonthill, his Abbotsford. Contemporary comment on the house comes mainly from the letters and reminiscences of departed house-guests, impressed but bewildered by what they had seen. But the Gothicization of Knebworth was not done primarily to offer a museum-showpiece for passers-through; it was done to provide an environment in which Bulwer-Lytton himself could live at ease.

Nevertheless he could not resist displaying his acquisitions, and this trait held for acquired knowledge as well. As Trollope delicately put it, 'He had read extensively, and was always apt to give his readers the benefit of what he knew. The result has been that very much more than amusement may be obtained from Bulwer's novels'. The historical novels, *The Last of the Barons* (1843) and *Harold* (1848), are replete with intrusive details of medieval artefacts. In *A Strange Story* (1862) the supplementary material threatens at times to smother the text. As the story reaches its climax there is a corresponding growth in the number and length of footnotes which offer readers a cure for snake-bite, speculation on the Apocryphal Book of Esdras, gleanings from various writers on science and the occult, as well as descriptions of such Australian peculiarities as creeks, boomerangs and shining cuckoos. Bulwer-Lytton had obviously read himself in well for his post as Secretary of State for the Colonies. In *My Novel* (1853) the autodidact Lenny Fairfield, educating himself out of his humble background into a position of remote if respected authority as a writer, is preferred to the much more active Randal Leslie, whose intriguing is close to the centres of political power and international affairs.

My Novel is the middle of a trio of 'Caxton' novels: *The Caxtons* (1849) and *What Will He Do With It?* (1858) are the others. The eponymous Caxton family, as introduced in the first of the series, is an engagingly diverse collection of individuals, eccentric or quirky by turns but capable of containment within the larger family unit.

The naming of Bulwer-Lytton's surrogate fictional family was significant: 'Caxton' is accentually equivalent to 'Lytton', his maternal name to which he gave more and more prominence over his patronym Bulwer as his life progressed. The printer Caxton appears as a character in *The Last of the Barons*; a large historical canvas by Daniel Maclise depicting King Edward IV visiting the Caxton press at Westminster occupied pride of place at Knebworth. The printer was a contemporary of Sir Robert Lytton, the first of the name to own the house. The coincidence would have been important to Bulwer-Lytton as he grew to sympathize more and more with the literary strengths represented by Caxton than with the more active virtues of Sir Robert Lytton, who fought with Henry VII at Bosworth. Their relative merits are rehearsed in fictional form in *The Caxtons*, where both ancestors are given the name Caxton. The assertively titled *My Novel* is presented as the work of the assumed author Pisistratus Caxton, not of the real author Bulwer-Lytton; the series of essays contributed to *Blackwood's Edinburgh Magazine* during the 1860s in which Bulwer-Lytton commented on life and letters were gathered under the title *Caxtoniana*.

My Novel, the most achieved of his later works, starts in the tradition of Fielding, with an introductory chapter at the beginning of each book in which the supposed author discusses the progress of his writing with members of his family. The story is set in the uneasy years before the first Reform Bill, beginning with parish pump politics in rural England before moving to aristocratic London. In Audley Egerton, the successful statesman whose life is blighted by a secret betrayal of friendship, one can recognize the Eugene Aram type. He is contrasted with Harley L'Estrange, the blameless friend. There are several such opposed pairings in the book: Egerton and L'Estrange, the socially incorruptible exile Riccabocca and the scheming Duke of Peschiera, and the studious Lenny Fairfield and the place-seeking Randal Leslie. Riccabocca's years in England with his daughter Violante and faithful servant Giacomo is a reworking of Prospero's story, the archetypal account of the public man who turns away from the world for the privacy of his study.

Although the novel is set in the turbulent years of Captain Swing and rural unrest, this is no more than hinted at, and the social tension is reduced to a misunderstanding about the refurbishment of the long-unused village stocks: is their repair for the purpose of making them picturesque or useful? The theme of Lenny Fairfield's essay, and of *My Novel* generally, revolves around Bacon's dictum that 'Knowledge is power'. Fairfield's Bacon and Riccabocca's Machiavelli are the ostensible theorists governing the book's world, but their ideas are tested and modified by pragmatism and good-feeling. It is a novel of compromise. Even Richard Avenel, the returned emigrant who has made good, has his American republican brashness softened by contrast with English gentility. The closing scenes of the book, describing the run-up to an election in the tradition of Dickens's Eatanswill or Samuel Warren's *Ten Thousand a Year*, show matters being eventually arranged through committee-room wheeling and dealing which Bulwer-Lytton would have us believe is commendable compromise and good sense.

Bulwer-Lytton's project of revealing the secret and subtle sides of human nature as announced in *Falkland* found its fullest expression in his occult fiction. The occult is an element in *Godolphin*, *Zanoni* (1842) and, especially, *A Strange Story* (1861), but there is a clear indication of his attitude to occult areas of experience in *The Last of the Barons*. Adam Warner in that novel, one of Bulwer-Lytton's recluses, is regarded with suspicion by his neighbours because he has devoted his life to a mysterious and dimly understood engine; he has, in fact, invented a primitive steam-engine some three centuries before Watt. The noisy and powerful contrivance, the driving-force of Victorian technology, seems devilish and supernatural to the uninformed. Bulwer-Lytton implies that occult phenomena are but the imperfectly comprehended operations of nature or the human mind and susceptible of explanation on material and rational grounds. This is the bearing of his short story 'The Haunted and the Haunters'. In a letter written near the end of his life to the London Dialectical Committee appointed to investigate spiritualism he stated it more directly: 'So far as my experience goes, the phenomena, when freed from the impostures with which their exhibition abounds, and examined rationally, are traceable to material influences the nature of which we are ignorant'.

A Strange Story is a crucial work in the tradition of nineteenth-century supernatural fiction, not so much for any intrinsic quality as for the moment at which it was published. In the early 1860s spiritualism and its attendant manifestations were beginning to penetrate the English consciousness, and the more materialist theories of apparitions and seemingly supernatural phenomena which had predominated earlier in the century were being superseded. The protagonist of Bulwer-Lytton's novel is a materialist doctor. Fenwick's medical training is central to the story; although the ostensible main plot is his love for Lilian, the motivation of the text is his progressive realization that he is wrong in his materialist rejection of the spiritual, and he is brought eventually to admit the existence of first the supernatural and finally the soul as his understanding is enlarged. The defeat of Fenwick's scepticism and his eventual acceptance of a transcendental area of experience begins with the scene in which Sir Philip Derval demonstrates to him the possibility of a trance-like visionary state more intense than anything that might be induced by mesmerism, in which 'there is extraordinary cerebral activity, a projectile force given to the mind, as distinct from the soul, by which it sends forth its own emanations to a distance in spite of material obstacles' (ch. 31). While in this state Fenwick sees into a human brain; it is surrounded by an aura of three different colours and he is led to suspect that these correspond to the three levels of human life, intelligence and the soul. These three levels also indicate the range of the novel's action. The adept uses occult powers to a merely animal end – to avoid death; Fenwick finds his theoretical view of the nature of man being challenged; his wrongful arrest for the murder of Derval is a challenge to his probity; and the wasting sickness of Lilian is a testing both of his sensibility and of his knowledge of himself. Lilian falls prey to 'mental alienation', 'brooding over images delusively formed within', but her recovery of mental vigour offers Fenwick a full life grounded in strictly human experience. Like the god-fearing Dr Faber who comes to Fenwick's aid, she offers an alternative to the transcendental experiments of Margrave and Derval. This is most strikingly apparent when Fenwick almost succumbs to the temptation of trying the force of Margrave's wand. 'There came over me an increased consciousness of vital power; a certain exhilaration, elasticity, vigour, such as a strong cordial may produce on a fainting man' (ch. 61). He is on the point of summoning spirits which, it is obvious, have a real and independent existence, but is recalled to this life by the voice of Lilian and, Prospero-like, he throws the wand into the lake.

A *Strange Story* ends with an affirmation of the conventional Christian duality of body and soul. Whether the orthodoxy of the ending or the exploration of belief of the greater part of the text is more indicative of the age is moot, but Fenwick himself moves from outright sceptical materialism to a direct encounter with the occult, after which his acceptance of Christianity is a comfortable compromise. He has, nevertheless, had brief contact with the hidden world of spirits that exist independently of humanity. This transcendental world is accessible to the adept through conjuration, which may take the form of wand-waving, as in *A Strange Story*, or of the table-rapping and planchette-writing which were coming in from America at just this time. This relatively late work by Bulwer-Lytton marks the arrival of the new supernaturalism in fiction.

Another quester who comes into contact with a hidden world is the narrator of *The Coming Race* (1873), the most interesting of Bulwer-Lytton's final trio of novels – the others are *Kenelm Chillingly* (1873) and *The Parisians* (1873). *The Coming Race* tells of a descent into a subterranean country peopled by the Vril-ya, beings who have developed a society in which all defects of comprehension and achievement have been eliminated. At first fascinated by the efficiency of this new world and its apparent imperviousness to emotional disruption, the narrator comes to the realization that humanity needs the variety of imperfection. The novella is Bulwer-Lytton's most elaborate apology for change, for the inherently stable world of the Vril-ya is shown as intolerable. It is the culmination of many of his works, the titles of which alone indicate the end of an order: *The Last Days of Pompeii*, *The Last of the Barons*, *Harold, or The Last of the Saxon Kings*. These works are not apocalyptic; their sense of an ending is informed by the possibility of a new order which will succeed.

A Strange Story is a supernatural novel which anticipates the occultism of the late nineteenth century. For a novelist who wrote with direct reference to the classic supernatural apparition story one must turn to Joseph Sheridan Le Fanu (1814–73). His work includes novels, short stories, poetry and journalism – he was the owner and editor of a number of Dublin publications, including during the 1860s the *Dublin University Magazine*, one of the leading periodicals of its day. As a novelist he made a false start to his career in the 1840s with two historical novels, *The Cock and Anchor* (1845) and *The Fortunes of Torlogh O'Brien* (1847), set respectively in the early eighteenth and late seventeenth centuries. The former is in the Ainsworthian mode, with a strong plot and one of the earliest fictional treatments of the Irish capital; *Torlogh O'Brien* imitates Scott, with its protagonist being caught up in the great historical events of his time – the arrival of King James in Ireland and his defeat by Williamite forces. There followed an interval of sixteen years before the publication of Le Fanu's next novel, *The House by the Churchyard* (1863), set in an eighteenth-century Dublin village and with a meandering but engaging plot which is more inclusive than linear. It includes a powerful short story of the supernatural in Chapter 12, 'an authentic narrative of the ghost of a hand'. Such ghost stories were Le Fanu's forte, and he wrote some of the most remarkable examples of the form. But his use of the explicitly supernatural is limited to these shorter pieces; in his novels the supernatural is generally referred to as a possibility but not actually admitted. This is so even in *Uncle Silas* (1864), the motivating force of which is the exposure of Maud Ruthyn to terror. Even though many of the characters in the novel are, like Le Fanu himself, adherents of Swedenborg's teachings, it is confined to a strictly materialist world. Swedenborgianism suggests an added spiritual dimension to the notably remote and restricted environment of the novel. The isolated condition of the characters seems to reflect the situation of nineteenth-century Anglo-Irish landowning families, marooned in their 'big houses' among an unsympathetic and culturally differentiated peasantry, although the setting of *Uncle Silas* is, in fact, in Derbyshire, apparently a concession to an English readership.

Maud Ruthyn, while no Swedenborgian herself, is surrounded by those associated with its doctrines: her painfully distant father, her friend and confidant Dr Bryerly, and her eventual antagonist, Silas himself. In the final paragraph of the novel, when Maud speaks as a retrospective narrator rather than as an involved protagonist, she does speak in Swedenborgian terms:

The world is a parable – the habitation of symbols – the phantoms of spiritual things immortal shown in material shape. May the blessed second-sight be mine – to recognize under these beautiful forms of earth the ANGELS who wear them; for I am sure we may walk with them if we will, and hear them speak!

Maud's earnestness here is oddly out of key with her conduct in the preceding narrative; this coda tells us more about how to read the book than it does about her beliefs and character. The world of *Uncle Silas* is a parable, and symbolic to an unusual degree, and the spiritual universe of Swedenborgianism, with its hierarchical distribution of angels, informs the topography of the novel. When Maud finds Dr Bryerly glancing through a book taken from the library shelves in her home, it is Swedenborg's *Heaven and Hell*; the particular passage to which our attention is drawn is one describing how evil spirits congregate together, separate from the good. There is an earthly correspondence to this in the location of Bartram-Haugh, the abode of Silas, Dudley his son, Wyat the servant, Madame de la Rougierre, and Dickon. Bryerly's selected text indicates not only the sinister tendencies of the people gathered around Maud at Bartram-Haugh but also enhances their status by linking them with supernatural beings. Throughout *Uncle Silas* the human is constantly being moved towards the ghostly, so that the ontological security of Maud is challenged simultaneously by the transcendentalism of Swedenborg and the evil of her uncle.

Silas occupies the role of a supernatural apparition in the novel; just as the apparition in a ghost story proper is generally delayed for as long as possible, so the introduction of Silas is held back until nearly half-way through the book of which he is dominant character. Although not present in the earlier scenes he is kept in Maud's consciousness: letters arrive from him, the story of his past is told by Lady Knollys, and his portraits make a forceful impression. There are two of these, and they ensure that Silas is present incorporeally almost from the outset. The ambivalence of his status is succinctly caught when Lady Knollys, gazing down at the miniature of him, comments '"A very singular face" – as one might who was looking down into a coffin.' The divisions between life and death and between the corporeal and the spiritual are constantly eroded.

Maud's journey towards Bartram-Haugh is described in detail, for it is a signal that she is moving into an unknown and alien environment – compare Pip's first visit to Satis House in *Great Expectations*. Awaiting her is Uncle Silas, the story of whose disreputable past she has already heard from Lady Knollys, told against the background noise of a storm:

And so it was like the yelling of phantom hounds and hunters, and the thunder of their coursers in the air – a furious, grand, and supernatural music, which in my fancy made a suitable accompaniment to the discussion of that enigmatical person – martyr – angel – demon – Uncle Silas – with whom my fate was now so strangely linked, and whom I had begun to fear.

(ch. 26)

This paragraph, keying in the story of Silas, marshals the constituents of the book's experience. The enveloping condition is composed of metaphorical phantoms and supernatural music, while in the foreground is the figure of Uncle Silas whose enigmatical nature is caught in the successive emendations 'person – martyr – angel – demon – Uncle'. At the centre of all this is Maud's perception or 'fancy', and the state towards which the whole text moves is there in the last word: 'fear'.

Uncle Silas, actively malevolent, exists as a function of Maud's vulnerability, a vulnerability which springs at once from her susceptibility to adolescent romanticizing before his portrait and actual subordination to him in his presence. The essentially passive Maud loses the supportive structures of her family and home and is cast into a world in which she can only sense, not make sense of, events. Her whole experience at Bartram-Haugh is one in which the actions and motivations of those around her are mysterious; the real world becomes occult to her, and is redeemed only by the transcendental Swedenborgianism of the book's final paragraph.

Wylder's Hand, published in the same year as *Uncle Silas*, also features a character intermediate between life and death. It concerns the murder of Mark Wylder by Stanley Lake, and his subsequent concealment of the crime by his arranging to have letters apparently from Wylder posted from various addresses. The discovery of Wylder's body, obviously dead for some considerable time, raises a conflict between two sets of observed facts: his apparent actions are belied by his death. *Wylder's Hand* differs markedly from *Uncle Silas* in that its focus of interest is the elucidation of a mystery, rather than the bewilderment or tensions caused in any one individual. The narrator, De Cresseron, very much on the periphery of events, introduces the idea of concealment or distortion of reality at the very outset of his involvement with Wylder:

... and now, remembering how the breaking of that seal resembled, in my life, the breaking open of a portal through which I entered a labyrinth, or rather a catacomb, where for many days I groped and stumbled, looking for light, and was, in a manner, lost, hearing strange sounds, witnessing imperfectly strange sights, and, at last, arriving at a dreadful chamber – a mad sort of superstition steals over me.

(ch. 1)

As with the last paragraph of *Uncle Silas*, this conveys the nature of the experience to be encompassed by the text rather than the progress of the narrator. The status of De Cresseron is so indeterminate that he slips out of the narrative a third of the way through, leaving the rest to be told omnisciently until his reappearance at the climax. It is left to the arrangement of events and their relation to one another to define the story. In *Uncle Silas* the necessary effect of terror is achieved by the suggestions of the supernatural which are directed at Maud Ruthyn. In *Wylder's Hand* attention is directed towards the external world rather than towards the mediating narrator, and the disorientation is intellectual rather than mental.

Le Fanu continued to produce novels until his death in the early 1870s, among them *All in the Dark* (1866), *The Tenants of Malory* (1867), *Haunted Lives* (1868), *The Wyvern Mystery* (1869), and *The Rose and the Key* (1871), but none of them has the power of *Uncle Silas* or *Wylder's Hand*. It may be that the disorientation and sheer loneliness, presented particularly in the former, is a reflection of the bewildered alienation felt by the Anglo-Irish in the third quarter of the nineteenth century as they came to feel more and more cast off from mainland Britain. But for a clearer depiction of that condition we must turn to an Anglo-Irish novelist whose work tended not towards fantasy and the supernatural but to comic realism: Charles Lever.

'Lever's novels will not live long' was Trollope's dismissive opinion in 1876, four years after Lever's death. Time seems to have borne out his judgment. The once popular early works, *Harry Lorrequer* (1839), *Charles O'Malley* (1841), *Jack Hinton, the Guardsman* (1843), *Arthur O'Leary* (1844) and *Tom Burke of 'Ours'* (1844), have labelled him a dealer in carefree anecdotage. These novels developed an appropriate form of their own, a sort of 'military picaresque', in which a young officer meets with a variety of adventures and intrigues in the garrison or in wider society. His experiences have often only a tangential relationship to his professional calling; the military background serves only to provide a neutral and unconstraining context. Although Ireland or Irishmen figure largely in these novels, they are not regional fiction in the mode initiated by Scott. Their emphasis is more on a heady and diverting succession of incident than on conveying a sense of their setting.

The late 1830s and early 1840s favoured the ebullience of Lever's early fiction. Ireland was emerging from the quarter-century or so of cultural somnolence into which it had slipped after the Act of Union in 1800 and the Emmet rebellion in 1803. Following Catholic Emancipation in 1829 – an act which had for Ireland the signal importance of the 1832 Reform Act in Britain – there ensued a decade or more of confident stability and Dublin began to recover something of the air of a capital city. One index of this was the emergence of a periodical press, led by the monthly *Dublin University Magazine* (1833–77) which aimed to emulate that which *Blackwood's Edinburgh Magazine* was achieving for Scotland. The new assertiveness meant that there was a new opportunity for works which explored the nature of Irishness and the Irish condition, as Galt and Lockhart had done for Scotland. Indeed, ever since Maria Edgeworth's *Castle Rackrent* (1800), published in the year of the Union, Irish fiction had had some heuristic intent. Lady Morgan, the Banims, William Carleton and Samuel Lover each displayed or interpreted Ireland to a predominantly English readership. Various causes might be advanced for this, ranging from the economic – the more lucrative market was to be found in England – to the psychological – there was a need to proclaim a national sense of difference while the Act of Union remained in force.

Lever, however, saw in the difference an opportunity for comedy, as he explained in a letter when planning his third book: 'My idea of Jack Hinton . . . is of an *exceedingly English* young guardsman coming over to Ireland in the period of the Duke of Richmond's viceroyalty, when every species of rackety doings was in vogue. The contrast of the two countries as exhibited in him and in those around him form the tableaux of the book'. Lever is interested in the national misunderstandings only in so far as they can be exploited for comic effect, and he conceives of the novel in terms of 'tableaux' – a succession of self-contained and almost static moments linked only by the first-person narrator.

Lever's career as a novelist began while he was away from Dublin. In 1827, at the age of twenty-one, he graduated from Dublin University and left Ireland to travel in America and Europe and to study medicine. During the thirties he was a doctor either in the Irish provinces or in Brussels, from where he began publishing *Harry Lorrequer* as a serial in the *Dublin University Magazine*. The reception afforded this and his other early writings persuaded him to abandon his medical career in favour of a literary one, and he returned to Dublin to take up the editorship of the *Dublin University Magazine* early in 1842. He also entertained Thackeray who was in Ireland gathering material for his *Irish Sketch-Book* (1843), and accepted the dedication of that work when it appeared. This connection, more than anything he had written in his own books, outraged many Dublin literati. Samuel Ferguson, a prominent contributor to the *Dublin University Magazine*, severed his links with the publication while Lever remained as editor. In Ireland at a time when national energies had been diverted from political resentment into a cultural assertiveness fuelled by a mix of romantic anti-quarianism and scholarly initiative, Thackeray's supercilious note was felt acutely. The learned activities of the Royal Irish Academy and the Irish Archaeological Society reflected the desired self-image of the educated Irishman; it was their recovery of the manu-script materials of old Irish literature which was to underpin the Irish literary renaissance fifty years later. One outlet for these energies was *The Nation*, a weekly newspaper established in 1842 which catered to the more positively nationalist elements of Irish opinion. It was in the pages of *The Nation* that William Carleton attacked Lever in 1843 for caricaturing Irishmen and, what was worse, doing it for the delight of English readers. In 1845 Lever left the *Dublin University Magazine*'s editorial chair, moved away from Ireland, and changed the temper of his work. This was first dis-cernible in *St Patrick's Eve* (1845) with its descriptions of peasant hardship. It was followed by *The Knight of Gwynn* (1847), set at the time of the Union nearly half a century earlier and published just at the time when that Union was coming under active review as a movement for repeal gathered momentum. This might have been an important work, but as usual Lever is too concerned with the characters in the foreground to shed any light on the historical background. By its end the novel's attention has wandered so far from Ireland that the climactic set-piece is the Battle of Aboukir. But Lever's attitude to Ireland in his fiction did change during the 1840s, when the particular trauma of the great famine (1845–8) was added to the wave of international revolutionary upheaval. By the time he wrote *Roland Cashel* (1849) he felt sufficiently sure of his position to insert a cameo of one Elias Howle, clearly intended for Thackeray:

'This inspired Cockney' determined to try a new phase of the subject; and this was not to counsel nor console, not to lament over nor bewail our varied mass of errors and misfortunes, but to laugh at us. To hunt out as many incongruities – many real enough, some fictitious – as he could find; to unveil all that he could discover of social anomaly; and without any reference to, or any knowledge of, the people, to bring them up for judgment before his less volatile and more happily circumstanced countrymen, certain of the verdict he sought for – a ready laugh.

Lever here comes close to throwing stones in his own glasshouse. Nevertheless it indicates a growing concern with the depiction of Ireland and the Irish for a readership which was predominantly

English and, what is more, becoming more and more resistant to Irish subject-matter, however presented. His solution was to deracinate his characters. The later novels, after 1850, are set largely on the Continent among the expatriate society in which Lever himself lived. The travelling Irish on leisurely grand tours or engaged in some foreign employment are divorced from their national context. They become innocents abroad, acceptable as individuals because of their diminished political or social significance. This makes for a peculiarly weightless fiction; the reality to which his novels refer is too often the dislocated environment of a foreign land. Of course, it was the real world for a considerable number of Victorians, among them Lever himself.

Principal among Lever's novels during the 1850s were *The Daltons* (1852), *The Dodd Family Abroad* (1854), *The Martins of Cro' Martin* (1856), *The Fortunes of Glencore* (1857) and *Davenport Dunn* (1859). He contributed the notably unsuccessful *A Day's Ride; A Life's Romance* (1863) to Dickens's *All The Year Round*; it caused such a falling off in circulation that Dickens was obliged to commence *Great Expectations* ahead of schedule to stop the rot. But during the 1860s Lever's principal periodical outlet was *Blackwood's Edinburgh Magazine*, in whose pages he was the most prominent Irish contributor of the decade – a notable achievement at a period when, as Trollope noted at the beginning of *Castle Richmond*, there was an overt hostility to Ireland and all things Irish in Britain. As well as the novels first published serially in *Blackwood's* – *Tony Butler* (1865) and *Sir Brooke Fossbrooke* (1866) – Lever contributed a series of essays written in the *persona* Cornelius O'Dowd. These were akin to Bulwer-Lytton's Caxton essays, but more discursive and light-hearted.

Lever's last novel, *Lord Kilgobbin* (1872), must stand as his most remarkable achievement. It was written in Trieste, where Lever had been appointed British Consul in 1867. From that city Lever meditated on the state of his native Ireland, as would another expatriate, James Joyce, do there forty years later. Lord Kilgobbin is an ageing country widower living in genteel decrepitude with his daughter Kate. They have dwindled into a state of inertia in the midland plains of Ireland, representatives of a condition which Lever, speaking as 'O'Dowd', had noted ten years earlier. 'What an inexhaustible mine of conservatism is Ireland! how persistently she stands fast when she doesn't go backward!' As usual in Lever's work, the stasis is disturbed by a foreign element, but in *Lord Kilgobbin* the foreign element is introduced into an Irish setting in the person of Nina Kostalergi, Kilgobbin's foreign-born niece. Her presence sets in train a series of events involving Kilgobbin's son, Dick, and Joe Atlee, a writer for the press of the day, Donogan, a darkly romantic nationalist conspirator, and two English officers touring unenthusiastically through Ireland. These latter-day Jack Hintons, however, cannot avoid becoming implicated in the affairs of the country; Atlee, on the other hand, distancing himself by travelling as an emissary of Lord Danesbury to Constantinople, rises ever higher.

The Kilgobbins and their cousin, the redoubtable Miss Betty O'Shea, find themselves moulded by the vicissitudes and circumstances of history which has assigned them the role of landlords. Lord Kilgobbin steers a middle course between efficiency and repression, and indeed is an Irish equivalent of Mr Brooke in *Middlemarch*, published the same year as *Lord Kilgobbin*. Lever's novel anticipates the alienation of the landed class in Ireland, a theme which was to be more fully explored in the novels of Somerville and Ross. The Kilgobbins are isolated from their countrymen precisely because they are anchored tangibly to Ireland: they own land. The barrier is not religion or nationality, for they are Catholic and Irish. Their position has become anomalous because of their distance from the administrative centres of Dublin and, especially, London. The instability of their position is emphasized by the constant menace of agrarian disturbance. On Betty O'Shea the effect is dramatic:

The growing unfertility of the land, the sturdy rejection of the authority of the Church, manifested in so many ways by the people, had led Miss O'Shea to speculate more on the insecurity of landed property in Ireland than all the long list of outrages scheduled at Assizes, or all the burning haggards that ever flared in a wintry sky. Her notion was to retire into some religious sisterhood, and away from life and its cares, to pass her remaining years in holy meditation and piety.

(ch. 54)

Her departure from the country and its problems is only one instance of what is a widespread tendency at the end of the novel. Atlee pursues his fortunes among the English, Walpole the English officer takes up a post in South America, Donogan and Nina elope to North America, and Lord Danesbury, his fingers burned by his Irish experiences, returns with relief to Turkey. At one stage even Dick seriously considers going to Australia. The only ones to stick unfalteringly to Ireland are Kate and her father, and at the end of the story their fortunes are little altered from what they were at the outset. Their attachment to Ireland, passive rather than passionate, endures in a situation that threatens to make them redundant.

10

FANTASY AND NONSENSE

Gillian Avery

While the nonsense writing of the Victorians might well have stemmed from the long tradition of nursery rhymes which have always flourished in England as nowhere else, it is more difficult to account for the unique vein of fantasy writing and literary fairy-tales at that period. England has never been particularly rich in native folk-tales compared with, say, France, Italy and Germany which have produced, notwithstanding, little in the way of original fantasy for children. One can only suggest that the encapsulated life led by so many young Victorians stimulated imagination. Middle-class children of the last century lived remote from the adult world and indeed from the company of other contemporaries, relying for amusement upon brothers and sisters, and the memoirs of the period are full of accounts of elaborate imaginary games. Eliza Keary in 1882 described just such a childhood when she wrote an appreciation of her sister Annie who grew up to write children's stories of her own, and Kenneth Grahame and his brothers and sister, as can be seen from *The Golden Age* (1895) and *Dream Days* (1898), inhabited imaginary worlds that were far more real to them than their sedate Thames Valley surroundings. Charles Lutwidge Dodgson devised complex games for his ten brothers and sisters and the family launched several Dodgson periodicals, *The Rectory Umbrella* being the best known as well as the longest lived.

By the 1840s fairy-tales were emerging from the banishment to which they had been consigned by rationalists who complained they did not teach anything specific, and by moralists who condemned them because they were not true; in 1844 Emily Pepys, then aged ten, was marvelling in her journal at the few books her mother had possessed in childhood. She was particularly surprised that she had not known *The Child's Own Book* (a popular collection of fairy tales first published in 1830 which also included stories such as Goody Two-Shoes, Philip Quarll, and a retelling of Gulliver's adventures in Lilliput). *German Popular Stories*, Edgar Taylor's translation of the Grimm brothers' tales, had appeared in 1823, and in 1846 the first translations of Hans Andersen. In 1843 Sir Henry Cole, a distinguished civil servant, under the pseudonym of 'Felix Summerly' initiated *The Home Treasury* series 'to cultivate the Affections, Fancy, Imagination and Taste of Children'. As the father of a family of eight he deplored the unavailability in suitable form of the traditional tales. Instead young minds were assailed by a battery of information books of which the works of 'Peter Parley' (the American Samuel Griswold Goodrich) were typical. Dickens was another defender of fairy-tales, and in his essay 'Frauds on the Fairies' in *Household Words* for 1 October 1853 he wrote: 'It would be hard to estimate the amount of gentleness and mercy that has made its way among us through these slight channels. Forbearance, courtesy, consideration for the poor and aged, kind treatment of animals, the love of nature, abhorrence of tyranny and brute force – many such good things have been nourished in the child's heart by this powerful aid.'

The early literary fairy-stories tended to be moralistic, a tradition which had begun in the eighteenth century with laboured allegories of which those composed by Sarah Fielding for *The Governess* (1749) are a fair example. Thus in *The Hope of the Katzekopfs* (1844) by Francis Paget (1806–82), a story well-known in early Victorian nurseries, and the first full-length fantasy for children, Fairy Abracadabra and the grave old man Discipline teach the spoiled prince, Eigenwillig (self-will), enslaved to the wicked imp Selbst (self-love), the need for self-discipline. Though the opening few chapters are boisterous pantomime as they describe the Katzekopf court and the havoc created there by the child that his parents are too lazy and too doting to discipline, the later chapters have the solemnity of a religious allegory. This type of tale was to remain in fashion throughout the century. Christina Rossetti (1830–94) produced an unpleasant example in 1874, *Speaking Likenesses*, where Flora who falls asleep during a birthday party which she has spoilt by her discontent, finds herself in the company of children whose physical shapes show their various disagreeable moral characteristics. Mrs Molesworth (1839–1921), whose attitude was always that of the benevolent but dictatorial governess, in her best-known book *The Cuckoo Clock* (1877) does not allow Griselda to embark upon fairy adventures with the cuckoo unless she has behaved well during the day. Alice Corkran's *Down the Snow Stairs* (1887) takes a wilful and self-centred child on various purifying adventures to find the Blue Rose that will heal the little brother who has been made ill through her own thoughtlessness. All these stories are preoccupied with punishment and retribution, and one might note here the underlying note of cruelty so often present. When, for instance, the Fairy Abracadabra is finally moved to take over the management of the Katzekopf heir, she pulls him after her through a keyhole, turning him into an attenuated thread which she rolls up into a ball and kicks through nettles, thistles and furze. George MacDonald introduced blood and violence into fantasies for adults and children alike; and although usually in his children's books he took a far less negative attitude, in *The Wise Woman* (1875) he created two repellent children and punished them with ingenious cruelty; while Edward Knatchbull-Hugessen, first Lord Brabourne (1829–93), without making any pretence of writing improvingly, produced a number of volumes of fairy-stories notable for their macabre descriptions of the activities of ogres.

Nonsense is often associated exclusively with Lear and Carroll, but though they undoubtedly made it into a minor literary art, the elements were already there in the English nursery rhymes, and in folk-literature generally. A rhyme such as

> I would, if I cou'd,
> If I cou'dn't, how cou'd I?
> I cou'dn't, without I cou'd, cou'd I?
> Cou'd you, without you cou'd, cou'd ye?
> Cou'd ye, Cou'd ye?
> Cou'd you, without you cou'd, cou'd ye?

which appeared in *Mother Goose's Melody* (c 1765) with the title 'A Logical Song, or the Conjuror's Reason for not Getting Money', is the sort of word-play that appealed to Carroll, and that he could vastly improve:

> They told me you had been to her,
> And mentioned me to him,
> She gave me a good character,
> But said I could not swim.

The following surreal rhyme, which occurs in the same collection and is said to have originated with the mummers, is, with its anthropomorphized objects, more in Lear's style:

> The sow came in with a saddle,
> The little pig rock'd the cradle,
> The dish jump'd a-top of the table,
> To see the pot wash the ladle;
> The spit that stood behind the wall
> Call'd the dishclout dirty troll;
> 'Ods-plut!' says the gridiron,
>   'Can't ye agree!
> I'm the head constable,
>   Bring 'em to me.'

And the zany extravagance of an Irish tale 'Tom of the Goatskin' has parallels in every folk-literature. Here a poor widow, lacking the clothes to put on her son, keeps him in the ash-pit by the fire, and 'according as he grew up, she sunk the pit deeper.' Lewis Carroll's father himself extemporized in the same style when he wrote to his young son: 'Then what a bawling & tearing of hair there will be! Pigs & babies, camels & butterflies, rolling in the gutter together – old women rushing up chimneys & cows after them – ducks hiding themselves in coffee cups, & fat geese trying to squeeze themselves into pencil cases . . .'

The eighteenth century produced a small quantity of literary nonsense. The example most often cited is the piece about the Great Panjandrum which begins 'So she went into the garden to cut a cabbage to make an apple-pie,' said to have been composed by Samuel Foote (1720–77) to test the memory of a veteran actor. This is in fairly familiar nursery-rhyme style. Far more original and out of due time are Horace Walpole's *Hieroglyphic Tales* written between 1766 and 1772 to amuse the little niece of a friend, and belonging in spirit more to the Victorian than to the Augustan age. In his introduction he commented how strange it was that 'There should have been so little fancy, so little variety, and so little novelty in writings in which the imagination is fettered by no rules, and by no obligation of speaking truth,' and he proved capable of invention more extravagant than Lear's or Carroll's, introducing, for instance, a pistachio nut drawn by a ladybird and an elephant, and a princess who 'was extremely handsome, had a great deal of wit, and spoke French in perfection,' but she had never been born. There was also Rudolf Erich Raspe (1737–94) – briefly befriended by Horace Walpole when he fled to England from his debts – whose *Baron Munchausen* (1785) lifted the tall story to the level of nonsense. The account of the baron tying his horse in deep snow to a church steeple is well-known, but it is sober compared to other exploits. On one occasion, for instance, he decides that the best way to get into an enemy fortress as a spy is to leap on to a cannon-ball as it is fired:

> But when I was half-way there it occurred to me that I was acting very rashly. 'It is all very well,' thought I, 'To get inside the fortress, but how shall I get out afterwards? And what will happen to me in there?'
>   As these thoughts passed through my mind, I perceived a bullet directed from the fortress against our camp passing a few feet from me. Without further hesitation I leaped upon it, and returned to our army.

In each of the Munchausen adventures there is a similar sequence of ideas pursued ruthlessly to the end, and there is also the violence that is a characteristic of nonsense as it later became formalized by Lear and Carroll. They were the first to see the potential of nonsense, and their highly individual realizations are now regarded as the norm.

Edward Lear (1812–88) was the twentieth and penultimate child of a stockbroker who went bankrupt. He was rejected by his mother and brought up by an elder sister. He was a delicate child with poor sight, suffering at an early age from epilepsy and terrifying fits of depression – the Morbids, as he styled them. His first attempts at earning money were from selling drawings, and it was through the illustrations of birds that he made at the Zoological Gardens that he came to the attention of Lord Stanley, heir to the Earl of Derby and President of the Zoological Society. Invited to Knowsley Hall in 1832 to make drawings of the animals in the private menagerie he rapidly endeared himself to the children of the household, whom he entertained with his drawings and extemporized verse, and was soon treated as a member of the family. Indeed in 1837 when his health deteriorated alarmingly, Lord Stanley (who had by now succeeded to the earldom) dispatched him to Italy. He was to spend very little time in England after that, wandering round Mediterranean countries, dependent for income on the watercolours, mostly landscapes, that he produced in such quantity. Diffident, self-deprecating, he formed extravagant attachments to young men who went their own way and forgot about him, and he felt himself to be barred by reason of poor health and his epilepsy from marriage with the one woman whom he seriously courted.

The Book of Nonsense appeared in 1846; an enlarged edition in 1861. This is a compilation of the limericks which he had devised for the Stanley children, illustrated with his own drawings. (He did not invent the limerick form which appears to have been first used in two little picture books, *The History of Sixteen Wonderful Old*

Women and *Anecdotes and Adventures of Fifteen Gentlemen* published in 1820 and 1821 respectively. Fifty years later Lear acknowledged that the limerick 'There was an old Man of Tobago' from the latter book had inspired his own.) The title page of *The Book of Nonsense* bore the rhyme:

> There was an Old Derry down Derry,
> Who loved to see little folks merry;
> So he made them a book, and with laughter they shook
> At the fun of that Derry down Derry.

But even in those early years his verses seem full of foreboding, of apprehension about what the world at large might choose to do to him. Many of the limericks are haunted by the lurking presence of 'They' who mock, deride or are openly hostile to the subjects.

> There was an Old Man with a gong,
> Who bumped at it all the day long;
> But they called out, 'O law! you're a horrid old bore!'
> So they smashed that Old Man with a gong.

And the subjects themselves are eccentric, lonely figures, frequently with some feature such as a grotesquely long nose or a globular figure – the sort of outcast, in short, that Lear in his darker moments felt himself to be. The culmination is more often than not violent or tragic: an aspect which children undoubtedly find attractive but which reflected his own insecurity and deep-seated melancholy.

> There was an Old Man of Cape Horn,
> Who wished he had never been born;
> So he sat on a chair, till he died of despair,
> That dolorous Man of Cape Horn.

Nevertheless, as Elizabeth Sewell points out in *The Field of Nonsense* (1952), they still outwardly keep the rules of nonsense in that there is no overt emotion shown over the catastrophes, which are treated with the robust ruthlessness found in nursery rhymes. The humour lies in the way the victims brush aside the disasters with bland composure.

> There was an Old Man of the Nile,
> Who sharpened his nails with a file;
> Till he cut off his thumbs, and said calmly, 'This comes –
> Of sharpening one's nails with a file.'

The most light-hearted of his verses appear in *Nonsense Songs, Stories, Botany and Alphabets* (1871), though even here, as in 'Calico Pie' there are hints of the desolation and sense of loss that were to haunt the last poems.

> But they never came back to me!
>   They never came back!
>   They never came back!
> They never came back to me!

He had by this time developed a far more finished style and his limericks seem halting in contrast to the sophisticated rhythms of 'The Owl and the Pussy-Cat' and 'The Jumblies'. The oppressive 'They' are absent, and characters like the Duck and the Kangaroo, the Daddy Long-Legs and the Fly, the Nutcrackers and the Sugar-Tongs, the Broom, the Shovel, the Poker and the Tongs embark on expeditions and holiday jaunts unrebuked – for the Nonsense Songs reflect the restless wandering of Lear's middle years. Moreover the expeditions are largely happy ones, and though in 'The Daddy Long-Legs and the Fly' he touches upon the alienation that he felt in his own life – the Daddy Long-Legs is tormented by the length of his legs and the Fly by the shortness of his own – there is the prospect of a happy outcome, an escape:

> Then Mr Daddy Long-Legs
>   And Mr Floppy Fly
> Rushed downward to the foamy sea
>   With one sponge-taneous cry;
> And there they found a little boat,
>   Whose sails were pink and gray;
> And off they sailed among the waves,
>   Far, and far away.
> They sailed across the silent main,
> And reached the great Gromboolian plain;
> And there they play for evermore
>   At battlecock and shuttledore.

In this and in 'The Jumblies' we get glimpses of that haunting dream-landscape with its resonant names that was to be such a conspicuous feature of the last poems, *Laughable Lyrics* (1877). Despite the title of the collection, the themes are almost without exception tragic, treating of desertion, loneliness, loss, and the victims no longer react, as in the limericks, with nonchalance. Since emotion is introduced and pity evoked, they are no longer strictly nonsense, which is essentially a dispassionate game with words, and become something that is very near poetry. 'The Dong with a Luminous Nose' with its Tennysonian reverberations describes an endless, hopeless search for a beloved:

> And now each night, and all night long,
> Over those plains still roams the Dong;
> And above the wail of the Chimp and Snipe
> You may hear the squeak of his plaintive pipe
> While ever he seeks, but seeks in vain
> To meet with his Jumbly Girl again;
> Lonely and wild – all night he goes, –
> The Dong with a Luminous Nose!

'The Pelican Chorus' (for which Lear, who was an accomplished amateur musician, composed the music) laments the departure of a daughter; 'The Courtship of the Yonghy-Bonghy-Bo' (for which he also composed music) describes a hopeless courtship which leaves both protagonists desolate; Mr and Mrs Discobolos on top of their wall work themselves into such a pitch of frenzy about the possible fate of their children that to blow themselves up with dynamite seems the only release. None is sadder than 'Incidents in the Life of my Uncle Arly,' included in the posthumous *Nonsense Songs and Stories* (1895), with its reiterated lament 'But his shoes were far too tight', and its summary of a fruitless lonely life which is perhaps how Lear in moments of despair saw his own:

> On a little heap of Barley
> Died my aged Uncle Arly,
>   And they buried him one night; –
> Close beside the leafy thicket; –
> There, – his hat and Railway-Ticket; –
> There, – his ever-faithful Cricket; –
>   (But his shoes were far too tight.)

Lear and Lewis Carroll are sometimes bracketed together, but though their work has similarities, they approached nonsense from differing standpoints. Lear was a humorist, essentially the sad clown who finally became unable to prevent his emotions from spilling into his writing. He was also a poet; G. K. Chesterton said of him that he presented his unmeaning words and amorphous creatures 'with the romantic prelude of rich hues and haunting rhythms'. In his seemingly effortless invention of nonsense characters and nonce words to describe their behaviour, he was, as Roger Lancelyn Green pointed out in *Tellers of Tales* (1969), blessed with a facility that most possessors leave behind in early childhood.

Carroll's approach, in contrast, is one of ruthless rationality pushed to its furthest extremes. The *Alice* books are free from emotion; they are based on word-play, puns, and ideas that are pursued to a logical conclusion. At the Mad Tea-Party Alice puzzles about the story the Dormouse is telling, of three little sisters who lived at the bottom of a treacle-well and learned to draw treacle:

'You can draw water out of a water-well,' said the Hatter; 'so I should think you could draw treacle out of a treacle-well – eh, stupid?'

'But they were *in* the well,' Alice said to the Dormouse, not choosing to notice this last remark.

'Of course they were,' said the Dormouse: 'Well in.'

Carroll's invention was more disciplined than Lear's; he uses many nursery-rhyme characters, other characters evolve out of words or phrases – the Mock Turtle (from the soup), the Mad Hatter (as mad as a hatter), the bread and butter fly. Conversation and argument play a far larger part than narration; only when a situation is dialectically explored does he proceed to the next episode. Nor was he at heart a humorist; he lacked Lear's ability to laugh at himself; he was, as Elizabeth Sewell says, 'a brilliant player of a particular game, but that is not at all the same thing.'

Charles Lutwidge Dodgson (the pseudonym was formed by partially Latinizing and then reversing his two Christian names) was born in 1832 at Daresbury in Cheshire, where his father had a living. The family moved to the rectory of Croft in Yorkshire when Charles was eleven; he was sent at first to the grammar school in Richmond and then to Rugby. In school holidays he began to produce a series of family magazines and his contributions even then demonstrated his flair for comic verse. He went up to Christ Church, Oxford in 1851, reading classics and mathematics and was nominated for a Studentship (Fellowship) there the following year, this giving him a small income and the right to reside in the college for the rest of his life, providing that he did not marry and that he took Holy Orders. (In fact, though he was ordained deacon, he never proceeded to the priesthood.) And at Christ Church he stayed all his life, eventually becoming Mathematical Lecturer.

In 1855 Henry George Liddell became Dean of Christ Church and in 1856 took up residence. There were then four Liddell children, Harry, Lorina, Alice (aged nearly four) and Edith. Dodgson, who had early become a keen amateur of photography, met the little girls for the first time in the spring of that year, when he was helping a friend photograph the cathedral from the Deanery garden. He put in his diary 'I mark this day with a white stone.' His friendship with the children prospered and he photographed Alice a number of times, both by herself and in groups with her sisters. In May 1862 he began taking them on boating trips on the Thames, and on 17 June there was an expedition to picnic at Nuneham Courtenay when the whole party was caught in a violent downpour – an episode that was commemorated in the episode of 'the Pool of Tears' in *Alice*. Another trip on 3 July was rained off and to compensate for the disappointment he organized an expedition upriver to Godstow the next day, adding in his diary a few months later 'On which occasion I told them the fairy-tale of *Alice's Adventures Underground* which I undertook to write out for Alice.' The story was continued on at least one other afternoon and was written out in fair copy that winter and presented to Alice in November 1864, inscribed 'A Christmas Gift to a Dear Child in Memory of a Summer Day.' Other families had by this time also seen it, including George MacDonald's children, and he was urged to publish it. A friend introduced him to Tenniel who agreed to do illustrations, and Dodgson slightly reworked the original material, removing some of the private jokes and adding the 'Pig and Pepper' and the 'Mad Tea Party' episodes. After delays and mishaps (Tenniel insisted on the whole of the first edition being scrapped as he was dissatisfied with the quality of the printing) the book, now bearing the title *Alice's Adventures in Wonderland*, finally appeared in November 1865 (but with the date 1866 on the title-page).

Long before the book's publication Dodgson's friendship with the Liddell children had ceased. The reason for the break is not known since the relevant page was torn out of Dodgson's diary. Clearly it was a source of great grief and it has been suggested that in his subsequent friendships with little girls he was always seeking for someone to take Alice's place. But in neither of the Alice books does a sense of loss obtrude, nor, for all that they are named after her, does the real Alice Liddell appear, except perhaps in the last few lines of *Wonderland* when Alice's sister muses on what the future holds for Alice the grown woman, and in *Looking Glass* when the account of Alice gathering scented rushes 'with flushed cheeks and dripping hair and hands' seems to recall a real boating expedition. Both books are sustained exercises in nonsense, a juggling with words in which flesh and blood has no place.

Though children tend to prefer *Wonderland* as more realistic, with Alice's puzzled references to her own life, her lessons, her friends, and her cat; to the purist *Through the Looking Glass* (1871) is

the better book. Both *Alice*s are contained within the framework of
a dream, but whereas the episodes of the first are organized with
corresponding inconsequence, the second is a tightly controlled
account of the reverse manner in which life must proceed on the
other side of a looking glass and also of the moves in a chess game
in which Alice ends by becoming a queen. In this the nonsense is
more ruthless and violent than in the first Alice. Humpty Dumpty,
one of the book's most formidable and memorable characters,
finishes in pieces, but not before he has indicated to Alice that she
would have done better to leave off her life at seven years old:

> 'I never ask advice about growing,' Alice said indignantly.
> 'Too proud?' the other enquired.
> Alice felt even more indignant at this suggestion. 'I mean,' she said, 'that
> one can't help growing older.'
> '*One* can't, perhaps,' said Humpty Dumpty; 'but *two* can. With proper
> assistance, you might have left off at seven.'

We also see Alice prepare to eat the pudding to which she has been
introduced, and the Walrus and the Carpenter devour the trusting
little oysters whom they have taken out for a walk:

> 'Now, if you're ready, Oysters dear,
>   We can begin to feed.'
>
> 'But not on us!', the Oysters cried,
>   Turning a little blue.
> 'After such kindness, that would be
>   A dismal thing to do!'
> 'The night is fine,' the Walrus said.
>   'Do you admire the view?
>
> 'It was so kind of you to come!
>   And you are very nice!'
> The Carpenter said nothing but
>   'Cut us another slice.'

Looking Glass also contains 'Jabberwocky', perhaps Carroll's most
inventive piece of nonsense. (Like 'The Walrus and the Carpenter'
it was original, not a parody as was most of his verse.) He had
written the first verse in 1855, copying it into a scrapbook, and was
to use many of the nonsense words (some of which, like
'jabberwocky' itself and 'chortle' have passed into common usage)
in *The Hunting of the Snark*. Indeed, he lingered on it with pleasure,

making Humpty Dumpty analyse it and provide a gloss for Alice's benefit.

The characters in both the *Alice*s – the Duchess, the March Hare, the Mad Hatter, the Cheshire Cat, the White Knight, Humpty Dumpty, Tweedledum and Tweedledee – are part of the texture of the English culture; quotations from them – 'Large as life and twice as natural', 'Jam to-morrow and jam yesterday – but never jam today', 'It was the *best* butter' – have become clichés; the Carroll parodies are far more familiar than the originals and are parodied in their turn. Only a handful of children's books have survived their generation and fewer still have attracted the serious attention of non-specialists. The fact that Lear and Carroll and Kenneth Grahame have achieved this recognition must in part be due to the fact that though they might have been stimulated in the first place by the existence of a child audience, they wrote entirely to please themselves, instead of following accepted ideas of what was thought appropriate for children. Carroll indeed went further than either of the other two, unconsciously no doubt, in departure from the accepted ethic of the day. Many of the poems he parodied are religious; the Isaac Watts hymns that he mocked ('How doth the little, busy bee' and ''Tis the voice of the sluggard') were part of most children's Sunday, indeed to some Watts's *Divine and Moral Songs* had almost sacramental significance; conversions were attributed to them; children died repeating them. Certainly it was an extraordinary contradiction to what we know of Carroll that he should choose to parody so much Christian verse; a pedantic, scrupulous precisian, he was more sensitive than most to irreverence and quick to rebuke even the most innocent manifestation. But one feels that rather than a deep-seated rejection of the Christian beliefs he professed, it may have been the passion of the game he was playing that seized him and stifled all power of detachment. He had, after all, implied in the conversation between Alice and Humpty Dumpty, that Alice would have done well to die at seven. And Alice Liddell – and there is no doubt about his deep feeling for her – was always indissolubly linked with the Alice of the stories. Indeed, the dedication verses of *Looking Glass* begin:

> Child of the pure unclouded brow
> And dreaming eyes of wonder!
> Though time be fleet, and I and thou
> Are half a life asunder,
> Thy loving smile will surely hail
> The love-gift of a fairy-tale.

His own attitude to the Alice books is curious. He never discussed the characters or the contents; he seemed to have rewritten them in his mind and have forgotten their anarchic nature, the violence, the frightening transformations and the irreverence, and spoke of them as though they were sedate and soothing Sunday books. To one correspondent he said that he hoped they had given 'real and innocent pleasure . . . to sick and suffering children.'

The first *Alice* is often regarded as a watershed in the history of children's books, the beginning of undidactic entertainment, the supreme example of nonsense; but though it had reached the status of a classic by 1871 when the sequel was published, nobody on its first appearance appeared to think it any different from other books being reviewed at the same season. Reviewers dwelt as much on the Tenniel drawings as on the text, and though few of them were hostile, even fewer took it seriously; a patronizing blandness was the usual tone and the writer then passed on swiftly to the next book. Most referred to it as a 'fairy-tale', which it is not. Indeed Carroll seems to have no literary antecedents. Once he had created the genre it seemed absurdly easy and scores of writers tried to imitate it, with stories of children being carried off to dreamlands, but though they might achieve a passable punning style the brilliant logical organization eluded them – one suspects they did not even perceive it and their tales remained only feeble shadows of the original. The most successful imitator was George Edward Farrow (1862–?1920), who in *The Wallypug of Why* (1895) and *The Little Panjandrum's Dodo* (1899) did achieve idiosyncratic characters and an abundance of pseudo-Carrollian paradox.

The only other extended work of nonsense that Carroll attempted was *The Hunting of the Snark* (1876). He had begun with the final line – 'For the Snark *was* a Boojum, you see' – which had come unbidden to his mind, and composed the eight cantos or 'fits' to lead up to it. The mock-heroic epic (which Carroll called 'an agony in eight fits'), the voyage of the Bellman and his crew in pursuit of the shadowy and elusive Snark, has received much attention from critics who sought to find some hidden meaning in it. Some have asserted that the trial scene – in which the Snark's summing up comes to more 'than the Witnesses ever had said', and the defendant is found to have died many years before – was based on the Tichborne Case (1871–4) which broke most records for protracted legal proceedings. Others have suggested that it depicts 'existential agony', or that it is a parable about the search for material wealth, or a satire on the quest for social advancement.

Carroll himself insisted that he didn't mean anything but nonsense. It has a dreamlike, hallucinatory quality about it. The Snark, in fact, never appears except in the barrister's dream of a trial, for the one member of the crew to track it down

> softly and suddenly vanished away –
> For the Snark *was* a Boojum, you see.

By the time of *Sylvie and Bruno* (1889) and *Sylvie and Bruno Concluded* (1893) his genius had left him. The books are an uneasy and surreal compound of saccharine fairy-tale and philosophical musing. They began as a story for children, 'Bruno's Revenge', published in *Aunt Judy's Magazine* in 1867, which developed into a novel for adults. Two fairy children, Sylvie and Bruno, who converse in the baby language fashionable at that period, are watched by a human observer who is in the real world caught up in the love of his friend Arthur Forester (he later dies of fever) for beautiful Lady Muriel. Elizabeth Sewell sums up Carroll's attitude as: 'Here is real life, grave thoughts, beauty, love, God, railway journeys, epidemics, alcoholism, the Oxford Movement, and they are all suitable matter for Nonsense, but the game must now be sober and reverent.' Sewell's comment is: 'There can only be one result; the game dies, and instead the reader is left with a dreary, odious, and pretentious mixture of false sentiment, preaching and whimsy.'

By the time the reviewers had encountered the first Alice the genre of literary fantasy was reasonably well-established. Dickens's *A Christmas Carol* had been published in 1843, Ruskin's *The King of the Golden River* in 1851, Thackeray's *The Rose and the Ring* in 1855, Frances Browne's *Granny's Wonderful Chair* in 1857 and Charles Kingsley's *The Water-Babies* in 1863. *The Rose and the Ring* with its slapstick account of how Prince Giglio and Princess Rosalba fight their way through traditional fairy-tale vicissitudes before they can live happily ever after, owes something to the burlesque elements in *The Hope of the Katzekopfs*, but also shows how fairy-tale themes were now presumed to be a familiar part of nursery culture. Both Ruskin's and Frances Browne's books are strongly influenced by the Grimm tales. Little is known of Frances Browne (1817–79) except that she was born in Donegal and was blind from an early age. *Granny's Wonderful Chair* which begins 'In an old time, long ago, when the fairies were in the world . . .' contains within a frame story six tales where diligence and kindliness and honesty are rewarded in true fairy style. But direct didacticism is absent and she writes of an enchanted pastoral world where colours are brighter, sounds clearer and scents sweeter, finishing with a lament that 'great wars, work and learning have passed over the world since then and altered all its fashions.'

The King of the Golden River has an Austrian setting. Ruskin himself regarded it as uninventive, 'a fairly good imitation of Grimm and Dickens, mixed with some true Alpine feeling of my own.' But in this story of two greedy brothers who are punished and a younger one of childlike generosity who is rewarded, he did create two highly original characters, the brazen-nosed, red-cheeked South-West Wind who devastates the fertile Styrian valley in return for the brothers' inhospitality (Richard Doyle made a memorable illustration of him for the first edition), and the King of the Golden River, who forms himself out of molten gold from a mug which the brothers have put in the furnace. But Ruskin, a novice at story-telling, was unsure how to handle these secondary characters, and each makes only one brief appearance.

The Water-Babies, one of the very few Victorian children's stories as well-known now as it was in its own day, is a very curious survival. Its pages are scattered with references to ancient contro-versies, intensely personal fads and ferocious prejudices. There is Kingsley's insistence on washing and cleanliness, his concern for sanitation and for exploited children, his passion for natural history through which he feels humankind can be redeemed, his theories on education, his resentment about his own upbringing, his views on medicine, the stupidity of academics and intellectuals, on cheap sweets and the children's books of his day, all set down haphazard with gusty vehemence. He lets off squibs at the expense of the Darwin and Huxley school, he tells his readers what he thinks of the Irish and the Americans, about 'frowzy monks' and the absurd new fashion of dining at eight, and how one's horse's comfort must be put before one's own. The only coherent narrative occurs in the opening pages. The little chimney-sweeper, Tom, sets out on a fine midsummer morning with his master Grimes to sweep the chimneys at Harthover Place, loses his way in the maze of flues and comes down into the bedroom of little Ellie. Then, pursued over the moors (for no particular reason) by all the denizens of Harthover Place, he scrambles down a cliff face and – to mortal eyes – appears to drown in the stream below. But the reader knows that he has become a water-baby and there follows his purification through water, with the help of the fairies Mrs Bedonebyasyoudid and Mrs Doasyouwouldbedoneby (who might be said respectively to represent Law and Love). This is the book's main theme. Kingsley, who was always a muddled thinker, here abandons all pretence of logical progression and the point he is trying to make is unclear. Though it would appear that Tom is going through a purging process to fit him for heaven (Kingsley, staunch Protestant that he was, would have been outraged if the word 'purgatory' was mentioned), at least two critics have suggested that the book is a masturbation fable and that Tom is being prepared for union with Ellie. Kingsley starts up scores of hares and never pursues them; he is forever digressing and losing his way; such narration as there is is held up while with great enjoyment he goes galloping off on some hobby-horse, or composes long lists in the manner of Rabelais. He was unsure where he stood as regards truth and fantasy. He thought that all right-minded children should have a sense of wonder and believe in fairies, which he vehemently asserts do exist; he also wanted to tell them of the marvels of nature, and he presents both as universal truths, overlooking the fact that readers might treat his account of the hatching of dragonflies in the same spirit as his account of water-babies. But for all this *The Water-Babies* engages the reader because of the richness of the texture, the infectious, boyish pleasure that Kingsley took in all his material, and the sheer scale of his ingenuity and invention.

Excepting only Carroll, and he wrote nonsense rather than fantasy, George MacDonald (1824–1905) was by far the most original and most influential of the Victorian fairy-tale writers. His reputation does not depend so much on the quality of his writing, for, as C. S. Lewis says, this is undistinguished, at times fumbling. 'Bad pulpit traditions cling to it; there is sometimes a nonconformist verbosity, sometimes an old Scotch weakness for florid ornament . . . sometimes an over-sweetness picked up from Novalis . . . What he does best is fantasy – fantasy that hovers between the allegorical and the mythopoeic. And this, in my opinion, he does better than any man.' And Rolland Hein speaks of his insight into the ultimate truths of existence, his symbolic exploration of its significance and his vision of the beauty of holiness.

Born in Huntly, Aberdeenshire, he lost his mother when he was eight, of the tuberculosis that was to afflict so many of his own children. It was an experience that profoundly affected him and many of his fantasies turn on a search for maternal affection. He was educated at King's College, Aberdeen, and at some stage in early manhood he seems to have been employed cataloguing books in a great house in the north of Scotland that has never been identified. And the image of a great house and its library constantly reappears. We meet it in his earliest fantasy, *Phantastes* (1858) and in the last, *Lilith* (1895), and it forms the background for his best children's book, *The Princess and the Goblin* (1872).

He entered a Congregationalist theological college in 1848, and in 1850 became minister to a congregation in Arundel, Sussex. But two years later he was in trouble with the deacons who accused him of heresy (he had suggested in a sermon that heathens might find salvation) and of being tainted with German theology. He resigned in 1853 and thereafter he had to support his family (he eventually had eleven children of his own together with two adopted ones) by lecturing, tutoring, occasional preaching and writing. In his leanest years his poverty was very great, and only financial help from friends saw him through. He was a prolific writer of novels of the 'kailyard' type. C. S. Lewis wrote of that 'world of granite and heather, of bleaching greens beside burns that look as if they flowed not with water but with stout, the thudding of wooden machinery, the oatcakes, the fresh milk, the poverty, and the passionate love of hard-won learning.' But there is little of the Scots landscape or legend about his fairy-tales; rather they reflect German romanticism and the stories of E. T. A. Hoffmann (1776–1822, the author of *The Nutcracker*). Always a profound admirer of Novalis (Friedrich Leopold von Hardenberg – 1772–1801), some of whose poems he translated in 1876, he prefaced *Phantastes* with a long quotation about the nature of fairy-tales, and *Lilith* ends: 'Novalis says, "Our life is no dream, but it should and will perhaps become one."'

Phantastes, which is also influenced by *The Faerie Queene*, relates how a young man, Anados (Greek, meaning 'pathless') finds his way into fairyland and his dreamlike and often erotic adventures there. (In this early work MacDonald seems to have used exotic imagery as a screen for the exploration of his own emotions.) Here the mother-figure who is also a grandmother – an important feature of most of his fairy-stories – makes her first appearance:

A wondrous sense of refuge and repose came upon me. I felt like a boy who has got home from school miles across the hills, through a heavy storm of wind and snow. Almost, as I gazed on her, I sprang from my seat to kiss those old lips. And when, having finished her cooking, she brought some of the dish she had prepared, and set it on a little table by me, covered with a snow-white cloth, I could not help laying my head on her bosom, and bursting into happy tears. She put her arms round me, saying 'Poor child; poor child!'

Lilith is a more coherent and tightly organized work, constructed after the fashion of *The Pilgrim's Progress*, but with the adventures repeated in reverse as Mr Vane comes back through all the lands into which he has passed by stepping through a mirror. Lewis wrote of *Phantastes* that its impact upon him when he was sixteen was like the first sight of Beatrice was to Dante, but it is *Lilith* with its witch-queen, its city of Bulika which she holds in terror, its animals and particularly the benevolent panther from which the Narnia saga much more obviously derives, though the strange, haunted, dreamlike landscape that MacDonald achieved eluded his disciple. Auden found *Lilith* the more satisfactory story: 'There seems no particular reason, one feels, why Anados should have just the number of adventures he did – but Mr Vane's experiences and his spiritual education exactly coincide.' This is perhaps to claim too much for the construction of *Lilith*, which was a book of MacDonald's old age. The symbolism is clearly theological, therefore we are more aware of inconsistencies and unresolved questions than in *Phantastes* whose purpose is shadowy. There are many elements in it that we recognize from earlier work, the preoccupation with death, with water as a life-giving, spiritual force, with the sanctity of childhood. But here the children, the Little Ones, are in a state of arrested development, and are finally led by Mr Vane in a bloody crusade against the evil Bulikans. The book is touched with the pessimism that afflicted him in those years – towards the end of his life he could not even bring himself to speak; and the note of cruelty that is discernible in so much of his fantasy is more marked.

Of his stories for children *The Princess and the Goblin* (1872) is generally regarded as the best. It is an account of a struggle between the forces of light, led by the little Princess Irene and the miner's son Curdie, and the forces of darkness – the goblins who live in the mountain below Irene's castle. Irene also represents faith and a spiritual state which Curdie and her nurse have not yet achieved; she alone can see the regal and radiant beauty of the great-great-grandmother who lives in a remote tower of the royal house, whereas they can see nothing more than a heap of musty straw and a withered apple. It is a gentle, kindly book, and MacDonald's grandmother/mother figure is seen at its happiest, all-powerful and tender, without the sentimentality of Anados's earth-mother, the unearthliness of North Wind in *At the Back of the North Wind* or the sternness of the Wise Woman in the book of that name. Its sequel, *The Princess and Curdie* (1882), is much darker and in its account of the evil state of Princess Irene's realm and its inhabitants seems to reflect MacDonald's despair over the condition of Victorian industrial society. The Princess and Curdie marry but have no children, and the king who succeeds them after their death brings about the destruction of the whole country.

At the Back of the North Wind (1872), though more original than either of these, lacks their pace and suffers perhaps from the over-sweetness of the central character, Diamond. It is a very ambitious book, in which MacDonald seeks to combine concern with moral and social problems with religious parable. Diamond, the son of a coachman who later becomes a London cab-driver, in the course of a dangerous illness is carried by the North Wind – at once a mother-figure and the Will of God – to the country at the back of the north wind, a country, MacDonald tells his readers, that both Herodotus and Dante (whom he refers to as 'Durante') have des-cribed, and that we recognize as purgatory. He learns to accept that good can come of ill (he sees, for example, the North Wind bringing about the loss of a ship) and returns to life a visionary. His shining goodness thereafter makes ordinary people turn against him and suppose him to be half-witted (an example of MacDonald's growing despair about humanity). By the end of the book he is dead:

I walked up the winding stair, and entered his room. A lovely figure, as white and almost as clear as alabaster, was lying on the bed. I saw at once how it was. They thought he was dead. I knew that he had gone to the back of the north wind.

MacDonald also wrote a number of short stories for children which were collected together in 1867 and published under the title of *Dealings with the Fairies*. Of these 'The Light Princess', with a heroine who lacks both physical and spiritual gravity, is the most light-hearted. It is immersion in water that brings about her regen-eration; similarly in *Lilith* the Little Ones are kept permanently in childhood because the rivers of their country have run dry. The collection also contains 'The Golden Key', which might be termed the children's version of *Lilith*, an account of the life's pilgrimage of two children who grow old as they journey and after passing through death into eternal life at last find the place of their quest, 'the country whence the shadows fall'. MacDonald influenced many subsequent writers, but only one writer of fiction succeeded in conveying sanctity with something of his eloquence. This was Dinah Maria Mulock (Mrs Craik, 1826–87) who in *The Little Lame Prince* (1875) movingly described, and with a lighter touch than MacDonald, how the crippled Prince Dolor, imprisoned at the top of a lonely tower by the uncle who has usurped his kingdom, overcomes his loneliness and disability with the help of a fairy cloak with which he can visit far-distant places.

Though MacDonald did not use Scottish legend in any of his fairy-stories, one contemporary did with great effect. Andrew Lang (1844–1921), chiefly remembered for his collections of fairy-tales, wrote a handful of original ones. *Prince Prigio* (1889) and *Prince Ricardo of Pantouflia* (1893) are fantasies in the *Rose and the Ring* style, but in *The Gold of Fairnilee* (1888) he wrote of the landscape and legend of the Scottish Border country. Set in the sixteenth century, it is written with a deeply-felt nostalgic affection for the countryside where he spent his boyhood, and also conveys vividly the uncertainties and perils in those years, when men went off to fight the English, and were borne back, stretched on their own shields. The Laird of Fairnilee dies thus, and his son Randal disappears on a midsummer eve, lured by the fairies. The countryside, from the Cheviot Hills to Carlisle, is searched, but all that can be found of him is his silver crucifix, which the fairies dare not touch. Of all the Victorian fairy-stories this one best succeeds in evoking a culture where fairies are a reality.

11

LATER VICTORIAN NOVELISTS

Patrick M. Yarker and Owen Knowles

Meredith, Hardy and Gissing (Patrick M. Yarker)

Pessimism. A History and a Criticism, by James Sully, published in 1877, was an acknowledgment of a mood that had been growing for a generation and was now almost general. It was no more than a mood, because few in England were prepared to be outright pessimists with all that that involved. Only one or two, such as James Thomson, whose *The City of Dreadful Night* (1874) reflected the teaching of Leopardi, were prepared to accept the full Continental doctrine. Yet scarcely any in the latter half of the century escaped its influence completely, and as the period wore on into the Decadence of the nineties it became more widespread. Sully suggested that it came partly from cynicism engendered by religious scepticism, and partly from 'a sense of the hollowness of the last century optimism'. Undoubtedly the collapse of religious authority and the discrediting of the optimistic monisms of the eighteenth century, with their Utilitarian offshoots, combined with the dead weight of scientific determinism to produce impossible tensions in those who tried to reconcile old habits of thought with the new circumstances. Yet, however blank the intellectual outlook, the belief prevailed that right and order would survive, and that man himself would supply the moral guidance evidently lacking elsewhere in the Universe. 'Meliorism', defined by Sully as 'the faith which affirms not merely our power of lessening evil – this nobody questions – but also our ability to increase the amount of positive good', was, with agnosticism, the characteristic doctrine of the period. The word is attributed to George Eliot, and the idea, with its onus of human responsibility, appealed to novelists. Even Hardy borrowed the name, though the possibility of improvement can be seen only far down the perspective of his thought.

*

George Meredith (1828–1900) appears at first sight to have little to do with pessimism. He had a fundamental vigour and zest for life, and might have said with Browning's David 'How good is man's life, the mere living!' He has been called a temperamental optimist. But his optimism was really only a determination to see the bright side of things; it was not a systematic view of life. For if there is a bright side, there must also be a darker one, and of this Meredith was fully aware. His novels, for all their high spirits, take a gloomy view of human nature. The only thing is that he presents this as a form of comic warning, implying that we are at liberty to take notice and do better. No more is implied, for to Meredith the 'shapeliness' of our life on earth is all that need concern us:

We do not get to any heaven by renouncing the Mother we spring from; and where there is an eternal secret for us, it is best to believe that Earth knows, to keep near her, even in our utmost aspirations.

(*Lord Ormont*, ch 14)

But to say 'it is best to believe . . .' implies that belief is a matter of arbitrary choice, and throws an air of sham over the whole thing. Meredith's earthbound optimism is something of an expedient, even, perhaps, a desperate clinging to the known in face of the unknown. He was called the reconciler of Wordsworth and Darwin, but this is hardly so. To Wordsworth Nature was the visible manifestation of a spiritual order of being, and his great power as a poet was his capacity to suggest both aspects in his words. In Meredith's poetry, however, Earth and Nature are realities, existing for themselves alone; even man appears only as a figure in the landscape. In his poem 'A Faith on Trial', or in 'The Woods of Westermain', and others in the volume of *Poems and Lyrics of the Joy of Earth* (1883), he set out a creed that makes no attempt to minimize the anomalies and frustrations of human life, and its final extinction. The well-known 'Dirge in Woods' (1870) has an Arnoldian cadence:

> Overhead, overhead
> Rushes life in a race,
> As the clouds the clouds chase;
> And we go,
> And we drop like the fruits of the tree,
> Even we,
> Even so.

On the Darwinian side, however, the picture was a little brighter. He believed that the emergence of consciousness marked the limit of Natural Selection, and that thereafter man must himself take a hand in the agonizing process of his creation. This prospect filled Meredith with exhilaration, for it restored the sense of man's co-operation with Nature. Imperfect and evolving, he must strive to follow his higher consciousness, for the older biological factors of evolution remain active. The predatory element, the 'scaly Dragon-fowl', is still apparent in man's nature as 'egoism', or the wilful assertion of the self in crass unawareness of the personalities and rights of others. Each man's task is to quell this primitive egoism which alienates him from the rest of creation and to cultivate awareness of life as a whole. The task is hard, but his efforts are not unaided. Even the bitterness of life can be a guide, administering a 'celestial hail of thwacks'. But above all, the universal harmony, manifesting itself in common sense and having as its instrument of correction the Spirit of Comedy, serves to maintain the essential balance between blood, brain, and spirit, by which harmony is achieved.

This is the theme of Meredith's novels: the regulation of human behaviour by the operation of the Comic Spirit. Wherever there is an aberration or want of proportion the Comic Spirit seeks to correct it. The novels all deal, in various ways, with this corrective process. In them egoism is shown in countless forms, though reduced in Meredith's comic world to a series of grotesque pos-turings and expedients, having in various degrees painful, even tragic, consequences, although remaining basically ridiculous. Seen in one light it is hardly an optimistic picture. The Comic Spirit presides over it with the 'sunny malice of a faun', waiting with suppressed glee for the next absurdity, which always comes. In 1877 Meredith gave his famous lecture *On the Idea of Comedy and of the Uses of the Comic Spirit*, explaining its function:

Men's future on earth does not attract it; their honesty and shapeliness in the present does: and whenever they wax out of proportion, overblown, affected, pretentious, bombastical, hypocritical, pedantic, fantastically de-licate; whenever it sees them self-deceived or hoodwinked, given to run riot in idolatries, drifting into vanities, congregating in absurdities, planning shortsightedly, plotting dementedly; whenever they are at variance with their professions, and violate the unwritten but perceptible laws binding them in consideration one to another; whenever they offend sound reason, fair justice; are false in humility or mined with conceit, individually, or in bulk – the Spirit overhead will look humanely malign and cast an oblique light on them, followed by volleys of silvery laughter.

(*An Essay on Comedy*, 1897, pp 89–90)

This detached view of life, uncommon among Victorians, perhaps owes something to Meredith's unusual upbringing. The Merediths were of Welsh extraction, but the family history really begins with his grandfather, Melchizedek Meredith (1763–1814), a well-known tailor and naval outfitter in Portsmouth. His portrait as 'the Great Mel' in *Evan Harrington* is no doubt authentic, and the novel reflects, with varying fidelity, much of the family background. George Meredith's father was the youngest of the Great Mel's seven children. When he was seventeen the Great Mel died, much in debt, leaving him, like Evan Harrington himself, to carry on the business, for which he had no inclination. Unlike Evan, however, he did not wed an heiress, but married the daughter of a local innkeeper. It was a successful match, and George Meredith, their only child, was born on 12 February 1828.

It is a curiosity of Meredith's life that these simple facts of his birth and parentage remained virtually unknown until after his death in 1909. Indeed, he took active steps to conceal them, and allowed romantic rumours concerning his origin to proliferate. But even more remarkable is the fact that in the Countess de Saldar in *Evan Harrington* (she was a portrait of his aunt Louisa, whose husband became a friend of the King of Portugal) he showed, with rich comedy, the absurdity of one whose extravagant horror of her tailoring origin led her into impossible shifts to conceal it. Whatever the explanation of this paradox, Meredith was clearly uneasy about his connection with trade and sought to sever it as soon as he could. It is possible that this inner uncertainty explained the 'faked' social values that E. M. Forster detected in his novels (*Aspects of the Novel*, 1949, p 86).

The second factor from his childhood that influenced his later life was his two years at the Moravian school at Neuwied on the Rhine. This school, dedicated to the principle of individual freedom, had a wide reputation, and boys from all over Europe were to be met there. Thus from the provincial milieu of the high-class tailoring business in Portsmouth Meredith was translated to a cosmopolitan centre alive with European liberalism. For in 1842, when he went there, the ferment that seethed up in 1848 was already active, and Meredith was greatly affected by it. It was said that he lived perpetually in the spirit of 1848. He returned to England with a taste for German literature that led him to Carlyle, and a zeal for revolutionary politics that soon gained him many friends of similar outlook.

Among these were Edward Peacock, son of Thomas Love

Peacock, and his sister, Mary Nicolls, whose sailor husband had been drowned shortly after their marriage. Meredith, then twenty-three, fell passionately in love with this tragic and beautiful daughter of the legendary friend of Shelley. She was seven years older than he, but after a furious courtship they were married, and the disastrous story partly recorded in *Modern Love* began. They lived at first with Peacock at Lower Halliford, but when their son Arthur was born, this further invasion proved too much, and they had to go. Peacock exerted a lasting influence on Meredith, to be seen not only in some of his more crotchety characters, but also in certain dialogue-scenes, such as the 'Animated Conversation at a Luncheon-Table' in *The Egoist*, which might almost belong to one of Peacock's books.

His first essay in narrative fiction, however, was in a different genre. *The Shaving of Shagpat* (1856) was an oriental tale, owing something to *Vathek* and to Southey's *Thalaba the Destroyer*, as well as to *The Arabian Nights*, but having elements of comedy that were Meredith's own. He denied intentional allegory, but this tale of a hirsute enchanter who holds a city in superstitious subjection by means of a single hair, and of the efforts of Shibli Bagarag, the barber, to shave him, and so become 'Master of the Event', doubtless reflects his ideas of rationality and freedom. It was followed by *Farina. A Legend of Cologne* (1857), a less successful parody of the Gothic tale of terror.

In the meantime his marriage was becoming impossible. Both were highly-strung and uncompromising, and a series of domestic disasters and difficulties with lodgings made things worse. In 1858 Meredith's wife ran away with Henry Wallis, the Pre-Raphaelite painter, for whose *Death of Chatterton* Meredith had posed. They went to Wales, where she bore Wallis a son, and then on to Capri. Arthur Meredith remained with his father, and though she returned the following year, Meredith never saw his wife again. She died friendless in 1861, and in the next year Meredith published *Modern Love*, a sequence of fifty sixteen-line 'sonnets', in which he probed the anatomy of an unhappy marriage with skill and experience. He concludes that there was no avoidable blame:

> The wrong is mixed. In tragic life, God wot,
> No villain need be. Passions spin the plot:
> We are betrayed by what is false within.
>
> (no. 43)

The effect of the disaster had already appeared, however, in *The*

Ordeal of Richard Feverel (1859), a book in which Meredith's bitterness is clearly visible beneath the surface. For, though treated as a comedy, the book ends in disaster for the innocent, and has an undercurrent of resentment, springing from the fact that Sir Austin Feverel's wife has run off with a poet. This warps his nature so that he resolves to bring up his son without knowledge of sexual love until he himself should choose him a partner. But Richard falls in love with Lucy, a farmer's niece, abducts and marries her. His father, however, so plays on his filial affection that, torn between this and his love for Lucy, he causes her much needless suffering and a tragic death. The book has many shortcomings, chiefly a lack of unity and motivation, but it contains the elements of much of Meredith's later work. Sir Austin is the first of his egoists, and his egoism destroys the natural harmony, with disastrous consequences. The irony, sustained throughout, is some of the harshest that Meredith ever developed. It was, for example, Sir Austin's own half-hearted affair with Lady Blandish that frustrated his 'System' by awakening romantic notions in Richard; his success in separating Richard from Lucy brought about what he most feared for his son (though advocating for others) 'to drag him through the sinks of the town'; in the end he realizes that Lucy is an admirable daughter-in-law, but it is then too late. Lucy dies, and Richard is left to endure the full agony of realization.

Meredith's irony depends on his attitude to his characters; it is not irony of situation, representing the grimness of human fate, but irony of folly, comic irony (though sometimes grim enough). For this reason Meredith never shrank from comment in his own person, or through the medium of an imaginary arbiter such as 'the Philosopher'. This is sometimes tedious, and he erred, too, in placing too great a reliance on the tone. The result is that his novels exist at several removes from life, and their effort is mainly intellectual. Although the movement towards realism was getting under way when he wrote, he had no bent for it. As W. E. Henley put it, his characters are not human beings but 'compendiums of humanity' (*The Academy*, vol xvi, 1879, p 369), so that his comic world, though far from ordinary life, is, in its own way, true.

The next novel, *Evan Harrington* (1861), is far more in the spirit of comedy than its predecessor. The Countess Louisa, for example, is in the broad tradition of matronly humour, though her social snobbery was a more recent emergence. In her assumption of a foreign manner that leads her to address her sisters as 'You English' she is of the order of pretenders who almost deceive themselves.

'We must honour Papa, even though we cannot, of course, acknowledge him' is the measure of her candour and family affection. She maintains her impossible position, both in her own and others' eyes, with immense resource and powers of generalship that proclaim Meredith's respect for the formidable capacity of women, even at a time when he still smarted from its effects. His books contain many masterful women – Rhoda Fleming, Vittoria, Diana Warwick, Carinthia Fleetwood; even the less forceful, such as Clara Middleton in *The Egoist*, have a determination not to be brooked, and one recognizes the force of Sir Willoughby Patterne's complaint, 'I am favoured by fortune from my birth until I enter into relations with women!' (ch. 40). For the women have an egoism of their own before which the male kind, otherwise rampant, is rebuked. The Countess Louisa is, in her many-sidedness, one of the best of Meredith's women characters, though her position is different from those of the others. There is little else in *Evan Harrington* to approach her. The book was published serially in *Once a Week*, with illustrations by Charles Keene, and was given by the reviewer in *The Saturday Review* 'a front place in literature that is . . . not destined to endure' (vol xi, 1861, p 77).

Meredith was now on intimate terms with Swinburne and the Rossettis and rented a room from them at 15 Cheyne Walk. He had formed two other friendships that influenced his novels. The first was with Janet Duff-Gordon, who inspired his more sympathetic heroines such as Rose in *Evan Harrington*, and the second was with Frederick Maxse, a naval officer who had distinguished himself in the Crimea. He was to be the model for the hero of *Beauchamp's Career*. About this time Meredith became literary adviser to Chapman and Hall, in which position he had some influence on younger novelists.

The next novel, *Emilia in England* (1864), afterwards called *Sandra Belloni*, repeated some of the comic features of *Evan Harrington* in the three Pole sisters, daughters of a merchant, who aspire to 'Fine Shades' of 'Nice Feeling' – perhaps owing something, too, to Ruskin's ideal view of the merchant in *Unto This Last*. They are contrasted with the simple ardour of Emilia, daughter of an itinerant Italian musician and possessor of a fine natural voice. *Rhoda Fleming* (1865), however, was a departure from Meredith's earlier vein. This story of a girl seduced by a young egoist has been said to give 'a curious impression of having been written in collaboration with Hardy' (S. Sassoon, *Meredith*, 1948, p 73); but Dahlia Fleming is unlike Tess. Her sister Rhoda is the one to carry on the 'Woman's Battle' of the original title. However, Meredith's approach to the theme, critical of the marriage custom, ironical about the need for the girl to be made an honest woman at all costs, is certainly more that of the late rather than the mid Victorian period. *Vittoria* (1866), sequel to *Sandra Belloni*, is Meredith's tribute to Mazzini and the 'Spirit of 1848'. Emilia, now a trained singer, gives her voice to the cause of freedom by singing a revolutionary song in the Opera House at Milan as a signal for the revolt against Austria.

In 1864 Meredith had married Marie Vulliamy, daughter of a neighbour, and this second marriage was to be as happy as the first had been wretched. The only shadow was the growing estrangement from Arthur, who was sent away to the Pestalozzi school in Switzerland for his health and seldom saw his father thereafter. A son, William Maxse, was born, and the Merediths moved to Flint Cottage, Box Hill, where the novelist spent most of his remaining years.

The Adventures of Harry Richmond (1871) was his first production at Flint Cottage and was serialized in *The Cornhill Magazine* with illustrations by George du Maurier. Written in the first person, as Harry's narrative of the struggle between his father and grandfather, each trying to save him from the other, the book owes much to Dickens, but develops, though it does not sustain, an exuberance of its own. Richmond Roy, the father, reputedly the son of a Royal Duke, a charlatan and poseur of egregious audacity, captivates Harry, and finally gains his understanding and loyalty. Though full of comment on contemporary questions, the book does not develop a purpose in the manner of the earlier novels. 'Uncurbed by philosophical reservations, George Meredith had been able to allow his imagination free scope', said an admirer. It may be, though, that Meredith's genius needed such a curb. *Beauchamp's Career* (1876), which he told John Morley was 'philosophical- political, with no powerful stream of adventure', certainly provided one. In 1867 Maxse retired from the Navy and stood as Radical candidate for Southampton, and thereafter uttered a series of reforming pamphlets. Meredith helped in his election campaign which failed, and produced his own pamphlet in the 'Up at Midnight' dialogues in *The Graphic*. It was the time of the Paris Commune, which Meredith greeted with an Ode. These activities were the background of the novel, which is diversified by uncertain but passionate amours, and such scenes as that (as E. M. Forster put it) 'of one old man whipping another from the highest motives' (*Aspects of the Novel*, 1949 edn, p 87). It is Meredith's best-constructed novel.

But narrative was not his main interest. His eye was on the drama of the big scene, and his stories too often repeat the same features – the jealous influence of an older man on a younger, the blighting of true love by wrong-headedness, the impossible passion for an ideal beauty. These elements serve only to connect the set pieces. His essay on Comedy is largely an account of the comic drama, with the emphasis on Molière and Congreve, and the success of his next book, *The Egoist* (1879), rightly regarded as his masterpiece, has something to do with its organization on the lines of a play. The narrative is far simpler than in earlier books and is developed in a series of dialogues. The characters are fewer than usual, and are grouped around the central figure, Sir Willoughby Patterne, gaining depth when, like Clara Middleton, they stand in open conflict with him, losing it as they move towards the circumference. Sir Willoughby is essential egoism. His monomania is no mere crochet, like that of Sir Arthur Feverel and others. In them there is always a spark of genuine feeling, a heart capable of being touched. But Willoughby has no heart; he has nothing at the centre at all. Outward appearances, the cutting of an appropriate figure, are all that he understands. He sees others only in terms of his own reputation.

'Egoism', a word dating from the late eighteenth century, was one of the key terms of the nineteenth. It bred an antonym, 'altruism', first used by Comte to provide an alternative to the principle of self-interest, long thought the chief motive in human affairs. Under Comte's influence a new ethic developed, in which egoism was the negative and altruism the positive morality. Meredith, however, does not present egoism in these terms in the book. Willoughby's self-centred assumptions about Clara are exasperating, but comically so, for we see that he injured no one but himself. Egoism, we understand, is the alienating principle, and if an individual chooses it, he must bear his resulting isolation. It was Meredith's most optimistic novel, and this, perhaps, was what he referred to when he told Stevenson, 'It is a Comedy with only half of me in it, unlikely therefore to take either the public or my friends' (*Letters*, ed. W. M. Meredith, 1912, vol I, p 297). He was mistaken, but there was point in his remark. In another sense it may have been what he put in unnecessarily, rather than what he left out, that was rejected. W. E. Henley, friend of both Meredith and Stevenson, reviewed the book in terms that might apply to Meredith generally:

His pages so teem with fine sayings, and magniloquent epigrams and gorgeous images, and fantastic locutions, that the mind would welcome dulness as a glad relief. He is tediously amusing; he is brilliant to the point of being obscure; his helpfulness is so extravagant as to worry and confound. His ingenuity and intelligence are always misleading him into treating mere episodes as solemnly and elaborately as a main incident; he is ever ready to discuss, to ramble, to theorize, to dogmatize, to indulge himself in a little irony, or a little reflection, or a little artistic misdemeanour of some sort.

(*The Athenaeum*, 1 November 1879, p 555)

The Egoist is freer from these faults than are most of the novels, but the indictment stands, and in some of the later books these faults were seriously aggravated.

The Tragic Comedians (1880) was based on the affair between Ferdinand Lassalle, the German socialist, and Helene von Donniges, as a result of which Lassalle fell in a duel. *Diana of the Crossways* (1885) also relied to some extent on historical personages, in this case Lady Caroline Norton and Lord Melbourne. Its theme, however, that of a married woman estranged from her husband, was becoming increasingly important with the triumph of feminism, and was to be the main concern of novels in the nineties. Meredith's last three works, *One of Our Conquerors* (1891), *Lord Ormont and His Aminta* (1894) and *The Amazing Marriage* (1895, but begun in 1879) all approach it in different ways. His son Arthur died in 1891, estranged from him as his mother had been. This perhaps revived something of Meredith's former outlook, for these novels all deal with broken marriages, now, in accord with the new spirit, carried to the full length of desertion and adultery. But the target of his attack was less personal than social, for each shows that modern society fosters egoism, with consequent wretchedness to the individual, and, in spite of the continued comic treatment, a gloomy outlook for mankind.

When Meredith died in 1909, his fame was at its height. Wilde, who had included a number of epigrams on Meredith in *The Decay of Lying*, also said:

One incomparable novelist we now have in England, Mr. George Meredith. There are better artists in France, but France has no one whose view of life is so large, so varied, so imaginatively true. There are tellers of stories in Russia who have a more vivid sense of what pain in fiction may be. But to him belongs philosophy in fiction. His people not merely live, but they live in thought.

(*The Soul of Man Under Socialism*)

It is true that Henry James complained bitterly about *Lord Ormont*, possibly because in it a Jamesian situation is handled in an un-Jamesian manner (*Letters*, ed. P. Lubbock, 1920, vol I, p 224), but he also praised Meredith's 'big strong whiffs of manly tone and clear judgment' (quoted by J. Lindsay, *George Meredith*, 1956, p 372), and these qualities also appealed to R. L. Stevenson, who first met him in 1878, and ever thereafter 'served under his colours'. Stevenson loved his romance, his broad and active view of life, and admired his brilliant insight and analysis of character. Meredith's poetry made him 'drunk like wine', and he was fascinated by his style and poetic approach to reality.

Hardy reflected different aspects of the master's work. He received from him the myth-making element, the presentation of ideas in terms of life. More, he drew from Meredith his cosmic view of human life, presided over by eternal Spirits, who, without participating, manipulate events. Glimpses of the 'squatting imps' that Meredith described in the Prelude to *The Egoist*, waiting and watching, with 'ears at full cock, for the commencement of the comic drama of the suicide', are continually caught in Hardy's novels. But the difference is that, whereas in Meredith the activities of these imps of the Comic Spirit work for Harmony, and therefore the eventual good of mankind, Hardy's watchers are malignant, or, at best, indifferent to the good or suffering of men. Hardy's irony, therefore, is a tragic irony of events or destiny, rather than a comic irony of character and folly. Meredith's egoist is not a universal figure. We may all be egoists in our way, but we are all capable of chastening by the celestial thwacks. But to Hardy the ills from which men suffer are irremediable.

For Hardy absorbed far more of the pessimistic doctrine than did Meredith. He was the reverse of gloomy by nature, but he had a shrewder understanding than had Meredith of the negative aspects of Victorian expansion. His origins were no more lowly than were Meredith's, but his roots were far deeper in the soil. The son of a builder, he was born in 1840 at Lower Bockhampton, a small hamlet on the edge of what he came to call Egdon Heath. There were generations of farming tradition behind him. He had an instinctive feel for the immemorial way of life, regulated by the seasons, punctuated by secular or ecclesiastical festivals, and maintained by 'practices which had suffered no mutilation at the hands of time'. Moreover, in those ancient regions evidence is plentiful of occupation and husbandry since prehistoric times. Hardy's sense of the past was fostered by the propinquity of these earlier inhabitants, who had never really vanished from the scene.

But now he saw this long continuity interrupted. Unlike Meredith, Hardy felt the loss of religious faith, but it would be wrong to regard him as a nineteenth-century philosophical sceptic or convert to agnosticism. His view of religion was not unconnected with his sense of the continuity of Dorset life since pagan times. The Church had come, and given the familiar pattern of Christian worship to the land, but it had not altered the fundamental beliefs, chthonic and fatalistic, that governed the lives of the people. Hardy's position was that of a further stage of sophistication, analogous, perhaps, to the legacy of the Enlightenment within the Church itself, the rational aspect slowly obliterating the sacramental. He remained, as he said, 'churchy; not in an intellectual sense but in so far as instincts and emotions ruled' (F. E. Hardy, *The Later Years of Thomas Hardy*, 1930, p 176). He thought of taking Orders when he was twenty-five, but he was already aware of a distance from his fellow-worshippers in Westminster Abbey. He felt increasingly wistful, longing for what he could no longer share. When he left school in Dorchester, he was articled to a local architect and restorer of churches, and he remained in this profession until the success of *Far from the Madding Crowd* released him in 1874. This active concern with the fabric of churches, decayed but extant, has an appropriate quality.

So, too, have the stories of gruesome but incongruous contents of coffins and other instances of macabre comedy that his profession afforded, for whereas Meredith was enabled by his Epicurean outlook to see life as a comedy with overtones of pathos, Hardy was impelled to the opposite view. He saw life as tragic, but with aspects of comedy. His sense of humour was irrepressible, but it was always inclined to the sepulchral. It became increasingly grotesque, and eventually did not relieve the pessimism of his novels but emphasized it, giving his work the 'twilight' quality that Meredith deplored. His self-acquired love of the classics fostered his belief in fate. His reading of the philosophers, of J. S. Mill and of Herbert Spencer's *First Principles* with its emphasis on force and causality, or of Schopenhauer and von Hartmann who proclaimed the doctrine of the unconscious Will, merely formulated what he already instinctively believed. Whereas mankind has consciousness, the force that controls him has not. Blindly, this unconscious Will frustrates and confounds man's noblest endeavours and passes on, unaware of the havoc caused. The imps that Meredith saw attendant on the Comic Spirit were to Hardy the agents of this alien force.

Hardy's novels present this sombre pageant from below, in the setting of his native Dorset, or Wessex, as he called it. The 'regional novel' was well established in English fiction by 1870, but Hardy brought an intensity to both landscape and figures that gave them something of the quality of myth. The literary heritage of his rustics has often been noted. They have affinity with Shakespeare's 'rude mechanicals'; their stoicism is reminiscent of Wordsworth, their earthiness of Scott. William Barnes, the Dorset poet, contributed much to their speech and activities. But Hardy also knew them well. In 1883 he published an essay on 'The Dorsetshire Labourer', giving an unsentimental picture of

a number of dissimilar fellow-creatures, men of many minds; infinite in difference; some happy, many serene, a few depressed; some clever even to genius, some stupid, some wanton, some austere . . . each of whom walks his own way the road to dusty death.

From all these elements he fashioned something like a chorus to his drama. They act and are acted upon, but they live their lives according to the conditions that engulf them. Among themselves they are honest, kindly, tolerant; steeped in superstition, they have an instinctive sense of the workings of fate that preserves them from *hubris*. They find an earthy happiness in their limited aspirations, commenting shrewdly on their betters who fail to do so. Over them the Comic Spirit may be said to preside and their unconscious humour epitomizes the comic irony of life.

Like Meredith, Hardy was much concerned with class-distinctions, and his first novel, *The Poor Man and the Lady* (written 1867, but never published, and now lost) was on this theme. Meredith read it for Chapman and Hall and advised Hardy to concentrate on greater complication of plot. This advice was followed in *Desperate Remedies* (1871), the ramifications of whose action are reminiscent of Wilkie Collins. It is a novel of dark passages and 'moral obliquity'. It was attacked as immoral, but the country scenes were praised; so in his next novel, *Under the Greenwood Tree* (1872), moral issues were evaded, and the rustics of the Mellstock Quire have the scene almost to themselves, as they campaign against their replacement by an organ. The tale of Dick Dewey's courtship of Fancy Day is a slight one. It has a happy ending, but it lay in Fancy's power to give matters a different turn, and she all but did so. Love, to Hardy, was an additional affliction laid on already suffering humanity. Edmund Blunden drew attention to Swinburne's address to Aphrodite in *Atalanta in Calydon*, which Hardy had read with 'glad surprize':

> Was there not evil enough,
>   Mother, and anguish on earth
>   Born with man at his birth
> That thou, having wings as a dove,
> Being girt with desire for a girth,
>   That thou must come after these,
>   That thou must lay on him love?

This was Hardy's view. Love, more than any other human attribute, puts man at the disposal of the tragic powers. *A Pair of Blue Eyes* (1873) develops this theme. It is set in Cornwall, whither Hardy had been sent by his employer to design a new tower for St Juliot's Church, near Tintagel. While there he fell in love with Emma Gifford, the Rector's sister-in-law, and was idyllically happy for his whole stay in Cornwall, as one of his most famous poems relates:

> When I came back from Lyonesse
> With magic in my eyes . . .

In the novel the love story follows a very different course.

Leslie Stephen, the editor of *The Cornhill Magazine*, had liked *Under the Greenwood Tree*, and asked Hardy to write a serial novel for his magazine. The result was *Far From the Madding Crowd* (1874), Hardy's first financial success, and on the strength of it he and Emma Gifford married. The novel marks a stage, for it was his first attempt to develop Wordsworth's view that in rural life 'the essential passions of the heart find a better soil in which they can attain their maturity'. It is a vigorous account of the conflict of individuals with each other and with circumstances. The main characters, Gabriel Oak, Boldwood, Serjeant Troy, and Bathsheba Everdene, are drawn with bold strokes, emphasizing their independence, and setting them starkly against fate. Bathsheba is the first of his passionate women, capricious, wilful and proud. Her three lovers reflect different aspects of her nature. Troy has the romance of martial legend implied by his name. His scarlet is like the note of a trumpet; he woos her with his sword. But by this time the other face of romance was all too familiar. Troy is not heartless, but he is shallow, and, for all his swordsmanship, weak. He deserts Fanny Robin, who dies bearing his child, and, after his marriage to Bathsheba, deserts her too. Farmer Boldwood, outwardly stolid, shows in the end the destructiveness of passion. Oak is like his name, too, and his marriage to the widowed Bathsheba, when all passion is spent, is an acceptable triumph for 'that love . . . beside which the passion usually called by the name is as evanescent as a stream'. But this was Hardy's concession to the public; he originally meant Bathsheba's awakening to come too late. The malignant power of fate is palpable in the novel – and at one point visible, too. In a moment of repentance Troy plants Fanny's grave with flowers. Above it, the gutter of the church-tower ends in a gargoyle, with 'short, erect ears, eyes staring from their sockets, and its fingers and hands were seizing the corners of its mouth which they thus seemed to pull open to give free passage to the water it vomited'. That night it rained, and the spout from this grotesque orifice washed away the tokens of Troy's remorse. This charade, one of many in the novels, epitomizes much of Hardy's attitude to life and of his method of expressing it.

His imagination was keenly visual, and by startling images he brings the living scene before the reader with astonishing suddenness. In contrast, his prose comments are often laboured and self-conscious. He gave his own explanation of this:

It is, of course, simply a carrying into prose the knowledge I have acquired in poetry – that inexact rhymes and rhythms now and then are far more pleasing than correct ones.

(*The Early Life of Thomas Hardy*, p 138)

But the effect is often less pleasing than he supposed, and critics have complained of the 'inartistic knottiness' of his prose.

He wrote a further novel for Leslie Stephen, *The Hand of Ethelberta* (1876), 'a somewhat frivolous narrative', according to Hardy's preface, on the Meredithian theme of a butler's daughter who conceals her lowly origin for matrimonial ends. Very different was the next novel, *The Return of the Native* (1878), whose great protagonist is, of course, Egdon Heath. Hardy's descriptions of 'Haggard Egdon', instinct with a life alien to the social ways of men, are triumphs of his method. Egdon dominates the lives of all who live on its fringes. Not all are able to come to terms with its sombre presence; to some it is actively hostile. Only the rustics accept it without question. It is at once a symbol and a manifestation of the 'unwitting Will', blind, non-human, timeless. Its appeal is to an instinct deep in man's nature but, so Hardy believed, beginning to stir anew, for Clym Yeobright, who 'indirectly bore evidence that ideal physical beauty is incompatible with emotional development' can understand its grandeur, so inimical to 'the sort of beauty called charming and fair'. Curiously, Hardy chose to match this romantic concept with a classical form, giving the novel unity of place and action. Critics disliked it, however, and he was obliged to mitigate some of its gloom before it could be published.

His next novel was accordingly much lighter, taking some of its inspiration from comedy rather than from tragedy. *The Trumpet Major* (1880) is Hardy's most genial novel, having, in spite of its martial background, more affinity with *Under the Greenwood Tree* than with any other. It reflects his lifelong fascination with the Napoleonic Wars, which reached its climax in *The Dynasts*. The Hardys, who had been living at Sturminster, near Poole, had moved to London in 1878, taking a house near Wandsworth Common. In the winter of 1880 Hardy fell ill and remained incapacitated for some months, during which he dictated a novel to his wife. This was *A Laodicean* (1881), his least successful book. When he recovered, Hardy moved again to Dorset, settling in Wimborne. Here, in the year of a comet, he wrote *Two on a Tower* (1882), in which he sought 'to set the emotional history of two infinitesimal lives against the stupendous background of the stellar universe', as he said in the Preface. This theme had been in his mind for some years, and had already appeared in some of his lyrics, notably 'A Lunar Eclipse' and 'In Vision I Roamed' (1866). But, though possible in a short lyric, the theme is unsuited to a novel, where all the interest is naturally on the infinitesimal lives. But the loneliness of man haunted his imagination, and he turned increasingly to the epic theme of an individual against fate. *Far From the Madding Crowd* and *The Return of the Native* had been concerned with groups of people who act and react to the impulse of their natures. Now he began to consider the problem of one who tries to combat his nature, to overcome the passions and reverse their effect; the efforts, in other words, of the individual will to assert itself. But, in Hardy's view, the individual will is a figment; it is no more than a manifestation of the general Will in the individual life. Such efforts, therefore, are doomed. So long as they do not conflict with the general Will, the illusion of the individual will may persist and even appear triumphant. But in the end the reality will assert itself.

This is developed in *The Mayor of Casterbridge* (1886), Hardy's version of the theme of crime and punishment. Michael Henchard is an epic figure, standing among his fellows 'like a great tree in a wind'. He is also an attempt by Hardy to create a complex character, at odds with himself. The causes of both his rise and fall are to be found in his own nature to an extent not seen before in the novels. Chance, as always in Hardy, plays a large part in the plot. But from the first episode, in which he sells his wife and child, the defects of his character are clear. Later, his good qualities are equally apparent, but his fortitude and determination to overcome his faults, his honesty and courage, cannot wipe out the consequences of his action. Nevertheless, his strength and ruggedness are apt to a certain phase of development, and Henchard has twenty years of triumph. But they must needs give way before the new order, represented by Farfrae, with his modern methods. Thereafter, transformed to stubbornness and rigidity, they cause Henchard's ruin. There is thus a secular pattern in the novel, which increases the Lear-like aspect some have found in it.

The location of the book reflects Hardy's move to Dorchester in 1883, first into a house in the town itself and, finally, in 1885, to Max Gate, the house he designed for himself on the outskirts, which was to be his home for the rest of his life. The first book he wrote at Max Gate was *The Woodlanders* (1887), a transitional work that looks back to *Far From the Madding Crowd* (and even earlier) in its plot, but reflects Hardy's new preoccupations in its theme. The doctrine of the Unfulfilled Intention marks a variation of his thought and is explicit in his description of Hintock Wood:

Here, as everywhere, the Unfulfilled Intention, which makes life what it is, was as obvious as it could be among the depraved crowds of a city slum. The leaf was deformed, the curve was crippled, the taper was interrupted; the lichen ate the vigour of the stalk, and the ivy slowly strangled to death the promising sapling.

(The Woodlanders, ch. 7)

Another new preoccupation, which had already appeared in *The Return of the Native,* and was to be of great importance in *Jude the Obscure,* was with 'modern nerves' and their incompatibility with 'primitive feeling'. In this respect Grace Melbury is a forerunner of Sue Bridehead.

The next novel was *Tess of the d'Urbervilles* (1891), in which he returned to his epic theme. The doctrine of the Unfulfilled Intention here takes on a more bitter aspect as Hardy questions the process by which 'so often the coarse appropriates the finer thus, the wrong man the woman, the wrong woman the man'. This, he says, 'many thousand years of analytical philosophy have failed to explain to our sense of order'. *Tess* differs from the earlier novels in that it was motivated by a social purpose, which he showed by his defiant caption to the title, 'A Pure Woman'. Not only the dispensations of fate, or the depravities of mankind, but the polite conventions of society were the objects of his scorn. Frankness in fiction was, during the eighties and nineties, an issue of growing importance and concern. In writing of Tess's seduction and its consequences Hardy cannot be said to have made a new departure, for the theme was much exploited, and had been treated with greater freedom by earlier writers. But by making her the heroine, and showing everyone else up in a poor light beside her, he deliberately challenged the view, more Malthusian than Christian, that a girl who has an illegitimate child, though she may be pitied, cannot be forgiven. It was a view that had been under fire since the House of Lords Select Committee in 1881, but it was not yet routed, and Hardy suffered for his temerity.

He had never been thoroughly reconciled to novel-writing, though he had become resigned to it as 'a trade'. Poetry had always been his preoccupation; he returned to fiction only to earn a living. If, however, his novels were not acceptable to the public he saw no point in writing any more. After reading a review of *Tess* he wrote in his journal

Well, if this sort of thing continues no more novel-writing for me. A man must be a fool to deliberately stand up to be shot at.

(*The Later Years of Thomas Hardy*, p 7)

However, adverse criticism was not general, and it was understood that the book was a masterpiece. Hardy did not hesitate to expose himself as a target once more, and *Jude the Obscure* came out in November 1895. Although the protagonists are very different, it was in some ways a rewriting of *Tess*, with Tess's position between Alec d'Urberville and Angel Clare repeated in considerable detail by Jude's relations with Arabella and Sue. But the book is in a very different key. The 'modern nerves' that Hardy wrote of in *The Woodlanders* take possession of it; the concomitant 'primitive passions' are debilitated and fretful. 'We are horribly sensitive, that's what's wrong with us', cries Jude, and it is the keynote of the book, objectified in the gruesome figure of Little Father Time. Sue Bridehead has all the instability of Hardy's earlier women expressed in terms of nervous exhaustion. Henry James complained to Stevenson that, in *Tess*, 'the pretence of sexuality is only equalled by the absence of it' (*Letters*, vol I, p 194), but in *Jude* both sides of the equation are revised. Hardy wrote that he meant the book to convey 'the contrast between the ideal life a man wished to lead and the squalid real life he was fated to lead'. He referred to Jude's aspiration to scholarship, but the wider reference is made clear by Jude's grotesque symbolic initiation when he is hit on the cheek by a hog's pizzle, thrown by Arabella. Like Meredith's novels of the nineties, *Jude* deals with what Hardy called the 'marriage question'. It does so not in terms of primitive passions, nor of a man's struggle, like Henchard's, against fate, but in terms of social conventions. 'It is no use fighting against God!' cries Sue; but Jude corrects her: 'It is only against men and senseless circumstances'. In their 'irregular' life together they are continually obliged to keep up appearances, and avert the suspicion of landladies. It was properly the realm of the Comic Spirit; when presented as tragedy the effect is lugubrious.

Hardy wrote no more novels after *Jude*, not because of the press reviews, but because he had exhausted a form that was never congenial to him. In 1898 he published *Wessex Poems*, some of which had been written thirty years before. Poetry was his natural medium; 'I am only a learner in the art of novel-writing', he said after *Tess*, his thirteenth novel. Since 1870, when he visited Peninsular veterans at Chelsea, the idea of an epic on the Napoleonic Wars had been in his mind.

The Dynasts came out in three parts, in 1903, 1906, and 1908. In its Shelleyan complex of non-human Spirits it embodies the ideas of the unconscious Will that lie behind the novels. It looks at man's life from above, as the novels survey it from below. In *The Dynasts* men, even the greatest, are seen to be puppets, activated by strings. Only the Spirits have life.

Hardy's first wife died in 1912. For years she had entertained the delusion that her husband was her inferior, and the effect of this is apparent in *Jude*. Yet after her death he wrote a number of poems recalling their early days together in Cornwall and other memories of her. In 1914 he married his amanuensis, Florence Emily Dugdale, whose two volumes of his Journals and other biographical material are the main source of our knowledge of Hardy's personal life and thought. Hardy died in January 1928.

He is often called a poetic novelist, and the reference is not so much to his images as to his whole attitude to prose fiction. At a time when ideas of verisimilitude and psychological realism were in the ascendant, Hardy was as apt as Dickens to ignore the limitations of every day. 'It is not improbabilities of incident but improbabilities of character that matter', he wrote in 1886. But even if that were true, Hardy's characters have a quality of their own, and inhabit a world in which the elements have been brought into a new relationship, with meaningful conjunctions of events in a landscape vibrant with purpose.

Hardy took Matthew Arnold's phrase 'the imaginative reason' to define his approach to reality, suggesting the capacity to see 'into the heart of a thing'. A very different approach was adopted by George Gissing, whose novels, though they owed much to Meredith, are unlike those of either Meredith or Hardy. Gissing has always been known as a 'realistic' writer; yet his view of realism was qualified by a belief that objectivity is impossible, for the observer necessarily imposes his own personality on what he sees. Writing of Dickens's practice of 'modifying circumstances' he said

Our 'realist' will hear of no such paltering with truth. Heedless of Pilate's question, he takes for granted that truth can be got at, and that it is his plain duty to set it down without compromise; or, if less crude in his perceptions, he holds that truth, for the artist, is the impression produced on him, and that to convey this impression with entire sincerity is his sole reason for existing.

(*Charles Dickens*, p 73)

This view is close to Pater, and it is central to Gissing's approach to the novel. He agreed that the artist must modify his material; but he argued that this modification must be at the behest of his artistic conscience, and not to conform with a separately conceived moral theory or view of life. For this reason he rejected 'naturalism', such as that of Zola, which George Moore was following in England in *A Mummer's Wife* (1882). For the principle of naturalism was scientific, and, said Gissing, 'there is no science in fiction'. Similarly, his pessimism was not a positive belief, such as Hardy's, but an attitude forced on him by experience.

The theme of failure haunted the novels of the later nineteenth century. Meredith treated it in *The Ordeal of Richard Feverel*; Hardy brought it to a nadir in *Jude*, and saw in it the pattern of the future, for Little Father Time was 'the beginning of the coming wish not to live'. Gissing embraced this mood, consciously or unconsciously, until it seemed the ruling spirit of his life. 'Poor Gissing struck me as quite particularly marked out for what is called in his and my profession an unhappy ending', said Henry James. Gissing spoke almost exultantly of his 'futile work' and his 'futile life', and his most autobiographical novel, *New Grub Street*, has failure and loneliness as its theme. Unlike Reardon in that novel, however, he was not a failure, but he felt himself an alien in society and would not adopt its values. His life was marked by appalling errors of judgment whose consequences made him wretched. He existed in garrets and cellars, working incredibly long hours at his novels, always miserably poor, and came to regard such privations as a necessary part of a writer's apprenticeship. 'Has he starved?' he would ask, when introduced to a new author's work. Such was the nature of the times that poverty was not only an experience essential to a writer's development but was also, so it seemed to him, a guarantee that he had not compromised his artistic conscience by surrender to the commercial spirit which it was his duty to condemn. His attitude was greatly influenced by Dostoievsky, who, he said,

a poor and suffering man, gives us with immense power his own view of penury and wretchedness.

(*Charles Dickens*, p 222)

But it was an attitude ultimately derived from his own experience. Once, after walking in the slums, he wrote to Frederic Harrison:

I have involuntarily stood still and asked myself – what then is the meaning of those strange words, Morality, Decency, Intelligence, which I have somewhere heard? . . . here they mean nothing, nay their presence would be an intrusion of an utterly incongruous element.

(23 July 1880 – quoted in Korg, *George Gissing: A Critical Biography*, 1963, p 44)

This was the total alienation of life in the slums, to understand which it was necessary to experience it. Others also despaired of reform. W. Hale White, · whose novels, except for their nonconformist background, have much in common with Gissing's, wrote of Drury Lane and the Seven Dials in 1885:

The preaching of Jesus would have been powerless here; in fact no known stimulus, nothing ever held up before men to stir the soul to activity, can do anything in the back streets of great cities, so long as they are the cesspools which they are now.

(*Mark Rutherford's Deliverance*, ch. 2)

Gissing agreed. His first novel, *Workers in the Dawn* (1880), was an attempt to test contemporary theories, notably Positivism, against this touchstone. As they were all optimistic in some degree, they all failed leaving only the belief in art and human dignity.

Gissing was born in Wakefield in 1857, the son of a chemist who kept a small shop. He was a brilliant boy at school and in 1872 won a scholarship to Owens College, Manchester. There his brilliance continued and he seemed destined for academic distinction in classics when the first of his acts of folly occurred. He met a young prostitute, pitied her plight and resolved to reclaim her. He sold all his available possessions, but it was not enough, because, unknown to him, her main need was for gin and she had gone on the streets on its account. Eventually, to get money for her, he rifled the Common Room at College, was caught, convicted and sent to gaol. This unhappy story says something of the loneliness and desperation, as well as of the failure of judgment, that led him again and again to similar self-destructive courses. However, he was not friendless and was given a passage to America, where his experiences matched those of Whelpdale in *New Grub Street*. Returning in 1877, he settled in London, ekeing out a living for himself and his brothers and sisters by tutoring, working late into the night at his first novel. No one would publish it, but at twenty-one he inherited some money from his father's shop and published the book at his own expense. He sent a copy to Frederic Harrison, who was interested in the Comtist element in it and resolved to help the author. He engaged Gissing as tutor to his two sons and gave him many introductions. Although the legacy soon went, Gissing was assured of an income from tutoring. However, he had sent for the girl from Manchester and married her, thereby more than cancelling his advantage. Henceforth his domestic life was a succession of mean lodgings, made unbearable by the irredeemable character, increasing illness and ultimate insanity of his wife.

In these circumstances he wrote his next novel, *The Unclassed* (1884). Meredith read it for Chapman and Hall and recommended its acceptance. As the title suggests, it deals with a number of people, notably Osmond Waymark and his friend Julian Casti, who wish to reject the conventions of society, but find that they cannot. Waymark's circumstances closely follow Gissing's own, and his views are undoubtedly Gissing's:

The novel of every-day life is getting worn out. We must dig deeper, get to untouched social strata ... Not *virginibus puerisque* will be my book, I assure you, but for men and women who like to look beneath the surface, and who understand that only as artistic material has human life any significance.

(ch. 15)

It was a view held by an increasing number. George Moore's pamphlet *Literature at Nurse* (1885) bitterly complained of the limitations imposed on British authors, largely by Mudie's Library which could condemn a book to financial failure by banning it. In 1888 Henry Vizetelly was gaoled for publishing translations of Zola. Hardy found himself in trouble over *Tess* and *Jude* in the 1890s. Gissing himself was constantly obliged to bowdlerize his work in order to get it published at all. Yet the compulsion to depict the darker aspects of urban life as they were, in all their squalor and hopelessness, remained dominant.

Gissing's wife had become so impossible that he was obliged to put her in a nursing home. He never saw her again alive, although she continued a source of anxiety to him until she died in 1888. He now began a more settled life in a flat near Baker Street Station and his output of novels increased. Three were finished in 1885–6: *Isabel Clarendon*, *A Life's Morning* and *Demos*. The first two were a complete break from the subject of the slums, and are psychological studies involving intellectual and moral problems. *Demos*, however, was a return to his previous field, but with a significant difference. In *Workers in the Dawn* and *The Unclassed* his sympathies had been with the poor and his concern was to ameliorate their conditions. Now, however, he proposed to write 'a savage satire on working-class aims and capacities'. In particular, he attacked the Socialist reformers, who seemed to him to demand from the working class a degree of responsibility that they were unable to attain. Generations of drudgery, deprivation, and squalor had bred in them a narrow, grasping mentality which no mere improvement of circumstances could alter and which, if it were given responsibility and power, would produce a far worse state than the present. It was a view similar to that expressed in Hyacinth in Henry James's *The Princess Casamassima*, also in 1886. Gissing demonstrated it by endowing Richard Mutimer, a superior and independent workman, ardent for the Socialist cause, with an unexpected fortune and property in the north of England. He plans a model settlement on the principles of Robert Owen, but his inherent defects of character bring him to ruin and disaster. *Thyrza* (1887) deals with the same theme in the context of education. It is, however, a more sympathetic novel. Thyrza herself contradicts his theory of working-class incapacity, and there are many instances in the novel of this 'kindly sympathy' that elsewhere he failed to observe in the slums.

Early in 1888 Gissing got a telegram saying his wife was dead. He found her lying in a wretched room, almost devoid of furniture and bedding, with the various 'pledges' she had signed, to keep off the drink, pinned round the wall. The experience could not fail to plunge him to the depths and his next novel, *The Nether World* (1889), is his most savage indictment of the slums and their inhabitants and of the age that had brought them into being. Palliatives and reforms are pointless in this turbulent abyss, for the people remain wedded to their own damnation. All must be swept away, and a new start made by means of the 'Orphean magic' of 'music the civilizer'. However, the novel contains some of Gissing's most spirited accounts of lower-class life, and the Bank-holiday scene at the Crystal Palace is, with George Moore's Derby Day scene in *Esther Waters*, among the most animated and circumstantial descriptions of popular high-spirits since Dickens.

When *The Nether World* was written, Gissing visited Italy and Greece. As Virginia Woolf said, he 'never ceased to educate himself', and as his horizon broadened, the scope of his novels changed. *The Emancipated* (1890) is partly set in Italy, and deals to some extent with the contrast between the drab outlook of provincial England and the brighter, freer atmosphere of the Mediterranean. More than this was involved in the change, however. The book was the first of a series of novels of middle-class life, dealing with the impact of contemporary life on the individual consciousness – particularly that of sensitive people whose development was stultified by existing conditions and convention. This, in turn, meant that Gissing came to rely less on the realistic presentation of a contrived plot, and began to develop his story from the characters, whose motives he subtly analysed in a manner learned in part from George Meredith.

New Grub Street (1891) is the best-known of these novels, and in some respects is his finest work. It is strongly autobiographical, and is, perhaps, a little specialized in its account of those who haunt 'the valley of the shadow of books', the British Museum Reading Room. No single character represents Gissing. Reardon, martyred to his artistic conscience, deserted by his talent, agonizing over the poverty to which he has reduced his wife, who deserts him in his distress, is a projection of Gissing's own worst fears. Biffen shows his idealization of the artist. Biffen lives in a garret, taking pupils for a few shillings a week, and works at his realistic novel for its own sake, careless of reward, yet risking his life to rescue the manuscript from a fire. Courteous, cheerful and starving, he is a romantic expression of the artist's isolation from the commercial nineteenth century. His act of straightening a book on his shelves before committing suicide suggests Schopenhauer's view that suicide is an affirmation, not a denial, of the active will. On the other hand, Milvain, ever-practical opportunist, is an ironic comment on the temporizing shrewdness necessary for survival, which Gissing, being incapable of it, sometimes almost envied. Milvain owes something to Sir Willoughby Patterne. Amy, Reardon's wife, illustrates Gissing's insight into feminine motives; he was, said V. S. Pritchett, 'unusual among English male novelists in discerning the mental life of women' (*The Working Novelists*, 1963, p 62). Marian Yule is an equally perceptive study, though her role is more passive. Like many of the novels, *New Grub Street* abounds in minor characters, sketched in a few strokes. Gissing's regular technique of presenting the simultaneous action of several groups of characters, the narrative switching from one to another, successfully evokes the composite life of the metropolis. The struggle against poverty, having a demoralizing effect on all the characters, provides a unifying theme.

Born in Exile (1892) also deals with the efforts of an exceptional individual to find his true place in nineteenth-century society, but his difficulty is not primarily economic, but social. Godwin Peak, a man of humble origins but outstanding ability, observes that only parsons are exempt from the prohibition of the class-barrier in matrimony. Although, therefore, his scientific education and personal conviction make him an uncompromising atheist, he hides from his enlightened friends, and establishes himself in Exeter as a candidate for Orders. He is accepted as such in a cultured and well-to-do household, falls in love with one of the daughters and almost succeeds in gaining her acceptance. But he cannot subdue his conscience and detests the part he is forced to play. Eventually he is unmasked. This novel, and others among his later works preoccupied with the theme of hypocrisy and charlatanism, questioned the fundamental standards of society.

Whether an intellectual but poor man should marry from the class of society to which he aspires, and so reduce his wife to a poverty she is unprepared for, or whether he should marry from the lower classes and sacrifice companionship in order to gain a practical partner, is a question met in nearly all Gissing's novels. He was well aware of the perils of the latter course, which, indeed, Biffen expounds convincingly to Reardon in *New Grub Street*. Yet he could not overcome his dread of the former. About 1890 he met several women who interested him, among them Edith Sichel, George Eliot's disciple. But fear of his poverty kept him aloof from them, and eventually that year, desperate with loneliness, he repeated his former mistake, and married a woman he had met casually in the street. This second marriage was, if anything, more dreadful than the first, for there were two children, boys, whose presence increased the nightmare of their domestic life. Perhaps because he was deprived, or deprived himself, of the company of educated women, they began to occupy a growing place in his imagination. *The Emancipated* was concerned with the development of two such women – Cecily Doran, who chose a superficial cleverness, and Miriam Baske who, though beginning far deeper in bigotry and provincialism, possesses a genuine sensibility which comes to life under the guidance of Ross Mallard, an artist with something of Gissing's own outlook. The difficulties of intelligent women play an important part in *Born in Exile*. Now three books were written dealing specifically with women's role in society. *The Odd Women* (1893) deals in part with an institution founded on charitable principles to train women and girls for clerical work, to enable them to live independently. It was followed by *In the Year of Jubilee* (1894) and *The Whirlpool* (1897).

Dickens posed important critical problems for the later nineteenth century. His greatness was assured and all novelists owed him an immense debt; yet none could deny that his novels lacked the qualities of realism and moral toughness that had come to be so highly thought of. Gissing was devoted to Dickens, to whom he owed more than to any other single writer, but he was well aware of Dickens's distortions, and of the enfeebled morality that lay behind his stories and characters. Although these offended his conscience as a novelist, nevertheless he saw that it was wrong to condemn Dickens on their account. In his book *Charles Dickens: A Critical Study* (1898) he insisted that Dickens must be seen in the context of his time. The need to appeal to a middle-class audience had led him to 'idealize' his characters, so that Sarah Gamp, for example, was 'the Platonic *idea* of London's hired nurses early in Victoria's reign'. However, the humorous treatment made her acceptable, for

Humour . . . is inseparable from charity. Not only did it enable him to see this coarse creature as an amusing person; it inspired him with that large tolerance which . . . preserves a modesty, a humility, in human judgment.
(*Charles Dickens*, p 92)

This comment suggests Gissing's own sparse use of humour. Biffen, for example, is a humorous character; he is also an ideal one. The more realistic persons in *New Grub Street*, Yule, for instance, are presented with no humour at all.

Gissing finished the monograph on Dickens during a second visit to Italy, and followed it with a series of prefaces on Dickens's novels. Now separated from his wife, he at last found congenial company. His early friends, Morley Roberts and Eduard Bertz, had remained, and in 1896 he met H. G. Wells who was to be a close friend until Gissing's death. He also found at last, in Gabrielle Fleury, a young Frenchwoman who wrote for permission to translate *New Grub Street*, a woman companion. With her he settled at St Jean de Luz. Although far from wealthy, he was better off than he had been. *New Grub Street* brought him something of a popular reputation, and a number of shorter books, notably *The Town Traveller* (1898), sold well. *The Crown of Life* (1899), partly set in Russia, reflects the teaching of Tolstoy, to whom a copy was sent. *Our Friend the Charlatan* (1901) retells the story of Godwin Peak, but in an objective and unsympathetic manner.

Gissing was now in poor health, but there still remained to be written one of his best-known works, *The Private Papers of Henry Ryecroft* (1903). In its air of retirement and reflection it is different from any of its predecessors. It is partly autobiographical, making use once more of Gissing's early privations, yet Ryecroft is not Gissing; nor is he, like Reardon, a projection of Gissing's hopes and fears. His thoughts are his author's, yet he has a detachment and resignation that Gissing hardly attained. The book is presented in oblique form, as a series of papers edited from Ryecroft's literary remains, and this adds to the distance, and gives a reflective authority to the ideas, and a tolerant nostalgia to the account of the early hardships. Ryecroft does not, like Gissing, consider his life futile; he believes that wisdom comes with meditation, and that, beyond man's view, there is a 'Reason for all'. Gissing's own pronouncement was that *Ryecroft* was 'more an aspiration than a memory'.

The second visit to Italy in 1897 had produced *By the Ionian Sea* (1901), a pleasant account of his visit to Calabria. In it he mentions a deterioration in his health, and this soon accelerated. He was working on *Veranilda*, a not very successful historical novel of the sixth century, at his home in France when at Christmas 1903 he caught a cold which rapidly turned to pneumonia. He died on 28 December, Wells, who had been brought from England, being with him.

In perspective, Gissing can be seen as very much a transitional novelist. On the one hand, his attitude to contemporary conditions and his developing introspection, particularly his understanding of the unconscious motives that control everyday actions, suggest a twentieth-century sensibility. George Orwell wrote that he

was interested in individual human beings, and the fact that he can deal sympathetically with several different sets of motives, and make a credible story out of the collision between them, makes him exceptional among English writers.

(*The London Magazine*, June 1930, p 36)

Orwell regretted that he had never read *Born in Exile*, but as Gissing's most inward novel it provides some of the best illustrations of this point, for example, the account of Peak's first meeting with the man whom he hopes to impress:

Though his sympathy was genuine enough, Godwin struggled against an uneasy sense of manifesting excessive appreciation. Never oblivious of himself he could not utter the simplest phrase of admiration without criticizing its justice, its tone. And at present it behoved him to bear in mind that he was conversing with no half-bred sciolist. Mr Warricombe obviously had his share of human weakness, but he was at once a gentleman and a student of well-stored mind; insincerity must be very careful if it would not jar upon his refined ear. So Godwin often checked himself in the utterance of what might sound too much like flattery.

(*Born in Exile*, Part II, ch. 4)

The ambivalent attitude of Godwin Peak, a man so introspective that perpetual self-analysis has dissipated his integrity, and the reaction of others to his broken personality form the substance of the novel.

Technically, on the other hand, Gissing's affinities were with an earlier period. His narrative method was straightforward, with occasional confidences to the reader and no concessions to point of view or efforts at verisimilitude. His prose is mainly that of plain statement. His loyalty to the three-volume form meant that he was often needlessly expansive. Yet he was capable of great economy, sometimes implying a great deal of comment in a short passage of observation. A street-scene described makes a complete indictment of the social order. A chance remark yields an insight into both an individual personality and the twists of conventional attitudes. In *Born in Exile*, for example, an 'advanced' woman is embarrassed to have imparted an item from a Church newspaper:

'Please don't think,' cried Mrs Morton . . . 'that I read such papers. We never have such a thing in our house, Mr Peak. I have only been told about it.'

(*Born in Exile*, Part II, ch. 1)

Gissing's irony exists on many levels, and permeates the novels throughout. His indictment was always indirect. In the early novels he let the dreadful facts speak for themselves, setting them out in a dispassionate account that was ironic in itself. Later, he investigated the effect of these facts of life, both visible and invisible, on sensitive natures, and his irony became more overt and outspoken. It is bitter because he sees no hope of change; his characters must endure the burden of their circumstances. 'Realism', he said, 'is a matter of degree and the author's temperament', and his own pessimistic temperament led him to observe that the burden falls most heavily on those whose keener sensibilities make them most vulnerable. His books owe their peculiar grimness, said Virginia Woolf,

to the fact that the people who suffer most are capable of making their suffering part of a reasoned view of life. The thought endures when the feeling has gone. Their unhappiness represents something more lasting than a personal reverse; it becomes part of a view of life. Hence when we have finished one of Gissing's novels we have taken away not a character, nor an incident, but the comment of a thoughtful man upon life as life seemed to him.

(*The Common Reader*, Second Series, 1932, p 223)

Butler, Stevenson and Kipling (Owen Knowles)

Samuel Butler (1835–1902), Robert Louis Stevenson (1850–94) and Rudyard Kipling (1865–1936) do not, of course, form the most natural and inevitable of literary groupings. Though there are some broad comparisons to be made between them – for example, in the way that their reputations have fluctuated since their deaths – these seem ultimately less important than their differences: the quintessentially English Butler, R. L. S. the Scotsman in Samoa, and Kipling the chronicler of Anglo-Indian society. Nevertheless, all three are important presences in the last two decades of the Victorian period (when Stevenson and Kipling were two of the most widely read authors in Britain and America) and all are essential to our view of its changing character. Their very differences from each other can be illuminating: by implication, they suggest the variety within a literary period which was in the process of emancipating itself from mid-Victorian orthodoxies and constraints, becoming more innovative and cosmopolitan in character, and which found many serious writers redefining their position in relation to middle-class audiences or facing the demand for 'mass' popular reading. Through these three writers we can also gain very distinctive access to some of the wider movements at work in two literary decades when it is sometimes unusually difficult to distinguish the 'late Victorian' from the 'pre-Modern'; in effect, they can be used as valuable and representative case-studies to point to some of the important typical pressures, options and tensions alive in the restless 1880s.

In the concluding chapters of *The Way of All Flesh* (1903; but written up to thirty years earlier), and through the person of its central character, Ernest Pontifex, Samuel Butler offers what seems very close to being a self-portrait. And in so far as the novel is concerned generally with evolution and 'descent', it also conveys Butler's view of a species of middle-class novelist as formed and made by the nineteenth century:

> The book [by Pontifex] rang with the courage alike of conviction and of an entire absence of conviction; it appeared to be the work of men who had a rule-of-thumb way of steering between subservism on the one hand and credulity on the other; who cut Gordian knots as a matter of course when it suited their convenience; who shrank from no conclusion in theory, nor from any want of logic in practice so long as they were illogical of malice prepense, and for what they held to be sufficient reason. The conclusions were conservative, quietistic, comforting. The arguments by which they were reached were taken from the most advanced writers of the day. All that these people contended for was granted them, but the fruits of the victory were for the most part handed over to those already in possession. . . . In politics he is a Conservative as far as his vote and interest are concerned. In all other respects he is an advanced Radical.
>
> (chs 92/93)

What we meet here is not only a summary of the qualities making up the distinctively 'Butlerian' but a wider portrait of the 1870s' 'artist-as-Laodicean' who 'should only be hot in striving to be as lukewarm as possible'. The portrait offers a recognizable kind of middle-class writer activated by an interest in 'advanced' ideas, whose scepticism has been fostered by mid-century debate on scientific and religious matters – but a kind of writer with important differences from his predecessors. One implication of Butler's portrait is that the 'earnest' mid-century has thrown up a new kind of Ernest, a marginalized Ishmael-figure who now sustains an identity by detachedly acting out the rituals of the society to which he belongs but in which he only partially believes. The cultivated but mocking *pretence* of conformity and deference provides the materials by which the gentlemanly Ernest transforms himself into playful showman and irritant: he is self-consciously *Homo duplex*, 'wickedly' trading in paradox, and ready to exploit a duplicitous relation with his audience and its values. As a disengaged performer he sceptically negotiates a way between opposites – the advanced and the traditional, imaginative bohemianism and bourgeois conformity, aggressive malice and passive concession – though he appears to be able to use these opposites against each other and all of them as quietly offensive weapons against his audience. No wonder that Butler's Pontifex delights in being compared to such different figures as Pascal, Swift and the authors of *Essays and Reviews* (1860). Indeed, the use of plural voices and masks seems essential to the importance of being Ernest and the effects of mystification, disguise and role-playing sought by him. If some of Ernest's tones look back to the earnest mid-1850s, others unmistakably anticipate the inflexions of comic and ironic provocation associated with a new generation of writers – Meredith, Wilde, and Shaw. And each of the latter might be fairly described in terms which G. D. H. Cole uses of Butler: 'He had most of the Victorian obsessions, though he had them upside down. That, indeed, was how he enjoyed having things' (*Samuel Butler*, p 11).

The Way of All Flesh portrays the way in which through the pressures of heredity, upbringing and experience Ernest Pontifex came to be the type of writer he was, though the novel was not to be published until after Butler's death. To a contemporary audience, familiar only with the curious and fragmentary medley of his published writings, Butler's works must have presented bewildering evidence of a Pontifex-in-the-making, that is, of the shifting and contradictory commitments of a writer adept at making and remaking himself in a number of literary forms and living very variously, and sometimes quirkily, as the earnest prophet, enlightened amateur, puckish wit and perverse controversialist. Some of his non-fictional writings (on Shakespeare, Homer and Italian painting) suggest the versatile gentleman-scholar who combines historical enquiry with a Shavian delight in promoting theories just because they are unorthodox and run counter to established opinion. Still other of his writings are a reminder that Butler was the product of a clerical family, had undergone a variation of the Victorian crisis of faith while preparing for Holy Orders and had subsequently negotiated an independent, 'rule-of-thumb' way between the conflicting claims of faith and science. Early in his career he was to ponder, for example, the authenticity of the Christian 'evidences' in the light of Higher Biblical Criticism in an anonymous pamphlet on *The Evidence for the Resurrection* (1865) and much later, in 1896, composed a clerical *Life and Letters* devoted to his grandfather, Bishop Samuel Butler. Homage indeed to an eminent Victorian! On the other hand, the central public controversy of Butler's career – and one which came to involve a fair measure of personal acrimony – was with Charles Darwin, who was closely acquainted with the Butler family. In considerable earnestness and with some degree of obsessiveness Butler produced a series of works – *Life and Habit* (1877), *Unconscious Memory* (1880) and *Luck or Cunning* (1887) – which in his view effectively 'answered' on scientific grounds Darwin's doctrine of natural selection as the basis for variation and therefore evolutionary progress. Such answer as he provided was not a direct counter-statement so much as a restatement of Darwin's conclusions, based upon Butler's study of the evolution of evolutionary thought itself and couched in terms which he professed to have found in the superseded work of Erasmus Darwin and Lamarck. In Butler's hands the result was a version of 'creative' evolution which, with its stress on the importance of inherited memory transmitted from generation to generation as habit and constantly growing with the life of the species, could in some measure be reconciled with the potent 'unspoken teachings' of the ancestral Church and the unconscious influence of its traditions: '"we", "our souls", our "selves" or "personalities" . . . are but the *consensus* and full flowing stream of countless sensations and impulses on the part of our tributary "souls" or "selves"' (*Life and Habit*, ch. 7).

What many of these non-fictional writings tend to suggest is the degree to which Butler, like many other writers of the 1870s, was shaped by the terms and structure of mid-century sceptical debate and his writings overshadowed by dominating father-figures in the shape of Darwin and the Higher Biblical critics. What they do not really communicate is the extent to which Butler was able playfully to disengage himself from the terms of that debate, subject its articles of faith to ironic scrutiny and transform its issues into satiric and speculative fictions; nor do they in any way anticipate the frontal iconoclasm and autobiographical seriousness of *The Way of All Flesh*. The degree to which Victorian religious and scientific controversy fostered and nourished a distinctive literary Ishmaelite is more obvious in works which Butler's contemporaries also found to be more uncomfortable – *Erewhon* (1872; to be followed in 1901 by its sequel, *Erewhon Revisited*) and *The Fair Haven* (1873). Material from Butler's non-fictional essays feeds into all of these works, but that material is now fictionalized and made ironical through the use of speakers, masks and other novelistic devices. Literary games and puzzles are also much in evidence – narrations-within-narrations, mixed genres, Wildean inversions and the pretence of valid analogy – and they form part of a wider game in which the writer feeds off received beliefs obliquely and in such a way as to move beyond specific ideas to a sceptical revaluation of the processes and ends of 'earnest' rational enquiry itself. Hence, though *The Fair Haven* outwardly announces itself as a typical tract of the 1870s and is subtitled 'A Work in Defence of the Miraculous Element in Our Lord's Ministry upon Earth, both as against Rationalistic Impugners and Certain Orthodox Defenders', its more wicked intention is to use a clergyman's earnest defence of the historical accuracy of the Gospels as the occasion for a parody and ironic spoof of the terms of mid-century debate. And since material from Butler's own earlier life and writings is also incorporated – but often slyly inverted – in the defence provided by 'John Pickard Owen' and his brother, we should also anticipate a fair measure of authorial self-irony. 'There is only one way out of it –', Butler comments with mock disingenuousness, 'that the reader should kindly interpret according to his own fancies. If he will do this the book is sure to please him' (Preface to Second Edition, p xx).

This same sentiment might also be applied to *Erewhon*, the brilliantly inventive satiric fantasy by which Butler was chiefly known to his contemporary audience. While many of that audience may have recognized in the author of *Erewhon* a child of the Victorian bourgeoisie whose worries, fears and obsessions reflected their own, they were inevitably discomfited by the idiosyncratic and opportunistic naughtiness of the child. Indeed, the unsettling effect of *Erewhon* upon its contemporary audience may have had much to do with Butler's strategy of using his middle-class credentials to ruffle and undermine that very class of which by birth and up-bringing he was essentially a product. An intriguing mixture of compliance or what Pontifex calls 'subservism', playfulness and sly provocation can certainly be felt in the book's unusual combination of genres and speakers. *Erewhon* works within an elusive framework of Utopian fiction, visionary dream and Swiftian imaginary voyage. Published in the same year as Lewis Carroll's *Through the Looking Glass* (1872), *Erewhon* also occupies a geographical 'nowhere' as a way of indulging its own unique form of topsyturvydom, while its occasional visionary and hedonistic intuitions also anticipate William Morris's *News from Nowhere* (1891).

This shifting framework should warn the reader against making too simple and hasty a judgment. To be sure, Butler's work makes belligerent assault on humbug, hypocrisy and the power of stultifying custom in a wide range of Victorian institutions: Erewhon's Musical Banks expose the exhaustion of the Established Church, the College of Unreason and its 'hypothetics' the arid scholarship of Oxford and Cambridge, and Ydgrunism (Grundyism) the real object of worship among the Victorian middle-classes. Family life, the upbringing of children, the treatment of crime and illness are also among the book's clearly focused targets, and they are often used by critics to measure the points 'scored' by Butler against Darwin and others. But it should be remembered that *Erewhon*, as it emerges through Butler's shifting combinations of satiric fantasy and speculation, is much more than the sum total of its satiric targets. For example, certain aspects of Erewhonian life are treated with a minimum of satire and permit a vision of alternative possibility, one result being that the narrator (and Butler?) can identify with the handsome and athletic high Ydgrunites and claim that 'The example of a real gentleman . . . is the best of all gospels' (ch. 17). Again, as the embodiment of both attractive and unattractive alternatives to Victorian England, the imaginary Erewhon allows Butler to play with a very fluid and shifting mixture of utopian and dystopian intimations. This effect is most memorably realized in a remarkable *tour de force*, 'The Book of the Machines' (chs 23–6), in which Butler registers the impact of Darwinian theory upon the Victorian consciousness by way of a prophetic vision – which taps a number of the age's most deep-seated fears – of the growth of machines and mechanical con-sciousness. The description here is not without its comic touches, assigned as it is to the Erewhonian Mr Thims (Smith!). But its main effect lies elsewhere – in the extraordinary fusion of diverse speculative and satiric attitudes which characterizes Butler's res-ponse to Darwin and, on a wider scale, the contemporary myths of 'progress'. A remarkable instance of the degree to which Victorian literature and science could enjoy what Gillian Beer calls 'a shared discourse . . . [of] not only *ideas* but metaphors, myths and narrative patterns', Butler's 'Book of the Machines' also shows a writer speculatively attuned to the sheer multiplicity of 'Darwin's plots' (see G. Beer, *Darwin's Plots*, p 7), to their comic and satiric as well as their mythic and prophetic applications. Its style also, in its assimilation and digestion of Darwinian rhetoric, registers both fascinated excitement and qualifying disquiet. It is, perhaps, with episodes like this in mind that Daniel F. Howard comments:

Actually *Erewhon* is not . . . an indictment of middle-class English life but a representation of a complex of attitudes toward it, articulated in styles ranging from burlesque to straightforward didacticism. The book's intellectual targets have also seemed unclear. . . . The simple view is that he [Butler] had rejected a theist master for a scientific one; but actually *Erewhon* demonstrated a synthesis of the two, yet also reflects a deep-rooted scepticism about the validity of each . . . Thus, *Erewhon* confronts Butler's doubts about the central intellectual influences in his life – indeed in Victorian life.
(Quoted in *Victorian Fiction: A Second Guide to Research*, ed. G. H. Ford,
p 304)

The full measure of that confrontation was not to become evident until the publication of Butler's major and now 'classic' book, *The Way of All Flesh*. As a passionately angry and bitter attack upon the systematic conspiracy at the heart of Victorian middle-class life, it was to make a dramatic impact on numerous young writers in the two decades following its publication. Virginia Woolf speaks for many of her contemporaries, young men and women alike when, in her essay on 'Mr Bennett and Mrs Brown' (1924), she makes the famous claim that 'on or about December, 1910, human nature changed' and goes on to proclaim that 'the first signs of it are recorded in the books of Samuel Butler, in *The Way of All Flesh* in particular'. She was undoubtedly joined in her enthusiasm by writers as diverse as Shaw, D. H. Lawrence, E. M. Forster, James Joyce, Somerset Maugham and May Sinclair who all, in varying degrees, felt that Butler's book 'belonged' to the twentieth century and its youthful moderns. The varied reasons for that impact are not difficult to imagine. The book offers a retrospective look back in anger by a young man who sees himself as a damaged victim of an entire century and who, before he can realize himself as man and artist, must systematically unravel the social and religious mythologies which have made him what he is: out of this opposition to his culture's externally imposed restraints he attempts to forge new strategies for self-preservation and self-construction. This combination of frustration, anger, literal home-sickness, and restless self-concern undoubtedly struck young Edwardians with symbolic force, and helps to explain why this youthful Ishmael overshadows such later creations as Lawrence's Paul Morel and Joyce's Stephen Daedalus. Other features of the book undoubtedly contributed to its later potency: it announces itself as a protest and *cri de coeur* on behalf of youth against the supposed wisdom of an authoritarian patriarchy, as an audacious stirring up of hornets' nests and as a call to confront new urgencies ('The question of the day is now marriage and the family system', the older Edward proclaims).

The later Edwardian response does help to throw genuine light on the originality of *The Way of All Flesh* and on the way in which it came to determine the pattern of later *Bildungsromanen*. As a novel dramatizing the initiation into life and subsequent development of Pontifex, Butler's work has several unusual features, including a distinctive chronicle richness and patterned 'epic' design. The curious history of the book's composition and publication can help here. As most readers might suspect, it is one of the most directly personal of *Bildungsromanen*, in which Butler returns to the conflict with his overbearing father and unsympathetic family. *The Way of All Flesh* was written secretly and intermittently over a number of years (1873–84) and while the antagonism between father and son was still painfully alive. Butler subsequently withheld the (unrevised) work from publication to avoid giving embarrassment to members of his family who made thinly disguised appearances in the book. In one sense, then, *The Way of All Flesh* provided its author with the means to prolong a private quarrel, pay off old scores, and allow himself the luxury of uninterrupted self-exoneration. Potentially and actually explosive, the relationship between Butler and his father gives the novel much of its power as a piece of living testimony and helps to explain why *The Way of All Flesh*, unlike many other novels of this type, cannot end with a vision of harmonious social accommodation.

Whatever its origins in private anger, Butler's novel finally transcends (and shows Ernest transcending) merely personal motive. Indeed, *The Way of All Flesh* is fully as remarkable for its width and design as it is for its hard-edged satire. For one thing, the materials out of which Ernest must construct his salvation include not only the history of one family but a much wider context of Pontifex generations which gives the study its chronicle richness and historical sweep across the century. In addition, since the youthful Ernest is the representative product of what his age has made him, the novel needs to move beyond the family to engage with the educational and religious traditions of the whole era – hence, for example, the documentary richness of Butler's portrait of the evolving Evangelical movement. In its width and scope, the novel is enriched by all of those wider interests which Butler was pursuing during its ten-year composition, and we therefore should be prepared to meet an encyclopaedic richness which can embrace both Darwin and David Strauss as Victorian father-figures.

Elaborate pattern and design are also suggested at all levels of the novel. Scrupulously sensitive to the significance of the names of his characters (Pontifex as 'bridge-builder', Alethea as 'Truth'), Butler also suggests through these devices a larger symmetrical pattern of ideals and anti-ideals which Ernest needs to understand. Such patterned symmetry also underlies the way in which Ernest's actual family is supplanted by a new one, with his god-father and god-mother over-seeing his education and pointing Ernest to the importance of those cultural traces of a past history to which he needs to adapt in order to link himself with more vital moral and social traditions. We may suspect, too, that the unconventional design of *The Way of All Flesh* also emerges through a partly ironic treatment of more traditional styles and genres popular in the period. Butler's novel embraces a whole conspectus of literary genres – the family saga, the novel of religious crisis, the portrait of the artist, quest literature – but in doing so it invariably inverts their conventions and undermines their traditional ends. A literary hybrid, *The Way of All Flesh* 'adapts' itself through extensive satiric play with the species: at one extreme it conveys an ironic sense of Ernest as the 'hero' of picaresque romance, while at another it slyly mocks Christina's dreams by recounting them in the form of Victorian stage melodrama. Such effects are neither incidental nor accidental: though Butler happily rejected the heavily ironic idea of calling his hero 'Christian', he does not in the novel's design sacrifice the larger ironic possibilities of his original idea.

The final chapters of *The Way of All Flesh* find Pontifex in much the same position as was Butler in the 1880s. Though both literary gentlemen are deeply rooted in the period's history, they are also sceptically isolated, curiously islanded between the past and the unborn future, and – as writers – must needs await a sympathetic audience. In light of their position Butler's physical life-span has an ironic appropriateness which the author himself would have joyed. Butler's life almost exactly coincided with Queen Victoria's reign, and his death took place in the year following hers. A new reign began, in more than one sense, with the appearance in 1903 of *The Way of All Flesh*, a work which Shaw in a letter of that year called 'one of the great books of the world'.

Like Butler, though for very different reasons, Robert Louis Stevenson presents an awkward and difficult problem to modern critics and criticism. In part the difficulty lies in the extraordinary reversal of his critical reputation after his death and during those decades when Butler was being 'discovered', a period in which the romantic cult of R.L.S., 'Prospero of Samoa', was systematically dismantled by biographers who found that the heroic invalid and exile had, after all, feet of clay. 'Exaggerated praise and excessive reaction against it describe the pattern of his reception', comments Paul Maixner (*Stevenson: The Critical Heritage*, p 2). That pattern of reaction was underpinned by two other related factors – on the one hand, by the growing unfashionableness in the years after Stevenson's death of the kind of manly and picturesque 'romance of adventure' with which he is associated and helped to establish and, on the other, by a rising tide of reaction against the type of 'tartan history' promoted by his fiction. Though the popular mythologies devised by Stevenson still survive – Long John Silver, Treasure Island, Dr Jekyll and Mr Hyde – they often do so only in sadly diminished and misunderstood form.

If a fairer estimate of Stevenson is to be reached, it will probably have much to do with how sympathetically the modern reader can respond to the various problems associated with his commitment to the novel of romantic 'action'. These problems were much alive during Stevenson's own lifetime and, indeed, form part of one of the most representative debates of the 1880s between Henry James in 'The Art of Fiction' (1884) and Stevenson, whose full position can be found in 'A Gossip on Romance' (1882) and 'A Humble Remonstrance' (1884). Against James's view that the seriousness of the novel as an artistic form is intimately associated with its capacity to produce an 'intense illusion of reality' and 'solidity of specification', Stevenson offers a direct counter-argument: for the power of romance to allow readers a way of escape and trans-cendance beyond the commonplace, and through heightened action – 'the shock of arms or the diplomacy of life' – to restore them to the colour, intensity and vitality of the child-like primary emotions. The essence of such romance lies in the typical nature of its situations, its stress upon 'action' rather than 'character' and upon incidents which allow the reader to play at being the hero and through him to transform anxiety into meaningful action: '. . . we forget the characters, then we push the hero aside; then we plunge into the tale in our own person and bathe in fresh experience, and then, and then only, do we say we have been reading a romance'. Stevenson's counter-plea to James is in some ways quite modern-sounding, insisting as he does upon intensities beyond the capacity of the realistic and naturalistic novel of the time, the close alliance of literature and dreams (here reflecting Stevenson's own experience of translating his own dreams into writing) and upon the fictiveness of fiction: 'The novel which is a work of art exists, not by its resemblances to life, which are forced and material, as a shoe must still consist of leather, but by its immeasurable difference from life, which is designed and significant, and is both the method and the meaning of the work'. While Stevenson scores some palpable hits in the debate, his tone betrays a more problematic uncertainty than James's. And it is most problematic on those occasions when he tries to reconcile his high-sounding general claims for romance with the 'leather' available to *him*. In confronting the problem of how his ideals translate into the contemporary formulae and conventions available to him, Stevenson betrays an uneasy tendency to equate 'dreams' with 'day-dreams', the 'child-like' with the demands of children's fiction, and the conventions of romance with inspired 'puppetry'. Outwardly conceding little, Stevenson's argument often falters into hesitant apologia. After all, a fair amount of 'brute incident' is essential to the 'elementary' novel of adventure: 'Danger is the matter with which this class of novel deals; fear, the passion with which it idly trifles; and the characters are portrayed only so far as they realize the sense of danger and provoke the sympathy of fear'.

The problems raised by this debate of 1884 also involve another consideration – that of the highly talented writer who finds himself uncomfortably situated in the mushrooming literary market-place of the 1880s. As one of the most marketable commodities of the time, colourful and exotic romance was increasingly called upon to satisfy the needs of a new mass audience whose tastes were for fresh sensation, 'brute incident', and pleasing escapism. In particular, the 1880s saw the rapid expansion of the market for children's literature of a more secularized kind, such as appeared in *Young*

Folks, the periodical in which both *Treasure Island* and *Kidnapped* were serialized. Stevenson's relationship to these mass audiences and their tastes was tellingly ambiguous and changing. As a literary man-of-all-trades who had several collaborators during his career, he could sometimes cheerfully speak of himself as a mere tradesman and manipulator of formulae, a supplier of costume-drama which he called 'Tushery'; at other times as a writer who had no respect for 'that fatuous rabble of burgesses called "the public"'; and on still other occasions as a helpless victim of a popularity he had neither courted nor wanted. These conflicting attitudes constitute a critical problem in so far as their implied presence can often be felt *in* Stevenson's fiction and makes his work curiously difficult to judge. In his novels generally (and even in any *one* work) he presents himself as a writer who can cheerfully modulate from box-office 'Tushery' to high originality and back again or who simultaneously tries to engage both adolescent and 'grown up' readers. These incompatibilities were clearly in Henry James's mind in 1884, and they prompted him to pose the important question: how could they be squared with Stevenson's increasingly serious ambitions to refine the 'matter' of romance?

Moreover, as a writer whose attitudes to his art were shaped by an unusual mixture of inherited inclinations and acquired convictions, Stevenson might have found this question very difficult to answer. From childhood onwards Stevenson's imagination was instinctively fired by the kind of 'matter' that belongs to the fireside ghost-story and winter's tale. As a young child and constant invalid, he had spent hours on end reading and listening to 'bogey' tales told to him by his father and his nurse – tales of pirates, thieves and ghosts which were invariably coloured by an uncompromising Calvinistic belief in sin and supernatural evil. In Stevenson's case the child is father of the man in several ways, not least in suggesting the 'ardent and uncomfortable dreamer' of later life as well as the difficult and complicated man of Calvinist background as depicted in W. E. Henley's poem 'Apparition': 'A deal of Ariel, just a streak of Puck,/ Much Antony, of Hamlet most of all,/ And something of the Shorter-Catechist'. Later on, Stevenson's rebellion against the staid limits of Presbyterian Edinburgh (where he was trained as an engineer) and his subsequent ill-health led to a life of constant travelling to climates hospitable to his condition – the South of France, Switzerland, Southern England, North America and finally the South Pacific. Physical travel conceived as a form of action against the inevitable and as experienced by the solitary exile becomes deeply ingrained in the literature Stevenson later wrote. As James commented, 'Mr. Stevenson has, in high degree . . . what may be called the imagination of physical states, and this has enabled him to arrive at a wonderfully exact notation of his panting Lowland hero [in *Kidnapped*], dragged for days and nights over hill and dale, through bog and thicket . . .' (Janet Adam Smith, *James and Stevenson*, pp 157–8). From this perspective Stevenson's very early essays – *An Inland Voyage* (1878) and *Travels with a Donkey* (1879) – are strongly prophetic of 'the imagination of physical states' to come. However, combined with and superimposed upon these strong temperamental predilections were the later acquired convictions and ambitions of the literary man – among these the serious desire to render as epic a phase of Scottish history, an increasing interest in stylistic and technical experiment, and an urge to show how the native romance might 'grow up' as a modern form in emulation of Nathaniel Hawthorne's example in America. Indeed, Walter Allen in *The English Novel* (1954) has gone so far as to claim that Stevenson's 'distinctive contribution to the English novel is that he successfully married Flaubert to Dumas. . . . His redis-covery of the art of narrative, of conscious and cunning calculation in telling a story so that the maximum effect of clarity and suspense is achieved, meant the birth of the novel of action as we know it, and the measure of the work of later writers such as John Buchan and Graham Greene . . .' (p 336). This is an interesting attempt to create a tradition for Stevenson, though its final claim is, I think, more appropriate to Conrad than to Stevenson: in the latter's case, the 'marriage' is subject to some very severe strains and stresses.

That Stevenson's first exercise in 'the elementary novel of adventure', *Treasure Island* (1883), should also turn out to be his first notable success and a popular classic of children's literature is hardly anticipated by the circumstances of its composition: it was originally written to amuse his twelve-year-old stepson, with his father in attendance ('It was *his* kind of picturesque,' says Stevenson), and what emerged was something as 'original as sin'. This happy collaboration seems to be reflected in a tale whose combination of fireside story, adventure tale and well-played game shapes its underlying quality as a romance. The story's essential 'matter' is so delightful just because it is so familiar and perennial – a desert island, buried treasure, shipwreck, mutiny, pursuit-and-chase. What is more remarkable is Stevenson's adaptation of it to suit the first-person intensity of a boy's experience and as an enactment of his fears, wishes and dreams. The relation of the narrative to wish-fulfilling dreams is an interesting one. An older narrator begins the story and offers access to his past experience. Within a paragraph, however, the youthful Jim takes over the narrative, and the narrative in turn enacts the boy's colourful dreams and expectations according to the logic of wish-fulfilment: he enjoys the camaraderie of an all-male world, shows a mature competence where adults can fail, meets perils but suffers no injury, is confronted by blessedly clear-cut objectives, and experiences all of the unalloyed intensity of what Hazlitt in one of his finest essays calls 'the feeling of immortality in youth'. Not that Stevenson's story turns its back upon potential terrors inimical to youth's charmed existence. In its own colourful way *Treasure Island* is full of violent deaths, nightmarish claims upon Jim, as well as the suggestion of 'strange and tragic' events (ch. 7). But Stevenson is as skilful in defusing these unwelcome disagreeables as he is in indulging their potentiality. Those two essentials of romance, fear and danger, can invariably be transcended through the unthinking and reflexive actions of the boy-hero. Again, many potentially unruly complications are defused in the suggestion that they quicken 'the wildly beating heart' and add to the excitement of undreamt-of adventure, while other terrors are robbed of their force by the implication that they enact the rituals of sportive play. Full of brilliant pictorial effects and finally echoing to the screams of Long John's parrot, *Treasure Island* is, indeed, 'all as perfect as a well-played boy's game' (Janet Adam Smith, op. cit., p 154).

In both substance and technique the early *Treasure Island* is also important in indicating how a model of youthful romance was destined to develop, grow up and mature in Stevenson's later fiction. Jim looks forward to the older David Balfour and his more difficult initiation into life, Long John to a whole gallery of later characters whose unscrupulous and Satanic malice is inseparable from their dangerous charm, and the island itself to the evocative wildness and isolation of the Highland fiction. What *Treasure Island* does not anticipate is the movement towards a more specifically rooted historical romance, in which Stevenson mingles and merges colourful fictions with actual events in Scottish history. Two examples of that alliance, *Kidnapped* (1886) and its sequel *Catriona* (1893), show Stevenson moving decisively back in time to the Jacobite rebellion of 1745 and its post-Culloden aftermath, in particular to the events surrounding the Appin murder of 1752 and the subsequent trial of James of the Glens which forms the basis for the first part of *Catriona*.

These two novels also offer an interesting test-case by which to measure the 'grown up' seriousness and depth of a recognizable kind of Stevensonian romance. Is it truly historical fiction or popular national balladry? Does it belong essentially to the colourful traditions of R. D. Blackmore's *Lorna Doone* (1869) or aspire to something more ambitious? Like the testimony that comes from Stevenson himself, the evidence provided by the novels is disconcertingly contradictory. The movement towards Scottish history appears to have followed upon Stevenson's long-standing ambition to write serious historical fiction, partly in emulation of Sir Walter Scott and partly in reaction against Scott whom Stevenson (in a letter of 1874) convicted of 'snobbery, conservatism, the wrong thread in History, and notably in that of his own land'. Nor, it seems, was there any want of committed enthusiasm in Stevenson's research into the '45 and in his meditations upon an appropriate literary Scots dialect. On the other hand, his own acute self-criticism after writing *Kidnapped* needs to be taken into account and it may suggest the degree to which Stevenson, as a historical novelist, flatters to deceive:

I began it partly as a lark, partly as a pot-boiler; and suddenly it moved, David and Alan stepped out from the canvas, and I found I was in another world. But there was the cursed beginning, and a cursed end must be appended . . . So it had to go into the world, one part (as it does seem to me) alive, one part merely galvanized: no work, only an essay. . . . [My] *Kidnapped* was doomed, while still in the womb and while I was yet in the cradle, to be the thing it is.

(*Letters*, vol II pp 41–2)

Stevenson's distinction between the 'alive' and the 'merely galvanized' goes right to the heart of one problem in both *Kidnapped* and *Catriona* – the tendency of 'romance' and 'history' to be two separate and discrete sources of interest (and actually signalled in *Catriona* by the move from Scotland to Holland). More seriously, both novels raise in acute form the question of whether Stevensonian romance, with its bold pictorial characterization, physical gusto, episodic action, and neat happy ending, can carry the weight of a really serious historical vision. To be sure, in *Kidnapped* the characters are historically circumstanced and situated, but very typically so and in response to the most popular kind of romantic fable which determines that Alan Breck will be the dashing, bonny, resourceful Highlander and doomed Jacobite, and David the canny, circumspect and 'civilized' Lowlander. There is here more character interest than has previously appeared in Stevenson's romance as well as an appealing image of male friendship. But, as Andrew Noble has suggested, such a simple, patterned relationship is a frail basis indeed upon which to build a symbolic national portrait and may point to the deeper truth that 'Stevenson was typically Victorian . . . [in] valuing Scott's historical fiction for its anodyne power' ('Highland History and Narrative Form in Scott and Stevenson' in *Robert Louis Stevenson*, ed. A. Noble, p 138).

Kidnapped and *Catriona* bear some likeness to the adolescent condition itself: both aspire to be politically and historically grown up, but both can as easily revert to what the author sees as a 'cradle' condition. For Stevenson's most original and powerfully unified work we need, I think, to look elsewhere, and in particular to three works – *Dr. Jekyll and Mr. Hyde* (1886), *The Master of Ballantrae* (1889) and the unfinished *Weir of Hermiston* (1896). Though the first differs from the two later works in being an example of Victorian urban Gothic, all three maintain rich links with 'bogey' tales and share illuminating similarities. In the first place, all of them show Stevenson moving away from the simple linear structure of romance towards what in 'A Humble Remonstrance' he calls 'the well-written novel' which 'echoes and re-echoes its one creative and controlling thought' through incident, character and style. *Dr. Jekyll* is the most striking example of such a resonant echo-chamber. Based as it is upon Jekyll's final realization of what he calls 'the profound duplicity of life', the story approaches that climax through a whole range of more commonplace insinuations of contrast, twinship, opposition and metamorphosis: one is not surprised to find that even characters' names punningly echo the theme of partnership ('If he be Mr. Hyde . . I shall be Mr. Seek'). This kind of design is also closely linked to Stevenson's experimentation with methods of indirect narration, particularly the use of multiple third-person accounts which diffuse, refract and echo what can also at appropriate points be rendered as intense first-person experience. *The Master of Ballantrae*, for example, allows the content of a disturbing 'winter's tale' – in which after the Stuart rebellion one son of the Durie family, a Satanic visitant and incubus, 'takes possession' of his brother, both of them finally perishing and being buried together – to be narrated by the family's matter-of-fact steward, who in turn pieces together his account from various memoirs. In its indirect methods (which combine the homespun with the richly stylized) the novel suggests not so much the combined tradition of Dumas and Flaubert as an important debt to both Emily Brontë's *Wuthering Heights* and Marryat's *The Phantom Ship*. The background presence of these two works, and especially the latter, with its use of the Flying Dutchman legend and intimations of supernatural evil, may also help to explain Stevenson's turning towards richly poetic Scottish folk-lore, tragic ballad and patterned fable.

These developments lead Stevenson in turn into unusual moral and psychological territory, marked by an ambivalence and fatalistic pessimism very different from the overall mood of *Kidnapped* or *Catriona*. Situated on the shifting frontier between the domestic and the lawless, these three novels are sometimes disturbingly close to patterned nightmare in their stress upon the uncanny in life and the deep-seated anxiety produced by it. Recognizably the product of that strangely contradictory individual of W. E. Henley's portrait, they show the studiously ascetic or puritan consciousness (conceived as a 'fortress of identity') undermined by dark and disturbing forces which are unfamiliar but also 'known' to it, or dramatize the relationship between conventional moral opposites in terms which bond together a vital amoral energy with its pallid complement. Out of such ambivalences Stevenson's parable for his age, *Dr. Jekyll*, was born. Set in London, in the all-male world of the professional classes, it is so disturbing, as G. K. Chesterton pointed out, because 'the real stab of the story is not in the discovery that one man is two men; but in the discovery that two men are one man . . .' (*Robert Louis Stevenson*, p 72) and that the 'respectable' man fulfils some of his most innate and natural drives through the actions of his dark shadow-self.

After the publication of *Dr. Jekyll* Stevenson wrote to J. A. Symonds: '*Jekyll* is a dreadful thing I own; but the only thing I feel dreadful about is that damned old business of the war in the members. This time it came out; I hope it will stay in, in the future.' In so far as *Dr. Jekyll* develops from a 'bogey' tale, moves beyond the vision of simple conflict to assert the union of antagonistic forces, it can also stand as a parable of Stevenson's own development. Indeed, his often frustrating struggle to reconcile his own needs as a serious writer with the popular conventions available to him might be seen to create the very conditions for the 'damned old business' to 'come out' so pressingly. What also emerges in the process is that to Stevenson we partly owe the persistence in the late nineteenth century and beyond of a rich and potent alternative to realistic traditions. With Hardy, Stevenson shared an antipathy to

Jamesian realism and slice-of-life naturalism and looked elsewhere for his sources of inspiration. The case for Hardy's importance in this alternative tradition has been made time and time again, but for Stevenson the case is still in the process of being made.

In the late 1880s, when Stevenson was approaching the height of his popular success, the young and unknown Rudyard Kipling was working as a reporter for *The Civil and Military Gazette* in India. Within six or seven years the prolific Kipling would become the most widely read and celebrated writer of the 1890s. Though he refused the Poet Laureateship in 1895 at the age of thirty, he was to be adopted as the decade's unofficial laureate. The famous 'Recessional' was published in *The Times* on the day after Queen Victoria's Diamond Jubilee in 1897; another historical moment, the American invasion of the Philippines, was marked by 'The White Man's Burden' (1897). Though Kipling took passage from India in 1889, India as country and symbol was to remain with him throughout the decade, culminating in the final homage offered through *Kim* (1901) and *Just So Stories* (1902). The latter year marks the date from which Kipling became a more permanent resident in England.

Kipling's early writings form part of a much larger body of literature to have emerged from India during the last two decades of the Victorian period when the Raj was at its zenith. But it is Kipling who occupies the Anglo-Indian world most fully and intimately, and it is his work that overshadows much of the British colonial fiction to follow. Kipling's background and Anglo-Indian origins are obviously key facts in approaching the writer. He was born in 1865, seven years after the Mutiny and in an India which through the establishment of a permanent Raj strongly dedicated to the Imperial Idea was regarded by prophets and advocates of imperialism at home as a unique experiment in the government of alien peoples. Kipling's early life was in many ways typical of its time and moment. His well-connected and cultured parents left England in the hope of repairing their failing fortunes in India, and outwardly Kipling's early life followed the pattern traditionally followed by many Anglo-Indian boys of the time: after a happy early childhood in India he was sent to England as a six-year-old for his serious schooling. As one of Kipling's later stories vividly indicates ('Baa, Baa, Black Sheep'), the first protracted stage of this education was deeply traumatic, with Kipling and his sister being desperately unhappy lodgers in the home of a Southsea family. Rescue finally came for the beleaguered child in the form of a transfer to the United Services College at Westward Ho! in Devon, where Kipling was introduced to the boarding-school life which he later recreated in *Stalky and Co*. There is a break in the traditional pattern here, since Kipling did not go on to University or train for an army career like most of his peers, but instead at the age of sixteen returned to Lahore where his father had secured a position in the City Museum. It is from this time that Kipling's reimmersion into Indian life and his connection with journalism dates. While later working for the *Pioneer*, the most important English-language daily in India, he wrote a series of stories which were published by the Railway Library in India and sold at railway stations for one rupee. In several unusual ways the young man and writer had been 'made in India'.

That most of Kipling's Indian works appeared just prior to a time when the entire Imperial Idea was increasingly under suspicion and when the very meaning of the term 'imperialism' was to acquire its present pejorative meanings gives them a special historical significance. But this same fact also explains the dramatic reversal in Kipling's popularity in the 1910s and the subsequent hostility to his work as being damagingly trapped within the strident jingoism, pugnacious territorial ambitions and popular racial myths of an earlier time. The turbulent history of Kipling criticism shows how easy it is to gather dismissive evidence against a writer who speaks of 'new-caught sullen peoples / Half devil and half child' who make up those 'lesser breeds without the Law', and of the Englishman's noble but foredoomed mission in the following terms: 'Watch Sloth and heathen Folly / Bring all your hope to naught'. Later critical reactions were to range from violent opposition to Kipling's 'toryism' as 'a lower-middle-class-snarl of defeated gentility' (Lionel Trilling) through Orwell's criticism that Kipling failed to see empire as 'primarily a money-making concern' to the note of polite dissent aroused even in his admirers at the spectacle of 'the deformation Mr Kipling the artist has at times undergone at the hands of Mr Kipling the man of action' (Bonamy Dobrée).

Charges like this still form an important crux in Kipling criticism. In his role as a public spokesman during the late 1890s Kipling was quite clear where he stood as a devotee of the Five Nations and a British colonialism whose function, so he felt, should be essentially Roman in nature, bringing order, peace and stability to the unenlightened. Were that the complete picture, however, Kipling would be a considerably more manageable and tidy presence than he in fact is. In some respects the grounds of the Kipling debate have shifted to include a wider and altogether untidier range of evidence – the case for a 'good' Kipling, his remarkable freedom of movement between Eastern and Western religions, and his nearness to Joseph Conrad. It has also come to include the fact that Kipling stands behind the traditions of both 'naïve' colonial literature *and* its predominantly satiric and self-questioning forms.

Indeed the scores of Kipling's Indian tales – as found in several volumes from *Plain Tales from the Hills* (1888) to *The Day's Work* (1898) – are remarkable for their seemingly instinctive and restless variety. One helpful way of indicating this variety is to note the co-presence of two very different emphases at work in the tales. On the one hand, there often seems to be a strong similarity of purpose between Kipling and Stevenson (a writer whom the former read and much admired). All of the things most admired by Stevenson – strong narrative action, typicality of situation, and the conjunction of literature and dreams – can also help to delineate facets of Kipling's literary encounter with colonial India. For the latter, of course, there was the romance of his present time and moment – the mission of Empire itself, with its heroic possibilities, images of male camaraderie and recurring tests upon manhood. Does not a combination of David Balfour and Alan Breck lead in a direct line to the resourceful Stalky? If Kipling was prone to take romance into some idiosyncratic areas, such as glamorization of machinery, he can also be seen as extending its traditional possibilities: he follows Stevenson – and with him, Poe, Dumas and *The Arabian Nights* – in valuing the exotic faraway India as a necessary setting for 'bogey' tales (as in 'A Phantom Rickshaw' and 'A Strange Ride') and in order to make an imaginative entry into the East to a degree allowed to no other writer of the time. Yet throughout Kipling's Indian tales there is an equally strong counterpull which, strange as it may seem now, made them appear crudely 'ugly' to some of his audience. This second stress is determinedly anti-romantic in its emphasis on the mundane 'regular working of the Empire' – its dull military, administrative and social routines, casual violences, disease, boredom, the endless rhythm of service and leaves, and the marriage market of Simla society. In numerous stories action is replaced by stagnation and fixity, the possibility of heroic ritual by routine, and the celebratory impulse of romance by a bare re-portorial naturalism. No doubt some of these stories engage with the commonplace as a way of drawing attention to the unsung heroes of Empire, but many of them insistently deflate and de-glamorize as well. What is emphasized has often less to do with the white man's burden than with what Oscar Wilde described as 'jaded second-rate Anglo-Indians ... in exquisite incongruity with their surroundings' (*Nineteenth Century*, 1890).

The proximity and interplay of these two stresses help to account for some of Kipling's very best tales in the 1880s and to explain their remarkable variety of form and perspective. But we should not, in the first place, underemphasize the provocative and irreverent 'infant monster'[1] who makes a more prominent appearance than many critics are prepared to allow. Conrad described Kipling as having a productive squint. We may rather feel that he shared with Samuel Butler a lively dislike of sham and a tendency to question even those beliefs which were dear to him. The youthful Kipling seems too acute a spectator not to want to measure the debits and credits of Empire and to look at exceptions to the rule which 'are decently shovelled out of sight' ('The Drums of Fore and Aft'). His early tales give him access to what would later become a traditional subject of the colonial novel – the English middle classes transplanted onto foreign soil where their social and racial customs stand in revealing contrast to their surroundings. The creator of Mrs Hauksbee or the cartoon-like Anthony Barr Saggott in 'Cupid's Arrows' (one of the very 'best' men, but socially 'like unto a blandishing gorilla') is no respecter of persons or the customs of the tribe. Nor, despite sharing some of Butler's attraction for High Ydgrunites, can Kipling always muster much sympathy for the seemingly endless procession of young, unfeeling public schoolboys who come to India direct from the rugby pitch, the 'same hard-trained, athletic-sports build of animal' who keeps 'his pores open and his mouth shut' ('The Brushwood Boy'). Time and time again in Kipling's stories we are halted in our steps by pressures running counter to simple expectations. Several of them, like 'Lispeth' or 'Beyond the Pale', provide variations on the theme

---

[1] This picturesque description of Kipling belongs to Henry James (letter to R. L. Stevenson, January 1891). James's admiration for the early Kipling was to be severely qualified as the decade wore on. Writing to Grace Norton at the end of 1897, he admitted to being sadly disappointed: 'In his earliest time I thought he perhaps contained the seeds of an English Balzac; but I have given that up in proportion as he has come down steadily from the simple in subject to the more simple – from the Anglo-Indians to the natives, from the natives to the Tommies, from the Tommies to the quadrupeds, from the quadrupeds to the fish, and from the fish to the engines and screws.'

that East and West cannot meet, but either lament that fact ('Love heeds not caste nor sleep a broken bed. I went in search of love and lost myself') or compassionately show an Indian woman's betrayal by an Englishman of 'superior clay': 'It takes a great deal of Christianity to wipe out uncivilized Eastern instincts such as falling in love at first sight' ('Lispeth'). In other, more sentimental tales like 'Wee Willie Winkie' we can feel a fugitive impatience on Kipling's part with the very romance it sustains: the heroic infant of the Raj is confronted by Pathans who know that, were the child to be harmed, the regiment to whom he is a 'God' will 'fire and rape and plunder for a month till nothing remains'. Clearly, Kipling is not averse to occupying the yawning gaps between the poetry and the prose of colonial endeavour.

In Kipling's finest Indian stories – including 'In the House of Suddhoo', 'The Head of the District', 'The Bridge-Builders', and 'The Man Who Would Be King' – the art of complicating inference and ambiguity tends to work through whole narrative structures, producing what has been called the 'art of double dialogue'. This selection of stories would indicate the fuller range of Kipling's skills, including his use of frame devices, bold symbolism, and shifting perspectives and counterpointings. It also suggests a writer ambitiously generalizing upon the meaning of the colonial encounter and in a way that was to determine much of the shape and substance of later colonial fiction – in particular, through his use of East and West in confrontation as a severe test and challenge upon Western liberal ideals in the presence of alternative gods. The large opposites with which Kipling works might be seen by comparing 'In the House of Suddhoo' with 'The Bridge-Builders', the first located in the symbolic house of India, the second centred upon a typical symbol of the colonialist's missionary 'work'. But the second tale, for example, also contains numerous opposites within its structure. It begins with a soaring description of what the bridge, as a piece of constructed order and design, signifies for its builder, Findlayson. Characteristically, the tale itself then bridges out to embrace the two sides of the river separated by the unpredictable Mother Gunga as well as the bridge's ambiguous significance as a link with the history of heroic imperial endeavour *and* with an uncertain Indian future. The central bridge in the story's narrative involves Findlayson's passage, during a flood and under the influence of medicinal opium, from the gods of his work to the strange embodiments of Mother Gunga's voice ('They have chained my flood, and my river is not free any more'), a passage signalled by Findlayson's movement from the support of his English assistant to that of another, the Lascar Peroo. Geographically, imaginatively, and as Kipling's version of a passage to India, the tale will *not* remain static. If a point of fixture is reached, it is on the island where, undergoing his strangely solitary vision and feeling himself to be the last survivor after the Deluge, Findlayson sees differently and more widely. Like Decoud in Conrad's *Nostromo*, Findlayson is removed from the world of men, islanded, and made to look at the 'night of time'. Unlike Decoud, however, he appears to be granted not only a vision but a beneficent blessing upon his work as an Anglo-Indian enterprise ('Go, my children! Brahm dreams – and till he wakes the Gods die not'). Yet the vision fades as quickly as it had appeared and the story's end reverts to the seeming confusions and inconsequentialities of the day's work. Was it a vision or a waking dream? Like Keats's ode, the story comes to rest in a state of suspension between possibilities.

Appearing in a volume entitled *The Day's Work* (1898), 'The Bridge-Builders' is not wholly characteristic of the predominant kinds of tone and address to be found in Kipling's work of that time. Even the infant monster soon comes to feel, it seems, that popularity carries onerous responsibilities, and, in particular, the duty to undertake the roles of prophet, spokesman and didact. From 1892–3 (and largely coinciding with the beginning of a four-year period spent in Vermont) Kipling's work shows overt signs of being shaped by – and wanting to shape – popular attitudes to Queen, Country and Empire. The effect upon his poetry in the mid-1890s can be seen in its movement towards, on the one hand, the declarative, oratorial and hymn-like, and, on the other, the 'singable slang' of the barrack-room. At its best Kipling's poetry adds a new dimension to the stock of popular Victorian hymnology and balladry; but at its worst it comes uncomfortably close to emulating the coarse-grained rhetoric of Mr Raymond Martin M.P., whose address to the school so embarrasses Stalky and friends in 'The Flag of their Country'. Other, slower developments were taking place in Kipling's fiction, notably a movement towards children's writing and the world of childhood conceived as a proving ground for responsible adulthood and as offering lessons in life under 'the Law', a concept that begins to accrete its varied significances in *The Jungle Book* (1894), *The Second Jungle Book* (1895) and *Stalky and Co*. By 1899 the problem posed by Kipling to a small but growing minority of critics was not only that his 'virtues' could well be seen as another's 'vices', but that his writing seemed to have hardened and solidified to the point where it was in some danger of parodying itself. In that year Henry James was to protest in a letter to Charles Eliot Norton: 'I can't swallow his loud, brazen patriotic verse – an exploitation of the patriotic idea. . . . Two or three times a century, yes; but not every month.'

There does not appear to be any simple or single reason for these changing stresses in Kipling's writing. In his turning towards the world of child and school we can in part detect a gathering nostalgia for his own past in India and Westward Ho! But equally powerful were Kipling's world travels of the early 1890s and the impact made upon him by the scale of the Empire and the largeness of the Imperial dream. By 1895 he identified himself squarely with Lord Salisbury's home and foreign policies and may well have felt the urge to distinguish British colonial policies (legitimized, so he felt, by their responsibility to 'the Law') from the crudely exploitative colonial activities of other European powers.

These and other growing convictions help to explain the expanding social and political dimensions of 'the Law' in Kipling's work, a concept which, while it links closely with the Imperial mission, is fed from many other sources – the Bible, public school values, the Victorian work ethic, and traditional patriotic feeling. In some of its manifestations Kipling's version of 'the Law' as a co-operative social ideal can also be likened to the early Conrad's belief in a 'few simple notions' (loyalty, fidelity and trust) which are sanctioned by tradition and nourished by the strict hierarchy of ship-board life, a hierarchy accepted by all in their best interests: common to both, at some points, is a stress upon the honourable discipline of work, fidelity to the group, and vigilant devotion to the facts of daily life. But in most essential matters, including the kind and degree of their commitment to such a code, the two writers seem very different, and especially so in 1899 when *Stalky and Co.* and *Heart of Darkness* were both published. The message from Conrad's African jungle stands in strange contrast to Kipling's voice from the jungle in *The Jungle Book*:

Because of his age and his cunning, because of his gripe and his paw,
In all that the Law leaveth open, the word of the Head Wolf is Law.
Now these are the Laws of the Jungle, and many and mighty are they;
But the head and the hoof of the Law and the haunch and the hump is Obey!

Warm homage, nostalgic hymn, meditative richness – all of these come together in *Kim* (1901), a remarkable climax to Kipling's

Indian writings and a synthesis of influences from many parts of his life. Begun during the first few months of the Boer War in South Africa where Kipling was serving as a war correspondent, the novel and its vision of Empire are probably deepened by that experience. Through Kim Kipling looks back affectionately on his own early years in India and also offers a tribute to his father, John Lockwood Kipling, who helped in the actual writing and shaping of the story. In a more general sense the novel can be regarded as Kipling's fullest homage to India and the Imperial design. Kim (Kimball O'Hara) plays a central part in this affectionate celebration. As an orphan born originally of Irish parents, he has become a waif of the Indian streets, 'Little Friend of all the World', and with the power of disguise to allow him entry into all sides of Indian life, a world rendered in the novel with astonishing width and detail. In being neither fully Indian nor conventional sahib Kim stands at the meeting points between two cultures and exists in response to a question ('Who am I?'). In the fictional portrait which follows 'the Law' is never explicitly invoked, but Kim is Kipling's most attractive embodiment of it: with the practical skills of a Stalky, the attentiveness of Mowgli, the courage of Wee Willie Winkie, he makes up the book's vision of a human, social and political ideal. Its human and social dimensions are most warmly realized in Kim's friendship with the Tibetan Lama, whose *chela* he becomes and with whom he undertakes a parallel quest. But all of Kim's social and political involvements later in the book serve to bind the link between two cultures: his participation in the Great Game of espionage (which also draws upon English and Indians) helps to support and strengthen the shared interests which for Kipling make up the essence of the Imperial Design.

Many of the book's most important features again recall Stevenson (*Kidnapped* in particular) and the characteristics of Stevensonian romance. Much of the colourful material of *Kim* belongs to the elementary novel of action – adventures on the road, the dreams of youth to participate in the adult world, the young man 'coming into his kingdom' and the joint quest to unravel secrets. In its effect, too, *Kim* splendidly fulfils Stevenson's requirement that the romance should 'bathe' the reader in fresh experience, whether it be the experience of a third-class compartment on an Indian train, the streets of Lahore or the soaring Himalayas. Kipling's novel also offers an example of romance grown up, attentive to resonance, and having a distinctive shape which emerges from its sense of patterned opposites between youth and age, East and West, practical worldliness and Buddhistic withdrawal, the Great Game and the Lama's Great Wheel. The Lama's quest and its conclusion begin and end the novel, giving its journey the dimension of a religious and philosophic quest. Yet that ancient quest design is complicated by a second one more characteristic of modern India, that of the Great Game itself as a manifestation of *Realpolitik*. The competing and interlocking tensions between the two provide the material for Kim's education and gradual growth into manhood: he finally emerges as a unique fusion of opposites, Kim Sahib.

Original, uneven, inconsistent, pugnacious – the 'Victorian' Kipling is all of these things and would continue to be so during the remainder of his writing career. If the Nobel Prize he received in 1907 also marks the moment when his reputation began to wane, it certainly does not signify that Kipling was to be a spent force, and almost a half of the volumes in the sizeable Collected Edition of his works belong to the post-1902 period. It is because of, rather than despite, his unevenness and angular awkwardness that Kipling is such an interesting figure, more interesting than many other writers who are more guardedly measured and impersonal. His involvement with affairs of the day accounts for an unusual range of varying public tones, some louder than others: as Yeats might say, out of his quarrel with others he often built a powerful rhetoric. But it is equally true to add that out of his own powerful self-quarrel he fashioned much of his finest work. That is why Kipling would have understood the imaginative and social conditions which went into the making of Ernest Pontifex, *Homo duplex*, and Dr Jekyll. The epigraph to Chapter 7 of *Kim* ('The Two-Sided Man') suggests no less than this:

> Something I owe to the soil that grew –
> More to the life that fed –
> But most to Allah Who gave me two
> Separate sides to my head.
>
> I would go without shirts or shoes,
> Friends, tobacco or bread
> Sooner than for an instant lose
> Either side of my head.

12
TENNYSON (and FITZGERALD)

John Killham

In a poem called 'Poets and Critics' (1892, but written long before),
Tennyson wrote:

> What is true at last will tell:
> Few at first will place thee well;
> Some too low would have thee shine,
> Some too high – no fault of thine . . .

When the lines were published three weeks after his death in
October 1892 at the age of eighty-three, his own reputation was
extremely high; but by 1922 Thomas Hardy in *Late Lyrics and
Earlier* was recording a melancholy truth when he wrote in 'An
Ancient to Ancients':

> The bower we shrined to Tennyson,
> > Gentlemen,
> Is roof-wrecked; damps there drip upon
> Sagged seats, the creeper-nails are rust,
> The spider is sole denizen; . . .

Part of the mood of the years following the First World War is
expressed by W. H. Auden and Christopher Isherwood in their
play, *The Ascent of F6* (1936). Ransom is reading from Dante the
famous lines, the sense of which Tennyson incorporates in his poem
'Ulysses': 'Consider your origin: ye were not formed to live like
brutes, but to follow virtue and knowledge.' His comment upon
them is: 'Virtue and Knowledge! One can picture Ulysses's audience: a crook speaking to crooks . . . Who was Dante, to speak of
Virtue and Knowledge? It was not Virtue those lips, which in-
voluntary privation made so bitter, could pray for; it was not
Knowledge; it was Power. Power to exact for every snub, every
headache, every unfallen beauty, an absolute revenge . . .' For many
of the post-War generation idealism had become suspect and
patriotism a sham. Virginia Woolf's portrait of Mr Ramsay in *To the
Lighthouse* (1927), marching about the garden reciting 'The Charge

of the Light Brigade' is meant to illustrate a case of hypertrophy of the will, while that of Sir William Bradshaw in *Mrs Dalloway* (1925) is a condemnation of the English disease of wanting to dominate people in the name of order, discipline, duty – ideals which certainly commended themselves to Tennyson. In the circumstances it is hardly surprising that a good deal of his poetry should have struck readers of the between-wars period as being out of touch with reality and betraying a lack of self-knowledge. In the thirties Pound parodied his most popular poems in sharp satires upon Big Business supposedly by Alfred Venison, a barrow-poet. Joyce brings him into *Ulysses* (1922) as Alfred Lawn Tennyson 'gentleman poet', and most amusingly deflates Enoch Arden and King Arthur by showing 'the eternal question of the life connubial' in a very realistic light, quite opposed to Tennyson's exalted dream-pictures of love and marriage. And Faulkner has Hightower in *Light in August* (1933), a man who has ruined his life and deserted his responsibilities, find solace in reading Tennyson:

Soon the fine galloping language, the gutless swooning full of sapless trees and dehydrated lusts begins to swim smooth and swift and peaceful. It is better than praying without having to bother to think aloud. It is like listening in a cathedral to a eunuch chanting in a language which he does not even need to not understand.

Hightower's state at the time is one of withdrawal, an abdication from ordinary living brought about by constant preoccupation with a dead heroic past.

These modern views of Tennyson are not just, but their exaggeration does draw attention to the curious juxtaposition in much of his poetry of an exalted, dreamy idealism and of violence, suggestive perhaps of the urgency with which the ideal is sustained in face of real-life materialism. *Maud* (1855) and the two 'Locksley Hall' poems (1842 and 1886), not to speak of the *Idylls of the King*, will illustrate the point. In the poem 'Merlin and the Gleam' (1889) Tennyson allegorically represents his lifelong concern with an ideal of conduct as a 'Gleam' which he followed despite its nearly disappearing in face of death. The 'Gleam' stood for 'the higher poetic imagination', by which he meant the employment of art in the service of ideals. Although he was not alone in believing that artists had a responsibility to inspire and sustain the public in an age when values were in doubt, he himself underwent so much mental anguish in arriving at the religious faith he thought necessary as a basis for morals that whatever we may think of some of his poetry as poetry, it is always interesting if only because it expresses so copiously and variously the Victorian sense of the relaxation in the hold over men's minds of the Christian faith, and the consequent need to elevate its moral behests to the status of an ideal. Nowadays we can hardly subscribe to the opinion that he was one of the greatest poets in the language, but many readers of his best things will echo Disraeli's opinion that 'if not a great poet', he is 'a real one'.

In 'Poets and their Bibliographies' (1885) Tennyson apostrophizes Virgil, Horace and Catullus, concluding:

> You should be jubilant that you flourish'd here
> Before the Love of Letters, overdone,
> Had swampt the sacred poets with themselves.

This must be every true poet's sentiment, even if it could be shown that scholars wished only to further the proper appreciation of his self-approved work. With Tennyson there is particular reason for expressing it because having published under his own name *Poems, Chiefly Lyrical* (1830) and *Poems* (1833) – he had appeared anonymously in 1827 in *Poems by Two Brothers* – he felt that they suffered from mawkishness and metrical irregularity. As a consequence he printed very little until 1842, when two volumes of *Poems* were published, the first consisting largely of poems from 1830 and 1833 volumes, but considerably revised. (A third was never republished in an authorized edition at all, though some that were not republished in 1842 reappeared in later collections.) A long poem, 'The Lover's Tale', which Tennyson proposed to include in the 1833 volume but withdrew on grounds of its faultiness was revised in 1868 but was again withheld from publication. Eventually he was driven to publish it in 1879. This sort of diffidence and uncertainty has made Tennyson's work particularly need the services of a bibliographer, and it is now best, as so much that he did not mean to be published has been, that a comprehensive edition should appear.

Tennyson's poetical career began early, among his ten brothers and sisters at home in the crowded rectory at Somersby in Lincolnshire (see *Unpublished Early Poems by Alfred Tennyson*, 1932 and *The Devil and the Lady*, ed. C. Tennyson, 1930). But it was at Trinity College, Cambridge, that he entered a circle of friends who encouraged him by admiration for his talent and their enthusiastic concern with liberal politics and religious problems. The attachment between the poet and Arthur Henry Hallam, son of the historian, was particularly close. They planned to join forces in writing a volume of poems, but Hallam eventually contented himself with encouraging his friend in the publishing of *Poems, Chiefly Lyrical* and enthusiastically reviewing them. They were both members of the Apostles, or 'The Cambridge Conversazione Society'; together they travelled in the long vacation of 1830 to the Pyrenees to aid General Torrijos's expedition: and in 1832 Hallam became engaged to Tennyson's sister, Emily. Hallam had all the qualities of intelligence and sensibility which were bound to win the admiration of the moody young Tennyson, and they were accompanied by an optimism and fortitude which he particularly needed in face of the criticism (not all of it harsh by any means) his early volumes received. The completely unexpected death of Hallam in 1833 left him to strive against an innate pessimism and doubt, and the 'ten years' silence', until the *Poems* of 1842, was spent not merely in polishing his already published work, but in coming to terms with grief, loneliness and indigence, a process resulting in a great deal of new and varied verse. Some of this went into the second 1842 volume, but many lyrics in a single verse-form dealing with the feelings and reflexions occasioned by Hallam's death lay in manuscript until they were ordered and expanded to form *In Memoriam A.H.H.*, published in 1850.

Order has been brought into the Tennyson canon by Christopher Ricks's edition of the poems (1969, but now in process of revision).

The early work shows two impulses operating, one subjective and 'aesthetic', the other seeking identification with the larger life of common men. Paradoxically it was Arthur Hallam, whom Tennyson saw as one admirably fitted for public life, who probably encouraged the first tendency. In a review of Tennyson's volume of 1830 (*The Englishman's Magazine*, 1831; in *Tennyson: The Critical Heritage*, ed. J. D. Jump, pp 34–49), Hallam very clear-sightedly attributed the difference between the greater masters of poetry (Homer, Dante, Shakespeare) and Keats or Shelley to developments in civilization which had forever extinguished the 'unreservedness of communion' between poets and readers:

Those different powers of poetic disposition, the energies of Sensitive [sensuous], of Reflective, of Passionate Emotion, which in former times were intermingled, and derived from mutual support an extensive empire over the feelings of men, were now restrained within separate spheres of agency . . . Hence the melancholy, which so evidently characterizes the spirit of modern poetry; hence that return of the mind upon itself, and the habit of seeking relief in idiosyncrasies rather than community of interest.

The modern poet of sensation, Hallam stated, cannot be expected
to exercise authority over public opinion; he must try to maintain art
as a preserve in which feeling can survive out of reach of those who
wish to expel it in favour of their utilitarian ends.

Many of Tennyson's early poems show that Hallam understood
very well one side of his temperament. 'The Poet's Mind' (1830:
1842)[1] shows a fine contempt for the dull Philistine. Poem after
poem celebrates in melodious if occasionally rather free rhythms,
the exquisite pleasure (to the sensitive mind) of mourning a dying
swan, or Oriana killed by a glancing arrow, or even the dying year:

> The air is damp, and hush'd, and close,
> As a sick man's room when he taketh repose
>   An hour before death;
> My very heart faints and my whole soul grieves
> At the moist rich smell of the rotting leaves,
>   And the breath
>   Of the fading edges of box beneath,
> And the year's last rose.
> Heavily hangs the broad sunflower
>   Over its grave i' the earth so chilly;
> Heavily hangs the hollyhock,
>   Heavily hangs the tiger-lily.
> ('Song: A Spirit Haunts the Year's Last Hours', 1830: 1842)

Another series of poems treats of the opposite pleasure of love, both
cool ('The Sea-Fairies', 1830: 1853) and warm ('Fatima', 1833:
1842). Yet another combines them, and we have, as J. S. Mill
observed, 'not mere pictures, but states of emotion, embodied in
sensuous imagery': 'The Lady of Shalott' is one of these, and the
near-symbolist 'Mariana' is another. All these poems show
Tennyson's satisfaction with the role of music-maker, the artist of
song. His parade of feeling inevitably affronted critics like 'Christopher North' and J. W. Croker, but there were others than Hallam
to praise even his precious word-pictures of 'Victorian' young
ladies.

But Hallam does not tell all the story. 'The Poet' (1830: 1842)
advances a quite different notion of the artist's function. It is to
use the 'vagrant melodies' of his song to carry 'the winged shafts
of truth', to create a sunrise in which Freedom's glance will melt

---

[1] The date of first publication in the 1830 and 1833 volumes is followed by that of
first republication. This does not mean that no further changes in the texts were
made.

rites and forms like snow. Pretentious this doubtless is, and premature the claim that the poet saw through life and death and his own soul to the meaning of the eternal will; but it shows that Tennyson was quite accessible to the call, first uttered by W. J. Fox when discussing the 1830 poems in *The Westminster Review*, to go beyond a 'facility of impersonation' and put his art to use. At the same time, poems like 'Supposed Confessions of a Second-rate Sensitive Mind' (1830: 1884) and 'The Palace of Art' (1833: 1842) hardly supported any pretension on Tennyson's part to solve the metaphysical problems of the age. The dreadful conclusion of 'The Palace of Art', a poem which displays Tennyson's skill in word-painting, is that withdrawal from real life into an aesthetic preserve is the greatest sin of which the artist can be guilty. 'Oenone' (1833: 1842) takes the rejection of mere beauty into classical myth, associating it with sensuality and a fearful outcome in (the Trojan) war; it thus anticipates the *Idylls of the King* which also makes the erotic the type of sin and weakness by which social decline is brought about.

Some of Tennyson's early poems like 'Recollections of the Arabian Nights' (1830: 1842) and 'A Dream of Fair Women' (1833: 1842) strongly suggest that he sometimes did not rely on his verbal artifice merely, but drew upon private fantasies. The 'Ode to Memory' (1830: 1842) suggests that he well knew that his strength lay in his ability to re-enter the world of his childhood, which was blessed with colour and excitement afforded by books and a sense of freedom in the security of a home which was in reality far from serene. If this is correct, then it is not difficult to imagine how disturbing must have been the realization that the way of the pure artist might be sinful; 'The Palace of Art' presents the sense of guilt and isolation:

> A spot of dull stagnation, without light
>   Or power of movement, seem'd my soul,
> Mid onward-sloping motions infinite
>   Making for one sure goal.

> A still salt pool, lock'd in with bars of sand,
>   Left on the shore; that hears all night
> The plunging seas draw backward from the land
>   Their moon-led waters white.

'The Lady of Shalott' (1833: 1842), on the other hand, although it may show in allegory the possible fate of the artist who cannot bear too much reality, lavishes so much artistry on the pathetic figure of the Lady that one may connect it with the impulse to compose lyrics (like 'Mariana' (1830: 1842) for instance) achieving an inspired blend of pathos, colour, symbolic landscape and musical refrain to produce rare effects of feeling or mood rather than any detachable meaning. At this time Tennyson's poetic encompassment of reality may be measured by 'The May Queen', 'The Miller's Daughter' (1833: 1842) and 'The Gardener's Daughter' (1842, but an earlier version was written by 1833), the last being two idylls of courtship and marriage, admirably suited to the Victorian taste for sentiment and pastoral.

The death of Hallam was a severe blow, not merely because their friendship sustained Tennyson in his loneliness and melancholy, but also because he had intellectual strength with which to meet the religious doubts which at that time Tennyson was experiencing. In 'Supposed Confessions' he had already written:

> How sweet to have a common faith!
> To hold a common scorn of death!
> And at a burial to hear
> The creaking cords which wound and eat
> Into my human heart, whene'er
> Earth goes to earth, with grief, not fear,
> With hopeful grief, were passing sweet!

Now he seriously asked himself whether life was worth living. Being a poet he began very quickly to put his feelings into poems, some of which appeared first in the second volume of *Poems*, 1842. One, 'The Two Voices', deals directly with the thought of suicide, which is rejected because life speaks within him of hope:

> Moreover, something is or seems,
> That touches me with mystic gleams,
> Like glimpses of forgotten dreams . . .

The conclusion is confident, and pre-figures the confidence of some of the poems Tennyson wrote much later in life, but there was still a long way to go. Other poems written or revised after Hallam's death are not so positive. Thus he revised 'The Lotos-Eaters' of 1833 to make escape into indolent dreaming have its justification in the sufferings of mankind, sufferings to which the gods are indifferent. Tennyson's talent for luxurious description now found its perfect outlet, and the poem is deservedly famous. It is an excellent example of a favourite Victorian poetic form, the dramatic monologue, in which very often (as in Browning), a saving irony plays over the supposed speaker's sentiments. In 'The

Lotos-Eaters' Tennyson could securely express his own yearnings for release from suffering, confident that his readers would recognize the Homeric and Lucretian parallels and exempt him from the charge of escapism. He resorts to the same device in 'Tithonus' (begun in or before 1833 but not published until 1860), which dramatizes the myth of the mortal to whom Aurora gave immortality, but not immunity from the sufferings of old age. The loss of youth is the respect that makes calamity of so long life. Tithonus begs Aurora for release, pleading that all living things enjoy the boon of death:

> The woods decay, the woods decay and fall,
> The vapours weep their burthen to the ground,
> Man comes and tills the field and lies beneath,
> And after many a summer dies the swan.

At first sight 'Ulysses' might seem, as Tennyson himself asserted, to express a contrary belief, the need for going forward into life despite the pains of age and the inevitability of death, just as in 'The Two Voices' he had written:

> 'Tis life, whereof our nerves are scant,
> Oh life, not death, for which we pant;
> More life, and fuller, that I want.

But we cannot help noticing that Ulysses resembles the lotos-eaters in his willingness to give up thoughts of wife and son, together with his ordinary duties as governor of the isle; nor can we ignore the valedictory associations of the great deep upon which he means to sail:

> The long day wanes: the slow moon climbs: the deep
> Moans round with many voices. Come, my friends,
> 'Tis not too late to seek a newer world.

The concern is as much with death as in the 'Morte d'Arthur': the hungry heart of Ulysses is bent upon the gleam of an untravelled world, and the restless pursuit of experience will never end until it arrives there and gains a peace that passes understanding. Arthur too finds a sort of death by water, but his passing to the idyllic island-valley of Avilion is described in more portentous imagery, for which the modern 'frame' serves as apology. The 'Morte d'Arthur' does not reach the level of the classical monologues. Its colour and glitter are splendid in their way, but the poem is too contrived and pictorial to involve our deeper feelings. The conclusion suggesting that Arthur reappears in 'the modern gentleman' is an example of

Tennyson's remarkable lack of a sense of bathos, evident in a number of poems. But it shows that his apprehension that the ideals he aspired to could not survive under the conditions of the modern world was, at this point in his career, restrained by hope that in the end they would reassert themselves in new forms. (Tennyson's interest in the Arthurian story also appears in a stanza of 'The Palace of Art'; and in the two poems 'Sir Galahad' and 'Sir Launcelot and Queen Guinevere', first published in 1842, but very probably written, like 'The Lady of Shalott', at Cambridge or soon after.) 'Locksley Hall' expresses anxiety and revulsion at the signs of the times, and hopes that all will be well: the moving irony of 'Ulysses' is replaced by another sort altogether, one dependent upon attributing yearning for withdrawal and peace (between nations this time) to a character whose near-hysterical utterances in face of disappointment are meant to betray to the reader their inadequacy. Unfortunately the final resolve to enter fully into the modern age sounds equally hollow:

> Not in vain the distance beacons. Forward, forward let us
> range,
> Let the great world spin for ever down the ringing grooves
> of change.

In 'The Golden Year' (1846) Tennyson later shows his consciousness of the fact that he was naturally disposed to handle the long-ago or the far future; contemporary problems relating to the condition of England in an age of industrialism and urbanization glanced at in 'Locksley Hall' were really outside his range. Characteristically he put his hope in gradualism (see, for example, 'You ask me why . . .', 'Of old sat Freedom on the heights', 'Love thou thy land'); his poetry on modern subjects written when the pain of his loss had quietened took the form of 'idylls' like 'Audley Court' and 'Walking to the Mail', or *vers de société* like 'The Talking Oak', 'Amphion' and 'The Day Dream'. Clearly Tennyson was searching for a new manner, perhaps in the hope of achieving popularity. 'Dora' affects an austere plainness; 'Will Waterproof's Lyrical Monologue' and 'The Vision of Sin' display an unexpected flair for facetious rhyming. In all this variety of work there is nothing very impressive, save for 'Break, break, break' which with 'Tears, idle tears' from *The Princess*, eloquently expresses his passion for the past, the past of his youth before experience of death or the past immortalized in the literature which described a golden age. It is as if he were deliberately avoiding the serious vein (which all the while was being released in the future *In Memoriam*) and cultivating the pretty, the charming, the sentimental. Poems like 'Godiva', 'The Lord of Burleigh' and 'Lady Clare' were perfectly adapted to the popular taste. 'Will Waterproof's Lyrical Monologue' may supply a clue to the reason for it in its hints of a fear of the critics and an 'eternal want of pence'.

The most ambitious of the poems in this new, lighter vein is the one which follows *Poems*, *The Princess*, first published in 1847, but revised in subsequent editions. This must strike the modern reader as a most curious undertaking for the poet of 'Ulysses' and 'Tithonus'. But it has for subject that very question which in his review of the 1830 volume W. J. Fox had wished Tennyson might think worthy of his powers if he truly aspired to the role he had outlined in 'The Poet', namely, the education of women. True to his resolve to cultivate the lightness of touch which he admired in older poets and apparently felt necessary as a counter to his natural seriousness, he embarked upon a tale of the absurd lengths a headstrong princess went to preserve her university of women from the interference of men. The story is much more fantastic than *Love's Labour's Lost*, and freely combines medieval and modern, a state of affairs justified by the pretence that it is told by a succession of undergraduate narrators to amuse themselves and some ladies on a picnic. (The 'modern' note is struck by the holiday amusements of the Mechanics Institute, particularly the 'strange experiments' wherein sport 'went hand in hand with Science': but it is harmonized with elements drawn from distant times and places, so that a strange air of unreality is lent to the scene, an effect reproduced in the tale itself by the 'weird seizures' of the Prince.) What begins as genial satire turns into sympathy for the Princess's cause. Although the prince who had tried to overset her scheme is defeated, she tends him and is won over to marriage. Was ever woman in this humour woo'd? The 'strange diagonal' the story takes shows clearly that Tennyson believed that in marriage the sexes fulfil not only one another's needs, but also nature's evolutionary plan: if marriage is to be meaningful, women must be freed from the restrictions they have suffered under in the past. There is in Tennyson a feminine streak which both makes him sympathetic to the women's cause and also underlies that dependency, even inadequacy, out of which his best poems come to be written. The lyrics 'Tears, idle tears', 'Now sleeps the crimson petal', 'Come down, O maid', which find a place in *The Princess*, all express in different ways his need and his characteristic inactivity, his submissiveness. He does not act, he waits, and his best poems are those which express expectancy or resignation.

In Memoriam, published in 1850, also ends with a marriage and the anticipated birth of a child which will prove 'a closer link/ Betwixt us and the crowning race' which, 'no longer half-akin to brute', will in the far future supplant the humanity whose present ignorance of the meaning of life brings the agonizings over death recorded in the earlier 131 sections of the poem. Those sections, seen from the concluding standpoint of 'colossal calm', appeared

> As echoes out of weaker times,
> As half but idle brawling rhymes,
> The sport of random sun and shade.
>
> (Concluding stanzas)

The confident conclusion occurs 'some thrice three years' after the dark day of Hallam's death; the passage of three Christmases is marked by poems in the series (XXX, LXXVIII and CV); but in fact nearly seventeen years had passed between that day and the publication of the poem, and for many of the poems the date of composition is a matter of speculation. But some were written right through the period in which Tennyson was producing the light-hearted work just described.

The poem finds its unity in the stanza form, from which Tennyson summons constant variations of effect, and in its subject, death. But it lacks the sort of structure found in 'Lycidas' or 'Adonais' or 'Thyrsis', all of which in various ways find, through an act of imagination, a means of moving away from the mere fact of death into a deeper sense of how to live. Critics have found pastoral elements in *In Memoriam* and have claimed for it the status of an elegy, but although many of the individual poems record the beauty of English landscape and season and relate to one another on occasion (through subject or imagery), they remain 'brief lays' and 'short swallow-flights of song'. They move away from sorrow over the death of Hallam to general speculations on what death may bring, and then return to Hallam again. But they never transcend the preoccupation with time and mortality, which takes ever-new forms as thoughts occur to the poet. The conclusion is itself a new departure. T. S. Eliot's comparison with a diary is just, for the poems are poignant personal responses to new grounds for hope or despair offered by particular occasions – anniversaries, books read, visits made. There is no total transformation wherein the doubts are swept away by a sudden recognition that it is life, not death, that counts. Tennyson's conclusion puts hope in lives yet to come, not in life here and now.

Although *In Memoriam* has no organic development, but only a switch from despair to an evolutionary hope, individual poems have an imaginative power very unlike anything else that Tennyson wrote. The narrow limits of the octosyllabic lines, arranged in rhyming quatrains, force him into a disciplining of his usual largeness, occasionally even slackness, of utterance; but he is not cramped by the restrictions of his stanza. Occasionally he sustains a thought through a long period:

> Till now the doubtful dusk reveal'd
>   The knolls once more where, couch'd at ease,
>   The white kine glimmer'd and the trees
> Laid their dark arms about the field:
>
> And suck'd from out the distant gloom
>   A breeze began to tremble o'er
>   The large leaves of the sycamore,
> And fluctuate all the still perfume,
>
> And gathering freshlier overhead,
>   Rock'd the full-foliaged elms, and swung
>   The heavy-folded rose, and flung
> The lilies to and fro, and said
>
> 'The dawn, the dawn', and died away;
>   And East and West, without a breath,
>   Mixt their dim lights, like life and death,
> To broaden into boundless day.
>
> (XCV)

Some of the poems have an air of conscious pastiche:

> When rosy plumelets tuft the larch,
>   And rarely pipes the mounted thrush . . .
>
> (XCI)

But while all of them show conscious artistry and rely upon musical phrasing, many succeed in conveying powerful impressions of despair, grief, resignation and hope. They are often occasioned by a scene, a visit, a departure, and Tennyson fuses the feeling with the objects that prompt it. It is this which gives the poems merit, rather than any consistent conclusion on the problem with which the poet is beset. For although at times he felt life to be so intolerable that death would be a relief, at others he was filled with dread at the thought that his life would end. *In Memoriam* exhibits his fear and doubt in the way it considers any possibility whatever that might bear on the meaning of death. Although he can occasionally feel that his intuition that he can never die is sufficient, he tries to find evidence to support him in the science which is opposed to intuition. Inevitably, the poem shifts from position to position, and even the introductory stanzas are less expressive of faith in the Christian revelation than a prayer for enlightenment by way of more scientific knowledge of a sort which will permit mind and soul to be reconciled; and this despite the fact that

> We have but faith: we cannot know;
> For knowledge is of things we see . . .
>
> (Introductory stanzas)

Tennyson differs fundamentally from Arnold, whose *Empedocles on Etna* shows that the logical consequence of seeing man to be free, free that is from any natural or divine restriction on his actions, could be to impose upon him an intolerable burden. Arnold went on to consider ways in which men could guide their actions by taking thought on their own nature, and ensuring that all its sides were developed harmoniously. Tennyson, on the other hand, broods upon the ways in which man may develop his nature in conformity with an ideal which has the same inner sanction as the belief that death cannot be the last word and that life is therefore purposive. His ideal conforms to what Nietzsche termed the Aryan myth, as opposed to the Hellenic one of Prometheus, and involves the idea of sin and the repression of some human drives to the end that others may develop. *In Memoriam* illustrates afresh what was implicit in 'The Palace of Art'.

> Arise and fly
> The reeling Faun, the sensual feast;
> Move upward, working out the beast,
> And let the ape and tiger die.
>
> (CXVIII)

> Let him, the wiser man who springs
> Hereafter, up from childhood shape
> His action like the greater ape,
> But I was *born* to other things.
>
> (CXX)

After *In Memoriam* Tennyson becomes more and more concerned with an ideal of conduct which is to raise the spirit of man to its high destiny, and incidentally, more and more critical of lapses from it.

Tennyson was appointed Poet Laureate in 1850. The 'Ode on

the Death of the Duke of Wellington' (1852) was a convenient means not only of gratifying his dislike of France and Louis Napoleon, expressed in a number of poems of this time, but also for praising one who embodied his ideal of selflessness and duty. It illustrates Tennyson's habit of surprising his readers by some new development, this time in composing a splendid occasional poem in the 'Pindaric' form. In *Maud* (1855) he surprised them even more. Here was the Laureate apparently attacking the morality of the nation of shopkeepers through the transparent mask of a frenzied young man whose father had committed suicide on being ruined by his fraudulent partner. (Fraud was also the subject of 'Sea Dreams'.) Gladstone was at a loss to understand why Tennyson should imagine that the Crimean War could be regarded as a means of achieving 'the effectual renovation of society'. Later he came to see that the words of a withdrawn man restored by love to 'oneness with his kind' were not to be attributed to the poet himself; but there are so many poems expressing dislike of the age that it is hard to believe that Tennyson did not have to invent too much. *Maud* is one of Tennyson's most carefully contrived poems, even though built around 'O, that 'twere possible', a lyric composed not long after Hallam's death: and the censorious passage is well fitted to its context. Self-obsession is, Tennyson suggests, a disease which conduces to a particular sensitivity to the inadequacies of society, though sufferers only hug it to themselves and do nothing. The cure comes with action, even if it takes the form it does. The main interest in the poem is, however, the development through an extraordinary range of lyric-forms of changing feelings as scepticism is followed by love, temporary collapse and recovery. *Maud* is something of a *tour de force*, combining the wildness of 'Locksley Hall' with the melancholy of 'Mariana', but also advancing the narrative, setting scenes and suggesting character. It is extravagant, admittedly, and seems more so when particular poems are taken out of context. Nevertheless, it is one of Tennyson's most successful long poems and is his particular representation of the effect upon a susceptible mind of the workings of a society which made money and position its principal concern. Not that realism is the important thing, at least in the usual sense; psychological realism there certainly is. The story part of the poem has its weaknesses from the standpoint of a political criticism, but it served Tennyson well in affording him situations of despair and exaltation which he was specially well-equipped to handle lyrically. It contrasts very forcibly with the narratives of 'Enoch Arden' and 'Aylmer's Field' (1864), which, instead of a first-person, lyric treatment, have the stately march of Tennysonian blank verse, not dissimilar to that used in a specimen translation of the *Iliad* made about the same time. Although the incidents described in both poems are said to have taken place many years before, they are really no less modern and ordinary than those in *Maud*. 'Aylmer's Field', in fact, is more explicitly Victorian in its condemnation of the pride of wealth and family than *Maud*, and the date 1793 which stands at the beginning is clearly meant as an admonishment to the likes of Sir Aylmer who might read the poem in 1864. Both poems have passages which are conventionally Christian in their standpoint, but Tennyson is really appealing for recognition that true nobility may be found at social levels below that which claims that virtue as a right of birth. 'Lady Clara Vere de Vere' anticipates 'Aylmer's Field':

> Kind hearts are more than coronets,
> And simple faith than Norman blood.

'Enoch Arden' surrounds the self-sacrifice of a sailor who finds his wife and family happy with a second (and richer) husband and father with the exalted music appropriate to the heroic poem. Alone and unrecognized, death dawns upon him; but he keeps his counsel.

> For thro' that dawning gleam'd a kindlier hope
> On Enoch thinking 'after I am gone,
> Then may she learn I lov'd her to the last.'

Enoch follows his gleam as faithfully as Ulysses, and the light of the ideal is made to fall upon the simple annals of the poor. The modern ear catches ironies where none were intended, for it will not suffice to transfer a modern tale into the place properly occupied by the heroes of myth. Tennyson was trying to impose his vision upon his characters, instead of entering imaginatively into their lives in the manner of a novelist. Mrs Gaskell had told a very similar story of a returned lover's sacrifice only a year before (in *Sylvia's Lovers*); and a novelist could have handled the action of 'Aylmer's Field' much more convincingly by spending more time on the characterization, and consequently the motivation. Only by turning to dialect could Tennyson honestly represent the very unidealistic attitudes to life of working people, and in a series of poems realize the grim humour and doggedness of real countrymen. How to give practical expression to his idea in regular poems remained a problem to the end of his life.

His most ambitious attempt was *Idylls of the King*, twelve books of a long poem dealing with incidents from the Arthurian cycle. His interest in the legends given such wide currency by Caxton's edition of Sir Thomas Malory's *Morte D'Arthur* is evident from his own 'Morte d'Arthur' of 1842 (adapted to the new poem as 'The Passing of Arthur') and several lyrics. His plan for a long poem on the subject was made as early as 1833, and it seems that he planned to turn it into an allegory of the intellectual tendencies of the nineteenth century. But in the end the poem, parts of which were published separately over the years between 1859 and 1885, had only a 'parabolic drift'; much of it followed the main lines of Malory's account, although, as the title suggests, only selected incidents were given. The love of Lancelot and Guinevere which led to the downfall of the Round Table, and which Malory could yet not feel it in him to condemn, is made by Tennyson the rift within the lute which progressively destroys the harmony upon which the Round Table depends. The Idylls vary considerably in treatment. 'Lancelot and Elaine' is a rapid and plain narrative of the incidents leading up to the death from unrequited love which formed the subject of 'The Lady of Shalott'. But other Idylls depart from this plainness of style and subject in several ways as Tennyson feels that simplicity or grandeur are involved. Simplicity he often renders by an attention to homely detail which makes his characters most unromantically present to the reader's eye, as if they were actors in costume. (G. M. Hopkins called the *Idylls* 'Charades from the Middle Ages'.) The Earl Doorm episode in 'Geraint and Enid' is typical:

> He spoke: the brawny spearman let his cheek
> Bulge with the unswallow'd piece, and turning stared...

Grandeur, on the other hand, is frequently sought in mist and vapour, darkness and glaring lights ('The Coming of Arthur', 'Guinevere', 'The Passing of Arthur').

The sinfulness of Lancelot's relationship with Guinevere is brought home to the reader not only by the encouragement it lends to thoroughly wicked women like Vivien and Ettare and the sorrows of innocent ones like Enid and Elaine, but also by Arthur's reaction once their guilt is known:

I hold that man the worst of public foes
Who either for his own or children's sake,
To save his blood from scandal, lets the wife
Whom he knows false, abide and rule the house: . . .
I cannot take thy hand; that too is flesh,
And in the flesh thou hast sinn'd; and mine own flesh,
Here looking down on thine polluted, cries
'I loathe thee . . .'

('Guinevere')

Although Swinburne may have been wrong to insist that Arthur
himself ought to have been shown as equally guilty of sexual impro-
priety (because the accounts vary), he voiced a feeling shared by
other readers that Tennyson had deliberately removed all tragic
interest from the fatal love of Lancelot and Guinevere. (The same
can be said of his account of Tristan and Isolt.) To make matters
worse, the Dedication speaks of Prince Albert as 'Scarce other than
my king's ideal knight'; and the epilogue to Queen Victoria connects the faith and loyalty, the lack of which led to the last battle in
the West in which Arthur was wounded and conducted out of life,
with the faith and loyalty to the crown on which the imperial
greatness of England depended:

The loyal to their crown
Are loyal to their own far sons, who love
Our ocean-empire with her boundless homes
For ever-broadening England, and her throne
In our vast Orient . . .

The 'parabolic drift' of the poem is certainly not in doubt, for
Tennyson makes plain that Camelot, Arthur and the Round Table
have an ideal and even supernatural status. Yet they are not spiritual
and timeless: they are sometimes very real and substantial, and their
overthrow demands that we think of them as under the dominance
of passing time, of Mutability, the condition of real existence to
which the Victorians were exceptionally sensitive. The resultant
'drift' is therefore accurately termed not allegorical, but parable-
like: and it may strike some readers that the parable really amounts
to an admonition to the nation to remember that 'the old order
changeth, yielding place to new': that if Arthur could refuse tribute
to Rome because it had become weak, others could do the same if
Britain allowed irreverence and disloyalty to sap her faith in herself.

The hints that Arthur is akin to Christ and that the doubtfulness
of his title should not diminish faith in his right to rule suggest that
Tennyson was not unwilling to surround the idea of nationhood

with an aura of holiness. Arthur's disapproval of the quest for the Holy Grail, which Galahad attains only at the cost of never returning to the practical duties of the Round Table, suggests that for the majority true religion is shown more by unity in practical purposes than in the private pursuit of a beatific vision which in the spring-time of Christendom was the highest reward of faith. (Compare the early 'St Simeon Stylites', published in 1842.) The *Idylls*, read symbolically, connect private life with national life; animality, sin, is a threat to the commonweal. It is not difficult to see why Kipling should have received Tennyson's praise as that of a general to a private, nor why in our own century Virginia Woolf and others should have associated him with their suspicion that Proportion has a formidable sister whose name is Conversion. (The pitch at which his fluent blank verse holds the reader in contemplation of the pure and illicit loves of Arthur's court may explain Faulkner's reaction.)

But to bring a charge of jingoism against Tennyson, citing his later poems like 'The Revenge' and 'The Defence of Lucknow', as well as 'Riflemen, Form', 'The Charge of the Light Brigade' and *Maud* as additional evidence, would not really be just. (See Tennyson's own answer in the epilogue to 'The Charge of the Heavy Brigade at Balaclava'.) He is certainly a patriotic poet: the conclusion of *The Princess* illustrates his life-long prejudice against the French. Several of the plays he wrote in the seventies and eighties (*Queen Mary, Harold* and *Beckett*, for example) after completing the bulk of the *Idylls* ('Balin and Balan' had yet to appear, in 1885) deal with English historical subjects. Nevertheless, taking the *Idylls* in conjunction with other late poems, one can see that Tennyson, still beset with doubts and difficulties over religious faith, was attempting in the *Idylls* to associate religion and the aspirations of society in such a way that each supported the other. His idealism could not rest in either alone since his doubts, if not about the existence of a divine power, then about its proper claims upon its believers, were still great, and what he saw of the reality of English life filled him with deep concern. His last volumes of poems (*The Holy Grail and Other Poems*, 1869; *Ballads and Other Poems*, 1880; *Tiresias and Other Poems*, 1885; *Locksley Hall Sixty Years After, etc.*, 1886; *Demeter and Other Poems*, 1889; *The Death of Oenone, Akbar's Dream and Other Poems*, 1892), varied as they are, contain a good number dealing with religious faith and with social conditions: some are full of foreboding, like the epilogue to the *Idylls*.

'The Higher Pantheism' (1869), read at the first meeting of the Metaphysical Society, has a ring of desperation about it, its ugly rhythms and trite sentiment fully meriting Swinburne's parody. 'Lucretius' (1863), a return to the dramatic monologue, is inferior to the early ones, but like 'Tiresias' (1885) and 'Demeter and Persephone' (1889), is an example of the skill with which the old poet could combine scholarship with his own leading ideas. 'Lucretius', though careful in its use of Epicurean doctrine, makes the erotic fantasies of the Roman poet express something of Tennyson's own strong belief in the reality of sin, its association with the animal part of man's nature, and the need of faith to overcome it. 'Tiresias' is an obvious counterpart to Tennyson's view of himself as a prophet earnestly trying to persuade men to a life of self-sacrifice in the interest of national survival. 'The Ancient Sage' (1885) expresses Tennyson's own religious doctrine in the person of Lao-tse. It shows, as does 'The Higher Pantheism', into how simple a form that doctrine had developed (or declined) since *In Memoriam*. Comparisons have been made between *In Memoriam* and the Christian existentialism of Kierkegaard, and between 'The Higher Pantheism' and the neo-Platonism of Plotinus: some resemblance between his belief and German transcendentalism certainly exists, but 'The Ancient Sage' shares Tennyson's faith that we have within us occasional gleams from the wholly spiritual world, or the Nameless: the physical world in time is but a shadow. This intuition is what Tennyson had always fallen back on and no other source for it is really necessary. In 'The Ancient Sage' it is asserted confidently, even jubilantly; and the young sybarite who feels that all is vanity is advised to

> leave the hot swamp of voluptuousness
> A cloud between the Nameless and thyself
> And lay thine uphill shoulder to the wheel . . .

But another late poem, 'Vastness' (1889), tells a very different story –

> What the philosophies, all the sciences, poesy, varying voices of prayer?
> All that is noblest, all that is basest, all that is filthy with all that is fair?
> What is it all, if we all of us end but in being our own corpse-coffins at
> last,
> Swallow'd in Vastness, lost in Silence, drown'd in the deeps of a
> meaningless Past?

The faith that death is not final is uttered in a single faint line at the end. 'Locksley Hall Sixty Years After' (1886) is equally despondent: although it is a dramatic monologue, it must surely register some part of Tennyson's own conviction that there is very little reason to think that the best is yet to be. Progress is now only to be feared: science has no charms for a people who have lost the sense of wonder with which their grandfathers greeted its successes of sixty years before. The poem is as rhetorical as its predecessor and is not likely to win its way by its charm of numbers, but detestation of mass-building, the popular press and lying politicians is put across with crude effectiveness. Other poems in the late volumes show Tennyson's sense of the cruelty and indifference of much that men say and do ('Rizpah', 'Romney's Remorse', 'Despair', 'St Telemachus', 'The Dead Prophet').

Not everything in the last volumes is gloomy. Poems like 'To Vergil', and 'Frater Ave atque Vale' (in memory of his poet-brother, Charles) are free from the chill recollection that art and life are both brief, now that astronomy and geology have become 'terrible muses' ('Parnassus'). There is room for humour and hope – and finally for the poem 'Crossing the Bar', which so faithfully represents the conclusion of Tennyson's struggle to achieve a faith that would conquer death.

Tennyson's verses 'To E. FitzGerald' were meant to accompany the poem 'Tiresias' as a gift to commemorate his friend's seventy-fifth birthday: but as the 'postscript' says, they never met FitzGerald's eyes, for the poet of the 'golden Eastern lay' died on 14 June 1883, nine months before the birthday in question. It is very probable that if he had lived, FitzGerald would have been embarrassed by them, although Tennyson had been his friend since 1835 at least. It is not simply that FitzGerald was averse to his personal life being made public, as Tennyson, like some other Victorians, was (see his poems 'To——, after reading a Life and Letters' and 'The Dead Prophet'). The recollections included in the complimentary lines of 'old Fitz' surrounded – and surmounted – by pigeons as he sat in the garden of his house called Little Grange outside Woodbridge, Suffolk, of his spare diet and Tennyson's one-time trial of it and its consequences, of the admiration his *Rubáiyát of Omar Khayyám* had earned 'from our best/In modern letters', all these are innocent enough and are as charmingly expressed as any of the occasional verses in which Tennyson is so effective. Rather it is that Edward FitzGerald was singularly averse to putting himself forward as a poet or writer worthy of the sort of esteem which he thought belonged to original artists. Throughout his whole literary life he was utterly self-effacing. It was only by chance that his authorship of the *Rubáiyát* became known. Tennyson had something of this, too (*In Memoriam* was first published anonymously), but it is entirely characteristic of FitzGerald that he should have heaped praise upon Tennyson in his 'Euphranor', and have persuaded him to publish again in 1842, after a virtual silence of ten years: while he, for his part, though ready to print at his own expense, and glad to have the praise of friends and well-wishers, consistently avoided the limelight, refusing to allow any 'puffing' by his 'publisher', Quaritch, and even keeping his name from the title-page of all his works save the *Six Dramas of Calderon Freely Translated*.

Tennyson's verse-letter throws light upon both men. It is entirely characteristic, for instance, that Tennyson should take the occasion of FitzGerald's death to speak again of his preoccupation with personal survival, his trust that death was not the 'deeper night':

> The deeper night? A clearer day
> Than our poor twilight dawn on earth –
> If night, what barren toil to be!
> What life, so maim'd by night, were worth
> Our living out? Not mine to me
> Remembering all the golden hours
> Now silent, and so many dead,
> And him the last.

It reveals, too, that Tennyson knew why FitzGerald would not in all likelihood approve the gift of 'Tiresias', an old poem in MS especially refurbished to serve the occasion; but only accept it

> Less for its own than for the sake
> Of one recalling gracious times,
> When, in our younger London days,
> You found some merit in my rhymes,
> And I more pleasure in your praise.

In the postscript he tells us that

> I fancied that my friend
> For this brief idyll would require
> A less diffuse and opulent end,
> And would defend his judgement well,
> If I should deem it over nice ...

Even before the 'younger London days' FitzGerald had shown signs of restiveness before Tennyson's diffuseness and opulence – both men were extraordinarily consistent through their lives. Of four stanzas (later deleted) which introduced 'A Dream of Fair Women' he wrote in 1833: 'This is in his best style: no fretful epithet, nor a word too much.' Later that year he mentions that Tennyson 'is chiefly meditating on the purging and subliming of what he has already done, and repents that he has published at all yet. It is fine to see how in each succeeding poem the smaller ornaments and fancies drop away, and leave the grand ideas single.' But even when the 1842 volumes appeared, FitzGerald saw much of 'his great fault of being too full and complicated', and wished he had published the new work separately. 'The other will drag it down.' Still, 'with all his faults' (and he was equally severe on another thing he thought Tennyson had no talent for, namely, trifling and badinage), 'he will publish such a volume as has not been published since the time of Keats: and which, once published, will never be suffered to die.' He thought it 'The last of old Alfred's best': believing that criticism between friends should be above all things critical, he found objection to much of the work published after 1842, save perhaps for *Maud*, which though in the vein of Browning, was far superior to that poet's detestable productions in the 'gurgoyle' manner. *In Memoriam*, though full of the finest things is, he thought, 'monotonous, and has the air of being evolved by a Poetical Machine of the highest order.' He thought the *Idylls* 'pure, noble and holy', but it was the dialect poem 'Northern Farmer: New Style' with its coarse yet humorous portrayal of human self-interest which moved him. These were FitzGerald's 'crotchets', but they seem less eccentric today.

Towards the end of his life many people thought him eccentric, and in the matter of his dress he may have been. All his life he had an assured income, for although he was the seventh child (among eight), his family, which descended on his mother's side from the fourth Earl of Kildare, was wealthy. From the age of nine Edward, born Purcell, bore his mother's name. At the university, or soon after, he adopted the plain style of living Tennyson refers to. He offered financial assistance to both Thackeray and Tennyson, the last of whom in the forties suffered that eternal want of pence that the son of a disinherited Lincolnshire rector might expect to enjoy, particularly if he took up no occupation other than writing poetry. FitzGerald avoided the extravagant way of life between Brighton and Portland Place which his mother found natural to her aristocratic taste. Although he visited London frequently and stayed with friends a good deal, he spent most of his life in various lodgings at no great distance from his birthplace, near Woodbridge in Suffolk: only for the last nine years of his life had he a permanent home of his own. He studied the ways and speech of countrymen and seamen, and avoided the gentry. It is not surprising that a man of such tastes should prefer his friend's Lincolnshire farmer to his Round Table, and should attribute his decline from poignant lyric into ideal 'epic' to wealth, adulation, a wife, lack of occupation and separation from common life at one or other of his retreats at Farringford or Aldworth.

FitzGerald regarded himself not as a genius like Tennyson, but as a man of taste, one who lived by cultivated feelings which found their gratification in friendship, music, painting – and literature, not much of which was appearing in modern times. He was decidedly not a recluse. When his friends (and among them he counted Thackeray and Carlyle) could not be in his company, he wrote letters which served as substitutes for conversation: and he was sometimes fearful that his friends, when they met him again, would find the real thing inferior to the surrogate. His letters form a valuable part of his production. Nor was he a scholar, in the narrow sense. In his extensive reading his attitude can perhaps be best described as that of a gentleman; he read to please his own taste. He was deeply suspicious of German aesthetics, because he thought books ought to serve right thinking and acting. He kept a commonplace book, and in it noted good things read and heard alike, though when he came to publish his *Polonius: A Collection of Wise Saws and Modern Instances* (1852) he could not always identify the quotations. His *Euphranor: A Dialogue on Youth* (1851, revised 1855 and 1882) gives an excellent impression of his mind: it pictures young men at their pleasures in Cambridge, and thereby distils the doctrine that the aim of education should be to breed men of sense, taught to be practical and energetic as well as sufficiently read in books to be able to carry on good conversation. FitzGerald carried this spirit into his reading. Like Dr Johnson, he did not always care to read a book through; if parts of it were flat or redundant, he would (literally) cut them out, thus reducing the call on shelf-space, doubtless a convenience to so unsettled a man. His reading in ancient authors did not cease after his time up at Cambridge. He read enthusiastically wherever the fancy took him – and eventually it took him outside Greek and Latin and into Italian, German, Spanish and Persian. He made, and had printed, his own translations of the *Agamemnon* (1869), a conflation of the Oedipus plays (1880, 1881), and published translations of six plays of Calderon (1853): two more were privately printed in 1865.

In all this work he sought to do for others what he regularly did for himself – to transfuse the spirit of the original. His *Agamemnon* – a 'per-version', as he called it, a tragedy 'taken from Aeschylus' – attempted to free the drama from all that impeded its 'accelerating interest from beginning to end', and to 'make the Poet free of the language which reigns over that half of the world never dreamt of in his philosophy'. He was under no delusion that such a taste could be truly achieved by other than 'some Poet, worthy of that name, and of congenial Genius with the Greek.' He felt that meantime he could best introduce an English reader to the play by what Dryden called 'metaphrase', that is, by transfusing its soul at the expense of the exact form of its body. So, he confesses, he used great licence only that he might be more faithful.

It is entirely characteristic of FitzGerald that he should have had printed a retrenched version of Crabbe's *Tales of the Hall*, the most genial of that poet's verse-tales, in which he saw qualities akin to Jane Austen's, and that he had it in mind to publish an edition of Dryden's Prefaces. He delighted in the thews and sinews of the language, in humour and good sense: Tennyson was almost certainly right in his rueful anticipations about the reception 'the diffuse and opulent end' of his 'Tiresias' would have had.

FitzGerald is known today principally for his *Rubáiyát of Omar Khayyám*, although he himself preferred his version of *Salámán and Absál, An Allegory, Translated from the Persian of Jámí*. (His other translation from Persian, Attar's *Mantik uttair*, entitled *The Bird Parliament*, was not published in his lifetime. Like *Salámán*, it was written before the *Rubáiyát*.) The *Rubáiyát*, or quatrains, of FitzGerald's *Omar* are commonly thought of as exotic, but the unaffectedness of the language (and the humour) should not be lost sight of:

> Ah, make the most of what we yet may spend,
> Before we too into the Dust descend;
> Dust into Dust, and under Dust to lie
> Sans Wine, sans Song, sans Singer, and – sans End!

Of course, the allusions to tavern and temple, to 'Kaikobád the Great, or Kaikhosrú' and the rest, not to speak of the close-gathered stanza with its triple, occasionally quadruple, rhymes in imitation of the original, do cast a powerful Eastern spell, just as the

Bible occasionally does: the stanzas on the Potter and the pot have obvious biblical associations not likely to be lost on Victorian readers, and certainly not on Browning (whose 'Rabbi Ben Ezra' has the same metaphor, used in a contrary sense). Although nominally a translation, it is really an English poem in its own right, and could nowadays be quite aptly called an 'imitation' in Robert Lowell's sense. It made a great impression on Ruskin (who addressed a letter to its anonymous author, begging for more, which took ten years to reach him), on Rossetti and Swinburne (who bought the brown-paper wrapped copies from a remainder-box) and on the many others who bought the next three editions.

The first edition has only 75 quatrains, while the fourth has 101, which is nine less than the second. Between 1859 and 1879, between the first and fourth editions, FitzGerald made considerable changes in the wording of the stanzas, and in the order in which they occur. This alone would suffice to show that he followed his usual practice of allowing himself considerable freedom on his adaptation of the originals, which consisted of an MS in the Bodleian Library, a copy sent him by his friend and mentor, E. B. Cowell, from Calcutta, and for the second edition (1868) an edition published in Paris in 1867 by J. B. Nicholas. He omitted many amatory and vinous stanzas, 'mashed' others together, and gave a sort of progression, imperfect though it is, from morning to evening. It is therefore vain to charge him with inaccuracy. He *was* an amateur and he did make mistakes, but the translations which have followed his achieve what interest they have because they throw light on FitzGerald's poem. By that light one sees that he is surprisingly close to many of the original quatrains, yet has managed to replace their abruptness by lines which, with a few exceptions in which the syntax is tortured, run very easily. The phrasing is carefully managed to bring pauses *within* the lines. This avoids the monotony which end-stopped lines with recurring rhymes are prone to suffer from, and strengthens the impression of a speaking voice which the colloquialisms supply. Really, the *Rubáiyát* is a dramatic monologue, and its swerves in thought or 'argument' both serve and are served by the metre. (FitzGerald's metrical skill is also evident in *The Bird Parliament*, which shows a command of the eighteenth-century manner in the heroic couplet.) Some inversions and archaisms occur, but they contribute to the impression of antiquity, while the imagery is as Persian as anyone could wish, even though FitzGerald did not care to mention a leg of mutton among the sufficiencies of life in stanza XII (Fourth edition).

FitzGerald's poem achieved its success because it appealed to a public perplexed in the extreme by the constantly-debated problems of faith and conduct which deepened every year after 1859 (in which *The Origin of the Species* was also published). FitzGerald himself had passed through a period of religious doubt and felt the power of modern science (particularly geology) to throw down old beliefs. He was quite aware of the 'wickedness' of the *Rubáiyát* (even *Fraser's Magazine* would not publish the least 'wicked' of them), but believed Omar's doubts to be shared by most reflective people in his day, even if, like him, they were still Christians. 'Omar' does not question the existence of God, only his inscrutability and his neglect of man's urgent need of illumination: so he remonstrates, appeals, even chides. He does not follow his own recommendation to leave thought about life and death alone, and his resort to the pleasure of the moment does not derive from natural sensuality but from bafflement of the intellect. Still, the poem does look forward to Pater and Swinburne; yet the enthusiasm for the poem in the nineties does not alter the fact that it offers very little in the way of self-indulgent delights, and from a present-day standpoint compares more interestingly with Tennyson, Arnold and Browning than with, say, the early Yeats, Dowson or Wilde. Its humour and lightness of touch in dealing with such serious issues contrasts strikingly with the later work of Tennyson, whose poem 'The Ancient Sage', with its emphasis on sin, individual experience, private intuition and renunciation, shows another sort of response to the decline of Christian faith.

13

THE BROWNINGS

Isobel Armstrong

The Brownings were eccentrics, both in their art and in their personal lives. Their marriage has come to seem one of the most romantic happenings of mid-Victorian literary life and yet it was remarkable for its oddity: it was the marriage, at forty, of an aggressive blue-stocking and pampered gentleman's daughter – egocentric, prejudiced, perceptive and clever – to a rather raw and unsuccessful poet some years younger than herself and socially very much her inferior. Robert Browning was the son of a bank clerk, of respectable but humble origin. He had become involved with the radical politics and Unitarian thinking of W. J. Fox (whom he once called his literary godfather) and his circle, had then moved into the theatrical world (thus making his social position more dubious than ever), writing plays which were not popular successes, even if they were not quite complete artistic failures. It was a rakish affair, indeed, and one can only admire the resilience and adventurousness of this pair as they freed one another. Elizabeth Barrett escaped from the restrictions of an oppressive father and an at least partly self-induced neurotic sickness; Browning escaped from the narrowness of life as the only son of unwisely admiring parents. Both of them, though late in life, made a bid for an existence which was emotionally mature and productive. But in order to achieve this they chose the difficult life of the exile or the expatriate, in virtually permanent residence in Italy, creating for themselves the conditions in which artistic eccentricity could thrive because they were necessarily cut off from the language, the social pressures and commitments of their country and therefore of the readers for whom they continued to write. Neither became a European writer – although Mrs Browning, in unread poems such as *Casa Guidi Windows*, perhaps attempted to be one; and yet neither is as central to Victorian culture as, say, Carlyle or Tennyson. The dangers of this lack of involvement are beautifully suggested by Mrs Browning in *Aurora Leigh* in a passage which says a good deal about the strange dissociation of living in a foreign land; the freedom and the alienation is expressed here:

> It's sublime,
> This perfect solitude of foreign lands!
> To be, as if you had not been till then,
> And were then, simply that you chose to be:
> To spring up, not be brought forth from the ground,
> Like grasshoppers from Athens, and skip thrice
> Before a woman makes a pounce on you
> And plants you in her hair! – possess, yourself,
> A new world all alive with creatures new,
> New sun, new moon, new flowers, new people – ah,
> And be possessed by none of them! no right
> In one, to call your name inquire your where . . .
> – Such most surprising riddance of one's life
> Comes next one's death; it's disembodiment
> Without the pang.

This 'riddance' of English life in 1846 had by far the greatest effect on the poetry of Robert Browning. It could be said that exile encouraged that eccentricity and waywardness of language to be found in his early work. The idiosyncratic freedom and independence of Browning's very sophisticated poetic experiments creates special difficulties for a critic; it is difficult to discover a central project in his work or any driving preoccupations. It seems all Gothic frolic with minor historical figures, the poetry of an antiquarian with surprising streaks of energy, violence and intellectual sophistication. What trajectory can one discover among such diverse works as a poem about a medieval quack philosopher (*Paracelsus*, 1835), or about an extremely minor poet caught up in the political struggles of pre-Dantean Italy (*Sordello*, 1840), a series of plays which are anything from the austere studies in political loyalty in *Strafford* (1837) to the overheated love-story unexpectedly embodied in a play with all the conventions of Victorian melodrama (*A Blot in the Scutcheon*, 1843), monologues spoken by mad dukes, Italian Renaissance painters, characters from Shakespeare and biblical characters? *Men and Women* (1855), written in Italy, makes great demands on its readers.

Though there are now signs that the work of deconstruction and of feminist and Marxist criticism is changing the nature of Browning criticism in a very productive way, it is still common to find the nineteenth-century descriptions and categories evolved to discuss Browning's poetry in critical use. It is still hard to get away from 'philosophy' and Browning's fascination with a sort of metaphysical tetrad – Love, Art, Beauty, Evil, categories which can be traced back to such works as Mrs Sutherland Orr's *Handbook* to the poetry of Browning. Her study was admirable in its day, but the rigorous concentration on prose meaning makes the fact that Browning wrote poetry almost irrelevant. Again, we use Browning's own categories, subjective and objective poetry, which he introduced in his essay on Shelley. Or again, we talk about Browning's dramatic power and psychological insight as if they were the most important things about his poetry, while it is arguable that Browning was often remarkably deficient in both. In any case, such an approach ignores the shading of the monologues from dramatic particularity to straightforward philosophical debate to the expression of undaunted, impersonal lyric feeling and throws a misleading emphasis on the lyrics and love poems as dramatic expressions of feeling.

It is arguable, however, that the break with England gave both Brownings their opportunity. It gave them a detachment and freedom from their culture which enabled them to mount a critique of it, though in very different ways. The great poems of 1855 in *Men and Woman*, and *Aurora Leigh* (1856) would not perhaps have emerged in the form they took without the 'riddance' of English life, and this exile provides the terms in which to understand both poets. The difficulties of Browning's poetry in particular become clearer. The cultural critique mounted by the poets is more immediately evident in the work of Elizabeth Barrett Browning. An account of some of the ambitious elements in her poem, *Aurora Leigh*, indicates the experimental nature of her work and helps one to understand the unconventional nature of both poets' writings.

Aurora Leigh is a strange blend of open-mindedness and thoroughly reactionary thinking. It bears the mark of Elizabeth Barrett Browning's daring, learnedness, outspoken intelligence – and some of her prejudices. Its verse is sometimes prolix and slack, but it is a quite remarkable work. It was a deliberately experimental poem, a novel in verse, a novel which might be described as the first consciously feminist novel because it is explicit about the needs of women and antagonistic to male assertiveness ('How arrogant men are!'), even though Elizabeth Barrett Browning was not sympathetic to politically organized women's protests. Aurora Leigh is a poetess, brought up by her aunt after her father's death in Italy. She falls in love with her cousin Romney but will not marry him, partly because she does not wish to be economically beholden to him and partly because of his reforming political beliefs, which she considers cold and abstract – he 'lives by diagrams'. Romney decides to marry a poor girl for ideological reasons. Marion Erle, however, is abducted and raped. Aurora finds her and her child in Italy and cares for them. She is finally reconciled with Romney when his social experiments with the poor have failed. He has become blind and the poem ends with their union after Marion Erle has refused to marry Romney, recognizing that he wished to marry her for abstract reasons.

Some of Elizabeth Barrett Browning's prejudices are manifested in Aurora's disgust with the poor and her firm belief that mechanical political reform is irrelevant to social problems. However, these prejudices are narrated as a retrospect, for the poem does not move into the present until the beginning of its third book, and it is arguable that they are the product of Aurora's young aggression and immaturity. For the heroine of the poem is not a pleasant person – often aggressive, violently opinionated and insensitive. It testifies to Elizabeth Barrett Browning's refusal of convention that she does not make Aurora a 'womanly' woman. The assertive voice of the poem becomes a way of refusing orthodox feminine roles. Aurora is a fiercely critical intellectual. Her struggle to find a voice as a city poet and her attack on the appropriation of poetry by male writers are aspects of a determined independence.

But the remarkable quality of the poem is not so much the creation of an assertive heroine as its recognition that women are entangled in notions of property and possession which are fundamentally economic. Aurora's struggle for financial independence is paralleled with that of Marion Erle, who is far more deeply subject to economic tyranny. From the very first, when her mother attempts to sell her to a potential seducer, her powerlessness and her role as object is understood. The epitome of powerlessness is the rape, and here Elizabeth Barrett Browning is bold, for in her subsequent description of this trauma Marion Erle speaks of herself metaphorically as a sacrificial figure on analogy with the crucified Christ. But the parallel takes an unexpected turn. The rape is a virtual death after which she is thrown into the pit like a corpse.

> – then they leave it in the pit,
> To sleep and find corruption, cheek to cheek
> With him who stinks since Friday.

> (VI. 1196–8)

'With him who stinks since Friday' is repeated vehemently, with the clear implication that the stinking corpse is the dead unrisen Christ who does not rise but putrefies, as a dead Christian religion putrefies in the society which creates the conditions for Marion's rape. In her wanderings she throws away the image of the Virgin Mary hung round her neck by villagers in protection as a useless weight.

> How heavy it seemed: as heavy as a stone;
> A woman has been strangled with less weight.
>
> (VI. 1256–7)

For Marion 'man's violence,/Nor man's seduction, made me what I am'. In this context it is the woman who is the Christ figure.

Throughout the poem there are meditations on the possibilities for action on the part of women in a world where they are not free to determine their lives. Aurora's mother is painted after her death, and Aurora describes the hauntingly ambiguous portrait in terms of the contradictory stereotypes assigned to women – Muse, Psyche, Medusa, the Virgin, Lamia. The portrait

> was by turns
> Ghost, fiend, and angel, fairy, witch, and sprite,
> A dauntless Muse who eyes a dreadful Fate,
> A loving Psyche who loses sight of Love,
> A still Medusa with mild milky brows
> All curdled and all clothed upon with snakes
> Whose slime falls fast as sweat will; or anon
> Our Lady of the Passion, stabbed with Swords
> Where the Babe sucked; or Lamia in her first
> Moonlighted pallor, ere she shrunk and blinked
> And shuddering wriggled down to the unclean.
>
> (I. 153–63)

These varying images of woman recur in the poem, tested out in different contexts in order to explore and analyse contemporary myths.

It is to be expected that Browning's far less popular *Men and Women*, published a year before *Aurora Leigh*, would have some relation to its concerns. The relationship is not immediately apparent, however, and to understand it it is necessary to go back to the start of his career.

His first poem, *Pauline*, was published in 1833 and reviewed in the same year by W. J. Fox, the only critic who took any notice of it, in the Unitarian journal he edited at that time, the *Monthly*

Repository. Browning published several early poems in this periodical, in particular 'Johannes Agricola' and 'Porphyria's Lover' in 1836, the first experimental dramatic monologues he wrote. Browning's association with this periodical is important, for the *Monthly Repository* was the most radical middle-class journal in existence then, both in its politics and religious views. Fox advocated fundamental political reform and the redistribution of wealth, a changed political and intellectual status for women, a new aesthetics which would evolve a democratic poetry (he published the working-class poet, Ebenezer Elliot, in his pages), and introduced reviews of the German Higher Criticism which was investigating the historical authenticity of the Bible and exploring new accounts of hermeneutics and the interpretative process. Even to read the *Monthly Repository* today is to be surprised by its *avant garde* views. Browning was in possession of advanced ideas which percolated to British intellectuals only gradually in the 1840s and 1850s.

Browning did not exploit the possibilities of what critics call the dramatic monologue (but which he tended to call the 'dramatic lyric') until he went to Italy. His early poems were a series of huge metaphysical, philosophical and historical constructions. They are brilliant and underrated, but the two *Monthly Repository* monologues pre-figure the forms he finally adopted. 'Porphyria's Lover' indicates how he was experimenting and in what way the dramatic monologue becomes vital to his broad aesthetic, intellectual and political projects.

'Porphyria's Lover' is the utterance of obsession with a sinisterly neat, enclosing rhyme-scheme which is not immediately apparent in the poem's flow. Porphyria visits the speaker, emerging out of a stormy landscape which reflects the lover's emotional mood of bitterness and despair into an enclosed room. The pair are in the situation of the lovers in Keats's *The Eve of St Agnes*, a poem which echoes the pattern of *Romeo and Juliet*, except that the roles of Porphyria and Madeline are reversed, and Porphyria seduces the lover. The end is murder. Porphyria is strangled with her own golden hair and the lover makes love to the corpse as Porphyria has made love to him. The final lines are a shock. The lover remarks that he has not moved all night 'And yet God has not said a word!' The reader realizes that the poem is not the description of immediate events but a narrative in the speaker's mind.

Why this strangely deviant and macabre interest in the psychology of insanity and sexual murder? The lover's will to possession – 'That moment she was mine, mine, fair,/Perfectly pure and good' – and his belief in an omniscient God of law seems like an expression of aberrant psychology for its own sake. It is when we turn this expressive psychology around and scrutinize it not as subjective feeling but as the object of analysis that the strategies of the dramatic lyric and their importance become clear. The extremity of the feeling forces this act of analysis upon the poem, which is subjective feeling and externalized objective experience simultaneously. Fox had argued in the _Monthly Repository_ that drama was the true democratic form because its external nature enabled free interpretative thought to play round action. If that logic is pursued here, understanding beyond the reach of the poem's speaker begins to emerge. The initial landscape is seized by human violence which forces it to correspond with its mood. The woman is seen in terms of property, breaking one legal tie to be overwhelmed by the urge for possession. As the dead body is itemized, Porphyria becomes 'it' to the speaker and the speaker 'its love', the love belonging to Porphyria and the love possessing her. A legal God is the logical consequence of these ideas of property. The terrible privacy of fantasy reconstructs the social order in a disturbed and distorted form. It is no consolation that this may be fantasy – and we are in doubt about this to the end – for it represents the murderous impulses inherent in society's own fictions. Brilliantly, Browning establishes a political base to a diseased romanticism through the strategy of the monologue form.

The virtuosity of this form was often disguised from his contemporaries, who saw his poetry as the product of an uncontrolled and subversive mind. A perceptive remark by Matthew Arnold, perceptive because it was written in 1848, well before Browning had produced the poems most people regard as typical of him, suggests what kind of poet he seemed to be. Comparing him with Keats, Arnold puts Browning firmly in the mainstream of Romantic poetry:

As Browning is a man with a moderate gift passionately desiring movement and fulness, and obtaining but a confused multitudinousness, so Keats with a very high gift is yet also consumed by this desire . . . neither understand that they must begin with an Idea of the world in order not to be prevailed over by the world's multitudinousness.

(_Letters . . . to Arthur Hugh Clough_, ed. H. F. Lowry, 1932, p 97)

Arnold's remark, I suspect with more insight than he knew, suggests so much that is true – the greedy, swamping physicality of

Browning's poetry and the lava-like quality of the language and structure of the poems. But he did not see the intellectual or philosophical stresses and distresses behind Browning's work or its political implications. For Browning began life as a Romantic poet with aesthetic, political and philosophical preoccupations similar in kind to those of the earlier Romantics before him, passionately desiring the world's multitudinousness indeed, but passionately believing also in the possibility of discovering a *unifying* Idea of the world. He wrote three poems before 1840 in this high Romantic mode, diffuse and confused indeed, but two of which (*Pauline* (1833) and *Sordello* (1840)) compare favourably with the mature work of Keats and Shelley. What follows is a gradual retreat from Romantic form and Romantic philosophy, and the rest of Browning's poetry is a toughly ardent criticism of high Romantic politics and idealism, particularly of Romantic views of freedom, the imagination, and the belief in feeling as a necessarily energizing power. A high Romantic optimism gives way to a guarded and occasionally raucously ironical scepticism. What Arnold does not suggest is Browning's self-consciousness, for he eventually explored experience in terms of the mind's self-enclosed *fictions*, as he had begun to do in 'Porphyria's Lover'. To '*begin*' with an 'Idea of the world' would have been anathema to him. In fact, what Browning does in his post-Romantic phase is to find more and more precise ways of expressing the psychological perplexities of the *pursuit* of order and meaning amid the moving fullness of the world's multitudinousness. There is no nihilistic acceptance of chaos in his poetry, as some people have claimed, but he proclaims no discoveries. Abt Vogler's momentary discovery of harmony and unity is the most provisional and fleeting of orders, created as it is out of extemporized notes. Browning's palace of sound is evanescent and fragments almost as soon as it is created. The pleasure domes of the unifying imagination in *Kubla Khan* are positively solid by comparison with it.

In the poems written after his departure to Italy in 1846 Browning can be seen restricting and delimiting the areas of experience explored in his poems. The huge, inclusive metaphysical constructs of the earlier work disappear and everything he wrote was on a smaller scale and took a wayward and eccentric form – lyrics so fragmented by fits and starts and spurts of feeling that they seem to break apart, monologues embodying strange situations and full of obliquities of meaning. Yet such poems as 'By the Fire-side', 'Childe Roland', 'Andrea Del Sarto' and 'Fra Lippo Lippi' are

Browning's major work and they constitute the critique of contemporary culture which was being made concurrently by his wife.
The restriction of his material is a way of concentrating and
clarifying his meaning; the eccentric form is actually a liberation, a
way of exposing values by testing them out in extreme and curious
contexts. In this account of Browning's work I shall discuss mainly
the achievement of *Men and Women* (1855). But in order better to
place these achievements it is necessary to look briefly at *Pauline*
and that transitional drama, *Pippa Passes* (1841).

Browning's early poems have dark elements, obsessed as they are
with disintegration, betrayal, guilt and failure, but they attempt to
offer a positive Idea of the world in the face of these things, an Idea
which is seen as applicable to the life of the whole society. *Pauline*,
discovering as it does the imagery of schizophrenia, is best called an
expressionist poem, Browning's *Erwartung*. It is a study of disintegration. The speaker describes an orgiastic grasping of experience, physical, emotional and intellectual, without any attempt
to establish a creative order. He is simply invaded by the world's
multitudinousness and all experience takes on a destructive life of
its own – 'I seemed the fate from which I fled':

> I am made up of an intensest life,
> Of a most clear idea of consciousness
> Of self...
> And to a principle of restlessness
> Which would be all, have, see, know, taste, feel, all –
> This is myself.

The speaker emerges whole, with his utopian beliefs in freedom
and perfectibility almost unscathed.

> Sun-treader, I believe in God and truth
> And love.

This is an address to Shelley and in it Browning reaffirms all his
hopes of 'perfecting mankind', hopes abandoned in the earlier part
of the poem. Browning's early passion for Shelley, whose beliefs he
interpreted in the most optimistic way and whose vegetarianism and
atheism he embraced with enthusiasm, manifests itself in this poem.
But *Pauline* is still swamped in its own subjectivity. Despite its
efforts to analyse the boundless possibilities of 'the unshaped images which lie/Within my mind's cave'. The complexity and subtlety of psychological processes, processes which he later objectified
and tried to build into the very structure of his poems, overwhelm
Browning here.

With *Paracelsus* and *Sordello* the attempt to convey the world's multitudinousness is made on a grander and grander scale so that with *Sordello* it includes the political and artistic life of a whole society, virtually of a whole culture. And yet as the scale becomes larger, there is an increasing recognition of randomness and disorder in all our affairs and of the difficulties of seeing the world as a meaningful whole.

A poem in dramatic form, *Pippa Passes* (1841), is Browning's last attempt to explore the problems of meaningful order and action on a large scale directly in terms of politics and teleology. Pippa, the poor factory girl, moves past four tenuously related groups of people more privileged than she at crucial moments of moral decision and seemingly affects the course of their lives by her lyrical songs. She breaks into the stagey eroticism of Ottima and Sebald who have murdered Ottima's husband only to find that they are freed neither from hate ('Now he is dead I hate him worse') nor from the growing staleness of their relations with one another, into the deliberations of the artist, Jules, who has been tricked into marrying the daughter of a prostitute, into those of the would-be political assassin, into the conversation of prostitutes, into a scheme for her own moral corruption being concocted by a servant of the Monsignor. The incidents seem arbitrarily chosen and randomly put together, the disorganized product of Browning's imagination overflowing as a froth of poetry and prose, much as Pippa describes the sun boiling over and spurting its light into the new day at the beginning of the poem. But here is the world's (or society's) multitudinousness. The public and private – love and art, church and state – are inextricable from one another. The 'formless' structure seems to be deliberate, for it asks the question of the poem: *is* there order, *is* there consequential pattern, in human actions? How meaningfully does Pippa impinge upon the decisions of others, and how far can we assent to her own conviction of preordained pattern and determined action? – 'With God, whose puppets, best and worst,/Are we'. Can we indeed derive an Idea of the world from the scattered events of the poem? The answers are left ambiguous and complex. Pippa is exploited, though she believes she is free. No one is aware of her as a hidden factor in their lives, and it is arguable that her song simply pushes people further towards exploiting one another. Pippa's song pushes Sebald into action but it does not alter his egocentric longing for purity, his desire to be free of the *guilt* of his crime rather than the crime itself; Jules decides to marry Phene but only because he decides to treat her like one of his own sculptures and he retreats into isolation and into the sterile freedom of his own idealized art. Every character acts on an intuitive response to Pippa's songs, but in every episode the quality of the feeling behind the impulse is suspect. The certainties have disappeared.

After the philosophical strenuousness of the early poetry it could look as if Browning simply gave up in his later work and accepted the arbitrary chaos of the world's multitudinousness, celebrating the life of feeling and impulse, the extreme of randomness. Not so. In the lyrics written after his departure for Italy Browning evolved a form and a language which could enact a haunting, exasperated pursuit of pattern and meaning. In the monologues he found a form where he could explore the human need to create and rehearse an image of the world and of the self, the need to create fictions. Direct treatment of political and social issues and institutions disappears, though a political and cultural critique is there indirectly through the structure and content of the monologue. It is the first two episodes of *Pippa* which carry over into Browning's later poetry. In the Ottima and Sebald episode we recognize the macabre, over-loaded feeling of poems such as 'The Laboratory' (1844) or 'In a Gondola' (1842) or the emotions of Guido in *The Ring and the Book*. The Jules and Phene episode looks forward to poems about the artist such as 'Andrea del Sarto' (1855), 'Fra Lippo Lippi' (1855) and 'Abt Vogler' (1864). These things now emerge indirectly, subsumed under Browning's preoccupation with art and with the life of the emotions, particularly with situations where feeling has turned in on itself and become corrosive. Browning became a psychological poet, not in the sense that he understood character, but in the sense that he explored the processes of perception and introspection. These create the fictions which are the distorted forms of cultural myths.

To give some sense of the achievements of Browning's maturity I shall look at some well-known poems from *Men and Women*: 'Love among the Ruins', 'Childe Roland', 'Two in the Campagna', 'Love in a Life', 'Fra Lippo Lippi', 'Cleon' and 'Karshish', and then briefly at *The Ring and the Book*, his last important work.

'Love Among the Ruins', written the day after 'Childe Roland', must have seemed important enough to Browning to be placed as the first poem in *Men and Women*. It is not altogether clear why this should have been so if one reads the poem as the simple celebration of a lovers' meeting. Two lovers meet on the ruins of an unnamed once great city – Rome, Babylon, Jerusalem. They are aware of the archaeology of a bygone culture and its violence but shut out

history, and the male speaker declares, 'Love is best'. And yet, characteristically, the critique lurking in the poem emerges through the
celebration of sexuality and the lover's certainties. It is achieved by a
remarkable structural ploy. The poem is made up of long and short
lines, and as a reading proceeds it becomes clear that the short lines act
as a subversive, mocking irritant to the smoothness of the harmonious
anapaests they follow. More remarkably still, the long lines can be read
with perfect sense if the short lines are excluded, and this occurs
throughout almost the whole poem. So two poems emerge, one which
excludes the energy of the short lines and one in which the short lines
insist on intruding on the completeness of the lovers' idyll. In one,
history and its violence, a greedy will to power and economic gain,
presses upon the present and threatens it. In the other poem, however, a
one-sided private passion excludes the social and political forces which
have created the present in which it exists and pretends to self-sufficing
completeness. Thus two fictions compete with one another, one about a
barbaric past and the other about self-sufficient love. 'Peace or War':
the last line of the first stanza suggests that the antithesis of the poem is
between the peace of love and the violence of war. The best way of
indicating the violent, ironic energy of one, and the bland lassitude of
the other, is to quote the two 'versions' of the text:

(1)

Where the quiet-coloured end of evening smiles,
On the solitary pastures where our sheep
Tinkle homeward through the twilight, stray or stop,
Was the site once of a city great and gay,
Of our country's very capital, its prince
Held his court in, gathered councils, wielding far
          Peace or War.

(2)

Where the quiet-coloured end of evening smiles,
          Miles and miles
On the solitary pastures where our sheep
          Half-asleep
Tinkle homeward through the twilight, stray or stop,
          As they crop
Was the sight once of a city great and gay,
          (So they say)
Of our country's very capital, its prince
          Ages since
Held his court in, gathered councils, wielding far
          Peace or War.

As the poem proceeds and the two texts struggle with each other it becomes clear that 'Peace or War' is too simple an opposition. If the past society lacks affective experience, the lovers' extra-historical, extra-cultural stance lacks energy. It becomes clear that the opposition between a privatized world and a public world of action is a *false* opposition. In this context 'Love is best' is a cultural myth which is deeply suspect and unsustaining. It is a damaging myth which constitutes self and society as fractured, disabling both. Moreover, it is a myth which assumes male dominance in the past – 'All the men!' – and an equal relationship between men and women in the present. But the lover's girl is silent, waiting for the climactic meeting with the lover. The significance of this poem to the title of Browning's volume, *Men and Women*, becomes clearer. The speaker assumes the equal importance of both genders. But there is an imbalance in 'Love Among the Ruins', which is about men – and only secondly, women. Both the early interests of the *Monthly Repository* and Elizabeth Barrett Browning's preoccupations with the powerlessness of women emerge in the virtuosity of the first poem in Browning's major volume.

'Childe Roland' is in many ways a companion poem to 'Love Among the Ruins'. But where 'Love Among the Ruins' is torn between uneasy affirmation and an equally uneasy scepticism, 'Childe Roland' belongs to a different symbolic world. Harold Bloom sees the poem as the culmination of romantic *aporia* in which all teleological and existential certainty collapses.

The crude, violent symbolism of 'Childe Roland' is typical of Browning only in its grotesquerie, for Browning did not often use the indeterminateness of symbol in his work. Nevertheless, its preoccupations are central to his poetry and it is rightly seen as an important poem. Created out of a hint from *King Lear*, it is Childe Roland's account of a last desperate quest for the mysterious dark tower. It is like a more terrible and concentrated *Pauline*, another description of disintegration conveyed through hysterical imagery of overwrought physical horror. Sexual hatred and disgust emerges destructively as the knight confuses vermin and babies.

> – It may have been a water-rat I speared,
> But, ugh! it sounded like a baby's shriek.

It is a miasmic poem created through ambiguous language. As soon as the quest begins, the knight is convinced that the leering old man's directions are false, and yet he leaves the 'safe way' for the 'ominous tract' which, '*all agree*', hides the dark tower. He sees the whole quest as a progress, a series of definite steps and achievements, in linear terms. He has been given an 'Idea of the world', a fiction of on-going progress and achievement, which he attempts to impose on his experience, but his experience constantly resists this formulation, constantly breaks out against such a notion with a raw violence. For what the knight does is to walk a psychological treadmill, repeating the same experience in a multitude of different and ever more violent ways. The imagery is all circular, even though it may look superficially as though some progress has been made. A river is crossed, but the knight's experience is no better on the other side – 'Now for a better country. Vain presage!' A landscape changes, but things are the same – 'And just as far as ever from the end!' An appalling conflict, a 'mad brewage', has taken place, but penned in a hollow where no footsteps can be seen leading out of or into the fight.

> Whose savage trample thus could pad the dank
> Soil to a plash? Toads in a poisoned tank,
>   Or wild cats in a red-hot iron cage.
>
> The fight must so have seemed in that fell cirque.
>   What penned them there, with all the plain to choose?
>   No footprint leading to that horrid mews,
> None out of it.

Toads in a poisoned tank, wild-cats in a red-hot cage, these are the tortured images of a person who is trapped in anguished fears and fantasies as the notion of linear achievement actually creates a prison for him. The knight sees his quest in terms of an escape from the self, the search for some revelation from without. But as he is forced into the solitude of the quest, with hints of guilt and betrayal in the masculine band of peers, he is forced to confront himself and to go deeper and deeper into the disordered regions of his being, the caves of the mind discovered in *Pauline*. Revelation of a kind is granted the knight when he recognizes the nature of his 'quest'. The plain dissolves into a bowl of mountains (another circular image of the cage) and he realizes that 'progress' is impossible – 'you're inside the den'. With this acceptance the knight accepts the irrational violence and hate of the poem as his violence and hate. 'Den' is a thoroughly appropriate image here – dens and violence go together. As he blows his horn comes the realization that he is upon the dark tower without having recognized it, so different is it from his preconceptions. The discovery of meaningfulness, or meaninglessness, never happens as it is expected to happen.

But what is the dark tower? Some people see it as a kind of milestone marking the knight's end and they see the whole poem as a symbolic account of a man facing death. But the dark tower, phallic, ugly ('round and squat', at any rate unprepossessing), opaque and mysterious ('blind as the fool's heart') and yet unique, stands possibly for that fiction of the self which each person blindly assumes to exist in order to see himself as a living, active entity at all. It is that irreducible nub of being which we irrationally intuit and which enables us to feel that we are uniquely 'I'. And yet here it is displaced, outside the self, a threatening admonitory presence. It is impossible to literalize the dark tower, and yet the suggestion of the poem is that it *has* been literalized, as goal, as phallic power. This has organized the knight's experience as continual self-testing and the quest for objectives, even though it drives him to disintegration. For this is not simply an existential poem. It registers psychological violence, but it is the violence created by a world of masculine values. No women enter the poem. Shaping its hatred and anxiety is another coercive myth, the fiction of male power. The blast on the horn is an act of celebration and of defiant fear, celebration because a unifying power has been provisionally discovered, fear because chaos can come again. The world's multitudinousness is threatening, contradictory and inchoate.

Most of Browning's love-lyrics are puzzled and puzzling, agnostic about the experience of loving. A poem like 'Meeting at Night' (1845), with its rhythms of mounting orgasmic excitement and swift, thrusting *achieved* sexual passion is a rarity among these lyrics. 'Meeting at Night' is a celebration of sheer physical feeling:

> As I gain the cove with pushing prow,
> And quench its speed i' the slushy sand . . .
> And blue spurt of a lighted match,
> And a voice less loud, thro' its joys and fears,
> Than the two hearts beating each to each!

– but Browning's lyrics generally combine the passionately cerebral with an intense physicality. The happy ease in eagerness of 'Meeting at Night' (like 'Childe Roland', an account of a journey, but this time a journey full of certainty), appears, when it does appear in the other poems, shot through with disappointment or scepticism. The blue spurt of the match (like Abt Vogler's palace of sound), a sudden illumination, incandescent but transitory, could be an image for love as it is seen in other lyrics. There is the rejection of love in 'A Woman's Last Word' (1855) where the refusal to quarrel is seen as a rejection of love because it is a refusal to communicate at all. There is 'A Lover's Quarrel' (1855), which turns upon a subtle reversal of the implications of spring and winter imagery. In the 'blocked-up' snow of winter the lovers existed in happy isolation, literally playing games – they pretend to be sailors, the man paints a charcoal moustache on the woman's face – and now they have quarrelled and now that it is spring the man simply feels that he must 'bear with it', rejecting change for fantasies of fulfilment in the frozen past. As he imagines a meeting in a crypt beneath the snow, he is 'blocked-up' indeed, incarcerated in memory. The Shelleyan cave of the mind, like the den of 'Childe Roland', has modulated to an eerier place, a crypt. This lyric, with its combination of the domestic and the macabre, intellectuality and a sort of ravenousness for the sensuous, is characteristic of Browning's mature love-poems. So is the use of contradiction between metre and rhythm to express a complexity of mood – the rhythms of exasperation and pain drive across the playful, tripping metre.

'Two in the Campagna' is another poem about failure or incompleteness in love. It is an attempt to define an elusive and subtle feeling which seems the key to the whole meaning of the relationship between two lovers, a feeling which constantly evades definition, the meaning and pattern which the speaker attempts to impose upon it – 'Where does the fault lie?'. All that he can do is to write a poem about a feeling about a feeling which mimes the attempt to catch at the 'living and moving' reality of experience. Ultimately the search brings him no further discovery, no 'Idea of the world', only reinforced knowledge of the teasing incompleteness of love and of his own inability to define it:

> Just when I seemed about to learn!
>   Where is the thread now? Off again?
>   The old trick! Only I discern –
>   Infinite passion, and the pain
> Of finite hearts that yearn.

But a kind of secondary knowledge has been gained: he knows about incompleteness and about the necessity to seek for structure in the 'world's multitudinousness', to be 'off again'.

In this poem Browning's language marvellously renders the fluidity of experience. His way of missing out grammatical connectives of all kinds, of breaking up sentences, of jerking from tense to tense, of letting adjectives clot together with the raw immediacy of a sensation becomes highly expressive here. The first stanza, for instance, catches the reader in an intricate web of tenses which opens up all kinds of doubts, possibilities, and uncertainties, particularly as the whole of the stanza is framed as a question and the poem opens on a passionately complex, doubting note:

> I wonder do you feel today
> As I have felt since, hand in hand,
> We sat down on the grass, to stray
> In spirit better through the land,
> This morn of Rome and May?

It is a comparison of past and present, but the clauses determining past and present have such an uncertain grammatical and logical status that the comparison becomes complicated. The woman and the speaker are repeating the experience of a May-time walk, pausing to reflect upon the things ahead of them (straying in spirit), but by asking 'do you feel today/As I *have felt since* . . .?' Browning adds a further straying in spirit, introspection about that past event *felt in the past* and possibly to begin again with the impetus of the repeated experience. We seem to have come in on the poem in the middle of a continuous striving with introspection. The last line of the stanza returns to present time, but with a trailing subordinate phrase, so that the perplexities introduced after the first line seem still governing the present – everything is still open.

'For me, I touched a thought . . .' The introspection does begin again and what follows is one of Browning's most brilliant renderings of a random but intense associative thought-process in terms not of the content of the thought but of what it feels like to think. Linked indissolubly with the visual straying in spirit, the process is seen in sharply physical terms. To *touch* a thought gives the thought the force of a sensation and in another image, comparing the process with the random complexities of the spider's web, Browning suggests how the mind spins its own perplexities and throws out its own threads of feeling and thought to escape from the very complexities it creates, thus creating further involutions of uncertainty – 'yonder weed/Took up the floating weft'. The thread of thought strays arbitrarily outwards from blind green beetles in an orange flower to the quiet Campagna; and the poet's speculation strays outwards, too, to the large questions of love and freedom and spontaneity and will, but he is led insistently back to the same painful sense of loss and incompleteness and faced at the end of the process with same endless process of definition. When 'the good minute' goes the self is left still spinning at the centre of the web. In a letter to Ruskin Browning spoke irritably of his failure to 'make out' his thoughts with his language and explained that the difficulty arose because his poetry was 'a putting of the infinite within the finite' (*The Life and Work of John Ruskin*, ed. W. G. Collingwood, 1893, vol I, p 200). If 'the infinite' here means the suggestion of endless, random experience with endless possibilities, Browning has expressed it in this poem both through language and form. The perplexity of the poem is created as much by what it does not say – in the gaps and leaps of the syntax and the associative process – as by what it says. Like so many of Browning's lyrics this poem is circular and returns to its beginning, an unbroken continuum of experience which is always open to redefinition.

The endless process of redefinition implied in 'Two in the Campagna' suggests that relations of love subsist on the perpetual creation of new fictions because 'infinite passion' is always in excess of the finite object. Perhaps the willingness to commit energy to the unceasing production of fictions *is* love. In spite of its agnosticism, this poem gives a content to the statement 'Love is best' in 'Love Among the Ruins'. The silent woman of 'Two in the Campagna' calls forth this activity. 'Love in a Life', a fragile, two-stanza lyric, is less certain of the fiction-making activity and is a much more circumspect analysis of romantic love:

Love in a Life

I

Room after room,
I hunt the house through
We inhabit together.
Heart, fear nothing, for, heart, thou shalt find her –
Next time, herself! – not the trouble behind her
Left in the curtain, the couch's perfume!
As she brushed it, the cornice-wreath blossomed anew:
Yon looking glass gleamed at the wave of her feather.

II

Yet the day wears,
And door succeeds door;
I try the fresh fortune –
Range the same chance! She goes out as I enter.
Spend my whole day in the quest, – who cares?
But 'tis twilight, you see – with such suites to explore,
Such closets to search, such alcoves to importune!

The rhyme scheme (ABCCCABC) clusters a triple rhyme at the centre of each stanza and returns to it in the last line. Coinciding with the rhyme cluster is the sense of each stanza, which searches for the 'heart' of the experience (stanza 1) or its 'centre' (stanza 2). But then the 'heart' or the 'centre' of the experience is postponed as the rhyme scheme opens out into repetition in the last three lines, and the search for the loved woman repeats itself again in a repetition which is never complete. In one way this is a subjective lyric expressing a totally committed desire as the lover searches endlessly for the centre of his experience, which is always displaced, for the woman is never known except by her effect on the closed environment of the house – a moving curtain, perfume, an evanescent image in the mirror. Yet this is one of those poems, like 'Porphyria's Lover' and 'Love Among the Ruins', which hints at a way of reading which begins to grasp problems the speaker cannot see. Thus the expressive moment becomes the material for investigation. Subjective expression reverses into the status of object and yields a rather different account of itself. One begins to notice the strangely impersonal verb 'inhabit' following the slightly predatory overtones of 'hunt'. The 'trouble' is not only the movement of the curtain, but also psychological 'trouble'. In the line 'Heart, fear nothing, for, heart, thou shalt find her', the first 'heart' momentarily implies a shortening of 'sweetheart' but the lover is actually addressing himself. The possibility that the lover's understanding of the effects of the woman's presence are effects of his own mind is never absent from the poem – the trouble in the curtain, the amazing organic blossoming of the plaster cornice wreath. But the mind itself is determined by what is outside. It is as if the physical ordering of the space he inhabits orders the lover's experience into ever-divided areas, one closed off from the other, and constituently organizes sexual relationships in terms of division and alienation. This small poem manages to suggest simply through the material details of furniture and space the lushness and concealments which create the 'trouble' of Victorian sexual relationships. Love here may be a fiction, the lover's pursuit of his own echoes, which have effaced the woman he pursues.

I have emphasized the achievement of Browning's lyrics (and I think they are the most interesting, if not the best things he wrote) because it is usual for the dramatic monologues to be given the greater share of critical attention. Perhaps this is because in them he is most clearly an innovator, but it may be that the monologues are the easiest of all his poems to understand. Certainly he continued to exploit the monologue both in *Men and Women* and in *Dramatis Personae* (1864). Some of the monologues, of course, are more dramatic than others; some of them, like 'A Death in the Desert' (1864), simply put theological ideas in a dramatic setting, or, like 'Bishop Blougram's Apology' (1855) and 'Mr. Sludge, "The Medium"' (1864), they sport with ideas, looking at the strange possibilities inherent in what by then were familiar Romantic notions and declining them as decadent Victorian religion. The dazzling intelligence of those monologues lies in the choice of a dramatic situation which will amplify and multiply the implications of the idea – a trick medium claims the prerogatives of the Romantic poet, the created world of the imagination: a time-serving bishop rests his weary conservatism and absolute institutions on an assent to intuitional feeling. Some of the monologues re-create in a condensed form the obsessions of Browning's early work. There is the mad duke of 'My Last Duchess' (1842) who cannot love without so possessing and destroying the identity of his wife that he literally kills her and lives with her dead substitute, a work of art. This recalls Jules in *Pippa Passes*. The Bishop ordering his tomb at St Praxed's (1845) still grasps insatiably, to 'have, see, know, taste and feel, all' at the very edge of death, taking to a lurid extreme the violent need to possess the world's multitudinousness expressed in *Pauline*. Some of the best monologues are those where Browning returns to his restless preoccupation with the need to impose a shape on experience, a need so great that the speakers continue to see their lives as meaningful wholes, even if the explanation they offer is patently the wrong one. 'Andrea Del Sarto', with its Chekhovian ironies, 'Fra Lippo Lippi' and 'Caliban Upon Setebos' are monologues of this kind. In 'Fra Lippo Lippi', in particular, Browning's early worries about the artist's audience, the feeling that creation is not completed until it is shared, expressed in *Paracelsus* and *Sordello*, reappears. Indeed, the monologue form allowed Browning to demonstrate the processes of communication in their essence, for the silent listener to whom the monologue is addressed as silently governs the way the nature of an experience is formulated. The most interesting achievement of the monologue-form is its way of being a study in the subtle reciprocal action and interaction between speaker and listener so that any Idea of the world which emerges depends on the two people encapsulated in the poem. It is as if Browning's large, baffled preoccupation with the nature of thought and action and its relation to the external world and to society is expressed indirectly and with wonderful simplicity and concentration through the conditions imposed by the form of the monologue itself. In the monologues he found a model for expressing the problems he explored in so many ramifications in the early poems. The dramatic form of the monologue, the utterance of a single speaker *presenting* himself to someone else, immediately raises the problem of interpretation and the fictive representations of the speaker – of which the speaker is unaware, or half aware. The monologues are certainly expressions of belief and feeling, but they become problematical when it is seen that they raise questions beyond the reach of the speaker, which he cannot see. Thus the monologue becomes a sceptical form for analysing belief and the coercive nature of ideology as subjective experience is reversed into being the object of analysis. But that analysis must be guarded, for it too is open to the hermeneutic problem of the text – it is an attempt at interpretation.

'Fra Lippo Lippi' seems like a robust defence of the aesthetic and emotional freedom of the artist, but when his listeners are taken into account the painter's manner seems more like robust defensiveness. He is defending a splendidly celebratory view of art as a reanimating power, art which is thoroughly democratic, based as it is on the portrayal of the actual, not an ideal world:

> you've seen the world
> – The beauty and the wonder and the power
> The shapes of things, their colours, lights and shades,
> Changes, surprises, – and God made it all!
> – For what? . . .

> Art was given for that;
> God uses us to help each other so,
> Lending our minds out.

But the tone of his celebration and its passionate praise of the living and moving world is significantly different from the aggressive bravado of the rest of the poem. Fra Lippo Lippi cannot sustain the quality of this feeling and presents himself blusteringly as the typical bohemian artist, or rather, the popular view of the bohemian artist – promiscuous, hedonistic and flagrantly against all orthodoxies. The reason for this is the presence of the watch, sceptically listening to his explanations. Lippi passionately believes himself to be a popular artist and is one, but when faced with an element of his audience, he loses confidence, distrusting their belief in him and ingratiates himself with his listener:

> Yes, I'm the painter . . .
> What, brother Lippo's doings, up and down,
> You know them and they take you? like enough!
> I saw the proper twinkle in your eyes –
> Tell you, I liked your looks at very first.

He protects a defensive image of himself and yet this is superimposed on another image of the painter he would like to be. On the other hand, the painter he would like to be is conditioned always by the painter he acts.

The category Browning found for many of his monologues, 'Dramatic Romances', is indicative of their status as fictions. Lippi's tale is a romance about his life as a poor boy, forced to undergo repressive monastery life for the sake of food. He talks compulsively about himelf, avidly constructing the myth of the bohemian, society's outsider. There is something collusive about this, for Lippi, Renaissance painter or not, is confirming a Victorian myth of the alienated artist and actually endorsing the uneasy status of art. The way back to acceptance for him is through realism, a faithful depiction of the life around him, but his notion of realism is undermined by an uncertainty about what that is. It is certainly not didactic art, but at some points he implies that realism consists simply in reproducing society's detritus, a 'half-stripped grape bunch', 'barrel-droppings, candle-ends'. Again he is never sure how much he is engaged on the simple reproduction of life's energy or how much he is a powerful agent in the creation and interpretation of it. Browning is thinking about the debate on painting and truth initiated by John Ruskin in *Modern Painters*. Lippi constantly undermines his own artistry by speaking of his art in terms of 'daubing' and 'splashing' as if he is defensive about the 'truth' of his art and in doing so opens up the question of what 'truth' is. Browning's monologue makes him thoroughly cornered, literally by the philistine surveillance of the watch and metaphorically because he is forced into a false position. His bluster half protects against, half conforms to an account of art as marginal and untruthful. How far he has been pushed into this corner by an ideological account of art is an open question. The poem opens up questions beyond the control of Lippi's representation of himself.

Karshish is a scientist, seemingly exempt from all but disinterested scientific practice, and appears to be the polar opposite of Lippi. In effect, however, the same questioning of assumptions and categories goes on here. If Lippi is a subversive being subverted by the processes of the monologue, Karshish is an empiricist outflanked by the empiricism of the monologue form. Just as 'Fra Lippo Lippi' is both a celebration and critique of a view of art, 'Karshish' is a celebration and critique of a view of science and of a scientific, positivist account of religious experience.

The scientist's experimental passion includes not only the properties of the physical world, as Karshish finds that 'Judea's gum-tragacanth/Scales off in purer flakes . . . exceeds our produce', but also extends to the medical man's sceptical analysis of a phenomenon, the risen Lazarus; though the man who induced the 'cure' of Lazarus is dead, Lazarus is fifty years old. ''Tis but a case of mania – subinduced/ By epilepsy', Karshish theorizes, and supports his theory by educing Lazarus's indifference to practical matters, including the Roman armaments which are building up to defeat his country. Karshish sees all this with the superior objectivity of the scientist who is exempt from national and political boundaries, but cannot see why Lazarus should be indifferent to these. As he considers the case of Lazarus, attempting to assimilate the phenomenon into his own categories and forms of thought, these categories are strained to breaking point. Among the problems Karshish as speaker cannot see fully is the scientific definition of insanity. What is madness? Is it simply a term for psychological conditions which cannot be culturally assimilated? Christian experience is for him a form of madness. Or is the empiricism of Karshish so limited that its concepts cannot evolve categories for states of mind and belief outside it? Is his passion for experiment a way of gaining power over the world? If madness is a form of fiction-making, what of his own categories? At the end of the monologue Karshish makes an imaginative leap, or an attempt at one, displacing the idea of power with the idea of love – 'So, the All-Great were the All-Loving too'. It is a Christian experience, but interestingly it is expressed in terms of a positivist fiction, a God projected from human love. The end of the monologue is equivocal; Karshish may have evolved a transforming idea, but it is arrived at through rational humanist thought rather than through comprehending an experience radically different from his own.

'The Epistle of Karshish' is placed at a crucial historical moment for Western European thought, enabling Browning to explore the Christian and the scientific myth. In 'Cleon' he extends his exploration of forms of thought and cultural conditions by placing Cleon, an intellectual and polymath writing to his patron prince at the end of Greek culture, just before the advent of Christianity. Cleon is obsessed with the decadence and complexity of his tradition. His fatigued perception of the isolation of the self-conscious intellectual from the energy of pure unconscious being is one of Browning's most intense studies of the myth of alienation prefigured in 'Love Among the Ruins'. A dry abstract language is matched to the sceptical condition which becomes more greedily aware of physical life the more it sees itself as external to it. This is one of the most exacting of the monologues but its analysis of the dryness of the ever-reflective mind as a modern condition is powerful. Cleon lives in a hierarchical slave-society and the contradictions of the master – slave relationship, in which the master becomes ever more exhausted by his power, are strikingly perceived. The poem returns one to the first volume in the poem and its analysis of contemporary myths with renewed understanding. There are enabling and disabling myths. Cleon is in the grip of one which determines that impoverishment is seen as the heart of knowledge which can only divide consciousness. The ironies of his sense of impoverishment emerge when he is fastidiously shocked that 'actually living' can be confused with '*knowing* [my italics] how . . . to live!' He is a man with an 'Idea of the world' in Arnold's terms (and Browning may have had Arnold in mind), which actually incapacitates him for 'the world's multitudinousness'.

Men and Women is a deliberately composite and fragmented work, as if to indicate that no one fiction or idea of the world will organize experience. It is a study of modern myths, of art, science, sexuality and consciousness, and their problematical status. His exile enabled him to explore the assumptions of his culture with a political and intellectual boldness he never achieved when he returned to England. Perhaps Browning never reached a poetry of such comprehensiveness and intensity again.

The poems of *Men and Woman* and of *Dramatis Personae* (1864) will always be the poems people read, but they have more meaning when they are related to their raw material, Browning's early work, and that, too, grows in stature. But what of the later work? Apart from a strange renewal of power in *Parleyings with Certain People of Importance in Their Day* (1887), the pattern is uneven after *The Ring and the Book* (1868). There are erratic flashes of strange intensity in poems such as *Fifine at the Fair* (1872), but in general Browning lost his way of giving such concentrated form to his agnostic puzzlement.

Some people end Browning's effective poetic achievement with *Dramatis Personae*, but *The Ring and the Book* can claim to be his last important work. This vast collection of monologues is a sustained and dazzling exploration of the overwhelming question which is asked in different ways in so many of Browning's poems: What is the status of the act of interpretation? Is it a fiction scrutinizing other fictions? This time it is asked on a huge scale and involves the beliefs and institutions of a whole society. Debating the Roman murder case of 1698 when Guido Franceschini stabbed his wife, Pompilia, every speaker – citizens, Pope, lawyers, participants – rests his interpretation of the events on different kinds of judgment. Each monologue qualifies another, defining and redefining the nature of interpretation. Judgment becomes anything but pure. In the last monologue of the poem, the violent despairing speech of Guido before his execution, one is persuaded to ask whether accounts of human action are ever adequate. Thus the extremities of violence he represents:

> Nor is it in me to unhate my hates, –
> I use up my last strength to strike once more
> Old Pietro . . .
>   . . . and I grow one gorge
> To loathingly reject Pompilia's pale
> Poison my hasty hunger took for food.

The metaphysical scale of the early poems has returned, but with all the concentration and intensity learned in the intervening time.

I have tried to show that Browning is a major poet rather than to take up and demolish the familiar case against his poetry – his vulgarity, coarseness and violence. Whatever the immediate impact of his poetry, one cannot fail to recognize in it a controlling intelligence, often exasperating but more often performing with a virtuosity both brilliant and profound. His poetry is a daring play with concepts and passions and not least dares to make a fundamental analysis of cultural politics. One person at least recognized his power when his contemporaries failed to acknowledge it – his wife. 'My cricket chirps against thy mandolin', she wrote in *Sonnets from the Portuguese* (IV). These sonnets, with their rather bookish Shelleyan imagery ('Straightway I was 'ware,/So weeping, how the mystic Shape did move/Behind me . . .'), their occasional 'emotionalosity', compared with the arresting intensities and intricacies of Browning's love poems (for instance with that tiny essay in adoration, 'Song'), and yet one feels in them the pressure of real bewilderment, uncertainty and wonder, particularly in Sonnets X, XX, XXII, XXIX, XXX, XL. And occasionally she will discover a grandly bizarre image to match the extravagance of her feeling. One reads these poems for their attempt to forge a new language for feeling:

> and distort
> Thy worthiest love with worthless counterfeit:
> As if a shipwrecked Pagan safe in port,
> His guardian sea-god to commemorate,
> Should set a sculptured porpoise, gills a-snort,
> And vibrant tail, within the temple-gate.

'Who loves *me?*' Aurora Leigh cries with passionate self-pity. Elizabeth Browning understood what it was like to be a woman who made violent emotional demands on the world and yet despised the 'luxury of emotion', and she is particularly perceptive about the difficulties of mediating powerful emotion. It may be that neither of the Brownings' major poems would have been achieved without their marriage. Marriage and Elizabeth Barrett, as well as the departure for Italy, certainly shaped the perceptions of Browning's early poems. The self-important public figure of Browning's later years, the extraordinarily conventional man who was, puzzlingly, such a great artist (portrayed in Henry James's *The Private Life*) seems to have given up the enthusiasms and boldness which were the life of his early work.

HOPKINS

Norman H. MacKenzie

During the lifetime of Gerard Manley Hopkins (1844–89) only a handful of special friends so much as knew that he was an active poet. Even within this closed circle there were some who turned with distaste from his work as freakish or disrespectfully headstrong. When Robert Bridges sent the popular Victorian poet, Coventry Patmore, his beautifully transcribed album of Hopkins's verse, starting with 'Pied Beauty', and including now-celebrated poems such as 'The Windhover', 'The Wreck of the Deutschland', 'The Leaden Echo and the Golden Echo', 'Binsey Poplars', and 'God's Grandeur', Hopkins received a completely negative, dispiriting response from his fellow Catholic:

My Dear Mr. Hopkins, – I have read your poems – most of them several times – and find my first impression confirmed with each reading. It seems to me that the thought and feeling of these poems, if expressed without any obscuring novelty of mode, are such as often to require the whole attention to apprehend and digest them; and are therefore of a kind to appeal only to the few. But to the already sufficiently arduous character of such poetry you seem to me to have added the difficulty of following *several* entirely novel and simultaneous experiments in versification and construction, together with an altogether unprecedented system of alliteration and compound words; – any one of which novelties would be startling and productive of distraction from the poetic matter to be expressed.

(Hopkins, *Further Letters*, 2nd edn, 1956, p 352)

Fortunately for us, Hopkins continued to evolve his rhythm, structure and diction from his own concepts of first principles instead of discreetly modifying prevailing fashion. Only a few of his poems were published during the nineteenth century. Even the first edition of 1918 sold with unenthusiastic leisureliness, but since 1930 Hopkins has come into his own: his intense perceptiveness, the fibrous strength of his textures, his success in 'breaking the feet' of the traditional English iambic – all these lent impetus to modern poets confronting a rather different world from his own. Hopkins remains unique, without obvious predecessors or followers who could be described as belonging to his 'school'. He was godfather rather than parent to many of the vigorous poets of the first half of this century. The growth of his reputation has been marked by the progressively fuller and more careful editions of his works, which now run to six large volumes: the *Poems* (which includes original compositions and translations in Welsh, Latin and Greek); three volumes of his *Letters*, lively with debates on poetic form and astute judgments of contemporary writers; a volume of his *Sermons and Devotional Writings*, strangely different from the pulpit literature of his age, different too from the Thomism of most Catholics because he preferred the individualistic philosophy of Duns Scotus; and finally the splendidly edited *Journals and Papers*. (See Bibliography p 535 for details and the short titles by which they are cited.) Embedded in his first diary are not only his earliest attempts at verse, set in revealing contexts, but also his Ruskinesque drawings. Knowing the Rossettis and Holman Hunt, he seriously considered becoming an artist himself. (For his sketches, see *Journals*, pp 453–5 and the plates which follow.) In music, lack of training prevented his attaining any fluency in performance or composition, but from the tunes which he wrote for various poems, mostly by his friends, experts can deduce a melodic inventiveness. (See *Journals*, pp 457–97 for reproductions of his music, and commentary by Dr John Stevens.)

Hopkins's journals extend from the year he entered Oxford up to February 1875. The earliest diaries record his perceptive speculations about the affinities between words of similar sound, both within English (standard and provincial) and in related languages. His own original hypotheses were based upon a sense of a word's innermost 'scape': he tended to follow the lead of those etymologists whose proposed derivations lent most vitality to a term. Philology in the mid-Victorian age, if less scientific, was more exhilarating than in later years. Many scholars believed that particular consonant clusters preserved basic Sanskrit roots, each of which had resulted in whole family-trees of descendants. Thus English words beginning with *fl–* were thought to preserve a root meaning to fly or flow. (W. Fowler, *The English Language*, 1857, p 109.) Hopkins offers conjectures about some twenty words beginning with *fl–*, differentiating subtly the gradations represented by *flick*, *fleck* and *flake*, and tentatively coupling with them *flitch*. When

therefore we encounter 'flitches of fern' in his 'Inversnaid' (1881)
we might well associate the phrase with the 'flakeleaves light' of
'Epithalamion' rather than invoke a crude kitchen image. Moreover,
in English dialect use, another word 'flitch' was a variant of the verb
'to flit', while a third homophone, used around Oxford, was a
variant of the adjective 'flick' meaning 'pert, lively, quick'. All these
associations tend to colour the term in 'Inversnaid'. Hopkins's
philological interests continued throughout his life (see for example, *Letters*, vol III, pp 280–6), and once he had found something
to say, his knowledge of the ancestry of words helped him to concentrate a great density of meaning into a short space.

More profoundly shaping his work came the concept for which
he invented the word *inscape*. Many streams of thought contributed
to its evolution. Ruskin, for example, in his *Modern Painters* continually searched for the scientific 'Law' or inner organization
which accounted for a specific appearance in a certain type of cloud
or landscape or tree. (See N. H. MacKenzie, *Hopkins Among the
Victorians*, in *English Studies Today: Third Series*, ed. G. I. Duthie,
1964, pp 159–65.) Philosophers from Plato to the Schoolmen of
the Middle Ages had theorized about the *potential* and the *actual*,
about *form* and *matter*. Hopkins uses the word *inscape* in his *Journals*
with some flexibility. Less precisely applied, it may merely point to
the recurring outward pattern shared by all members of a species,
or repeated in man-made things such as the successive tie-beams of
a barn roof. But in more typical passages Hopkins is referring to the
sum of the special qualities within an object which give a sensitive
observer an insight into its distinctive nature. After he discovered,
with strange exhilaration, the *Opus Oxoniense* of Duns Scotus (to
whom he shows moving gratitude in his sonnet 'Duns Scotus's
Oxford'), he looked more and more for the moment of vision, of
interior perception into an object's being (the result of the *instress* or
energy pulsing from its individual or specific qualities), as opposed
to the superficial, confused knowledge with which most people rest
content. All his best poems seem the product of such vision: they try
to reconstruct in the intricacy of intermingling phrases the *inscape*
which he has discovered. (See W. A. M. Peters, *Gerard Manley
Hopkins*, 1948, ch. 1 for many examples of *inscape* and *instress*; the
most detailed and philosophical treatment of *instress* is by
L. Cochran, *Hopkins Quarterly*, vol 6, no. 4, 1980, pp 143–76.)

While an undergraduate at Oxford Hopkins fell first under the
spell of the Tractarians (or Puseyites), who represented the ritualistic fringe of the High Anglican Church. Deeply in earnest himself,

exacting in every matter of conduct or conscience, he began to question the authenticity of the English Church, like many another student in the years following the publication of Newman's *Apologia pro Vita Sua* (1864). At length, after much mental turmoil (reflected both in his diaries and current poems), he decided in 1866 to enter the Church of Rome. His conversion created a dissonance between himself and his family, still apparent in a sonnet written in Ireland nearly twenty years after this event: 'To seem the stranger lies my lot' (*Poems*, p 101; *Oxf. Auth.*, p 166). The tension was increased when he decided to abandon all thought of art or poetry as a career, perhaps even as a relaxation, in order to give himself wholly to the Jesuit priesthood.

Those who believe that Hopkins might have become a greater poet if he had not turned priest should classify and weigh his undergraduate poetry. The most ambitious pieces are certainly secular, but they are heralds of failure, fragments which he never succeeded in worrying into completion: *Richard*, a blank verse narrative, *Floris in Italy*, a verse play. His future powers are more nearly anticipated in those poems of 1864–6 torn by uncertain faith or reaching after the spiritual ideal – 'Heaven-Haven', 'The Half-way House' and 'Nondum'. The best is 'The Habit of Perfection':

> Shape nothing, lips; be lovely-dumb:
> It is the shut, the curfew sent
> From there where all surrenders come
> Which only makes you eloquent.
>
> Be shellèd, eyes, with double dark
> And find the uncreated light:
> This ruck and reel which you remark
> Coils, keeps, and teases simple sight.
>
> (*Poems*, p 31; *Oxf. Auth.*, p 81)

The senses can seldom have been dismissed more sensitively or (in the best meaning of the word) sensuously. The originality of phrase and metaphor in which he afterwards excelled is here predicted by words like *the shut, curfew* (St James, ch. 3, vv. 5–6, warns us that the 'tongue is a fire', apt to escape control); *ruck* and *reel* have the direct appeal of the robust dialect words favoured by William Barnes, whose Dorset poetry Hopkins admired.

Hopkins left Oxford with a hard-earned First in 1867, and having finally decided on his vocation, he ceremonially burned his poems. The long training for the Jesuit priesthood followed. During the two years of his novitiate, spent in the quiet of Manresa House whose richly wooded grounds seemed an extension of the adjoining Richmond Park, he lived a life of meditation and devotional reading such as his 'Habit of Perfection' had aspired to, voluntarily isolated from the reading or composition of literature in a community severed from the 'ruck and reel' of national events. Then came three years of study in Lancashire – scholastic philosophy and ethics, mathematics and mechanics. Though he found sparse leisure for reading poetry or reviews, he drew inspiration from three beautiful rivers, the great hills and noble fells (*Letters*, vol I, p 26; vol III, pp 234–5, 238).

Since his entry into the Jesuit order Hopkins had in five years written no spontaneous poetry, only verse produced at the direct request of a superior – such as Greek iambics to welcome a new Bishop (not extant) or poems to honour the Virgin Mary, including 'Ad Mariam' and 'Rosa Mystica' in which Swinburne's melodious modes were used for sacred purposes. A landmark was reached in 1873 with his appointment for a year as Professor of Rhetoric at Manresa House, to teach some twenty advanced Jesuit students – a post which drove him to a fresh study of English literature and the reading of newly published volumes, e.g. by Matthew Arnold and Browning. A few pages of his notes have survived, on 'Rhythm and Other Structural Parts of Rhetoric' along with a fragment of a lecture on the distinction between 'Poetry and Verse' (*Journals*, pp 267–90). These notes, though highly technical, reveal ideas about poetry which he was soon to put into effect. He emphasizes that poetry is a branch of speech, meant to be heard – a conviction which he applied most emphatically to his own productions (*Journals*, pp 267, 289; *Letters*, vol I, pp 46, 79, 263, 272). And he speaks of alliteration as being used 'thickly in modern English verse: one may indeed doubt whether a good ear is satisfied with our verse without it' (*Journals*, p 284).

The theological study which followed (1874–7), culminating in his ordination as priest, was in an environment which he found lyrically beautiful, overlooking the Welsh valley of the Elwy. It was in Wales that the final goad into poetry came in December 1875, when he was given official approval to write an ode on an event which had moved him deeply because it dramatized the new persecution of Catholics in central Europe, making England by contrast seem receptive to the Faith. Driven from Germany through the Falk Laws, five Franciscan sisters, tertiaries who cared for the poor and sick, had been sailing to a new life in America when their ship, the *Deutschland*, veered in a fierce snowstorm to its death on a submerged sandbank, too far from the English coast for their peril to be observed.

13

Into the snows she sweeps,
Hurling the haven behind,
The Deutschland, on Sunday; and so the sky keeps,
For the infinite air is unkind,
And the sea flint-flake, black-backed in the regular blow,
Sitting Eastnortheast, in cursed quarter, the wind;
Wiry and white-fiery and whirlwind-swivellèd snow
Spins to the widow-making unchilding unfathering deeps.

14

She drove in the dark to leeward,
She struck – not a reef or a rock
But the combs of a smother of sand: night drew her
Dead to the Kentish Knock;
And she beat the bank down with her bows and the ride
of her keel;
The breakers rolled on her beam with ruinous shock;
And canvas and compass, the whorl and the wheel
Idle for ever to waft her or wind her with, these she endured.
                    (*Poems*, pp 55–6; *Oxf. Auth.*, p 113)

While *The Times* and the German Reichstag demanded to know why rescue attempts were delayed thirty hours, and editorials in other papers questioned the captain's competence (e.g. *Illustrated London News*, December 11, *Saturday Review*, December 18 1875), Hopkins saw God extracting good from cruelty and suffering. All denominations had been shaken by the Presidential address to the British Association of Professor Tyndall (1874), identifying some religious views of Nature as surviving forms of primitive 'superstition' – Hopkins (*Letters*, vol III, p 127) read a slightly abridged version – and by John Stuart Mill's *Three Essays on Religion* (1874), which discerned no moral design or sense of justice in the Contriver of the cosmos. The Jesuit journal, *The Month*, was much concerned over agnostic assaults on religion and the persecutions in Europe. Hopkins the priest no longer harboured the doubts which had filled his undergraduate poem 'Nondum' with echoes of *In Memoriam*. Here he discerns, hidden behind the braggart Death and the roaring night, the unacknowledged Master of all, setting limits to the surge. God is hailed as

> The recurb and the recovery of the gulf's sides,
>   The girth of it and the wharf of it and the wall;
> Stanching, quenching ocean of a motionable mind;
> Ground of being, and granite of it: past all
>   Grasp God, throned behind
> Death with a sovereignty that heeds but hides, bodes but abides;
>   (*Poems*, p 62, stanza 32; *Oxf. Auth.*, p 118)

Those less familiar with Hopkins will most easily enjoy the narrative stanzas (11–17), but fully annotated editions or the *Reader's Guide* should clear up most perplexities in the other portions. God is acknowledged as in the *inscape* of everything He has made; but we are usually blind to the divine instress except in the presence of great beauty – Hopkins mentions his favourite scenes, 'lovely-asunder Starlight' and the 'dappled-with-damson west' (stanza 5) – or under the impact of the power strokes delivered by storm and lightning (stanza 6). Yet in the confusing paradox of a world breached by the Fall and distorted by evil, the love of God can still operate through elements which the poet describes as 'endragonèd' (suggesting the biblical arch-enemy of mankind) or issuing from 'cursed quarter'.[1] The lightning is also God's love: He is winter as much as spring, trying always to draw or drive men from their deluding self-sufficiency. In the final stanzas the poet's imagination passes beyond his vision of the King advancing over the wild waters to receive His witness, the tall nun: he prays for His re-coronation in England, an exile restored.

Looking back on the stanzas quoted above, in stanza 13, line 5, to interpret 'the sea flint-flake' we have to ask ourselves how much of the inscape (or individuating characteristics) of a flint-flake are meant to be applied to an apparently completely different object, water. Everybody knows that flakes of flint were used in Stone Age implements for cutting, and in Hopkins's *Journals* (p 148) this is the predominant quality carried over: 'great waves . . . flinty sharp'. But on a bleak December day the dark glaze of the sea would also resemble the glassy grey-black sheen of a flint, and the shifting little hollows which catch the eye in restless water might have reminded the poet of the shallow depressions which dimple nodules of flint. All these perceptions and more are conveyed by a single compound verb to knowledgeable readers – provided they are themselves alert

---

[1] See *Sermons*, p 60 – 'it would have been no Paradise if it were liable to drought and storm'; also pp 90–2 on the imperfect providence which permits disasters such as wrecks.

to the inscapes of nature, or can use encyclopaedias (or museum displays) imaginatively. But with stanza 32 no such compression is attempted as the poet tries to make us aware of the *instress* or unifying energies involved when the ocean beats against its containing cliffs. To mirror these ceaseless rounds of attack and repulse the poet needs the span of three lines, with seven words to encapsulate the action. Each contributes a phase of the interplay between sea and rock, while together they inscape the unruly human mind, prone to perpetual instability under its gusty moods and even to occasional violent outbreaks. Faith in the divine ruler can restrain our storms, while even the most self-confident of Bismarcks or sea-captains may learn his limitations if he pits himself against the laws of nature.

It is, of course, possible to parallel a few of this poem's metaphors or phrases in the work of Hopkins's contemporaries. Swinburne's *Erechtheus*, published while Hopkins was composing the 'Deutschland', carries similar imagery of sea and wreck – even lines with cognate rhythms (see Swinburne, *Collected Works*, 1924, vol II, pp 353, 389, 399). Browning's Pope in *The Ring and the Book* may refer to the truth being flashed in a single lightning stroke, or to the purgatorial gloom,

> Where God unmakes but to remake the soul
> He else made first in vain.
>
> (X. 2119 ff)

But in total effect 'The Wreck of the Deutschland' has no precedents in its rhythmic versatility, while its finest lines – including most of the long-drawn hexameters which end the stanzas – forge words into new and memorable units. The ambiguities of the ode retard but enrich even the modern student to whom sprung rhythm presents fewer vocal entanglements, but to Hopkins's fellow Jesuits the poem was unforgivably hobbled and knotty. (See N. H. MacKenzie, *Hopkins*, 1968, pp 24–35.)

Having erected this memorial to strengthen faith, the poet naturally wished it to be seen, and unaware how far he had ventured ahead of general comprehension, he submitted the ode to the Jesuit journal, *The Month*. It was reluctantly refused. When that journal had been founded, its first editor had been warned by Newman that '*Catholics* are not a reading set' (29 June 1864; quoted in *The Month*, vol 101, January 1903, p 3) and required no predominantly literary review. Furthermore the Jesuits, following the lead of their founder, St Ignatius, had throughout their history avoided prominence and

mistrusted brilliance, because earthly fame might lead a priest into
the sin of pride. The Society, as Hopkins frankly explained to a
friend urging the printing of his poems, valued literature only as a
means to their main end, the advancement of the faith, and poetry
'has seldom been found to be to that end a very serviceable means'
(*Letters*, vol II, p 93). Hopkins completely accepted this evaluation
as in the best interests of his Church, of his own highest nature and
even of his poetry. His decision may seem regrettable to many who
imagine that Victorian literature would have been leavened by his
germinal innovations. We can only observe that among those contemporaries favoured with access to his work, most Catholics found
it too unorthodox in literary terms, while to most Protestants it had
the added deterrent of being too orthodox in Catholic terms.
Victorian reviewers would certainly have pilloried Hopkins, a man
who already shrank under the reputation of eccentricity. Robert
Bridges's long delay in editing his poems brought one distinct gain,
as Mellowan has observed: it postponed their appearance until
1919, 'one of the most propitious years in which such "new" poetry
could have been brought before the public, since only in the 1920s
was a criticism developed which was appropriate for it. Hopkins was
not so much born before his time, as before his critics' (*Modern
Philology*, vol LXIII, 1965, p 51).

There was nothing personal in the Jesuit rejection of his verse,
since they published his 'Silver Jubilee' along with a sermon by
Father John Morris, S. J. that same year. But this was a somewhat
inferior 'popular' piece in his own estimation, written to honour a
bishop (*Letters*, vol I, p 77). After a further elegy, on 'The Loss of
the Eurydice' (April 1878), had been declined by *The Month*, and
the Rector of Stonyhurst had ruled that his 'May Magnificat' was
below standard for display before the college's statue of the Virgin
the following month, Hopkins ceased even to divulge to close
colleagues that he ever wrote poetry on his own.

Fortunately the dampening effect of the Church-centred conservatism of his rectors was to some extent offset by a growing
correspondence with two poets, Bridges and Dixon, with whom he
interchanged detailed mutual criticism. Of immense value for the
preservation of his poetic self was his friendship with Robert
Bridges, whom he had known at Oxford. Different though they
were in cast and calling, the two men were drawn into gradually
mellowing harmony by their common pursuit of perfection in verse.
Even before Hopkins had announced that he would no longer seek
publication, nor permit it unless it came about through his

superiors, Bridges as early as 1879 prepared an album in which to mount the autograph poems which Hopkins sent him, thus preserving them from the casualness of their author. And within a few years he also transcribed them into another album for private circulation among his friends, first scrupulously sending the book to Hopkins for checking and emendation.

That there were to begin with foolish misunderstandings on both sides we can see despite the destruction of Bridges's share of this fascinating correspondence (*The Letters of Gerard Manley Hopkins to Robert Bridges*). While Hopkins was studying theology (and incidentally privately learning Welsh) in the pastoral seclusion of Wales, the poet Bridges was facing the ugly duties of house-, and later casualty-physician in St Bartholomew's Hospital, London. His official report discloses that he had to see 30,940 patients in a single year! Hopkins, from graduation to the close of his life, seems to have lived under mental and physical tension which rendered even minor crises exhausting. It is ironic to find him writing from the peace of St Beuno's to St Bartholomew's: 'Dearest Bridges, – You have no call to complain of my delay in writing, I could not help it: I am not a consulting physician and have little time and now I am very very tired, . . . and "scarce can go or creep"' (*Letters*, vol I, p 32). 'While others dance and play' – an adjoining phrase which he suppressed in this unidentified quotation from Haydn's popular song – hints at his delusions concerning Bridges's leisure ('My mother bids me bind my hair', from *Twelve Canzonets*). Bridges on his side at first showed cloven prejudices against his friend's Order. These Hopkins parried with humorous echoes, such as when he writes to Bridges (describing some fervent Anglicans), 'The Puseyites are up to some very dirty jesuitical tricks' (*Letters*, vol I, p 58). Bridges was overharsh in castigating the 'oddities' to which Hopkins himself confessed, but Hopkins needed such reactions to keep eccentricity in check. Missing the chastening effect of a public upon a writer's experiments, he valued the comments of Bridges and Dixon: 'a poet', he said, 'is a public in himself' (*Letters*, vol I, p 59). While he demanded absolute clarity in the verse of his friends, Hopkins himself needed to be told from time to time that some poem of his own resisted decipherment. If Bridges's taste was sometimes too classically circumspect to respond to audacities of phrase, such as 'leaves me a lonely began' ('To seem the stranger'), Hopkins was in artistic matters sufficiently self-assured in the rightness of his general practices to tell Bridges, for example, that his strictures upon 'The Wreck of the Deutschland' were mere bilgewater (*Letters*, vol I, pp 50, 46–7). So too when towards the end of his life he developed new theories of musical composition, he firmly defended the music he had set to Collins's 'Ode to Evening': 'If you do not like it it is because there is something you have not seen and I see. That at least is my mind, and if the whole world agreed to condemn it or see nothing in it I should only tell them to take a generation and come to me again' (*Letters*, vol I, p 214). In practice, however, where his poetry was involved he was apprehensive of its being so much as seen by literary reviewers like Andrew Lang, and in the early stages of a new venture he needed encouragement 'as much as crops rain' (*Letters*, vol I, pp 218–9).

In their prosodic experiments Hopkins and Bridges were friendly rivals. Both had independently begun to develop Miltonic inversions before they exchanged poems (*Letters*, vol I, p 38). Hopkins borrowed from music the term 'counterpoint' to describe the reversal of two successive feet, as in the opening trochees of the iambic pentameter line:

$$/ \ x|/x \ | x \quad /| \ x \ /| \ x \quad /|$$
Generations have trod, have trod, have trod

('God's Grandeur')

Here the iambic plod at the end attains an onomatopoeic fitness because of the disturbed metre in the first two feet. 'Sprung Rhythm', however, was a bold step well beyond simple counterpointing or the substitution of trisyllabic for disyllabic feet. We may trace the new rhythm 'haunting his ear' back to those lecture notes already referred to, made for his Manresa students in 1873–4, where he showed himself moving away from the simplicities of reigning prosodists with their generalized patterns of standard stressed and standard unstressed syllables. Hopkins's subtle ear caught infinite nuances: 'no two weak accents in a word are exactly equal'. He had recognized a metrical foot as capable of having four or five syllables, 'grouped about one strong beat' (*Journals*, p 271), and further anticipated the note on 'Sprung Rhythm' with which he afterwards prefaced the experimental 'Wreck of the Deutschland' (first published in *Poems of Gerard Manley Hopkins*, ed. W. H. Gardner and N. H. MacKenzie, 1967, pp 255–6) by pondering on the way in which a sensitive reader might increase the emphasis upon the stressed syllable of a long word to balance its family of unstressed syllables (*Journals*, p 271). He had quoted lines in which an accented monosyllabic foot has replaced a trochee or iamb – another characteristic of 'Sprung Rhythm':

/ ×|/ ×|/ | /
Toad that under *cold stone*

/ × | / ×| /×|/
Days and nights has thirty one

(*Macbeth* IV. i. 6)

where editors have been tempted to amend *cold* into *coldest* to 'preserve' the rhythm. In a line of 'Sprung Rhythm', as he developed it from 'The Wreck of the Deutschland' onwards, a metrical foot anywhere may consist of a single accented syllable, or have any reasonable number of unstressed syllables (not merely one or two) following the stress. But although in theory the five-stress lines of a sonnet could be constructed with unlicensed abandon, Hopkins's fine ear tested the balance of his phrases one against the other, marrying sense and sound in a manner impossible with conventional prosody. In the most characteristic 'sprung' lines the voice 'springs' from one stress to another, across a gap left by the omission of a slack syllable redundant to the meaning. Thus in 'Inversnaid'

/ /
A windpuff-bonnet of fawn-froth

Turns and twindles over the broth

/ /
Of a pool so pitch-black, fell-frowning,

It rounds and rounds Despair to drowning.

(*Poems*, p 89; *Oxf. Auth.*, p 153)

the two final stresses in lines 1 and 3 have no intervening slacks. We can reduce them to conformity and commonplace by substituting

/ × / / × /
tawny for *fawn*, and *frightful* for *fell*.

It is unfortunate that Hopkins's surviving journals break off in the middle of a story just ten months before the wrecking of the *Deutschland* exploded him back into poetry, but the ones we have are invaluable as a background to his verse. They preserve thousands of acutely worded notes (for he is a connoisseur of precise or uncommon words in his prose also) on the inscapes of waterfalls and ash trees, skies cloud-moulded or pierced with stars, quaint dialect words or pronunciations, comments on the architecture of churches or the merits of individual pictures in an Academy Exhibition. Entering his incessant discoveries in his journals reinforced his memory, so that as he composed poems or sermons his language was saved from the ruts by myriads of direct impressions. The prose entries form an invaluable commentary on his verse. Thus under April 21 and 22 1871 he records exceptional cloudscapes: 'the sky a beautiful grained blue, silky lingering clouds in flat-bottomed loaves, others a little browner in ropes or in burly-shouldered ridges swanny and lustrous, more in the Zenith stray packs of a sort of violet paleness . . . Later/moulding which brought rain: . . . April 22 – But such a lovely damasking in the sky as today I never felt before . . . slanted flashing "travellers", all in flight, stepping one behind the other, their edges tossed with bright ravelling' (*Journals*, p 207). Six years later the instress of a resplendent autumn sky reminded him of many of these metaphors. As he returned in holiday mood from fishing in a Welsh valley 'half an hour of extreme enthusiasm' resulted in 'Hurrahing in Harvest' (1877):

> Summer ends now; now, barbarous in beauty, the stooks rise
> Around; up above, what wind-walks! what lovely behaviour
> Of silk-sack clouds! has wilder, wilful-wavier
> Meal-drift moulded ever and melted across skies?
>
> (*Poems*, p 70; *Oxf. Auth.*, p 134)

How the opening line, and even the title, have been tautened from their first draft: '*Sonnet in Harvest* – It is harvest; now barbarous in beauty . . .'[1] All nature is buoyant as the clouds. The stooks (Hopkins relishes the dialect word) rise as though about to float; the poet's heart soars with elation; the azurous hills are 'hung' (he discarded 'strong' and 'grand' in search of a fresh exactitude). The mountains combine the lifting grace of the stallion with the gentleness of the violet:

> And the azurous hung hills are his world-wielding shoulder
> Majestic – as a stallion stalwart, very-violet-sweet! –

a male/female image-cluster which Bridges considered an affectation, but which for Hopkins caught the very inscape of the weighty hovering hills, strength married to tender beauty. The final tercet of the sonnet is reminiscent of Plato's *Phaedrus* in which Socrates explains how the soul may grow wings, but may lose them; how the philosopher, admiring the beauty of the world and recol-

---

[1] The misprinting from 1930 till the fourth edition of line 1 as 'the stooks arise' destroyed the leap of the sprung rhythm.

lecting the divine beauty which is its prototype, is raised with an enthusiasm like the spreading of new wings in flight, only to find himself impotent to leave the ground (246A–250C). So too Hopkins is honest enough to end his sonnet in what some might think anticlimax, the sober reservation in '*half hurls*':

> These things, these things were here and but the beholder
> Wanting; which two when they once meet,
> The heart rears wings bold and bolder
> And hurls for him, O half hurls earth for him off under his feet.

Although to the end of his short life Hopkins could be beckoned into corresponding excitement (see, e.g., his 'Ashboughs', *Poems*, p 185; *Oxf. Auth.*, pp 177–8, copied onto the same sheet of paper as four 'sonnets of desolation', probably in 1887–8), he also suffered throughout frequent periods of deflation, such as preoccupies a sonnet contemporary with 'Hurrahing in Harvest', 'The Caged Skylark':

> As a dare-gale skylark scanted in a dull cage,
>   Man's mounting spirit in his bone-house, mean house, dwells –
>
>   That bird beyond the remembering his free fells,
> This in drudgery, day-labouring-out life's age.
>
> > (*Poems*, p 70; *Oxf. Auth.*, p 133)

The alliteration and assonance point up the incongruities: the *skylark* is *scanted* ('constricted' – Hopkins rescues the sense of spatial limitation, still familiar in the adjective *scant* but neglected in the verb); the *dare-gale* bird is now *dull*; once able to soar or *drop* to its nest, it now *droops*. So too each human soul, 'flesh-bound' in 'bone-house' (a kenning dating from *Beowulf* (ll. 2508, 3147)) is seen as 'distressed', barred in, 'day-labouring' like the blind Milton, condemned to earth-bound drudgery like Samson in the prison-house of his enemies. (See Milton's *Samson Agonistes*, ll. 573, 1338, 1393; and *Sonnet*: 'On his Blindness'.) Milton is a perpetual influence upon Hopkins in vocabulary and rhythm.

Written during that same fertile year, 1877, 'The Windhover' has become the most famous of his sonnets, its infinite suggestiveness attracting innumerable interpretations. It is ironic to find dogmatists trying to pontificate, from the embrasures of their fixed minds, what its *only* correct reading must be.

We may detect signs in it of many submerged contrasts: between the poet's timid heart hiding from conflict and the blast-defiant kestrel; between the pretty plumes of a bird dead-still and the stirring magnificence of one in which courage and action are seen to combine ('buckle') with its animal ('brute') beauty; between the hawk's aerobatic control in curving, flashing flight and the muscle-taxing endurance of the ploughman steering the share down its straight path, turning dull rust into sun-reflecting metal; between the blue-bleak coals, conserving their ebbing heat, and their fiery brilliance when they sacrifice all they have left in self-destroying splendour.

A more important antithesis became less evident during the sonnet's revision: the windhover is only the dauphin, not the King: a much-loved favourite ('minion'), not the centre of feudal loyalty. The dawnbird hints at, but is outshone by, the Dayspring Himself, the Sun of Righteousness, 'a billion/Times told lovelier, more dangerous'. The contemplation of created things leads the Jesuit priest to the Creator himself, just as (in 'God's Grandeur') the clouds at sunrise are construed as the shining wings of the Comforter, and the stars in 'The Starlight Night' as chinks letting the brightness of heaven escape, like knot-holes in a barn through which the lights of the harvest-home feast can be seen (ll. 13, 14).

After his ordination in 1877 Hopkins was given a succession of posts as the Society tried to find the most suitable niche for him. For a while he was stationed in London, his main duties being preaching at the West-End Jesuit Church in Farm Street. Then followed parish duties in Oxford, Lancashire and Glasgow. To this brief portion of his life, less than four years, belong such well-known nature poems as 'Binsey Poplars', 'Inversnaid', and 'Spring and Fall: To a Young Child'. No real girl seems to have underlain this last beautiful lyric:

> Márgarét, áre you gríeving
> Over Goldengrove unleaving?
> Leáves, líke the things of man, you
> With your fresh thoughts care for, can you?
> Áh! ás the heart grows older
> It will come to such sights colder
> By and by, nor spare a sigh
> Though worlds of wanwood leafmeal lie;
>
> *(Poems*, p 88; *Oxf. Auth.*, p 152)

Other poems centre on people rather than the inscapes of the natural world. 'At the Wedding March' touches, as Hopkins seldom did in his mature poems, on the love between man and woman. 'Felix Randal' pictures a boisterous blacksmith at his 'random grim forge, powerful amidst peers', contrasting in every way with the sensitive and rather delicate little poet. An outstanding young Irish lad in the barracks near Oxford is the subject of 'The Bugler's First Communion'. Father Hopkins's admiration for fine boyhood or masculine strength and beauty emerges clearly in such pieces, and when combined with a few like admissions in confession notes made while he was an austere Anglican, this suggests to some that one possible source of the strain under which he laboured as teacher and priest was his determination not to allow his response to those in his charge to sway him from the detached impartiality expected of a Jesuit. While this common reflection of all-male society in school, Oxford and Jesuit communities gives him the status of hero among some avowed followers of Walt Whitman, there are others so unsympathetic to the Church that they view his adherence to the strictest sexual ideals as the product of harmful and timid restraints (see, e.g., John Robinson, *In Extremity: A Study of Gerard Manley Hopkins*, 1978, pp 89– 103).

His sermons also date from these central years. As with his verse, Hopkins tended to follow his own unique bents, sometimes to the amusement or disapproval of fellow Jesuits whose aesthetic side lay dormant. The sermons abound in energetic concepts and phrases, as when he suggests that Eve, thinking 'God her lord and landlord was envious and grudging, a rackrent', decided to 'seize crown-property', only to find herself turned out of Paradise with Adam in 'the first and most terrible of evictions' (*Sermons*, pp 66–7).

The theological writings printed with his sermons mostly belong to the final stage of his Jesuit training, his year as a Tertian, a period free from routine professional duties, given over entirely to the deepening of devotional life. During this spell he made notes towards a commentary upon the *Spiritual Exercises of St Ignatius*. Since his work is profoundly Ignatian, this section of the book (pp 122–209) provides serious students of his poetry with considerable guidance.

After his tertianship Hopkins was given advanced teaching posts – first at Stonyhurst College, and then, when the Jesuits were asked to rescue from failure the Catholic University College in Dublin, as Professor of Classics there from 1884 to his death in 1889. Ireland amidst her struggles towards independence was no haven of peace for any Englishman; the Catholic bishops who had mismanaged the College had insisted on stripping it of its library before handing over to the Jesuits, thus handicapping both students and staff. Moreover, Hopkins was passing through a spiritual experience of deep aridity: many have compared it to the Dark Night of the Soul which saints and mystics have attempted to describe. Among his papers after his death were found the intense personal 'sonnets of desolation' (as they are sometimes called). 'No worst, there is none' contains one of the most memorable sestets in English literature:

> O the mind, mind has mountains; cliffs of fall
> Frightful, sheer, no-man-fathomed. Hold them cheap
> May who ne'er hung there. Nor does long our small
> Durance deal with that steep or deep. Here! creep,
> Wretch, under a comfort serves in a whirlwind: all
> Life death does end and each day dies with sleep.
> (Poems, p 100; Oxf. Auth., p 167)

The unnerving image with which this opens illustrates Cochran's definition of *instress*: 'the intrinsic tension upholding the unity of being ... and distinguishing and individualizing that being'. Here someone facing spiritual disintegration, the loss of treasured assumptions on which his security has stood, is depicted as a solitary climber clinging in despair to the lip of a precipitous drop, dragged by the heels towards a shattering abyss. Another begins with self-charity, a mood very different from self-pity: 'My own heart let me more have pity on'. The desperation of a spirit which has exhausted all its own resources has nowhere been put more tersely than in the lines:

> I cast for comfort I can no more get
> By groping round my comfortless than blind
> Eyes in their dark can day or thirst can find
> Thirst's all-in-all in all a world of wet.
> (Poems, p 102; Oxf. Auth., p 170)

How is it that Hopkins seems to brand his name on every poem, scarcely a maverick line being found among his mature compositions? A student of Victorian literature seeking to contrast him with his contemporaries might go far towards an answer by placing one of his impressive later poems, 'Spelt from Sibyl's Leaves', alongside 'Childe Roland to the Dark Tower Came' by Browning, and Tennyson's 'Lucretius'. All three are mature works, and though not equally typical of their authors, they are made more comparable by a certain community of subject. Here we can merely begin the analysis.

Spelt from Sibyl's Leaves

Earnest, earthless, equal, attuneable, | vaulty, voluminous,
 . . . stupendous
Evening strains to be tíme's vást, | womb-of-all,
 home-of-all, hearse-of-all night.
Her fond yellow hornlight wound to the west, | her wild
 hollow hoarlight hung to the height
Waste; . . .

(*Poems*, p 97; *Oxf. Auth.*, p 175)

The unusual verse movement arrests attention. Hopkins created this sonnet out of eight-foot lines for the same reason which made him afterwards extend three other sonnets by means of codas – 'Tom's Garland', 'Harry Ploughman' and 'That Nature is a Heraclitean Fire'. He was striving to match in English the more dignified weight of the sonnet in Italian – to him one of the most perfect structures in all literature (*Letters*, vol II, pp 85–98). Over two-thirds of his major work went into sonnet-craftmanship: he seldom had leisure or impetus for longer poems. Moreover, he felt that Tennyson and Browning became shapeless and less artistic when they spread themselves. 'Just think the blank verse these people have exuded', he wrote (*Letters*, vol I, p 111). Hopkins poured into his poems only the essence, usually fractioned off at high temperature. And since he defined poetry as 'speech framed to be heard for its own sake and interest even over and above its interest of meaning', he filled it with 'repeating figures' (*Journals*, p 289) to make it musical and memorable. His poems almost invariably have rhyme, preventing their stanzas from unravelling into amorphous lengths when heard instead of seen.

As for diction, all three poets coin and compound in their own fashion: each has his favourite words. Hopkins loved consonant clusters, vigorous Anglo-Saxon monosyllables, with lively dialect words such as *pashed* or *degged* for flavour; but he knew the art of injecting a single polysyllable into a line heavy with monosyllables.

Óur tale, O óur oracle. | Lét life, wáned, ah lét life wind
Off hér once skéined stained véined varíety |upon, áll on
 twó spools; párt, pen, páck
Now her áll in twó flocks, twó folds – black, white; | right,
 wrong; reckon but, reck but, mind
But thése two; wáre of a wórld where bút these | twó tell,
 each off the óther;

(*Poems*, p 98, ll, 10–13; *Oxf. Auth.*, p 175)

Browning's vast vocabulary, however, included most of Hopkins's regular words, even if he used them differently and often hurried them down with less propriety or care for sound. It is a fallacy, too, to think that sprung rhythm led Hopkins into conversational cadences. Browning might simulate informal talk and Tennyson rhetorical speech, but with Hopkins the syntax and word-play are usually too elaborate to suggest the ordinary speaking voice. With great deliberation he fits every word – a fragment of mosaic – into a place which it alone can fill. The seven adjectives through which Hopkins seeks to come to terms with the devouring threat of evening (l. 1) each invite extensive commentary. We are given pause not by the rarity of some of these words, rather by the intense imagination with which they are applied: thus *equal* may remind us of the impartial, levelling quality of gathering darkness which made earlier scholars guess that *evening* might be cognate with the adjective *even* (see Johnson's Dictionary, ed. Todd, 1827.); *vaulty* reflects the way in which the shallow bowl of the sky may gain height as night comes on, its deep arch being here identified with that of a cosmic burial crypt (cf. 'or night, still higher', 'The Wreck of the Deutschland', stanza 26). The compounds describing night in line 2 – *womb-of-all, home-of-all, hearse-of-all night* – have classical models among the innumerable Greek words in *pan-* and *pam-*, or in the *De Rerum Natura* (V. 259), where Lucretius writes of the earth as 'omniparens, eadem rerum commune sepulcrum'. Hopkins avoided the commonplace *womb . . . tomb* antithesis (used, e.g., in Shakespeare's Sonnet 86, Swinburne's *Erechtheus*, Tennyson's *Lucretius*, l. 243: 'the womb and tomb of all'). His *hearse-of-all* applied to enveloping night is more original and graphic: it refers to a type of 'hearse' still to be found in old cathedrals – a canopied framework, lit with hundreds of little tapers, mounted high above the bier of someone lying in state. Phrases in Hopkins bear closer inspection than those of most poets.

Towards the end of this sonnet there is an adaptation of a Welsh device with which Hopkins frequently harmonized his verse: *hér once skéined/stained véined/varíety*. This imitates *cynghanedd sain*, in which a line is divided into three sections, the first two linked by rhyme and the second two by alliteration. (See W. H. Gardner, *Gerard Manley Hopkins*, vol II, pp 143–58.) Closer approximations to Welsh alliteration (where a series of successive consonants may be repeated in identical order) are found in this poem: *west, waste; tool, tale; bleak, black; waned, wind*. These pairs also illustrate another device which he admired, 'vowelling off', or the 'changing of vowel down some scale' (*Journals*, p 284). He had luxuriated in them in 'The Wreck of the

Deutschland', stanza 8, where we encounter *lash, lush, (plush); kept, capped; flesh (Gush), flush, flash* all in the narrow space of five lines.

Finally, the sprung rhythm of 'Spelt from Sibyl's Leaves' establishes it as Hopkins's own make. The lines vary sensitively in pace and weightiness. Readers who do not trouble to give each half-line its four necessary stresses (the first line has a foot-long pause after 'voluminous') miss the intricacy of the effect. Note the drawn-out monosyllabic feet in line 2: 'tíme's | vást' – usually demoted to a trochee as though it were no more than

'Évening stráins to be tímeless'.

Occasionally, as in the last line, the accents provided may seem eccentric: 'thóughts agáinst thoughts ín groans grínd' – where *in* is given pre-eminence above the two flanking words. But read as marked, the line seems distorted by the torture it describes. Once again Hopkins's *Letters* are full of illumination for us. 'Of this long sonnet above all remember what applies to all my verse, that it is, as living art should be, made for performance and that its performance is not reading with the eye but loud, leisurely, poetical (not rhetorical) recitation, with long rests, long dwells on the rhyme and other marked syllables, and so on. This sonnet should be almost sung: it is most carefully timed in *tempo rubato*' (*Letters*, vol I, p 246).

Among the finest of his last poems is another extended sonnet, 'That Nature is a Heraclitean Fire . . .', (1888), which looks to the resurrection for the converting of this discordant mixture called 'man' – 'This Jack, joke, poor potsherd, | patch, match-wood, immortal diamond' (*Poems*, p 106; *Oxf. Auth.*, p 181) – into pure and entire diamond. In a frank poem, written a few weeks before his final illness, 'The Shepherd's Brow . . .', he enlarges upon the laughable pretensions of mankind. Here the heroic struggles of his 'terrible sonnets' such as 'Carrion Comfort' are viewed through a Swiftian reducing-glass:

> But man – we, scaffold of score brittle bones;
> Who breathe, from groundlong babyhood to hoary
> Age gasp; whose breath is our *memento mori* –
> What bass is *our* viol for tragic tones?
> He! Hand to mouth he lives, and voids with shame;
> (*Poems*, p 107; *Oxf. Auth.*, p 183)

When Hopkins died in 1889, only 44 years old, the obituaries which praised his talent as an artist and critic showed no awareness that he was a poet. If he had lived to a riper age, we may assume that he would have continued to wrestle words, rhythm and verse-forms into new approximations to his thought, but there is little evidence that his rather restricted range of subjects would have expanded. He showed no wish to pass beyond the age-old circumvallating walls of the Catholic faith, though one of his fellow Jesuits, paying him tribute remarked: 'If I had known him outside, I should have said that his love of speculation and originality of thought would make it almost impossible for him to submit his intellect to authority' (*Letters and Notices*, vol XX, March 1890, p 173). If many Catholics now regard him as the one truly satisfying English poet, his fascination is also felt by those to whom his beliefs seem mistaken and his feelings sometimes misplaced.

During the last quarter of the century since his death national awareness of the poet in Britain has noticeably increased. The founding of an influential Hopkins Society in 1969, with representatives all over the world, led to such recognition of his status as the unveiling, amid much publicity, of a monument to him in the Poets' Corner of Westminster Abbey in December 1975, on the centenary of the wrecking of the *Deutschland*. Today the members of the International Hopkins Association include not only English critics in Britain, Ireland and North America, but active scholars in Holland, France, Spain, Italy and (most numerous) Japan. His poetry and prose are becoming increasingly available in other languages, but translators freely acknowledge the impossibility of recapturing his virtuosity with words and rhythms, or the intensity of imaginative suggestion which have together earned him the wide respect he now enjoys.

15

THE ROSSETTIS AND OTHER CONTEMPORARY POETS
James Sambrook

The Pre-Raphaelite Brotherhood was formed in 1848, that year of revolutions, by three painters, Dante Gabriel Rossetti (1828–82), Holman Hunt (1827–1910) and J. E. Millais (1829–96), a sculptor Thomas Woolner (1825–92), and three comparative nonentities whose main function appears to have been to bring the number up to a mystic seven. They had disbanded by 1853, and only Hunt stuck doggedly for the rest of his life to the original aims of the Brotherhood. These aims were – in revolt against academic rules of lighting and composition derived ultimately from Raphael – to paint always direct from the natural object, to use 'the bright colours of nature', and to choose subjects from contemporary life or to give all the realism of a contemporary scene to those historical and literary subjects which they took chiefly from Shakespeare, Keats and the Bible, or – in Rossetti's case – from Dante and Malory. They followed one of the innumerable paths 'back to nature'. In their case they sought nature by means of a minute particularization.

The Pre-Raphaelite Brotherhood founded a literary organ, *The Germ: Thoughts towards Nature in Poetry, Literature and Art*, which survived for four issues (January–May, 1850). This journal carried some admirable early poems by Dante Gabriel Rossetti, his sister Christina and Coventry Patmore, but in its pages appeared also two winsome cantos by Woolner of the work he later expanded into a *Maud*-like monodrama, *My Beautiful Lady* (1863):

> I love My Lady; she is very fair;
> Her brow is wan, and bound by simple hair:
> Her spirit sits aloof, and high,
> But glances from her tender eye
> In sweetness droopingly.
>
> (i, 1–5)

The last line adequately describes Woolner's style. The work (which was popular in its day) is interesting now only as a document from a sexually repressed society where sad love-longing is sublimated into idealism. It is a verbal equivalent of some of Arthur Hughes's paintings.

Despite *The Germ* and despite the fact that parallels may be discovered between some P.R.B. paintings and some mid-Victorian poetry, we shall find that 'Pre-Raphaelite' is not a very meaningful term in *literary* history. Rossetti had literary disciples and associates who picked up briefly from him a certain style of Romantic archaism. This is not 'Pre-Raphaelitism' in the original sense, and, in any case, the differences among these disciples are more important than the similarities.

Dante Gabriel Rossetti's income came from painting; he published verse in periodicals but did not make any collections until fairly late in life, with *Poems* (1870, expanded 1881) and *Ballads and Sonnets* (1881). Many of these poems had been written as early as the 1840s, and of those the longest is the unfinished narrative, 'The Bride's Prelude' (1881). This poem's medievalism 'of lozenged arm-bearings', 'of chevesayle and mantelet' is straight from Chatterton and Keats, but the narrative method of accumulating minutely observed descriptive details corresponds in some way to Millais' and Hunt's crab-like labour over their anecdotal canvases inch by painstaking inch – at the cost of any central emphasis in the work. But Rossetti's poem has a remarkable and finely realized cloistral, airless atmosphere:

> The room lay still in dusty glare,
>   Having no sound through it
> Except the chirp of a caged bird
> That came and ceased: and if she stirred,
> Amelotte's raiment could be heard.
>
> (151–5)

This is the effect of his elaborate, mysterious, tense, agoraphobic water-colours such as 'The Wedding of St. George' (painted 1857) or 'Sir Galahad at the Ruined Chapel' (1859).

Such paintings confirm Rossetti's declaration that 'imaginings . . . envelop me from the outer world'. He never finished his oil 'Found' (begun 1853) which was his one attempt to paint a contemporary subject in the vein of Hunt's 'The Awakening Conscience'. The subject of a dramatic verse-monologue 'Jenny' (begun 1848) is comparable to that of 'Found', but the distinctive

quality of the poem lies in the flickers of imaginative strangeness
that brighten this study of a prostitute:

> When, wealth and health slipped past, you stare
> Along the streets alone, and there,
> Round the long park, across the bridge,
> The cold lamps at the pavement's edge
> Wind on together and apart,
> A fiery serpent for your heart

(150–5)

and her client, the poet,

> Like a toad within a stone
> Seated while Time crumbles on . . .
> Even so within this world is Lust

(282–97)

rather than in the pathos of its social commentary. 'The Burden of
Nineveh' (1850) has a thoughtful, dry, ironic criticism of Mam-
monized English society; the Italian Revolution of 1848 prompts
'On Refusal of Aid between Nations', and is referred to in a
passionate Browningesque dramatic monologue, 'A Last Confession'; but all these are untypical of Rossetti's work as a whole.

Rossetti was half-Italian by birth. He wrote poems in Italian and
his first large book was of English translations from pre-Petrarchan
lyric poets, *The Early Italian Poets* (1861, rearranged as *Dante and his
Circle*, 1874). These translations might be regarded as a scholarly
counterpart to Pre-Raphaelitism; Petrarch was to European lyric
poetry as Raphael was to figure-painting; so that, by going to
Dante's *Vita Nuova* and the courtly love poems of the Sicilian
School, Rossetti was returning to the fresh dawn of art. In the prose
tale 'Hand and Soul' (*The Germ*, 1850) a thirteenth-century painter
has a vision of heaven where he worships a Beatrice-like figure who
is a symbol not of Theology (as Beatrice was) but of Art. He
'became aware that much of that reverence which he had mistaken
for faith had been no more than the worship of beauty'. Then he is
commanded to paint a mystical lady who is the image of his own
soul. God does not require the artist to moralize, but only to be true
to his inner experience.

The Beatrice figure reappears in Rossetti's best known poem
'The Blessed Damozel' (1850, later extensively revised), which he
intended as a complement to Poe's 'The Raven' (1845). Rossetti
sketches his setting in the manner of two men he excessively
admired – John Martin (1789–1854), the wild, apocalyptic painter,

and Philip James Bailey, author of the popular hyper-drama *Festus* (1839):

> It lies in Heaven, across the flood
>   Of ether, as a bridge.
> Beneath, the tides of day and night
>   With flame and darkness ridge
> The void, as low as where this earth
>   Spins like a fretful midge.

(stanza 6)

This is grand, the names of Mary's heavenly seamstresses *are*, as the poet claims, 'five sweet symphonies', the aureate diction glitters, and one is reminded of the exquisite, but factitious, work of the Greek poets of Alexandria. Rossetti's conception of an after-life where the Blessed Damozel weeps in frustrated longing to be united with her lover – rather than with God – is not even remotely Christian. Heaven provides decorative, fancifully exotic and archaic 'furnishings' for the plaints of parted lovers. Rossetti consistently uses religion as an aesthetic mine. Significantly, he gave the title *Songs of the Art Catholic* to a manuscript collection of his verses which he sent to his friend William Bell Scott in 1847.

The Beatrice of Rossetti's life was Lizzie Siddal, to whom he was half-heartedly engaged for ten years before he dutifully married her in 1860. After less than two years of married life she poisoned herself with laudanum, and Rossetti in a fit of remorse buried his unique manuscript volume of poems in her coffin, whence it was exhumed seven years later for the poems to be included in the 1870 volume. He never laid her ghost, and in the 1860s and 70s painted four posthumous portraits of her as 'Beata Beatrix'. At the time of that marriage, though, he was infatuated with Jane, the wife of his friend William Morris. He had painted her in 1857 as Guenevere in the Oxford Union fresco which he described as follows:

Sir Lancelot prevented by his sin from entering the Chapel of the San Grael. He has fallen asleep before the shrine full of angels, and between him and it rises in his sleep the image of Queen Guenevere, the cause of all.

(Letters, vol I, 337)

Jane Morris continued to fascinate Rossetti to the end of his life. For sexual satisfaction he went to the vulgar and vital Fanny Cornforth, who was following the oldest profession in the notorious Argyll Rooms when he met her in the 1850s. She sat for 'Found' and for many of the later 'epicurean' half-length portraits intended

for the Renaissance palaces of Northern plutocrats when Rossetti,
alive to his market, had become a somewhat flashily sensual type of
Bradford Titian.

The guilt and the idealism of these personal relations appear in
the sonnet sequence 'The House of Life', which represents a not
altogether successful attempt to spiritualize love, using Dante's
imagery and notions but lacking Dante's religion. So Rossetti rises
no higher than religiosity in 'Heart's Hope' (sonnet v in the final
version of the sequence, 1881), 'The Kiss' (vi), 'Secret Parting'
(xlv), and 'Love's Redemption' in its 1870 version – it was revised as
'Love's Testament' (iii) in 1881:

> O Thou who at Love's hour ecstatically
>   Unto my lips dost evermore present
>   The body and blood of Love in sacrament;
> Whom I have neared and felt thy breath to be
> The inmost incense of his sanctuary.

This has a certain incantatory power, but the image remains vague
and the idea vaguer.

This is not always the case. 'Silent Noon' (xix) has the Millais or
Hunt qualities of fresh, crisp, static particularity. In its small way it
approaches the one undoubted masterpiece of Pre-Raphaelite
painting, 'The Blind Girl' by Millais:

> Your hands lie open in the long fresh grass, –
>   The finger-points look through like rosy blooms:
>   Your eyes smile peace. The pasture gleams and glooms
> 'Neath billowing skies that scatter and amass.
> All round our nest, far as the eye can pass,
>   Are golden kingcup-fields with silver edge
>   Where the cow-parsley skirts the hawthorn-hedge.
> 'Tis visible silence, still as the hour-glass.
>
> Deep in the sun-searched growths the dragon-fly
> Hangs like a blue thread loosened from the sky.

The painter's sharp perception and grasp of detail crystallize and
communicate honestly an intense experience. So too in 'Sudden
Light':

> I have been here before,
>   But when or how I cannot tell:
> I know the grass beyond the door,
>   The sweet keen smell,
> The sighing sound, the lights around the shore,

and in that fine rendering of exhausted sorrow, 'The Woodspurge'. Both these poems appeared among the Songs appended to the incomplete version of 'The House of Life' in *Poems* (1870).

Rossetti's most memorable poetry, like Wordsworth's, explores the landscape of memory; but all too often for Rossetti memory is a nightmare of remorse. He recognizes his failure to sustain his idealism in life, and is haunted by guilt over lost opportunities and failures in art due to lethargy, over visits to the Argyll Rooms, over Lizzie's death and over his love for Jane Morris. Remorse deepens into self-disgust and disintegration of personality:

> Look in my face; my name is Might-have-been;
> I am also called No-more, Too-late, Farewell;
> ('A Superscription', xcvii, 'The House of Life')

> God knows I know the faces I shall see,
> Each one a murdered self, with low last breath.
> 'I am thyself – what hast thou done to me?'
> 'And I – and I – thyself,' (lo! each one saith,)
> 'And thou thyself to all eternity!'
> ('Lost Days', lxxxvi)

Four sonnets, written in 1868 and called collectively 'Willowwood' (xlix–lii), most poignantly speak for a man divided against himself. Here the past invades the present. Dumb, lonely figures – representing the lost days – stand beneath the trees, and the corpse of the wife rises to the surface of the hidden river. The images, at once personal and archetypal, convey a powerful sense of remorse brooding over the dead days. This 'thicket' image in 'Willowwood' – 'the rustling covert of my soul' – is almost obsessive in Rossetti's work. It appears most strikingly in the pen-and-ink drawing 'How they met themselves', where two lovers in a wood (the models were Lizzie and himself on their honeymoon in Paris, 1860) meet their menacing *doppelgängers* who warn of impending death. Around them the leaves and branches press down closely.

It is this sinister, demonic region where love meets death, rather than the angelic sphere of 'The Blessed Damozel', that Rossetti re-creates most convincingly. The image of the fatal woman runs through his painting from the Guenevere of 1857 to the last version of Proserpine in the year of his death; both were painted from Jane Morris. In the sonnet for his oil painting 'Pandora' (Jane Morris again) he sees 'In Venus' eyes the gaze of Proserpine'; love and death are united. In sonnet xlviii of 'The House of Life' a veiled woman reveals herself as 'Death-in-love'. The finest of Rossetti's several Coleridgean ballad imitations, 'Sister Helen' (1853, but much revised later), tells of a witch torturing and killing her false lover by melting a waxen image. Significantly, when Rossetti re-handles the matter of *Paradise Lost* and the *Iliad* in his ballads 'Eden Bower' and 'Troy Town' (1870), it is to compress it into the utterances of those mischief-working sirens, Lilith and Helen.

Rossetti once praised the Scottish painter W. D. Kennedy (1813–65) for re-creating 'the landscapes we have known in our dreams' (*Collected Works of D. G. Rossetti*, 1887, vol II, 496). These are Rossetti's landscapes in, for instance, 'Love's Nocturn' (1870):

> Vaporous, unaccountable,
>   Dreamworld lies forlorn of light . . .
>
> There breath perfumes; there in rings
> Whirl the foam-bewildered springs;
>   Siren there
> Winds her dizzy hair and sings . . .
>
> The black firwood sets its teeth.
> Part the boughs and look beneath, –
>   Lilies share
> Secret waters there, and breathe.
>   (8–9, 25–8, 102–5)

Perhaps the most intensely imagined work of Rossetti's is 'The Orchard-Pit', written about 1871 in prose and partly in verse, but unpublished in his lifetime. (In its present state it conveniently illustrates Rossetti's method of 'working up' a poem from a prose draft, just as some artists work up a painting from detailed sketches.)

> Piled deep below the screening apple-branch
>   They lie with bitter apples in their hands:
> And some are only ancient bones that blanch,
> And some had ships that last year's wind did launch,
>   And some were yesterday the lords of lands.
>
> In the soft dell among the apple-trees,
>   High up above the hidden pit she stands,
> And there for ever sings, who gave to these,
> That lie below, her magic hours of ease,
>   And those her apples holden in their hands.

This in my dreams is shown me; and her hair
   Crosses my lips and draws my burning breath;
Her song spreads golden wings upon the air,
Life's eyes are gleaming from her forehead fair,
   And from her breasts the ravishing eyes of Death.[1]

Men say to me that sleep hath many dreams,
   Yet I knew never but this dream alone:
There, from a dried-up channel, once the stream's,
The glen slopes up; even such in sleep it seems
   As to my waking sight the place well known.

Rossetti turns his back on society, progress, the Condition of England question, and all public themes in order to prowl through the rustling coverts of his soul and flush out the spectres of the pre-conscious mind. Albeit narrowly and neurotically he continues, with a genuine imaginative power, to work the introspective vein prospected by the great Romantic poets at the beginning of the nineteenth century.

The religious enthusiasm of the Rossetti sisters, Christina (1830–94) and Maria, more than compensated for the indifference of their brothers. William, the agnostic, was irritated by Christina's 'perpetual church-going and communions, her prayers and fasts, her submission to clerical direction, her oblations, her practice of confession' (*Poetical Works of C. G. Rossetti*, ed. W. M. Rossetti, 1904, p lv). From the 1840s both sisters attended the famous, heady, High Church services at Christ Church, Albany Street in London, and were excited by the spectacle of attractive young women from good families devoting themselves to austerity, discipline and virginity in the Anglican sisterhood founded nearby by Dr Pusey. Maria joined a sisterhood as soon as she thought her family duties permitted this, and Christina from the 1860s was an associate of the Highgate Penitentiary devoted to the reformation of prostitutes. Neither sister ever married.

Christina strikes her characteristic note as a poet in 'An End' (*The Germ*, 1850), written when she was seventeen. It begins 'Love, strong as Death, is dead' and concludes:

---

[1] It was Rossetti's uncle, J. W. Polidori, who told the famous story of Shelley at Geneva in 1816 suddenly shrieking and rushing from the room. Polidori had, with cold water and ether, to restore him to normality. It transpired that as Shelley had been staring at Mary Shelley he had been shocked into uncontrollable horror by seeing a vision of a woman he had once heard of who had eyes for nipples. See *Diary of Dr. John William Polidori*, ed. W. M. Rossetti, 1911, p 128.

> To few chords and sad and low
> Sing we so:
> Be our eyes fixed on the grass
> Shadow-veiled as the years pass,
> While we think of all that was
> In the long ago.

In her first published collection, *Goblin Market* (1862), which was widely recognized as revealing a new major woman poet to succeed Mrs Browning who had died in the previous year, and in the later collections of her voluminous lyrical verse, *The Prince's Progress* (1866), *A Pageant* (1881), *Poems* (S.P.C.K., 1893) and *New Poems* (1895), Christina strikes these few chords again and again. However, they are not her only notes. There are nonsense verses, such as 'If a Pig wore a Wig', in her collection of nursery rhymes, *Sing-Song* (1872) (though much of her writing for children – particularly in the prose stories – is gruesome and minatory). There is a slightly laboured playfulness in 'No, Thank You, John' and a delicate wit in 'The Queen of Hearts'. A simple clear note of sensuous rapture is heard in 'Maiden-Song', 'A Bride Song' and 'A Birthday' (*Macmillan's Magazine*, 1861):

> My heart is like a singing bird
> Whose nest is in a watered shoot;
> My heart is like an apple-tree
> Whose boughs are bent with thickset fruit;
> My heart is like a rainbow shell
> That paddles in a halcyon sea;
> My heart is gladder than all these
> Because my love is come to me.

More often, though, Christina images the joys of the senses as forbidden fruits – as in the opening lines of her richly imagined *Goblin Market*, a poetic fairy-tale unobtrusively informed by the Christian doctrines of the Fall and Atonement, and sharpened by psychological insight into the nature of guilt and self-sacrifice.

Renunciation of the Flesh, the World and the Devil is the subject of a tensely dramatic dialogue, 'The Three Enemies' (1862), but nearly all her verse, early and late, is in a sense a dialogue between the resolved soul and created pleasure. There are echoes from Albany Street when she writes of the nun's vocation in dramatic monologues such as the splendidly passionate 'The Convent Threshold' (1862) or 'Soeur Louise de la Miséricorde' (1881). In the fourteen sonnets entitled 'Monna Innominata', with epigraphs from Dante and Petrarch, and the twenty-eight entitled 'Later Life' (both 1881) she tells how earthly love dies to be reborn as love of Heaven. The nightmare images of her sonnet 'The World' (1862) reveal a very horror of the flesh. The effort that her renunciation of earthly loves cost her is sometimes apparent. 'Noble Sisters' and 'Sister Maude' (1862, but omitted by Christina from subsequent editions) are allegories of a conflict within the divided personality: one sister drives away the other sister's lover. In 'Up-Hill' (*Macmillan's Magazine*, 1861, and the first poem to bring consider- able public attention to Christina) the familiar Pilgrim's Progress figure becomes an emblem of world-weariness in a particularly sinister way:

> Does the road wind up-hill all the way?
> Yes, to the very end.
> Will the day's journey take the whole long day?
> From morn to night, my friend.
>
> But is there for the night a resting-place?
> A roof for when the slow dark hours begin.
> May not the darkness hide it from my face?
> You cannot miss that inn.

In her second lyric under the title 'The Heart Knoweth its own Bitterness' (written 1857, but not published in full until 1895) Christina, by contrast, is not the weary pilgrim but a splendidly passionate creature, distraught in a world that can provide no satisfaction for her love:

> To give, to give, not to receive!
>   I long to pour myself, my soul,
> Not to keep back or count or leave,
>   But king with king to give the whole.
> I long for one to stir my deep –
>   I have had enough of help and gift –
>   I long for one to search and sift
> Myself, to take myself and keep.
>
> You scratch my surface with your pin,
>   You stroke me smooth with hushing breath:–
> Nay pierce, nay probe, nay dig within,
>   Probe my quick core and sound my depth.
> You call me with a puny call,
>   You talk, you smile, you nothing do:
>   How should I spend my heart on you,
> My heart that so outweighs you all? . . .

> Not in this world of hope deferred,
>> This world of perishable stuff:–
> Eye hath not seen nor ear hath heard
>> Nor heart conceived that full 'enough':
> Here moans the separating sea,
>> Here harvests fail, here breaks the heart:
>> There God shall join and no man part,
> I full of Christ and Christ of me.

Hymns and prayers account for an ever increasing proportion of her verse in later years. They consist, as we should expect, of highly rigorous self-examinations as she treads the hard, up-hill road to Christ. With age and sickness her cry 'Lord, I am waiting' grows ever more insistent; but she had been waiting ever since, at the age of fourteen, she had placed all her hopes in Heaven:

> filling there and satisfying
> Man's soul unchanging and undying,
> Earth's fleeting joys and beauties far above,
> In heaven is Love.
>
> ('Earth and Heaven')

Her introspection, unlike her brother's, is disciplined sternly to orthodox and intelligible religious ends.

The Pre-Raphaelite Brothers liked the ballad rhythms and medieval décor in *Poems* (1844) by Coventry Patmore (1823–96), and invited him to contribute to *The Germ* (1850). He wrote a brief succession of bright verbal vignettes, 'The Seasons':

> The crocus, in the shrewd March morn,
>> Thrusts up his saffron spear;
> And April dots the sombre thorn
>> With gems, and loveliest cheer.
>
> Then sleep the seasons, full of might;
>> While slowly swells the pod,
> And round the peach, and in the night
>> The mushroom bursts the sod.
>
> The winter comes: the frozen rut
>> Is bound with silver bars;
> The white drift heaps against the hut;
>> And night is pierced with stars.

This word-painting is good, but untypical. Patmore is remembered as the thrice-married celebrant and singer of the connubial sacrament; above all as the author of *The Angel in the House*

(1854–6) which sold a quarter of a million copies before its author's death. This verse-novel, prompted by Patmore's love for his first wife, tells in smooth but never tedious octosyllabics how Felix Vaughan, a respectable young gentleman with six hundred pounds a year, courts and marries Honoria, eldest daughter of the Dean of Sarum, without meeting any serious obstacle. Patmore mirrors the domesticity of the Victorian middle-class with a Betjemanic fidelity:

> Geranium, lychnis, rose array'd
> The windows, all wide open thrown;
> And some one in the Study play'd
> The Wedding-March of Mendelssohn.
>> (Bk I, canto i, 'The Cathedral Close', 2)

He dignifies the commonest tastes and sentiments of his readers – hence the poem's popularity – but more than this, he accompanies the unruffled narrative of commonplace incidents with a subtle psychological commentary:

> And ever her chaste and noble air
> Gave to love's feast its choicest gust,
> A vague, faint augury of despair.
>> (Bk I, canto vi, 'The Dean', 4)

> Why, having won her, do I woo?
> Because her spirit's vestal grace
> Provokes me always to pursue,
> But, spirit-like, eludes embrace.
>> (Bk II, canto xii, 'Preludes', 1)

Patmore, like Dante Gabriel Rossetti, pursues a love that can never be completely satisfied by its carnal object, but, unlike Rossetti, he can relate this pursuit of the ideal love easily (one is sometimes tempted to say, complacently) to life and to a total religious scheme of things. Accepting the sacramental doctrine that, in the words of Newman's *Apologia*, 'material phenomena are both the types and the instruments of real things unseen,' he sees sexual union in Christian marriage as the shadow of God's love for the human soul. This doctrine is expounded in 'The Wedding Sermon' which concludes *The Victories of Love* (1860–3, a sequel to *The Angel in the House*) and is further developed in the odes written at various times after the death of his first wife in 1862, and published as *The Unknown Eros* (1877–8).

Some of these odes, 'Eros and Psyche', 'Psyche's Discontent', 'Wind and Wave', display a frank sexuality that shocked many of Patmore's first readers. 'Pain' and 'De Natura Deorum' which describes the joys of the wife:

> Ah, Child, the sweet
> Content, when we're both kiss'd and beat!

appear to have traces of sado-masochism, but Patmore would claim, with St Bernard of Clairvaux, that these image the soul's desire to submit fully to God. The sexual relation symbolizes the spiritual. In 'Sponsa Dei' Patmore expresses with a craggy directness this idea that, as man is to woman, so God is to the soul, an ardent, tyrannical lover:

> Who is this only happy She,
> Whom, by a frantic flight of courtesy,
> Born of despair
> Of better lodging for his spirit fair,
> He adores as Margaret, Maude, or Cecily? . . .
>
> What if this Lady be thy soul, and He
> Who claims to enjoy her sacred beauty be,
> Not thou, but God; and thy sick fire . . .
> A reflex heat
> Flash'd on thy cheek from His immense desire,
> Which waits to crown, beyond thy brain's conceit,
> Thy nameless, secret, hopeless longing sweet,
> Not by-and-by, but now,
> Unless deny Him thou!

This is the culmination of the philosophy of *The Angel in the House*. The Mariolatry that appears in some other odes (e.g. 'Deliciae Sapientiae de Amore' and 'The Child's Purchase') can be attributed to Patmore's conversion to Roman Catholicism in 1865, on his second marriage. Some earlier, tender odes – 'The Toys', 'Tired Memory', 'Departure' and, most notably the delicate and tremblingly beautiful 'The Azalea' – convey in direct, simple terms the widower's lonely sadness. There is a repellently different tone in the bitter, reactionary political odes such as '1867', referring to Disraeli's Reform Act:

> In the year of the great crime,
> When the faobles and their Jew,
> By God demented, slew
> The Trust they stood twice pledged to keep from wrong.

In the face of creeping democracy Patmore hurls his impotent invective and stands aside:

> Here, in this little Bay,
> Full of tumultuous life and great repose,
> Where, twice a day,
> The purposeless, glad ocean comes and goes,
> Under high cliffs, and far from the huge town,
> I sit me down.
> For want of me the world's course will not fail:
> When all its work is done, the lie shall rot;
> The truth is great, and shall prevail,
> When none cares whether it prevail or not.

He turns away to meditate, in characteristically disciplined, energetic and grave Pindarics, upon the religion that had provided him with the intellectual convictions and the imaginative symbols by which he had idealized Victorian domestic life and love.

It was Patmore who brought to wide notice the poetry of the Dorset schoolmaster and parson William Barnes (1801–86), whose dialect poems also were admired by and influenced Hopkins and Hardy. For all the deliberate provinciality, indeed rusticity, of his poetic diction, Barnes was a man of wide learning: he studied Hebrew, Welsh, and Persian prosody; his pioneering *Philological Grammar* (1854) was based on the comparative study of no fewer than 64 languages; he advocated the revitalizing of English by eliminating words from Greek and Latin and introducing new words of Anglo-Saxon provenance; he affirmed that the Dorset dialect of his own day was close to the speech of King Alfred and was 'purer and more regular than that which has been adopted as the national speech'.

His early verse, the unremarkable *Poetical Pieces* (1820) and *Orra, a Lapland Tale* (1822), was written in 'national English', as were two later volumes of *Poems* (1846 and 1868); but his most distinctive poetry is to be found in the three volumes of *Poems of Rural Life in the Dorset Dialect* (1844, 1859 and 1862). Though he justified his choice on scholarly grounds, Barnes chose Dorset dialect primarily because it 'is my mother tongue, and is to my mind the only true speech of the life that I draw'. As it happens, Dorset rural life in his day was marked by widespread poverty, on the causes of which he occasionally comments in poems of social concern (rather than protest), such as his eclogues 'Two Farms in Woone' and 'The Common a-took in', but mostly he portrays only the socially harmonious aspects of rural life and labour. One of his characteristic modes is the short descriptive poem that might best be described as a lyrical georgic: 'Vellèn o' the Tree', 'Out at Plough', 'Hay

Carrèn', 'A haulen o' the Corn', 'Milkèn Time', etc. Barnes makes common life vocal; he is particularly good at catching and holding moments of fellowship and contentment, whether he is celebrating village festivals, as in 'Gwain to Feair', 'Harvest Hwome', and 'Keepèn up o' Chris'mas', or merely the end of an ordinary day's labour, as in 'Zun-zet', 'Evenèn in the Village', or 'Day's Work a-done', where there is a hint of the spiritual innocence of Blake's Echoing Green:

> And oh! the jäy our rest did yield,
>   At evenèn by the mossy wall,
> When we'd a-work'd all day a-vield,
>   While zummer zuns did rise an' vall,
>   As there a lettèn
>   Goo all frettèn,
> An' vorgettèn all our twiles,
> We zot among our childern's smiles.

Barnes employs the language of Dorset country folk to express the wholesomeness and decorum of a communal village life that is tied to the seasons, but he writes also on the seasons of human life, with his poems on rustic wooing, contented marriage, children, and bereavement. 'Woak Hill' describes the widower leaving the house where he had lived with his wife:

> When sycamore leaves were a-spreadèn,
>   Green-ruddy, in hedges,
> Bezide the red doust o' the ridges,
>   A-dried at Woak Hill:
>
> I packed up my goods all a-sheenèn
>   Wi' long years o' handlèn,
> On dousty red wheels ov a waggon
>   To ride at Woak Hill.

As he departs he calls the dead wife and fancies that she accompanies him to his new home:

> I call'd her so fondly, wi' lippèns
>   All soundless to others,
> An' took her wi' aïr-reachèn hand,
>   To my zide at Woak Hill.
>
> On the road I did look round, a-talkèn
>   To light at my shoulder,
> An' then led her in at the door-way,
>   Miles wide vrom Woak Hill.

Here is the 'holy simplicity' that Palgrave singled out as Barnes's most distinctive quality.

This quality emerges too in the unaffected and unselfconscious delight with which he dwells on colour, light, and movement in his word-paintings of the Dorset natural scene, as in 'The Water Crowvoot':

> O small-feäc'd flow'r that now dost bloom
> To stud wi' white the shallor Frome,
> An' leäve the clote to spread his flow'r
> On darksome pools o' stwoneless Stour,
> When sof'ly-rizèn aïrs do cool
> The water in the sheenèn pool,
> Thy beds o' snow-white buds do gleam
> So feäir upon the sky-blue stream,
> As whitest clouds, a-hangèn high
> Avore the blueness o' the sky.

Hopkins said of Barnes: 'He is a perfect artist and of a most spontaneous inspiration; it is as if Dorset life and Dorset landscape had taken flesh and tongue in the man'. 'My orcha'd in Linden Lea', probably Barnes's best known poem on account of its setting by Vaughan Williams, breathes the inner serenity and spiritual liberty of a truly natural pastoral:

> 'Ithin the woodlands, flow'ry gleäded,
> By the woak tree's mossy root,
> The sheenèn grass-bleädes, timber-sheäded,
>   Now do quiver under voot;
> An' birds do whissle over head,
> An' water's bubblèn in its bed,
> An' there vor me the apple tree
> Do leän down low in Linden Lea.

It has the freshness and simplicity of folk-song, so much so that one scarcely notices the ingenuity of the refrain, structured as it is by the Welsh prosodic device of *cynghanedd*, a pattern of consonantal repetition.

Like Barnes, Robert Stephen Hawker (1803–75) was a Westcountry clergyman whose earliest verse was published in the 1820s. Hawker's *Tendrils* appeared in 1821, and his best known poem, the rousing Trelawny ballad 'The Song of the Western Men', in 1826. Apart from this ballad, his verse, which was usually published in small pamphlets, went largely unnoticed. The only sizeable collection made in his lifetime was *Cornish Ballads and Other Poems*

(1869). His *Footsteps of Former Men in Far Cornwall* (1870) is a gathering of prose biographical sketches of Cornish 'characters', whose eccentricities were, in many cases, matched by those that Hawker himself developed in his forty years as a patriarchal, almost missionary, vicar of the isolated, uncivilized parish of Morwenstow in North Cornwall. He had known the Tractarians in his undergraduate days at Oxford. At Morwenstow he sought to revive what he took to be the usages of the ancient Celtic Church, but his most significant innovation was the Harvest Festival, connecting church ceremonial with the land.

Like Barnes, Hawker is a local poet, but in a locality where every rock and ruin is instinct with legend. Folklore prompts, for instance, the simple, lively ballad, 'Featherstone's Doom', about the Cornish wrecker whose troubled spirit is doomed to live beneath Blackrock, near Bude, and twist a rope of sand. But more often he writes of the Christian legends and local saints – in, for instance, 'The Sisters of Glen Nectan' (which he accused Wilkie Collins of plagiarizing), 'The Doom Well of St Madron' (Arthurian), 'The Saintly Names' and 'St Nectan's Kieve'. In 'Morwenna Statio' and 'The Vine' he makes ecclesiological tours of his own parish church reading sermons in its stones, but he loved the shrine more than the pulpit. To Sabine Baring-Gould's antiquarian query about the burial-place of St Morwenna he replied:

What! Morwenna not lie in the holy place at Morwenstow! Of that you will never persuade me – no, never. I know that she lies there. I have seen her, and she has told me as much, and at her feet ere long I hope to lay my old bones.

'A Rapture on the Cornish Hills' records a mystical experience, but far more distinctive is 'Aishah-Schechinah' (1860) which is a meditation upon the mystery of the Incarnation:

> The zone, where two glad worlds for ever meet,
>   Beneath that bosom ran:
> Deep in that womb the conquering Paraclete
>   Smote Godhead on to man.

Hawker translated the Hebrew words of his title as 'The Woman Numinous', and refers often in his works to the 'Numyne', which he defines as 'the Spiritual or Etherial Element . . . Within its texture the other and grosser elements of Light and Air, ebb and flow, cling and glide. Therein dwell the forces, and thereof Angels and all Spiritual Things receive their Substance and Form'.[1]

---

[1] Hawker, like R. W. Dixon and, no doubt, many other Christians perturbed by the assertions of scientific materialism, obtained religious comfort from the scientific theory of a luminiferous ether, propounded by Sir David Brewster (1781–1868), inventor of the kaleidoscope.

This definition occurs in one of the many learned footnotes to his longest poem, *The Quest of the Sangraal* (1864), a blank verse narrative with a Cornish setting. Of all the many Victorian retailers of the Grail story Hawker is most fully alive to the Christian truth of the legend. Whereas Tennyson represents the quest as a morbid, enthusiastic mysticism that will destroy the system of rational virtue in the Round Table, Hawker sees it as the fullness of spiritual vitality. Tennyson's Arthur is full of gloomy foreboding; Hawker's Arthur is the first to raise the cry 'Ho! for the Sangraal, vanished vase of God!' For Hawker the Grail is a specific object, 'The vessel of the Pasch, Shere Thursday night', as well as an emblem of life and fertility and an awesome sign of God's indwelling with men. So he writes of Joseph of Arimathea:

> He dwelt in orient Syria: God's own land . . .
> His home was like a garner, full of corn
> And wine and oil: a granary of God . . .
> All things were strange and rare: the Sangraal
> As though it clung to some etherial chain,
> Brought down high heaven to earth at Arimathèe.
>
> (ll 88, 91–2, 95–7)

(There is a comparable directness and lack of affectation in the devotional drinking-song, 'King Arthur's Waes-hael', added among the appendices to *The Quest of the Sangraal*.) Like Tennyson, Hawker speaks to his contemporaries and offers, in the last lines of his poem, an allegory of the spiritual history of modern Britain, but his work is far more 'medieval' in its heartfelt faith and its unforced symbolism than anything produced by Tennyson or by any contemporary except Christina Rossetti, who uses little medieval décor, and Patmore, who uses hardly any.

William Morris (1834–96) was born into the Victorian plutocracy, but nostalgia for an imagined, changeless medieval world was the chief urge of his busy life from the boyhood when he rode through Epping Forest in a toy suit of armour to the maturity when he recounted *A Dream of John Ball* in the pages of the Socialist journal he had founded. As an Oxford undergraduate he joined Edward Burne Jones, Richard Watson Dixon and others who had felt the backwash from the Tractarians and had resolved to form a celibate Brotherhood, the 'Order of Sir Galahad', to conduct a 'Crusade and Holy Warfare' against the materialism and rationalism of the age. They read *The Germ*, founded, in imitation, *The Oxford and Cambridge Magazine* (1856), and were inspired by Dante Gabriel Rossetti with artistic and literary ambitions.

Morris's first collection of verse, *The Defence of Guenevere* (1858), was dedicated to Rossetti and includes at least four poems directly inspired by Rossetti's 'medieval' water-colours of 1854–7. Morris uses painterly techniques to convey feeling through the pose of a figure or the placing of significant detail:

> I look'd down on the floor,
> Between my feet . . .
>   less and less
> I saw the melted snow that hung in beads
>   Upon my steel shoes; less and less I saw
> Between the tiles the bunches of small weeds.
>
>   ('Sir Galahad, a Christmas Mystery')

Other pieces deploy the devices of traditional ballads, with just a little too obtrusive an antiquarianism:

> He had a coat of fine red gold,
>   And a bascinet of steel;
> Take note his goodly Collayne sword
>   Smote the spur upon his heel.
>
>   ('Welland River')

In this picturesque, 'medieval' world re-created from Malory and Froissart Morris found an escape from the ugliness and commercialism of contemporary society, and discovered, too, a violence that, perhaps in his case, compensated for his middle-class environment. Such violence may be found in the more intensely imagined pieces – 'The Defence of Guenevere' itself, 'Sir Peter Harpdon's End', 'Concerning Geffray Teste Noire' and 'The Haystack in the Floods':

> Right backward the knight Robert fell,
> And moaned as dogs do, being half dead,
> Unwitting, as I deem: so then
> Godmar turn'd grinning to his men,
> Who ran, some five or six, and beat
> His head to pieces at their feet.

Sometimes the piety of the Age of Faith appears as an ironic appendage:

> 'Swerve to the left, son Roger,' he said,
>   'When you catch his eyes through the helmet-slit,
> Swerve to the left, then out at his head,
>   And the Lord God give you joy of it.'
>
>   ('The Judgment of God')

The cool, 'flat' tone in which Morris narrates an episode even as brutal as the conclusion of 'The Haystack in the Floods' reveals the sensibility of the designer rather than, say, the moralist. His main occupations from 1861, when he founded his decorative art firm, were in the applied arts of design, where his work supplemented that of Owen Jones and Pugin to bring about a revolution in public taste. But, significantly, Morris himself very rarely designed three-dimensional objects; his talent was as a designer of flat, and usually repetitive, patterns for fabrics and wallpapers (see P. Floud 'William Morris as an artist: A new View' and 'The Inconsistencies of William Morris', *The Listener*, 7 and 14 October 1954).

The literary equivalent to this talent appears as a kind of verbal tapestry in the verse romances of his middle years, *The Life and Death of Jason* (1867) and a retelling of two dozen medieval and classical stories in *The Earthly Paradise* (1868–70). In these any central significance is dispelled by the meticulous attention to visual detail. 'The Hill of Venus' (*Earthly Paradise*), for instance, is a kind of pageant-poem which closely corresponds in content, organization and style to any typical Burne-Jones frieze with its procession of pale, androgynous figures. In the introductory verses to *The Earthly Paradise* Morris asks his readers to 'Forget six counties overhung with smoke', and proclaims himself the 'idle singer of an empty day' who strives

> to build a shadowy isle of bliss
> Midmost the beating of the steely sea.

This gesture of 'aesthetic withdrawal' reappears in the languid, sweetly melancholy morality play, *Love is Enough* (1872), where the five receding planes of action constitute a kind of Chinese box of dreams 'dreamed within another dream'.

Morris claimed that his discovery of the Icelandic sagas, which taught men to endure stoically the worst of this world rather than dream of a better, served to wake him from his dreams to a sense of reality. In two renderings of the Sigurd story and one of the *Laxdaela Saga* – as, too, in *The Pilgrims of Hope* (1885–6), a Socialist narrative poem with a contemporary setting – the theme of a husband despised by a wife who has taken a more splendid lover may conceivably echo the relationship between Jane Morris and Rossetti. The cantering measure of *The Story of Sigurd* (1877) is at least brisker than the variously languid metres of *The Earthly Paradise*, but there is hardly any more emotional urgency. In his later years he turned increasingly to prose, and between 1888 and his death wrote eight somniferous, pseudo-medieval romances in archaic English.

Two of these were among the books printed splendidly at Morris's Kelmscott Press in the 1890s. The Kelmscott books, like the tiles, fabrics and wallpapers of Morris and Co., were supplied to a narrow luxury-market when, paradoxically, Morris's political activities were directed towards the creation of an equal, classless society. His Socialism grew out of his views upon the relationship between art and society which originated in his reading Ruskin at Oxford, but he went far beyond Ruskin in claiming that the regeneration of art could come about only after the overthrow of the capitalist, competitive economic structure which underlay contemporary ugliness and squalor. In the expository prose of two collections of essays, *Hopes and Fears for Art* (1882) and *Signs of Change* (1888), and other scattered lectures and essays in his Socialist journal *The Commonweal* (founded 1885) Morris analyses social ills with pungency and economy, but his complementary imaginative work, *News from Nowhere* (1890), which beautifully and wistfully paints a Rousseau/Godwinesque – anarchist – pastoral – arts-and-crafts ideal society, is only a compensatory dream, not far removed in tone and function from his medieval romances.

Morris was a man of action. His work in decorative arts and crafts and in politics has played some part in cultural developments of the twentieth century, and, indeed, in helping to define 'culture' for us, but his poetry represents only one, and not the most important, aspect of his personality and achievement.

Richard Watson Dixon (1833–1900) was a member of the Oxford Brotherhood of Rossetti's disciples and the originator of *The Oxford and Cambridge Magazine*, but, unlike Morris and Burne-Jones, he persisted in the first intention of all three to enter the Anglican ministry. Much of the verse in his first collection, *Christ's Company* (1861), reflects the ritualizing, 'aesthetic' afterglow of the Tractarian Movement. In hagiographical pieces such as 'The Holy Mother at the Cross' and the lengthy 'St John' (as, too, in *S. John in Patmos*, 1863) he dresses and somewhat muffles a strictly orthodox body of Christian doctrine in Keatsian vestments. More esoteric are the inner landscapes of 'The Soul's World' and 'Despair', or those mysterious, half-apprehended visions of sin in 'The Wizard's Funeral' and 'Dream':

> With scarlet corded horn,
> With frail wrecked knees and stumbling pace,
> The scapegoat came:
> His eyes took flesh and spirit dread in flame
> At once, and he died looking towards my face.

In the lyrics appended to *Historical Odes* (1864) the mood is of regret and resignation, perhaps connected with the ending of his intense intellectual and emotional life within the Brotherhood – the state that he had once called 'meteorosophia'. His feelings are expressed directly in 'To Summer' and 'Ode on Departing Youth', but more obliquely in 'Inscience':

> The wind, like mist of purple grain
> Arises o'er the Arab plain;
> Strange constellations flashing soar
> Above the dreadful Boreal shore.
>
> But never purple cloud I see
> Swelling above immensity;
> And never galaxy doth peer
> Through the thick mists that wrap me here.

From 1875 to his death he worked obscurely in North-country vicarages upon his large-scale, learned and often witty, anti-Froude *History of the Church of England*. His long *terza-rima* narrative poem, set in the tenth century, *Mano* (1883), has an imaginative coherence and depth which, like that of Hawker's *The Quest of the Sangraal*, comes from the combination of scholarship and religious insight. In his privately printed *Odes and Eclogues* (1884) and *Lyrical Poems* (1887) there are plaintive, introspective odes on 'Conflicting Claims' and 'Advancing Age', and other poems, notably 'The Spirit Wooed', 'The Fall of the Leaf' and a handful of songs which look at external nature in a distinctively innocent, fresh and unselfconscious way. See, for instance, the end of 'Winter Will Follow':

> And yet again the bird that sings so high
> Shall ask the snow for alms with piteous cry,
> Take fright in his bewildering bower, and die.

From 1878 he had been corresponding with Hopkins, and the comfort and encouragement he gave to Hopkins was a significant indirect contribution to English poetry. Dixon, indeed, was the only contemporary who came close to a full understanding of Hopkins's verse, because he had known the kind of spiritual struggles which underlay it. Hopkins found in Dixon's verse, 'an extreme purity, a directness of human nature, and absence of affectation which is most rare', and added, 'I feel in reading him what a gentleman he is and it brings on the feeling that I am a blackguard' (*Letters of G. M. Hopkins to R. Bridges*, ed. C. C. Abbott, p 139). Dixon received even less public attention than Hawker (whose mind and career his resembled – except in their more colourful aspects). The high praise he earned from Hopkins and Bridges is a tribute to the saintliness of the man and the truth of his vision, rather than to the skill of the artist, for Dixon never fully mastered the techniques of versification – a failure that is all the more glaring when he is set beside his friends, Rossetti, Swinburne, Hopkins and Bridges.

Algernon Charles Swinburne (1837–1909), while an Oxford undergraduate, wrote poems, such as 'Queen Yseult', 'Joyous Garde' and 'Lancelot', that read like addenda to *The Defence of Guenevere*, but he quickly passed, comet-like (with his tiny body and glory of flame-coloured hair) out of the orbits of Rossetti and Morris. His verse tragedies, *The Queen Mother* and *Rosamund* (1860), are ill-conceived imitations of George Chapman. By contrast, *Atalanta in Calydon* (1865), is the most spirited and least academic of the Victorian attempts to imitate Greek tragedy. The rush and lilt of the famous first chorus, 'When the hounds of spring are on winter's traces', splendidly achieve the intensity of Dionysian rapture. However, the implacable and inscrutable God whose purposes are questioned in biblical cadences in the fourth chorus, 'Who hath given man speech?', is Hebraic rather than Hellenic, while the appeal from the tyranny of that 'supreme evil God' to 'the holy spirit of man' is the libertarian humanism of the nineteenth century. The rich and intoxicating rhythms of this play may be compared with the flatness of Morris's rime royal in 'Atalanta's Race' in *The Earthly Paradise*: Swinburne's rhythms express, or rather embody, youth, vigour, defiance, the great and general idea of liberty.

The third chorus of *Atalanta in Calydon*, 'We have seen thee, O Love', hails the 'perilous goddess' Aphrodite as mother of love and death. In the tragedy *Chastelard* (1865, but begun at Oxford in 1860) Mary Stuart appears as 'Fair fearful Venus' who

> reddens at the mouth with blood of men,
> Sucking between small teeth the sap o' the veins,
> Dabbling with death her little tender lips.

(V, ii)

Vampire figures are not uncommon in Romantic literature, but they are rarely as egregious as Swinburne's or as obviously linked to overt sexual abnormalities, for at his poetic prime Swinburne, apart from being a chronic drunkard, was a masochist who liked to be whipped by two ladies in a brothel in St John's Wood. Between 1861 and 1881 he worked with loving care upon his epic of flagellation, *The Flogging Block* (unpublished).

That a man's weaknesses may be the condition of his poetic vigour seems to be the case in *Poems and Ballads* (1866), where Swinburne works out his sado-masochistic impulses in heady lyrical verse, and, in passing, tilts at the grey, repressive eunuch-morality of Christians – followers of the 'pale Galilean'. The libertarian feeling that underlay *Atalanta in Calydon* explodes here into a tuneful riot of variegated but cerebral lechery. A recurrent imagined situation is of submission to a cruel, lustful, destructive woman – Dolores ('daughter of Death and Priapus/Our Lady of Pain'), the Empress Faustine, Lucrezia Borgia in 'A Ballad of Life' or the Venus of Tannhaüser in 'Laus Veneris'. There is Lesbian cannibalism in 'Anactoria', where Sappho exclaims,

> That I could drink thy veins as wine, and eat
> Thy breasts like honey!

The cult of the androgyne appears in four 'Hermaphroditus' sonnets, influenced by the 'charming monster' in Théophile Gautier's *Mademoiselle de Maupin*. Medieval necrophilia is the subject of 'The Leper'. In the Proserpine poems Swinburne's sense of sexual isolation develops into a defiant, and of course melodious, fatalism:

> Pale beyond porch and portal
>   Crowned with calm leaves, she stands
> Who gathers all things mortal
>   With cold immortal hands
>   ('The Garden of Proserpine')

> For there is no God found stronger than death; and death is a sleep.
>   ('Hymn to Proserpine')

Swinburne had preached the doctrine of aestheticism in his review of Baudelaire's *Fleurs du Mal* in *The Spectator* (1862), had related it to his own *Poems and Ballads* in his defence of that work, *Notes on Poems and Reviews* (1866), and had given prominence to the slogan 'Art for art's sake' in his critical study, *William Blake* (1868). In the 'Prelude' to *Songs before Sunrise* (1871) he announces a new 'public', political purpose in his work. He had been an admirer of Mazzini and a dedicated republican from his Oxford days, and in this volume he commemorates the Italian liberation movement. Nevertheless, his prostrated hero-worship and loving attention to the sufferings of the persecuted are, psychologically, not completely out of keeping with *Poems and Ballads*. However, the effort at sublimation makes atheism, not sexual deviation, the foremost motif. The 'Hymn of Man', a companion of the earlier 'Hymn to Proserpine', hurls the language of the Bible back into the teeth of God:

Thou are smitten, thou God, thou art smitten; thy death is upon thee, O Lord.
And the love-song of earth as thou diest resounds through the wind of her wings –
Glory to Man in the highest! for Man is the master of things.

In 'Hertha', 'Genesis' and 'Christmas Antiphones' Swinburne again preaches this Positivist religion of humanity.

The best of Swinburne is in the volumes of 1865 to 1871. Undistinguished sequels to the successes of those years appeared in *Erectheus* (1876), more exactly imitating Greek tragedy than *Atalanta in Calydon* did, and the vast *Bothwell* (1874) and *Mary Stuart* (1881), fluently versifying Froude to complete the trilogy begun by *Chastelard*. The best things in *Poems and Ballads, Second Series* (1878) are a set of distinguished translations from Villon and the premature elegy on his idol Baudelaire, 'Ave atque Vale' (written 1867). In this last Swinburne distantly and faintly echoes the heady excitements of his own 'Fleurs du Mal', the *Poems and Ballads* (1866), while recognizing Baudelaire's far profounder conception of the nature of evil:

> Thou sawest, in thine old singing season, brother,
>   Secrets and sorrows unbeheld of us:
>   Fierce loves, and lovely leaf-buds poisonous,
> Bare to thy subtler eye, but for none other
>   Blowing by night in some unbreathed-in clime;
>   The hidden harvest of luxurious time,
> Sin without shape, and pleasure without speech;
>   And where strange dreams in a tumultuous sleep
>   Make the shut eyes of stricken spirits weep;
> And with each face thou sawest the shadow on each,
>   Seeing as men sow men reap.

Swinburne was drinking himself to death, but in 1879 he was taken home by Theodore Watts-Dunton and restored to sobriety and social respectability – to live out his remaining thirty years as the hermit of Putney and to write another twenty books of verse and critical prose.

Swinburne wrote too much. His great agglomerations of words leave too little for the mind to grasp. Even his best work is marred by what he called 'a tendency to the dulcet and luscious form of verbosity'. Our general impression in reading his published verse – that sound predominates over sense – is confirmed by his manuscripts. His drafts of 'Ilicet' in *Poems and Ballads* (1866) show that in his hunt for the correct five-syllable adjective in the verse 'Of the old unalterable gods' he rejected in turn 'unprofitable', 'unperishable', 'unfathomable', 'inexorable', 'unconquerable' and (indeed) 'inevitable'. Such care is evidence, though, of a very fine ear for the tonal values of words. Swinburne, for all the great bulk of his writings, has little to say, but he never forgets his own declaration that the poet's 'first and last duty is to sing', and, in a sense, the melody of his lyrical poems *is* their meaning. Thus the persona of the nightingale is well-chosen in 'Itylus':

> Sister, my sister, O fleet sweet swallow,
>> Thy way is long to the sun and the south;
>> But I, fulfilled of my heart's desire,
>
> Shedding my song upon height, upon hollow,
>> From tawny body and sweet small mouth
>> Feed the heart of the night with fire.

James Thomson (1834–82) died in poverty, having sustained a precarious and dipsomaniac existence as schoolmaster, clerk and hack-journalist (1860–75) for Charles Bradlaugh's 'Atheistic-Republican-Malthusian' *National Reformer*. In the pages of that journal he thumbed his nose at God with such pieces as 'The Story of a Famous Old Firm' (1865) and 'Christmas Eve in the Upper Circles' (1866), and occasionally contrived the more penetrative satire that is found in 'Proposals for the Speedy Extinction of Evil and Misery' (1871). This last essay is founded upon Swift's *Modest Proposal*; Thomson suggests that current ills should be cured by universal suicide. Such grim ridicule of the Victorian idea of progress perplexed the perfectibilian secularists who were his friends.

Thomson's verse, printed in various journals, went unnoticed until, near the end of his life, he published two collections in 1880 and 1881. The initials 'B.V.' (Bysshe Vanolis) over which he published much of his verse proclaimed his admiration for Shelley and for the melancholy German who wrote under the pen-name Novalis; but, except in such trifles as 'The Lord of the Castle of Indolence' (1860) where he imitates his poet-namesake and Keats in *their* imitations of Spenser, Thomson is not an obtrusively 'literary' poet, as, for instance, Morris and Swinburne are.

The 'banjo-music' (in Edmund Blunden's phrase) of the Cockney conversation-pieces, 'Sunday at Hampstead' (1866) and

'Sunday up the River' (1869), and the ghost-story shivers of 'In the Room' (1872), where dingy lodging-house furniture chatters around a suicide's corpse, are inconsiderable, but 'The Doom of a City: a Fantasia' (written 1857, before he had turned atheist, published posthumously) is worth attention, if only because it is Thomson's longest poem. Its action opens in a real city where the narrator paces at night

> through desert streets, beneath the gleam
> Of lamps that lit my trembling life alone,
>
> (Part I, l. 26)

This episode may owe a hint to the admirably atmospheric nightscape of 'Glasgow' in *City Poems* (1857) by Alexander Smith (1830–67). (Wordsworth, of course, had already provided the Victorians with the frightening image of man 'single in the wide waste of the city'.) But the action of Thomson's poem soon moves to a dream-city where the narrator hears God's judgments against a London that is in danger of going the way of Tyre, Carthage and Venice, because its enormous wealth rests upon bitter social and economic inequalities, gambling, greed, fraud, and so forth. The poem is a commonplace allegory, preaching the gospel according to Carlyle –

> Finite souls and all things live by progress solely,
>   All *are* but what they *do*.
>
> (Part III, l. 619)

– but there is something of an original imaginative vision in the dream-cityscape, which conveys powerfully a nightmare sense of sterility and futility.

In his one great poem, 'The City of Dreadful Night' (published serially in *The National Reformer*, 1874), he combines the real city and the dream into an image that evokes the condition of solitary man in urban surroundings, while at the same time it performs its chief function in objectifying the poet's own religious despair and sense of psychological disintegration. Arnold had known that the inescapable city was a breeding ground for 'this strange disease of modern life'. Thomson displays the ravages of this disease, not as 'sick hurry and divided aims', but, more sensationally, as the divided selves and the 'Infections of incurable despair' (xv, l. 21) of the various inhabitants of his city. One of these city-dwellers is the traveller through the desert (iv) who has seen his better self, corpse-like, carried off by his dead mistress, leaving the other 'viler' self to stride on in fear and anger into the city. Another is a deformed, bestial, crawling figure (xviii), who seeks to retrace the thread of his life and become 'An infant cradled on its mother's knee', an infant who would scream 'if it saw this loathsome present me'. Others are the frail form (ii) who endlessly revisits, like a purposeless machine, the places where Faith, Hope and Love died, and the necrophiliac in his luxurious surroundings (x) uttering a melodious dirge. The city is a condition of mind such as that displayed in the later, overtly personal poem 'Insomnia' (1882); it is the hell of Thomson's own consciousness:

> The City is of Night, but not of Sleep;
> There sweet sleep is not for the weary brain;
> The pitiless hours like years and ages creep,
> A night seems termless hell. This dreadful strain
> Of thought and consciousness which never ceases,
> Or which some moments' stupor but increases,
> This, worse than woe, makes wretches there insane.
>
> (i, ll. 71–7)

Some passages seem to offer what is in some sense a 'criticism of life'. In a grimly ironic parody of the Positivists' view of intellectual history (xx), the angel (theism), the warrior (science) and the un-armed man (nihilism) fall in turn before the sphinx Necessity. A Messiah-like figure preaches in the great cathedral (xiv–xvi)

> Good tidings of great joy for you, for all:
> There is no God; no Fiend with names divine
> Made us and tortures us . . .
> I find no hint throughout the Universe
> Of good or ill, of blessing or of curse;
> I find alone Necessity Supreme.
>
> (xiv, ll. 40–1, 73–5)

and in the last section of the poem the Titanic 'Patroness' of the city, a figure modelled on Dürer's 'Melencolia', offers her 'con-firmation of the old despair'. But in drawing this strange and awesome female Thomson, in fact, is obeying the command given to the artist in Rossetti's 'Hand and Soul', that is, to paint the image of his own soul. Thomson's passion and vision, like Rossetti's, serve an intense subjectivism. Both use poetry to grapple with inner experience rather than to address audiences. Believing that art is dream rather than a public-address system, they manage to illuminate significantly some of the general neuroses of their age.

16

ASPECTS OF THE FIN DE SIÈCLE

Bernard Bergonzi

Towards the end of the nineteenth century many writers felt that
literature and art had moved into a new phase, and that, even
though Queen Victoria continued to be very much alive, the
Victorian era was already passing away. Although there was, and
is, agreement that the change took place, critics remain divided
about the best way of describing this phase of cultural history, and
about the point in time when it began to emerge. To talk simply of
the 'nineties' is tempting: the period was indeed remarkably
compact, with a very characteristic literary flavour, and its
mythology has survived for over seventy years. The 'nineties',
whether qualified as 'naughty' or 'mauve' or 'yellow', can still exert
a striking appeal, as is evident in the vogue for Beardsley prints
and *art nouveau* decoration. And yet to refer to a single decade in
this way can be misleading, since many of the essential attitudes of
the nineties had their roots in the eighties or even the seventies;
specifically, the Aesthetic Movement, which is sometimes referred
to as though it were synonymous with the innovations of the
nineties, was essentially a manifestation of the previous decade; as
early as 1881 Oscar Wilde was caricatured in the Gilbert and
Sullivan opera, *Patience*. The word 'Decadence' has a broader
application, but suffers from its ambiguity; some of the time it
suggests a combination of physical lassitude and psychological and
moral perversity – as exemplified, for instance, in J-K. Huysmans's
novel, *À Rebours*, which was much admired in the nineties –
although more properly it should refer only to language. Arthur
Symons wrote in the Introduction to *The Symbolist Movement in
Literature* (1899), 'the term is in its place only when applied to
style; to that ingenious deformation of the language, in Mallarmé,
for instance, which can be compared with what we are accustomed
to call the Greek and Latin of the Decadence.' A few years before
Symons had been happy to use 'decadence' in the broader and

looser sense, as in his poem, 'Intermezzo', which describes the dancer 'Nini Patte-en-l'Air' as the 'Maenad of the Decadence'.

I have decided in this essay to use the phrase *fin de siècle*, which clearly points to the preoccupations of the last years of the nineteenth century, without being limited to a single decade, and which can cover such particular manifestations as 'aestheticism' and 'decadence'. From the early nineties onward, *fin de siècle* was something of a catch-phrase; there is a characteristic instance in Wilde's *The Picture of Dorian Gray*, published in 1891:

> '*Fin de siècle*,' murmured Lord Henry.
> '*Fin du globe*', answered his hostess.
> 'I wish it were *fin du globe*,' said Dorian with a sigh. 'Life is a great disappointment.'
>
> (ch. XV)

In the poem just referred to, Symons attributes to Nini Patte-en-l'Air,

> The art of knowing how to be
> Part lewd, aesthetical in part
> And *fin-de-siècle* essentially.

Holbrook Jackson quotes various other entertaining instances of the phrase in his book, *The Eighteen Nineties* (first published in 1913 and still an indispensable guide to the period). It occurs more portentously in Max Nordau's *Degeneration*, of which the English translation appeared in 1895; writing with ponderous, pseudo-scientific assurance, Nordau uses the phrase *fin de siècle* to define and dismiss practically everything that was significant in late-nineteenth century art and literature: Wagner, Ibsen, Zola, the French symbolists, were all seen as symptomatic of a prevalent mental and physical degeneration. The English translation of *Degeneration* was something of a *succès de scandale*; it ran through several impressions in 1895, no doubt because it coincided with the trials of Oscar Wilde, but was quickly forgotten. Bernard Shaw attacked the book at length in *The Sanity of Art*.

The phrase *fin de siècle* was applied to a wide range of trivial behaviour, provided it was sufficiently perverse or paradoxical or shocking. Yet insofar as *fin de siècle* refers to a serious and consistent cultural attitude, it had two essential characteristics: the conviction that all established forms of intellectual and moral and social certainty were vanishing, and that the new situation required new attitudes in life and art; and the related belief that art and morality were separate realms, and that the former must be regarded as wholly autonomous; hence the aesthetic doctrine or 'art for art's sake'. As I have remarked, it is difficult to define the point at which these attitudes begin clearly to emerge. If the *fin de siècle* represented a break with established Victorian attitudes, then the break was not particularly clean: in a literary sense there are lines of development that link the *fin de siècle* poets with the major Romantics – with Blake, with Coleridge and with Keats. Arthur Hallam's review of Tennyson's early poems – whose influence was acknowledged by Yeats – was an important intermediary: Hallam praised a poetry of pure images, without any admixture of rhetoric, in a thoroughly protosymbolist fashion. One writer has attempted to pin down the emergence of the doctrine of aestheticism:

The actual doctrine appears first in Swinburne's review of Baudelaire's *Fleurs du Mal* in the *Spectator* for September 6th, 1862 (reprinted in Swinburne's *Works*, Volume XIII, p 419) and in Pater's essay on Winckelmann, which was published in the *Westminster Gazette* in 1867. Swinburne's *William Blake* (1868) gave prominence to the phrase 'art for art's sake' and five years later the phrase was embodied in the provocatively enigmatic conclusion to Pater's *Renaissance*.

(Ian Fletcher in *Romantic Mythologies*, ed. I. Fletcher, 1967, p 181)

The mention of Walter Pater takes us clearly within the ambience of the *fin de siècle*. For over thirty years Pater was one of the most influential of English writers, both for his manner of writing and for what was supposed to be his essential message. Oscar Wilde in *De Profundis* refers to reading Pater's *The Renaissance* (originally titled, in the first edition of 1873, *Studies in the History of the Renaissance*) in his first term at Oxford, calling it 'that book which has had such a strange influence over my life'. Arthur Symons, in a memorial essay written after Pater's death, said that *The Renaissance* 'even with the rest of Pater to choose from, seems to me sometimes the most beautiful book of prose in our literature'. James Joyce, in many passages in his early books, *Dubliners* and *A Portrait of the Artist as a Young Man*, reveals a consciousness that has been saturated in Pater's prose. W. B. Yeats, looking back in the nineteen-twenties to his companions of the nineties, wrote:

If Rossetti was a subconscious influence, and perhaps the most powerful of all, we looked consciously to Pater for our philosophy. Three or four years ago I re-read *Marius the Epicurean*, expecting to find I cared for it no longer, but it still seemed to me, as I think it seemed to us all, the only great prose in modern English . . .

(*Autobiographies*, 1955, p 302)

Such valuations are hard for the present-day reader to accept, since he is accustomed to a prose that is expressive rather than musical, and he is likely to echo Max Beerbohm's complaint about Pater:

I was angry that he should treat English as a dead language, bored by that sedulous ritual wherewith he laid out every sentence as in a shroud – hanging like a widower, long over its marmoreal beauty or ever he could lay it at length in his book, its sepulchre.

(*Works and More*, 1946, p 115)

Beerbohm's point is well taken, and yet it is in a sense unfair to Pater; his prose makes its effects cumulatively, and its appeal can grow with familiarity; one also becomes aware of a curious counterpointing between Pater's elaborately cadenced, ritualistic prose, and his sceptical, relativistic, even iconoclastic intelligence.

From an art-historical point of view, *The Renaissance* is an important work, since Pater was one of the first English writers to deal in an analytical and historically conscious fashion with some of the major artists of the Italian Renaissance, thus anticipating the later, more systematic researches of Berenson and other scholars. At the same time Pater ranges widely, in a way that illustrates the cultural time-travelling and eclecticism that typified the aesthetic movement of the seventies and eighties. At one end of the scale he writes about two thirteenth-century French stories, and at the other he discusses the eighteenth-century German antiquarian, Johann Winckelmann. The most famous lines in *The Renaissance* – indeed, in all of Pater's work – form the celebrated purple passage about the Mona Lisa, which Yeats rather perversely arranged in *vers libre* to print as the first exhibit in the *Oxford Book of Modern Verse*. It is unfortunate that this passage has come to be regarded merely as a virtuoso stylistic exercise; it occurs as the climax of Pater's essay on Leonardo, and is carefully led up to and prepared for by the developing strategy of the essay. Furthermore, what Pater says about the Mona Lisa is at least as important as the way he says it. For him she is a symbol of the modern consciousness that is burdened by a multiplicity of knowledge and experience; she is an embodiment of the timeless frequenting of many cultures that modern historical knowledge has made possible; she anticipates *The Waste Land* and the *Musèe Imaginaire*:

She is older than the rocks among which she sits; like the vampire, she has been dead many times, and learned the secrets of the grave; and has been a diver in deep seas, and keeps their fallen day about her; and has trafficked for strange webs with Eastern merchants: and, as Leda, was the mother of

Helen of Troy, and, as Saint Anne, the mother of Mary; and all this has been to her but as the sound of lyres and flutes, and lives only in the delicacy with which it has moulded the changing lineaments, and tinged the eyelids and the hands. The fancy of a perpetual life, sweeping together ten thousand experiences is an old one; and modern philosophy has conceived the idea of humanity as wrought upon by, and summing up in itself, all modes of thought and life. Certainly Lady Lisa might stand as the embodiment of the old fancy, the symbol of the modern idea.

In the almost equally celebrated 'Conclusion' to *The Renaissance*, Pater continues to stress the 'modern idea': 'to regard all things and principles of things as inconstant modes or fashions has more and more become the tendency of modern thought'. Here we see the authentically *fin de siècle* note. As an historical relativist Pater was sceptical about the possibility of ultimate values and truths; human life was fleeting and uncertain, and instead of pursuing abstractions, man should constantly strive to refine and purify his sensations and impressions:

Every moment some form grows perfect in hand or face; some tone on the hills or sea is choicer than the rest; some mood or passion or insight or intellectual excitement is irresistibly real and attractive to us – for that moment only. Not the fruit of experience, but experience itself, is the end. A counted number of pulses only is given to us of a variegated, dramatic life. How may we see in them all that is to be seen in them by the finest senses? How shall we pass most swiftly from point to point, and be present always at the focus where the greatest number of vital forces unite in their purest energy?

To burn always with this hard, gemlike flame, to maintain this ecstasy is success in life. In a sense it might even be said that our failure is to form habits: for, after all, habit is relative to a stereotyped world, and meantime it is only the roughness of the eye that makes any two persons, things, situations seem alike. While all melts under our feet, we may well grasp at any exquisite passion, or any contribution to knowledge that seems by a lifted horizon to set the spirit free for a moment, or any stirring of the senses, strange dyes, strange colours, and curious odours, or work of the artist's hands, or the face of one's friend. Not to discriminate every moment some passionate attitude in those about us, and in the very brilliancy of their gifts some tragic dividing of forces on their ways is, on this short day of frost and sun, to sleep before evening.

The traditional *carpe diem* theme is reinforced by a profound, modern scepticism which rejects any 'theory or idea or system which requires of us the sacrifice of any part of this experience'. The moral antinomianism that Pater's 'Conclusion' seemed to be advancing was found deeply subversive; and Pater, who in his personal life was an orderly, withdrawn, somewhat timid scholar, removed it from the second edition of *The Renaissance*: 'As I conceived it might possibly mislead some of those young men into whose hands it might fall.' He finally restored the 'Conclusion', slightly modified, to the third edition of his book, with the added comment, 'I have dealt more fully in *Marius the Epicurean* with the thoughts suggested by it.'

Marius the Epicurean, published in 1885, is nominally a novel, but Pater's talents for fiction were limited, and there is little sense of character or dramatic interplay in *Marius*. The central figure is a Roman gentleman living in the second century A.D., a conscientious, rather solemn young man, who attempts to live according to the best principles of paganism, as outlined in the Epicurean philosophy. *Marius the Epicurean* is subtitled, 'His Sensations and Ideas', and although Marius's attitude to life is continuous with that presented in the 'Conclusion' to *The Renaissance*, his Epicureanism is a very high-minded affair, far removed from mere sensuous hedonism; Marius cultivates the pleasures of the mind and spirit rather than of the senses. But the insufficiency of Epicureanism weighs increasingly on Marius, and he is drawn to an enchanting community of early Christians. He is captivated by the beauty of their ritual, and the sweetness and light of their beliefs, and he dies in their care, without having been formerly converted. Provided one does not expect the normal satisfactions of fiction from *Marius* and gives oneself time to adapt to its infinitely leisurely cadences, *Marius* can be read as a work of a genuine, if muted, charm, where action is at a minimum, but where the reader is slowly borne along by the billowing movement of Pater's prose and caught up by degrees into Marius's unfolding consciousness. Although Pater endeavours to make the historical detail correct, it is evident that an earnest nineteenth-century enquirer lies beneath Marius's Roman exterior, and that the Roman Empire of the Antonines thinly conceals the late-Victorian British Empire. The book develops at length the historical superimpositions hinted at in the description of the Mona Lisa.

Pater's major writings reveal another crucial element in the *fin de siècle* state of mind: the mistrust of theory and system, and the corresponding stress on sensation and impression, led in the nineties to a taste for the brief concentrated lyric, and, in prose, for the short story. In the twentieth century the tendency became more systematic, in the 'images' and 'epiphanies' and other moments of fragmentary illumination in the literature of the Modern

Movement. *Marius* had a more immediate effect in projecting the attractiveness of ritual as a way of life, independently of religious affiliation. Yeats remarked of it:

I began to wonder if it, or the attitude of mind of which it was the noblest expression, had not caused the disaster of my friends. It taught us to walk upon a rope tightly stretched through serene air, and we were left to keep our feet upon a swaying rope in a storm.

(Autobiographies, p 302)

There was one writer who absorbed Pater's lesson not wisely but too well, who achieved a tragic celebrity with relatively slender talents, and whose name is still a veritable symbol for the whole *fin de siècle* period and state of mind. This, of course, is Oscar Wilde: he is difficult to place in literary history, since, as he admitted, he devoted his genius to his life rather than his art. Wilde survives as a figure of pure and fascinating mythology, where the works inevitably seem secondary to the legend of the man. The essential judgments were made, sharply but justly, soon after Wilde's death by Arthur Symons, who was the finest critic of his day:

His intellect was dramatic, and the whole man was not so much a personality as an attitude. Without being a sage, he maintained the attitude of a sage; without being a poet, he maintained the attitude of a poet; without being an artist, he maintained the attitude of an artist. And it was precisely in his attitudes that he was most sincere.

(Studies in Prose and Verse, 1904, p 125)

Admittedly, Wilde wrote copiously in verse and prose, but the more one reads through his collected works the more one is conscious of its largely derivative quality. Most of the verse draws heavily on a variety of Victorian poets, while his most famous piece of fiction, *The Picture of Dorian Gray*, though a lively story, is a pale imitation of Huysmans's *À Rebours*. The dialogues first published in Wilde's book, *Intentions*, 'The Critic as Artist' and 'The Decay of Lying', offer a witty and accessible source of ideas about art that were fundamental to symbolist aesthetics and which have been developed in the literature and criticism of the twentieth century. Yet they are all taken over from other critics: 'Reading *Intentions* one finds here a bit of Arnold, here a patch of Pater or William Morris, and, in this unlikely company, even Carlyle' (Ruth Z. Temple in *Edwardians and Late Victorians*, ed. R. Ellmann, 1960, p 42).

If one wishes to find out what is most enduring in Wilde's work one is likely to turn to his comedies, *Lady Windermere's Fan*, *A Woman of No Importance*, *An Ideal Husband* and *The Importance of*

Being Earnest, which were produced between 1892 and 1895. All are excellent pieces of theatre and splendidly witty. Yet the first three tend to be melodramatic and contain a rather uneasy mixture of farce and morality: *The Importance of Being Earnest* is Wilde's comic masterpiece, and indeed one of the great comedies of the English theatre. Its qualities have been well described by Ian Gregor in an important article on Wilde's comedies ('Comedy and Oscar Wilde', *Sewanee Review* vol LXXIV, 1966, pp 501–21); he says of this play, 'what he gives us is a completely realized idyll, offering itself as something irrevocably *other* than life, not a wish-fulfilment of life as it might be lived'. For the rest, some of Wilde's shorter tales preserve their self-conscious charm; and among the poems, 'The Ballad of Reading Gaol' stands out as an impressive achievement, although it is over-long and suffers from Wilde's tendency to turn the elements of tragedy into a repetitive decoration. To quote Symons again:

In this poem, where a style formed on other lines seems startled at finding itself used for such new purposes, we see a great spectacular intellect, to which, at last, pity and terror have come in their own person, and no longer as puppets in a play.

(op. cit., p 124)

Symons himself was one of the most interesting figures of the *fin de siècle* period. He was born in 1865 and emerged in the eighties as a self-taught but learned young literary man, who was widely read in several languages. In addition to his distinction as a critic, he was a prolific minor poet, a translator, an essayist on all forms of art and an *entrepreneur* of foreign literary influences. In this last respect Symons was of crucial importance, notably as the author of *The Symbolist Movement in Literature* (1899), a book which discussed the work of such French poets as Rimbaud, Verlaine, Laforgue and Mallarmé. This book had a decisive influence on the development of twentieth-century poetry in English. It was dedicated to Yeats who became a close friend of Symons in the nineties; Symons, who was very much at home in Paris literary circles, introduced Yeats to Mallarmé and other French Symbolists and to their work, thereby expanding and reinforcing Yeats's existing interest in poetic symbolism, which he had developed from his reading of Blake and his dabblings in magic and the occult. Yeats himself influenced Symons away from mere 'decadence' as a literary concept, towards a quasi-occult understanding of symbolism, reinforced with a Paterian sense of ritual; in the introduction to *The Symbolist*

Movement Symons wrote that literature 'becomes itself a kind of religion, with all the duties and responsibilities of the sacred ritual'. A few years later, T. S. Eliot as an undergraduate at Harvard was to find Symons's book extremely fruitful:

I myself owe Mr Symons a great debt. But for having read his book I should not, in the year 1908, have heard of Laforgue and Rimbaud; I should probably not have begun to read Verlaine, and but for reading Verlaine, I should not have heard of Corbière. So the Symons book is one of those which have affected the course of my life.

> (Quoted in F. O. Matthiessen, *The Achievement of T. S. Eliot*, 1959, pp 27–8)

Yeats and Symons were associated in a group of poets calling themselves the Rhymers' Club that met during the nineties; in Yeats's words, the Club 'for some years was to meet every night in an upper room with a sanded floor in an ancient eating-house in Fleet Street called the Cheshire Cheese'. The Rhymers, as their name denoted, aimed at the unpretentious pursuit of pure song, purged of Victorian rhetoric or moralizing, and their habit of meeting regularly in such surroundings was an attempt to combine French literary café life with Johnsonian conviviality. These poets were later to be mythologized by Yeats as the 'tragic generation': two of the Rhymers, Ernest Dowson and Lionel Johnson, were to die in their thirties, and another, John Davidson, committed suicide in 1909 at the age of forty-three. Symons, although he lived to be nearly eighty, was afflicted by madness in his later years. The Rhymers did not have the temper of literary revolutionaries, but they aimed to break with the recent past in a way that has been memorably described by Yeats:

The revolt against Victorianism meant to the young poet a revolt against irrelevant descriptions of nature, the scientific and moral discursiveness of *In Memoriam* – 'When he should have been broken-hearted', said Verlaine, 'he had many reminiscences' – the political eloquence of Swinburne, the psychological curiosity of Browning, and the poetical diction of everybody. Poets said to one another over their black coffee – a recently imported fashion – 'We must purify poetry of all that is not poetry', and by poetry they meant poetry as it had been written by Catullus, a great name at that time, by the Jacobean writers, by Verlaine, by Baudelaire. Poetry was a tradition like religion and liable to corruption, and it seemed that they could best restore it by writing lyrics technically perfect, their emotion pitched high, and as Pater offered instead of moral earnestness life lived as 'a pure gem-like flame' all accepted him for master.

> (*The Oxford Book of Modern Verse*, p ix)

As I have remarked, the brief concentrated lyric could serve as the literary crystallization of a Paterian sensation; the most obvious stylistic influences at work in such poetry were the Elizabethan lyric and the short poems of Verlaine. Even now, so long after they wrote, it is not easy to get the poets of the nineties in critical focus. It is tempting to mythologize them as men, as Yeats did, and to regard their verses as infinitely poignant human records; alternatively, one can dismiss them as poseurs of patently limited talent, whose literary achievement is minuscule, when it is not wholly unnoticeable. Looked at as objectively as possible, the poets of the nineties do have certain definable qualities in their favour. They were at their best extremely skilful craftsmen, who could bring off subtle and striking rhythmic effects, and who were surprisingly successful in importing a Verlainian music into their poems. And by following the example of Baudelaire they were able to enlarge the subject-matter of poetry, even though Baudelaire was systematically misunderstood in the nineties as a romantically decadent celebrant of 'sin' rather than as the tormented Catholic moralist that he was later to appear to T. S. Eliot. At all events, the sensibility of the nineties was inclined to write about prostitutes, or other sources of casual amour: 'the chance romances of the streets, the Juliet of a night', in Symons's words. However much the poets may have romanticized these matters, by touching on them at all they were acknowledging an element in the social reality of Victorian London that had not, so far, received much literary recognition. Despite the narrowness of their poetic means, poets such as Dowson and Symons broadened the spectrum of poetic material in a way that anticipates Eliot, and which shows the influence not merely of French poetry, but of French fiction. Where they were weakest was in the resources of their diction. Dowson's well-worn (and hard-wearing) anthology favourite. 'Non sum qualis eram bonae sub regno Cynarae', illustrates these consider-ations:

> Last night, ah, yesternight, betwixt her lips and mine
> There fell thy shadow, Cynara! thy breath was shed
> Upon my soul between the kisses and the wine;
> And I was desolate and sick of an old passion,
>   Yea, I was desolate and bowed my head:
> I have been faithful to thee, Cynara! in my fashion.
>
> All night upon mine heart I felt her warm heart beat,
> Night-long within mine arms in love and sleep she lay;
> Surely the kisses of her bought red mouth were sweet;
> But I was desolate and sick of an old passion,
>   When I awoke and found the dawn was gray:
> I have been faithful to thee, Cynara! in my fashion . . .

It is evident that Dowson's Swinburnian or Pre-Raphaelite diction is strained to breaking point in his attempt to convey a novelistic complexity of the erotic life. But I would argue that the poem's achievement is that it can take the strain: Dowson's intentions are reinforced by a remarkable verbal energy that underlies the seemingly debilitated surface of the poem and by his virtuoso manipulation of rhythm.

Symons treats of a similar theme, more succinctly and equally musically, in 'Leves Amores II', a poem which conveys an intensely 'realistic' experience with all the immediacy demanded by twentieth-century poetics:

> The little bedroom papered red,
> The gas's faint malodorous light,
> And one beside me in the bed,
> Who chatter, chatters, half the night.
>
> I drowse and listen, drowse again,
> And still, although I would not hear,
> Her stream of chatter, like the rain,
> Is falling, falling on my ear.
>
> The bed-clothes stifle me, I ache
> With weariness, my eyelids prick;
> I hate, until I long to break
> That clock for its tyrannic tick.

Symons was an intensely visual poet, who often anticipates the effects demanded by the Imagists of c 1912; as for instance, in 'At Dieppe: After Sunset', written in 1890:

> The sea lies quieted beneath
> The after-sunset flush
> That leaves upon the heaped grey clouds
> The grape's faint purple blush.
>
> Pale, from a little space in heaven
> Of delicate ivory,
> The sickle-moon and one gold star
> Look down upon the sea.

Symons was a passionate frequenter of the music-halls of London and Paris, and he constantly celebrates them in his verse. His interest in ballet-girls was not merely amorous; he was a great exponent of the *fin de siècle* interest in the dance as a momentary fusion of art and ritual, a pure expressive image lifted out of discourse and the flux of everyday life. This topic has been discussed by Frank Kermode in *Romantic Image* and pursued in detail in 'Poet and Dancer Before Diaghilev', an essay which combines theatrical and literary history (included in Kermode's *Puzzles and Epiphanies*, 1962).

Another of the Rhymers, Lionel Johnson, has left an unflattering comment both on Symons's proto-Imagist methods and his propensity for sordid subjects:

[Symons] is a slave to impressionism, whether the impression be precious or not. A London fog, the blurred, tawny lamplights, the red omnibus, the dreary rain, the depressing mud, the glaring gin-shop, the slatternly shivering women: three dexterous stanzas telling you that and nothing more. And in nearly every poem, one line or phrase of absolutely pure and fine imagination. If he would wash and be clean, he might be of the elect.
(Quoted in *Literary Essays of Ezra Pound*, ed. T. S. Eliot, 1960, p 365)

Johnson was a poet of more austere temperament than Dowson or Symons; his indulgence was alcohol rather than harlots. Like his contemporaries, Johnson was a disciple of Pater, but he followed the implications of *Marius the Epicurean* to their logical conclusion and joined the Roman Catholic Church. Catholicism was very much in the air in the nineties: Dowson also became a Catholic, of an intensely aesthetic, wistful kind, though he does not seem to have shared Johnson's attachment to reading the Fathers of the Church and otherwise speculating on doctrinal niceties (graphically described by Yeats in the *Autobiographies*). Aubrey Beardsley was converted to Catholicism towards the end of his short life, and Oscar Wilde became a Catholic on his death-bed. Another convert was the poet John Gray, not one of the Rhymers, who was a close friend of Wilde and who was falsely alleged to be the original of Dorian Gray: he interestingly broke the *fin de siècle* pattern of the 'tragic generation' by becoming a priest and not dying young. Gray ended his days in 1934 at the age of sixty-eight as a well-loved parish priest in Edinburgh. The temper of this aesthetic Catholicism is well illustrated in two poems on the same theme by Dowson and Johnson, which also serve to contrast the temperaments of the two poets:

Benedictio Domini

Without, the sullen noises of the street!
The voice of London, inarticulate,
Hoarse and blaspheming, surges in to meet
The silent blessing of the Immaculate.

Dark is the church, and dim the worshippers,
  Hushed with bowed heads as though by some old spell,
While through the incense-laden air there stirs
  The admonition of a silver bell.

Dark is the church, save where the altar stands,
  Dressed like a bride, illustrious with light,
Where one old priest exalts with tremulous hands
  The one true solace of man's fallen plight.

Strange silence here: without, the sounding street
  Heralds the world's swift passage to the fire:
O Benediction, perfect and complete!
  When shall men cease to suffer and desire?

Dowson

The Church of a Dream

Sadly the dead leaves rustle in the whistling wind,
Around the weather-worn, gray church, low down the vale:
The Saints in golden vesture shake before the gale;
The glorious windows shake, where still they dwell enshrined;

Old Saints by long dead, shrivelled hands, long since designed:
There still, although the word autumnal be, and pale,
Still in their golden vesture the old saints prevail;
Alone with Christ, desolate else, left by mankind.

Only one ancient Priest offers the Sacrifice,
Murmuring holy Latin immemorial:
Swaying with tremulous hands the old censer full of spice,
In gray, sweet incense clouds; blue, sweet clouds mystical:
To him, in place of men, for he is old, suffice
Melancholy remembrances and vesperal.

Johnson

Both poems convey a Paterian feeling for liturgy, but where Dowson is fervid and aspiring, Johnson is cold and melancholy. Johnson was, if anything, a more accomplished verbal artist than Dowson or Symons, but compared with theirs, his poetry, which dwells on religious topics or fragments of Celtic legend (although born a Welshman, Johnson transformed himself into an honorary but patriotic Irishman), is somewhat stiff and lacking in human interest. He is seen at his best in such accomplished anthology pieces as 'By the Statue of King Charles at Charing Cross' and 'The Dark Angel'.

In attacking Symons for his taste for low urban subjects, Johnson was drawing attention to another poetic preoccupation of the *fin de siècle*: if a tormented eroticism was one way of extending the range of poetry, a fascination with the multifarious life of the modern city was another. London was not, of course, a completely untouched poetic subject; Tennyson momentarily caught the anomic quality of urban life in a superb image in *In Memoriam*:

> He is not here; but far away
> The noise of life begins again,
> And ghastly thro' the drizzling rain
> On the bald street breaks the blank day.

Wordsworth treated London positively in 'Sonnet Written on Westminster Bridge' and negatively in the middle books of the *Prelude*; and there are dark visions of London life in Blake and the Augustan satirists. Yet the great exemplar for the *fin de siècle* poets was Baudelaire, whose poems about Paris had shown the intense but sombre poetic possibilities of the huge modern metropolis. A more romantic source of urban imagery was Whistler and other painters; Wilde wrote in 'The Decay of Lying':

Where, if not from the Impressionists, do we get those wonderful brown fogs that come creeping down our streets, blurring the gas-lamps and changing the houses into monstrous shadows? To whom, if not to them and their master, do we owe the lovely silver mists that brood over our river, and turn to faint forms of fading grace curved bridge and swaying barge?

He had already shown a similar response in his poem, 'Impression du Matin', published in 1881:

> The Thames nocturne of blue and gold
> Changed to a Harmony in grey:
> A barge with ochre-coloured hay
> Dropt from the wharf: and chill and cold
>
> The yellow fog came creeping down
> The bridges, till the houses' walls
> Seemed changed to shadows and St Paul's
> Loomed like a bubble o'er the town.

Among the Rhymers there were similarly romantic treatments of the urban scene; Richard Le Gallienne's 'A Ballad of London' indulges in the characteristic *fin de siècle* preference for the artificial over the natural:

> Ah, London! London! our delight,
> Great flower that opens but at night,
> Great City of the midnight sun,
> Whose day begins when day is done.

> Lamp after lamp against the sky
> Opens a sudden beaming eye,
> Leaping alight on either hand
> The iron lilies of the Strand . . .

Symons wrote copiously about London – his third book of poems, published in 1894, is appropriately called *London Nights* – and his treatment ranges between the romantic and the intensely realistic; he is usually most effective when he is most purely descriptive:

> The grey and misty night,
> Slim trees that hold the night among
> Their branches, and, along
> The vague Embankment, light on light.

One of the most striking of the poets associated with the Rhymers was John Davidson, a melancholy Scotsman of philosophical inclinations – he was one of the first people in England to be interested in Nietzsche – whose treatment of urban themes was realistic to the point of grimness. Perhaps Davidson's best known poem is 'Thirty Bob a Week', the monologue of an impoverished clerk hopelessly struggling to keep up appearances and make ends meet:

> For like a mole I journey in the dark,
> A-travelling along the underground
> From my Pillar'd Halls and broad Suburbean Park,
> To come the daily dull official round;
> And home again at night with my pipe all alight,
> A-scheming how to count ten bob a pound.

T. S. Eliot wrote interestingly about his admiration for this poem:

I am sure that I found inspiration in the content of the poem, and in the complete fitness of content and idiom: for I also had a good many dingy urban images to reveal. Davidson had a great theme, and also found an idiom which elicited the greatness of the theme, which endowed this thirty-bob-a-week clerk with a dignity that would not have appeared if a more conventional poetic diction had been employed. The personage that Davidson created in this poem has haunted me all my life, and the poem is to me a great poem for ever.

(*John Davidson: A Selection of His Poems*, ed. M. Lindsay, 1961, pp xi–xii)

Davidson coldly appraised the newer aspects of the spreading metropolis in 'A Northern Suburb':

> In gaudy yellow brick and red,
>   With rooting pipes, like creepers rank,
> The shoddy terraces o'erspread
>   Meadow, and garth, and daisied bank.
>
> With shelves for rooms the houses crowd,
>   Like draughty cupboards in a row –
> Ice-chests when wintry winds are loud,
>   Ovens when summer breezes blow.

In such poems as these Davidson suggests a poetic equivalent to the fiction of George Gissing. In a late poem, written not long before he died, Davidson turned to the fairly well-worn subject of the Thames and treated it in a way that is both realistic and richly textured:

> As gray and dank as dust and ashes slaked
> With wash of urban tides the morning lowered;
> But over Chelsea Bridge the sagging sky
> Had colour in it – blots of faintest bronze,
> The stains of daybreak. Westward slabs of light
> From vapour disentangled, sparsely glazed
>
> The panelled firmament; but vapour held
> The morning captive in the smoky east.
> At lowest ebb the tide on either bank
> Laid bare the fat mud of the Thames, all pinched
> And scalloped thick with dwarfish surges. Cranes,
> Derricks and chimney-stalks of the Surrey-side,
> Inverted shadows, in the motionless,
> Dull, leaden mirror of the channel hung.

The poets associated with the Rhymers were not the only ones who expressed a *fin de siècle* sensibility. I have already referred to John Gray, the author of *Silverpoints* (1893), a slender volume designed with infinite preciousness by the artist Charles Ricketts; Gray's poetry was of a matching preciousness – Lionel Johnson dismissed him as a 'sometimes beautiful oddity' – although some of it has a curious distinction; like Symons, Gray was very familiar with the French Symbolists, and translated some of their verse, usually in a more restrained and laconic fashion than Symons. (For a further account of Gray, see my introduction to his *Park: A Fantastic Story*, reprinted in my *The Turn of a Century*, 1973, pp 114–23. For a comparison of Gray and Symons as translators from the French, see

Ruth Z. Temple, *The Critic's Alchemy*, 1953, pp 322–30.) Another Catholic, Francis Thompson, continues to be well-known, at least on the strength of his 'Hound of Heaven': Yeats remarked of him in relation to the Rhymers, 'Francis Thompson came once but never joined'. Thompson's life of indignity and suffering makes him a signal embodiment of the late-nineteenth-century myth of the *poète maudit*, and his Catholicism was more existential and less Paterian or aesthetic than that of his contemporaries. In literary respects, too, his perspective was somewhat different from theirs; his models were the Metaphysicals, particularly Crashaw, and Shelley, whom he saw, curiously, as fulfilling their promise. The influence of these poets is evident in 'The Hound of Heaven', which remains a vigorous if over-forceful record of spiritual adventure. In 'In No Strange Land' Thompson writes more calmly of mystical experience:

> O world invisible, we view thee,
> O world intangible, we touch thee,
> O world unknowable, we know thee,
> Inapprehensible, we clutch thee!
>
> Does the fish soar to find the ocean,
> The eagle plunge to find the air –
> That we ask of the stars in motion
> If they have rumour of thee there?

Another poet chiefly remembered as the author of a famous anthology piece is W. E. Henley; the poem is, of course, 'Invictus':

> Out of the night that covers me,
> Black as the Pit from pole to pole,
> I thank whatever gods may be
> For my unconquerable soul.

The rhetoric now seems a little stagey and unconvincing, though the poem's defiant spirit reflects Henley's own life-long struggle against physical disability. His most interesting work is the early sequence of poems called 'In Hospital', which dates from the eighteen-seventies; its exact descriptive realism gives it a surprisingly modern flavour. Henley also experimented with *vers libre*, and in his 'London Voluntaries' he treated a familiar topic, although in a more rhapsodic spirit than most of the Rhymers would have thought appropriate. Although his verse reflected something of the *fin de siècle*, in his role as publicist, critic and editor, Henley was decidedly out of sympathy with anything that smacked of aestheticism or decadence. He favoured a robust, extrovert attitude in literary matters, and in politics he was a vehement imperialist. Henley was a friend of R. L. Stevenson, with whom he collaborated in several works, and as editor of the *Scots Observer*, the *National Observer*, and the *New Review*, he sponsored such new arrivals on the literary scene as Kipling and Wells. The nineties was a great period for literary magazines: *The Yellow Book*, which ran from 1894 to 1897, is generally regarded as the quintessential expression of the *fin de siècle* spirit, although this was only true, if at all, of the first four numbers, of which Aubrey Beardsley was art editor; after the *débâcle* of Wilde in 1895, Beardsley was removed from his post, and *The Yellow Book*, although unchanged in appearance, became a sober middle-of-the-road publication. The spirit of the nineties was better captured in *The Savoy*, which was edited by Arthur Symons, and, although it ran for only a few months during 1896, it was described by Holbrook Jackson as 'the most ambitious and, if not the most comprehensive, the most satisfying achievement of *fin de siècle* journalism in this country' (*The Eighteen Nineties*, 1950, p 47). Beardsley's drawings were prominent in *The Savoy*, which also published one of his occasional ventures into literature, the consciously decadent romance, *Under the Hill*. A prominent contributer to the early *Yellow Book* was Max Beerbohm; his love of witty paradox and his preference for the artificial as against the natural – his essay, 'The Pervasion of Rouge' is characteristic – made him thoroughly *fin de siècle*, but he always wrote in a spirit of ironical, mocking detachment, and his essays have lasted better than the work of his more fervid contemporaries. The wealth of literary periodicals in the nineties meant that the short story as a literary form was encouraged, and excellent work was done in this medium by Kipling and Wells and James. Closer to the *fin de siècle* spirit were English disciples of Maupassant like Hubert Crackanthorpe and Ella D'Arcy.

Considered as a literary period the eighteen-nineties was rich and various, and much of its best work was written outside the ambience of the *fin de siècle* mood. A comprehensive survey of the period would certainly acknowledge, for instance, in poetry, Kipling's *Barrack-Room Ballads*, Housman's *A Shropshire Lad* and Alice Meynell's *Poems*, as well as the poets I have discussed. In fiction, the major achievements of the nineties included Gissing's *New Grub Street*, Stevenson's *Weir of Hermiston*, George Moore's *Esther Waters*, James's *Spoils of Poynton* and *The Awkward Age*, and Hardy's *Tess of the d'Urbervilles* and *Jude the Obscure*. The last-named of these does, in fact, embody a good deal of the *fin de siècle* state of mind, notably in the presentation of the neurasthenic 'new woman', Sue Bridehead, and in the grotesque child, 'Father Time'. H. G. Wells's *The Time Machine* is a highly distinguished piece of fiction which, as I have argued elsewhere (*The Early H. G. Wells*, 1961) is pervaded by *fin de siècle* feelings, little as one would normally associate them with Wells. And the picture would need to be completed by some consideration of Shaw's achievement in *Plays: Pleasant and Unpleasant*.

Yet to concentrate on what I have tried to isolate, however imperfectly, as the *fin de siècle* mentality is to stress what from Pater onward was known as the 'modern' and to emphasize those elements in late-nineteenth century literary theory and practice that were to be picked up by the Modern Movement in the early twentieth. In one sense the activity exemplified by the Rhymers did not last beyond the end of the century. As Yeats put it:

Then in 1900 everybody got down off his stilts; henceforth nobody drank absinthe with his black coffee; nobody went mad; nobody committed suicide; nobody joined the Catholic church; or if they did I have forgotten.
(*The Oxford Book of Modern Verse*, p xi)

(Yeats, in his habitual mythologizing, *had* forgotten: Symons went mad and Davidson committed suicide.) And yet in a deeper sense, the continuities between Pater and Joyce, and between Symons or Davidson and Eliot, are apparent. Yeats himself, who has appeared in this essay as a commentator rather than a creative participant, is the supreme example of a great writer of our century who was nurtured in the nineties, and who transcended the *fin de siècle* spirit without abandoning it. But that is a matter for another chapter and another volume.

17

THE VICTORIAN THEATRE

Cecil J. L. Price

The Victorian theatre made a comparatively small contribution to nineteenth-century literature. The output of plays was enormous, for there were far more theatres in existence than had ever been known before, and, with the growth of population and improvement in public transport, large audiences to fill them. All kinds of entertainment were presented from 'legitimate' theatre (straight plays, unaccompanied by music) to equestrian dramas, melodrama, punning farce, and music-hall sketch. The demand was great, and many of the suppliers were either resident dramatists at the playhouses or non-resident hacks. Their financial rewards were generally meagre, and were supplemented by acting. They were forced to bring out plays quickly, and found it easier and more profitable to dramatize a novel or translate a French melodrama than to attempt anything original. Even creating a new play was largely a matter of devising situations for the stock scenes and machinery of the theatre concerned, as well as for particular members of its company acting well-defined characters like the heavy father, Irish boy, soubrette, walking gentleman, or dastardly villain.

An amusing but significant picture of the dramatist's lot at the beginning of the period was drawn by Dickens in *Nicholas Nickleby* (1838–9), a year after Victoria's accession to the throne. Crummles and his band of players were highly coloured but not very untrue to life, and the manager's method of obtaining a new attraction was only too typical. Nicholas was asked to translate and adapt a French play for him, to introduce a dance for the 'Infant Phenomenon', and to bring the scenes to a close 'with a picture'. By the standards of the day and of the next thirty years, this was a comparatively simple demand for a piece of dramatic fretwork. Conditions like these did not favour the dramatist and it was only in the seventies that they really began to improve.

In the intervening period they were strongly affected by the low social position of the theatre. Attendance at the old patent houses, Drury Lane and Covent Garden, was still socially possible, and Victoria herself encouraged the work of Charles Kean, manager of the Princess Theatre; but the minor theatres, homes of melodrama and burlesque, were left to the 'fast' and the raffish. Arthur Machen put the position clearly: 'In the days of Thackeray, the theatre lived not for itself, but as a symbol of gaiety' (*Far Off Things*, 1923, p 60), and we have to remember that the word 'gay' had a strongly pejorative sense and was obviously at the other extreme from the prevailing admiration for earnestness. Refinement, respectability and religious zeal all kept people away and the theatre suffered, as Matthew Arnold suggested (*Letters of an Old Playgoer*, 1919, pp 23–4), because it did not attract an audience really representative of the society of its day. Opera alone retained social favour, partly because of the idea that music could only have an elevating effect and partly because of Victorian delight in the ostentatious (See A. Hauser, *Social History of Art*, 1951, vol II, p 809).

The theatres had their hardest struggle for existence in the fifties and early sixties, but gradually began to win favour again and by the end of the century had done much to consolidate their position as centres of artistic excellence. The general quality of plays was higher and the financial reward greater. If a play were a London success, it was sent on tour throughout the country and brought in even more money. Syndicates were formed to promote and control productions, and introduced new problems for the dramatist, but, at least, a successful playwright could now give time and thought to his work. In its turn the public was willing to give more time and thought to the productions, and the standards of reviewing in the newspapers rose considerably. Ibsen became known here, and the stage began to rival the pulpit.

Yet if the common man of our own day were to be asked what he knew of the Victorian theatre, he would mention first *Maria Marten* and *Sweeney Todd*. In the popular imagination they epitomize the nineteenth-century desire for the sensational as well as some of the lurid means of satisfying it: the murder and the dream in the one; 'I'll polish them off', in the other. Pressed again our informant might recall *The Bells* as a play always associated with Henry Irving, though it was really an adaptation of Erckmann-Chatrian's *Le Juif Polonais*. Only after further thought would Wilde, Shaw and Pinero come to mind, and the last two might well be seen to have contributed more to the twentieth- than to the nineteenth-century theatre.

The common man would be right, for though the eighties and nineties saw the production of a few splendid comedies that are among the glories of our dramatic literature, the period as a whole was dominated by the melodrama. If, then, we are to look for a dramatist who is truly representative of the period, we must select Dion Boucicault (1820–90), whose literary contribution is almost nil but who influenced the theatre of his time very considerably.

He is credited with 145 plays, many of them adaptations or written in collaboration with novelists and actors. The best of his early attempts was in comedy, *London Assurance* (1841), and its style – imitating, at some distance, *The School for Scandal* – is indicated in the name of one of its characters, Lady Gay Spanker. The dialogue moves briskly through a complicated plot; character is sufficiently noted to allow the players to give an illusion of a kind of life; and the whole play has a characteristic jauntiness. Boucicault went on to make a reputation as an adapter of French melodrama. The best-remembered is *The Corsican Brothers*, which gave Charles Kean splendid acting opportunities of a spectacular kind. Kean's passion for detail and his delight in tableaux and 'strong' scenes affected Boucicault considerably, but with this difference: he reconstructed in detail contemporary rather than historical themes, believing as he did that the public was most interested in 'the actual, the contemporaneous, the photographic' (See F. Rahill, *The World of Melodrama*, 1967, p 184). He thought about the negro problem in the United States and wrote *The Octoroon* (1859), in which the heroine generously committed suicide rather than allow her white lover to suffer from his association with her. This is presented against an 'authentic' background of slave auctions and lynching, as well as the exciting spectacle of a steam-boat exploding in flames.

From the literary point of view Boucicault's greatest successes were his highly romantic pictures of Irish country life in *The Colleen Bawn* (1860) and *The Shaughraun* (1875). There were 'sensation scenes' in them, but much of the interest lay in language, character and sentiment – W. S. Gilbert, for example, mentions in *Patience* 'The pathos of Paddy as rendered by Boucicault'. Middle-class people were still stilted and stunted, but the country folk had undoubted vitality. Some of the phrases remind us of Synge. Danny the boatman says of Eily:

The looking glass was never made that could do her justice; and if St. Patrick wanted a wife, where could he find an angel that 'ud compare with the Colleen Bawn. As I row her on the lake, the little fishes come up to look at her; and the wind from heaven lifts up her hair to see what the devil brings her down here at all – at all.

(Act I, scene i)

If this reminds us of Christy Mahon's phrases about Pegeen, some lines in *The Shaughraun* recall Pegeen's interview with the Widow Quin:

Mrs. O'Kelly Run in quick, before he sees you, and I'll take the churn.
Claire Not I! – I'll stop where I am. If he was the Lord-Lieutenant himself I'd not stir or take a tuck out of my gown.

(Act I, scene i)

Boucicault acted the parts of Myles na Coppaleen and Conn the Shaughraun himself and gave them an unusual gusto. In so doing he transformed the stock character of the Irish boy (long amusing for his Irish 'bulls') into a fiery and quick-witted schemer. Boucicault cannot be ignored, if only because Synge, Shaw and O'Casey were strongly influenced by, or reacted against, his example.

Another playwright who was to influence his successors considerably – though in a more literary way – was T. W. Robertson (1829–71). It is easy to exaggerate his achievement, for it marks only the beginning of a movement away from the broad effects of melodrama and farce towards a more subtle realization of everyday life upon the stage. Allardyce Nicoll quotes approvingly one of Boucicault's remarks: 'Robertson differs from me, not fundamentally, but scenically; his action takes place in lodgings and drawing rooms – mine has a more romantic scope' (*A History of Late Nineteenth Century Drama, 1850–1900*, 1946, vol I, p 120). This seems to me only partly true. The more romantic scope of the setting and action meant that a rhetorical and declamatory manner was still appropriate: exaggeration and high-flown speeches were condoned. Robertson worked towards a greater naturalism, with very brief speeches carefully lined. The contrast between the two styles may be seen in Pinero's *Trelawney of the 'Wells'* (1898), where Tom Wrench represents Robertson, and the old-style actors complain of Tom's play that 'there's not a speech in it, my dear – not a real speech; nothing to dig your teeth into' (Act IV).

Of course, Robertson's earliest work is in the old vein, and even in *David Garrick* (1863), where he begins to show some faint signs of individuality, there is much that is conventional. The dialogue is largely made up of questions and exclamations, and the central scene is one in which Garrick pretends to be drunk. As a portrayal of a great actor the play has no psychological interest; but it is unusual for its time in detailed stage directions and the naturalistic set with its clutter of ornaments, books and furniture.

In *Society* (1865) Robertson realizes his aims far more surely. Chodd junior declares that his cheque book can buy him anything, and has to be brought to realize that a wife is not always gained by such simple means. Maud is in love with the well-born but unfortunate Sidney Daryl, and her mother strongly opposes the match (and supports Chodd) until she learns that Sidney has not only been secretly bringing up her dead son's daughter, but has been elected to parliament and has succeeded to a title. This sounds stagey enough, but *Society* is original in the way it indicates the love between Maud and Sidney: in place of the usual declamatory raptures, muted tones suggest passionate feeling.

In *Caste* (1867) Robertson took another social theme, but handled it with greater subtlety. The serious point of view is as moderate in tone as one would expect from a dramatist who is trying to move away from the melodramatic; and it is put forward by the hero, George:

Caste is a good thing if it's not carried too far. It shuts the door on the pretentious and the vulgar; but it should open the door very wide for exceptional merit. Let brains break through its barriers, and what brains can break through love may leap over.

(Act III)

A more comic outlook is expressed in the encounter between George and Eccles:

Eccles (*sighing*) Ah, sir, the poor and lowly is often 'ardly used. What chance has the working man?
George None when he don't work.
Eccles We are all equal in mind and feelings.
George (*aside*) I hope not . . . allow me to offer you this trifling loan.
Eccles Sir, you're a gentleman. One can tell a real gentleman with half a sov – I mean with half an eye – a real gentleman understands the natural emotions of the working man.

(Act I, scene i)

For Eccles a gentleman is one who has money to give away. Shaw's Doolittle, Burgess, and Snobby Price share in the character and the point of view.

Eccles is a petty thief and gambler, but he is no melodramatic villain. Robertson's concentration is upon contrast, but of the meditative, comic and sentimental type. Polly defends her father with the words, 'He has his faults, but his good points, when you find 'em, are wonderful.' So Eccles does not change his ways, but cheerfully accepts the invitation to go to 'Jersey, where spirits are cheap', so that he can drink himself to death in a year. The audience must accept him as he is, even in the final tableau: 'Eccles falls off the chair in the last stage of drunkenness, bottle in hand. Hawtree, leaning one foot on the chair from which Eccles has fallen, looks at him through eyeglass.' There is no moralizing here, merely a quizzical glance at the toper.

Robertson's plays are altogether less strident than those of Boucicault and other dramatists of his day. Of course, he often depends on the emotional shorthand of the theatre, particularly the accepted clichés of conventional themes. Look at the exchange between the Marquise de St Maur and Esther:

Marquise (rising) You are insolent – you forget that I am a lady.
Esther You forget that I am a mother. Do you dare to offer to buy my child – *his* breathing image, *his* living memory – with money? There is the door – go.

(Act III)

Usually the tone was more restrained, as suited 'cup and saucer' comedy. He was able to suggest a natural situation, too, by keeping several dialogues in motion at the same time, and by interrupting a straight narrative by one character with the preoccupations of another.

In *Caste* and his later plays (*Play*, 1868; *School*, 1869; *War*, 1871) he is most successful in the comic scenes. The titles suggest an absorption in social ideas that is not entirely justified. He is acute enough to make some good points in passing, but he is usually more interested in effective theatre than in forceful thinking. With this qualification in mind, we may agree with the critic who said that his plays 'are entitled to a place with the novels of Trollope as sober records of mid-Victorian England' (E. Reynolds, *Early Victorian Drama, 1830–1870*, p 92).

Another writer who made a very personal contribution to the Victorian theatre was W. S. Gilbert (1836–1911). Robertson encouraged him in his writing, but Gilbert's work owed far more to the extravaganzas of J. R. Planché (1796–1880) and the farces of H. J. Byron (1834–84). Gilbert's serious plays, such as *The Palace of Truth* (1870), *Sweethearts* (1874), *Broken Hearts* (1875) and *Dan'l Druce the Blacksmith* (1876) are forgotten, but one of them, *Pygmalion and Galatea* (1871), was a great success in its own day and reads well. It possesses that mingling of light irony and more melancholy feeling which was to be characteristic of his masterpieces, the libretti for the Savoy operas. The dramatist's art is rather confined in the operatic medium, but Gilbert skilfully provided variety of interest in spectacular entrances and contrasting choruses. Thirteen comic operas were produced between 1875 and 1896, and a number of them are still extraordinarily popular. They have given more phrases and characters to the common stock of English quotation than all the other Victorian plays combined.

Two of the comic operas were outstanding in their satirical wit: *H.M.S. Pinafore* (1878) and *Patience* (1881). The first took off vigorously the nautical drama of the early part of the nineteenth-century. The 'Ruler of the Queen's Navee' is not a good-hearted jolly Jack Tar but a man whose soul has been 'fettered to an office stool'. The sentimental Little Buttercup has (like most middle-aged ladies in the Victorian theatre) a shameful secret to disclose: in her youth she practised baby-farming. The Captain, too, teaches the 'principle that a British sailor is any man's equal, excepting mine.' Yet all this is deftly handled with the lightest of touches. In *Patience* much the same methods are used to laugh at pretentious aestheticism, but Gilbert is careful to balance the arguments. The chorus of twenty lovesick maidens is set off against the chorus of blustering dragoons. The accusation against the aesthetes that 'the meaning doesn't matter if it's only idle chatter of a transcendental kind' is compared with the reproach to the philistines, 'Of course you will pooh-pooh whatever's fresh and new, and declare it's crude and mean.' Yet the final effect is an amusing burlesque of the ideas of Oscar Wilde in his early phase: if we wish to understand them, we must 'cling passionately to one another, and think of faint lilies'.

In *The Mikado* Gilbert reached his highest achievement. Mock gravity and complicated humour mark Ko-ko's

self-decapitation is an extremely difficult, not to say dangerous thing to attempt; . . . it's suicide and suicide is a capital offence.

(Act I)

Witty ingenuity is to be found in his handling of feminine rhyme in 'Taken from a county jail.' The patter-songs (like 'I've got a little list') are brilliantly executed, and Gilbert's remarkable ability in mixing pathos with absurdity is evident in 'Willow, tit-willow'. Against the ferocity of the Mikado himself and his judicial 'object all sublime' are placed the artless prattle of the 'Three little maids from school', and the sentiment of 'A wandering minstrel I'. Real depth of feeling is not to be expected here or in his other comic operas: they are brilliantly limited to what will delightfully entertain.

It is strange to reflect that Gilbert is the only writer to use verse with complete success in the Victorian theatre. It is true that his range was confined to the comic, ironic and sentimental, and would have been scorned by poets whose ambitions lay in historical tragedy. Yet he knew his theatre; they did not show that they knew theirs. R. H. Horne (1803–84) and J. W. Marston (1819–90) had tried to imitate the most sublime moments of the Elizabethans and failed. Tennyson's *Becket* (1893) gave Irving an acting part but is of little interest otherwise. W. B. Yeats (1865–1939) brought out *The Countess Cathleen* (1892) and *The Land of Heart's Desire* (1894), but their blank verse and commonplace metaphor made them slow and wordy, poeticized closet-drama rather than true verse-plays.

The dramatists who still remain to be considered all achieved their theatrical success in prose comedy. The nearest in spirit to Gilbert's flippant and satirical jesting is Oscar Wilde (1854–1900), especially in his one undisputed masterpiece, *The Importance of Being Earnest*. His earlier plays, however, are more akin to those of Pinero and H. A. Jones.

The fact that they turn upon the disclosure of a shameful secret might be of much psychological interest in the study of Wilde himself, were this device not so common in the Victorian theatre. He also brings into these pictures of fashionable society that other well-worn figure, a woman with a past – Mrs Erlynne (*Lady Windermere's Fan*, 1892), Mrs Arbuthnot (*A Woman of No Importance*, 1893) and Mrs Cheveley (*An Ideal Husband*, 1895). In fact, he is content to make use of the usual human furniture of the comedies of his day and of some of its more melodramatic conventions, but he is different from many of his contemporaries in being more interested in dialogue than character and in wit rather than situation. This sometimes leads to an uneasy sequence of ideas that weakens the theme.

An obvious example of this is to be found in *A Woman of No Importance*. Mrs Arbuthnot's secret was that she had been seduced by Lord Illingworth and that Gerald, her son by him, knows nothing of his parentage. Mrs Arbuthnot only divulges the information at the end of Act III, when Gerald threatens to shoot Illingworth. At this point the audience is entirely on Gerald's side, and is pleased when it learns, in the following act, that he is to marry the wealthy Hester. In the plot of the play Gerald and Hester stand for right thinking and Mrs Arbuthnot represents right feeling: in theatrical terms, they must be adequately rewarded. For Wilde this was the mechanical part of the play, but in inserting his celebrated epigrams he sometimes forgot that what the witty characters said was at odds with their role. An illustration may be found in Illingworth's statement, 'Nothing is serious except passion' (Act I), though his character, as it is developed, seems to suggest that he thinks nothing at all is serious.

Even though the persiflage of the aristocrats remains much longer in the memory than the correctness of hero and heroine, we are sometimes conscious that the wit itself owes something to old devices. Definition is one of them, and there are long rallies on the subject of the ideal husband at one point and on the secret of life at another. At times mechanical contrivance is too obvious:

Illingworth What do you call a bad man?
Mrs. Allonby The sort of man who admires innocence.
Illingworth And a bad woman.
Mrs Allonby Oh! the sort of woman a man never gets tired of.

(Act I)

The humour here lies in the adjectives, since they are merely the opposite of what is expected. Exchange them and the replies are commonplace. The trick was a useful one but Wilde used it too often.

A Woman of No Importance has much less unity of tone and effect than *The Importance of Being Earnest* (1895) and has never been so successful on the stage. The latter shows the same command of form, but this time the handling of the theme is masterly. Illingworth had said that the problem of poverty in the East End was 'the problem of slavery. And we are trying to solve it by amusing the slaves' (Act I). No such acknowledgement of the real world and its troubles is to be found in *The Importance of Being Earnest*, and its reasoning is unclouded by sincerity. Pleasure alone matters; ideals are merely fancies. Gwendolen displays these feelings perfectly in Act I:

We live, as I hope you know, Mr. Worthing, in an age of ideals. The fact is constantly mentioned in the more expensive monthly magazines, and has reached the provincial pulpits, I am told; and my ideal has always been to love some one of the name of Ernest.

The challenge is put out gaily and draws attention to Wilde's delight in absurdity and twisted logic:

Algernon Please don't touch the cucumber sandwiches. They are ordered specially for Aunt Agatha. [*Takes one and eats it.*]
Jack Well, you have been eating them all the time.
Algernon That is quite a different matter. She is my aunt.

But the most famous example of brilliant flippancy is the scene between Lady Bracknell and Jack concerning his appearance in a handbag.

Wilde's summary verdict on the play was a just one: 'I like the play's irresponsibility and its *obiter dicta*, but it is essentially an acting play' (*Letters*, ed. R. Hart-Davis, 1962, p 786). Its vitality in the theatre is remarkable, and its appeal is to the comic side of the intellect. Shaw thought it heartless and a proof of Wilde's perversion, but while we inhabit the world it portrays we are aware only of the joy we obtain from the run of the dialogue and the soaring wit. Within those limits style alone matters; persiflage is all.

A. W. Pinero (1855–1934) made an early reputation as a writer of farce. The best was *Dandy Dick* (1887), which, in spite of the facetiousness at the expense of the aitchless lower classes, had a neat plot and a number of warmly funny characters and situations. He could laugh quite safely at some of the old stage clichés:

Sheba Shall we grant them a dignified interview?
Salome Yes. Curl your lip, Sheba.
Sheba You curl your lip better than I – I'll dilate my nostrils.

(Act II)

When he turned to social satire, he was less successful, and plays like *The Times* (1891) compared unfavourably in tone and effect with, say, *New Man and Old Acres* (1869) by Tom Taylor and A. W. Dubourg. He is much better in the handling of sentiment. In the first act of *Trelawney of the 'Wells'* (1898) the consequential actors and actresses of the old school are seen bidding farewell to their young colleague, Rose. Mr and Mrs Telfer, the leaders, are particularly ludicrous in their pomposity, but at the end of the play face a very uncertain future with a courage that lifts them from caricature into life. Naturally, they deplore the efforts of Tom Wrench (who represents T. W. Robertson) to catch the accents of ordinary speech and are bewildered when he says he wants to 'fashion heroes out of actual, dull, every-day men' (Act I). Pinero then proceeds to show us that these ordinary stage-folk really have a quiet heroism about them in their acceptance of their fate and their warmth of heart. These qualities give them an imaginative life denied to the wealthier people they meet. Courage, too, marks Sophy in *The Gay Lord Quex* (1899), more especially in the brilliant third act. She is an independent self-made young manicurist and thinks she can protect her foster-sister Muriel against Quex. She finds herself out-manoeuvred and Quex forces her to write a letter that he can hold against her. We recognize this as an old theatrical trick, but then see that Pinero's later development of the situation springs from character. Sophy realizes that she is betraying Muriel, so she makes the quixotic gesture of tugging the bell-rope, knowing that it may bring the servants and compromise her reputation. Quex admires her spirit and answers her gesture by giving up the letter. All this is most effectively worked out, with changes of mood that are always acceptable. Sophy is ordinary, very ordinary, but she has some extraordinary qualities too. Pinero really interests us in her and can even show her spying at a keyhole without forfeiting our sympathy. He is a dramatist with considerable technical resource, and it is a pity that his dialogue now seems flat and, in the worst sense, too ordinary.

The theatrical progress of Henry Arthur Jones (1851–1929) is a little like that of Pinero, though his early reputation was gained in melodrama rather than farce. *The Silver King* (1882) had a long run and is still remembered for its celebrated line, 'Oh God! put back Thy universe and give me yesterday!' (Act II scene iv). Wilfred Denver made a fortune in the American mines and returned home to exact vengeance from men who had made it appear that he was a murderer. The theme lent itself to strong situations and Jones exploited them, but when he came to apply himself to more serious subjects, he found that he was unable to avoid a certain conventionality of outlook as well as a tendency to over-emphasis. These defects even mar what are probably the best of his twenty-four plays: *The Case of Rebellious Susan* (1894), *The Liars* (1897) and *Mrs. Dane's Defence* (1900). The three bear out the statement by Sir Richard (in *The Case of Rebellious Susan*) that women cannot 'break the seventh commandment, without leaving any ill effects upon society' (Act I). Susan has to forgive her unfaithful husband and forget the attentive young diplomat; Lady Jessica must give up the idea of an elopement; Mrs Dane must not expect to marry again. Jones puts his point of view in the mouth of Sir Daniel Carteret: 'The rules of the game are severe. If you don't like them, leave the sport alone' (*Mrs. Dane's Defence*, Act IV). But the pronouncement comes a little too pat and we have the uncomfortable feeling that Sir Daniel is not talking about sport but about blood-sport. Besides, after some brilliantly contrived situations, moments of real crisis, clever bursts of dialogue and one famous cross-examination, the endings are tame, even timid. Jones was a first-rate story-teller with a talent for edged dialogue, but he did not really understand character or ideas. For him Nora Helmer and Hedda Gabler had lived in vain.

This is not really surprising, for Ibsen's plays on social questions (*Pillars of Society*, 1875–7; *A Doll's House*, 1878–9; *Ghosts*, 1881; *An*

Enemy of The People, 1882), were slow to impress themselves on the English theatre. Their champion was William Archer (1856–24), who was able to influence taste both through his translations and his work as dramatic critic for several periodicals. His articles in the *London Figaro* (1878–81) interested George Bernard Shaw (1856–1950), and Shaw's daily reading in the British Museum (*Das Kapital* in French, and an orchestral score of *Tristan and Isolde*) piqued Archer's curiosity. They became close friends and were to raise the standards of theatrical criticism to a height seldom reached before or since. They also collaborated in two acts of a play: Archer thought up the plot and Shaw supplied the dialogue. Seven years later Shaw completed it alone for production. It was called *Widowers' Houses* (1892).

The occasion was of importance in theatrical history, for the play was put on by J. T. Grein (1862–1935), who was director of the Independent Theatre, an organization formed to give special performances of work of literary and artistic merit rather than merely commercial possibilities. Grein had attracted considerable attention in March 1891 when he had put on Ibsen's *Ghosts*: most critics had been abusive, hearing only the references to venereal disease and missing the profoundly moral point of the play. *Widowers' Houses* discussed a rather different kind of problem: who was to blame for the slums – landlords, the poor or society as a whole? Sartorius, the landlord, is a self-made man who has known poverty himself and is able to justify his methods without difficulty. The opposite point of view is put by his employee, Lickcheese:

Hardly a penny of that but there was a hungry child crying for bread it would have bought.

(Act II)

For two acts the debate has strong moral force, but it falls off in the third act where the question is resolved in rather stagey terms. Nevertheless, this 'blue book drama', as it was called, was ahead of its time in its searching discussion of the ethics of the ownership of slum property. The shrewdest comment upon it was written by Oscar Wilde: 'I like your superb confidence in the dramatic value of the mere facts of life' (*Letters*, ed. R. Hart-Davis, p 339). Encouraged by this, Shaw went on writing plays, though they were not produced, *The Philanderer* is dull (as Archer said it was), but it is not 'vulgar and worthless' (*Collected Letters of G. B. Shaw*, ed. Dan H. Laurence, 1965, p 711). *Mrs. Warren's Profession* is much more successful. Vivie is the 'new woman':

Praed Are you to have no romance, no beauty in your life?
Vivie I don't care for either I assure you.
Praed You can't mean that.
Vivie Oh yes I do. I like working and getting paid for it. When I'm tired of
working I like a comfortable chair, a cigar, a little whisky, and a novel
with a good detective story in it. . . .

(Act I)

Yet she is appalled to hear of her mother's (Mrs Warren's) secret:
that she was a prostitute and now draws a comfortable living from a
chain of brothels abroad. Mrs Warren defends herself much as
Sartorius had done. She had been born in poverty and had resolved
to better herself, but the path she had taken was not that recommended by Samuel Smiles: she preferred a brothel to the horrors of
a white-lead factory. Vivie can forgive her this, but not her
secretiveness and pretence of respectability, living one life and
believing in another. The reactions are interesting, though the
leading characters are highly unsympathetic. Shaw challenged the
romantic view that the fallen woman was a victim (as in *La Dame aux
Camélias*) of her own passionately generous nature and suggested
that sober truth indicated she was mercenary. Pinero's Paula (in *The
Second Mrs Tanqueray*) might be a scapegoat (see M. Meisel, *Shaw
and the Nineteenth Century Theatre*, 1963, pp 143–58), but Mrs
Warren could only be a calculating shopkeeper, ready to justify her
prices. So Shaw called the play 'a cold-bloodedly appalling one'
(*Collected Letters*, p 566). It would be very much worse, however, if
we believed in the characters. As it is, we accept them as puppets in
an intellectually exciting debate.

Shaw regarded these early days as 'dramatic pictures of middle-
class society from the point of view of a Socialist who regards the
basis of that society as thoroughly rotten economically and morally'
(*Collected Letters*, p 632). On the same occasion he made a strong
distinction between them and the four subsequent plays, which
were not 'realistic' but dealt 'with life at large'. In other words, he
moved now from a discussion of social evils to a delighted mockery
of accepted Victorian conventions.

Arms and the Man (1894) was the first of his plays to be given in
the West End, but ran for only eleven nights. It was quite well
received by the critics, and the American rights were bought by the
actor, Richard Mansfield. Shaw, however, had no means of
knowing that even this very modest degree of success was to be
denied him in the commercial theatre for another decade. It is easy
to understand why *Arms and the Man* was not more successful.

Jingoism was still common, and an attack on the romantic view of Ruritanian (actually Bulgarian) military men could well be taken as mockery of real heroes like 'the soldiers of the Queen'. Shaw seems to intend it to be just such a satire on inflamed patriotic feeling: the only good soldier is a sensible man who does not hazard his life without cause, who indulges in no heroics, and who finds chocolate as useful as cartridges. Bluntschli, who epitomizes this point of view, is a middle-class Swiss, eminently practical, and even apologetic about his efficiency. His attitude is contrasted with the heroic antics of Sergius, who has to learn to pronounce the true lesson of the play:

Oh, war! war! the dream of patriots and heroes! A fraud, Bluntschli. A hollow sham, like love.

(Act III)

The attitudinizing common in popular military plays of the day is dismissed. Aristocratic dowries are laughed at when Bluntschli bids for Raina's hand with the contents of his hotels. Stage conventions of all kinds are held up to ridicule. Even the device of demonstrating a character's ill-breeding by showing him or her listening at a keyhole is examined, and Bluntschli says, 'It's all a question of the degree of provocation' (Act III).

From this most good-humoured of comedies Shaw went on to create the second of his 'Four Pleasant Plays', *Candida* (1895). Here, too, he attacked romantic fustian and conventional situations. When her husband is away from home and Marchbanks, the young poet, is with her, Candida has no adulterous *affaire* with him but listens placidly while he woos her by the only method he knows – reading his poems. Similarly, in the bargaining scene, she points out that her eloquent husband is not the strong man he would wish to appear to be: his ready-made phrases prevent him from knowing the truth. She is not wholly dependent upon him; he is upon her.

By comparison with these two beautifully constructed plays, *You Never Can Tell* (1897) is something of a disappointment. The opening seems to suggest an attempt at the manner of *The Importance of Being Earnest*, and in the amusing prattle of the twins Shaw comes nearer to it than anywhere else in his work. He still shows his remarkable ability to write prose that leaps from the actor's tongue and to create characters like the waiter whose commonsense delights us, but the satire upon Victorian family life goes on too long, and Mrs Clandon, her husband, McComas and Bohun are uninteresting. Gloria, too, though triumphing over Valentine in their sex-combat, is unattractive.

In the same year Shaw wrote what is undoubtedly one of his best stage plays, *The Devil's Disciple*. The direction his thoughts were taking is to be seen in a letter to Ellen Terry:

A good melodrama is a more difficult thing to write than all this clever-clever comedy.

(Collected Letters, p 617)

When he set about writing, he cheerfully admitted that the new play was based on Adelphi Theatre tricks – 'the reading of the will, the heroic sacrifice, the court martial, the execution, the reprieve at the last moment' (A. Henderson, *George Bernard Shaw, Man of the Century*, 1956, p 473). Specific resemblances have also been found to Boucicault's *Arrah-na-Pogue* (1864) (A. Nicoll, op. cit., pp 90–1). Yet what is at once clear is that Shaw has given these stock situations a new force. Dick Dudgeon, the reprobate, does not know why he takes the parson's place and brings the threat of execution upon himself. It seems a wry jest, but he grows in moral stature as he faces the consequences. The contrast between his apparent bravado, Burgoyne's suavity and Judith's bewilderment is brilliantly conceived.

The last two plays that Shaw wrote in the Victorian period were *Caesar and Cleopatra* (1898) and *Captain Brassbound's Conversion* (1899). If they were by other nineteenth-century dramatists, they would be acclaimed as thoughtful and imaginative, but they are by Shaw at less than his best. He is much too discursive in them and appears to be aiming at something greater than he achieves. What is noticeable is that he was to return to some of the character-types and their relationships for two of his greater plays. The Caesar – Cleopatra association is to be revealed with greater insight in Undershaft and Barbara; Brassbound was to be transformed into Shotover.

Shaw had to wait until the famous seasons (1904–7) at the Court Theatre before the public had any real chance of seeing his plays in London. By that time he was ready to conquer the literary and theatrical worlds, and to bring his magnificent intelligence and superb prose to the creation of some of the finest comedies of the twentieth century. Yet his roots were in the earlier period and, theatrically speaking, he was certainly the most eminent of the Victorians.

BIBLIOGRAPHY

The place of publication of books mentioned in the text or bibliographies is London, unless otherwise stated.

General

The following is a list of some books of general interest on the Victorian period.

The New Cambridge Bibliography of English Literature, vol III (1800–1900), 1969.
Batho, E., and Dobrée, B., eds, *The Victorians and After*, revised 1950.
Faverty, F. E., ed., *The Victorian Poets, A Guide to Research*, 2nd edn, 1968.
Stevenson, L., ed., *Victorian Fiction, A Guide to Research*, 1964.
Briggs, A., *Victorian People*, 1954.
—— *Victorian Cities*, 1963.
—— *The Age of Improvement*, 1959.
Buckley, J. H., *The Victorian Temper*, Cambridge, Mass., 1951.
Burn, W. L., *The Age of Equipoise*, 1964.
Chadwick, O., *The Victorian Church*, Part I, 1967; Part II, 1970.
Cruse, A., *The Victorians and Their Books*, 1935.
Ensor, R. C. K., *England, 1870–1914*, Oxford, 1936.
Fairchild, H. N., *Religious Trends in English Poetry*, vol IV, 1957.
Holloway, J., *The Victorian Sage*, 1953.
Houghton, W. E., *The Victorian Frame of Mind*, New Haven, 1957.
Ideas and Beliefs of the Victorians (B.B.C. Talks), 1949.
Kitson Clark, G., *The Making of Victorian England*, 1962.
Somervell, D. C., *English Thought in the Nineteenth Century*, 1929.
Wellek, R., *A History of Modern Criticism*, vol IV, 1966.
Willey, B., *Nineteenth Century Studies*, 1949.
—— *More Nineteenth Century Studies*, 1956.
Williams, R., *Culture and Society, 1780–1950*, 1958.
Woodward, E. L., *The Age of Reform, 1815–1870*, 1938; with corrections, 1946.
Young, G. M., *Victorian England: Portrait of An Age*, 1937.
and the following periodicals:
Nineteenth Century Fiction [originally *The Trollopian*], Berkeley, California 1945– .
Victorian Poetry, Morgantown, West Virginia, 1963– .
Victorian Studies, Bloomington, Indiana, 1957– .

1. *Victorian Thought*

I *Primary Sources*

Bagehot, W., *Estimations in Criticism*, ed. C. Lennox, 2 vols, Edinburgh, 1908–9.

Carlyle, T., *Sartor Resartus*, 1833 [published anonymously].

—— *The French Revolution*, 2 vols, 1837.

—— *Critical and Miscellaneous Essays*, 2nd edn, 5 vols, 1840.

—— *Past and Present*, 1843.

—— *Cromwell's Letters and Speeches*, 3 vols, 1845.

—— *Latter-Day Pamphlets*, 1850.

Darwin, C., *On the Origin of Species by Means of Natural Selection*, 1859.

—— *The Descent of Man and Selection in Relation to Sex*, 2 vols, 1871.

Dickens, C., *Hard Times*, 1854.

Disraeli, B., *Coningsby*, 3 vols, 1844.

—— *Sybil*, 3 vols, 1845.

Essays and Reviews, 1860.

Froude, J. A., *History of England from the Fall of Wolsey to the Defeat of the Spanish Armada*, 12 vols, 1870.

—— *Thomas Carlyle*, new edn, 1896.

Huxley, T. H., *Collected Essays*, 9 vols, 1893–5.

Lyell, C., *Principles of Geology*, 3 vols, 1830–3.

—— *Geological Evidences of the Antiquity of Man*, 1863.

Macaulay, Lord, *Complete Works*, 12 vols (Albany edn), 1898.

Mill, J. S., *A System of Logic*, 2 vols, 1843.

—— *On Liberty*, 1859.

—— *Utilitarianism*, 1865.

—— *Autobiography*, 1873.

—— *Bentham and Coleridge*, with an introduction by F. R. Leavis, 1950.

Newman, J. H., *An Essay on the Development of Christian Doctrine*, 1845.

—— *Discourses on the Scope of University Education*, Dublin, 1852.

—— *Apologia pro Vita Sua* (the two versions of 1864 and 1865 preceded by Newman's and Kingsley's pamphlets), with an introduction by Wilfrid Ward, Oxford, 1913.

Pugin, A. W., *Contrasts or a Parallel between the Noble Edifices of the Middle Ages and Corresponding Buildings of the Present Day*, 1841.

—— *An Apology for the Revival of Christian Architecture*, 1843.

Ruskin, J., *Works*, eds E. T. Cook and A. Wedderburn, 39 vols, 1903.

Stanley, A. P., *Essays Chiefly on Questions of Church and State from 1850–1870*, 1870.

II *Critical Works*

Hutton, R. H., *Essays on Some of the Modern Guides of English Thought*, 1887. A judicious summing-up, after the battle, by an intelligent Anglican.

Church, R. W., *The Oxford Movement*, 1891.

Gooch, G. P., *History and Historians in the Nineteenth Century*, 1913. Thorough, indispensable and dull.

Robertson, J. M., *A History of Freethought in the Nineteenth Century*, 1929. Thorough, though at times intemperate.

Young, G. M., *Victorian England: Portrait of an Age*, Oxford, 1936. A masterly account in brief compass.

Willey, B., *Nineteenth Century Studies*, 1949. A learned and lucid, though unexciting, account of the development of thought from Coleridge to Matthew Arnold.

—— *More Nineteenth Century Studies*, 1956. A sympathetic account of Victorian agnosticism from a modern equivalent of a Broad Church point of view.

Holloway, J., *The Victorian Sage*, 1953. A very intelligent and original account, from a point of view combining the philosophical and the literary approach, of the 'Prophets' from Carlyle onwards. Ruskin is unfortunately omitted.

Houghton, W. E., *The Victorian Frame of Mind*, New Haven, 1957. A sensitive and useful study of everyday feelings and attitudes, 1830–1870.

Williams, R., *Culture and Society 1780–1950*, 1958. An interesting and original, though very one-sided and at times scornful, account of the relation of the thinkers to the society in which they lived.

Plamenatz, J., *The English Utilitarians*, Oxford, 1958. A first-class philosophical study.

Geyl, P., *Debates with Historians*, 1962. A masterly enquiry into the moral and political assumptions of Carlyle, Macaulay and others.

Rosenberg, J. D., *The Darkening Glass*, 1963. The best general study of the development of Ruskin's thought.

Burn, W. L., *The Age of Equipoise*, 1964. Perhaps the best general study of mid-Victorian life in every aspect.

Cockshut, A. O. J., *The Unbelievers*, 1964. A study of agnostic thought, 1840–90.

Bagehot, W., *Literary Essays*, ed. N. St John Stevas, 1965. Bagehot is unfailingly acute, witty and realistic.

Chadwick, O., *The Victorian Church*, Part I, 1966; Part II, 1970. An admirable study of the subject.

2. Faith and Doubt in the Victorian Age
(See also bibliography to *Victorian Thought*)

I *Primary Sources*

Arnold, Matthew, *St. Paul and Protestantism*, 1870.
—— *Literature and Dogma*, 1873.
—— *God and the Bible*, 1875.
Arnold, Thomas, *Sermons in Rugby Chapel (1832–40)*, 1878.
Clifford, W. K., *Lectures and Essays*, 2 vols, 1879.
Clough, A. H., *Prose Remains*, 1888.
—— *Poems*, eds F. L. Mulhauser, 2nd edn, 1974.
Dickens, Charles, *Little Dorrit*, 1855–7.
Disraeli, B., *Sybil*, 1845.
—— *Lothair*, 1870.
Eliot, George, *Scenes of Clerical Life*, 1858.
—— *The Mill on the Floss*, 1860.
—— *Felix Holt, The Radical*, 1866.
—— *Middlemarch*, 1872.
—— *Daniel Deronda*, 1876.
Froude, Hurrell, *Remains*, eds J. H. Newman and J. Keble, 4 vols, 1838–9.
Gaskell, Elizabeth, *North and South*, 1854–5.
Gosse, Edmund, *Father and Son*, 1907.
Hardy, Thomas, *The Return of the Native*, 3 vols, 1878.
—— *Collected Poems*, 4th edn, 1930.
Hare, Augustus, *The Story of My Life*, 6 vols, 1896.
Hopkins, G. M., *Poems*, 4th edn, 1967.
—— *Further Letters* (including correspondence with Coventry Patmore), ed. C. C. Abbott, 2nd edn, 1956.
Hughes, Thomas, *Tom Brown's Schooldays*, 1857.
Huxley, T. H., *Science and Hebrew Tradition*, 1893.
—— *Science and Christian Tradition*, 1894.
—— *Evolution and Ethics*, 1894.
Keble, John, *The Christian Year*, new edn, 1899.
Mallock, W. H., *The New Republic*, 1877.
Meredith, George, *Poems and Lyrics of the Joy of Earth*, 1883.
Mill, J. S., *Three Essays on Religion*, 2nd edn, 1874.
Newman, J. H., *Loss and Gain*, 2nd edn, 1848.
—— *The Present Position of Catholics*, 1851.
Pater, Walter, *Marius the Epicurean*, 1885.

Pattison, Mark, *Memories*, 1883.
Ruskin, John, *Praeterita*, 1885–9.
Seeley, Sir J. R., *Ecce Homo*, 1865.
Stanley, A. P., *Thomas Arnold*, 1844.
—— *Essays on Church and State (1850–70)*, 1870.
Stephen, Sir James, *Essays in Ecclesiastical Biography*, 2 vols, 1849.
Stephen, J. F., *Liberty, Equality, Fraternity*, 1873.
Stephen, Leslie, *Essays in Freethinking and Plainspeaking*, 1873.
—— *An Agnostic's Apology*, 1890.
Swinburne, A. C., *Collected Poetical Works*, 2 vols, 1924.
Thomson, James, 'The City of Dreadful Night' in *National Reformer*, 1874.
Tracts for the Times: by members of the University of Oxford, 6 vols, 2nd edn, 1839–41.
Trollope, Anthony, *Barchester Towers*, 1857.
—— *Ralph the Heir*, 1871.
Trollope, Frances, *The Vicar of Wrexhill*, 1837.
Ward, Mrs Humphry, *Robert Elsmere*, 1888.
—— *Eleanor*, 1900.
Ward, W. G., *The Ideal of a Christian Church*, 1844.
White, W. Hale, *The Autobiography of Mark Rutherford*, 1881.
—— *Mark Rutherford's Deliverance*, 1885.
Wilberforce, R. I. & S., *Life of William Wilberforce*, 5 vols, 1838.
Wiseman, Nicholas, Cardinal, *Essays on Various Subjects*, 3 vols, 1853.
Yonge, Charlotte M., *The Heir of Redclyffe*, 1853.
—— *Abbeychurch*, 1844.
—— *The Castle-Builders*, 1854.

II *Critical and Secondary Works*

Altholz, J. L., *The Liberal Catholic Movement in England*, 1960. A scholarly and extremely well-balanced account of the 'Rambler' and its contributors 1848–64. Brings out difficulties of newly resurgent Catholicism in reconciling authority with nineteenth century mass communications.
Annan, Noel, *Leslie Stephen*, 2nd edn, 1984. More than a biography. A widely-ramifying study of English intellectual life, and the development of agnosticism.
Balleine, G. R., *A History of the Evangelical Party in the Church of England*, new edn, 1951.

Brose, Olive, *Church and Parliament (1828–60)*, 1959. A sympathetic study of the modernization of the administration and finances of the Church of England in the Age of Reform.

Brown, Ford K., *Fathers of the Victorians*, 1961. An informative but somewhat hostile account of the 'Clapham Sect', and the social crusades of Wilberforce and others.

Chapman, Ronald, *Father Faber*, 1961. A useful biography of a famous Oratorian preacher and head of the Brompton Oratory.

—— *Faith and Revolt: Studies in the Literary Influence of the Oxford Movement*, 1970.

Cockshut, A. O. J., ed., *Religious Controversies of the Nineteenth Century*, 1966.

Cunningham, V., *Everywhere Spoken Against: Dissent in the Victorian Novel*, Oxford, 1975.

Gladstone, W. E., 'The Evangelical Movement' in *Gleanings from Past Years*, vol VII, 1879. Particularly interesting as showing the unexpected elements of continuity between the Evangelical and Oxford Movements.

Haight, G. S. *George Eliot. A Biography*, 1968. A full study based on extensive primary sources.

Huxley, Leonard, *Life and Letters of T. H. Huxley*, 2 vols, 1903. A good source for the study of Darwinian controversies.

Jay, Elizabeth, *The Religion of the Heart: Anglican Evangelicalism and the Nineteenth-Century Novel*, Oxford, 1979.

Leslie, Shane, *Henry Edward Manning*, 1921. A spirited account of the man who, more than any other, helped to turn an impoverished and handicapped Catholic community into a flourishing part of the national life.

Martin, B. W., *John Keble*, 1976. A sensitive study of one of the most important leaders of the Oxford Movement.

Reardon, B. M. G., *From Coleridge to Gore: A Century of Religious Thought in Britain*, 1971.

Sellers, I., *Nineteenth-Century Nonconformity*, 1977.

Thompson, D. M., ed., *Nonconformity in the Nineteenth Century*, 1972.

Ward, Bernard, *The Eve of Catholic Emancipation*, 3 vols, 1911. A full and fascinating study of the emergence of English Catholicism from centuries of exclusion and contempt.

Woolf, R. L., *Gains and Losses: Novels of Faith and Doubt in Victorian England*, New York, 1977.

Wright, T. R., *The Religion of Humanity*, 1986. The best full study of Comtean positivism, and its influence both on those who fully accepted it, and on those who were influenced more or less strongly.

3. *Matthew Arnold (and A. H. Clough)*

I *Matthew Arnold*

Works of Matthew Arnold, 15 vols, 1903–4. Vols 1–2 the poems, 3–12 the prose, 13–15 the letters and bibliography. Incomplete.

The Poetical Works of Matthew Arnold, eds C. B. Tinker and H. F. Lowry, 1950. Formerly the standard text, but shortly to be superseded by the forthcoming Poetical Works for Oxford Texts, ed. Miriam Allott and N. S. Shrimpton, with introduction and full commentary replacing the 1940 Tinker and Lowry commentary (see below).

The Poems of Matthew Arnold, ed. K. Allott, 1965, 2nd edn Miriam Allott, 1979. Annotated and contains material omitted from the standard text; the 1979 edn contains material omitted from the 1965 edn. *Matthew Arnold*, ed. Miriam Allott and Robert H. Super (The Oxford Authors, 1986).

Matthew Arnold. Selected Poems and Prose, ed. Miriam Allott, 1978, repr. 1985.

The Complete Prose Works of Matthew Arnold, ed. R. H. Super, Ann Arbor, 11 vols, 1960–1977. The definitive edition; finely edited, superbly annotated and indexed.

Five Uncollected Essays of Matthew Arnold, ed. K. Allott, Liverpool, 1953.

Essays, Letters, and Reviews by Matthew Arnold, ed. F. Neiman, Cambridge, Mass., 1960.

The Notebooks of Matthew Arnold, eds H. F. Lowry, K. Young and W. H. Dunn, 1952.

Letters of Matthew Arnold, 1848–1888, ed. G. W. E. Russell, 1895. Mainly family letters, with many omissions; unindexed. Will be superseded by the forthcoming complete edition of the letters, ed. C. Y. Lang, University of Virginia.

The Letters of Matthew Arnold to Arthur Hugh Clough, ed. H. F. Lowry, 1932. Excellent edition with a useful introduction.

The Portable Matthew Arnold, ed. L. Trilling, New York, 1949. Useful selection of poetry and prose with stimulating introduction.

Eliot, T. S., 'Arnold and Pater', *Selected Essays*, 1932.

Trilling, L., *Matthew Arnold*, 2nd edn, 1949.

Tinker, C. B., and Lowry, H. F., *The Poetry of Matthew Arnold: A Commentary*, 1940. Pioneering work, but to be used with caution. For the forthcoming Oxford commentary see under *The Poetical Works of Matthew Arnold* above.

Bonnerot, L., *Matthew Arnold – Poète: Essai de biographie psychologique*, Paris, 1947.

Brown, E. K., *Matthew Arnold: A Study in Conflict*, Chicago, 1948.

Holloway, J., *The Victorian Sage*, 1953.

Jump, J. D., *Matthew Arnold*, 1955.

Gottfried, L. A., *Matthew Arnold and the Romantics*, 1963.

Anderson, W. D., *Matthew Arnold and the Classical Tradition*, Ann Arbor, 1965.

Culler, A. D., *Imaginative Reason*, New Haven, 1966. A study of the poetry.

Madden, W. A., *Matthew Arnold*, Bloomington, Indiana, 1967.

Leavis, F. R., 'Arnold as Critic' (1938), *A Selection from Scrutiny*, Cambridge, 1968.

Honan, P., *Matthew Arnold: A Life*, 1981. The standard biography.

II *A. H. Clough*

The Poems of A. H. Clough, eds H. F. Lowry, A. L. P. Norrington and F. L. Mulhauser, Oxford, 1951. The standard text.

The Poems of Arthur Hugh Clough, ed. A. L. P. Norrington, Oxford, 1968. Based on the 1951 edn, with new notes and introduction.

The Correspondence of A. H. Clough, ed. F. L. Mulhauser, 1957.

The Poems and Prose Remains of A. H. Clough, ed. B. Clough, 1869. Vol 1 contains the life, selected letters and prose remains.

Selected Prose Works of A. H. Clough, ed. B. Trawick, Alabama, 1964. Badly edited and introduced, but contains new material.

Chorley, K., *A. H. Clough: The Uncommitted Mind*, Oxford, 1962. An interesting biography.

Houghton, W. E., *The Poetry of Clough*, New Haven, 1963. The best critical study.

Veyriras, P., *A. H. Clough*, Paris, 1964.

Biswas, R. K., *Arthur Hugh Clough: Towards a Reconsideration*, Oxford, 1972.

4. *Dickens*

The Clarendon Dickens, General editors, John Butt, Kathleen Tillotson and James Kinsley, Oxford, 1966– . Potentially the definitive edition. The following volumes have appeared so far: *Oliver Twist, Edwin Drood, Dombey and Son, Little Dorrit, David Copperfield, Martin Chuzzlewit, Pickwick Papers.*

Of the numerous reprint and paperback editions available the most comprehensive are those published in the Penguin English Library. All of the novels, together with a range of the shorter fiction, are included in this series. The textual editing of these volumes is unambitious, but their various introductions and notes are informative.

The Letters of Charles Dickens (Pilgrim edn), eds M. House, G. Storey and K. Tillotson, Oxford, 1965– . Twelve projected volumes, of which five, covering the years 1820 to 1849 have so far appeared.

The Letters of Charles Dickens, ed. W. Dexter, 3 vols, 1938.

Selected Letters of Charles Dickens, ed. D. Paroissien, 1985.

Forster, J., *The Life of Charles Dickens*, 1872–4. Authorized biography, which draws heavily on its author's relationship with his subject. (Latest edn, ed. A. J. Hoppé, 2 vols, 1966.)

Gissing, G., *Charles Dickens: A Critical Study*, 1898. As a committed realist, Gissing finds Dickens's use of coincidence, exaggeration, sentiment, etc., questionable, but his book is a fine examination of one novelist by another.

Chesterton, G. K., *Charles Dickens*, 1906. Energetic discussion, emphasizing extrovert qualities of the early novels. See also his *Appreciations and Criticisms of Charles Dickens's Works*, 1911.

Orwell, G., 'Charles Dickens', *Inside the Whale*, 1940. Examines contradictions in Dickens's social attitudes, while expressing delight in the singularity of his fictional imagination.

House, H., *The Dickens World*, 1941. Pioneering study of the relationship between the novels and their socio-historical background.

Wilson, E., 'Dickens: The Two Scrooges', *The Wound and the Bow*, 1941. Dickens's personal psychology as interpreted through the life and the works.

Lindsay, J., *Charles Dickens*, 1950. Marxist study of the relationship between the life, the society and the work.

Johnson, E., *Charles Dickens: His Tragedy and Triumph*, 1953. Standard modern biography. Chapters of criticism on each of the novels.

Ford, G., *Dickens and His Readers*, 1955. Valuable account of developments in the history of Dickens's reputation.

Butt, J., and Tillotson, K., *Dickens at Work*, 1957.

Miller, J. Hillis, *Charles Dickens: The World of His Novels*, 1958.

Ford, G. H., and Lane, L., eds, *The Dickens Critics*, 1961.

Collins, P. A. W., *Dickens and Crime*, 1962; *Dickens and Education*, 1963. Well-documented studies. More interesting biographically than critically.

Leavis, F. R., and Leavis, Q. D., *Dickens the Novelist*, 1970.

Collins, P., ed., *Dickens: The Critical Heritage*, 1970. Comprehensive collection of contemporary reviews.

Gold, J., *The Stature of Dickens: A Centenary Bibliography*, 1971. Can be updated by reference to A. M. Cohn and K. K. Collins, *The Cumulated Dickens Checklist 1970–79*, 1982.

Welsh, A., *The City of Dickens*, 1971. The relationship, structural and symbolic, as well as socio-historical, between the novels and their urban context.

Carey, J. *The Violent Effigy*, 1973. Short but stimulating general discussion, drawing on examples at random, but emphasizing the significance of Dickens's personality for his fiction.

Patten, R. L., *Dickens and His Publishers*, 1978.

Stone, H., *Dickens and the Invisible World*, 1979. Examination of selected novels in the light of their reflection of fairy-tale motifs and structures.

Cohen, J. R., *Charles Dickens and His Original Illustrators*, 1981. The fullest study to date of this topic. Extensive bibliography.

Horton, S., *The Reader in the Dickens World*, 1981. 'Reader-response' critical investigation that emphasizes multiplicity of potential interpretation. See also her *Interpreting, Interpreting* (1979), a similar exercise devoted entirely to *Dombey and Son*.

Page, N., *A Dickens Companion*, 1984. Valuable compilation of information, with individual chapters devoted to each of the full-length works, and sections devoted to dramatizations, filmography, topography, etc.

5. Surtees, Thackeray and Trollope

I Surtees

The novels are available in a series issued in a facsimile edition by the R. S. Surtees Society, Craddock near Cullompton, Devon. There is a paperback of *Mr. Sponge's Sporting Tour* in Oxford World's Classics.

Cuming, E. D., *Robert Smith Surtees, Creator of Jorrocks* by Himself and E. D. Cuming, 1924. The autobiographical notes expanded.

Watson, Frederick, *Robert Smith Surtees: A Critical Study*, 1933. Good on the various social strata represented in the novels.

Cooper, Leonard, *R. S. Surtees*, 1952.

Bovill, E. W., *The England of Nimrod and Surtees 1815–1854*, 1959. Social and agricultural historical background.

Dobrée, Bonamy, 'Robert Smith Surtees' in *Imagined Worlds*, eds M. Mack and I. Gregor, 1968, pp 157–70. Succinct and suggestive critical study.

Johnston-Jones, D. R., *The Deathless Train: The Life and Work of Robert Smith Surtees*, Salzburg, 1974.

Welcome, John, *The Sporting World of R. S. Surtees*, 1982. Biographical and critical, better on the former.

II Thackeray

Works, 17 vols, 1908. Introductions by George Saintsbury. With original and revised readings and additional material.

Works, 26 vols, 1910–11 (Centenary edn). Biographical introductions by Anne Thackeray Ritchie, with Leslie Stephen's memoir and many of Thackeray's drawings.

Letters and Private Papers, ed. G. N. Ray, 4 vols, Cambridge, Mass., 1946.

Bagehot, W., 'Sterne and Thackeray', *National Review*, 1864; *Collected Works*, ed. N. St J. Stevas, vol II, 1965, pp 278–312.

Trollope, A., *Thackeray*, 1879. (English Men of Letters Series.)

Cecil, Lord David, *Early Victorian Novelists*, 1934. A judicious estimate.

Dodds, J. W., *Thackeray, A Critical Portrait*, New York, 1941. 'Criticism with some biographical infiltration.'

Greig, J. Y. T., *Thackeray, A Reconsideration*, Oxford, 1950. Links criticism to biography. Not always sympathetic.

Stevenson, L., *The Showman of Vanity Fair*, 1947.

Ray, G. N., *The Buried Life*, 1952. Suggests originals for many of the characters.

—— *Thackeray*, 2 vols, New York, 1955 and 1958. The standard biography.

Tillotson, G., *Thackeray the Novelist*, 1954. Indispensable critical study.

Tillotson, K., *Novels of The Eighteen-Forties*, 1954. Has a most enlightening chapter on *Vanity Fair*.

Loofbourow, J., *Thackeray and the Form of Fiction*, Princetown, 1964. Concerned with parallels in form and time.

Dyson, A. E., *The Crazy Fabric*, 1965. Chapter on the complex ironies in *Vanity Fair*.

Tillotson, G., and Hawes, D., eds, *Thackeray: The Critical Heritage*, 1968. Extensive anthology of criticism in Thackeray's own time and just afterwards. Good introduction.

McMaster, Juliet, *Thackeray: The Major Novels*, Manchester and Toronto, 1971. Examines authorial presence, narrative technique, serialization.

Hardy, Barbara, *The Exposure of Luxury: Radical Themes in Thackeray*, 1984. On rank, money, nature and art, and love.

Carey, J., *Thackeray: Prodigal Genius*, 1977.

III *Trollope*

There is no complete edition. Nine titles are available in the Oxford Illustrated Trollope, but Oxford World's Classics series contains over 30 titles.

Letters, ed. N. John Hall, 2 vols, 1983.

James, Henry, *Partial Portraits*, 1888.

Sadleir, M., *Trollope: A Commentary*, 1927, revised 1945. The standard critical biography.

Cecil, Lord David, *Early Victorian Novelists*, 1934.

Brown, B. C., *Anthony Trollope*, 1950. A perceptive short study, especially good on Trollope's 'Englishness' and the influence of the Civil Service upon him.

Cockshut, A. O. J., *Anthony Trollope: A Critical Study*, 1955. The second part is an attempt to rehabilitate some of the later novels.

Helling, R., *A Century of Trollope Criticism*, Helsingfors, 1956. Surveys the course of Trollope's reputation.

Booth, B. A., *Anthony Trollope: Aspects of His Life and Work*, 1959. Informed critical judgments by a leading Trollope scholar.

Polhemus, R. M., *The Changing World of Anthony Trollope*, Berkeley and Los Angeles, 1968. Chronological study of the novels with emphasis on Trollope's changing view of the world. Excellent on 'Love and the Victorians'.

Smalley, D., ed., *Trollope: The Critical Heritage*, 1969. Companion volume to Tillotson and Hawes' *Thackeray*.

Roberts, Ruth, ap, *Trollope: Artist and Moralist* (in USA as *The Moral Trollope*), 1971.

Skilton, D., *Anthony Trollope and His Contemporaries: A Study in the Theory and Conventions of Mid-Victorian Fiction*, 1972.

Halperin, J., *Trollope and Politics: A Study of the Pallisers and Others*, 1978. Each novel treated separately – well-informed and well-defined.

Pollard, Arthur, *Anthony Trollope*, 1978. Survey of the Works.

Terry, R. C., *Anthony Trollope: The Artist in Hiding*, 1978. Topics such as commerce, society, the Press, Ireland, personal relationships.

Tracy, Robert, *Trollope's Later Novels*, 1978. Stresses formal skills as a novelist.

Edwards, P. D., *Anthony Trollope: His Art and Scope*, 1978. Wide-ranging, not always sympathetic.

McMaster, Juliet, *Trollope's Palliser Novels: Theme and Pattern*, 1979. Personal lives in the political novels.

Harvey, G., *The Art of Anthony Trollope*, 1980. Argues strongly for design and notes likenesses with some Elizabethan and Jacobean plays.

Letwin, Shirley, *The Gentleman in Trollope: Individuality and Moral Conduct*, 1982. Discrimination, diffidence and honesty as gentlemanly qualities.

6. The Brontës

Life and Works of Charlotte Brontë and Her Sisters, eds Mrs Humphry Ward and C. K. Shorter (Haworth edn), 7 vols, 1899–1900.

Novels and Poems of Charlotte, Emily and Anne Brontë, 7 vols, 1901–7 (Oxford World's Classics).

The Shakespeare Head Brontë, eds T. J. Wise and J. A. Symington, 20 vols, 1932–8. Definitive edition – Novels in 11 vols; Life and Letters in 4 vols; Miscellaneous and Unpublished Writings, 2 vols; Poems, 2 vols; Bibliography, 1 vol.

Legends of Angria, eds F. E. Ratchford and W. C. de Vane, New Haven, 1933. Compiled from early writings of Charlotte Brontë.

Complete Poems of Anne Brontë, eds C. K. Shorter and C. W. Hatfield, 1923.

Complete Poems of Charlotte Brontë, eds C. K. Shorter and C. W. Hatfield, 1923.

Complete Poems of Emily Brontë, ed. C. W. Hatfield, New York, 1941.

Gondal's Queen: A Novel in Verse by Emily Brontë, ed. F. E. Ratchford, Texas, 1955. Poems arranged as coherent reconstruction of the Gondal epic.

Gaskell, Mrs E. C., *Life of Charlotte Brontë*, 2 vols, 1857; 3rd edn 'revised and corrected'. The standard biography.

Transactions and Publications of the Brontë Society, Bradford (then Haworth), 1895–

Shorter, C. K., *The Brontës and Their Circle*, 1896. A pioneer piece of scholarship.

Woolf, V., '*Jane Eyre* and *Wuthering Heights*' in *The Common Reader*, 1925.

S[anger], C. P., *The Structure of 'Wuthering Heights'*, 1926. The first and invaluable analysis of structure.

Cecil, Lord David, *Early Victorian Novelists*, 1934. Chapters on Charlotte and Emily.

Ratchford, F. E., *The Brontës' Web of Childhood*, New York, 1941. The authoritative study of the juvenilia.

Lane, M., *The Brontë Story: A Reconsideration of Mrs Gaskell's 'Life of Charlotte Brontë'*, 1953.

Visick, M., *The Genesis of 'Wuthering Heights'*, Hong Kong, 1958; Oxford, 1959. Examines the relationship of the poems to the novel.

Gérin, W., *Anne Brontë*, 1959.
—— *Branwell Brontë*, 1961.
—— *Charlotte Brontë*, 1967.
   All three are the fullest biographies to date.
Martin, R. B., *The Accents of Persuasion*, 1966. A critical study of Charlotte Brontë's novels.
Ewbank, I–S., *Their Proper Sphere*, 1966. A study of the Brontë sisters as essentially female novelists of their times.
Craik, W. A., *The Brontë Novels*, 1968.
Allott, M., ed., *Charlotte Brontë: The Critical Heritage*, 1974.
Duthie, E., *The Foreign Vision of Charlotte Brontë*, 1975.
Hardy, B., 'The Lyricism of Emily Brontë' in *The Art of Emily Brontë*, ed. A. Smith, 1976.
Alexander, C., *The Early Writings of Charlotte Brontë*, 1983.

7. Mrs Gaskell and George Eliot

I *Mrs Gaskell*

Works (Knutsford edn), 8 vols, 1919–1920.
Letters, eds J. A. V. Chapple and A. Pollard, Manchester, 1966.

Chadwick, Mrs E. H., *Mrs Gaskell: Haunts, Homes and Stories*, 1913.
Sanders, G. de W., *Elizabeth Gaskell*, New Haven, 1929. Includes a detailed bibliography.
Haldane, E. S., *Mrs Gaskell and her Friends*, 1930.
ffrench, Y., *Mrs Gaskell*, 1949.
Hopkins, A. B., *Elizabeth Gaskell: Her Life and Work*, 1952.
Tillotson, K., *Novels of the Eighteen-Forties*, 1954. Contains a good discussion of *Mary Barton*.
Pollard, A., *Mrs Gaskell, Novelist and Biographer*, Manchester, 1965. A good critical discussion, sensitive and straightforward.
Wright, E., *Mrs Gaskell: The Basis for Reassessment*, 1965. Useful critical discussion, especially good on religious ideas and background.
Chapple, J. A. V., 'North and South: A Reassessment', *Essays in Criticism*, vol XVII, October 1967. Good on sensibility and detail.
Gérin, W., *Elizabeth Gaskell: A Biography*, 1976. The standard life.
Craik, W. A., *Elizabeth Gaskell and the English Provincial Novel*, 1975.
Lansbury, C., *Elizabeth Gaskell: The Novel of Social Crisis*, 1975.
Easson, A., *Elizabeth Gaskell*, 1979.
Chapple, J. A. V., (with J. G. Sharps) *Elizabeth Gaskell: A Portait in Letters*, Manchester, 1980.

II *George Eliot*

Works (Cabinet edn), 20 vols, Edinburgh and London, 1878–85.
Letters, ed. Gordon S. Haight, 9 vols, 1954–78 (cited as Haight).
Essays, ed. Thomas Pinney, 1963.

James, Henry, 'Daniel Deronda: A Conversation' in *Partial Portraits*, 1888. Reprinted by F. R. Leavis in *The Great Tradition* (see below). Subtle, amusing and still critically suggestive.

Kitchel, A. T., *George Lewes and George Eliot*, New York, 1933.

Leavis, F. R., *The Great Tradition*, 1948. A close and searching evaluation. To be read critically, not piously.

Willey, B., *Nineteenth Century Studies*, 1949. Good on the background of religion and philosophy.

Hardy, B., *The Novels of George Eliot*, 1959. Close analysis of language, narrative, plot and structure.

Harvey, W. J., *The Art of George Eliot*, 1961. A more theoretical discussion than Hardy's, but similar in conclusion.

Beaty, J., *Middlemarch from Notebook to Novel*, Illinois, 1960. On the genesis and revisions.

Hardy, B., *Critical Essays on George Eliot*, 1970.

Redinger, R., *George Eliot: The Emergent Self*, New York, 1975. Provocative, but not always reliable.

Showalter, E., *A Literature of Their Own: British Women Novelists from Brontë to Lessing*, 1977. Feminist studies.

Witemayer, H., *George Eliot and the Visual Arts*, 1979.

Jacobus, M., *Women Writing and Writing about Women*, 1979.

Hardy, B., *Particularities: Readings in George Eliot*, 1983. Includes discussion of Casaubon marriage, environments, feelings, concept of imagination.

Beer, G., *Darwin's Plots: Evolutionary Narrative in Darwin, George Eliot and Nineteenth-Century Fiction*, 1983.

Shuttleworth, S., *George Eliot and Nineteenth-Century Science: The Make-Believe of a Beginning*, 1984.

Hardy, B., *Forms of Feeling in Victorian Fiction*, 1985.

Beer, G., *George Eliot*, 1986. Important for context of Victorian feminism.

Haight, G. S., *George Eliot, a Biography*, 1968. The only exhaustive and full account of the life.

8. *Victorian Women Prose-writers*

I *Primary texts*

Braddon, Mary E., *Lady Audley's Secret*, 1862.
—— *Aurora Floyd*, 1863.
Brontë, Charlotte, *Shirley, a Tale*, 1849.
Broughton, Rhoda, *Cometh Up as a Flower*, 1867.
Butler, Josephine, ed., *Women's Work and Women's Culture*, 1869.
Caird, Mona, 'The Morality of Marriage' *Fortnightly Review*, February 1890.
Cobbe, Frances Power, 'Celibacy versus Marriage', February 1862; 'What Shall We Do With Our Old Maids?', November 1862; 'Criminals, Idiots, Women and Minors', December 1868 – all in *Fraser's Magazine*.
Egerton, George, (Mary Chavelita Dunne), *Keynotes*, 1893.
—— *Discords*, 1894.
Eliot, George, 'Silly Novels by Lady Novelists', 'Address to Working Men by Felix Holt' and 'Notes on Form in Art', all in *The Essays of George Eliot*, ed. Thomas Pinney, 1963.
—— *Adam Bede*, 1859.
—— *Felix Holt*, 1866.
Ellis, Sarah Stickney, *The Women of England, their Social Duties and Domestic Habits*, 1839.
Gaskell, Elizabeth, *North and South*, 1855.
—— *Sylvia's Lovers*, 1863.
Harkness, Margaret, (John Law), *A City Girl: A Realistic Story*, 1887.
Kavanagh, Julie, *Rachel Grey*, 1856.
Linton, Eliza Lynn, *The Girl of the Period and Other Essays*, 1883, reprinted from articles in *Saturday Review* 1867–75.
—— 'Wild Women', *Nineteenth Century*, July and October 1891 and March 1892.
Martineau, Harriet, *Illustrations of Political Economy*, 25 vols, 1832–4.
—— *Deerbrook*, 1892.
—— *Autobiography*, 1877.
Marx, Eleanor and Aveling, Edward, 'The Women Question', *Westminster Review*, January 1886.
Mitchell, Hannah, *The Hard Way Up, the Autobiography of Hannah Mitchell, Suffragette and Rebel*, ed. Geoffrey Mitchell, 1968.

Oliphant, Margaret, 'The Laws Concerning Women', April 1856; 'The Condition of Women', February 1858; 'Sensation Novels', May 1862; 'The Great Unrepresented', September 1866; 'Novels', August 1863; 'The Anti-Marriage League', January 1896; all in *Blackwood's Edinburgh Magazine*.

—— *Miss Marjoribanks*, 1866.

—— *Hester: A Story of Contemporary Life*, 1883.

—— *Autobiography and Letters*, ed. Mrs Harry Coghill with an introduction by Q. D. Leavis, 1974.

Ruskin, John, 'Of Queens' Gardens' in *Sesame and Lilies*, 1863.

Schreiner, Olive, *The Story of an African Farm*, 1883.

Sewell, Elizabeth, *The Experience of Life*, 1853.

Smith, Barbara Leigh, 'A Brief Summary in Plain Language of the Most Important Laws Concerning Women', 1854.

—— 'Woman and Work', 1857.

Taylor, Harriet, 'The Enfranchisement of Women', *Westminster Review*, July, 1851.

Thompson, William, *Appeal of One Half the Human Race, Women, Against the Pretensions of the Other Half, Men, to Retain Them in Political, and thence in Civil and Domestic Slavery*, 1825.

Tonna, Mrs (Charlotte Elizabeth), *Helen Fleetwood*, 1841.

—— *The Wrongs of Woman*, 4 vols, 1843–4.

Trollope, Frances, *Michael Armstrong, the Factory Boy*, 1839.

—— *Jessie Phillips*, 1844.

Ward, Mrs Humphry, 'An Appeal Against Female Suffrage', *Nineteenth Century*, May 1889.

—— *Marcella*, 1894.

—— *Sir George Tressady*, 1896.

Webb, Beatrice, *My Apprenticeship*, 1921.

Yonge, Charlotte M., *The Heir of Redclyffe*, 1854.

—— *The Clever Woman of the Family*, 1865.

II *Critical Works*

Colby, Vineta, *Yesterday's Women. Domestic Realism in the English Novel*, Princeton, New Jersey, 1974. On fiction by women during the first third of the nineteenth century.

Cox, R. G., 'Reviews and Magazines', *From Dickens to Hardy* (*The Pelican Guide to English Literature*, vol 6), 1958.

Foster, Shirley, *Victorian Women's Fiction: Marriage, Freedom and the Individual*, 1985. On Diana Mulock Craik, Charlotte Brontë, Elizabeth Sewell, Elizabeth Gaskell and George Eliot.

Goode, John, 'Margaret Harkness and the socialist novel', *The Socialist Novel in Britain*, ed. H. Gustav Klaus, 1982.

Jordan, Ellen, 'The Christening of the New Woman: May 1894', *Victorian Newsletter*, Spring, 1983.

Kestner, Joseph, *Protest and Reform. The British Social Narrative by Women 1827–1867*, 1985. A detailed, well-documented study of a wide range of writers.

Kovacévić, Ivanka and Kanner, S. Barbara, 'Blue Book into Novel: The Forgotten Industrial Fiction of Charlotte Elizabeth Tonna', *Nineteenth Century Fiction*, 25, 1970–71.

Killham, John, *Tennyson and 'The Princess': Reflections of an Age*, 1958. Useful account of the feminist movement in the first half of the nineteenth century.

Moers, Ellen, *Literary Women*, 1977. Original and thought-provoking account of 'representative' women writers including Jane Austen, Mary Shelley, Emily Brontë and George Eliot.

Newton, Judith Lowder, *Women, Power and Subversion: Social Strategies in British Fiction, 1778–1860*, Athens, Georgia, 1981. A study of the 'covert power of women' in novels from *Evelina* to *The Mill on the Floss*.

Nield, Keith, ed., *Prostitution in the Victorian Age: Debates on the Issue from Nineteenth-Century Critical Journals*, 1973.

Showalter, Elaine, *A Literature of Their Own*, 1977. Traces the development of a tradition of women novelists from the Brontës to Doris Lessing: an important and influential work.

Spencer, Jane, *The Rise of the Woman Novelist*, 1986. On the eighteenth-century women novelists.

Strachey, Ray, *The Cause: A Short History of the Women's Movement in Great Britain* (1928), 1978.

Stubbs, Patricia, *Women and Fiction: Feminism and the Novel 1880–1920*, 1979. A lively account of the 'new woman', particularly in the fiction of James, Meredith, Moore, Wells and Hardy.

Woolf, Virginia, *A Room of One's Own* (1928), 1945.

—— *Three Guineas* (1938), 1977. Classic feminist texts which address questions of women's writing, their education and their status, and warn of the dangers of sexual polarization.

Young, G. M., *Victorian England: Portrait of an Age* (1936), 1986. One of the best general studies of the period which also takes the 'woman question' as a recurrent theme.

9. Mid-Victorian Novelists

I *Disraeli*

Novels and Tales, ed. P. Guedalla, 12 vols, 1926–7.

Stephen, L., 'Mr Disraeli's Novels', *Hours in a Library*, 2nd series, 1876.

Harrison, F., *Disraeli's Place in Literature*, 1894.

Froude, J. A., *The Earl of Beaconsfield*, 1905; first published 1890. Lively if adulatory biography by one of the Great Victorians. The emphasis is on Disraeli's personality and on his achievements as Prime Minister. There is a good chapter on *Lothair*.

Speare, M. E., *The Political Novel*, Oxford, 1924. Argues that Disraeli created the political novel which he considers to be dominated by ideas rather than emotions. Some questionable generalizations but a useful comparison of Disraeli's thought with that of Carlyle.

Pritchett, V. S., 'Disraeli', *The Living Novel*, 1946.

Jerman, B. R., *The Young Disraeli*, Princeton, 1960.

Smith, S. M., ed., *Mr Disraeli's Readers*, Nottingham, 1966. Letters written to Disraeli and his wife by readers of *Sybil*. Introduction and commentary.

Blake, R., *Disraeli*, 1966. Important and detailed biography of Disraeli. It closely follows his political career but there are full references to the novels and some illuminating details of their composition, publication and reception.

Levine, R. A., *Benjamin Disraeli*, New York, 1968.

Schwarz, D. R., *Disraeli's Fiction*, 1979.

Braun, T., *Disraeli: The Novelist*, 1981.

II *Kingsley*

Life and Works, 19 vols, 1901–03.

Harrison, F., *Charles Kingsley's Place in Literature*, 1895.

Raven, C. E., *Christian Socialism 1848–1854*, 1920.

Brown, W. H., *Charles Kingsley. The Work and Influence of Parson Lot*, Manchester, 1924. Style occasionally florid, and the book uncritical and rather complacent, but the writer knew Ludlow and gives some useful facts of the Co-operative Movement's debt to the Christian Socialists.

Kendall, G., *Charles Kingsley and his Ideas*, 1947.

Vidler, A. R., *The Theology of F. D. Maurice*, 1948. Systematic study of Maurice as theologian and of Christian Socialism as the manifestation of his theology at one period of his life. Useful bibliography of Maurice's writings.

Martin, R. B., *The Dust of Combat, A Life of Charles Kingsley*, 1959. Fairly detailed biography with some literary criticism; a good bibliography of critical works on Kingsley. Sometimes inaccurate.

Smith, Sheila M., 'Truth and Propaganda in the Victorian Social Problem Novel', *Renaissance and Modern Studies*, vol VIII, 1964. References to Kingsley, Disraeli, Reade.

Allen, P. R., 'F. D. Maurice and J. M. Ludlow: A Reassessment of the Leaders of Christian Socialism', *Victorian Studies*, vol XI, 1968.

Hartley, A. J., *The Novels of Charles Kingsley: A Christian Social Interpretation*, 1977.

III *Collins*

There is no readily available collected edition of Collins's novels. His major novels have been published in recent years by Dover Publications or Oxford University Press.

Sayers, Dorothy, Introduction to *Great Short Stories of Mystery, Detection and Horror*, 1928.

Ellis, S. M., *Wilkie Collins, Le Fanu and Others*, 1931.

Eliot, T. S., 'Wilkie Collins and Dickens', *Selected Essays*, 1932. Includes illuminating discussion of the nature of melodrama.

Ashley, R., 'Wilkie Collins and the Detective Story', *Nineteenth Century Fiction*, vol VI, 1951.

Booth, B. A., 'Wilkie Collins and the Art of Fiction', *Nineteenth Century Fiction*, vol VI, 1951.

Robinson, K., *Wilkie Collins, A Biography*, 1951. A substantial biography with some sound literary criticism; particularly good on the relationship between Collins and Dickens.

Davis, N. P., *The Life of Wilkie Collins*, Urbana, Ill., 1956. Some extravagant claims for Collins as a novelist, but a detailed and well-documented biography.

IV *Reade*

Novels, 17 vols, 1895.

Phillips, W. C., *Dickens, Reade and Collins, Sensation Novelists*, New York, 1919. Does not sufficiently relate the vogue for 'sensation' to the society in which it arose, but includes an interesting account of nineteenth-century methods of publishing and selling novels to meet the demands of an increasingly varied range of readers, and the effect of these demands on the novels produced.

Hornung, E. W., 'Charles Reade', *The London Mercury*, vol IV, 1921.

Sutcliffe, E. G., 'The Stage in Reade's Novels' and 'Charles Reade's Notebooks', *Studies in Philology*, vol XXVII, 1930.

Elwin, M., *Charles Reade, A Biography*, 1931. A full and detailed biography; not much literary criticism. A sensible discussion of the relationship between the events of Reade's life and his literary, dramatic and journalistic work.

Turner, A. M., *The Making of 'The Cloister and the Hearth'*, Chicago, 1938. Exhaustive study of the sources of the novel, but little critical evaluation.

Rives, Léone, *Charles Reade, Sa Vie, Ses Romans*, Toulouse, 1940. Over-estimates Reade's importance as a writer, but a useful biography.

Burns, W., 'The Sheffield Flood: a Critical Study of Charles Reade's Fiction', *Publications of the Modern Language Association of America*, vol LXIII, 1948.

Smith, Sheila M., 'Propaganda and Hard Facts in Charles Reade's Didactic Novels', *Renaissance and Modern Studies*, vol IV, 1960.

V *Bulwer-Lytton*

Works, 37 vols, 1873–7.
The Life, Letters and Literary Remains of Edward Bulwer, Lord Lytton, 1883.

Lytton, 2nd Earl of (Victor A. G.), *The Life of Edward Bulwer, First Lord Lytton*, 2 vols, 1913.

Sadleir, Michael, *Bulwer and His Wife: A Panorama 1803–1836*, 1931. A detailed account of Bulwer-Lytton's early years and the society in which he moved.

Lytton, 2nd Earl of (Victor A. G.), *Bulwer Lytton*, 1948.

Dahl, Curtis, 'History on the Hustings: Bulwer-Lytton's Historical Novels of Politics', in *From Jane Austen to Joseph Conrad*, eds R. C. Rathburn and M. Steinmann, 1958.

Sanders, Andrew, *The Victorian Historical Novel 1840–1880*, 1974. Deals with Bulwer-Lytton's *Harold* and Charles Kingsley's *Hypatia* and *Hereward the Wake*.

Christensen, A. C., *Edward Bulwer-Lytton; The Fiction of New Regions*, Athens, Ga., 1976.

Eigner, Edwin M., *The Metaphysical Novel in England and America*, 1978. Includes Bulwer-Lytton alongside Dickens, Melville and Hawthorne.

VI *Le Fanu*

There is no readily available collected edition of Sheridan Le Fanu's novels; his major novels and stories have been published in recent years by Dover Publications.

Ellis, S. M., *Wilkie Collins, Le Fanu and Others*, 1931.

Browne, Nelson, *Sheridan Le Fanu*, 1951. A useful elementary study.

Begnal, Michael H., *Joseph Sheridan Le Fanu*, Lewisburg, 1971. An introductory monograph.

McCormack, W. J., *Sheridan Le Fanu and Victorian Ireland*, Oxford, 1980. Very thorough literary biography of Le Fanu relating his life and work to the Ireland of his day.

VII *Lever*

Novels, 37 vols, 1897–9.

Fitzpatrick, W. J., *The Life of Charles Lever*, 1884.

Stevenson, Lionel, *Dr Quicksilver; The Life of Charles Lever*, 1939. A clear and reliable literary biography.

Jeffares, A. Norman, 'Lever's *Lord Kilgobbin*', in *Essays and Studies 1975*, ed. Robert Ellrodt, 1975.

10. *Fantasy and Nonsense*

I *Primary Sources*

A Book of Nonsense, ed. Ernest Rhys, Everyman Paperback, 1967.

Browne, Frances, *Granny's Wonderful Chair*, Puffin Classic, 1985.

Carroll, Lewis, *Alice in Wonderland*, ed. Donald J. Gray, Norton Critical edn, New York, 1971. Contains *Alice's Adventures in Wonderland; Through the Looking Glass; The Hunting of the Snark*, together with background material and critical essays.

—— *Sylvie and Bruno*, 1889.

—— *Sylvie and Bruno Concluded*, 1893.

Corkran, Alice, *Down the Snow Stairs*, 1887.

Farrow, G. E., *The Wallypug of Why*, Gollancz Revival, 1968.

Kingsley, Charles, *The Water-Babies*, Gollancz Paperback, 1986.

Knatchbull-Hugessen, Edward, *Stories for my Children*, 1869.

—— *Crackers for Christmas*, 1883.

Lang, Andrew, *The Gold of Fairnilee*, Gollancz Revival, 1967.

Lear, Edward, *The Complete Nonsense*, ed. Holbrook Jackson, 1947.

MacDonald, George, *At the Back of the North Wind*, Puffin Classic, 1984.

—— *The Light Princess and Other Tales*: Being the complete fairy-stories of George MacDonald, ed. Roger Lancelyn Green, 1961.

—— *The Lost Princess [The Wise Woman]*, Dent Illustrated Classic, 1965.

—— *Phantastes* and *Lilith*, introduction by C. S. Lewis, 1971.

—— *The Princess and Curdie*, Puffin Classic, 1985.

—— *The Princess and the Goblin*, Puffin Classic, 1986.

Mulock, Dinah Maria (Mrs Craik), *The Little Lame Prince and his Travelling Cloak*, 1875.

Opie, Iona and Peter, eds, *The Oxford Dictionary of Nursery Rhymes*, Oxford, 1951.

Paget, Francis, *The Hope of the Katzekopfs*, 1844.

Rossetti, Christina, *Speaking Likenesses*, 1874.

Ruskin, John, *The King of the Golden River*, Dover edn, New York, 1974.

Thackeray, William Makepeace, *The Rose and the Ring*, Puffin Classic, 1964.

Victorian Fairy Tales, ed. Jack Zipes, 1987. Includes stories by principal writers of the period.

II *Critical Works*

Auden, W. H., Introduction to *The Visionary Novels of George MacDonald*, New York, 1954.

Avery, Gillian and Bull, Angela, *Nineteenth-Century Children*, 1965. Contains two chapters on fairy-stories.

Carpenter, Humphrey, *Secret Gardens*, 1985. Has chapters on Carroll, Kingsley and MacDonald.

Chesterton, G. K., 'In Defence of Nonsense', *The Defendant*, 1901.

Chitty, Susan, *The Beast and the Monk*, 1974. Biography of Kingsley.

Cripps, Elizabeth A., 'Alice and the Reviewers', *Children's Literature*, vol 11, New Haven, Conn., 1983.

Darton, F. J. Harvey, *Children's Books in England*, 3rd edn, ed. Brian Alderson, Cambridge, 1982. Still the best historical account.

Green, Roger Lancelyn, *Tellers of Tales*, revised edn, 1969. Has brief accounts of all the authors discussed in this chapter.

Hein, Rolland, *The Harmony Within*, Michigan, 1982. Short critical account of MacDonald's works.

Hudson, Derek, *Lewis Carroll*, 1954. Lavishly illustrated biography.

Huxley, Francis, *The Raven and the Writing Desk*, 1976. A study of nonsense.

Lewis, C. S., *George MacDonald: An Anthology*, 1946. Has valuable introductory essay.

MacDonald, Greville, *George MacDonald and his Wife*, 1924.

Noakes, Vivien, *Edward Lear, the Life of a Wanderer*, 1968. The definitive biography.

Prickett, Stephen, *Victorian Fantasy*, 1979.

Reis, Richard H., *George MacDonald*, New York, 1972.

Sewell, Elizabeth, *The Field of Nonsense*, 1952. The best critical account of nonsense, dealing particularly with Lear and Carroll.

Wolff, Robert Lee, *The Golden Key*, New Haven, Conn., 1961. A detailed critical account of MacDonald's writing.

11. *Later Victorian Novelists*

I *Meredith*

Works (Memorial edn), 29 vols, 1909–12.
Poetical Works, ed. Phyllis B. Bartlett, 2 vols, New Haven, 1978.
Notebooks, eds Gillian Beer and Margaret Harris, Salzburg, 1983.
Letters, ed. C. L. Cline, 3 vols, Oxford, 1970.

Ellis, S. M., *George Meredith: His Life and Friends*, 1919. Informative biography by a writer with intimate contacts in the Meredith circle of the time.
Kelvin, N., *A Troubled Eden: Nature and Society in the Works of George Meredith*, Edinburgh, 1961. A systematic study of Meredith's ideas.
Pritchett, V. S., *George Meredith and English Comedy*, 1969. Meredith as disengaged performer and wit, whose comic *forte* is the taming and deflation of romantic egotism.
Beer, Gillian, *Meredith: A Change of Masks. A Study of the Novels*, 1970. A lively and perceptive study, focused on Meredith's development as a consciously experimental novelist.
Williams, Ioan, ed., *Meredith: The Critical Heritage*, 1971.
Fletcher, Ian, ed., *Meredith Now: Some Critical Essays*, 1971.
Stone, D. D., *Novelists in a Changing World: Meredith, James, and the Transformation of English Fiction in the 1880s*, Cambridge, Mass., 1972. An interesting comparative study of two major writers seen against the background of a transitional period.
Wilt, Judith, *The Readable People of George Meredith*, Princeton, 1975. As challenging on general theoretic issues as it is on particular problems raised by Meredith's fiction.
Moses, J., *The Novelist as Comedian: George Meredith and the Ironic Sensibility*, New York, 1983. A lively and appreciative study of the 'unsafe' and 'maverick' Meredith.

II *Hardy*

Works (Wessex edn), 22 vols, 1912–22.
Works (New Wessex edn), 14 vols, 1974.
The selected edition of Hardy's major novels published by Oxford University Press promises to be definitive, *The Woodlanders* (1982) and *Tess of the d'Urbervilles* (1983) having already appeared.

The Complete Poems, ed. James Gibson, 1979.

The Complete Poetical Works, ed. Samuel Hynes, multivolume edition, Oxford, 1982– .

The Collected Letters of Thomas Hardy, ed. Richard Little Purdy and Michael Millgate, multivolume edition, Oxford, 1978– .

Thomas Hardy's Personal Writings: Prefaces, Literary Opinions, Reminiscences, ed. Harold Orel, 1966.

Literary Notebooks, ed. Lennart A. Björk, 2 vols, 1985.

Personal Notebooks, ed. Richard H. Taylor, 1979.

The Life and Work of Thomas Hardy, ed. Michael Millgate, 1984. This edition of what has previously been known as *The Early Life and Later Years of Thomas Hardy* (and published under Florence Emily Hardy's name) is based on Hardy's original manuscript and provides an authentic autobiographical work.

Lawrence, D. H., 'A Study of Thomas Hardy' in *Phoenix: The Posthumous Papers of D. H. Lawrence*, 1936. A brilliant 're-creative' reading, which reveals as much about Lawrence as it does Hardy.

Hardy, Evelyn, *Thomas Hardy: A Critical Biography*, 1954. Still useful for the intimacy of its detail and the critical opinions advanced.

Brown, Douglas, *Thomas Hardy*, 1954; revised edn, 1961. One of the first sustained attempts to set Hardy's fiction against a background 'agricultural rather than intellectual'.

Cox, R. G., ed., *Thomas Hardy: The Critical Heritage*, 1970.

Gregor, Ian, *The Great Web: The Form of Hardy's Major Fiction*, 1974. A fresh and original reading of the 'unfolding process' of Hardy's narratives.

Kramer, Dale, *Thomas Hardy: The Forms of Tragedy*, Detroit, 1975. Shows Hardy's subtlety and versatility as a creator of 'modern' tragedies.

Williams, Merryn, *A Preface to Hardy*, 1976. Clear, well-balanced introduction.

Grundy, Joan, *Hardy and the Sister Arts*, 1979. Hardy's interest in the 'composite Muse' – that is, pictorial and dramatic art, cinematic devices, music and drama.

Kramer, Dale, ed., *Critical Approaches to the Fiction of Thomas Hardy*, 1979.

Page, Norman, ed., *Thomas Hardy – The Writer and his Background*, 1980. Hardy and his work suggestively broached by way of larger issues – for example, Hardy and the English language, his relationship to Darwin, and attitudes to education.

Millgate, Michael, *Thomas Hardy: A Biography*, Oxford, 1982. Standard biography.

Casagrande, Peter, *Unity in Hardy's Novels: 'Repetitive Symmetries'*, 1982. 'Repetitive symmetries' within the single Hardy novel and as they underlie certain definable groups of novels.

Boumelha, Penny, *Thomas Hardy and Women: Sexual Ideology and Narrative Form*, Brighton, Sussex, 1982. A rewarding, but sometimes unduly difficult Althusserian reading of Hardy's novels. Historical and feminist in position.

Brady, Kristin, *The Short Stories of Thomas Hardy: Tales of Past and Present*, 1982.

III *Gissing*

Virtually all of Gissing's novels have been reprinted in modern editions by Harvester Press (Brighton, Sussex), each with a useful introduction and notes.

George Gissing and H. G. Wells: Their Friendship and Correspondence, ed. R. A. Gettmann, Urbana, Ill., 1961.

Letters to Members of his Family, eds A. and E. Gissing, 1927.

The Letters of George Gissing to Gabrielle Fleury, ed. Pierre Coustillas, 1964.

Letters to Eduard Bertz, 1887–1903, ed. A. C. Young, New Brunswick, N. J., 1961.

Gissing's Commonplace Book, ed. Jacob Korg, New York, 1962.

The Diary of George Gissing, Novelist, ed. Pierre Coustillas, Hassocks, Sussex, 1978.

Korg, Jacob, *George Gissing: A Critical Biography*, Seattle, 1963. Full-scale portrait of man and writer, knowledgeable and well-researched.

Tindall, Gillian, *The Born Exile: George Gissing*, 1972. Embraces both biographical material and his attitude to class, money, women, sex and marriage as reflected in the fiction.

Coustillas, Pierre and Partridge, Colin, eds, *Gissing: The Critical Heritage*, 1972.

Poole, Adrian, *Gissing in Context*, 1975. One of the best general critical studies of Gissing's fiction.

Collie, Michael, *George Gissing: A Biography*, Folkestone, 1977. Interesting for its insights into Gissing's 'bohemian nature' and its consequences for his life and art.

—— *The Alien Art: A Critical Study*, Folkestone, 1977. Traces the effect of Gissing's position as an outsider.

Halperin, John, *Gissing: A Life in Books*, Oxford, 1982. Sees Gissing as not only using his fiction as a release for obsessions with class, money and sex, but also re-enacting in his life inventions from the fiction.

IV *Butler*

Works (Shrewsbury edn), 20 vols, 1923–6. The only complete collected edition, though not always textually reliable.

Ernest Pontifex or The Way of All Flesh, ed. Daniel F. Howard, 1965. A reliable scholarly edition of Butler's best known work.

Letters between Samuel Butler and Miss E. M. A. Savage, 1871–1885, ed. Arnold Silver, New York, 1962.

The Correspondence of Samuel Butler with His Sister May, ed. Daniel F. Howard, Berkeley and Los Angeles, 1962.

Notebooks (Selections), eds Geoffrey Keynes and Brian Hill, 1951.

Jones, H. Festing, *Samuel Butler, Author of Erewhon (1835–1902): A Memoir*, 2 vols, 1919. Still the most comprehensive life and letters.

Muggeridge, Malcolm, *The Earnest Atheist: A Study of Samuel Butler*, 1936. Impatient with the myth of Butler as a 'pioneer rebel and inveigher against cant'.

Cole, G. D. H., *Samuel Butler and 'The Way of All Flesh'*, 1947. Good introduction.

Furbank, P. N., *Samuel Butler (1835–1902)*, Cambridge, 1948.

Willey, Basil, *Darwin and Butler: Two Versions of Evolution*, 1960. Sympathetic evaluation of the grounds of Butler's disagreement with Darwin.

Holt, Lee, *Samuel Butler*, New York, 1964. Standard survey and guide through Butler's varied writings.

Buckley, J. H., *Seasons of Youth: The Bildungsroman from Dickens to Golding*, Cambridge, Mass., 1974. Brings together Gosse's *Father and Son* and Butler's *The Way of All Flesh* in one of its chapters. Notable for its shrewd insights and sound judgments.

Norrman, Ralf, *Samuel Butler and the Meaning of Chiasmus*, 1986. Patterns of symmetry in his style, perceptions and thought.

V *Stevenson*

Works (Valima edn), ed. Lloyd Osbourne, 26 vols, 1922–23. Includes much material not published in previous collections, along with Prefatory Note by Fanny van de Grift Stevenson.

Works (South Seas edn), 32 vols, New York, 1925. The last collected edition and most complete on the letters.

The Collected Poems, ed. Janet Adam Smith, 1971.

The Letters of Robert Louis Stevenson to His Family and Friends, ed. Sidney Colvin, 2 vols, 1899; new edn, 4 vols, 1911.

Henry James and Robert Louis Stevenson: A Record of Friendship and Criticism, ed. Janet Adam Smith, 1948. A useful collection of letters and interchanges between the two writers.

RLS: Stevenson's Letters to Charles Baxter, eds De Lancey Ferguson and Marshall Waingrow, New Haven, 1956.

Daiches, David, *Robert Louis Stevenson: A Revaluation*, Glasgow, 1947. Brief and appreciative introduction, good on Stevenson's Scottish background and narrative skills.

Furnas, J. C., *Voyage to Windward: The Life of Robert Louis Stevenson*. Superlative biography.

Kiely, Robert, *Robert Louis Stevenson and the Fiction of Adventure*, Cambridge, Mass., 1964. The first full-scale attempt to explore the implications of Stevenson's aesthetic and its relation to his fiction.

Eigner, Edwin M., *Robert Louis Stevenson and the Fiction of Adventure*, Princeton, 1966. Stevenson's relation to nineteenth-century romance traditions, both British and American.

Swearingen, Roger G., *The Prose Writings of Robert Louis Stevenson: A Guide*, 1980. Descriptive bibliographical guide.

Calder, Jenni, ed., *Stevenson and Victorian Scotland*, Edinburgh, 1981.

Maixner, Paul, ed., *Robert Louis Stevenson: The Critical Heritage*, 1981.

Noble, Andrew, ed., *Robert Louis Stevenson*, 1983. Valuable collection of modern views on Stevenson's fiction, travel writing, literary debate with Henry James, and (in a fine essay by the editor) 'Highland History and Narrative Form in Scott and Stevenson'.

Hammond, J. R., *A Robert Louis Stevenson Companion: A Guide to the Novels, Essays and Short Stories*, 1984.

VI *Kipling*

Works (Uniform edn), 28 vols, 1899–1938.

Works (Sussex edn), 35 vols, 1937–9.

Rudyard Kipling's Verse: Definitive Edition, 1940.

Early Verse by Rudyard Kipling, 1878–1889: Unpublished, Uncollected, and Rarely Collected Poems, ed. Andrew Rutherford, Oxford, 1986.

Rudyard Kipling to Rider Haggard: The Record of a Friendship, ed. Morton Cohen, 1965.

'O Beloved Kids': Rudyard Kipling's Letters to his Children, ed. Elliot L. Gilbert, 1983.

Carrington, Charles, *Rudyard Kipling*, 1955; revised edn, 1978. The standard biography.

Tompkins, J. M. S., *The Art of Rudyard Kipling*, 1959; revised edn, 1965. Clear and informative general study.

Rutherford, Andrew, ed., *Kipling's Mind and Art*, Edinburgh, 1964. Compendium of modern Kipling criticism.

Green, Roger Lancelyn, ed., *Kipling: The Critical Heritage*, 1971.

Gilbert, Elliot L., *The Good Kipling: Studies in the Short Story*, Manchester, 1972. Energetic and forceful defence of Kipling on the grounds that he should be judged by his best work.

Gross, John, ed., *Rudyard Kipling, the Man, his Work and his World*, 1972.

Islam, Shamsul, *Kipling's 'Law': A Study of his Philosophy of Life*, 1975. A useful descriptive study of the slow formation of a concept central to Kipling's work.

Wilson, Angus, *The Strange Ride of Rudyard Kipling: His Life and Works*, 1977. A vivid and picaresque account of the man and his work, especially illuminating on Kipling's early years.

Birkenhead, Lord, *Rudyard Kipling*, 1978. Written in 1948, this biography was delayed for over thirty years by the refusal of Kipling's daughter to allow its publication. Neither an unkind nor even unattractive portrait, Birkenhead's work is simply a more authoritatively personal one than many others.

Page, Norman, *A Kipling Companion*, 1984.

12. *Tennyson (and FitzGerald)*

I *Tennyson*

Works with Notes by the Author, ed. (with Memoir) Hallam, Lord
Tennyson, 1913. A single volume printing of the Eversley edn,
9 vols, 1907–8.

Poetical Works, Including the Plays, 1953 (Oxford Standard Authors).
Has an appendix of suppressed poems.

The Devil and the Lady, by Alfred Tennyson, ed. C. B. L. Tennyson,
1930.

Unpublished Early Poems, ed. C. B. L. Tennyson, 1932.

None of the editions listed above contains Tennyson's contributions to *Poems by Two Brothers*.

Poems, ed. C. B. Ricks, 1969. Comprehensive, annotated.

Tennyson, Hallam, Lord, *Alfred Lord Tennyson: A Memoir, by his
Son*, 2 vols, 1897. Comparison with *Materials for a Biography of
AT*. 4 vols privately printed by Hallam, Lord Tennyson for his
children shows how freely the *Memoir* was adapted from the
poet's surviving papers.

—— *Tennyson and his Friends*, 1911.

Nicolson, [Sir] Harold, *Tennyson: Aspects of his Life, Character and
Poetry*, 1923.

Bush, D., *Mythology and the Romantic Tradition in English Poetry*,
Cambridge, Mass., 1937.

Paden, W. D., *Tennyson in Egypt; A Study of the Imagery in his Earlier
Work*, Lawrence, Kansas, 1942.

Tennyson, [Sir] Charles [C.B.L.], *Alfred Tennyson*, London and
New York, 1949.

Mattes, E. B., *In Memoriam: The Way of a Soul*, New York, 1951.

Johnson, E. D. H., *The Alien Vision of Victorian Poetry*, Princeton,
1952.

Killham, J., *Tennyson and 'The Princess'*, 1958.

—— ed., *Critical Essays on the Poetry of Tennyson*, 1960.

Buckley, J. H., *Tennyson: The Growth of a Poet*, Cambridge, Mass.,
1961. Uses the Tennyson materials at Harvard.

Richardson, J., *Pre-Eminent Victorian*, 1962.

Pitt, V., *Tennyson Laureate*, 1962.

Rader, R. W., *Tennyson's 'Maud': The Bibliographical Genesis*,
Berkeley, California, 1963.

Jump, J. D., ed., *Tennyson: The Critical Heritage*, 1967.
Sinfield, A., *The Language of Tennyson's 'In Memoriam'*, 1971.
Ricks, C., *Tennyson*, 1972.
Palmer, D. J., ed., *Tennyson*, 1973. In the *Writers and Their Background* Series.
Pattison, R., *Tennyson and Tradition*, Harvard, 1979.
Martin, R. B., *Tennyson: The Unquiet Heart*, 1980.
Gray, J. M., *Thro' the Vision of the Night*, Edinburgh, 1980. A study of source, evolution and structure of the *Idylls of the King*.
Sinfield, A., *Alfred Tennyson*, 1986. In the series *Re-reading Literature*.

II *FitzGerald*

Letters and Literary Remains, ed. W. A. Wright, 7 vols, 1903 (containing *More Letters* and *Letters to Fanny Kemble*, ed. Wright, 1895 and 1901).
Variorum and Definitive Edition of the Poetical and Prose Writings, ed. G. Bentham, New York, 1903. No letters, but includes items omitted in Wright.
Some New Letters . . . to Bernard Barton, ed. F. R. Barton, 1923. (Published as *Edward FitzGerald and Bernard Barton*, New York, 1924).
FitzGerald to his Friends, ed. A. Hayter, 1979. Selected letters with introduction and bibliography of older editions of letters.
The Letters of Edward FitzGerald, eds A. M. and A. B. Terhune, 4 vols, Princeton, 1980.

Allen, E. H., *Edward FitzGerald's Rubáiyát of Omar Khayyám*, 1899. Gives Persian original, literally translated.
Campbell, A. Y., 'Edward FitzGerald' in *The Great Victorians*, eds H. J. and E. Massingham, 1932.
Terhune, A. M., *The Life of Edward FitzGerald*, New Haven, 1947. Includes a list of FitzGerald's major works and editions in which they appear.
Arberry, A. J., *Omar Khayyám: A New Version Based upon Recent Discoveries*, New Haven, 1952.
—— *The Romance of the Rubáiyát*, 1959.
Graves, R., and Ali-Shah, Omar, *The Rubáiyát of Omar Khayyám*, 1967. A new translation from 'a twelfth-century manuscript of uncontradictable authority.' Revives the claim that Khayyám was a Sufi mystic, and the charge of inaccuracy in 'translation'.

13. *The Brownings*

I *Robert Browning*

Works, ed. F. G. Kenyon, 10 vols, 1912.
The Complete Works, ed. Roma A. King *et al*, Ohio, 1968–   .
Robert Browning: The Poems, 2 vols, eds J. Pettigrew and T. J. Collins, 1981.
The Poetical Works of Robert Browning, ed. I. Jack, Oxford, 1983–   .
The Letters of Robert Browning and Elizabeth Barrett Browning, 2 vols, 1899.
Letters, ed. T. L. Hood, New Haven, 1933.

Orr, Mrs Sutherland, *A Handbook to the Works of Robert Browning*, 1886.
Griffin, W. H. and Minchin, H. C., *The Life of Robert Browning*, 1911, revised, 1938.
Raymond, W. O., *The Infinite Movement*, Toronto, 1950.
Miller, Betty, *Robert Browning, A Portrait*, 1952.
DeVane, W. C., *A Browning Handbook*, revised, New York, 1955.
Drew, P., *The Poetry of Browning: A Critical Introduction*, 1970.
Ward, Maisie, *Robert Browning and His World*, 1968.
Armstrong, Isabel, *Robert Browning, Writers and Their Background Series*, 1974.
Honan, P. and Irvine, W., *The Book, The Ring and The Poet*, 1974.
Bloom, H. and Munich, A., eds, *Robert Browning: A Collection of Critical Essays*, 1979.
Tucker, jnr., H. S., *Browning's Beginnings: The Art of Disclosure*, 1980.
Slinn, E. Warwick, *Browning and the Fictions of Identity*, 1982.

II *Elizabeth Barrett Browning*

Poetical Works, 1904 (Oxford Standard Authors).
Letters, ed. F. G. Kenyon, 2 vols, 1897.

Taplin, G. B., *The Life of Elizabeth Barrett Browning*, New Haven, 1957.
Hayter, Alethea, *Mrs. Browning*, 1962.
Leighton, Angela, *Elizabeth Barrett Browning*, 1986.

14. *Hopkins*

The short titles used in references are given in brackets after the entry. All quotations from the published poems are taken from the fourth edition.

Poems, 1st edn, eds R. Bridges, 1918; 4th edn, eds W. H. Gardner and N. H. MacKenzie, 1967; final revision 1984 (*Poems*).

Gerard Manley Hopkins, Oxford Authors (complete poems and selected prose), ed. Catherine Phillips, 1986.

The Poetical Works of Gerard Manley Hopkins, Oxford English Texts, ed. N. H. MacKenzie. Full commentary and variant readings.

Letters . . . to Robert Bridges, ed. C. C. Abbott, 1935, revised 1955 (*Letters*, vol I).

The Correspondence of Gerard Manley Hopkins and Richard Watson Dixon, ed. C. C. Abbott, 1935, revised 1955 (*Letters*, vol II).

Further Letters of Gerard Manley Hopkins, including his correspondence with Coventry Patmore, ed. C. C. Abbott, 1938, 2nd edn, revised and enlarged, 1956 (*Letters*, vol III).

Note-books and Papers, ed. H. House, 1937, revised and enlarged as:

Journals and Papers, ed. H. House, completed by Graham Storey, 1959 (*Journals*).

Sermons and Devotional Writings, ed. C. Devlin, 1959 (*Sermons*).

Leavis, F. R., *New Bearings in English Poetry*, 1932.

—— *The Common Pursuit*, 1952.

Pick, J., *Gerard Manley Hopkins – Priest and Poet*, 1942.

Gardner, W. H., *Gerard Manley Hopkins – A Study of Poetic Idiosyncrasy in Relation to Poetic Tradition*, vol I, 1944; II, 1949; revised 1966.

Kenyon Critics, *Gerard Manley Hopkins*, New York, 1945.

Peters, W. A. M., *Gerard Manley Hopkins – A Critical Essay towards the Understanding of his Poetry*, 1948.

Weyand, N. and Schoder, R. V., eds, *Immortal Diamond – Studies in Gerard Manley Hopkins*, 1949.

Grigson, G., *Gerard Manley Hopkins*, 1955.

Winters, Y., *The Function of Criticism*, Denver, Col., 1957.

Heuser, A., *The Shaping Vision of Gerard Manley Hopkins*, 1958.

Ritz, J–G., *Robert Bridges and Gerard Hopkins. A Literary Friendship*, 1960.

Downes, D., *Gerard Manley Hopkins – A Study of His Ignation Spirit*, 1960.

—— *Victorian Portraits: Hopkins and Pater*, New York, 1965.

Keating, J. E., *The Wreck of the Deutschland – An Essay and Commentary*, Kent, Ohio, 1963.

Hartman, G. H., ed., *Hopkins – A Collection of Critical Essays*, Englewood Cliffs, 1966.

MacKenzie, N. H., *Hopkins*, Edinburgh, 1968, Writers and Critics Series.

—— *Gerard Manley Hopkins: A Reader's Guide*, 1981.

Milward, P., *A Commentary on 'The Wreck of the Deutschland'*, Tokyo, 1968.

Schneider, E., *The Dragon in the Gate*, California, 1968.

McChesney, D., *A Hopkins Commentary*, 1968.

Johnson, W. C., *Gerard Manley Hopkins: The Poet as Victorian*, Ithaca, 1968.

Thomas, A., *Hopkins the Jesuit: The Years of Training*, 1969.

Dilligan, R. J., and Bender, T. K., *A Concordance to the English Poems* [4th edn] *of Gerard Manley Hopkins*, Madison, 1970.

Mariani, P., *Commentary on the Complete Poems of Gerard Manley Hopkins*, Ithaca, 1970.

Fulweiler, H. W., *Letters from the Darkling Plain: Language and the Grounds of Knowledge in the Poetry of Arnold and Hopkins*, Columbia, Missouri, 1972.

Sulloway, A., *Gerard Manley Hopkins and the Victorian Temper*, 1972.

Bottrall, M., ed., *Gerard Manley Hopkins: Poems – A Casebook*, 1975.

Milward, P. and Schoder, R., *Landscape and Inscape: Vision and Inspiration in Hopkins's Poetry*, 1975.

Bergonzi, B., *Gerard Manley Hopkins*, Masters of World Literature, New York, 1977.

Milroy, J., *The Language of Gerard Manley Hopkins*, 1977.

North, J. S. and Moore, M. D., eds, *Vital Candle: Victorian and Modern Bearings in Gerard Manley Hopkins*, Waterloo, Ontario, 1984.

For comments on all books and articles up to 1969–70 see T. Dunne, *Gerard Manley Hopkins: A Comprehensive Bibliography*, Oxford, 1976.

15. *The Rossettis and Other Contemporary Poets*

I *General*

Beerbohm, M., *Rossetti and his Circle*, 1922. A series of 24 satirical water-colour drawings by a critic of exquisite analytic vision.

Praz, M., *The Romantic Agony*, 1933. Deals in some detail with Swinburne – especially his sado-masochism, but its analysis of certain kinds of beauty is relevant to the work of D. G. Rossetti, Morris and Thomson.

Hough, G., *The Last Romantics*, 1947. Chapters II and III contain the best modern criticism of D. G. Rossetti, the P. R. Brotherhood and William Morris.

Fredeman, W. D., *Pre-Raphaelitism. A Bibliocritical Study*. Cambridge, Mass., 1965. A good bibliography for D. G. Rossetti, but very patchy in its coverage of other painters and writers.

The Pre-Raphaelites and their Circle, ed. C. Y. Lang, 1968. Illustrated anthology with generous selections from the poetry of the Rossettis, Morris, Swinburne, Meredith and FitzGerald.

Stevenson, L., *The Pre-Raphaelite Poets*, 1972. A lively account of the Rossettis, Morris, Swinburne and others as 'the shock troops in the assault on bourgeois complacency'.

Sambrook, J., *Pre-Raphaelitism*, 1974. A collection of critical essays from 1850 to 1974.

Harding, J., *The Pre-Raphaelites*, 1977. A substantial collection of colour and black-and-white reproductions of work by twenty artists.

II *D. G. Rossetti*

Works, ed. W. M. Rossetti, 1911. Still the most complete edition. The table of contents conveniently provides a chronological outline of Rossetti's writings.

Dante Gabriel Rossetti: Poems, ed. O. Doughty, 1957.

Letters, eds O. Doughty and J. R. Wahl, 4 vols, 1965–7.

Dante Gabriel Rossetti and Jane Morris: Their Correspondence, eds J. Bryson and J. C. Troxell, 1976.

Doughty, O., *A Victorian Romantic, Dante Gabriel Rossetti*, 2nd edn, 1960. The most detailed and best balanced of the many *Lives* of Rossetti.

Surtees, V., *The Paintings and Drawings of Dante Gabriel Rossetti*, 2 vols, 1971. The major reference work on its subject.
Rees, J., *The Poetry of Dante Gabriel Rossetti: Modes of Self-Expression*, 1981. A fresh and lively exploration of Rossetti's originality.
Riede, D. G., *Dante Gabriel Rossetti and the Limits of Victorian Vision*, 1983. A comprehensive study of the relationship between Rossetti's poetry and his painting.

III *C. G. Rossetti*

Complete Poems, ed. R. W. Crump, 2 vols, Louisiana, 1979–85.

Bellas, R. A., *Christina Rossetti*, 1977. Handy short account.
Battiscombe, G., *Christina Rossetti, a Divided Life*, 1981. The best balanced account.

IV *Patmore*

Poems, ed. F. Page, 1949. Incomplete, but the standard modern edition.

Page, F., *Patmore, a Study in Poetry*, 1933. Amply fulfils its intention 'to expound a temper' rather than 'to collect a system'.
Patmore, D., *The Life and Times of Coventry Patmore*, 1949. An intimate biography.
Reid, J. C., *The Mind and Art of Coventry Patmore*, 1957. A learned and exhaustive study of Patmore's thought.

V *Barnes*

Poems, ed. B. Jones, 2 vols, 1962.

Dugdale, G., *William Barnes of Dorset*, 1953. Readable biography.

VI *Hawker*

Hawker, R. S., *Cornish Ballads and Other Poems*, ed. C. E. Byles, 1904.

Burrows, M. F., *Robert Stephen Hawker, a Study of his Thought and Poetry*, 1926. Pedestrian, but thorough.
Brendon, P., *Hawker of Morwenstow: Portrait of a Victorian Eccentric*, 1975. Lively biography.

VII *Morris*

Collected Works, ed. May Morris, 24 vols, 1910–15. Standard edition with valuable Introductions by the editor.
Collected Letters, ed. N. Kelvin, 3 vols, 1984– .
William Morris: News from Nowhere and Selected Writings and Designs, ed. A. Briggs, revised 1984. Handy selection in Penguin.

Henderson, P., *William Morris: His Life, Work and Friends*, 1967. A well-proportioned account of Morris's activities.
Thompson, E. P., *William Morris, Romantic to Revolutionary*, revised 1977. Mostly on Morris's political activities.
Faulkner, P., ed., *Morris: The Critical Heritage*, 1973. Selection of nineteenth-century critical writings on Morris.
Bradley, I., *William Morris and his World*, 1978. Copiously illustrated guide.
Faulkner, P., *Against the Age: An Introduction to William Morris*, 1980. The best brief introduction.

VIII *Dixon*

Poems by Richard Watson Dixon, a Selection, ed. R. Bridges, 1909.

Sambrook, J., *A Poet Hidden: the Life of R. W. Dixon*, 1962.

IX *Swinburne*

Poems, 6 vols, 1904.
Tragedies, 5 vols, 1905. These two collections are incomplete, but textually are more accurate than the 'Bonchurch' edn.
Algernon Charles Swinburne: The Complete Works, ('Bonchurch' edn), eds E. Gosse and T. J. Wise, 20 vols, 1925–7. Textually corrupt. It includes Gosse's tactful *Life* of Swinburne.
The Swinburne Letters, ed. C. Y. Lang, New Haven, 6 vols, 1959–62.
New Writings by Swinburne, ed. C. Y. Lang, New York, 1964.
Swinburne: A Selection, ed. Edith Sitwell, 1960. Contains the best of the verse, including *Atalanta in Calydon* entire. The introduction is full of creative understanding.

Cassidy, J. A., *Algernon C. Swinburne*, 1964. Sensible brief introduction.

Hyder, C. K., ed., *Swinburne: The Critical Heritage*, 1970. Anthology of early criticism of Swinburne, down to Max Beerbohm.

Henderson, P., *Swinburne, the Portrait of a Poet*, 1974. The best of the recent biographies of Swinburne.

McGann, J. J., *Swinburne, an Experiment in Criticism*, 1972. A quirky but enthusiastic and perceptive rehabilitation of Swinburne, cast in dialogue.

X *James Thomson ('B.V.')*

Poetical Works, ed. B. Dobell, 2 vols, 1895. Prefaced by a *Memoir*.

Poems and Some Letters, ed. Anne Ridler, 1963. The most substantial selection of poems.

The Speedy Extinction of Evil and Misery: Selected Prose of James Thomson (B.V.), ed. W. D. Schaefer, Berkeley, California, 1967.

Walker, I. B., *James Thomson 'B.V.': A Critical Study*, Ithaca, 1950. The most thorough and studious critical account of Thomson.

Schaefer, W. D., *James Thomson 'B.V.': Beyond 'The City'*, Berkeley, California, 1965. Contains an extremely useful bibliography. Makes enthusiastic claims for Thomson as a religious, political, social and economic thinker and literary critic.

16. *Aspects of the Fin de Siècle*

I *General*

Symons, Arthur, *The Symbolist Movement in Literature*, 1899, New York, 1958, with an introduction by Richard Ellmann.
—— *Studies in Prose and Verse*, 1904.
Jackson, Holbrook, *The Eighteen Nineties*, 1913. This is still the most comprehensive and detailed survey of the nineties.
Yeats, W. B., *The Oxford Book of Modern Verse*, Oxford, 1936.
—— *Autobiographies*, 1955.
Temple, R. Z., *The Critic's Alchemy: A Study of the Introduction of French Symbolism into England*, New Haven, 1953.
Kermode, F., *Romantic Image*, 1957. A short but immensely suggestive study of *fin de siècle* iconography and its relation to twentieth-century poetics.
—— *Puzzles and Epiphanies*, 1962.
Ellmann, R., ed., *Edwardians and Late Victorians* (English Institute Essays 1959), New York, 1960.
Hough, G., *The Last Romantics*, 1961. An outstandingly good study of the period.
Charlesworth, B., *Dark Passages: The Decadent Consciousness in Victorian Literature*, Madison, Wisconsin, 1965.
Fletcher, I., ed., *Romantic Mythologies*, 1967.
Stanford, D., ed., *Poets of the Nineties*, 1965. A quite representative modern anthology, but the editorial matter is not reliable.
Clarke, Austin, *The Celtic Twilight and the Nineties*, Dublin, 1969.
Evans, B. Ifor, *English Poetry in the Later Nineteenth Century*, 2nd edn, 1966.
Fletcher, I., ed., *Decadence and the 1890s*, 1979. A collection of essays placing the phenomenon of decadence in its cultural and ideological contexts.
Johnson, R. V., *Aestheticism*, 1969.
Lester, J. A., *Journey through Despair: Transformations in British Literary Culture 1880–1914*, Princeton, 1968.
Nelson, J. G., *The Early Nineties: A View from the Bodley Head*, Cambridge, Mass., 1971.
Perkins, D., *A History of Modern Poetry: from the 1890s to the High Modernist Mode*, Cambridge, Mass., 1976. A substantial work of literary history, tracing the continuities between the *fin de siècle* and modernism.

Small, I., ed., *The Aesthetes: A Sourcebook*, 1979.

Thornton, R. K. R., ed., *Poetry of the Nineties*, 1970. A Penguin anthology.

—— *The Decadent Dilemma*, 1983. Discusses art as well as literature.

Warner, E. and Hough, G., eds, *Strangeness and Beauty: An Anthology of Aesthetic Criticism 1840–1910*: vol I, *Ruskin to Swinburne*, vol II, *Pater to Symons*, Cambridge, 1983.

II *Particular Authors*

Beerbohm, Max, *Works and More*, 1946.

Cecil, D., *Max*, 1965.

Riewald, J. G., ed., *The Surprise of Excellence: Modern Essays on Max Beerbohm*, Hamden, Conn., 1974.

Davidson, John, *A Selection of His Poems*, ed. Maurice Lindsay, 1961.

Flower, D., ed., *The Poetical Works of Ernest Dowson*, 1967.

Flower, D. and Maas, H., eds, *The Letters of Ernest Dowson*, 1967.

Gray, John, *Silverpoints*, 1893.

—— *Spiritual Poems*, 1896.

Sewell, B., ed., *Two Friends: John Gray and André Raffalovich*, Aylesford 1963.

Henley, W. E., *Works*, 5 vols, 1921.

Buckley, J. H., *W. E. Henley*, Princeton, 1945.

Fletcher, I., ed., *The Complete Poems of Lionel Johnson*, 1953.

Pater, Walter, *Works*, 10 vols, 1910.

Fletcher, I., *Walter Pater*, 1959.

Seiler, R. M., ed., *Walter Pater: The Critical Heritage*, 1980.

Symons, Arthur, *Collected Works*, 7 vols, 1924.

Lhombreaud, R., *Arthur Symons*, 1963.

Thompson, Francis, *Works*, ed. W. Meynell, 3 vols, 1913.

Reid, J. C., *Francis Thompson: Man and Poet*, 1959.

Maine, G. F., ed., *The Works of Oscar Wilde*, 1948.

Pearson, H., *The Life of Oscar Wilde*, 1954.

Beckson, K., ed., *Oscar Wilde: The Critical Heritage*, 1970.

Ellmann, R., ed., *Oscar Wilde: A Collection of Critical Essays*, Englewood Cliffs, N. J., 1969.

17. *The Victorian Theatre*

[Selected] *Plays by Dion Boucicault*, ed. P. Thomson, Cambridge, 1984.

[Selected] *Plays by Tom Robertson*, ed. W. Tydeman, Cambridge, 1982.

Gilbert, W. S., *The Savoy Operas*, ed. D. Hudson, 2 vols, 1962–3.

[Selected] *Plays by Henry Arthur Jones*, ed. R. Jackson, Cambridge, 1982.

Hamilton, C., ed., *The Social Plays of A. W. Pinero*, vols I & II, repr. New York, 1967.

Shaw, G. B., *Plays, Pleasant and Unpleasant*, 2 vols, 1898.

—— *Three Plays for Puritans*, 1901.

—— *Collected Letters*, ed. Dan H. Laurence: vol I, 1874–97 (1965); vol II, 1898–1910 (1972).

Wilde, O., *Collected Works*, ed. R. B. Ross, vols I–VI, repr. New York, 1969.

—— *Letters*, ed. R. Hart-Davis, 1962.

Booth, M. R., ed., *English Plays of the Nineteenth Century*, vols I & II, *Dramas*; vol III, *Comedies*; vol IV, *Farces*; vol V, *Pantomimes, Extravaganzas and Burlesques*, Oxford, 1969–1976. An excellent selection.

Archer, W., *English Dramatists of To-Day*, 1882.

Shaw, G. B., *Our Theatre in the Nineties*, 3 vols, 1932.

Irving, L., *Henry Irving*, 1951.

Nicoll, A., *A History of English Drama*: vol IV, *Early Nineteenth-Century Drama*, 2nd edn, 1955; vol V, *Late Nineteenth-Century Drama*, 2nd edn, 1959. They contain a comprehensive coverage of the period.

Meisel, M., *Shaw and the Nineteenth-Century Theatre*, Princeton, 1963. An acute examination of the relationship.

Schoonderwoerd, N., *J. T. Grein, Ambassador of the Theatre*, Assen, 1963.

Rahill, F., *The World of Melodrama*, 1967.

Conolly, L. W. and Wearing, J. P., *English Drama and Theatre, 1800–1900. A Guide to Information Sources*, Detroit, 1978. Covers a wide range.

Stephens, J. R., *The Censorship of English Drama*, 1824–1901, Cambridge, 1980. Thoughtful.

Booth, M. R., *Victorian Spectacular Theatre (1850–1910)*, Oxford, 1981.

TABLE OF DATES

The following table provides a conspectus of the period, relating literature to other events of the time. It does not contain the dates of all the works of all the authors dealt with in the preceding pages. Dramatic works usually appear under the year of performance.

1832   Grey P. M.; Parliamentary Reform.

       Crabbe d. Goethe d. Bentham d. Sir Walter Scott d. Tennyson, *Poems* (Lady of Shalott, Lotos Eaters, &c); Disraeli, *Contarini Fleming*.

       Morse – telegraph.

1833   Factory Act ('Children's Charter'); Oxford Movement.

       Browning, *Pauline*; Carlyle, *Sartor Resartus*; Newman *et al*, *Tracts for the Times* (to 1841).

1834   Melbourne and Peel P.M.s; Tolpuddle Martyrs transported; Abolition of slavery in British Empire; Poor Law.

       Coleridge d. Charles Lamb d.

       Crabbe, *Poetical Works*.

       Faraday – electrical self-induction; Braille – alphabet for blind.

1835   Cobbett d.

       Dickens, *Sketches by Boz*, 1st ser.; Browning, *Paracelsus*; Wordsworth, *Yarrow Revisited*; Strauss, *Der Leben Jesu*; Gogol, *Dead Souls*.

       Donizetti, *Lucia di Lammermoor* (opera).

1836   Dickens, *Sketches by Boz*, 2nd ser., *Pickwick Papers*.

       First train in London.

1837   Accession of Queen Victoria.

       Carlyle, *French Revolution*; Dickens, *Oliver Twist*; Thackeray, *Yellowplush Papers*.

       Froebel's kindergarten; Pitman's shorthand.

1838   Anti-Corn Law League (Manchester); Beginnings of Chartism.

       Dickens, *Nicholas Nickleby*; Surtees, *Jorrocks' Jaunts and Jollities*.

       National Gallery; Liebig and beginnings of biochemistry.

1839   Chartist Riots; Anglo-Chinese Opium War.

Carlyle, *Chartism*; Sydney Smith, *Works*; Thackeray, *Catherine*.

Daguerre – photography; Turner, *Fighting Temeraire* (painting); Grand National at Aintree and Cesarewitch at Newmarket.

1840　Union of Canada Act; Penny Post; Queen's marriage to Prince Albert.

Browning, *Sordello*; Mérimée, *Colomba*; Poe, *Tales of the Grotesque*.

Kew Gardens; Houses of Parliament.

1841　Peel P. M.; New Zealand declared British; Sovereignty over Hong Kong; Livingstone in Africa; Delane – editor of *Times*.

Browning, *Pippa Passes*; Carlyle, *Heroes and Hero Worship*; Dickens, *Old Curiosity Shop*; Emerson, *Essays*.

Ross discovers Southern Continent; *Punch*; Bradshaw's *Railway Guide*; Cook's tours.

1842　Chartist Riots; Income Tax; Mines Act (no women or children under 10 underground); Copyright Act (42 years or 7 years after author's death).

Tennyson, *Poems* (Morte d'Arthur, &c); Wordsworth, *Poems*; Longfellow, *Ballads*.

Mudie's Circulating Library; Mendelssohn, 'Scottish' Symphony (op. 36).

1843　Natal British

Southey d. (Wordsworth succeeded as Poet Laureate).

Carlyle, *Past and Present*; Dickens, *Christmas Carol*; J. S. Mill, *Logic*; Macaulay, *Critical and Historical Essays*; Ruskin, *Modern Painters* (to 1860).

Brunel's Thames Tunnel; Thurber's 'typewriter'; Wagner, *Flying Dutchman* (opera); Donizetti, *Don Pasquale* (opera).

1844　Factory Act (restricts hours for women and children); Co-operative Movement (Rochdale Pioneers); Royal Commission on Health of Towns.

Dickens, *Martin Chuzzlewit*; Disraeli, *Coningsby*; E. B. Barrett (Browning), *Poems*; Thackeray, *Barry Lyndon*; Dumas, *Three Musketeers, Count of Monte Cristo*.

Chambers, *Vestiges of Creation*.

1845　Newman becomes Roman Catholic; Irish Potato Famine.

Disraeli, *Sybil*; Mérimée, *Carmen*.

Armstrong – hydraulic crane; British Museum; Liszt, *Préludes*; Wagner, *Tannhäuser* (opera).

1846 Repeal of Corn Laws; Railway boom; *Daily News* (ed. Dickens); Irish potato crop fails again; Russell P. M.

Brontës, *Poems*; G. Eliot, *Strauss's Life of Jesus*; Balzac, *Cousine Bette*; Melville, *Typee*.

E. Howe – sewing machine (U.S.A.); Mendelssohn, *Elijah* (oratorio); Berlioz, *Damnation of Faust*; Liszt, 1st Hungarian Rhapsody; Schumann, 2nd Symphony.

1847 Ten Hours Factory Act.

C. Brontë, *Jane Eyre*; A. Brontë, *Agnes Grey*; E. Brontë, *Wuthering Heights*; Tennyson, *The Princess*.

Simpson – chloroform.

1848 Communist Manifesto; Chartist petition; Revolution throughout Europe; Public Health Act.

Emily Brontë d.

A. Brontë, *Tenant of Wildfell Hall*; Dickens, *Dombey and Son*; Gaskell, *Mary Barton*; J. S. Mill, *Principles of Political Economy*; Thackeray, *Vanity Fair*.

Pre-Raphaelite Brotherhood; Millais, *Ophelia* (painting).

1849 Christian Socialism (F. D. Maurice and Kingsley).

Anne Brontë d.

Arnold, *Strayed Reveller*; C. Brontë, *Shirley*; Clough, *Ambarvalia*; Froude, *Nemesis of Faith*; Macaulay, *History of England* (to 1861); Ruskin, *Seven Lamps of Architecture*; *Household Words* (ed. Dickens).

Menai Bridge; Monier – reinforced concrete.

1850 Public Libraries Act; Roman Catholic hierarchy in Great Britain; Gorham Judgment in C. of E. (on baptismal regeneration).

Wordsworth d. (Tennyson succeeded as Poet Laureate).

Dickens, *David Copperfield*; E. B. Browning, *Poems* (Sonnets from the Portuguese, &c); Browning, *Christmas Eve and Easter Day*; Carlyle, *Latter-Day Pamphlets*; Kingsley, *Alton Locke*; Rossetti *et al*, *The Germ* (1–4); Tennyson, *In Memoriam*; Thackeray, *Pendennis*; Wordsworth, *The Prelude*; Hawthorne, *The Scarlet Letter*.

Natural Sciences School at Oxford; Clausius – 2nd Law of Thermodynamics; Millais, *Christ in the House of His Parents* (painting); Paxton's Crystal Palace; Schumann, 3rd Symphony.

1851   Napoleon III's *coup d'état* in France; Australian gold-rush;
        Great Exhibition, Hyde Park; Owens College, Man-
        chester.
        Kingsley, *Yeast*; Meredith, *Poems* (Love in a Valley);
        Ruskin, *Stones of Venice* (to 1853); Melville, *Moby Dick*.
        King's Cross station; Verdi, *Rigoletto* (opera); Corot, *Danse
        des Nymphes* (painting).
1852   Revival of Convocation (C. of E.); Derby and Aberdeen
        P.M.s.
        Arnold, *Empedocles on Etna*; Thackeray, *Henry Esmond*;
        H. B. Stowe, *Uncle Tom's Cabin*.
        Niagara Falls Bridge; Paddington Station.
1853   Arnold, *Poems* (Scholar Gypsy, Sohrab and Rustum);
        C. Brontë, *Villette*; Gaskell, *Ruth, Cranford*; Thackeray,
        English Humourists; Hawthorne, *Tanglewood Tales*;
        Le Nerval, *Les Chimères*.
        Verdi, *Il Trovatore; La Traviata* (operas).
1854   Crimean War (Balaclava, Inkermann); Dogma of the Im-
        maculate Conception; Northcote-Trevelyan Report on
        Civil Service.
        Dickens, *Hard Times*; Patmore, *Angel in the House*, Pt 1.
        Maurice's Working Men's College, London.
1855   Palmerston P.M.; Sebastopol captured; Florence Night-
        ingale in Crimea; Newspaper tax abolished; Livingstone
        discovers Victoria Falls.
        Charlotte Brontë d.
        Arnold, *Poems*, 2nd ser.; Browning, *Men and Women*;
        Gaskell, *North and South*; Kingsley, *Westward Ho*;
        Tennyson, *Maud*; Thackeray, *The Newcomes*; Trollope,
        The Warden.
1856   Treaty of Paris (ending Crimean War); Limited Liability
        Act.
        Froude, *History of England* (and to 1870);
        Patmore, *Angel in the House*, Pt 2; Reade, *It is Never Too
        Late to Mend*; Flaubert, *Madame Bovary*; Hugo, *Con-
        templations*.
        Bessemer's steel process.
1857   Indian Mutiny; Matrimonial Causes Act (divorce courts);
        Ritual cases in Church courts.
        C. Brontë, *The Professor*; E. B. Browning, *Aurora Leigh*;
        Buckle, *History of Civilisation in England*; Dickens, *Little*

Dorrit; Gaskell, *Life of C. Bronte*; Trollope, *Barchester Towers*; Baudelaire, *Les Fleurs du Mal.*

Transatlantic cable; National Portrait Gallery.

1858 Derby P.M.; Removal of Jewish disabilities.

Carlyle, *Frederick the Great*; Clough, *Amours de Voyage*; G. Eliot, *Scenes of Clerical Life*; Morris, *Defence of Guenevere*; Trollope, *Dr Thorne, The Three Clerks.*

Covent Garden Opera; Frith, *Derby Day* (painting); Manet, *Le Concert aux Tuileries* (painting).

1859 Palmerston P.M.; Franco-Austrian War over Italy.

De Quincey d. Leigh Hunt d. Macaulay d.

Dickens, *Tale of Two Cities*; FitzGerald, *Omar Khayyám*; G. Eliot, *Adam Bede*; Meredith, *Richard Feverel*; Mill, *On Liberty*; Smiles, *Self-Help*; Tennyson, *Idylls of the King* (to 1872); Thackeray, *The Virginians; All the Year Round* (ed. Dickens); Goncharov, *Oblomov*; Hugo, *Légende des siècles.*

Darwin, *Origin of Species*; Gounod, *Faust* (opera); Wagner, *Tristan und Isolde* (opera).

1860 Italian unification; Lincoln U.S. President; Food and Drugs Act.

Collins, *Woman in White*; G. Eliot, *Mill on the Floss*; Patmore, *Angel in the House*, Pt 3.; Peacock, *Gryll Grange; Essays and Reviews; Cornhill Magazine*, ed. Thackeray; Burckhardt, *Renaissance in Italy*; Boucicault, *Colleen Bawn.*

1861 American Civil War; Death of Prince Consort.

Mrs Browning d. Clough d.

Arnold, *On Translating Homer*; Dickens, *Great Expectations*; G. Eliot, *Silas Marner*; Meredith, *Evan Harrington*; Mill, *Representative Government*; Palgrave, *Golden Treasury*; Reade, *The Cloister and the Hearth*; H. Spencer, *Education*; Trollope, *Framley Parsonage.*

Pasteur's germ theory of disease; Morris's wallpapers and tapestries; Royal Academy of Music; Brahms, Piano Concerto no. 1.

1862 Colenso denies authenticity of Mosaic books.

Collins, *No Name*; G. Eliot, *Romola*; Meredith, *Modern Love*; C. Rossetti, *Goblin Market*; Ruskin, *Unto This Last*; Thackeray, *Philip*; Trollope, *Orley Farm*; Hugo, *Les Misérables*; Turgenev, *Fathers and Sons.*

Verdi, *La Forza del Destino* (opera); Sarah Bernhardt's debut in Paris; Cricket tour to Australia.

1863 Thackeray d.

Gaskell, *Sylvia's Lovers*; Huxley, *Man's Place in Nature*; Lyell, *Antiquity of Man*; Mill, *Utilitarianism*; Reade, *Hard Cash*; Renan, *La Vie de Jesus*.

Manet, *Déjeuner sur l'Herbe* (painting); Football Association.

1864 Landor d. Clare d. Surtees d.

Browning, *Dramatis Personae*; Gaskell, *Cousin Phillis*; Meredith, *Emilia in England* (later *Sandra Belloni*); Newman, *Apologia pro Vita Sua*; Tennyson, *Enoch Arden*; Trollope, *The Small House at Allington, Can You Forgive Her?*

'Pasteurization'; Geneva Convention (Red Cross); Bruckner, Mass No. 1 in D minor; Tchaikovsky, *Romeo and Juliet Overture*.

1865 Russell P. M.; Assassination of Lincoln; End of American Civil War.

Mrs Gaskell d.

Arnold, *Essays in Criticism*, 1st ser.; 'Lewis Carroll', *Alice in Wonderland*; Meredith, *Rhoda Fleming*; Swinburne, *Atalanta in Calydon; Pall Mall Gazette* and *Fortnightly Review*.

Lister – antiseptic surgery; Rimsky-Korsakov, 1st Symphony; Whymper climbs Matterhorn.

1866 Derby P. M.; Austria at war with Prussia and Italy; Dr Barnardo's Homes; Riots in Ireland.

Peacock d.

Collins, *Armadale*; Gaskell, *Wives and Daughters*; G. Eliot, *Felix Holt*; Reade, *Griffith Gaunt*; Swinburne, *Poems and Ballads*; Trollope, *The Belton Estate*; Daudet, *Lettres de Mon Moulin*; Dostoievsky, *Crime and Punishment*; Ibsen, *Brand*; Hugo, *Les Travailleurs de la Mer*; Verlaine, *Poemes saturniens*.

Nobel – dynamite; Mendel, laws of heredity; Smetana, *Bartered Bride* (opera); Henry Irving on London stage.

1867 Disraeli P.M.; Dominion of Canada; Second Reform Bill.

Arnold, *New Poems*; Bagehot, *English Constitution*; Carlyle, *Shooting Niagara*; Meredith, *Vittoria*; Trollope, *Last Chronicle of Barset*; Marx, *Das Kapital*, I; Ibsen, *Peer Gynt*; Zola, *Thérèse Raquin*.

Strauss, 'Blue Danube' Waltz.

1868 Gladstone P.M.

Browning, *The Ring and the Book*; Collins, *Moonstone*; Morris, *Earthly Paradise* (& 1869, 1870).

Wagner, *Die Meistersinger* (opera); Grieg, Piano Concerto in A minor; Brahms, *German Requiem*; Renoir, *Lise* (painting).

1869   Suez Canal; Irish Church disestablished.

Arnold, *Culture and Anarchy*; Mill, *On the Subjection of Women*; Tennyson, *Holy Grail*; Trollope, *Phineas Finn*; Flaubert, *L'Education sentimentale*; Verlaine, *Fêtes galantes*.

Brahms, *Hungarian Dances*; Wagner, *Das Rheingold* (opera); Galton and eugenics; Mendeleeff's periodic tables of chemical elements.

1870   Franco-Prussian War; Elementary Education Act; Dogma of Papal Infallibility.

Dickens d.

Arnold, *St Paul and Protestantism*; Dickens, *Edwin Drood*; Disraeli, *Lothair*; Newman, *Grammar of Assent*; Reade, *Put Yourself in His Place*; D. G. Rossetti, *Poems*.

Cramme's dynamo; J. D. Rockefeller, Standard Oil Co.; Wagner, *Die Walküre* (opera).

1871   Abolition of religious tests at Oxford and Cambridge; Trade Unions legalized; Newnham College, Cambridge; Stanley meets Livingstone; Bank Holidays established.

T. W. Robertson d.

Arnold, *Friendship's Garland*; Darwin, *Descent of Man*; G. Eliot, *Middlemarch*; L. Carroll, *Through the Looking Glass*; Meredith, *Harry Richmond*; Ruskin, *Fors Clavigera*; Swinburne, *Songs before Sunrise*.

Whistler, *Artist's Mother* (painting); Verdi, *Aida* (opera).

1872   Secret Ballot.

F. D. Maurice d.

Butler, *Erewhon*; Hardy, *Under the Greenwood Tree*; Ruskin, *Munera Pulveris*.

Edison's telegraph.

1873   Financial crisis in Europe and America; Sankey and Moody Revival meetings.

J. S. Mill d. Lytton d.

Arnold, *Literature and Dogma*; Mill, *Autobiography*; Pater, *Studies in the Renaissance*; Trollope, *Eustace Diamonds*; Tolstoi, *Anna Karenina*.

Cezanne, *Straw Hat* (painting); Remington typewriters.

1874   Disraeli P.M.,

Hardy, *Far From the Madding Crowd*; Thomson, *City of Dreadful Night*; Trollope, *Phineas Redux.*

Monet, *Impression: Sunrise* (painting); Wagner, *Götterdämmerung*; Verdi, *Requiem.*

1875   Britain buys Suez Canal shares.

Charles Kingsley d.

Tennyson, *Queen Mary*; Trollope, *The Way We Live Now.*

Bizet, *Carmen* (opera); Gilbert & Sullivan partnership; Tchaikovsky, 1st Piano Concerto.

1876   Bulgarian Atrocities.

G. Eliot, *Daniel Deronda*; Meredith, *Beauchamp's Career*; Morris, *Sigurd the Volsung*; Tennyson, *Harold*; Trollope, *The Prime Minister*; James, *Roderick Hudson.*

Edison's phonograph; Gauguin's landscapes at Salon, Paris; Brahms, 1st Symphony; Wagner, *Siegfried* (opera).

1877   Russo-Turkish War; Annexation of Transvaal.

Bagehot d.

Meredith, *Idea of Comedy*; Zola, *L'Assommoir*; Ibsen, *Pillars of Society.*

Rodin, *Bronze Age* (sculpture).

1878   Congress of Berlin; Irish Land League (Parnell); Salvation Army.

Browning, *La Saisiaz*; Hardy, *Return of the Native*; Swinburne, *Poems and Ballads* II.

London electric street lighting; Eddystone Lighthouse; Tchaikovsky, *Swan Lake* (ballet).

1879   Gladstone's Midlothian Campaign.

Browning, *Dramatic Idyls I*; Meredith, *Egoist*; Spencer, *Principles of Ethics*; Stevenson, *Travels with A Donkey*; Ibsen, *Doll's House.*

London telephone exchange; Australian frozen meat; Rodin, *John the Baptist* (sculpture).

1880   Gladstone P.M.; Transvaal declares itself a republic.

'George Eliot' d.

Browning, *Dramatic Idyls* II; Disraeli, *Endymion*; Gissing, *Workers in the Dawn*; Hardy, *Trumpet Major*; Tennyson, *Ballads and Other Poems*; Trollope, *The Duke's Children*; Dostoievsky, *Brothers Karamazov*; Maupassant, *Boule de Suif*; Zola, *Nana.*

Dvorak, 1st Symphony; Tchaikovsky, *1812 Overture.*

1881   Married Women's Property Act; Irish Land Act; Revised
        Version of New Testament.
        Disraeli d. Carlyle d.
        'Mark Rutherford', *Autobiography*; D. G. Rossetti, *Ballads
        and Sonnets*; Trollope, *Dr Wortle's School*; Ibsen, *Ghosts*;
        James, *Portrait of a Lady*; Verlaine, *Sagesse*.
        Monet, *Sunshine and Snow* (painting); Offenbach, *Tales of
        Hoffman* (opera).
1882   Phoenix Park murders in Dublin; British intervention in
        Egypt.
        Darwin d. D. G. Rossetti d. James Thomson (B.V.) d.
        Trollope d.
        Shaw, *Cashel Byron's Profession*; Swinburne, *Tristram of
        Lyonesse*; Maupassant, *Une View*.
        Daimler's petrol engine; Manet, *Le Bar aux Folies-Bergères*
        (painting); Brahms, Piano Concerto no. 2; Wagner,
        Parsifal (opera).
1883   FitzGerald d.
        Trollope, *Autobiography*; Lang &c., *Iliad*; Nietzsche, *Thus
        Spake Zarathustra*.
        Brahms, Symphony no. 3; Dvorak, *Stabat Mater* (oratorio);
        Royal College of Music.
1884   Third Reform Bill; Oxford English Dictionary (to 1928).
        Charles Reade d.
        Gissing, *The Unclassed*; Tennyson, *Becket*; Huysmans, *À
        Rebours*; Ibsen, *Wild Duck*; Mark Twain, *Huckleberry
        Finn*.
        Seurat, *Bathers at Asnières* (painting); Burne-Jones, *King
        Cophetua and the Beggar Maid* (painting).
1885   Salisbury P.M.; Fall of Khartoum.
        Meredith, *Diana of the Crossways*; Pater, *Marius the
        Epicurean*; Ruskin, *Praeterita*; Tennyson, *Tiresias*; Zola,
        Germinal.
        Gold in Transvaal; Degas, *Woman Bathing* (painting);
        Sullivan, *Mikado* (opera); Brahms, Symphony no. 4.
1886   Gladstone and Salisbury P.M.s.
        Gissing, *Demos*; Hardy, *Mayor of Casterbridge*; Kipling, *De-
        partmental Ditties*; Tennyson, *Locksley Hall Sixty Years
        After*; Ibsen, *Rosmersholm*; James, *Bostonians; Princess
        Casamassima*; Nietzsche, *Beyond Good and Evil*.
        Severn Tunnel; Canadian Pacific Rly. completed.
1887   Queen's Jubilee; Stanley discovers Lake Nyanza.

Gissing, *Thyrza*; Hardy, *Woodlanders*; Pater, *Imaginary Portraits*; Strindberg, *The Father*.

Verdi, *Otello* (opera).

1888   County Councils established.

Matthew Arnold d.

Arnold, *Essays in Criticism* II; Gissing, *A Life's Morning*; Kipling, *Soldiers Three; Plain Tales from the Hills*; Yeats, *Fairy and Folk Tales of the Irish Peasantry*; Strindberg, *Miss Julie*; Verlaine, *Amour*; Zola, *La Terre*.

Eastman's Kodak box camera; Dunlop's pneumatic tyre; Van Gogh's *Yellow Chair* and *Sunflowers* (paintings); Rimsky-Korsakov, *Scheherazade* (music); Football League.

1889   London Dock Strike.

Browning d. G. M. Hopkins d. Wilkie Collins d.

Browning, *Asolando*; Gissing, *The Nether World*; Pater, *Appreciations*; Swinburne, *Poems and Ballads* III; Tennyson, *Demeter*; Yeats, *Wanderings of Oisin*.

Dvorak, Symphony no. 4; Franck, Symphony in D minor.

1890   Beginnings of municipal housing.

Newman d.

Frazer, *Golden Bough* (to 1915); W. James, *Principles of Psychology*; Morris, *News from Nowhere*; Ibsen, *Hedda Gabler*.

Borodin, *Prince Igor* (opera); First 'tube' railway.

1891   Free elementary education.

Gissing, *New Grub Street*; Hardy, *Tess of the D'Urbervilles*; Henley, *Lyra Heroica*; Kipling, *The Light That Failed*; Shaw, *Quintessence of Ibsenism*; Wilde, *Picture of Dorian Grey*.

Tchaikovsky, *Nutcracker* (ballet).

1892   Gladstone P.M.

Tennyson d.

Gissing, *Born in Exile*; Henley, *Song of the Sword*; Kipling, *Barrack-Room Ballads*; Shaw, *Widowers' Houses*; Tennyson, *Death of Oenone*; Yeats, *Countess Kathleen*; Ibsen, *Master Builder*.

Toulouse-Lautrec, *At the Moulin Rouge* (painting).

1893   Independent Labour Party.

Davidson, *Fleet Street Eclogues*; Gissing, *The Odd Women*; Pinero, *The Second Mrs Tanqueray*; F. Thompson, *Poems* (Hounds of Heaven &c); Wilde, *A Woman of No Importance*.

Benz's four-wheel car; Manchester Ship Canal; *The Studio* (with Beardsley drawings); Dvorak, New World Symphony; Tchaikovsky, *Symphony Pathétique*; Verdi, *Falstaff* (opera).

1894 Rosebery P.M.; Death Duties.

Froude d. Stevenson d. Christina Rossetti d. Pater d.

Davidson, *Ballads and Songs*; Gissing, *In the Year of Jubilee*; Meredith, *Lord Ormont*; Moore, *Esther Waters*; Shaw, *Arms and the Man*; Swinburne, *Astrophel*; Yeats, *Land of Heart's Desire*.

Yellow Book (Beardsley art editor); Debussy, *L'Après-midi d'un Faun* (music); Edison's Kinetoscope Parlour, New York.

1895 Salisbury P.M.; Jameson Raid (into Transvaal).

Conrad, *Almayer's Folly*; Gissing, *Eve's Ransom*; Hardy, *Jude the Obscure*; L. Johnson, *Poems*; Meredith, *Amazing Marriage*; Wells, *Time Machine*; Wilde, *Importance of Being Earnest*; Yeats, *Poems*.

National Trust; Röntgen's X-rays; Freud's first work on psychoanalysis; Marconi's 'wireless' telegraphy; Mahler, Symphony no. 2; R. Strauss, *Til Eulenspiegel*.

1896 Morris d. Patmore d.

Housman, *A Shropshire Lad*; Pinero, *Benefit of the Doubt*; Chekhov, *Seagull*.

Nobel Prizes; Langley's flying machine; Morris & Burne-Jones' Kelmscott Chaucer.

1897 Queen's Diamond Jubilee; 2nd Colonial Conference; Workmen's Compensation Act.

Conrad, *Nigger of the Narcissus*; Davidson, *New Ballads*; Kipling, *Captains Courageous*; F. Thompson, *New Poems*; Shaw, *Candida*; Wells, *Invisible Man*; James, *Spoils of Poynton, What Maisie Knew*.

Ross discovers malaria bacillus; Klondike Gold Rush; Tate Gallery.

1898 Kitchener defeats dervishes at Omdurman; Anglo-French clash at Fashoda.

'Lewis Carroll' d.

Gissing, *Human Odds and Ends*; Hardy, *Wessex Poems*; Shaw, *Plays Pleasant and Unpleasant, Caesar and Cleopatra*; Wells, *War of the Worlds*

The Curies discover radium; Rodin, *Kiss* (sculpture).

1899 South African War; Board of Education.

Gissing, *Crown of Life*; Pinero, *Trelawny of the 'Wells'*; Tolstoi, *Resurrection*.

Elgar, *Enigma Variations* (music); Sibelius, Symphony no. 1.

1900   Relief of Ladysmith and Mafeking.

Ruskin d. Wilde d. Dowson d.

Conrad, *Lord Jim*; Henley, *For England's Sake*; Pinero, *Gay Lord Quex*; Shaw, *Three Plays for Puritans*; Wells, *Love and Mr Lewisham*.

Max Planck's quantum theory; Elgar, *Dream of Gerontius* (oratorio); Mahler, 4th Symphony; Sibelius, *Finlandia Overture*.

1901   Death of Queen Victoria.

1903   Butler, *The Way of All Flesh*.

INDEX

Figures in heavy type indicate main reference, those in italics bibliography.

Acton, William, 219; *Prostitution*, 219
Addison, Joseph, 117, 124
Ainsworth, Harrison, 243
All the Year Round, 104, 107, 262
Allen, Grant, *Woman Who Did, The*, 231
Allen, Walter, *English Novel, The*, 347
Anecdotes and Adventures of Fifteen Gentleman, 292
Archer, William, 494
Arnold, Matthew, viii, 7, 9, 14, 47, 48, **51–67**, **69–80**, 261, 326, 373, 386, 393, 417, 461, 469, 484, *506–7*; *Culture and Anarchy*, viii, 9, 14, 54–5, 71–5, *261*; *Empedocles on Etna, and Other Poems*, 56, *373*; *Essays in Criticism*, 55, 70–71, 74, 76, 78; *Essays in Criticism*, 2nd Series, 78–9; *Friendship's Garland*, 73; *God and the Bible*, 42, 71; *Irish Essays*, 73; *Letters to Clough*, 53, 57, 61, 64, 65, 75, *393*; *Literature and Dogma*, 52, 71–2; *Merope*, 57, 61, 69; *Mixed Essays*, 70, 72; *New Poems* (1867), 52, 57, 62; *On the Study of Celtic Literature*, 72, 78; *On Translating Homer*, 55, 78; *On Translating Homer: Last Words*, 77–8; *Poems* (1853), 56, 60; *Poems*, Second Series (1855), 57; *Popular Education of France, The*, 73; *St Paul and Protestantism*, 42; *Strayed Reveller, and Other Poems, The*, 57–8; 'Bacchanalia', 64–5; 'Balder Dead', 57, 61, 64; 'Buried Life, The', 64; 'Calais Sands', 57; 'Church of Brou, The', 64; 'Dover Beach', 57, 60, 62; 'Empedocles on Etna', 56–7, 59–61, 64, 68–9; 'Faded Leaves', 59; 'Forsaken Merman, The', 58; 'Function of Criticism at the Present Time, The', 74–6; 'Future, The', 59; 'Future of Liberalism, The', 73; 'Growing Old', 58; 'Heinrich Heine', 70; 'In Utrumque Paratus', 58; 'Memorial Verses', 59, 61, 63; 'Mycerinus', 58; 'New Sirens, The', 58; 'Obermann Once More', 56, 60, 62–3; 'On the Modern Element in Literature', 59, 76, 80; 'Resignation', 58; 'Rugby Chapel', 41, 63; 'Scholar-Gipsy, The', 57, 60–62, 64–5; 'Second Best, The', 63; 'Sick King in Bokhara, The', 58; 'Sohrab and Rustum', 56–7, 60–61, 64; 'Stanzas from the Grande Chartreuse', 60, 64, 66; 'Stanzas in Memory of the Author of "Obermann"', 59, 62; 'Strayed Reveller, The', 58; 'Study of Poetry, The', 78; 'Summer Night, A', 64; 'Switzerland', 59, 62; 'Thyrsis', 56, 62, 64, 70, *371*; 'To a Gipsy Child by the Sea Shore', 58; 'Tristram and Iseult', 59, 64; 'Yes! in the sea of life enisled', 60; 'Youth of Man, The', 59; 'Youth of Nature, The', 59
Arnold, R., 133
Arnold, Thomas, 26, 40–41, 42, 53, 55, 63–4, 66–7, *69*, 71, 77
Ashford, Daisy, 249
Athenaeum, 203
Auden, W. H., 55, 361
Aunt Judy's Magazine, 300
Austen, Jane, 26, 82, 134, 139, 162, 174, 181, 222, 384; *Emma*, 213
Aveling, Edward, 229

Bagehot, Walter, **16–17**, 117
Bailey, Philip James, 438
Baker, E. A., 135
Barbauld, Mrs. 202
Barnes, William, 319, 416, **448–50**, *538*; *Orra, a Lapland Tale*, 448; *Philological Grammar*, 448; *Poems of Rural Life in the Dorset Dialect*, 448;

Poetical Pieces, 448; 'My Orcha'd in Linden Lea', 450; 'Walter Crowvoot, The', 450; 'Woak Hill', 449

Baudelaire, Charles, 458, 459, 465, 471, 472, 476

Beardsley, Aubrey, 463, 474, 480

Beer, Gillian, *Darwin's Plots*, 341

Beerbohm, Max, 466, 480

Bentham, Jeremy, 10–11, 12–13

Bentley's Miscellany, 84

Blackmore, R. D., *Lorna Doone*, 349

Blackwood's Magazine, 105, 188, 203, 221, 243, 262, 274, 282, 284

Blake, Robert, 248, 251

Blake, William, 94, 449, 465, 470, 476

Blunden, Edmund, 460

Boucicault, Dion, 266, **485–6**, 488, 497; *Arrah-na-Pogue*, 497; *Colleen Bawn, The*, 485; *Foul Play*, 266; *London Assurance*, 485; *Octoroon, The*, 485; *Shaughraun, The*, 485–6

Braddon, Mary Elizabeth, 223–4, 262; *Aurora Floyd*, 223; *Lady Audley's Secret*, 223–4, 262

Bradlaugh, Charles, 25, 460

Bridges, Robert, 413, 421–3, 425, 456–7

Briggs, Asa, 101

Bright, Jacob, 214

Brontë, Anne, 145–51, **160–163**, 172, 513–14; *Agnes Grey*, 148, 150, 161–3; *Poems by Currer, Ellis, and Acton Bell*, 150; *Tenant of Wildfell Hall, The*, 150, 160–61

Brontë, Branwell, 145, 147, 149, 160, 186, *513–14*

Brontë, Charlotte, 126, 145–51, **151–9**, 160, 161, 170, 172, 175, 180, 188, 193, 204, 215, *513–14*; *Emma*, 159; *Jane Eyre*, 148, 150, 151–2, 153–7, 159, 213, 224, 236; *Moores, The*, 159; *Poems by Currer, Ellis, and Acton Bell*, 150; *Professor, The*, 149–52; *Shirley*, 148, 150, 152, 153, 157–9, 161, 202, 212–13, 214–15; *Villette*, 149–51, 153, 155, 156–7, 159, 236

Brontë, Emily, 145–51, 160, **163–72**, 204, *513–14*; *Poems by Currer, Ellis, and Acton Bell*, 150; *Wuthering Heights*, 147–8, 150, 160, 163–71, 183, 218, 351; 'Cold in the earth', 170–71; 'He comes with western winds', 172; 'No coward soul is mine', 170

Brontë, Maria Branwell, 146

Brontë, Patrick, 146

Browne, Frances, *Granny's Wonderful Chair*, 300

Browning, Elizabeth Barrett, **387–91**, 411–12, 443, *534*; *Aurora Leigh*, 227, 388, 389–91, 412; *Casa Guidi Windows*, 387; *Sonnets from the Portuguese*, 411

Browning, Robert, 52, 58, 63, 170, 256, 263, 308, 368, 382, 385, 386, **387–411**, 412, 417, 420, 429–31, 437, 471, *534*; *Blot in the Scutcheon, A*, 388; *Dramatis Personae*, 406, 410; *Fifine at the Fair*, 410; *Men and Women*, 263, 388, 389, 391, 395, 397, 399, 406, 410; *Paracelsus*, 388, 396–7, 406; *Parleying With Certain People of Importance in Their Day*, 410; *Pauline*, 391, 394–5, 399–400, 406; *Pippa Passes*, 395, 396–7, 406; *Ring and the Book, The*, 52, 397, 410–11, 420; *Sordello*, 388, 394, 396, 406; *Strafford*, 388; 'Abt Vogler', 394, 397, 401; 'Andrea Del Sarto', 394, 397, 406; 'Bishop Blougram's Apology', 406; 'By the Fire-side', 394; 'Caliban Upon Setebos', 406; 'Childe Roland', 394, 397, 399–402, 429; 'Cleon', 409; 'Death in the Desert, A', 406; 'Dramatic Romances', 408; 'Epistle of Karshish, The', 397, 408– 9; 'Fra Lippo Lippi', 394, 397, 406–9; 'In a Gondola', 397; 'Johannes Agricola', 392; 'Laboratory, The', 397; 'Love Among the Ruins', 397, 399, 404, 405, 410; 'Love in a Life', 397, 404; 'Lover's Quarrel, A', 402; 'Meeting at Night', 401; 'Mr Sludge, "The Medium"', 406; 'My Last Duchess', 406; 'Porphyria's Lover', 392, 394, 405; 'Rabbi Ben Ezra', 58, 385; 'Song', 411; 'Two in the Campagna', 397, 402–4; 'Woman's Last Word, A', 401

Buchan, John, 347

Bulwer, *see* Lytton

Bunyan, John, 28, 118, 151; *Grace Abounding*, 28; *Pilgrim's Progress, The*, 303

Burdett-Coutts, Angela, 105, 219

Burke, Edmund, 10, 55

Burne-Jones, Edward, 452, 454, 455

Burns, Robert, 79

Butler, Josephine, 219–20

Butler, Samuel, 46, 215, 335, **336–44**, 355, *529*; *Erewhon*, 339, 340, 341; *Erewhon Revisited*, 339; *Fair Haven, The*, 339; *Life and Habit*, 338 *Life and Letters*, 338; *Luck or Cunning*, 338; *Unconscious Memory*, 338; *Way of All Flesh, The*, 257, 336, 337, 339, 341, 342–4; 'Book of the Machines, The', 340–41

Butt, J. (and Tillotson, K.) 101, 107
Byron, George Gordon, Lord, 1, 59, 79, 151, 192, 240, 241, 242, 251
Byron, H. J., 488

Caird, Mona, 231
Carleton, William, 282, 283
Carlyle, Thomas, viii, 1–7, 10, **13–17**, 24, 46, 55, 73, 104–5, 133, 243, 245, 254, 256, 260, 310, 383, 387, 461, 469; *French Revolution, The*, 5, 104; *Latter-Day Pamphlets*, 6; *Nigger Question, The*, 6; *Past and Present*, viii; *Sartus Resartus*, 3–5, 243
Carroll, Lewis, 289–91; 294, **295–300**, 302; *Alice in Wonderland*, 295, 296–8; *Hunting of the Snark, The*, 297, 299–300; *Mother Goose's Melody*, 289–90; *Rectory Umbrella, The*, 287; *Through the Looking Glass*, 295, 296–8, 340; *Sylvie and Bruno*, 300; *Sylvie and Bruno Concluded*, 300; 'Jabberwocky', 297; 'Walrus and the Carpenter, The', 297
Cecil Lord David, 124, 156
Chateaubriand, François, A., 192
Chatterton, Thomas, 436
Chaucer, Geoffrey, 69, 79
Chesterton, G. K., 81, 99, 128, 294, 351
Christian Socialism, see Kingsley, Maurice, Ludlow, Osborne
Civil and Military Gazette, The, 352
Clarke, Marcus, 268
Clifford, W. K., *Lectures and Essays*, 43–4
Clough, Arthur Hugh, 41, 51, 56–7, 61, **65–70**, 75, *507*; *Amours de Voyage*, 65, 67, 69; *Bothie of Toper-na-Vuolich, The*, 70; *Correspondence of A. H. Clough, The*, 66; 'Dipsychus', 65, 68–70; 'Easter Day', 65–6; 'Epithalamium', 70; 'Latest Decalogue, The', 65, 70; '*Mari Magno* or Tales on Board', 69; 'Natura Naturans', 65, 70; 'Say not the struggle . . .', 65
Cobbe, Frances Power, 220–21
Cobbett, William, 28
Cockshut, A. O. J., 34; *Religious Controversies of the Nineteenth Century*, 34
Colby, Vineta, *Yesterdays Women*, 202, 204–5
Cole, G. D. H., 337
Cole, Sir Henry, *Home Treasury, The*, 288
Coleridge, Samuel Taylor, 2, 3, 10–11, 12–13, 53, 257, 465
Collins, Philip, 83
Collins, Wilkie, 107, 132, 249, **262–9**, 319, 451, *521*; *Armadale*, 264–5; *Black Robe, The*, 249; *Frozen Deep,*

The, 267; *Heart and Science*, 268; *Hide and Seek*, 264; *Law and the Lady, The*, 264; *Man and Wife*, 267–8; *Moonstone, The*,107; *New Magdalen, The*, 267; *No Name*, 265; *Woman in White, The*, 262–4, 266
Comte, Auguste, 45, 46, 315, 328
Congreve, William, 315
Conrad, Joseph, 139–40, 354, 355, 357; *Nostromo*, 357
Corkran, Alice, *Down the Snow Stairs*, 288
Cornhill Magazine, The, 23, 116, 159, 314, 320
Cox, R. G., 204
Crabbe, George, 69, 384
Crackanthorpe, Hubert, 480
Crashaw, Richard, 479

Dante, Alighieri, 364, 435, 436, 437, 439, 444; *Vita Nuova*, 437
D'Arcy, Ella, 480
Darwin, Charles, vii, 10, **18–22**, 308; *Descent of Man*, 19; *Origin of Species*, 19, 386
Davidson, John, 471, **477–8**, 481; 'Northern Suburb, A', 478; 'Thirty Bob a Week', 477
Davies, Hugh Sykes, 143
de Beauvoir, Simone, *Second Sex, The*, 230
Defoe, Daniel, 88, 188; *Robinson Crusoe*, 88
Dickens, Catherine, 85, 86, 105
Dickens, Charles, 1–2, 13–15, 28, 29, 31, 32, 51, 76, **81–110**, 112, 115, 116–18, 120, 121, 133, 143, 173, 174, 177, 180, 191, 193, 195, 238, 243–4, 247, 251, 261, 262, 263, 264, 266–7, 273, 288, 314, 325, 326, 330, 332–3, 483, *508–9*; Novels listed in chronological order, 83; *All The Year Round*, 284; *American Notes*, 91; *Barnaby Rudge*, 2, 15, 90–91, 104; *Bleak House*, 84–5, 87, 94, 98, 100–106, 109, 195, 261; *Christmas Carol, A*, 85, 300; *David Copperfield*, 83, 95, 99–100, 106, 121; *Dombey and Son*, 94–9, 100, 103, 105, 106, 109, 116; *Edwin Drood*, 81–2, 105, 107, 110; *Great Expectations*, 83, 95, 99–100, 104, 106–7, 270, 279, 284; *Hard Times*, 1, 13, 15, 95, 104–5; *Little Dorrit*, 30, 81, 84, 94–5, 100–101, 103–4, 105–6, 109; *Martin Chuzzlewit*, 91–3, 95, 96, 100, 251, 264; *Nicholas Nickleby*, 85, 89–90, 93, 102, 118, 243, 251, 483; *Old Curiosity*

Shop, The, 85, 90–91, 94; *Oliver Twist*, 84–5, 89–90, 93–4, 96, 102, 243, 251; *Our Mutual Friend*, 81, 84, 86, 94, 100, 105, 107–10, 118, 195; *Pickwick Papers*, 87–90, 91–2, 93; *Sketches by Boz*, 83, 87; *Tale of Two Cities, A*, 15, 91, 95, 104–5

Disraeli, Benjamin, 1, 8, 15, 27, 36, 117, **239–52**, 253, 273, 363, *520*; *Alroy*, 241; *Coningsby*, 15, 239, 243, 244–6, 251, 255; *Contarini Fleming*, 241, 248; *Endymion*, 239, 251; *Henrietta Temple*, 241; *Lothair*, 239, 248–9, 251; *Revolutionary Epic*, 241; *Sybil*, 1, 15, 28, 243, 246–7, 249, 251, 252, 267; *Tancred*, 239, 248; *Venetia*, 241; *Vindication of the English Constitution, A*, 242; *Vivian Grey*, 240–42, 248; *Young Duke, The*, 241–2

D'Israeli, Isaac, 239

Dixon, Richard Watson, 421, 422, 452, **455–7**, *539*; *Christ's Company*, 455; *Historical Odes*, 456; *History of the Church of England*, 456; *Lyrical Poems*, 456; *Mano*, 456; *Odes and Eclogues*, 456; *S. John in Patmos*, 455; 'Advancing Age', 456; 'Conflicting Claims', 456; 'Despair', 455; 'Dream', 455; 'Fall of the Leaf, The', 456; 'Holy Mother at the Cross, The,' 455; 'Inscience', 456; 'Ode on Departing Youth', 456; 'St. John', 455; 'Spirit Wooed, The', 456; 'Soul's World, The', 455; 'To Summer', 456; 'Winter Will Follow', 456; 'Wizard's Funeral, The', 455

Dodgson, Charles Lutwidge, *see* Carroll, Lewis

Don Quixote, 88

Donne, John, 21

Dowson, Ernest, 386, **471–5**

Dryden, John, 21, 54, 79, 384

du Maurier, George, 231

Dublin Review, 36

Dublin University Magazine, 277, 282, 283

Dubourg, A. W., 492

Dürer, Albrecht, 462; 'Melencolia', 462

Edgeworth, Maria, *Absentee, The*, 202; *Castle Rackrent*, 201–2, 282

Edinburgh Review, 203

Egerton, George, *Discords*, 231–2; *Keynotes*, 231–2

Eliot, George, 25, 27, 29, 31, 33, 46, 47, 48, 55, 173, 175, 177, 180, **185–97**, 202, 203, 216, 219, 261, 263, 268, 273, 232, 331, *515–16*; *Adam Bede*, 185–6, 188, 189, 197, 208, 216–18, 220, 263; *Amos Barton*, 28, 189; *Daniel Deronda*, 26, 194–7, 217, 224; *Felix Holt*, 25, 32, 186, 189, 192, 194–7, 225, 226; *Middlemarch*, 32, 194–6, 202, 217, 222, 224, 234, 285; *Mill on the Floss The*, 45, 191–3, 218; *Romola*, 188–9, 194–5; *Scenes of Clerical Life*, 177, 185, 188, 189, 191, 214; *Silas Marner*, 185, 194; 'Silly Novels by Lady Novelists', 216

Eliot, T. S., 51, 53–4, 63, 78, 372, 471–2, 474, 477, 481

Ellis, Mrs., 200, 234

Englishman's Magazine, The, 364

Erckmann-Chatrian, 484

Essays and Reviews, 20, 42, 46, 337

Essays of George Eliot, 225–6

Evans, Marian, *see* Eliot, George

Evening Chronicle, The, 87

Evidence for the Resurrection, The, 338

Examiner, 203

Faber, F. W., 8, 39

Farrow, George Edward, *Little Panjandrum's Dodo, The*, 299; *Wallypug of Why, The*, 299

Faulkner, William, 362

Ferrier, Susan, 202

Fielding, Henry, 82, 88, 111, 117, 118, 120; *Jonathan Wild*, 118

Fielding, K. J., 91

Fielding, Sarah, *Governess, The*, 288

FitzGerald, Edward, 90, **380–86**, *533*; *Agamemnon*, 384; *Bird Parliament, The*, 384–6; *Euphranor: A Dialogue on Youth*, 383; Oedipus plays, 384; *Polonius: a Collection of Wise Saws and Modern Instances*, 383; *Rubáiyát of Omar Khayyám*, 380–81, 384–6; *Salámán and Absál, An Allegory, Translated from the Persian of Jámí*, 384; *Six Dramas of Calderon Freely Translated*, 381, 384; 'Dream of Fair Women, A', 382; 'Euphranor', 381

Foote, Samuel, 290

Forster, E. M., 269, 310, 314–15, 341

Forster, John, 82–5, 87, 92–3, 96, 99

Fortnightly Review, 231

Foster, Shirley, 221

Fowler, W., 414

Fox, C. J., 16

Fox, W. J., 366, 370, 387, 391, 393
Fraser's Magazine, 5, 220, 252, 254, 259, 272, 386
Froude, Hurrell, 36; *Remains*, 35
Froude, James Anthony, vii, 6, 14, 17–18, 241, 456, 459; *Carlyle's Life in London*, vii; *Earl of Beaconsfield, The*, 241; *Thomas Carlyle*, 6

Gaskell, Mrs Elizabeth, viii, 1, 84, 87, 145, 150, 151, **173–85**, 186, 188–91, 193, 202, 215–16, 246–7, 225–6, 376, *515*; *Cousin Phillis*, 174, 183; *Cranford*, 87, 173, 178, 182–3, 185; *Letters*, 175–6; Life of Charlotte Brontë, 145, 174, 185; *Mary Barton*, 174–81, 184, 185, 214, 220; *North and South*, 26, 84, 173, 179–81, 184, 202, 209, 215; *Ruth*, 178–81, 184, 185, 208–9, 217, 219, 220; *Sylvia's Lovers*, 183–5, 225–6, 376; *Wives and Daughters*, 173, 183–4
Gibbon, Edward, 47
Gilbert, W. S., 463, 485, *488–90*; *Broken Hearts*, 488; *Dan'l Druce the Blacksmith*, 488; *H.M.S. Pinafore*, 489; *Mikado, The*, 489; *Palace of Truth, The*, 488; *Patience*, 485, 489; *Pygmalion and Galatea*, 488; *Sweethearts*, 488
Gil Blas, 88
Gissing, George, 177, **326–35**, 478, 480, *528–9*; *Born in Exile*, 331–2, 334–5; *By the Ionian Sea*, 333; *Charles Dickens: A Critical Study*, 326–7, 332; *Crown of Life, The*, 333; *Demos*, 329; *Emancipated, The*, 330, 332; *In the Year of Jubilee*, 332; *Isabel Clarendon*, 329; *Life's Morning, A*, 329; *Mummer's Wife, A*, 326; *Nether World, The*, 330; *New Grub Street*, 327, 328, 331, 333, 480; *Odd Women, The*, 231, 332; *Our Friend the Charlatan*, 333; *Private Papers of Henry Ryecroft, The*, 333; *Thyrza*, 329; *Town Traveller, The*, 333; *Unclassed The*, 328–9; *Whirlpool, The*, 332; *Workers in the Dawn*, 327, 329; *Veranilda*, 333
Gautier, Theophile, 458
Gladstone, W. E., 15, 20, 24, 80, 374
Godwin, William, *Caleb Williams*, 271
Goethe, Wolfgang von, 3, 58, 61, 68
Gosse, Edmund, 256, 260
Gosse, Philip, 48, 256; *Father and Son*, 48
Grahame, Kenneth, 298; *Dream Days*, 287; *Golden Age, The*, 287

Grand, Sarah, *Heavenly Twins, The*, 231
Gray, John, 474, **478–9**; *Park: A Fantastic Story*, 478; *Silverpoints*, 478
Gray, Thomas, 79
Green, Roger Lancelyn, *Tellers of Tales*, 294
Greene, Graham, 347; *Quiet American, The*, 65
Grein, J. T., 494
Grey, W. R., 219

Haight, G., *George Eliot, A Biography*, 31
Hallam, Arthur Henry, 363–6, 371–2, 465
Hallam, Henry, 15–16
Halevy, J., 194
Hardy, Thomas, ix, 20, 45, 47, 49, 183, 184, 202, 307, 313, **317–26**, 329, 351, 352, 361, 480, *526–8*; *Desperate Remedies*, 319; *Dynasts, The*, 322, 325; *Far from the Madding Crowd*, 318, 320, 322–3; *Hand of Ethelberta, The*, 321; *Jude the Obscure*, 323–6, 329, 480; *Laodicean, A.*, 322; *Mayor of Casterbridge, The*, 322; *Pair of Blue Eyes, A*, 320; *Oxen, The*, 49; *Poor Man and the Lady, The*, 319; *Return of the Native, The*, 47, 321–3; *Tess of the d'Urbervilles*, 178, 183, 228, 323–5, 329, 480; *Trumpet Major, The*, 322; *Two on a Tower*, 322; *Under the Greenwood Tree*, 319, 322; *Wessex Poems*, 325; *Woodlanders, The*, 323–4; 'Ancient to Ancients, An', 361
Hare, Augustus, 31, 33; *Story of My Life*, 30
Harkness, Margaret, *A City Girl: A Realistic Story*, 228–9
Harrison, Frederic, 253, 261, 327, 328
Hartman, E. von, 318
Hawker, Robert Stephen, 450–52, 456–7, *538*; *Cornish Ballads and Other Poems*, 450; *Footsteps of Former Men in Far Cornwall*, 451; *Quest of the Sangraal, The*, 452, 456; *Tendrils*, 450; 'Aishah-Schechinah' ('Woman Numinous, The'), 451; 'Doom Well of St Madron, The', 451; 'Featherstone's Doom', 451; 'Morwenna Statio', 451; 'Rapture on the Cornish Hills, A', 451; 'St Nectan's Kieve', 451; 'Saintly Names, The', 451; 'Sisters of Glen Nectan, The', 451; 'Song of the Western Men, The', 450; 'Vine, The', 451
Hemingway, Ernest, 194

Henley, W.E., **479–80**;
'Apparition', 346; 'In Hospital', 479;
'Invictus', 479; 'London
Voluntaries', 479
*History of Sixteen Wonderful Old Women,
The*, 292
Hoffmann, E. T. A., *Nutcracker,
The*, 303
Hogarth, Mary, 85
Homer, 57, 78, 364
Hopkins, Gerard Manley, 11, 38, 256,
379, **413–33**, 456–7, *535–6*; *Floris in
Italy*, 416; *Journals and
Papers*, 414–15, 417, 419, 423–5,
431; *Letters*, 414–15, 417, 418,
421–3, 430, 432, 456; *Poems*, 414,
416, 418–19, 424–30, 432;
Richard, 416; *Sermons and Devotional
Writings*, 414, 428; 'Ad
Mariam', 417; 'Ashboughs', 426;
'At the Wedding March,' 427;
'Binsey Poplars', 413, 427; 'Bugler's
First Communion, The', 428;
'Caged Skylark, The', 426; 'Carrion
Comfort', 432; 'Duns Scotus's
Oxford', 415; 'Epithalamion', 415;
'Felix Randal', 427; 'God's
Grandeur', 413, 423, 427; 'Habit of
Perfection, The', 416–17; 'Halfway
House, The,' 416; 'Harry
Ploughman', 430; 'Heaven-
Haven', 416; 'Hurrahing in
Harvest', 425, 426;
'Inversnaid', 415, 424, 427; 'Leaden
Echo and the Golden Echo,
The', 413; 'Loss of the Eurydice,
The,' 421; 'May Magnificat', 421;
'My own heart', 429;
'Nondum', 416, 418; 'Pied
Beauty', 413; 'Rosa Mystica', 417;
'Shepherd's brow, The', 432; 'Spelt
from Sibyl's Leaves', 430, 432;
'Spring and Fall: To a Young
Child', 427; 'Starlight Night,
The', 427; 'That Nature is a
Heraclitean Fire', 430, 432; 'To
seem the stranger', 416, 422; 'Tom's
Garland', 430; 'Windhover,
The', 413, 426; 'Wreck of the
Deutschland, The', 413, 418–20,
422–3, 431–2
Hopkins Soceity, 433
Horne, R. H., 490
Houghton, W. E., vii–viii
House, Humphry, 94, 104
Household Words, 84, 104, 288
Housman, A. E., 47, 480
Howard, Daniel F., 341

Hügel von, *Reality of God, The*, 42
Hughes, Arthur, 436
Hughes, Thomas, 257; *Tom Brown's
Schooldays*, 41
Hume, David, 16
Hunt, Holman, 414, 435–6, 439
Huxley, T. H., 10, 20, 44; *Evolution and
Ethics*, 44
Huysman, J. K., 463, 469

Ibsen, Henrik, 231, 464, 484, 493–4
International Hopkins Association, 433
Irving, Henry, 484, 490
Isherwood, Christopher, 361

Jackson, Holbrook, 464, 480
James, G. P. R., 117
James, Henry, 82, 108, 134, 140, 142,
143–4, 156, 157, 182, 183, 190, 202,
231, 268, 317, 324, 326, 329, 344,
345, 346, 347, 358, 412, 480;
Awkward Age, The, 480; *Portrait of a
Lady, The*, 231; *Princess Casamassima,
The*, 329; *Private Life, The*, 412;
Spoils of Poynton, 480; *Art of Fiction,
The*, 344
Jameson, Mrs, *Characteristics of
Women*, 210
Johnson, Edgar, 85, 86, 101, 107
Johnson, Lionel, 471, **474–6**, 478; 'By
the Statue of King Charles at
Charing Cross', 475; 'Dark Angel,
The', 475
Johnson, Samuel, 2, 54, 124, 383, 431
Jones, Henry Arthur, 490, **493**; *Case of
Rebellious Susan, The*, 493; *Liars,
The*, 493; *Mrs Dane's Defence*, 493;
Silver King, The, 493
Jones, Owen, 454
Jonson, Ben, 119, 120
Jowett, Benjamin, 20, 42
Joyce, James, 341, 342, 362, 465, 481

Kavanagh, Julia, *Rachel Gray*, 213–14
Kean, Charles, 484–5
Keary, Eliza, 287
Keats, John, 1, 22, 61, 62, 64, 79, 357,
364, 382, 393, 394, 435, 436, 460,
465; *Eve of St Agnes, The*, 392
Keble, John, 8, 33, 35, 37, 38
Kelvin, Lord, 19
Kempis, Thomas à, 192
Kennedy, W. D., 441
Kestner, Joseph, *Protest and
Reform*, 209
Kierkegaard, Sören, 379
Kingsley, Charles, 8, 247, **252–62**,
520–21; *Alton Locke*, 255–6, 258–60,

261, 267; *Cheap Clothes and Nasty*, 259; *Glaucus, or the Wonders of the Sea Shore*, 256; *Hereward The Wake*, 255; *Hypatia*, 260; *Two Years Ago*, 256, 260–61; *Water Babies, The*, 260, 300, 301–2; *Westward Ho!*, 256, 260; *Yeast*, 252–3, 254–6, 258, 260, 261, 267

Kipling, Rudyard, 113, 335, **352–60**, 480, *531*; *Barrack-Room Ballads*, 480; *Day's Work, The*, 354, 357; *Jungle Book, The*, 357, 358; *Just So Stories*, 352; *Kim*, 352, 359, 360; *Plain Tales from the Hills*, 354; *Second Junge Book, The*, 357; *Stalky & Co.*, 353, 357, 358; 'Beyond the Pale', 355; 'Bridge-Builders, The', 356, 357; 'Brushwood Boy', 355; 'Cupid's Arrows', 355; 'Drums of Fore and Aft, The', 355; 'Flag of their Country', 357; 'Head of the District, The', 356; 'Heart of Darkness', 358; 'In the House of Suddhoo', 356; 'Lispeth', 355, 356; 'Man Who Would be King, The', 356; 'Phantom Rickshaw, A', 354; 'Strange Ride, A', 354; 'Wee Willie Winkie', 356

Knatchbull-Hugessen, Edward, first Lord Brabourne, 289

Koestler, Arthur, 249

Laforgue, Jules, 470

Lamb, Anne Richelieu, *Can Women Regenerate Society?*, 210

Lang, Andrew, 423; *Gold of Fairnilee, The*, 306; *Prince Priglo*, 306; *Prince Ricardo of Pantouflia*, 306

Lawrence, D. H., 42, 175, 341, 342

Le Fanu, Joseph Sheridan, **277–81**, *523*; *All in the Dark*, 281; *Cock and Anchor, The*, 277; *Fortunes of Torlogh O'Brien, The*, 277; *Haunted Lives*, 281; *House by the Churchyard, The*, 278; *Rose and the Key, The*, 281; *Tennants of Malory, The*, 281; *Uncle Silas*, 278–81; *Wylder's Hand*, 281–2; *Wyvern Mystery, The*, 281

Le Gallienne, Richard, **476–7**; 'Ballad of London, A', 476–7

Lear, Edward, 289, 290, **291–4**, 295, 298; *Book of Nonsense*, 291–2; *Field of Nonsense, The*, 292; *Laughing Lyrics*, 293; *Nonsense Songs and Stories*, 294; *Nonsense Songs, Stories, Botany and Alphabets*, 293; 'Courtship of the Yonghy-Bonghy-Bo, The', 294; 'Daddy Long-Legs and the Fly, The', 293; 'Jumblies, The', 293; 'Owl and the Pussy-Cat, The', 293; 'Pelican Chorus, The', 294; 'They', 293

Leavis, F. R., 61–2, 104, 145, 151, 191

Leavis, Q. D., 235–6

Lever, Charles, 117, **281–5**, *523*; *A Day's Ride; A Life's Romance*, 284; *Arthur O'Leary*, 281; *Charles O'Malley*, 281; *Daltons, The*, 284; *Davenport Dunn*, 284; *Dodd Family Abroad, The*, 284; *Fortunes of Glencore, The*, 284; *Harry Lorrequer*, 281, 282; *Jack Hinton, the Guardsman*, 281; *Knight of Gwynn, The*, 283; *Lord Kilgobbin*, 284–5; *Martins of Cro'Martin, The*, 284; *Roland Cashel*, 283; *St Patrick's Eve*, 283; *Sir Brooke Fossbrooke*, 284; *Tom Burke of 'Ours'*, 281; *Tony Butler*, 284

Lewes, G. H., 151, 187, 193, 200, 260

Lewis, C. S., 302, 303

Liddell, Henry George, 295

Linton, Eliza Lynn, 231, 233

London Figaro, 494

Lowe, Robert, vii

Lowell, Robert, 385

Ludlow, John, 258

Lyell, Sir Charles, 18, 20; *Antiquity of Man, The*, 20; *Principles of Geology*, 18

Lytton, Edward Bulwer, 117, 118, 241, 243, **269–77**, *522–3*; *Alice*, 272; *Caxtons, The*, 273–4; *Coming Race, The*, 270, 277; *Deveraux*, 272; *Disowned, The*, 272; *England and the English*, 118; *Ernest Maltravers*, 272; *Eugene Aram*, 117, 118, 243, 270, 272; *Falkland*, 270, 271–2, 275; *Godolphin*, 272, 275; *Harold*, 270, 273, 277; *Kenelm Chillingly*, 277; *Last Days of Pompeii, The*, 270, 272, 277; *Last of the Barons, The*, 270, 273, 274, 275, 277; *My Novel*, 270, 273–5; *Parisians, The*, 277; *Paul Clifford*, 117, 243, 270, 272; *Pelham*, 117, 241, 270, 271, 272; *Pilgrims of the Rhine*, 270; *Rienzi*, 270, 272; *Strange Story, A*, 270, 273, 275–7; *What Will He Do With It?*, 273; *Zanoni*, 270, 275

Lytton, Strachey, G., 47

Macaulay, Thomas, Lord, 14, **15–18**, 20, 29, 44, 105; *History*, 15–17

MacDonald, George, **302–6**; *At the Back of the North Wind*, 304, 305; *Dealings with the Fairies*, 305;

Lilith, 303, 304, 305;
Phantastes, 303, 304; *Princess and Curdie, The*, 304–5; *Princess and the Goblin, The*, 303, 304; *Wise Woman, The*, 289
Machen, Arthur, 484
Macmillan's Magazine, 443–4
Mallarmé, Stéphane, 470
Malory, Sir Thomas, 376, 435, 453
Manning, Henry Edward, 27, 39–40
Marcet, Mrs, 202
Maria Marten, 484
Marryat, Frederick, *Phantom Ship, The*, 351
Marston, J. W., 490
Martin, John, 437
Martineau, Harriet, 151, 200, 201, **204–6**, 207, 237; *Autobiography I*, 200, 204, 205; *Autobiography II*, 201; *Deerbrook*, 204–6, 237; *Illustrations of Political Economy*, 204, 206, 207; *Ireland*, 204; *Life in the Wilds*, 204; *Manchester Strike, A*, 204
Marx, Eleanor, 229, 330
Maugham, William Somerset, 341
Maupassant, Guy de, 480
Maurice, Frederic Denison, **257–8**; *Christian Socialism*, 258; *Theological Essays*, 257
Mayhew, Henry, 259
Mazzini, Joseph, 458
Meredith, George, 45, 263, **308–17**, 318–19, 325–6, 328, 330, 337, *526*; *Adventures of Harry Richmond, The*, 314; *Amazing Marriage, The*, 316; *Beauchamp's Career*, 313, 314; *Diana of the Crossways*, 316; *Egoist, The*, 311, 313, 315–17; *Essay on Comedy, An*, 309, 315; *Evan Harrington*, 310, 312–13; *Farina*, 311; *Lord Ormont and His Aminta*, 308, 316; *Modern Love*, 311; *One of Our Conquerors*, 316; *Ordeal of Richard Feverel, The*, 263, 312, 326; *Poems and Lyrics of the Joy of Earth*, 308; *Rhoda Fleming*, 313–14; *Sandra Belloni (Emilia in England)*, 314; *Shaving of Shagpat, The*, 311; *Tragic Comedians, The*, 316; *Vittoria*, 314; 'Dirge in Woods', 308; 'Faith on Trial, A', 308; 'Woods of Westermain, The', 308
Meynell, Alice, 480
Mill, James, **10–11**, 200, 201; *History of India*, 11
Mill, John Stuart, 1, 2, 6, **10–13**, 24, 55, 73, 214, 220, 221, 256, 318, 365,

418; *Autobiography*, 11, 27; *Logic*, 10; *On Liberty*, 11, 73; *Principles of Political Economy*, 13; *Thoughts on Poetry*, 12; *Three Essays on Religion*, 418; *Utilitarianism*, 12
Millais, J. E., 435–6, 439
Milton, John, 426, 441
Mitchell, Hannah, *Hard Way Up, The*, 229
Molesworth, Mrs, *Cuckoo Clock The*, 288
Molière, 315
Monthly Magazine, The, 87
Monthly Repository, 204, 391–2, 393, 399
Moore, George, 326, 329, 480; *Esther Waters*, 229, 330, 480; *Literature at Nurse*, 329
More, Hannah, 202
Morgan, Lady, 282; *Woman and her Master*, 210
Morris, William, 261, 438, **452–5**, 457, 460, 469, *539*; *Commonweal, The*, 455; *Defence of Guenevere, The*, 453, 457; *Dream of John Ball, A*, 452; *Earthly Paradise, The*, 454, 457; *Hopes and Fears for Art*, 455; *Laxdaela Saga*, 454; *Life and Death of Jason, The*, 454; *Love is Enough*, 454; *News from Nowhere*, 340, 455; *Pilgrims of Hope, The*, 454; *Signs of Change*, 455; *Story of Sigurd, The*, 454; 'Atalanta's Race', 457; 'Concerning Geffray Teste Noire', 453; 'Defence of Guenevere, The,' 453; 'Haystack in the Floods, The', 453–4; 'Hill of Venus, The', 454; 'Judgment of God, The', 453; 'Sir Galahad, a Christmas Mystery', 453; 'Sir Peter Harpdon's End', 453; 'Welland River', 453
Mulock, Dinah Maria, *John Halifax, Gentleman*, 218–19; *Little Lame Princess, The*, 305

Nation, The, 283
National Reformer, The, 460
New Sporting Magazine The, 87, 111
New York Tribune, 210
Newman, John Henry, Cardinal, viii, 1, 2–3, **6–10**, 19, 27, 33, 36, 37, 38, 39–40, 55, 67, 77, 416, 420, 446; *Apologia Pro Vita Sua*, 7–9, 34, 67, 416, 446; *Development of Christian Doctrine, The*, 9; *Grammar of Assent, The*, 9; *Idea of a University, The*, 9; *Present Position of Catholics, The*, 38; *Tracts for the Times*, 3, 7, 34

Newton, Judith Lowder, *Women, Power and Subversion*, 203
Nietzsche, Frederick, 20, 373, 477
Nineteenth Century, 233, 355
Noble, Andrew, *Robert Louis Stevenson*, 350, 351
Nordau, Max, 464
Norton, Charles Eliot, 358

O'Casey, Sean, 486
Oliphant, Margaret, 200, 202–3, 220–23, 235–6, 243, 262, 263; *Hester*, 236–7; *Miss Marjorie Banks*, 222, 236
Orwell, George, 249, 334, 353; *1984*, 249
Osborne, Sidney Godolphin, 253
Oxford and Cambridge Magazine, The, 452, 455

Paget, Frances, *Hope of the Katzekopfs, The*, 288, 300
Palgrave, Francis Turner, 450
Pall Mall Gazette, 230
Palmerston, Viscount John Henry Temple, 27
Pankhurst, Christabel, *Great Scourge, The*, 231
Pater, Walter, 9, 326, 386, **465–9**, 470–71, 474–5, 481; *Marius the Epicurean*, 47, 465, 468–9, 474; *Renaissance, The*, 9, 465–8
Patmore, Coventry, 39, 69, 413, 435, **445–8**, 452, *538*; *Angel in the House, The*, 445–7; *Poems (1844)*, 445; *Victories of Love, The*, 446; *Unknown Eros, The*, 446; 'Azalea, The', 447; 'Child's Purchase, The', 447; 'De Natura Deorum', 446; 'Deliciae Sapientiae de Amore', 447; 'Departure', 447; '1867', 447; 'Eros and Psyche', 446; 'Pain', 446; 'Psyche's Discontent', 446; 'Seasons, The', 445; 'Sponsa Dei', 447; 'Tired Memory', 447; 'Toys, The', 447; 'Wedding Sermon, The', 446; 'Wind and Wave', 446
Pattison, Mark, ix, 42
Peacock, T. L., 251, 310–11
Pepys, Emily, *Child's Own Book, The*, 287
Petrarch, Francesco, 437, 444
Pinero, Arthur Wing, 484, 486, 490, **492–3**, 495; *Dandy Dick*, 492; *Gay Lord Quex, The*, 492; *Second Mrs Tanqueray, The*, 495; *Times, The*, 492; *Trelawney of the 'Wells'*, 486, 492

Pioneer, 353
Planché, J. R., 488
Plato, 425
Plotinus, 379
Poe, E. A., 437
Pollard, Arthur, 174, 176, 181
Pope, Alexander, 78–9
Pound, Ezra, 362, 474
Pre-Raphaelite Brotherhood, 435–7, 445; *and see* Burne-Jones, Edward, Morris, William, and Rossetti, D. G.
Pritchett, V. S., *Working Novelist The*, 115
Pugin, Augustus, 22, 28, 454
Punch, 116, 231
Pusey, Edward Bouverie, 36, 37

Quarterly Review, 203

Raspe, Rudolf Erich, *Baron Munchausen*, 290–91
Reade, Charles, 262, **265–9**, *521–2*; *Cloister and the Hearth, The*, 266; *Foul Play*, 266; *Free Labour*, 267; *Gold*, 267; *Griffin Gaunt*, 265; *Hard Cash*, 266–7; *It Is Never Too Late to Mend*, 262–3, 266–8; *Masks and Faces*, 267; *Peg Woffington*, 267; *Put Yourself in His Place*, 266–7; *White Lies*, 268
Reid, Mrs Hugo, *Plea for Women, A.*, 210
Rhymers' Club, The, 471–81
Richardson, Dorothy, 232
Richardson, Samuel, 82
Rimbaud, Arthur, 470
Robertson, T. W., **486–8**, 492; *Caste*, 487–8; *David Garrick*, 486; *Play*, 488; *School*, 488; *Society*, 487; *War*, 488
Robinson, John, *In Extremity: A Study of Gerard Manley Hopkins*, 428
Rossetti, Christina Georgina, 288, 313, 414, 435, **442–5**, 452, *538*; *Goblin Market*, 443; *New Poems*, 443; *Pageant, A.*, 443; *Poems*, 443; *Prince's Progress, The*, 443; *Sing-Song*, 443; *Speaking Likenesses*, 288; 'Convent Threshold, The', 443; 'Earth and Heaven', 445; 'End, An', 442–3; Heart knoweth its own bitterness, The', 444–5; 'Later Life', 444; 'Monna Innominata', 443–4; 'Noble Sisters', 444; 'Sister Maude', 444; 'Soeur Louise de la Miséricorde', 443; 'Three Enemies, The', 443; 'Up-Hill', 444; 'World, The', 444

Rossetti, Dante Gabriel, 22, 313, 385, 414, 435, **436–42**, 446, 452–3, 454, 457, 462, 465, *538*; *Ballads and Sonnets*, 436; *Early Italian Poets, The (Dante and his Circle)*, 437; *Letters*, 438; *Poems* (1870), 436, 440; *Songs of the Art Catholic*, 438; 'Blessed Damozel, The', 437, 438, 440; 'Bride's Prelude, The', 436; 'Burden of Nineveh, The', 437; 'Eden Bower', 441; 'Hand and Soul', 437, 462; 'Heart's Hope', 439; 'House of Life, The', 439, 440; 'Jenny', 436–7; 'Kiss, The'; 439; 'Last Confession, A', 437; 'Lost Days', 440; 'Love's Nocturn', 441; 'Love's Redemption' (rev. 'Love's Testament'), 439; 'On Refusal of Aid between Nations', 437; 'Orchard-Pit, The', 441–2; 'Pandora', 440; 'Secret Parting', 439; 'Silent Noon', 439; 'Sister Helen', 441; 'Sudden Light', 439; 'Troy Town', 441; 'Willowwood', 440; 'Woodspurge, The', 440
Rossetti, Maria, 442
Rossetti, W. M., 442
Ruskin, John, viii, 2, 13, 14, 21, **22–4**, 29, 31, 33, 42, 55, 215, 313, 385, 404, 415, 455; *King of the Golden River, The*, 300, 301; *Modern Painters*, 408, 415; *Munera Pulveris*, 23; *Praeterita*, 30; *Time and Tide*, 24; *Unto this Last*, 23, 313; 'Of Queen's Gardens', 215
Russell, Lord John, 16

Sadleir, M., 138, 140
Sainte-Beuve, C. K., 51, 63
Sand, George, 80
Savoy, The, 480
Schopenhauer, Arthur, 318, 331
Schreiner, Olive, 229; *Story of an African Farm, The*, 202, 230–31
Scott, Sir Walter, 124, 151, 159, 192, 319, 349
Scott, William Bell, 438
Scotus, Duns, 414–15
Seeley, Sir J. R., *Ecce Home*, 42
Sewell, Elizabeth, 292, 295, 300; *Experience of Life, The*, 213–14
Shakespeare, William, 57, 110, 151, 153, 319, 364, 370, 388, 431, 435
Shaw, George Bernard, ix, 107, 337, 341, 344, 464, 484, 486, 487, 492, **494–7**; *Arms and the Man*, 495–6; *Caesar and Cleopatra*, 497;

Candida, 496; *Captain Brassbound's Conversion*, 497; *Devil's Disciple, The*, 496–7; *Mrs Warren's Profession*, 494–5; *Philanderer, The*, 494; *Plays: Pleasant and Unpleasant*, 481; *Sanity of Art, The*, 464; *Widowers' Houses*, 494; *You Never Can Tell*, 496
Shelley, P. B., 1–2, 79, 241, 311, 364, 389, 394, 395, 460, 479
Showalter, Elaine, 218, 224, 230
Sinclair, May, 232, 341
Smalley, D., 134
Smith, Adam, 13
Smith, Alexander, 461; *City Poems*, 461
Smith, Barbara Leigh, 210–11, 212
Smith, Janet Adam, *James and Stevenson*, 347, 348
Smollett, Tobias, 82, 88, 111
Southey, Robert, 311
Spectator, The, 203, 458
Spencer, Herbert, 14, 318
Spencer, Jane, *Rise of the Women Novelists, The*, 201
Spenser, Edmund, 460; *Faerie Queen, The*, 303
Stanley, A. P., 20, 41
Stead, W. T., 230
Stephen, J. Fitzjames, 29, 121; *Liberty, Equality, Fraternity*, 46–7
Stephen, Leslie, 29, 252, 320–21
Sterne, Laurence, 117
Stevenson, L., 120
Stevenson, Robert Louis, 315, 317, 335, **344–52**, 480, *530*; *An Inland Voyage*, 347; *Catriona*, 348, 349, 350, 351; *Critical Heritage, The*, 344; *Dr Jekyll and Mr Hyde*, 350, 351; *Kidnapped*, 346, 347, 348, 349, 350, 351, 359; *Master of Ballantrae, The*, 350; *Travels with a Donkey*, 347; *Treasure Island*, 346, 347, 348; *Weir of Hermiston*, 350, 480; 'Gossip of Romance, A', 344; 'Humble Remonstrance, A', 344; 'Prospero of Samoa', 344
Stowe, Harriet Beecher, 264
Stubbs, Patricia, 230
Sully, James, 307
Surtees, Robert Smith, 87, **111–15**, *510*; *Ask Mamma*, 114; *Handley Cross*, 111; *Hawbuck Grange*, 113; *Hillingdon Hall*, 112; *Jorrocks' Jaunts and Jollities*, 110, 113; *Mr Facey Romford's Hounds*, 114; *Mr Sponge's Sporting Tour*, 113, 115; *Plain or Ringlets*, 114; *Young Tom Hall*, 111, 114

Swedenborg, Emanuel, *Heaven and Hell*, 278

Sweeney Todd, 484

Swift, Jonathan, 73, 117, 337, 460

Swinburne, Algernon Charles, 44, 65, 313, 320, 377, 379, 385, 386, 417, 420, 431, **457–60**, 465, 471, 472, *539*; *Atalanta in Calydon*, 320, 457, 459; *Bothwell*, 459; *Chastelard*, 457, 459; *Erechtheus*, 420, 431, 459; *Flogging Block, The*, 457; *Mary Stuart*, 459; *Notes on Poems and Reviews*, 458; *Poems and Ballads* (1866), 458–60; *Poems and Ballads, Second Series*, 459; *Queen Mother, The*, 457; *Rosamund*, 457; *Songs before Sunrise*, 458; *William Blake*, 458, 465; *Works*, 465; 'Anactoria', 458; 'Ave atque Vale', 459; 'Ballad of Life, A', 458; 'Christmas Antiphones', 459; 'Garden of Proserpine, The', 458; 'Genesis', 459; 'Hermaphroditus', 458; 'Hertha', 459; 'Hymn of Man, The', 43, 459; 'Hymn to Proserpine', 458; 'Ilicet', 460; 'Itylus', 460; 'Joyous Garde', 457; 'Lancelot', 457; 'Laus Veneris', 458; 'Leper, The', 458; 'Queen Yseult', 457

Symonds, J. A., 9, 351

Symons, Arthur, 463–5, **469–77**, 478–81; *London Nights*, 477; *Studies in Prose and Verse*, 469–70; *Symbolist Movement in Literature, The*, 463, 470; 'At Dieppe: After Sunset', 473; 'Intermezzo', 464; 'Leves Amores II', 473

Synge, J. M., 485–6

Taylor, Edgar, *German Popular Stories*, 288

Taylor, Harriet, 210–11, 212, 216

Taylor, Tom, 492; *New Men and Old Acres*, 492

Temple, Frederick, 20

Tennyson, Alfred, Lord, vii, ix, 15, 19, 21, 45, 49, 51–2, 63, 70, 110, 151, 260, **361–80**, 381–4, 386, 387, 429–31, 452, 465, 476, 490; *Akbar's Dream and Other Poems*, 379; *Ballads and Other Poems*, 378; *Beckett*, 378, 490; *Death of Oenone, The*, 379; *Demeter and Other Poems*, 379; *Harold*, 378; *Holy Grail and Other Poems, The*, 378; *Idylls of the King*, 362, 366, 376, 378–9, 382; *In Memoriam A. H. H.*, 19, 63, 364, 370–74, 379–80, 382, 418, 471, 476;

Locksley Hall Sixty Years After, etc., 378–9; *Maud*, 70, 260, 374–5, 378, 382, 435; *Poems* (1833), 363; *Poems* (1842), 363, 367; *Poems by Two Brothers*, 363; *Poems, Chiefly Lyrical*, 363; *Princess, The*, 200–201, 235, 370–71, 378; *Queen Mary*, 378; *Tiresias and Other Poems*, 378; 'Amphion', 370; 'Ancient Sage, The', 379, 386; 'Audley Court', 369; 'Aylmer's Field', 375; 'Balin and Balan', 378; 'Break, break, break', 370; 'Charge of the Heavy Brigade, The', 378; 'Charge of the Light Brigade, The', 361–2, 378; 'Come down, O maid', 371; 'Coming of Arthur, The', 376; 'Crossing the Bar', 380; 'Day Dream, The', 370; 'Dead Prophet, The', 380; 'Defence of Lucknow, The', 378; 'Demeter and Persephone', 379; 'Despair', 380; 'Dora', 370; 'Dream of Fair Women, A', 366; 'Enoch Arden', 375; 'Fatima', 365; 'Frater Ave atque Vale', 380; 'Gardener's Daughter, The', 367; 'Geraint and Enid', 376; 'Godiva', 370; 'Golden Year, The', 369; 'Guinevere', 376; 'Higher Pantheism, The', 379; 'Lady Clara Vere de Vere', 375; 'Lady Clare', 370; 'Lady of Shalott, The', 365, 367, 369, 376; 'Lancelot and Elaine', 376; 'Locksley Hall', 362, 369, 374; 'Locksley Hall Sixty Years After', 362, 380; 'Lord of Burleigh, The', 370; 'Lotos-Eaters, The', 368; 'Love thou thy land', 369; 'Lover's Tale, The', 363; 'Lucretius', 379, 429, 431; 'Mariana', 365, 367, 374; 'Maud', 362; 'May Queen, The', 367; 'Merlin and the Gleam', 362; 'Miller's Daughter, The', 367; 'Morte d'Arthur', 369, 376; 'Northern Farmer: New Style', 382; 'Now sleeps the crimson petal', 371; 'O, that 'twere possible', 374; 'Ode on the Death of the Duke of Wellington', 374; 'Ode to Memory', 366; 'Oenone', 366; 'Of old sat Freedom on the heights', 369; 'Palace of Art, The', 366–7, 369, 373; 'Parnassus', 380; 'Passing of Arthur, The', 376; 'Poet, The', 366, 370; 'Poets and Critics', 361; 'Poets and their Bibliographies', 363; 'Poet's

Mind, The', 365; 'Recollections of the Arabian Nights', 366; 'Revenge, The', 378; 'Riflemen, form', 378; 'Rizpah', 380; 'Romney's Remorse', 380; 'St Simeon Stylites', 378; 'St Telemachus', 380; 'Sea Dreams', 374; 'Sea-Fairies, The', 365; 'Sir Galahad', 369; 'Sir Launcelot and Queen Guinevere', 369; 'Song: A Spirit Haunts the Year's Last Hours', 365; 'Supposed Confessions of a Second-rate Sensitive Mind', 367; 'Talking Oak, The', 370; 'Tears, idle tears', 370–71; 'Tiresias', 379, 380–81, 384; 'Tithonus', 368, 370; 'To E. FitzGerald', 380; 'To Vergil', 380; 'To—, after reading a Life and Letters', 380; 'Two Voices, The', 367–8; 'Ulysses', 361, 368–70; 'Vastness', 379; 'Vision of Sin, The', 370; 'Walking to the Mail', 370; 'Will Waterproof's Lyrical Monologue', 370; 'You ask me why, tho' ill at ease', 369
Ternan, Ellen, 104
Thackeray, William Makepeace, 23, 31, 32, 38, 82, 115–31, 134, 137, 139, 151, 173, 174, 180, 191, 239, 243, 244, 283, 383, 484, 510–11; Book of Snobs, The, 116; Catherine, 116–18, 243; Dennis Duval, 116; English Humourists of the Eighteenth Century, The, 116–17, 122; Four Georges, The, 117; Great Hoggarty Diamond, The, 116; Henry Esmond, 116–17, 124–8; Irish Sketch-Book, 282; Letters, ed. G. N. Ray, 130; Lovel the Widower, 116; Luck of Barry Lyndon, The, rev as Memoirs of Barry Lyndon, The, 116–18, 127, 131; Newcomes, The, 116, 122–3, 126, 128–31; Pendennis, 116, 121–2, 126–30; Philip, 116; Rose and the Ring, The, 300, 306; Roundabout Papers, 116, 128; Vanity Fair, 114, 116, 118–21, 126–7, 130, 137, 180, 195, 224, 244; Virginians, The, 116–17, 121–2, 124, 126–8; Yellowplush Papers, 116; 'Codlingsby', 239; 'Novels by Eminent Hands', 117; 'Phil Fogarty, a Tale of the Fighting Onety-Oneth', 117
Thompson, Francis, 479; 'Hound of Heaven', 479; 'In No Strange Land', 479
Thompson, William, Appeal, 200
Thomson, James, (1700–48), 162

Thomson, James, (B.V.), 307, 460–62, 540; 'Christmas Eve in the Upper Circles', 460; 'City of Dreadful Night, The', 43, 307, 461–2; 'Doom of a City, The', 461–2; 'In the Room', 461; 'Insomnia', 462; 'Lord of the Castle of Indolence, The', 460; 'Proposals for the Speedy Extinction of Evil and Misery', 460; 'Story of a Famous Old Firm, The, 460; 'Sunday at Hampstead', 460; 'Sunday up the River', 461
Tillotson, G. (and Hawes, G.), 126–7, 128
Tillotson, Kathleen, 84, 99, 173; see also under Butt, J.
Times, The, 26, 352
Tolstoy, Leo, 195, 333
Tonna, Charlotte Elizabeth, 206–8, 214, 227, 244; Helen Fleetwood, 206, 208, 209, 220; Wrongs of Woman, The, 207
Tractarians, vii, 54, 66, 133, 415, 451, 452, 455; see also under Newman
Trilling, Lionel, 72, 139
Trollope, Anthony, 2, 31, 82, 113, 114, 115, 131–44, 244, 251, 263, 269, 273, 488, 511–12; Autobiography, 131–2, 136, 138–40, 142–4, 269; Barchester Towers, 132–3, 142–3; Belton Estate, The, 135; Can You Forgive Her?, 132, 135, 142; Castle Richmond, 132, 284; Claverings, The, 133, 135–6; Doctor Thorne, 132, 134, 136; Duke's Children, The, 132, 137–8, 142; Eustace Diamonds, The, 132, 136, 140; Framley Parsonage, 132, 139, 143; Kellys and the O'Kellys, The, 131; Lady Anne, 136; Landleaguers, The, 132; Last Chronicle of Barset, The, 132, 136–8; Macdermots of Ballycloran, The, 131; Orley Farm, 133, 136, 141–3; Phineas Finn, 132, 138; Phineas Redux, 132, 138, 143; Prime Minister, The, 132, 135, 137–8, 142; Ralph the Heir, 26, 132, 138; Small House at Allington, The, 131–2, 135, 142; Thackeray, 143; Three Clerks, The, 131, 143; Warden, The, 132–3, 139, 263; Way We Live Now, The, 133, 137
Trollope, Frances, 208–9, 214, 244; Jessie Phillips, 208–9; Michael

Vathek, 311
Verlaine, Paul, 471–2
Vizetelly, Henry, 329
Voltaire, 47

Walpole, Horace, *Hieroglyphic Tales*, 290
Ward, Bernard, *Eve of Catholic Emancipation*, 39
Ward, Robert Plumer, 241
Ward, W. G., 38, 67; *British Critic, The*, 38
Warren, Samuel, *Ten Thousand A Year*, 275
Watts, Isaac, *Divine and Moral Songs*, 298
Watts-Dunton, Theodore, 459
Webb, Beatrice, **227–9**; *My Apprenticeship*, 228; 'Choice of a Craft', 227
Wells, H. G., 333, 480–81; *Time Machine, The*, 481
Westminster Review, The, 10, 13, 203, 210, 216, 219, 229, 366
White, W. Hale, 31, 327; *Mark Rutherford's Deliverance*, 31, 327
Wilberforce, William, 29, 30
Wilde, Oscar, ix, 257, 316, 337, 386, 463–5, **469–70**, 474, 476, 480, 484, 490–92, 494; *De Profundis*, 465; *Ideal Husband, An*, 469, 490; *Importance of Being Earnest, The*, 257, 469–70, 490, 491, 496; *Intentions*, 469; *Lady Windermere's Fan*, 469, 490; *Letters*, 492, 494; *Picture of Dorian Gray, The*, 464, 469; *Woman of No Importance, A*, 469, 490–91; 'Ballad of Reading Gaol, The', 470; 'Critic as Artist, The', 469; 'Decay of Lying, The', 469, 476; 'Impression du Matin', 476
Wilson, Edmund, 107
Wiseman, Cardinal Nicholas, *Essays on Various Subjects*, 35–6
Wollstonecraft, Mary, 205, 230
Wood, Ellen Price, 262; *East Lynne*, 262
Woodham Smith, Cecil, 132
Woolf, Virginia, 199, 226, 232, 335, 341, 361, 378; *Room of One's Own, A*, 199; *Three Guineas*, 226; *To The Lighthouse*, 361
Woolner, Thomas, 435–6; *My Beautiful Lady*, 435–6
Wordsworth, William, 1, 11, 12, 27, 35, 58, 64, 79, 187, 188, 191, 308, 319, 364, 440, 461, 476
Wright, Edgar, 174
Wright, T. R., *Religion of Humanity, The*, 45

Yeats, W. B., 60, 386, 465–6, 469, 470–72, 474, 479, 481, 490
Yellow Book, The, 480
Yonge, Charlotte, M., 27, 35, 38; *Clever Woman of the Family, The*, 224, 225; *Daisy Chain, The*, 224; *Heir of Redcliffe, The*, 218, 224
Young England, 244
Young Folks, 345–6
Young, G. M., 209, 237

Zabel, M. D., 101
Zola, Emile, 177, 326, 329, 464